SAP PRESS Books: Always on hand

Print or e-book, Kindle or iPad, workplace or airplane: Choose where and how to read your SAP PRESS books! You can now get all our titles as e-books, too:

► By download and online access
► For all popular devices
► And, of course, DRM-free

Convinced? Then go to **www.sap-press.com** and get your e-book today.

SAP® Product Lifecycle Management

 **PRESS**

SAP PRESS is a joint initiative of SAP and Galileo Press. The know-how offered by SAP specialists combined with the expertise of the Galileo Press publishing house offers the reader expert books in the field. SAP PRESS features first-hand information and expert advice, and provides useful skills for professional decision-making.

SAP PRESS offers a variety of books on technical and business-related topics for the SAP user. For further information, please visit our website: *www.sap-press.com*.

Mario Franz
Project Management with SAP Project System (3rd Edition)
2013, 571 pp., hardcover
ISBN 978-1-59229-432-9

Eric Stajda
Document Management with SAP DMS (2nd Edition)
2013, 279 pp., hardcover
ISBN 978-1-59229-862-4

Jawad Akhtar
Production Planning and Control with SAP ERP
2014, app. 825 pp., hardcover
ISBN 978-1-59229-868-6

Stefan Glatzmaier and Michael Sokollek
Project Portfolio Management with SAP RPM and cProjects
2009, 355 pp., hardcover
ISBN 978-1-59229-224-0

Hanneke Raap

SAP® Product Lifecycle Management

Bonn • Boston

Galileo Press is named after the Italian physicist, mathematician, and philosopher Galileo Galilei (1564—1642). He is known as one of the founders of modern science and an advocate of our contemporary, heliocentric worldview. His words *Eppur si muove* (And yet it moves) have become legendary. The Galileo Press logo depicts Jupiter orbited by the four Galilean moons, which were discovered by Galileo in 1610.

Editor Emily Nicholls
Acquisitions Editor Katy Spencer
Technical Reviewer Eric Stajda
Copyeditor Julie McNamee
Cover Design Graham Geary
Photo Credit iStockphoto.com/13857545/Pgiam
Layout Design Vera Brauner
Production Graham Geary
Typesetting SatzPro, Krefeld (Germany)
Printed and bound in the United States of America, on paper from sustainable sources

ISBN 978-1-59229-418-3

© 2013 by Galileo Press Inc., Boston (MA)
1st edition 2013

Library of Congress Cataloging-in-Publication Data
Raap, Hanneke.
SAP product lifecycle management / Hanneke Raap. — 1st edition.
pages cm
ISBN 978-1-59229-418-3 — ISBN 1-59229-418-9 — ISBN 978-1-59229-601-9 —
ISBN 978-1-59229-602-6 1. Product life cycle. 2. SAP ERP. I. Title.
HF5415.155.R33 2013
658.5—dc23
2013015245

Contents at a Glance

Dear Reader,

Writing a book is sometimes like working with clay.

The project starts out with a vision and a basic knowledge of the simple ingredients and tools. It's often not until the project begins and the wheel starts spinning slowly does the magnitude of your goal become real. So you devote months to kneading the clay, and slowly discover that your hobby has become a labor of love when you weren't looking. When you finally slide your completed piece into the kiln, it's hard to let go.

From proposal to publication, this book is almost two years in the making. Hanneke Raap offered this project both the expertise and commitment needed to write "the book" on SAP Product Lifecycle Management, and quickly discovered how challenging such a project can be. Penning an 850-page compendium can be intimidating for any author team, let alone for a first-time author with a full-time senior consultant position with SAP and requisite travel schedule. In the last two years, she's balanced writing with living—she's coordinated a cross-country move and house hunt, celebrated an engagement, and made career advances, all while staying sane.

Product lifecycle management is broad. To initially conceive of such a topic in a way that the final product is both functional and accessible is a challenge; to periodically return to and reconsider the original vision can be painstaking—but ultimately rewarding—work. As Hanneke shaped and reshaped and reshaped again, and tolerated my own pokes and prods, the book began to take recognizable form as the complete resource on SAP Product Lifecycle Management that it was designed to be. Fresh from the kiln, the final product is ready as an everyday reference and guide.

Emily Nicholls
Editor, SAP PRESS

Galileo Press
Boston, MA

emily.nicholls@galileo-press.com
www.sap-press.com

Contents

7   Project Management   503

Contents

Acknowledgments

I would like to dedicate this book to my family and loved ones. Without your love and support, this book wouldn't have been possible.

First, to my fiancé, Freddie Tuinstra, who happily let me pursue my dream of becoming a published author and sharing my knowledge with readers. He sacrificed endless hours and many weekends by supporting me during the research, writing, and chapter delivery.

Second, to my parents, Albert Raap and Jelly-Raap Westerbrink, who gave me the best possible foundation. They taught me to work hard, be determined, share with others, and value my independence, and they allowed me to make my own decisions and mistakes from the moment I could talk. They showed me how to pursue my hopes and dreams.

Lots of love, too, to my sister, Ria Andringa, and her family, who show their love and support in many ways, make me feel proud, and keep me grounded. (My nieces don't seem to care about my being an author—they just want a kiss and a cuddle!)

The scope of this book was enormous, so I am very grateful to several colleagues who performed reviews in their specialized field: Karan Hon, Mark Wilson, Pieter van Daal, Lilliana Grbic, Brindusa Radulescu and Nicholas Nicoloudis. Thanks are due to David Iredale, Martin Burke, and Bruce McKinnon, who gave me confidence and always believed in my professional capabilities. Special thanks go to Jocelyn Dart, who inspired, guided, and coached me during the writing process.

Thanks also to everyone at Galileo Press, especially to my editors, Emily Nicholls and Katy Spencer, who subjected themselves to countless readings and provided invaluable feedback. Although we were in different time zones and continents, they were always just an email or phone call away, and their dedication helped us cross the finish line. I'd also like to thank fellow SAP PRESS author Eric Stajda for his technical review.

Finally I would like to thank the many customers and dedicated employees who have influenced my career; they have made my job rewarding by letting me understand their organizations and translate their business requirements into workable SAP business processes. I would like to mention Brabant Water, COA, International Criminal Court, Rodamco, NedTrain, Dutch Defence Organization, L'Oreal, Greater Wellington Regional Council, Christchurch City Council, Australian Defence Force, Australia Post, Coles, and Brisbane City Council in particular, among others.

SAP Product Lifecycle Management solutions provide all of the end-to-end business processes for effectively and efficiently managing the lifecycles of your company's products, programs, projects, and assets so you can succeed in today's dynamic and connected world.

1   Product Lifecycle Management

SAP Product Lifecycle Management (SAP PLM) provides you with integrated solutions to support all of your company's necessary end-to-end business processes. During the different stages of their lifecycles, software solutions can provide the required practices and advantages you need to succeed in today's rapidly changing world.

This book provides you with an overview of SAP's solutions to manage your company's products, projects, programs, and assets. It shares insight into the different solutions that SAP PLM offers and shows how your organization can benefit from implementing it. The book describes the supported business processes, functions, and features of the solutions so you can evaluate whether a solution is relevant for your organization. By implementing these solutions, you can leverage best practices and focus on your core business activities, ensuring that you stay ahead of the competition and are equipped to succeed.

1.1   Goal and Purpose of the Book

This book provides you with a comprehensive functional overview of SAP PLM. You'll learn about the benefits you can gain by implementing this integrated solution, which supports the decision-making process and gives you valuable information for drawing up a business case or other project initiation documents. The book also provides you with insights on how to benefit from implementation when solutions are introduced gradually in separate phases. Where possible, the supported business scenarios and processes are supplemented with examples of how other customers have implemented the product. After reading this book, you'll understand what SAP PLM is and which business processes are supported by which part of the solution.

This book provides you with knowledge about SAP and its product portfolio, along with insights about how SAP PLM fits into the picture and what is covered under the term *product lifecycle management*. It outlines the specifics of SAP PLM within the SAP Business Suite and gives you an overview of the newest features and functions within SAP PLM 7.02, such as the latest SAP NetWeaver Portal, SAP Project and Portfolio Management (PPM), SAP Governance Risk and Compliance (SAP GRC), products supporting innovation (e.g., code name "Edison" and SAP Product Development), and the latest available business intelligence (BI) tools (e.g., SAP 3D Visual Enterprise and product dashboards).

Any company that is using SAP PLM today should be able to understand its current SAP footprint and determine which parts of SAP PLM the company already uses (e.g., the SAP Materials Management [SAP MM], SAP Document Management System [SAP DMS], and SAP Engineering Change Management [ECM]), where future improvement possibilities lie, and which parts are irrelevant for its business. Businesses that are about to start an SAP implementation (with or without SAP PLM) need to know what functionalities are included in product lifecycle management, develop an understanding of the SAP terminology, and know how to find more information on specific topics such as SAP DMS and SAP PPM.

1.1.1 Target Audience

This book will be valuable for project team members (such as key users, super users, and project managers) who are about to start implementing SAP PLM in their organization. You'll be able to research and evaluate the functions and features offered by the different components within SAP PLM to determine which are relevant for your organization.

It's also valuable for customers that use SAP PLM today and are looking to optimize or extend their existing SAP PLM processes. Consultants, solution architects, and advisors within the product lifecycle arena will also find this information helpful because it provides insights into the expected benefits, integration, and concepts of the solution that can be leveraged during engagements.

1.1.2 Chapter Outline

This book walks you through each of the significant elements of SAP PLM. Each chapter gives you insight into the solution and which master data and business processes are delivered. Where possible, tips, tricks, and practical, real-world examples have been included to provide the information with appropriate depth and context to make it easier for you to digest. Bulleted lists, step-by-step processes, and valuable screenshots and figures help to illustrate the topic at hand. This book provides you with a complete functional overview of all the functionalities and tools offered within SAP PLM—from the initial product idea and product strategy tools, to SAP Product Data Management (SAP PDM), SAP Project and Portfolio Management (PPM), and delivering the product to your customers, to servicing it via maintenance and service. Along with all this, SAP PLM enables you to provide your organization with the appropriate product BI at any given time.

You can either read the book from cover to cover or simply focus on the chapters that are most relevant to your organization. This book roadmap will help you chart the solutions and elements that are discussed in each chapter.

Chapter 1: Product Lifecycle Management

The book starts off with an introduction to SAP and its product portfolio and discusses how SAP PLM fits into this picture. It explains the history of SAP ERP and SAP PLM, outlines trends and challenges that customers face today, and gives insight into how your organization might be able to benefit from implementing the SAP PLM solution. Note that if your company seeks to introduce the SAP PLM solutions gradually instead of all at once, you can find the benefits specific to the solution in their respective chapters.

Chapter 2: Product Management

This chapter focuses on the first stage of developing a product: the product strategy and planning phase. You'll learn how to manage your own product portfolio and how ideas and concepts for new products can be tracked, investigated, and followed up by activities for new product introductions and how processes for post-launching can be formalized. It includes the management of product compliance, risk, and policies as well as protecting product intellectual property.

Chapter 3: Product Data Management

Product-related data and project-related data know no departmental boundaries; it's collected throughout all phases of the product lifecycle, from when the first product idea is formed until the product is delivered to the customer. This data is used and changed continuously by various users along the supply chain. Within the SAP PLM and SAP ERP data model, different master data objects can be used to support all relevant parties with the necessary product information in a timely matter.

This chapter explains the main master data objects used within SAP PLM, such as the product master, routings, Specification Management and Recipe Management, SAP DMS, classification, and product costing. Lifecycle data management is a key part of an SAP PLM solution and should be considered its foundation. Downstream processes leverage integrated master data maintenance tools such as the product browser, the Engineering Workbench, and the Integrated Product and Process Engineering (iPPE) Workbench.

Chapter 4: Product Variants, Classification, and Collaboration

The first section focuses on how to manage complex, highly variable products through Variant Configuration, which gives you the functions to reflect those in a flexible way (i.e., with minimal master data maintenance effort) and the ability to configure the products according to individual customer requirements. The last section outlines the different end-to-end processes available for product data to enable effective and efficient product collaboration among the different stakeholders, such as product development and engineering.

Chapter 5: Maintenance and Customer Service

This chapter gives you an overview of the master data and the processes available through both the SAP Plant Maintenance (SAP PM) and SAP Customer Service (SAP CS) components. SAP PM is focused on the master data and maintenance processes of the technical objects (often referred to as company assets) for which you are responsible and are often for company-owned or leased assets. SAP CS focuses on the master data and processes available when performing maintenance activities in a customer environment, where activities can include customer contract management and invoicing the customer for these performed activities.

Chapter 6: Product Compliance

This chapter discusses the functionalities offered within SAP Environment, Health, and Safety Management (SAP EHS Management) component. SAP EHS Management helps you address global regulatory compliance as well as cost-effectively identify, manage, and mitigate global environment, health, and safety risks by taking an integrated approach to Operational Risk Management. The goal is to provide a reliable solution in a market environment with the increasing importance of corporate responsibility and sustainability.

Chapter 7: Project Management

A discussion of project and resource management capabilities will give you a solid understanding of the business processes that are covered, from a project's initiation to its delivery to the end user, whether this is an external customer or your own organization. This chapter explains how to ensure that you spend and distribute your limited resources wisely and in alignment with your company's strategy. This chapter teaches you how to gain insight into your project pipeline, how to provide the right information to make informed decisions during all phases of a project, and how to monitor costs and make accurate, up-to-date forecasts. Both the SAP Project System (SAP PS) and the web-based SAP Project and Portfolio Management (PPM) solutions are explained in detail.

Chapter 8: Product Quality and Product Change Management

Chapter 8 discusses two separate components: SAP Quality Management (QM) and SAP Engineering Change Management (ECM). Both are integrated, play a key role during all phases of a product's lifecycle, and are fundamental parts of the SAP PLM solution suite. QM capabilities ensure that your products conform to predetermined quality standards and allow you to perform quality checks during all of the different product phases and stages. ECM capabilities can be used when any changes need to be formalized and managed for a product, for other objects such as bills of material (BOMs) or routings, and for documentation.

Chapter 9: Relevant SAP PLM Additions

Chapter 9 covers two additional topics that are often part of an SAP PLM implementation: fleet management and mobility. SAP Fleet Management manages your company's diverse vehicle fleet. The second section provides a functional overview of the SAP Mobile Platform solution offering by explaining the current mobile solutions and applications as well as providing insight into the future direction of SAP Mobile Platform.

Chapter 10: Product Insights and Analytics

This chapter provides an overview of what SAP offers for product intelligence by explaining the searching capabilities, SAP Visual Enterprise, and the end-to-end reporting processes. Reporting on product data is discussed by first explaining the standard reporting options within SAP ERP, followed by how an organization can benefit from implementing additional reporting tools, such as the SAP NetWeaver Business Warehouse (SAP NetWeaver BW) and SAP BusinessObjects. It shows some examples of these reports and provides details about the standard content that is available for SAP PLM as of this book's publication date.

Chapter 11: Conclusion

This chapter provides summary and take-away points for each of the chapters and includes information on what you should be able to do after you've read the book.

1.2   SAP

When you're considering when or how to use an SAP solution, it's useful to understand the background and future of SAP in terms of its strategy and mission. Because SAP PLM and product development is part of the book, this section briefly describes how the organization is structured and managed so you can understand how SAP innovates and develops new products.

As the market leader in enterprise application software, SAP helps companies of all sizes—including small businesses and midsize companies—and of all industries to simply run their businesses better. From product idea to product development, from strategy to execution, from project initiation to project execution and closure, SAP software aims to empower people and organizations to work together more efficiently and use business insight with the objective of staying ahead of the competition in today's challenging business environment.

The software products SAP offers today have been developed and enhanced over the years based on decades of experience and a strong focus on research and development. Products have gone from a client server-based technology to enterprise service architecture. SAP's product strategy leverages in-memory, cloud, and mobile technologies in a way that builds on the existing application platform to minimize disruption. Through orchestration, all SAP solutions offer master data management, business process management, and unified lifecycle management.

The overall management, primary research, development activities, and corporate administration functions take place at SAP's headquarters in Walldorf, Germany. Other offices in more than 50 countries around the world ensure that SAP stays close to its customers and their needs. The subsidiaries perform various tasks such as the distribution, research and development, and sales of SAP's products, as well as providing SAP services (such as customer support, marketing, and administration) on a local basis.

The company and its functional areas are managed both globally and regionally. Because certain information is accessible on a regional level, it can be useful to understand how SAP has been split into the following geographical regions:

▶ Americas (America, Canada, Latin America)

▶ APJ (Asia, Pacific, and Japan)

▶ EMEA (Europe, Middle East, and Africa)

After you've bought an SAP solution, understanding where to go for additional information improves your chances of successfully implementing and running the solution. Let's briefly explore the community and its stakeholders.

SAP Ecosystem and Partners

SAP's ecosystem offers a complete and consistent framework for customers, partners, and individuals to innovate rapidly, improve return on investment (ROI), and grow. SAP offers global and local partnership categories for every strategic business area and customer need in all market segments.

SAP's partner program offers a set of business enablement resources and program benefits to help partners, including value-added resellers (VARs) and independent software vendors (ISVs), to be profitable and successful in implementing, selling, marketing, developing, and delivering SAP solutions to existing and new customers. Service partners support SAP customers during of the stages within the lifecycle of an application, such as the selection, implementation, and go-live phases of SAP products. These service partners usually have extensive SAP knowledge and years of experience and can take part in a qualification process to prove their expertise in certain SAP products or solutions, which can lead to being awarded Special Expertise Partner status. SAP also partners with other software companies and integrators to define standard interfaces. These interfaces can be used to integrate additional products seamlessly into SAP solutions (for example, the partnership with Microsoft to integrate the Microsoft Office offerings and the partnership with Adobe for the SAP Interactive Forms by Adobe).

Another important part of SAP's ecosystem is the reference customer. These are customers who have successfully implemented SAP solutions and are willing to share their experiences within the SAP community. The exchange of information takes place through visits, phone calls, presentations, and interviews.

User Groups

SAP customer companies and partners have formed independent, nonprofit SAP user groups who exchange SAP product knowledge and user experience among their members, influence SAP product releases and direction, and provide insight into the market needs. The largest user groups are the Americas' SAP Users' Group (ASUG), the German-speaking SAP User Group (DSAG), the SAP Australian User Group (SAUG), and the UK & Ireland SAP User Group. In 2007, an overarching SAP user group was formed—the SAP User Group Executive Network (SUGEN)—to further the information exchange and best practice sharing among SAP user groups and to coordinate the collaboration with SAP for strategic topics.

Conferences

Each year in the spring, SAP runs SAPPHIRE in both North America and Europe to inform customers in an open and exciting atmosphere about the major product changes and the strategic directions of the company. SAP TechEd is held during the fall, when consultants and software development partners get to hear about product additions, changes, and strategic directions from a technical perspective.

Virtual Communities and Product Information

Apart from contacting your area SAP branch for information or to request a product demonstration, you can find a lot of information about SAP products and services online. Visit the SAP websites (*www.sap.com* and *help.sap.com*) or become a registered member at the SAP Service Marketplace (*http://service.sap.com*).

However, as soon as you become an SAP customer, you become part of the most comprehensive and consistent ecosystem in the industry. You can tap into the knowledge of communities and harness the value of SAP partner solutions and services. You can share knowledge and experiences, alongside other developers, consultants, integrators, and business analysts who have joined to gain and share knowledge about SAP solutions and technologies. Expert blogs, discussion forums, exclusive downloads and code samples, training materials, and a technical library are all available to you.

You can participate in the SAP Community Network, by going to the website *www.scn.sap.com*, where you can join the communities relevant for you and your organization. SAP communities have been set up around the following three core capabilities:

▶ Industry-focused excellence, to find and deploy solutions specific to your own industry and business needs. There are currently 11 active Industry Value Networks available (e.g., Banking, Chemicals, Consumer Products, High Tech, Public Sector, Retail).

▶ Community-powered results, which allows you to connect with the right people, organizations, and resources to deliver fast results to your organization.

▶ Orchestrated co-innovation, to effectively work together and influence SAP developments and next-generation solutions.

1.3 The SAP Product Portfolio

Let's briefly explore the solutions offered by SAP, putting special emphasis on the solutions within the SAP PLM area and how they fit into the overall product offerings. This section gives insight on how and where to find information on new releases of SAP products and explains the different phases an SAP release goes through. The maintenance and support activities SAP offers are briefly explained, including an introduction on the central tool for support and maintenance activities — SAP Solution Manager.

1.3.1 SAP Business Suite and SAP ERP

SAP Business Suite offers a flexible software solution targeted at large companies with a high number of users and processes that are constantly changing. It provides comprehensive business applications that allow you to manage your entire value chain and the most critical business processes. SAP Business Suite provides your organization with consistent results throughout the entire company network and gives you the flexibility needed in today's dynamic market situations through an open, integrated solution for the entire value chain to meet constant, new demands from your customers. It consists of a number of different products, which enables cross-company processes.

SAP Business Suite software supports core business operations ranging from supplier relationships to production, warehouse management, sales, and all administrative functions, through to customer relationships. It's important to understand how SAP PLM fits into the SAP Business Suite solution, so this section outlines the different elements of the solution in some more detail, as shown in Figure 1.1.

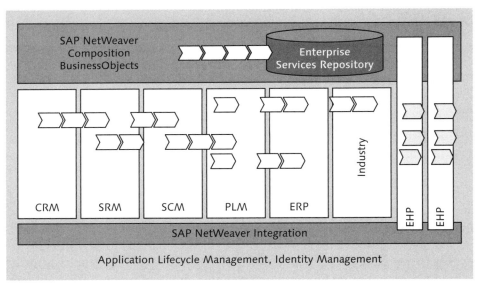

Figure 1.1 SAP Business Suite

The core application of SAP Business Suite, SAP ERP (which stands for Enterprise Resource Planning) is a set of business applications that support all of the essential business processes of an enterprise. SAP ERP supports mission-critical, end-to-end business processes for finance, human capital management, asset management, sales, procurement, and other essential corporate functions. The solution is divided into three main areas—logistics, finance, and human resources—which are further split up into the different components (formerly known as applications). SAP ERP is used to manage internal and external resources, such as products, tangible assets, money, materials, and people. Its purpose is to capture business activities, inform all business functions inside the boundaries of the organization, and manage the connections to outside stakeholders, such as customers, vendors, and contractors. SAP ERP forms the core of the solution.

SAP ERP also supports industry-specific processes by providing industry-specific business functions that can be activated selectively in your SAP ERP environment. After activation, the industry solution provides specific master data objects and business processes and extends existing business processes with additional functions and features. Since the release of SAP ERP and SAP NetWeaver, you can activate multiple industry solutions, whereas just one industry solution could be active prior to SAP NetWeaver. Examples of available industry solutions include banking, high-tech, oil and gas, utilities, chemicals, healthcare, retail, consumer products, and the public sector.

Another important SAP Business Suite application, Customer Relationship Management (SAP CRM), provides a comprehensive platform for marketing, sales, and service professionals to obtain complete customer intelligence that they can use to effectively manage customers and customer-related processes. SAP CRM enables multichannel customer interactions—including via the Internet, smartphones, and social media—and also offers a dedicated communications infrastructure that helps to connect all users anytime, anywhere.

The SAP Supplier Relationship Management (SAP SRM) application automates, simplifies, and accelerates procure-to-pay processes for goods and services. Centralized sourcing and contract management activities can be improved in all industries through SAP SRM, and it allows you to interact with suppliers throughout multiple channels.

SAP Supply Chain Management (SAP SCM) focuses on the collaboration, planning, execution, and coordination of the entire supply network, which empowers you to adapt your supply chain processes within an ever-changing competitive environment. Your supply chains can be transformed into open, configurable, responsive supply networks in which customer-centric, demand-driven companies can sense and respond more intelligently and more quickly to demand-and-supply dynamics across the globe.

SAP PLM provides you with a complete solution for all of your product- and asset-related processes during all stages of their lifecycle. The product is supported from the first product idea, through manufacturing, and delivery to the customer, to product maintenance and service and the final stage of decommission and disposal, and includes the supporting process throughout the extended supply chain. It facilitates creativity and frees the process of product innovation from organizational constraints. SAP Project and Portfolio Management (PPM) capabilities, whether they are internally focused or customer-focused projects, support the project lifecycle from project initiation, to planning and execution, to project closure.

The SAP BusinessObjects portfolio covers a variety of demands for companies small to large with solutions for business users who need to analyze and report information, make informed strategic and tactical decisions, build business plans, and manage risk and compliance. The SAP BusinessObjects portfolio includes analytic applications that are designed to help business users reach strategic goals, deliver predictable results, and make sound decisions. SAP BusinessObjects BI and SAP solutions for information management applications support companies to provide trusted information to every member of a business network, helping them to respond faster and make better decisions. The SAP BusinessObjects portfolio also includes Enterprise Performance Management (SAP EPM) and Governance, Risk, and Compliance (SAP GRC) solutions, which help customers to manage profitability, risk and compliance, and systems and processes.

Solutions for Sustainability

SAP solutions for sustainability help enable organizations' sustainability initiatives. They include the measurement of sustainability key performance indicators (KPIs); energy and carbon management; product safety; and environment, health, and safety management to help customers pursue a sustainable business strategy. In 2010, SAP acquired TechniData, a leading supplier of compliance management solutions. The acquisition allowed SAP to offer more of the content and strategic services that customers require in this field. This has resulted in a faster return on customers' investment, providing a holistic and integrated portfolio of sustainability solutions that help customers implement, measure, and report sustainability activities across the full enterprise. These solutions include the following:

- **SAP Advance Metering Infrastructure**
  Provides integration for utilities and is aimed at energy suppliers.

- **SAP Sustainability Performance Management**
  Sets sustainability goals and objectives, measures and communicates performance, and reduces data collection costs and errors.

- **SAP Carbon Impact OnDemand**
  Helps accurately measure, profitably reduce, and confidently report on greenhouse gas emissions and other environmental impacts.

- **SAP Environment, Health, and Safety Management (SAP EHS Management)**
  Addresses regulatory compliance and helps companies efficiently comply and protect their people and plant by taking an integrated approach to all aspects of risk and compliance (see Chapter 6).

- **SAP Manufacturing Integration and Intelligence (SAP MII)**
  Provides the tools and content to help customers track and identify opportunities for energy reduction in manufacturing.

SAP NetWeaver

From a technological viewpoint, SAP ERP is based on the SAP NetWeaver technology platform that is embedded in an open and flexible service-oriented architecture (SOA), which can connect SAP and non-SAP applications using Web Services to protect your IT investments. The SAP NetWeaver technology platform integrates information and business processes across diverse technologies and organizational structures and provides the technical foundation for SAP applications. In addition, it delivers a portfolio of enterprise technology that allows you to extend your applications to reach more people and to adopt new processes, devices, and consumption models. A good example is the SAP NetWeaver Business Warehouse (SAP NetWeaver BW), which provides you with a comprehensive tool to extract and analyze data captured within your SAP PLM environment. SAP NetWeaver helps you improve team productivity and business integration, enables you to simplify and manage your IT environment, and reduces operational costs so that IT resources are free to focus on business innovation.

1.3.2 The Current SAP Solution Portfolio

Apart from the SAP Business Suite and the sustainability offerings, which are mainly used by large organizations, SAP also offers several other products to deliver solutions on-premise, on-demand, and on-device to small and midsized companies:

▸ SAP Business One is a comprehensive, integrated SAP ERP application with an interface similar to Microsoft Windows. It's distinguished by simple navigation and drilldown options, innovative Drag&Relate functions, and integration with Microsoft Word and Excel.

▸ SAP Business ByDesign is a complete and adaptable on-demand business solution designed to liberate midsize companies from the restrictions of traditional IT.

▸ SAP Business All-in-One is the brand name for vertical (industry-specific or country-specific) solutions that are based on the technology of SAP Business Suite and were developed in conjunction with SAP's partners. It's focused on small companies with few employees and relatively stable processes, which can use preconfigured SAP systems.

Duet and Alloy

Business users need direct access to people, processes, and information to work efficiently—without having to give up familiar applications or master complex software. Duet software and Alloy software provide direct access to SAP Business Suite software using familiar Microsoft Office and IBM Lotus Notes software. This often leads to improved business user productivity and decision making, and increased compliance with corporate policies.

SAP Mobile Solutions

SAP has different applications and solutions available in the mobile space. Mobility is an exciting topic because it is currently one of the main focus areas within SAP. The acquisition of Sybase and Syclo, both companies with decades of experience with mobile solutions and integration to SAP, has led to the substantial growth and improvement of the product portfolio in this area. The first mobile solution map was published in October 2012, which also provides the future outlook to enabling a single SAP Mobile Platform. Chapter 9 explains the mobility topic and SAP offerings relevant to SAP PLM in more detail.

SAP HANA

Although not yet added in the overview illustration (Figure 1.1), SAP's latest product, SAP HANA is worth mentioning. SAP HANA is a flexible, data-agnostic, in-memory appliance that combines SAP software components optimized for hardware provided and delivered by SAP partners. With SAP HANA, organizations can instantly analyze their business operations, using huge volumes of detailed transactional and analytic information from virtually any data source. In addition to revolutionizing customers' access to data, SAP HANA provides the foundation for building new, innovative applications. These applications will leverage the in-memory database and calculation engine within SAP HANA, allowing customers to conduct complex planning, forecasting, and simulation based on real-time data.

1.3.3   The SAP Business Suite Release Strategy

SAP Business Suite offers additional functions and features by releasing SAP enhancement packages (EHPs), as shown in Figure 1.2. The introduction of enhancement packages has caused a revolutionary shift in innovation, which makes it possible for customers to start using new functionality almost as soon as it becomes available, without any disruptions to their current business activities. With this new concept, it becomes unnecessary to perform a full-scope upgrade project, including the relevant project steps, which in turn reduces costs significantly during the innovation process.

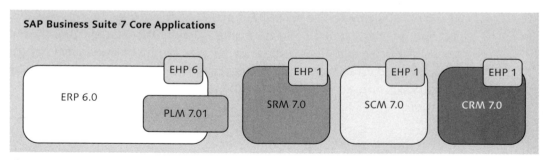

Figure 1.2 SAP Business Suite and Enhancement Packs

> **Note**
>
> This book is written based on the latest SAP ERP release (ERP 6 EHP 6) and the latest releases of SAP PLM 7.02.

The new release strategy provides the following benefits:

▶ Gain stability and access to innovation

▶ Upgrade only the enhancements applicable to your business

▶ Reduce risk and downtime

▶ Speed implementation and test less

▶ Reduce training effort

An enhancement package is optionally installed and activates software innovations for SAP ERP 6.0, including UI simplifications, functional enhancements, and enterprise services. SAP enhancement packages are built on top of each other. You simply select and activate the functionality that your company requires, and the functionality your business doesn't need will remain dormant. You can activate additional functionality through the Switch Framework tool, which is available in the SAP Implementation Guide (IMG) using Transaction SPRO (the transaction used to access all SAP configurations).

SAP releases (except content releases) and corresponding enhancement packages are generally introduced into the market in two shipment phases: restricted (via the SAP Ramp-Up program with a limited group of customers) and unrestricted (in which the product becomes available to all customers).

To find more information about enhancement packages, you can visit the SAP Service Marketplace (*http://service.sap.com/businesssuite*) and follow the links to the enhancement package infocenters *http://service.sap.com/rampup*). Through the Product Availability Matrix in the SAP Service Marketplace (*http://service.sap.com/pam*), SAP regularly publishes information about SAP solutions, the latest releases, the release type (standard release, pilot release, standard-related custom development project release, or custom development project release), availability of the product, maintenance stages and periods, upgrade paths, and technical information.

1.3.4 SAP Solution Manager

To support maintenance activities, such as installing enhancement packages or loading SAP notes (which contain information and sometimes programs updates) to fix a known problem, SAP recommends that you use SAP Solution Manager.

SAP Solution Manager enables customers to manage their SAP applications efficiently throughout the complete solution lifecycle. To accelerate implementation and upgrade projects, SAP provides SAP Solution Manager content for SAP applications and SAP NetWeaver. SAP Solution Manager add-ons offer extensions you can deploy flexibly to activate functionality specific to focus groups and integration packages to leverage third-party functionality.

SAP Solution Manager provides you with the following functions and features:

- SAP Business Suite content, to accelerate implementation and upgrade
- Change Control Management
- Testing
- Service Desk functions to manage IT and application support
- Diagnostics to identify, analyze, and resolve problems (e.g., root-cause analysis)
- Centralized and real-time solution monitoring of systems, business processes, and interfaces
- Service-level management and reporting to support strategic IT decisions
- Administration activities

For more information on SAP Solution Manager, please see the SAP corporate website at *http://www.sap.com/platform/netweaver/components/solutionmanager/index.epx* or *http://service.sap.com/upgrade* (requires logon). These resources provide details on SAP upgrade offerings, application-specific upgrade information, and upgrade news.

1.4   Product Lifecycle Management

After explaining the concept and definition of product lifecycle management, we'll walk you through its brief history to continue exploring the current trends and challenges this area faces. We'll conclude with the benefits from implementation of SAP PLM in general and explain which end-to-end business processes are covered through the SAP PLM solution offering and how they fit within the SAP PLM solution map.

1.4.1 What Is Product Lifecycle Management?

Product lifecycle management is the process of managing the entire lifecycle of a product from its conception, through design and manufacture, to service and disposal. The exact order of events and tasks varies according to the product and industry, but the main processes are represented in Figure 1.3.

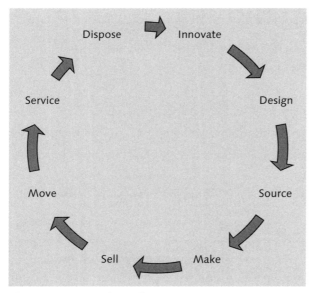

Figure 1.3 Basic Product Lifecycle

In a nutshell, the product lifecycle includes the following steps:

1. During the innovation phase, the product is specified and the concept is designed.

2. During the design phase, design details are worked out and validated, analyses are performed, and tools are designed.

3. During manufacturing, the components or ingredients are sourced, and the plan or recipe is developed. This is when the product is either built, assembled, or processed, and during this phase, several tests and quality checks can be performed to ensure the product is of the right quality.

4. After the product is sold and delivered, support and maintenance services can take place.

5. Eventually, the product can be replaced or disposed of.

The SAP PLM end-to-end processes are further broken down into implementable steps, which will all be discussed in more detail over the course of this book. Before addressing the functions and features of the different software solutions offered, it's important to understand the history and evolution of SAP PLM solutions. Figure 1.4 shows how the entire product lifecycle is supported—from idea, to customer delivery, to eventually retirement.

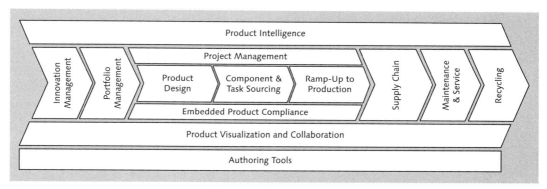

Figure 1.4 Product Lifecycle of SAP PLM Integrated Product Development

Traditionally, processes set up to support product development occurred in a sequential matter and had department-focused silo solutions specifically tailored to product data management activities such as design, research, and costing. SAP ERP systems focused on sales and distribution, the production process, and servicing the product on the SAP Enterprise Asset Management (SAP EAM) system. Figure 1.5 shows the relationships between these systems in relation to the product lifecycle management steps.

The task of traditional product data management systems was to be the interface between technical and business information processing systems, linking computer-aided design software on the technical side (CAx systems such as CAD, CAE, CAM, and PDM) to procurement and production on the business side (such as SAP ERP systems). This trend refocused product data management systems exclusively on development. The information flow in this traditional process is in one direction only and treats departments as individual silos. The result was that when, for example, the development department had suggestions for improvements or changes, the marketing department and even the customers were not informed of them. That is, changes along the value chain were not communicated to the involved stakeholders—only to the executor of the next step in the sequence. Figure 1.6 shows an example of a typical traditional product data management process.

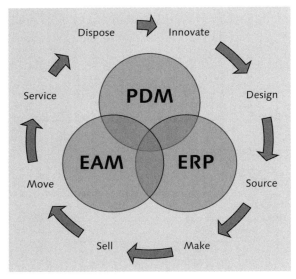

Figure 1.5 Traditional Product Data Systems

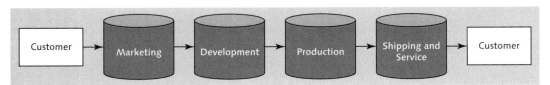

Figure 1.6 Example of Traditional Product Development Process

This approach made it almost impossible to ensure that the customers received the product or service they sought. Furthermore, this process doesn't correspond to any real product development process because different departments actually develop and produce in parallel and work interdependently, rather than in sequence. Product data was usually maintained in several places, across different systems, and without proper validations or integration. This approach also led to a lack of communication between internal and external employees, a lack of visibility and process control, and a lack of data transparency and consistency.

In today's rapidly changing and adaptive world, this view is no longer sustainable. Most companies aren't prepared to invest time and money in the interface between development and engineering on the one hand, and operative areas (such as production, sales and distribution, and services) on the other. Seamless integration between these applications makes far more sense.

SAP's lifecycle data management provides you with the tools to solve these problems and gives you solutions to support the product data throughout its entire lifecycle. Regardless of which department starts with a new product or product idea, as soon as product data is created, it can be reused in all of the downstream processes. It offers you an integrated product development process that is built upon and adds to the existing functions for planning, optimizing, and executing business processes. These include new areas of activity and groups of users in product development. It provides you with a single source of the truth when it comes to product data, with the focus on lifecycle data management. Figure 1.7 shows the conceptual shift from specialized data management to lifecycle data management.

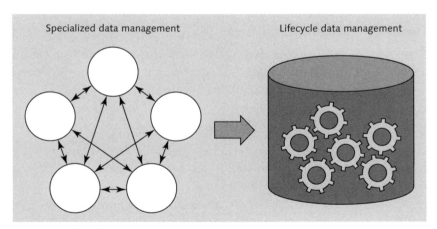

Figure 1.7 Lifecycle Data Management

Through collaboration, you can ensure that everyone participates in completing specific tasks, wherever employees are and no matter where they work. The product-related and project-related data knows no departmental boundaries and is collected throughout all phases of the product lifecycle. This data is used and changed continuously by various users along the supply chain, which is supported with controlled change management processes. These change management processes let you define validity parameters and release changes, and understand the impacts on the downstream processes that have already begun (e.g., during the production process). Data exchange over the Internet can be used because this is the key technology for global networking. The number of cross-company scenarios and processes that use the Internet is growing each day. In this approach, information flows between all of the different parties involved in product development, and changes are communicated appropriately.

The product development process is no longer narrowly focused on development and computer-aided design models but instead focuses more broadly on the complexity of the process and its activities, such as market studies, customer surveys, and development requests. Usually, a large number of documents have to be managed, such as marketing plans, logs, and specifications.

SAP PLM is aimed at all industries that need to manage their products, project, programs, and assets effectively. It's focused on both the discrete industries (e.g., high-tech, automotive, aerospace or plant engineering, and construction) and on the process industries (e.g., oil and gas, chemicals, and pharmaceuticals).

1.4.2 Current Trends and Challenges

Product development is influenced by a variety of complex factors that mainly result from globalization and the nature of product development. Consider these global trends and how they have impacted product development:

- **Increased pace of innovation**
  An ever-changing customer need and market environment makes innovation a key competitive differentiator. Organizations need to drive innovation on products, services, and processes as well as shorten innovation cycles by evaluating customer needs, understanding market opportunities, and aligning the product portfolio strategy with business execution. So the innovation process needs to be effectively managed and continuously tracked.

- **Global operational competitiveness**
  To stay competitive, businesses need to be faster, leaner, and more productive than ever before. Organizations need to improve development efficiency to increase profitability and reduce time to profit by reducing time to market and increase efficiencies in design, manufacturing, and service. They should also

focus on continuous product cost management, reduce component costs, and introduce more flexible and dynamic development collaboration networks

▶ **Increasing product compliance and corporate regulations**
Governments and other institutions are pressing for compliance with various regulations, such as the U.S. Sarbanes-Oxley Act (SOX), the European Union's Waste Electrical and Electronic Equipment (WEEE) directive, the European Community regulation on chemicals and their safe use (Registration, Evaluation, Authorization and Restriction of Chemical substances, known as REAC), and U.S. Food and Drug Administration requirements for improved tracking and drug pedigree information. This trend emphasizes why organizations need to establish a sustainable product strategy for environmental health; reduce risk by focusing on compliance controls, documentation, and visibility; introduce a sustainability "culture"; and design sustainable and compliant products. This approach can avoid compliance violations from development, manufacturing, sales, service, or recycling criteria.

▶ **Networked economy**
New channels and more demanding customers have led to an increase in new products. These products must be tailored to meet the customer's needs. The reality is that every company lives within many business networks and can play different roles in each. Global communication and partnerships must be formed to create win-win situations in which collaboration and the sharing of information are critical success factors.

▶ **Adaptive business networks**
Companies in today's competitive environment want a clear path forward that will increase both efficiency and adaptability to improve profitability. Having long been successful in improving efficiency, SAP is applying its three decades of business and IT experience to helping customers increase their adaptability. The result is the adaptive business network, a concept created through hundreds of discussions with customers and years of research by SAP.

While business networks are constantly changing, the key questions for every participant should be, "What is my defendable differentiation? What do I do better than my competitor? What is the core that my business should focus on?" Companies are looking at their business environment and seeing the following trends:

▶ **Customer power shift**
First of all, recent years have seen an enormous shift of power from the suppli-

ers to the customer. Customers increasingly understand the global market and demand market transparency through the accessibility of information. The wealth of supply creates many options for customers impacted by globalization and technology. The competition has intensified, and products are increasingly commoditized especially within industries that supply services and manufactured goods (as is currently happening within the mobile handset industry). As a result, however, customers—both consumers and businesses—have a newfound influence on design, delivery of products and services, and business models.

▶ **Workforce dynamics and global workforces**

Two things are happening here. First—and related to increasing globalization—companies are spreading work around the globe, taking advantage of time zones and specialization to compete. Examples of companies delegating work around the globe include GE, Siemens, and, of course, SAP. Even *The Wall Street Journal*, where we read about many of these stories, has editorial control handled in New York, Hong Kong, and Brussels, making the publication more current but also more international. Companies are focusing more on their core business, which leads to a shift in the type of work within enterprises and the way it's performed. This shift is changing the way companies compete and create value, and it's only just beginning to change.

▶ **Intensified competition**

Mergers and acquisitions (M&A) trends, technology trends, customer trends, and a host of other factors are combining to create a perfect storm of competition in many—or maybe all—industries. Companies are competing on the basis of cost structure, prices, design, innovation, customer service, capabilities, brands, cultural adaptability, and so on. The result is both new, radical delivery and commercialization models. This means every business—and especially the larger, established ones that are SAP's core customers— must find new and powerful ways to innovate and differentiate as rapidly and efficiently as possible. In many cases, it comes down to agility—the ability to rapidly detect and respond to threats and opportunities. Another key outcome SAP has seen is the emergence of robust, far-reaching business networks—in other words, the networked economy.

▶ **Increased risk**

Businesses in every sector have come under more pressure due to the increase and stricter regulations in the wake of September 11, 2001, corporate scandals, trade disputes, environmental issues, the global financial crisis, and other catalyzing events. Regardless of size, enterprises that want to participate in the global economy will face the same challenges as they grapple with new regulations. A 2011 PriceWaterhouseCoopers study asserts that only 65% of executives are confident that they are complying with foreign regulations.

Disruptive technology remains an ever-present agitator. As an example, the world continues to see an explosion in digital information, and, by extension, information technology. The growth in information technology has been driven by lower communication costs, an exponential growth of computing power, and an improving price-performance ratio for storage. Today's IT conversations are marked by talk about cloud computing and its implications, which is just one example of how disruptive technology is reshaping our world and our customers' businesses. But there is no question that it's happening and that it, too, is changing how companies compete.

Different companies have different answers to the question about core and context based on their specific strengths. Some companies (e.g., contract manufacturers) are focusing their efforts on doing what they do most efficiently and creating operational excellence. Others, such as airlines or utility companies, realize that their assets are the foundation of their success and do everything they can to maintain a high performance in these assets.

SAP calls these different strategies "value creation models." It believes that great companies focus on one (or, at the most, two) of those models at a time.

Companies such as Nestle, BMW, and Hewlett-Packard are responding to the challenge by continuously innovating and delivering the right products and services of the right quality at the right time and at the right price. They are aiming for the value creation model Product and Service Leadership. The Product and Service Leadership model can be achieved by integrating all product-related and service-related processes and representations to set up a flexible, dynamic, and effective global network. This Product and Service Leadership framework/approach breaks down the walls between marketing, research and development, procurement, manufacturing, logistics, sales, and service and strives for profitable, market-leading products.

SAP PLM enables Product and Service Leadership through its service-enabled platform, SAP NetWeaver. Companies create value for their customers through tangible products, services, or combinations of both, depending on the industry.

A successful modern company designs, develops, and delivers its offerings as a collaborative effort among all stakeholders involved within its global network of brand owners, suppliers, and distributors. Interconnecting all product-related and service-related stakeholders in a single business network provides the necessary shift from silo to parallel collaboration between different business departments such as marketing, R&D, procurement, manufacturing, logistics, and service. This new framework and cross-functional collaboration is the secret behind today's profitable, industry-leading offerings. The entire ecosystem can constantly fine-tune processes and products to respond to ever-changing customer needs and market demands.

1.4.3 Benefits of Using SAP PLM

By supporting all product lifecycle processes, SAP PLM can provide consistent, relevant information on demand at any time, from any place, across all departments, and across the extended supply chain. A holistic approach to SAP PLM streamlines your company's processes, multiplies efficiency, and empowers a fast response to changes in products, markets, or competitors. It can reduce development time (and thereby lower costs) in many ways, including running processes in parallel instead of sequentially. Therefore, an SAP PLM solution must be designed to impact your organization's bottom line.

When considering implementing and optimizing SAP PLM products, it's important to understand how and where your company will benefit from the SAP PLM solutions. You should be able to anticipate your ROI. To help you build a solid business case, this section offers an overview of potential benefits from using SAP PLM. First we'll introduce general benefits, and second, some measurable benefits based on benchmarks of other customers who have implemented the SAP solution. These have been added merely to provide you with insight to the possible benefits that have been achieved by actual customers. There is no guarantee that your company will perform equally, as every customer has its own specific circumstances and opportunities to optimize business.

To meet the demand of such product-driven companies, SAP offers a set of end-to-end processes that empowers customers to become Product and Service Leaders in their product and service offering by tapping into these benefits:

▶ Reduced time-to-market

▶ Reduced development, infrastructure, and product costs

- Improved product design, quality, and prices
- Increased customer satisfaction and market share
- Consistent, centralized, role-specific, and context-driven access to the information, applications, tools, and services needed to accomplish their daily work at any moment and on any Internet-enabled device for all stakeholders
- Streamlined processes that multiply efficiency and empower a fast response to changes in products, markets, and competitors' situations
- Parallel processing
- Improved ability to develop and introduce new products that meet customer needs to increase new product sales and shorten time to market
- Higher new product quality
- Faster responsiveness to changing demand and supply chain signals through increased visibility into suppliers' processes
- Reduced operating costs by reducing errors and network, cycle times, and direct materials costs
- Better understanding of the capacity of an organization and its suppliers
- Optimization of profit during order fulfillment by carefully distributing products across the most attractive channels
- Creation of new streams of revenue through services that extend the customer relationship after the sale
- Improved decision making at all levels of the organization through powerful and flexible analytics capabilities to cover such areas as portfolio management, occupational health, product safety, product quality, and enterprise asset management
- Lower total cost of ownership (TCO) through an open and robust infrastructure that provides easy integration of operational systems, such as CAD applications, SAP ERP, SAP CRM, SAP SRM, and SAP SCM solutions

Let's consider specific examples of the values and quantitative benefits affecting revenue, operating cost, and working capital achieved by enterprises that have implemented the SAP PLM solution:

- Reduced time to market by using a complete solution to manage and retrieve all product-related information from concept through design, production, and product obsolescence. Example: a 40% improvement in product change cycle times.

▶ Reduced cost-to-market by evaluating program and project progress and supporting investment and divestment decisions for products. Example: a 15-30% reduction in unnecessary prototypes.

▶ Reduced risk exposure and cost of engineering changes by providing an integrated set of capabilities to monitor, implement, and control engineering changes from customer-requested changes to projects, products, and engineering changes against released production orders. Example: an engineering review process reduced by 83%, from 12 days to 2 days.

▶ Delivered products tailored to individual needs. Also, improved knowledge of available parts and components to reduce costly design and engineering work, and the ability for vendors to enter niche markets. Example: a 25% productivity increase in design engineering.

▶ Increased revenue. Examples:
   ▸ Increase in new product sales by 2–20%
   ▸ Improved time to market by 20–30%
   ▸ Improved quality of new products by 20–40%

▶ Reduced operating cost. Examples:
   ▸ Reduced errors and rework by 6–26%
   ▸ Reduced cycle time reduction by 30–50%
   ▸ Reduced direct material costs by 2–5%

▶ Affected working capital. Examples:
   ▸ Reduced inventory levels by 3–5%
   ▸ Improved capacity utilization by 6–10%
   ▸ Reduced warranty and returns allowances 10–20%

1.4.4   Solution Map for SAP PLM

To understand which tools and processes SAP supports in SAP PLM, use the specific business map shown in Figure 1.8, which demonstrates how implementing each solution can deliver value to your business.

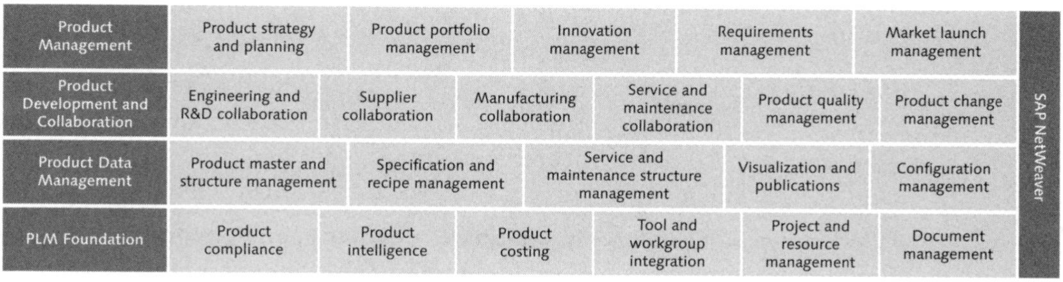

Product Management	Product strategy and planning	Product portfolio management	Innovation management	Requirements management	Market launch management
Product Development and Collaboration	Engineering and R&D collaboration	Supplier collaboration	Manufacturing collaboration	Service and maintenance collaboration	Product quality management	Product change management
Product Data Management	Product master and structure management	Specification and recipe management	Service and maintenance structure management	Visualization and publications	Configuration management
PLM Foundation	Product compliance	Product intelligence	Product costing	Tool and workgroup integration	Project and resource management	Document management

Figure 1.8 SAP PLM Business Process Map

The SAP PLM business process map distinguishes between four separate process categories (Product Management, Product Development and Collaboration, Product Data Management, and PLM Foundation) in which the main processes have been placed.

This book covers all of the topics and processes mentioned in the solution map for SAP PLM:

▸ **Product Management (Chapter 2)**
Product management, which is supported by product portfolio analysis and management, includes getting the planning and decision-support capabilities to align high-level product plans and objectives with corporate strategies. The associated regulations, risks, and legal support need to become visible when developing product and technology roadmaps. Though innovation is a creative process, you can support it by identifying opportunities for innovation, managing those opportunities, and ultimately measuring the value the innovation activities provide your organization. A foundation is provided so customer requirements of many types can be tracked and provide you with the right information to act accordingly within a continuously changing market.

▸ **Product Development and Collaboration (Chapter 7 and Chapter 8)**
Product development and collaboration is a key capability consisting of business processes that engage multiple roles and communities of practice across the enterprise and business network to drive continuous product innovation, product development and performance, and product quality.

▸ **Product Data Management (Chapter 3, Chapter 4, and Chapter 5)**
All product-related data can be managed along the entire lifecycle. This includes the development and planning phase, technical document management, parts management, and product and process structure management.

Classification and Variant Configuration are fully supported so you can optimize master data and include company specifics. For discrete industries, BOMs and routings can be used to support product manufacturing. For process industries, for example, Specification Management and Recipe Management are offered to facilitate product development. As-built and as-maintained structures are provided for the product service and maintenance phases.

▶ **PLM Foundation (Chapter 3, Chapter 6, Chapter 7, and Chapter 10)**
The PLM Foundation contains all of the fundamental main processes within SAP PLM. The product compliance process describes how to properly maintain regulations surrounding products and how to comply with the product regulations that govern labeling, product safety, and hazardous and dangerous goods management. It also covers product costing capabilities to give you insights into cost during the different stages within a product, so you can best calculate price information. Project and resource management supports all phases from project idea to execution so your company can make informed decisions on how to spend money, locate resources, prioritize projects, allocate realistic time frames, and align projects with your company's long-term strategy. SAP Document Management System (SAP DMS) allows you to store and update documents for all kinds of objects in SAP. Examples of tasks you can accomplish with the SAP DMS include storing technical drawings against a material master, linking a blueprint deliverable to a project, and assigning a quality assurance report to a product trial.

> **Note**
>
> The SAP PLM Solution Map is a cross-industry solution map. The most recent version can be found at *http://www.sap.com/solutions/businessmaps* on the CROSS-INDUSTRY BUSINESS MAPS page. Here you can also find other cross-industry maps, such as Customer Relationship Management (CRM) and SAP NetWeaver.

1.4.5 Solution Map for SAP ERP

Several of the components that are offered and covered under the SAP PLM Solution Map are also covered by the SAP ERP Solution Map under the process categories Product Development and Collaboration, Enterprise Asset Management, and Operations Cross Functions, which have been highlighted in Figure 1.9. It's important to understand the overlap and know how to find more information about the solution or topic because this will help you understand if the introduction of a new solution or function requires any follow-up activities (such as the procurement of additional software licenses or hardware) or if it's part of your current footprint. It also helps you navigate SAP resources.

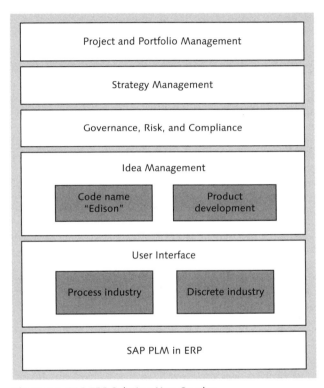

Figure 1.9 SAP ERP Solution Map Overlap

1.5   Summary

By now, you should have a clear understanding of what to expect from this SAP PLM resource. You can either read the book from cover to cover or simply focus on the chapters that are relevant for your organization. This first chapter has put SAP in context by giving a brief introduction to SAP as a company, and explaining its strategy, structure, and extensive SAP community. We've explained the current overall product portfolio in which SAP PLM is positioned to provide you with an understanding of the different solutions offered under the SAP PLM Solution Map. Last, the chapter introduced product lifecycle management as a concept, offered a brief history of the space, described the current trends and challenges companies are facing, and listed some important benefits customers can expect when implementing SAP PLM.

The first topic which we will be addressing in the upcoming chapter will be product management. We introduce the New Product Development and Introduction pyramid—which divides the NPDI processes into three main areas: innovation, product planning and management, and functional execution—and the associated SAP solutions.

When you're developing a new product, you can support the initial stages it goes through by mapping out product strategies; setting up a governance, risk, and compliance framework; defining and monitoring product portfolios and executing those defined strategies; and monitoring its progress.

2 Product Management

This chapter focuses on the first stage of developing a product: the product strategy and planning phase. You'll learn how to develop the company's product strategies, set up an SAP Governance, Risk and Compliance (SAP GRC) solution to protect your intellectual property, and manage corporate risks. This chapter explains how to manage your product and project portfolio and how ideas and concepts for new products can be collected and analyzed, as well as how the process for new product introductions can be addressed and formalized for the post-launch processes.

Figure 2.1 shows the New Product Development and Introduction (NPDI) pyramid as developed by SAP Solution Management, which breaks NPDI into three critical capabilities: innovation strategy, planning and management, and functional execution. We've outlined the chapter to align with this pyramid:

- ▶ Section 2.1 explains innovation strategy and focuses on product and strategy planning—the first two tiers of the NPDI pyramid.
- ▶ Section 2.2 focuses on product innovation and requirements management, which is part of idea management and product development.
- ▶ Section 2.3 covers the functional execution of managing and supporting market launch.

The end-to-end process of product data management is called continuous product and service innovation; it covers the detailed steps according to the following areas as introduced within the NPDI pyramid. Figure 2.2 maps the responsibilities, workflows, or processes against the responsible departments.

- ▸ **Strategy and Planning**
  Performed by marketing, covering product intelligence, strategy management, and initiative planning.

- ▸ **Managing Innovation**
  Performed by research and development covering idea management and concept management.

- ▸ **Program and Project Management**
  Performed by operations covering the different processes of project management.

- ▸ **Portfolio Management**
  Performed by product management covering product profitability analysis.

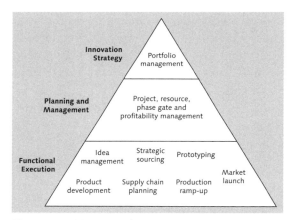

Figure 2.1 NPDI Pyramid

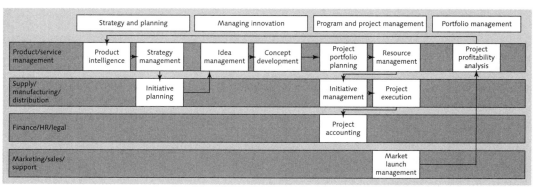

Figure 2.2 Continuous Product and Service Innovation

This chapter will explain all the processes and their implementable steps, with the exception of SAP Project Management, which will be explained in more detail in Chapter 7.

Let's turn our attention first to product strategy and planning.

2.1 Product Strategy and Planning

The product strategy and planning phase is covered by multiple SAP solutions. Table 2.1 provides an overview of the SAP product strategy and planning solutions. The first row explains the main function of the product, and the second row lists the product and release on which the following section is based.

Function	Product strategy and planning	Product roadmap	Product risk management	Product IP management
Product	SAP EPM Strategy Management Release 10.0	Future releases	SAP Risk Management; Release 10.0	SAP GRC Access Control and Process Control; Release 10.0

Table 2.1 Product Strategy and Planning Solutions

2.1.1 SAP Strategy Management

Product strategy and planning is also known as strategy management. A common theme among customers who want to use strategy management is a desire to close the gap between strategizing and executing the strategy. One contributing factor of this gap is that employees often don't understand how the company's strategy affects them or how their decisions impact others. As a result, decisions are made and actions are taken that are misaligned—or even in direct conflict with—the organization's direction.

Another possible reason for the gap is often that the management systems and processes in place don't adequately empower employees in the decision-making process, especially in terms of how their decisions align with the company's strategy. Too often, strategy is managed with inadequate tools that require too many manual steps and updates in spreadsheets, presentations, Word documents, and email. Ultimately, strategy management in general can help improve alignment with execution by providing an enabling platform.

The SAP Strategy Management solution is part of SAP Enterprise Performance Management (SAP EPM). The following benefits can be derived from using the SAP Strategy Management solution:

▶ Improved organizational alignment and clear accountability with insight regarding intelligently managing resources to ensure individuals understand how they can impact strategic goals and how they impact others

▶ Improved visibility into and control over the factors that affect your organization via an easy-to-use tool that supports scorecards, strategy management, and metrics management with drilldown capabilities

▶ Greater agility via more effective communication and understanding of changing strategic goals, initiatives, priorities, risk and interdependencies that enable you to respond quicker to changing business needs

▶ Improved analytics resulting in superior visualization so decisions can be made with confidence in a timely manner and so everyone works off the same data

▶ More accurate planning, which takes less effort because of the direct integration with SAP Business Planning and Consolidation (SAP BPC)

▶ Ability to demonstrate how an organization is performing toward its strategic goals by providing insights on strategic performance and areas that require action

▶ Supported distribution of administrative tasks to multiple people throughout the organization instead of just the IT staff to promote self-service so that every user can configure the application, perform user setup, and update KPIs and initiative creation with role-based, extended access

SAP Strategy Management offers functions for all three pillars of strategy management, which are represented in Figure 2.3.

1. **Goals and objectives**
   Improving performance, goal, and objective development must involve more stakeholders, be done interactively, get updated frequently, and tie to organizational operations and initiatives. You can define short-, medium-, and long-term strategies and communicate and cascade these strategies organization-wide to the right stakeholders. The application provides visualization of the strategy through strategy maps and strategy trees or by setting up a custom diagram, so you can motivate your employees toward organizational objectives.

2. **Initiatives**

   Project and initiative participants need better insight into the strategic relevance to make informed decisions and execute them in the right context. Through initiative management, you can manage execution towards goals, prioritize critical programs and resources to achieve objectives, highlight interdependencies, and drive accountability.

3. **Key performance indicators (KPIs)**

   Organizations need metrics that everyone trusts from a common source, complemented with the ability to drill down and personalize the views based on an individual's needs. The application allows you to drill down and set up exception analysis and provides multidimensional metrics for which you can either collect data automatically where available or set up manual data entry with workflow (e.g., customer satisfaction numbers). When using SAP GRC, you can integrate SAP Risk Management in the form of risk indicators.

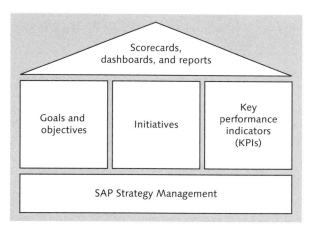

Figure 2.3 Three Pillars of Strategy Management

Across the top of Figure 2.3, you'll notice the "roof"—the ability to analyze the data via scorecards, dashboards, and reports. These can be used to support operational and strategy reviews, so you can measure, monitor, and manage progress. All of the data used comes from the same trusted source, which supports collaboration to provide the information in the right context. This allows you to create and communicate trustworthy management and executive reports quickly and in a standardized way.

SAP Strategy Management Business Process

A best practice for closed-loop performance management is the (Robert) Kaplan & (Dave) Norton Strategy Management approach, branded as the Palladium Execution Premium Process (XPP). What differentiates this approach from others (such as TQM, Six Sigma, and Malcolm Baldrige) is its focus on linking strategy formulation and managing the execution of the strategy.

SAP Strategy Management has solutions for every step in the process and has been designated as a Palladium Kaplan-Norton Balanced Scorecard Certified™ Software product, which indicates that it supports balanced scorecards that typically contain a mix of financial and nonfinancial objectives and associated performance measures.

SAP Strategy Management can be broken down into the following business process, as represented in Figure 2.4.

Figure 2.4 SAP Strategy Management Business Processes

Step 1: Develop the Strategy

The strategic management process begins with strategy development. During this step three areas need to be covered:

▶ **Identify mission (purpose) and vision (aspirations).**
Although this might seem obvious, it's important to understand what business you're in and why and to clarify the organization's purpose (mission), values, and aspirations (vision). These statements guide the rest of the strategy formulation process.

▶ **Conduct strategic analysis.**
You need to do a complete comprehensive analysis of the operating and competitive environment and any major changes that have occurred since the last planning process was undertaken to determine the key issues the company is facing and to identify risks to the organization. Accurate information about the profitability of products and customers is essential in this step, and you can use SAP BPC to get this information, particularly on actual versus plan data. Apart from understanding financial risks, you need to also look at both strategic risk (associated with your business objectives, such as growing revenue, containing

costs, or entering new markets) and execution risks (associated with the day-to-day tasks required to execute your strategies) to get a complete overall picture. You should define risk thresholds and risk tolerances for individual and combined risks, including your response strategies. Visibility into the rules and regulations that affect your industry, your region, and your operations plays an important role here and will lead to the development of an appropriate compliance framework and set of controls.

▶ **Formulate the strategy.**
When formulating the strategy, you'll understand what niche you serve, how you differentiate yourselves, and which key processes lead to this differentiation. You can determine the required human capital resources necessary and the enabling technology. Simply said, it will give you a clear understanding of how to best compete.

The strategy plan or diagram provides a means of communicating and explaining to all stakeholders the organizational mission and supporting objectives to achieving it. Figure 2.5 offers a fictitious strategy plan, showing the relationship between various strategic objectives critical to achieving the plan and telling the story of how together they help the organization achieve its overall mission. It's important to reflect the organization's intention accurately and make sure that it's worded in a way that is relevant and meaningful to the organizational stakeholders.

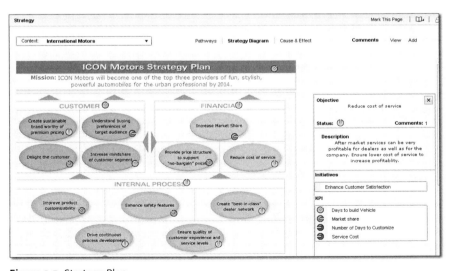

Figure 2.5 Strategy Plan

Step 2: Translate the Strategy

During this step, three areas need to be covered:

▶ **Map objective relationships and organize in strategic themes.**

Translating the strategy defined in step 1 involves defining objectives, KPIs, and initiatives. These can be included in the SAP Strategy Management system repository. The strategy itself is represented in a strategy map that typically contains around 25 objectives spread across 4 or 5 perspectives (usually financial, customer, internal process, and learning and growth) representing the different organizational viewpoints, and grouped into 4 to 6 strategic themes. The themes and context in which they are represented are completely configurable to your organizations requirements and could represent geographies, departments, business units, or any other type of segmentation you want to use.

Figure 2.6 shows an example of a strategy map in the overall context called INTERNATIONAL MOTORS, which has been configured based on this company's requirements.

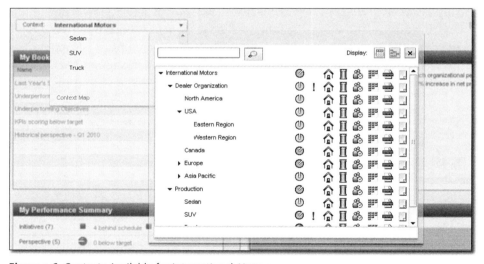

Figure 2.6 Contexts Available for International Motors

You can add *hotspots* to the strategy map, which when opened can provide more details on the objectives (e.g., the owner), description, associated KPIs, and any key risk indicators (KRIs) when using SAP Risk Management. This makes the strategy map more dynamic.

Next, a balanced scorecard is created that contains the objectives with measures and targets assigned to them. The strategy should address all aspects that influence the organization's success. The balanced scorecard helps by organizing the strategy into layers of different perspectives: financial, customer, internal processes, and learning and growth, of which Figure 2.7 is an example.

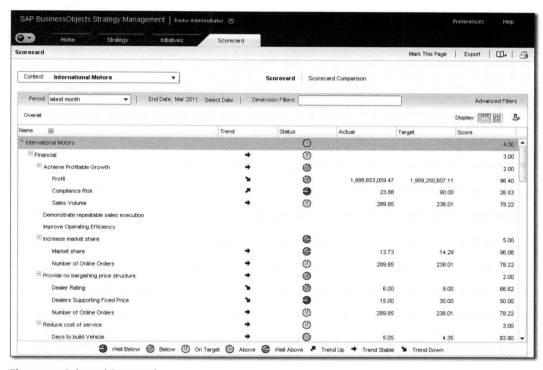

Figure 2.7 Balanced Scorecard

▶ **Adjust corporate objectives with embedded risk indicators and heatmaps.**
When you use SAP Risk Management, which defines and documents the policies and procedures necessary to address relevant risks and compliance issues, you can map the KRIs defined in SAP Risk Management to objectives in SAP Strategy Management and use the risk heatmaps.

▶ **Manage prioritized initiatives that have clear ownership and interdependencies.**
In the following step (align the organization), initiatives are created and associated with objectives. Initiatives are the strategic actions that need to occur to

achieve the performance goals. An initiative should include the high-level tasks critical to its success, the interdependencies between these tasks, and an indication of progress. At this time, you can assign cross-organizational or cross-functional teams to perform these tasks. All of the information about the initiative allows collaboration, helps identify bottlenecks, and enables proactive corrective action.

Figure 2.8 shows an overview of the initiatives that have been defined for the company INTERNATIONAL MOTORS, including MILESTONES OF FIRST INITIATIVES, that shows the interdependencies in a fishbone diagram. The initiative management capabilities in SAP Strategy Management aren't intended to replace lower-level project management applications but are intended to enable the management of high-level strategic initiatives easily from a single application.

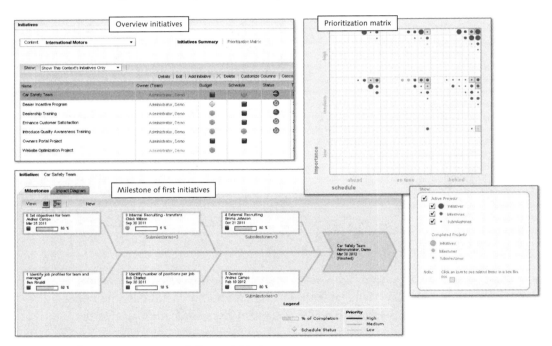

Figure 2.8 International Motors Initiatives

► **Visualize multi-year strategy and areas of focus.**
You can visualize your multi-year strategy and areas of focus by using the pathway, as shown in Figure 2.9. Well-defined pathways help organizations remain

true to their long-term vision to help ensure they will ultimately be successful in achieving it. Generally, it's best not to assign indicators of success or failure to pathways, as doing so automatically diverts attention away from the strategy itself, and people tend to get stuck in the details.

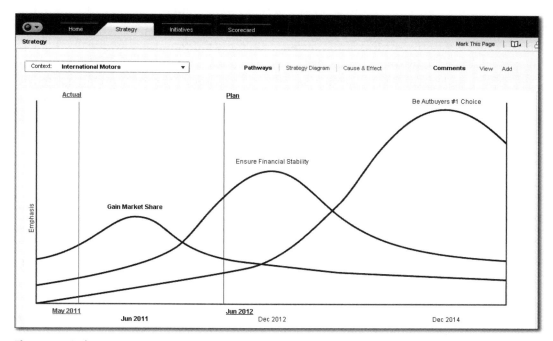

Figure 2.9 Pathway

Step 3: Align the Organization

You should include both the business units and shared services units in the overall corporate strategy and the business processes. The alignment step includes the following actions:

▶ **Vertically and horizontally align organizations with hierarchies of contexts.** Strategy is usually defined at the individual business unit level, cascading down from the overall corporate strategy. The corporate-level strategy defines how the strategies of the individual business units can be integrated to develop synergies otherwise unavailable to each individual business unit. This leads to each business unit owning its scorecard, which consists of objectives local to it, objectives that support higher level corporate objectives, and objectives that support other business units.

▶ **Align support units with overall strategy for maximum impact.**
It's important not to overlook the role of support units, such as IT or facility management, in the strategy. These support units should align their strategy and operations with those of the business units they support to ensure the most efficient use of the resources and capabilities available. Ideally, the support units and the business units negotiate and agree on the service level, which will lead to the viewing of the support units as service providers contributing to the organization's performance. The negative impacts of the unavailability of these services due to unplanned events should be considered, so SAP Risk Management plays a role because risk scenarios should be developed, exposure determined, and historical losses analyzed. Note that integration with SAP GRC is necessary to cover both areas.

▶ **Drive consistency and communicate strategy.**
Alignment of the business processes toward the company's strategy is important. Especially because the employees who are working on process improvements should understand the strategy and align their daily activities to this strategy. Communication and training play a key role when making sure the employees understand the strategy and motivating them to act upon it.

▶ **Assign ownership and accountability.**
Using the KPI library means that the definitions, objectives, and KPIs are shared and measured in the same manner across the organization. A KPI may have a common definition but be measured differently for a given context. Or an objective may exist in multiple contexts but be measured by different KPIs. Assigning objectives, KPIs, and initiatives to the responsible owner, such as a business unit or a project team, will provide clear ownership and will drive accountability. Figure 2.10 shows examples of ownership for an initiative and a KPI.

▶ **Reveal contributions and problem areas using comparisons.**
By using scorecards, you can easily compare business or support units performance, either against overall performance or against benchmarks. To compare against benchmarks, you need to set up a context representing the benchmark and compare performance to it in the same way you would with any other context.

Figure 2.10 Accountability

Step 4: Plan Operations

During the planning phase, the objectives are translated into specific plans that require resources and inputs. After the key process for improvement has been identified, the operating plan should be created, which consists of the following components: a sales forecast, marketing expenses, workforce plans, administrative expenses, and capital expenditures. Source KPI (actual and target) and initiative (actual and budget) data can be provided via integration with SAP BPC. During execution, performance results are monitored and actions are defined to improve operations as well as revise strategic plans based on new information and lessons. During execution, other applications under SAP EPM can be used to support monitoring and to help the organization do the following:

▶ Build proactive monitoring into business processes and strategies.

▶ Report risk exposure as well as specific incidents and losses.

▶ Monitor and evaluate response effectiveness and completeness.

Step 5: Monitor and Learn

The integration between SAP Strategy Management and SAP Risk Management allows you to adjust planning attempts to identify the risks that affect the plans and then show the range of possible outcomes based on varying levels of risk. It's important to develop appropriate risk responses, and resolution strategies for the top risks need to be in place. These should include process controls, procedures for transfer of responsibility, and approval cycles. Automatic controls can help ensure policies are followed, while eliminating human error and testing effectiveness can be done on a regular basis.

This monitor and learn step represents the transition from planning to executing strategy to ensure that progress is monitored on a regular basis. Routine reviews of both operations and strategy take place, in which information and insights from SAP Strategy Management are used as a basis. Systematically tracking implementation progress and alerting stakeholders effectively identifies both problems and failures, as well as showing bright spots and successes, so stakeholders can identify what is working well in one area and consider these methods for other groups. Generally, operational reviews focus on short-term performance and responses to issues requiring immediate attention, whereas strategic reviews focus on discussions about KPIs and progress on initiatives that are part of the business unit's balanced scorecard. During the operational and strategic review meetings, problems, barriers, and challenges are analyzed.

To monitor progress, organizations should associate KPIs with each objective. KPIs are quantifiable performance measures explicitly linked to an objective and a relevant and useful means of measuring performance, which provides stakeholders with a common set of metrics to measure performance and drive consistency. KPIs should include three critical components:

► **Actual**
  The organization's current status.

► **Target**
  The predetermined benchmark the organization wants to achieve.

► **Performance gap**
  The delta between actual and target.

Both leading and lagging indicators of performance should be incorporated. Leading indicators are drivers of future performance (such as employee morale and brand recognition), whereas lagging indicators measure end results and are the outcome of past actions (such as revenue, costs, and market share). You can visually portray the impact a specific initiative has had on a KPI. Scorecards provide an intuitive, high-level overview of ongoing progress to help employees easily and quickly understand the current performance status. Scorecards are ideal for casual users who are not interested in the details.

Dashboards, on the other hand, provide a visual of the most important information needed to achieve one or more objectives and are used to visually communicate progress on multiple key metrics. Dashboards become truly valuable when you drill down into dimensions to identify the source of issues. For example, you can drill into greater levels of KPI detail when using SAP Strategy Management and complementary SAP BusinessObjects BI tools.

Within SAP Strategy Management, you can start a discussion and capture findings within the appropriate context. By using scoreboards and other visual insight tools, you have a quick overview of performance and can identify the source of the issue "anomaly." Figure 2.11 gives an example of starting a discussion from within SAP Strategy Management that contains the link to the context.

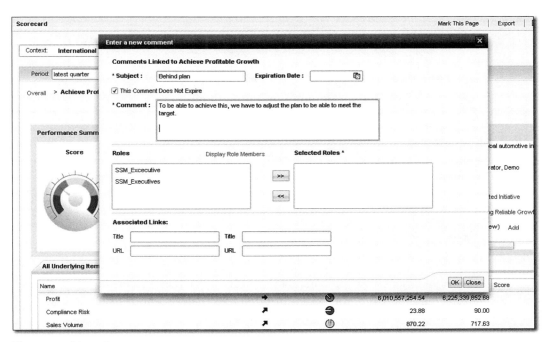

Figure 2.11 Discussion

To perform more detailed analysis and set up drill-down capabilities into KPIs, you need to integrate other SAP EPM applications, as well as use additional quantitative and qualitative data concerning external factors. To enable this, organizations must translate strategy into quantifiable terms. Even "soft" or intangible objectives (e.g., "Establish customer intimacy" or "Improve employee satisfaction") need to be made measurable or SMART (specific, measurable, achievable, realistic, and time-specific). Measure them periodically, and compare the results against the levels sought by management. Figure 2.12 shows you how you can drill down on a KPI.

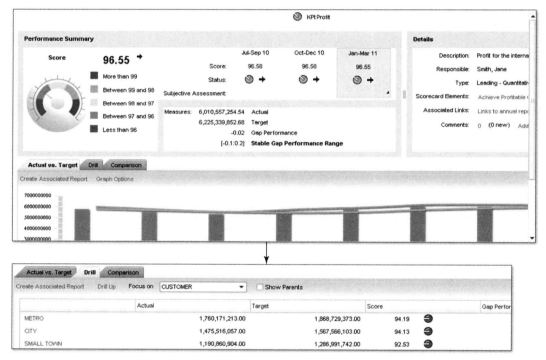

Figure 2.12 Drilling Down on KPI

The reviews can be supported by SAP Strategy Management by electronically assembling review documents as PDF files. In PDF files, screenshots can be used, annotated, and even embedded in other external documents such as Microsoft Office documents or SAP BusinessObjects Dashboards visualizations.

Risk monitoring can take place by the use of dashboards, which help to answer the following key questions:

▶ What and where are the top risks?

▶ How much have risk levels changed for key activities/opportunities?

▶ Have incidents and losses occurred?

▶ Are we assessing risks in accordance with our policies?

Automatic monitoring of KRIs allows you to, for example, automatically send process owners an email when thresholds get crossed. Effective risk management should also document "occurred risks" or "external events" along with causes, related costs, and owners, which in turn helps to better estimate risks in the future. You can also create and manage subjective assessments associated with KPIs and objectives, which provide an effective way to communicate potential risks.

Step 6: Test and Adapt

Periodically, the executive team will need to meet to determine whether the strategy is working or needs revising. Testing and adapting the strategy means you're constantly alert to internal and external factors that require attention and you're revising the strategy to account for these factors. If revising the strategy is deemed necessary as a result of this meeting, the strategy within SAP Strategy Management will need to be updated (including updating the lower-level planning solutions).

As a result, we begin another lap around the cyclical model, starting at step 2: translate the strategy.

We recommend that you provide additional what-if analysis, which involves two steps:

1. **Use scenario modeling.**
   Through scenario modeling, you can see the impacts of changes by setting a minimum base and a high and low case based on adjustments made to various inputs such as market growth, costs, and exchange rates. Monte Carlo simulation, for example, takes this even further and looks at a broader range of scenarios. Using this technique, you can assign probabilities to various outcomes, which means you can estimate the uncertainly of a given forecast; for example, we can be 70% certain of a minimum outcome of zero escalations.

2. **Add and prioritize initiatives based on current performance.**
   In the main INITIATIVES area, you can add new and update existing initiatives. You can quickly enter or edit the description, owner, progress, and expenditure as well as which objectives this initiative supports. Note that when integrated with SAP BPC, the actual and budget values can be automatically updated and pulled from other operational systems, where integration to SAP products in this area such as SAP Project System (SAP PS) and or SAP Project and Portfolio Management (PPM) are fully supported. You can also set links to external documents or websites and notify team members when they get assigned to an initiative.

2.1.2 SAP Governance, Risk, and Compliance

Governance, risk, and compliance is one of those topics that, when not addressed appropriately, can lead to disastrous problems, including brand management damage and negative exposure for your organization.

Customers find that implementing a governance, risk, and compliance solution can be very time-consuming and resource-intensive and still expose the organization to undue risk. But SAP can provide you with a framework that leverages existing system data and provides you with an integrated approach to governance, risk, and compliance. These issues can be addressed by using SAP GRC technology, which allows you to better manage your risk, compliance, and other initiatives by automating previously manual and time-consuming tasks and by leveraging accumulated knowledge from numerous installations. The purpose and scope is to operate in an open architecture to allow integration to third-party applications and use of any device (such as iPhone, iPad, Blackberry, Android devices, etc.) to access data. In an SAP-dominant environment, a true advantage of using the SAP GRC application is its out-of-the-box integration.

Figure 2.13 shows the importance of an integrated approach to the governance, risk, and compliance convergence.

SAP GRC provides processes for the following areas: SAP Risk Management, SAP Compliance Management, SAP Policy Management, SAP Access Control, and SAP Process Control. It also provides functions regarding SAP Global Trade Services and Nota Fiscal Electronica (SAP NFE), which are outside the scope of this book. Performing audits or audit management is done in conjunction with SAP GRC solutions, but this process is more an operational execution process and so will be described in more detail in Chapter 6.

Besides the SAP NFE (which is an electronic invoicing solution for Brazil), all of these products are used in SAP PLM and will be explained in more detail in the rest of this section (with the exception of audit management, which is discussed in Chapter 6). However, before we can go into the details of each of these processes, we need to briefly describe the compliance framework and the central master data model used within SAP GRC areas. Before doing this, we'll describe an integrated example of the use of several SAP GRC products to help you understand the integration between the products. The use and implementation of the SAP GRC products has been described with the assumption that you use SAP ERP as the main backend system, but be aware that these products also can be implemented in conjunction with other products or even as stand-alone solutions.

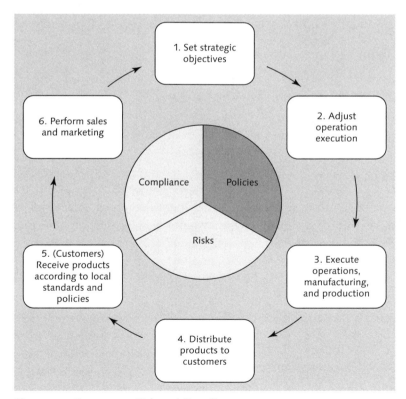

Figure 2.13 Governance, Risk, and Compliance

Let's consider an example of an integrated approach and an example of a risk in which SAP Risk Management, SAP Access Control, SAP Process Control, and central functions are used in an integrated manner. Figure 2.14 shows an integrated approach, where all different parts of the SAP GRC solution are being used to detect and prevent fraud related to the procure-to-pay process.

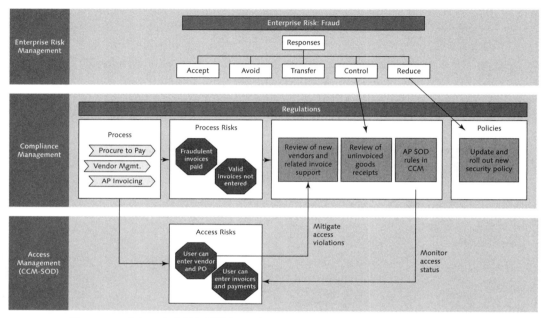

Figure 2.14 Integrated SAP GRC Example

Within SAP Processes Control, this company has identified a significant risk of fraud during the procure-to-pay process within vendor management and booking invoices processes. Two process risks have been identified:

▶ Fraudulent invoices paid
▶ Valid invoices not entered

Two access risks have been identified:

▶ When user can enter a vendor and a purchase order
▶ When user can enter invoices and payments

Several types of risk responses are possible to mitigate the risk, such as accept the risk, avoid it, transfer it, control it, or reduce it. Within the example, the company has chosen a mixed approach to control the risk by introduction of access and process controls and monitoring them and to reduce the risk through updating the security policy.

- **SAP Access Control**
  The controls include the use of SAP Access Control, which can be used to prevent most segregation of duties (SoD) conflicts, which are often stipulated in SoD regulations such as the Sarbanes-Oxley (SOX) act and the Gramm-Leach-Bliley Act (GLBA). Where SoD violations are identified, one or more mitigating controls are put in place. You can, for example, put a control in place to check when a user has access to enter both the vendor and a purchase order. Another control can be to check whether a user can enter both invoices and payments. In addition, an automated control can be set up to monitor the status of the access risk in SAP Access Control when linked to existing controls within SAP Process Control.

- **SAP Process Control**
  Process controls can be assessed or tested to ensure appropriate design and effectiveness. Process controls can be linked to access controls and monitored together.

- **Policies**
  To reduce the risk of fraud, the security policy can be managed within the common SAP Policy Management component, which can include acknowledgments or quizzes to determine policy effectiveness.

In any given organization, it's possible that several different compliance groups are responsible for managing compliance of various regulatory requirements and policies. The organization of these groups will drive how these initiatives are managed within SAP Process Control. Usually, companies start with a decentralized approach, where they operate in separate silos and use independent solutions, and neither data nor processes information is shared among them. When they mature in their compliance management processes, they start to streamline activities and to centralize and share master data by sharing the same central organization structures, central processes, or central control structure.

Table 2.2 gives the benefits of the different compliance management maturity models, starting with independent solutions for compliance at the top of the table, and moving to a more mature, integrated, and centralized solution at the bottom. Based on your choice of compliance model, the following benefits can be expected when moving from one model to the next model. The benefits actually accumulate; that is, the benefits from the previous framework are also still valid when you move to the next model.

Compliance Model	Benefits
Independent solution	▸ Separate methodologies and compliance management practices ▸ Several IT solutions
Silos	▸ Reduced IT costs ▸ Faster adoption of new requirements ▸ Visibility of all compliance initiatives from a single source ▸ Common training materials for all teams using the solution
Hybrid	▸ Reduction of data redundancy and multiple maintenance activities ▸ Shared control evaluations reduces number of tests and assessments ▸ Reporting across similar compliance initiatives possible
Centralized	▸ Global/central compliance office that aligns compliance initiatives with corporate strategy ▸ Centralized data management further drives operational efficiencies and consistency ▸ Running centralized reporting across all initiatives and doing centralized testing and monitoring of the controls across all projects/initiatives

Table 2.2 Benefits of Compliance Models

Figure 2.15 shows the impact each compliance management maturity model has on the master data and the efforts required to maintain it.

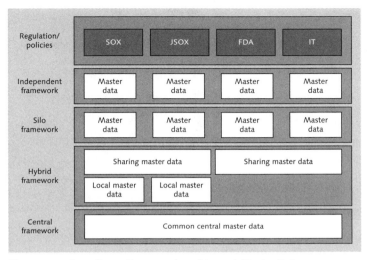

Figure 2.15 Compliance Framework and Impact Master Data

2.1.3 Central Master Data GRC

Central master data is relevant for the entire company. Table 2.3 gives you a high-level view of the master data objects used in SAP GRC 10.0 solution. Although not intended to represent all possible master data objects, it should give you an understanding of which master data objects are used in SAP GRC and in the different parts of the solution.

SAP Process Control— Risk Management	SAP GRC	SAP Access Control
▶ Organization ▶ Regulation* ▶ Process ▶ Subprocess/activity ▶ Risk* ▶ Control	▶ Organization* ▶ User* ▶ Role* ▶ Subprocess/activity* ▶ Business process* ▶ Control* ▶ Control extensions: Risk/user/action	▶ Business unit ▶ User ▶ Role ▶ Business process ▶ Subprocess ▶ Mitigation control ▶ Risk/user/action ▶ Access risk* ▶ Access rule*

Table 2.3 Central Master Data

> **Note**
>
> The master data objects for organization, processes, and control structures are shown with an asterisk because as central objects, they are shared to support a more integrated approach to governance, risk, and compliance. Control extensions are used to expand the control entity so it can be used for different purposes.

Organizational hierarchy represents your company's organizational structure for the purposes of internal controls. It impacts analysis and reporting requirements. Organizational structures can be based on legal entities, geographical entities, functional or business units, or other structures used within your company such as profit centers, divisions, and plants. The example in Figure 2.16 shows the hierarchy and corresponding details.

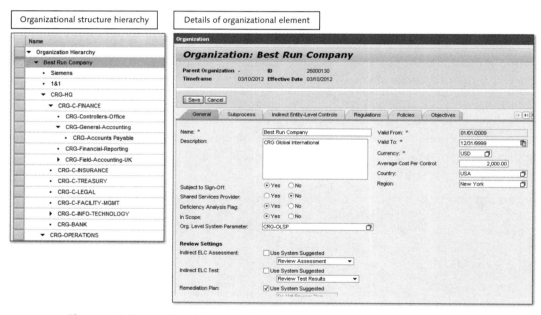

Figure 2.16 Organizational Structure Hierarchy

A *process* refers to a predetermined sequence of steps that needs to be undertaken to produce a specific business outcome, including the business decisions that have to be undertaken and the flow of materials and information. The *central process hierarchy* represents the structure of your processes and subprocesses with the related control objective/risk and account group assignment. These processes and subprocesses are displayed hierarchically in Figure 2.17 and in an example in Figure 2.18.

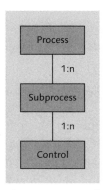

Figure 2.17 Central Process Hierarchy

Process Structure	
Date 03/11/2012 🔲 Apply Advanced Create ▲ Open Delete Ac	
Name	**Type**
▼ Process Structure	
▶ Financial Accounting (FAS 133)	Process
▶ Financial Close Process	Process
▶ Good Manufacturing Practice	Process
▼ Health & Safety	Process
▼ Monitoring EH&S Laws and Regulations	Subprocess
▪ H&S - Health and Safety Mgt Checklist	Control
▪ H&S - Monitoring of Submissions	Control
▶ Competence Training and Awareness	Subprocess
▶ Emergency Preparedness and Response	Subprocess
▶ HR and Payroll	Process
▶ Information Technology	Process
▶ IT General Controls	Process
▼ Logistics	Process
▼ Marine Chartering	Subprocess
▪ LOG - 10 + 2 Compliance	Control
▶ Nomination Setup, Monitoring, etc.	Subprocess
▼ NPDI	Process
▪ Product Development	Subprocess

Figure 2.18 Process Structure Example

To start immediately with the implementation of automated rule functionality, you may find it useful to set up the following processes: financial close, procure-to-pay, order-to-cash, and system configuration. This is because SAP Process Control includes delivered rules to support automated testing and control monitoring for these processes. So you can choose either to use these as samples and tailor them based on your own specific requirements or to start from scratch.

The *account group hierarchy* shown in Figure 2.19 represents the relationship of accounts with related assertions and risks. You should create account groups that are relevant for your company's compliance initiatives and designate them as significant for tracking and reporting and document the reason behind this.

Then you need to define financial assertions that are relevant to your account groups and assign the risk to the financial assertions. Financial assertions are declarations made by management about the significant accounts reported on their financial statements. According to SOX, an account is significant if there is a reasonable possibility that a misstatement in the account would have a material impact on the financial statements. For the purposes of SOX, the Public Company Accounting and Oversight Board (PCAOB) in the standard No.5 (AS5) as of August 2007 names the financial assertions as completeness, existence or occurrence, rights and obligations, valuation or allocation, presentation, and disclosure. You can use as-is or configure Business Configuration Sets (BC Sets) to provide these financial assertions.

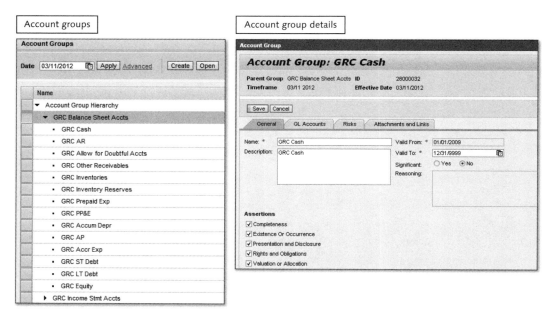

Figure 2.19 Account Group Hierarchy and Details

The *control objective hierarchy* represents your company's control objectives and related risks. They can be created through the compliance structure work center and have validity dates to support time-dependent reporting. After creation, they should be assigned to the subprocesses to indicate control objectives that should be supported by controls within the subprocess. The left side of Figure 2.20 shows an example of an objective hierarchy. Later, risks and parent control objectives will be assigned to individual controls to indicate which objectives are actually met and which risks are actually mitigated by controls within the subprocess. The difference between what should be supported/mitigated and what is actually supported is the basis for the gap reporting.

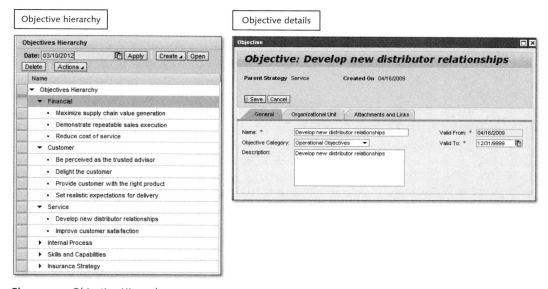

Figure 2.20 Objective Hierarchy

Risk and Risk Classifications

Catalogs enable you to collect data (KRIs) for risks, opportunities, and responses in a uniform way, which allows you to better analyze and report on the data. Figure 2.21 shows examples of these catalogs. You can use KRIs as early warning signals (e.g., lending exposure versus limits, customer complaints, systems availability).

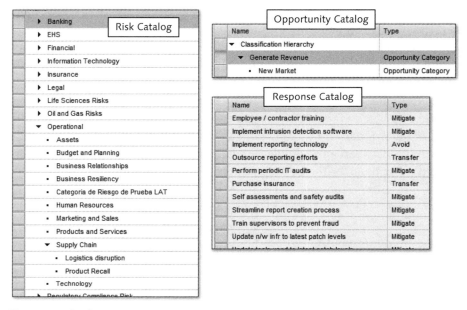

Figure 2.21 Catalogs

Policy and Regulations

Regulation master data is relevant to the regulation and is organization-dependent. Within each regulation, the process and subprocess assignments are made to an organization and include the following:

▶ Organization-dependent processes

▶ Organization-dependent subprocesses

▶ Organization-dependent controls

There are several policy- and regulation-related terms you should know:

▶ **Regulation**
This term refers to legislation that constitutes or constrains rights and allocates responsibilities, which can be followed by sanctions when businesses don't comply. A regulation is a legal restriction imposed by the government authority, self-regulation of an industry such as through a trade association, social regulations (norms), or market regulations.

▶ **Policy**

This term is a set of principles used as a guide for action, especially in a government or business. It's government policy to identify, reduce, or eliminate risks to its property, interests, and employees; to minimize and contain the costs and consequences in the event of harmful or damaging incidents arising from those risks; and to provide for adequate and timely compensation, restoration, and recovery.

Figure 2.22 shows how a regulation and policy is classified, including example data.

▶ **Procedures**

This term refers to a series of actions necessary for accomplishing a particular goal.

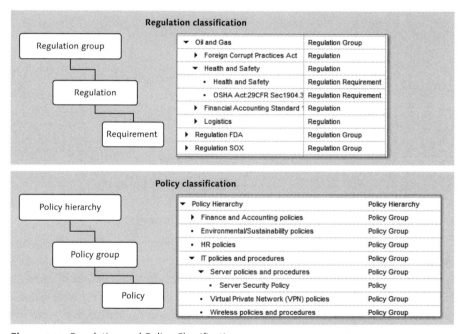

Figure 2.22 Regulation and Policy Classification

Master Data Creation Process

The creation of master data is supported with the process shown in Figure 2.23. Because it's a standard process, we won't go into substantial detail here.

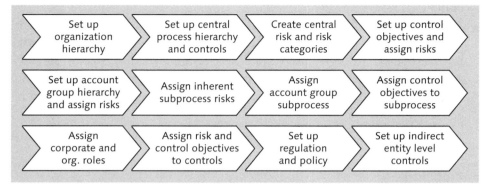

Figure 2.23 Creation of Master Data

Content Lifecycle Management

A common function (together with SAP Policy Management and the ad hoc issues) is Content Lifecycle Management (CLM), which enables mass import, export, and editing of master data content. It supports third-party content deployment through comparison to existing customer content. This external content can be imported when first starting to use the SAP GRC solution, based on data from legacy systems, or it could be used when content is developed and made available via third parties. After you have imported the data into CLM, you can review it, mass edit the data, resolve any conflicts that might exist with the current data, and decide what to deploy to SAP Risk Management and SAP Process Control.

2.1.4   Product Compliance and Policy Management

Product governances and compliance is covered in the two common functions available within the SAP GRC solution: SAP Policy Management and ad hoc issues management. SAP Compliance Management provides documentation of compliance structures and related compliance initiatives. Scoping your activities based on their risk focuses control evaluation efforts on those control activities with the greatest likelihood of failure and potential negative impacts on your organization. You can evaluate compliance by setting up self-assessments and management assessments through custom surveys and testing activities or automated tests using business rules. If exceptions are identified during these evaluations, issues are created and assigned for remediation, and users determine appropriate next steps.

SAP Policy Management

SAP Policy Management provides end-to-end management of corporate policies aligned with SAP Risk Management and SAP Compliance Management, including creation, localization, distribution, and acknowledgement. SAP Policy Management is a common function available to SAP GRC customers using Process Management and/or SAP Risk Management.

The supported process for SAP Policy Management is represented in Figure 2.24 and described in the following set of steps.

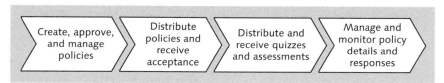

Figure 2.24 SAP Policy Management Process

1. **Create, approve, and manage policies.**
   During this first step, create the policy and attach the actual policy if necessary. You determine the scope of the policy by assigning it to the organization, processes or activities, and stakeholders involved, including linking the policy to control(s). When using SAP Risk Management, you can also assign controls or risks to the policy. Figure 2.25 shows an example of a policy.

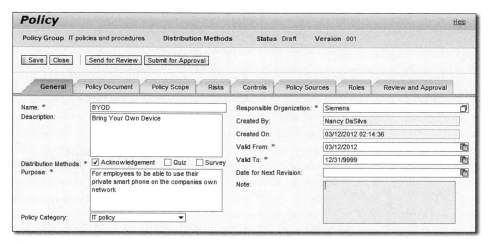

Figure 2.25 Policy

2. **Distribute policies and receive acceptance.**
   In this step, you can distribute the policy to those affected via email. If desired, you can monitor their formal acceptance or acknowledgement. Because policies may be widely distributed through your organization, a logon isn't required to receive the policy or to acknowledge receiving it.

3. **Distribute and receive quizzes and assessments.**
   You can assess the policy recipients' understanding of the policy by giving them questionnaires or quizzes via email.

4. **Manage and monitor policy details and responses.**
   The policy details and follow-up actions can be monitored, like the results of the acknowledgement step, and assessments will be stored and can be used to report against.

Ad Hoc Issues

Another common function is ad hoc issue management. This function lets you identify, remediate, and track issues that aren't the result of scheduled compliance evaluations. Examples are external audit findings, issues discovered by inspections, and problems reported by individuals who aren't part of the formal compliance process.

Figure 2.26 shows the ad hoc issue management process and the steps are described in the following list.

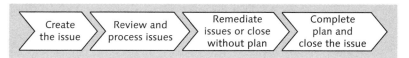

Figure 2.26 Ad Hoc Issue Management Process

1. **Create the issue.**
   You identify and create the issue, as shown in Figure 2.27. You can fill out details such as the associated business entities (e.g., organizations), assign a source (configurable) of the issue risks (such as opportunity, incident, response, KRI), or configure regulations and control, which is specifically important when it comes to enterprise risk management. When you create an issue regarding compliance, it's important to assign it to a control, process, subprocess, regulation, and organization. When the details are incomplete, a

review process step takes place; when the details are complete, remediation starts immediately.

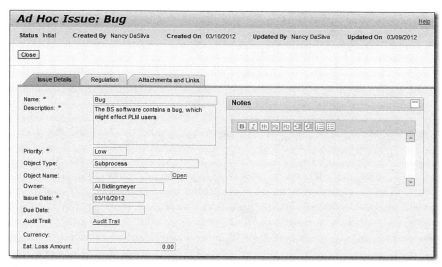

Figure 2.27 Ad Hoc Issue

2. **Review and process issues.**
   If the data is incomplete after the identification of an issue, it will be sent to an issue administrator for review, completion, and assignment.

3. **Remediate issues or close without plan.**
   The remediation can take place, which is very similar to the remediation as discussed in SAP Process Control.

4. **Complete plan and close the issue.**
   This step eventually leads to the issue being closed.

2.1.5 Product Risk Management with SAP GRC

A *risk* is defined as an event that may result in a significant deviation from a planned objective that results in an unwanted, negative consequence. A risk is defined by three parameters:

▸ Existence of a threat for a business process

▸ Likelihood of occurrence

▸ Impact on the business process/product/service

Through the SAP Risk Management process you can identify, mitigate, and monitor critical business risks that may have a negative impact on an organization's performance, goals, and objectives. Via enterprise risk management, you can prioritize scarce resources to mitigate the company's highest risk areas. The complete picture of risk management, in general, is to reach your company's objectives by putting a business model(s) in place that provides processes, products, and services in alignment with those objectives. During all business activities, the company needs to ensure its compliance to both external regulations and laws and its internal policies.

> **Note**
>
> Risks are often confused with hazards. Whereas a risk relates to the likelihood that being exposed to the hazard will cause harm, a *hazard* is a source or a situation with a potential for harm in terms of human injury or ill health, damage to property, damage to the environment, or a combination of these. Risks may have a positive or negative impact.

This section focuses specifically on product risk management, and it will be described with product risk management as guidance (though remember that SAP GRC does cover risks in all areas).

SAP GRC technologies provide an integrated or holistic approach to enterprise risk management to understanding and managing all the different types of risks an organization faces. The main purpose of SAP Risk Management is to improve the quality of decision making by making risks and their interdependencies insightful and therefore decreasing the likelihood that your organization gets surprised by events that, in hindsight, could have been predicted and prevented. It provides a common risk framework and risk management information system.

Data Model for SAP Risk Management

Before going into the supported SAP Risk Management process, it's important to understand the data model of SAP Risk Management, which appears in Figure 2.28. On the right-hand side, you see all of the master data catalog objects. Starting with the OBJECTIVE HIERARCHY (top right), which represents on the top level numerous strategies, on the next level, the strategic initiatives are followed by the objectives. The ACTIVITY HIERARCHY represents all of the risk-bearing business activities, such as processes, initiatives, projects, and new products, which can be grouped in activity categories. The risk and opportunity classification contains the basic entities of SAP Risk Management and can be used to categorize risk and opportunities. All of these master data objects were explained in more detail earlier in the chapter.

On the left side of Figure 2.28, you see the actual application data objects (such as the ORGANIZATION STRUCTURE) and a shared master data element between SAP Risk Management and SAP Process Control: the business ACTIVITIES and the RISKS AND OPPORTUNITIES, which are shaded. The relationships between the catalog objects and the real objects are represented by dotted lines. When identifying risks, you can either assign them to an activity or to an organizational unit, where when using activities, they help structure the SAP Risk Management data and provide an additional reporting dimension.

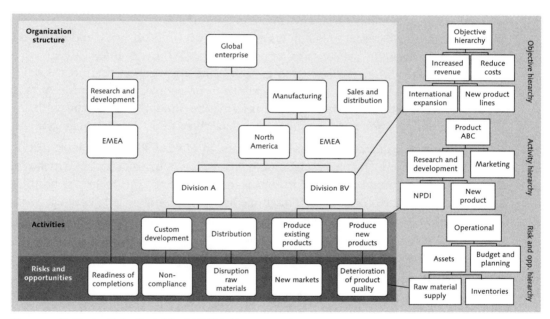

Figure 2.28 Master Data Model for SAP Risk Management

Let's consider the SAP Risk Management process, which is shown in Figure 2.29 and described in the steps following.

Figure 2.29 SAP Risk Management Process

1. **Perform risk planning.**

   During the risk planning process, you determine which business activities need to be reviewed, the risk threshold levels set up, and SAP Risk Management participants defined. You set the goals, objectives, strategies, scope, and parameters of the activity or part of the organization to which SAP Risk Management is being applied. You also specify the nature of the decision that needs to be made as a result of the SAP Risk Management activity. The depth and breadth of the SAP Risk Management activities needs to be defined, including specific inclusions and exclusions.

   It's important to understand both the external and internal context for the SAP Risk Management activity. External context can, for example, include the business environment, social environment, and regulatory environment. You can identify the external stakeholders and the key business drivers, and perform a SWOT (strengths, weaknesses, opportunities, and threats) analysis. When diving into the internal context, things such as the organization's culture, its stakeholders, its structure, and the capabilities of people, system, process, and capital must be understood. This information should provide you with the right information to set up the master data objects for SAP Risk Management.

   An example of a business activity relevant within SAP PLM is the introduction of a new product. During planning, you develop your risk criteria, which represent the criteria against which risk is to be evaluated. This forms the basis for the rest of the process, and it might be useful to subdivide the chosen activity/process/project into smaller parts to provide a logical framework that helps ensure significant risks aren't overlooked. This can, for example, be a project work breakdown structure, product introduction plan, or a process map.

2. **Identify and analyze the risk.**

   When identifying a risk, it's important to understand the drivers, the events that could cause the risk to occur, the impact, and the consequences if the risk were to occur. This information can be summarized in a Risk Bow Tie Model, shown in Figure 2.30. The left-hand side shows the drivers of a risk, and the right-hand side shows the impact.

   A risk can be assigned to an organizational unit directly or via the use of an activity to the organizational unit. Figure 2.31 provides an example.

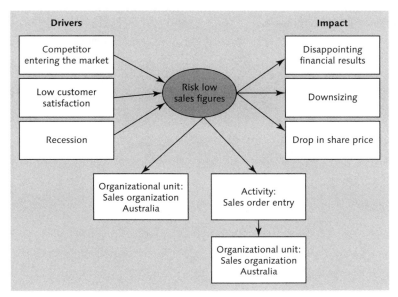

Figure 2.30 Example of Risk Bow Tie Model

After risks have been identified, you can perform analysis. Approaches used to identify risk include checklists, judgments based on experience, records, flow charts, brainstorming, system analysis, scenario analysis, and system engineering techniques.

SAP Risk Management offers surveys (Activity Survey, Risk Survey, and Risk Indicator Survey), which can be a useful way to collect risk information necessary for decision making. During risk analysis, the sources of the risk, their consequences, and the likelihood that those consequences may occur should be analyzed. You can perform three types of analysis:

▶ **Inherent risk analysis**
The likelihood and impact of the risk with the existing response measures in place.

▶ **Residual risk analysis**
The likelihood and impact of the risk with additional response measures put in place.

▶ **Planned residual risk analysis**
The target likelihood and impact required for the risk level to be acceptable.

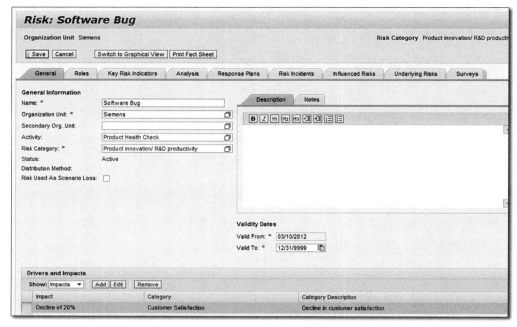

Figure 2.31 Example of Risk and Impacts

A risk level matrix is generally used to convert the likelihood and impact of the risk into risk levels, which in turn help prioritize risk and provide a means of linking the risk with an appropriate management action. Figure 2.32 provides an example.

Risk impact + risk probability = risk level

Analysis

Create ▲ | Analysis: 03/11/2012 - New ▼ | Undo New Analysis | Analysis Profile

Analysis Type	Probability (%)	Probability Level	Probability Score	Total Loss	Impact Level	Impact Score	Expected Loss	Risk Level	Risk Score
Inherent Risk	95	Certain	100	50,000.00 EUR	Insignificant	10	47,500.00 EUR	Low	55

Risk Matrix

Risk Level		Risk Impact				
		Insignificant	Minor	Moderate	Major	Catastrophic
Risk Probability	Certain					1
	Likely				3	3
	Possibily			1	4	1
	Unlikely		1	1		
	More					

Figure 2.32 Risk Matrix

Techniques used during risk analysis are structured interviews with experts or other multidisciplinary groups of experts in the subject area, individual evaluations using questionnaires, and models and simulations. Risk grouping and risk-intern relationships can be used to perform scenario analysis (a scenario is a story used to describe plausible future risk and associated impacts) and Monte Carlo analysis (assigning variables at random, originated in casinos to determine variables for betting games).

To plan and perform assessments and tests, you have to understand the four different types of evaluation procedures that are available for evaluation purposes:

- Assessment
- Manual tests
- Automated control compliance test
- Automated control monitoring

The risk assessment process is supported as shown Figure 2.33; recall that it's a subprocess of SAP Risk Management process step 2: identify and analyze risk.

Figure 2.33 Plan and Perform Assessments and Tests

- **Planning a risk assessment**
  Through the planner, you can schedule an assessment, which can be done either as one assessment or a periodic plan. The planner will guide you through the different steps necessary to create the plan, which are ENTER PLAN DETAILS • SELECT ORGANIZATION • SELECT OBJECT(S) • REVIEW • CONFIRMATION. Figure 2.34 shows the first two steps.

- **Performing assessments and tests**
  In this step (Figure 2.35), you actually perform assessments and tests.

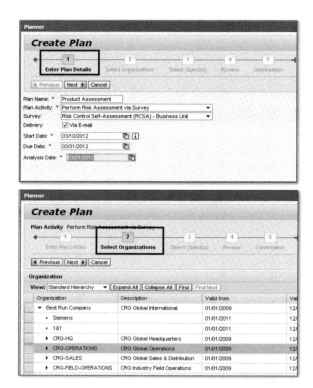

Figure 2.34 Create Assessment Plan: Steps 1 and 2

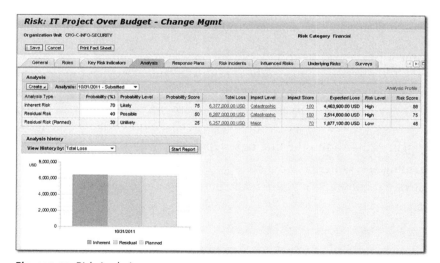

Figure 2.35 Risk Analysis

► **Testing strategy**

Based on the risk level determined during the assessment, you can set up a test strategy method, which determines the test strategy and level of evidence (see Figure 2.36).

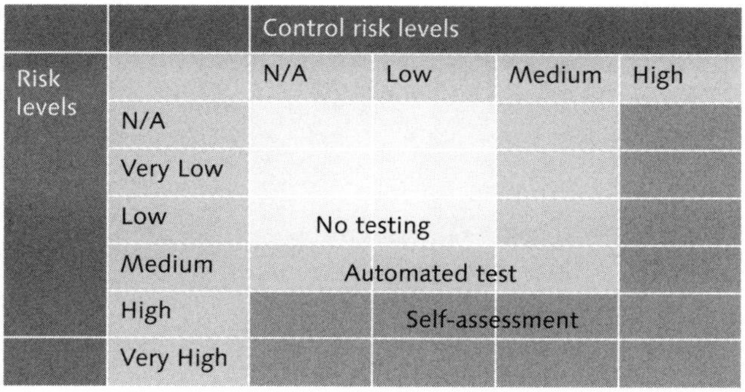

Risk levels	Control risk levels			
	N/A	Low	Medium	High
N/A				
Very Low				
Low	No testing			
Medium	Automated test			
High	Self-assessment			
Very High				

Figure 2.36 Level of Evidence Resulting in the Test Strategy

3. **Create a risk response.**

After identifying and analyzing the risk, you need to determine the necessary response to this risk, also referred to as the *decision measure*. You can use a response available in the catalog, add a new response, and/or assign a control to a risk, which is either a process step or task performed as part of the routine business operations with the purpose of mitigating the risk. Figure 2.37 shows an example of the response plans in place for the risk PROJECT OVER BUDGET; you'll find them in the RESPONSE PLANS tab.

Possible options for treating risks with negative outcomes include the following:

► Risk reduction by changing the likelihood

► Avoidance by deciding not to start or carry on with the activity due to its risk

► Transferring or sharing risk with another party, which can be done by the use of contracts, insurances, or by partnerships and joint ventures to spread responsibility and liability

► Accepting or retaining the risk; you can choose to accept the risk partly by sharing the risk with another party, such as when there is a failure to identify, share, or treat the risk

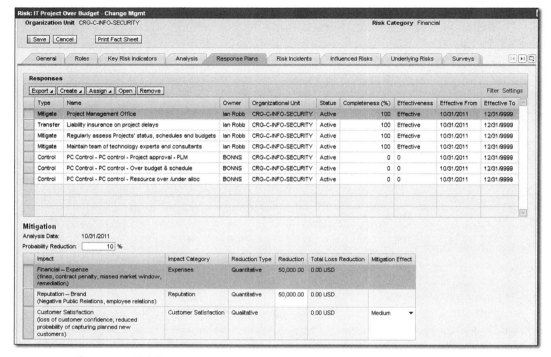

Figure 2.37 Risk Responses

4. **Monitor risks.**

During risk monitoring, you implement response actions, monitor the effectiveness and completeness of the response actions, identify corrective actions, and communicate the status of a risk by providing reports on the status of a risk and invoking contingency plans. Figure 2.38 shows an example of a risk heatmap, which shows how the identified risk has been grouped into risk levels. You can set up automatic exception reporting, so when an exception occurs for a defined KRI, the stakeholders responsible will be notified of this exception. When the end of life for a risk has been reached, the risk and all its outstanding activities can be closed.

This SAP Risk Management model and supported process is just an overview and introduction to give you an idea of the functionality available within the standard software. Much more could have been written about this topic, but that exceeds the scope of this book.

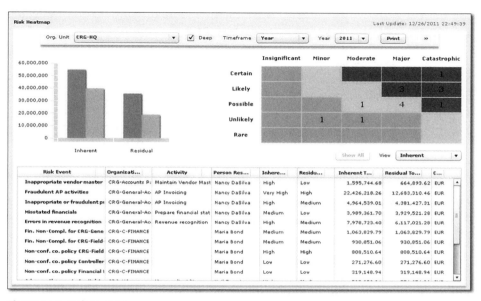

Figure 2.38 Risk Heatmap

2.1.6 Product Intellectual Property Management with SAP GRC

Product intellectual property (IP) management represents the development and tracking of the product-related intellectual property pipeline and the management of high-value patent portfolios and their associated licensing agreements. Product IP management is supported by access, security, and audit control for documents, content, files, models, and other information that are the product-related intellectual property of an enterprise, which is covered by the SAP BusinessObjects products SAP Access Control and SAP Process Control under the business process called enterprise risk and controls management.

Enterprise Risk and Controls Management

Enterprise risk and controls management incorporates direct processes for helping organizations manage their enterprise risks and control initiatives. The solution aligns the business units that are responsible for managing these initiatives by providing a standardized, central solution that automates and monitors key risks and controls at the business level. The solution uses both SAP Risk Management and SAP Processes Control. SAP Process Control applies a risk-based approach to setting up a control environment and identifying the most effective and efficient controls needed to achieve compliance.

Figure 2.39 shows the high-level business process. The boxed area takes place in SAP Risk Management, as described in more detail in Section 2.1.7, and the SAP Process Control steps are documented in more detail next.

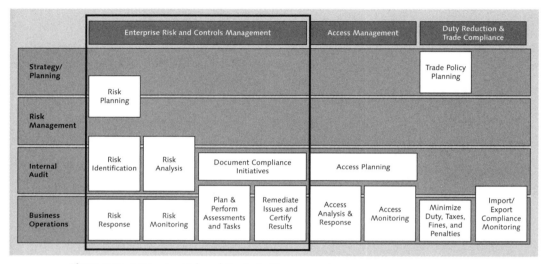

Figure 2.39 Enterprise Risk and Controls Management

The following benefits can be gleaned from the effective use of SAP Access Control and SAP Process Control:

▶ Most comprehensive set of capabilities available; integrated and closed-loop solution covering all steps to manage, monitor, and analyze SAP GRC processes

▶ Proactive monitoring across KRIs and compliance effectiveness

▶ SAP GRC solutions delivered with industry-specific risk, compliance and process content

▶ Proven solutions

Some possible benefits are specific to SAP Access Control:

▶ Minimize time to compliance by quick, effective, and comprehensive access risk identification and by eliminating existing access and authorization risks

▶ Continuous access management, which improves productivity of end users, reduces costs for role maintenance, avoids business interruptions with faster emergency responses, eases compliance, and avoids authorization risk

▶ Effective management oversight by analytical capabilities and internal audit capabilities

SAP Access Control

SAP Access Control is a risk-based access and authorization management solution through which you can efficiently manage access risk by providing users with the right access to the system. It documents and provides analysis functions to ensure SoD and prevent excessive unauthorized access rights because both have been identified as top contributors to fraud and audit findings. Security role management, user access management, and emergency access management help you ensure compliance for thousands of users, roles, and processes in real time to allow risk management in a proactive manner, ensuring compliance with security policies and restriction of critical permissions. This results in an improved ability to protect information and prevent fraud while minimizing the time and costs involved in the management of access risk.

The SAP Access Control application is a suite made up out of four main components—Risk Analysis and Remediation (RAR), Compliant User Provisioning (CUP), Superuser Privilege Management (SPM), and Enterprise Role Management to provide a comprehensive and integrated solution for managing access to all of your enterprise systems—and a fifth important component, SAP NetWeaver Identity Management (SAP NetWeaver ID Management). These are shown in Figure 2.40. Let's look at these first four in more detail.

Risk Analysis and Remediation (RAR) is a fully automated security audit and SoD analysis tool designed to recognize, analyze, and resolve all issues related to regulatory compliance. You can identify risks and assign them to functions, which in turn can be associated with a business process. Its automatic analytic capabilities can produce both summary and detailed reports in real time for selected users, user groups, roles, and profiles, as well as for critical actions, critical permissions, critical roles, and profiles. This allows you to stop security and controls violations before they can occur, which significantly reduces the compliance time, costs, and risks.

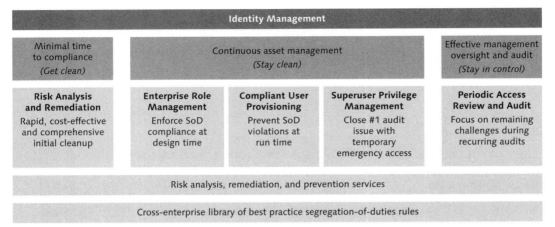

Figure 2.40 SAP Access Control and Authorization Management

Compliant User Provisioning (CUP) is an automated end-to-end user request, approval, and user administration solution that is web-based and workflow-configurable with proactive SoD compliance checking. It gives you the means to allow administrators of enterprise systems to automate the user-creation process, to manage the various types of business risks and reduce their workload, and therefore reduce costs. Figure 2.41 gives you an example of an access request.

The SAP Workflow Engine allows you to automate and accelerate user administration throughout the entire lifecycle from the hiring to the retirement of an employee by a dynamic configurable workflow. Its integration with RAR prevents SoD violations and helps to ensure corporate accountability and compliance to laws and regulations such as SOX and provides auditable tracking for auditors. An event such as a new employee hire or a job change can automatically trigger sequences in separate systems, which can be performed by business users without any involvement from system administrators.

CUP can be used for the following:

▶ Risk maintenance

▶ Control maintenance

▶ Mitigation activities

▶ User maintenance

▶ Role maintenance

▶ Requesting super user access

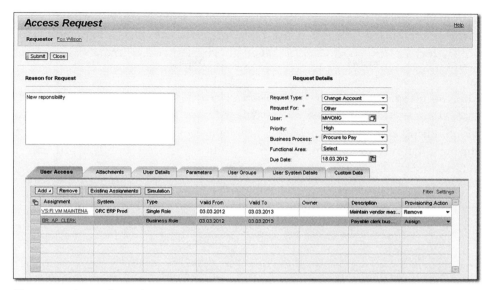

Figure 2.41 Access Request

As you can see in Figure 2.42, when you're using CUP with SAP Risk Management, you can report on all of the risks that are a result of access violations.

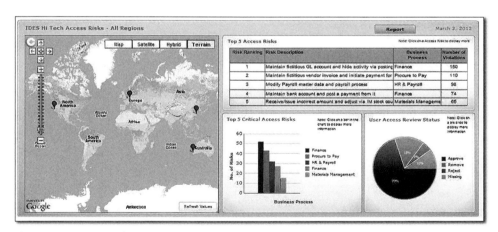

Figure 2.42 Access Risk Overview

Enterprise Role Management automates role definition and role management. It provides you with the capability to define, develop, test, and maintain roles consistently across the entire enterprise. It simplifies documenting and maintaining role management through a single maintenance from a single location, which often results in lower maintenance costs, provides compliance and audit traceability for security checks and avoids authorization risk, eliminates errors and enforces best practices, and provides easier knowledge transfer.

You can use the *Superuser Privilege Management* (SPM) component to track and trace the activities performed by a privileged user. A *privileged user* is often provided during emergencies to solve a problem or extraordinary situation such as during a cutover or implementation. Within SAP Access Control, this user is referred to as a *firefighter*.

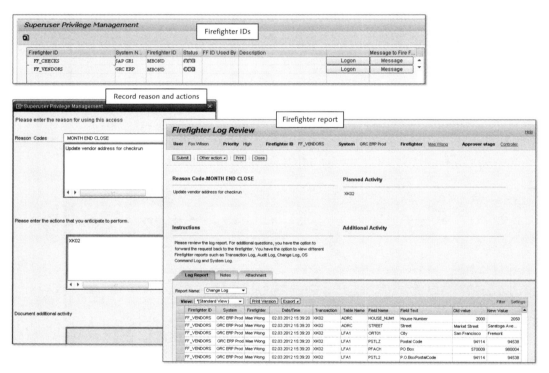

Figure 2.43 Firefighter IDs

This role has super user privileges, which means the user has broad access, with sometimes even access to all possible transactions (such as with the SAP role SAP_ ALL). Via SPM, these rights are provided by a controlled and auditable environment, which can help you solve one of the top open audit issues. Via the firefighter role, you use pre-assigned firefighter IDs, which include the correct access restriction and are only valid during the period you specify. Also, all field-level changes are tracked in an audit log. (Figure 2.43 shows examples of these.) This avoids business obstructions with a fast emergency response, reduces the time necessary to undertake a compliance audit, and reduces the time to perform critical tasks.

SPM can be used with and integrated into CUP, where an approver approves and grants access for the firefighter ID.

SAP NetWeaver Identity Management (SAP NetWeaver ID Management) solutions provide the key infrastructure to manage user accounts in multiple backend systems. SAP Access Control currently provides integration with SAP NetWeaver ID Management solutions for enterprise-wide compliant provisioning. When integrated with an SAP NetWeaver ID Management solution, there are two possible scenarios:

▶ **SAP Access Control-driven provisioning**
Where the request is created in SAP Access Control, risk analysis and approval are completed in SAP Access Control, SAP content is provisioned from SAP Access Control, and non-SAP provisioning information is sent to SAP NetWeaver ID Management for provisioning. This flow is shown in Figure 2.44, with the first step being done within SAP Access Control and the SAP NetWeaver ID Management solution handling the non-SAP provisioning information.

Figure 2.44 SAP Access Control Workflow

▶ **SAP NetWeaver ID Management-driven provisioning**
When a request is created in SAP NetWeaver ID Management, a request information is sent to SAP Access Control for risk analysis and approval, SAP content is provisioned from SAP Access Control, and non-SAP provisioning information is sent to SAP NetWeaver ID Management for provisioning.

SAP Process Control

SAP Process Control applies a risk-based approach to setting up a control environment and identifying the most effective and efficient controls needed to achieve compliance. SAP Process Control lets you document your compliance initiatives, plan and perform assessments and tests, remediate issues, and certify results data. SAP Process Control and SAP Risk Management provide an end-to-end process for enterprise risk and controls management.

Before explaining the functions, features, and data model for SAP Process Control, it's important to understand the solution-supported compliance models and which benefits you gain per model, including the effect on your SAP Process Control processes and data.

Consider these benefits of SAP Process Control:

▶ **Visibility**
You can achieve continuous visibility across compliance initiatives via accountability and standardization of processes, with comprehensive reports and dashboards to monitor effectiveness across systems.

▶ **Efficiency**
You can achieve automation of control activities, simplification of integrated processes, and delivered rules—even across complex environments—to increase efficiency.

▶ **Confidence**
With unified controls, you can adapt to changing business needs to increase agility, ensure audit integrity, and, by continuous monitoring, build confidence in effective compliance initiatives.

SAP Process Control Data Model

Figure 2.45 shows the data model used within SAP Process Control in the latest version of SAP GRC 10.0. Note that the control can only see the risks assigned to the subprocess and that financial assertions are assigned indirectly to the control via the risk. Keep in mind that the previous versions of SAP Process Control have different data models because the focus of SAP Process Control has been shifted to a risk-based approach. The reason for changing the data model and SAP Process Control processes to focus on the areas of greatest risk is because regulatory standards such as SOX and agencies such as the SEC and Public Company Accounting Oversight Board (PCAOB) emphasize the importance of auditing higher risk areas;

they focus on incorporating a top-down approach for audit planning and provide auditors with a range of alternatives for addressing lower risk areas to ultimately determine the nature, extent, and timing of control evaluations.

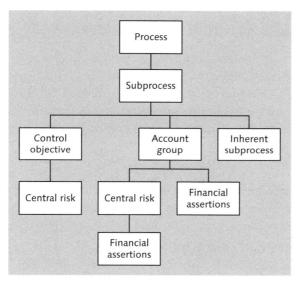

Figure 2.45 SAP Process Control Data Model

A business process consists of assessing, testing, and monitoring results data with related issues and a remediation plan, when necessary. Within the assessment surveys, you maintain the Question Library and surveys for all types of surveys. These will be used later in the individual compliance initiative planner for survey tasks. Each compliance initiative may have different survey types configured. Test plans are either manual or automated.

SAP Process Control roles and authorizations models extend SAP's user and roles management from SAP NetWeaver to provide additional flexibility to the end users. They are maintained in three areas: the SAP NetWeaver backend, SAP Process Control, and SAP NetWeaver Portal.

SAP Risk Management Financial Compliance

To perform SAP Risk Management financial compliance, a top-down risk-based approach (TDRA) is used within SAP Process Control. Figure 2.46 shows the steps involved in a risk-based financial compliance cycle, and they are described in the following list.

Figure 2.46 Top-Down Risk-Based Approach

1. **Material analysis**

   During material analysis, you identify the in-scope organization, processes and subprocesses, and the significant accounts and significant assertions; you determine which account groups and which assertions are affected. You have to consider the materiality, the likelihood of errors or frauds, the accounting and reporting complexities, and subjectivity. You can download consolidated account group templates and upload balances.

2. **Risk assessment**

   ▶ Identify risks of financial misstatements: During this step, you determine what could go wrong to determine the sources and likelihood of misstatements.

   ▶ Identify significant affected locations and processes: During this step, you determine the significant locations and processes that would be affected by the risk.

3. **Control risk assessment**

   ▶ Assess the financial reporting risks: Rate the risk by considering the impact and the likelihood of the risk for material misstatement in the financials.

   ▶ Identify controls to address financial reporting risk: Identify the controls that can mitigate the risk.

4. **Test strategy**

   ▶ Evaluate control operating effectiveness: Evaluate whether the chosen controls are effective and efficient, make sure you consider the control risk factors to determine the nature, and extend the timing of the control evaluations.

   ▶ Perform surveys and manual tests: Surveys and tests ensure compliance with SOX 404 requirements. SAP Process Control provides standard procedures to monitor, evaluate, and report on controls and subprocesses.

SAP Process Control includes four types of evaluations: assessments, manual tests, automated control compliance tests, and automated control monitoring.

An *assessment* is a survey-based evaluation. Surveys consist of questions developed by the organization and stored in the question library. Each time a survey is triggered, it is circulated to the involved stakeholders, which are the internal control manager, the audit manager, the process owners, and the controls owners. Standard SAP Process Control surveys can be used for the following purposes:

- Assessing whether the designed controls and subprocesses are appropriate
- Assessing the effectiveness of the controls and the subprocesses
- Assessing company-wide controls

SAP Process Control provides the types of assessment surveys shown in Table 2.4.

Type	Used By	Purpose	Roles
Control design assessment	Internal auditors, the SOX team, or control owner	To conduct periodic assessments of the design of controls	<ul><li>Perform assessment: control owner</li><li>Review assessment: subprocess owner</li></ul>
Subprocess design assessment	Internal auditors, the SOX team, or control owner	To conduct periodic assessments of the design of business processes	<ul><li>Subprocess owner</li><li>Process owner</li></ul>
Self-assessment	Control owner	To evaluate controls; often used as a way to monitor controls and identify and remediate issues before a formal test of effectiveness is performed	<ul><li>Perform assessment: control owner</li><li>Review assessment: subprocess owner</li></ul>
Indirect entity-level control assessment (also known as company-level or pervasive controls)	Multiple organizational owners	Conducted at a higher level in the organization than transactional control activities, which is performed by persons knowledgeable of how entity-level controls affect overall compliance	<ul><li>Organizational owner</li><li>Internal control manager</li></ul>
Sign-off assessment	Multiple organizational owners	To document the approval of the compliance results, including the accountability trail	<ul><li>Multiple roles, based on organizational model</li></ul>

Table 2.4 Assessment Surveys

To perform an assessment survey, you first need to set up questions and survey templates in the library. Within the question library, you set up a reusable and editable catalog of generic compliance questions, which can be used when building a survey questionnaire (see Figure 2.47).

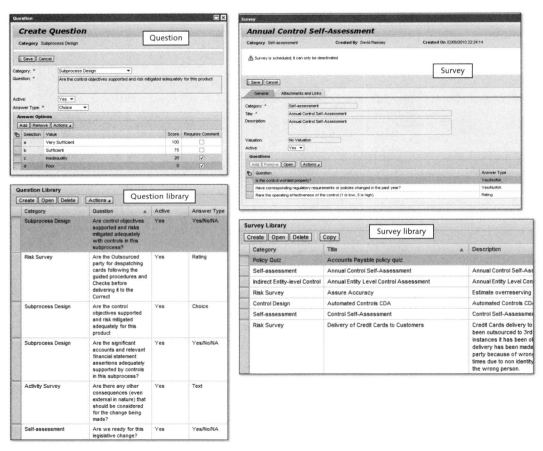

Figure 2.47 Question and Survey

The process for the survey completion consists of the following steps, where the assessment is a required step and all the other steps are optional:

1. Assessment: Create a manual test plan. Test steps and required step, sampling methodology, and initial sample size. Set up what to do in case of a step failure.

2. Validate the assessment.

3. Process issues.

4. Process the remediation plan.

5. Validate the issues.

6. Reassess.

You can configure the task receiver of the evaluation performance and evaluation, but there are roles responsible for these activities by default as mentioned in Table 2.4. With regard to manual tests (offline forms and databases), auditors and reviewers can use SAP Interactive Forms by Adobe, which provides a process to manage test plans, perform the tests, and report issues. They can be used either in an online mode, via download capabilities, or in an offline mode, which might be useful when Internet access is unavailable or unreliable. Datasheets provide access to all information related to a control or subprocess to give you a single point of view of all information, which you can export, share, and print. The sections on the datasheet include master data, control objectives and risks, account groups, related attachments and links, parent hierarchy of control, assessment surveys, manual test plans, evaluation results, test of effectiveness result, control design assessment results, and remediation plans.

During the review of the assessment, you can identify an issue when an evaluation or test fails. An issue represents an exception, or a potential or actual problem. After the issue is reviewed, you can implement a remediation plan to resolve the issue. The plans can be submitted via an offline Interactive Form by Adobe.

As mentioned during our discussion of SAP Risk Management, the probability and the impact of the risk drives the testing strategy of the control. You get a complete overview of the risks, the in-scope controls, and the test strategy via the *risk and control matrix report* (central report, shown in Figure 2.48). This report shows the risks, specific in-scope controls, and the testing strategy. Flexible selection criteria provide you the means to focus on your area of responsibility or interest.

Automated Assessments: Automated Rules Framework

There are several reasons to consider going to an automation of controls: to handle repeatable controls; to improve quality of work and free up auditors from tedious work; to self-document; to reduce efforts, cost, and reliance on external resources; and to speed up the process and improvement of Knowledge Management (KM).

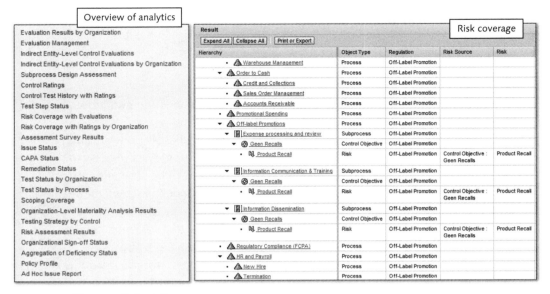

Figure 2.48 Analytics

To set up automated assessment, you need to use the Automated Rules framework. Several content and out-of-the-box solutions are delivered. This is just a short introduction to automation to give you an understanding of the solution, so please see the SAP BusinessObjects help files for more information.

Aggregated Deficiencies

Aggregation of Deficiencies (AoD) enables users to assess control deficiency levels for each failed control and/or to assess an aggregated deficiency level for a group of failed controls. This feature was introduced in SAP Process Control 3.0. You can decide to use either a top-level approach, where the AoD is only done at the corporate level, or a bottom-up approach, where AoD is done in two steps—first an AoD at organization levels, and then an AoD analysis on the corporate level. There are different levels for SOX and SOX Japan:

▸ **Material weakness**

A deficiency or combination of deficiencies in internal control over financial reporting that there is a reasonable possibility that a material misstatement of the company's annual or interim financial statements won't be prevented or detected on a timely basis.

▶ **Significant deficiency**
A deficiency or combination of deficiencies in internal control over financial reporting that is less severe than a material weakness, yet important enough to merit attention by those responsible for oversight of the company's financial reporting and should be reported to audit committees.

▶ **Deficiency**
A deficiency or combination of deficiencies, in internal control over financial reporting that is less severe than a significant deficiency but still important enough to report to audit committees.

Through continuously monitoring transactions within the SAP Process Control, you can identify and correct errors, waste, abuse, policy violations, and potential fraud. They require an in-depth analysis of transactions, which in turn provides you with an improvement in quality and time to execute business processes, increases insights into your business activities, and increases margin contribution.

SAP Global Trade Services

SAP Global Trade Services involves controlling the cost and risk of international trade by ensuring compliance with global regulations, accelerating trade activity, and minimizing duties. Via SAP Global Trade Services, you can continuously and automatically monitor your transactions to accomplish three key goals:

▶ Better manage global trade operations

▶ Ensure ongoing compliance

▶ Optimize the cross-border supply chain

By using SAP Global Trade Services, you can reduce errors and revenue leakage, deter fraud and abuse in transactions, and improve audit efficiency.

2.1.7 SAP Strategy Management and SAP GRC Architecture

SAP Strategy Management and SAP GRC are built on open standards such as Java 2 Platform, Enterprise Edition (J2EE) to easily fit into your existing IT environment and complement your organization's current applications. The primary objective of dynamic product development is to support usability and allow for mobility for all functions. Figure 2.49 shows the solution architecture of the landscape for SAP Strategy Management and SAP GRC.

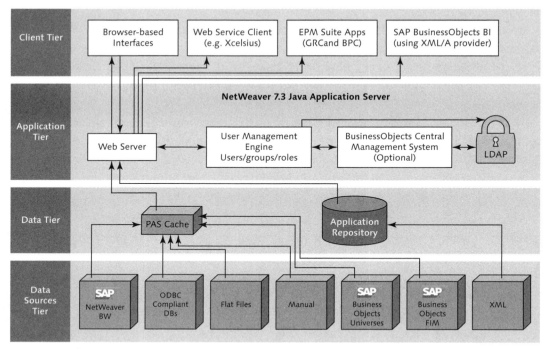

Figure 2.49 SAP Strategy Management Architecture and SAP GRC

2.2 Planning and Management

The Planning and Management tier of the NPDI pyramid is supported by SAP Product and Portfolio Management (PPM). You can also use the subsidiary PPM–Portfolio Management for project management and scheduling purposes. The workflows for all three of these are shown in Figure 2.50.

This section will explain the portfolio management capabilities of the PPM solution in more detail from the context of product management, including product innovation management. Organizations that don't manufacture, produce, or sell products can use PPM–Portfolio Management to manage a different type of portfolios to focus on the assets they are responsible for, for example, or to set up a portfolio for internal projects. Chapter 7 describes the project management, scheduling capabilities, and product development collaboration of PPM in more detail.

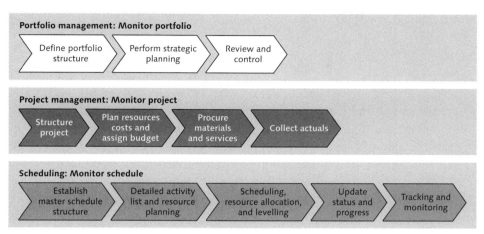

Figure 2.50 Overview of PPM

PPM focuses on identifying, evaluating, and managing the "family" or, as defined in the solution, the portfolio of products that a company offers and maintains. You can compare product investment alternatives based on market demand, competitive pressures, cost rollups, project sales and profitability estimates, overall resource needs, status reporting, and other inputs to determine which ideas and products to invest in, to expand, and to sustain. Apart from focusing on the introduction of future product portfolios, you can also analyze existing product portfolios and provide insights into market and sales opportunities, costs and risks, and therefore the competitive strength of the current and future business. The definition of target groups, degrees of individualization, sales channels, and other strategy-level design approaches takes place at the end of the process.

SAP PPM 5.0 is the latest release and has evolved based on and from a collection of the following older product versions:

▶ Cross Application Resource and Portfolio Management (xRPM)

▶ SAP Resource and Portfolio Management (SAP RPM)

▶ Collaboration Projects and Folders (c-projects and c-folders)

The following benefits focus on using the PPM–Portfolio Management capabilities:

▶ **Alignment with corporate objectives**
You can align your product portfolio with your corporate objectives.

▸ **Maximized portfolio value**
By selecting, winning, and retaining the most promising portfolio items, you ensure a balanced portfolio with acceptable risk, changing business objectives, and various investment types. Collecting feedback on product lifecycle fuels future innovation initiatives.

▸ **Transparency and informed decisions**
PPM–Portfolio Management provides a complete and up-to-date view of the entire company portfolio, enabling informed decision making to promote optimal distribution of valuable company assets, such as capital and resources. Insights about overlapping projects, risks, and resource bottlenecks become available sooner, so adjustments can be made.

▸ **Integration**
PPM–Portfolio Management can be fed with information from existing project management, human resources, and financial systems to provide an overview of the project portfolio and resource availability, which could potentially speed up the data collection process and makes the data more reliable. Integration between SAP solutions is a given, and integration to other common third-party products such as Microsoft Project and Primavera are also supported by certified and standard interfaces.

▸ **Governance**
You can consistently enforce corporate, IT, and other policies across the enterprise by using rigorous process controls, authorizations, approval procedures (e.g., for funding), gateways and templates, workflows, and backups by role-specific workflow as required in many standards, such as the American SOX accounting standard (specifically sections 302 and 404).

▸ **Tighter risk mitigation**
Through flexibility to adjust operations to changing client demands and government and industry regulations, risk is mitigated.

2.2.1 PPM Data Model

The first step in the PPM–Portfolio Management process is to define a portfolio structure. You can use several portfolio master data objects in PPM, which can be used to represent a portfolio, as shown in Figure 2.51. This data model accommodates methods and models, such as Six Sigma, Phase-Gate, Critical-Path, and Product and Cycle-Time Excellence (PACE). We'll briefly explain each object in the data model now.

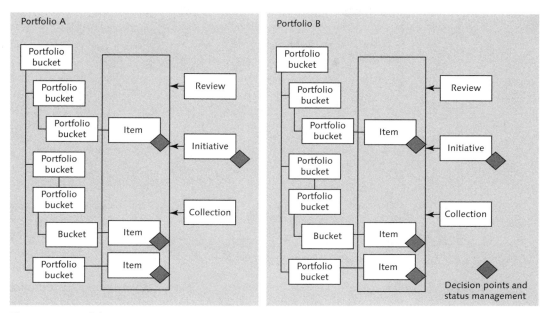

Figure 2.51 Portfolio Master Data

A *portfolio* is a range of investments held by an organization or a range of products or services offered by an organization; it forms the cornerstone of PPM. You can choose to set up organizational, functional, or regional portfolios. Cross-portfolio functions are limited and include resource planning and some overall reporting; however, most PPM functions are performed and created at the portfolio level. Examples are the creation of a collection, a review, and an initiative, which are all done at the portfolio level, across multiple buckets. You should keep these principles in mind when you're defining company portfolios. You can, for example, define a portfolio for new product introductions, a services portfolio, or an IT initiatives portfolio. Figure 2.52 shows how you can switch from one portfolio IPD: PRODUCT PORTFOLIO to another defined portfolio.

As shown in Figure 2.52, the overall structure of the portfolio is reflected in a hierarchy of *buckets*. The portfolio bucket is used for filtering and analysis. Each portfolio item needs to be assigned to a portfolio bucket at the lowest level. It provides a container for portfolio items, each with a separately managed budget.

Figure 2.53 gives you an example of the portfolio item as defined within the NPDI FOR CONSUMER PRODUCTS portfolio.

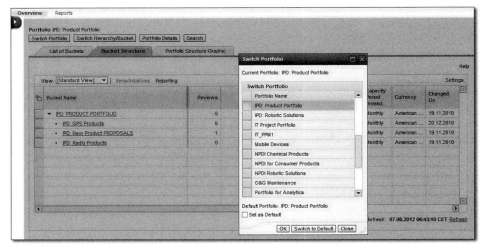

Figure 2.52 Portfolio Overview

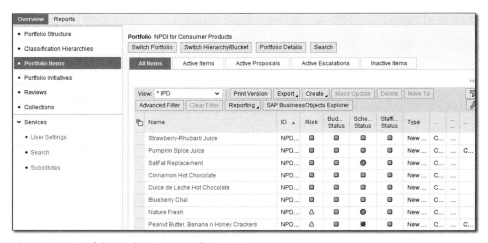

Figure 2.53 Portfolio Bucket Structure for NPDI Consumer Products

Through *portfolio items*, you can represent project or product proposals, product initiatives, projects, concepts, or services. The process that a portfolio item has to follow depends on the portfolio type and is reflected in decision points and their related statuses. These will need to be configured based on your company's specific requirements. Within the item, you can use questionnaires or scoring models to determine critical success factors (which need to be configured).

Figure 2.54 gives you an example of the dashboard that shows all of the initiatives within a portfolio. As you can see, it provides you with a good overview of which items need attention based on traffic lights; these draw attention to exceptions or problems covering specific areas, such as budget status or risk.

Figure 2.54 Portfolio Items Overview

Figure 2.55 gives you an example of a portfolio item that represents the proposal for a new cookie product. As you can see, the sequential steps are shown, starting with R&D READY. These are the different phases, or decision points, through which a portfolio item type must pass: PACKAGING READY, TRIALS COMPLETE, QUALITY SIGN-OFF, PRODUCT READY.

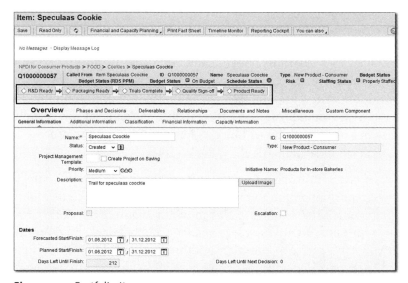

Figure 2.55 Portfolio Items

Figure 2.56 shows how to set up and use a questionnaire within an item (but also within other data in PPM). The questionnaire will be used to determine the value of a field within the item. In the example in Figure 2.56, the probability of technical success is determined based on the questionnaire answers.

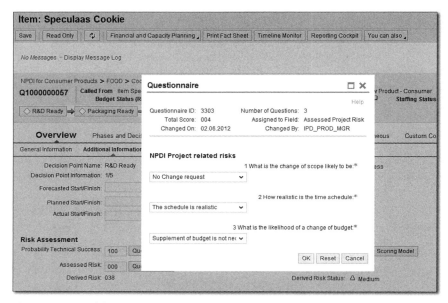

Figure 2.56 Portfolio Item with Questionnaire

The *review* object represents a periodic review of selected items in a portfolio at a predefined time, such as a quarterly, bi-annually, annually, or ad hoc review. Portfolio reviews enable portfolio managers to make fact-based decisions. The portfolio items within a review are evaluated and compared within a scoreboard. A review like the one shown in Figure 2.57 is created at bucket level and is applicable to select items or initiatives within the bucket. The review process is described in more detail in Section 2.2.2.

A *collection* represents a set of related portfolio items with a common strategic goal. It has its own reporting option to provide portfolio managers the flexibility to monitor the performance of a collection, as shown in Figure 2.58. Collections can, for example, represent initiatives, a seasonal launch plan, or a brand or program. Although you can't create a collection with items that belong to multiple portfolios (called cross-portfolio collections) because all items need to belong to the same portfolio, you can include items from different buckets.

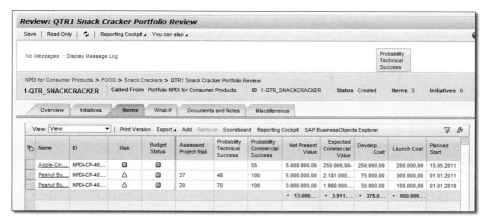

Figure 2.57 Portfolio Review

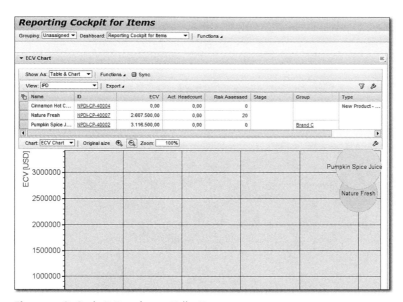

Figure 2.58 Cockpit Based on a Collection

The *initiative* object represents an operational initiative that can include several portfolio items, with its own phases and decision points/status management to monitor the process of the initiative as a whole. It can be used for strategic planning—both financial and capacity—and is maintained at the bucket level. It can be assigned to different items, belonging to different portfolio buckets, as long as they are within the same portfolio. It could, for example, represent the planning and development of new products. Via dashboards, you can visualize the overview and the status information for all initiatives as shown in Figure 2.59. Figure 2.60 shows a drinks and beverages initiative being run—going through the product readiness, lead market, global market phases, and so on.

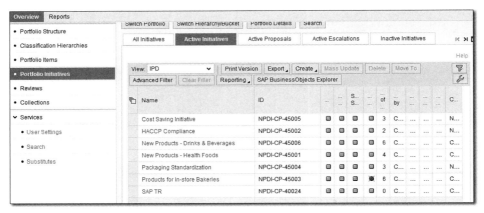

Figure 2.59 Initiatives Overview

Figure 2.60 Drinks and Beverages Initiatives Example

Classification and Portfolio Hierarchies

To use an additional structure beyond the existing portfolio structure, you can use a portfolio hierarchy via the classification function. This allows you to use an additional structure and assign existing items and initiatives to it. Figure 2.61 shows how the portfolio is set up based on different types of products, whereas the classification hierarchy is set up regionally. You can now perform functions and reporting from both perspectives.

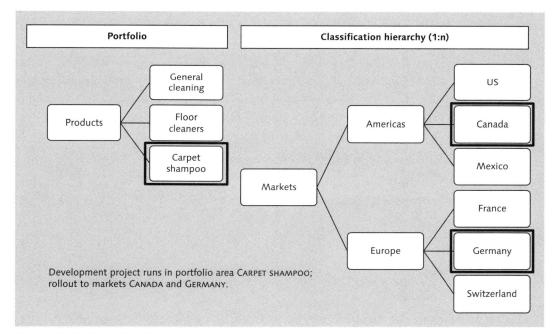

Figure 2.61 Portfolio Classification

Business Partners

Within the portfolio objects, employees might be assigned as responsible employees, approvers, stakeholders, or resources. PPM uses the *business partner* concept to cater to these employees. They can be created manually in the application or can be uploaded from HR systems such as SAP ERP Human Capital Management (SAP ERP HCM) or others. The business partners assigned to the portfolio elements (portfolio, bucket, or item) are the ones with access to the specific elements. SAP standard will copy all of the roles assigned at the portfolio level to the lower-level items, but any changes can be made through the administration functions by the portfolio administrator, item administrator, portfolio manager, or resource manager when required.

Enriching PPM

Within each object, more detailed information can be captured and configured based on your company's needs. Examples of configuration options are portfolio types and project types; however, a number of additional system enrichment options are available for integrating your own business-relevant data. This book doesn't lend itself to discussing all of the available options in detail because its focus is to provide you with an overview. A more detailed book on this topic is available: *Project Portfolio Management with SAP RPM and cProjects* by Stefan Glatzmaier and Michael Sokollek (SAP PRESS, 2009).

2.2.2 Processes in Portfolio Management

PPM–Portfolio Management provides four main processes with which you can define, manage, and monitor your portfolios:

- Define portfolio structure
- Strategic portfolio planning
- Review and control portfolio objects
- Monitor portfolio

These processes available within PPM–Portfolio Management are described in detail in the following sections. Other supported processes within PPM are described in Chapter 7.

Define Portfolio Structure

This process is focused on creating and changing the product portfolio. The setup portfolio structure will be used as the basis for the execution of the business processes to allow you to perform strategic planning and to review, control, and monitor your portfolio. To use this process, follow these steps:

1. **Define a strategy.**
   Your company's strategy needs to be reflected by and translated to an appropriate portfolio structure so you can set up the structures and assign them to the appropriate business owners.
2. **Identify opportunities.**
   Opportunities for new products or new projects can be collected within PPM. They can be generated as new portfolio items from scratch or via code name "Edison" or SAP Product Definition as collection tools. After the right status has been reached, these ideas flow through to PPM as portfolio items and/or as a project.
3. **Analyze risk and rank opportunities.**
   By using the review object, you can compare and review several portfolio items with each other and prioritize and align them with your company's objectives. A review can be an ad hoc activity—for example, after a campaign of idea collections—or a periodic planned activity (annually, bi-annually, quarterly, or monthly). The review uses the scoreboard and an accompanying score model to determine the parameters and their weight, which will be used during the comparison of the different initiatives.

   As soon as you choose and configure the appropriate score model in the solution, the scoreboard will show you the values used for the comparison as well as the results for prioritization. This process step enables the key stakeholders to make fact-based decisions. Figure 2.62 shows an example of prioritization based on the model for NPDI RISKS.

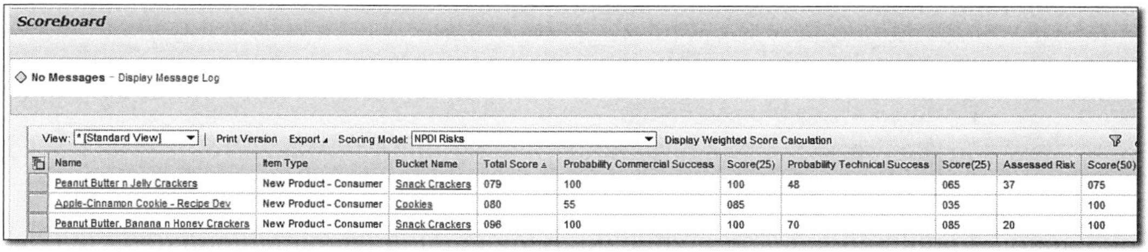
Scoreboard

No Messages - Display Message Log

View: * [Standard View] | Print Version Export Scoring Model: NPDI Risks Display Weighted Score Calculation

Name	Item Type	Bucket Name	Total Score	Probability Commercial Success	Score(25)	Probability Technical Success	Score(25)	Assessed Risk	Score(50)
Peanut Butter n Jelly Crackers	New Product - Consumer	Snack Crackers	079	100	100	48	065	37	075
Apple-Cinnamon Cookie - Recipe Dev	New Product - Consumer	Cookies	080	55	085		035		100
Peanut Butter, Banana n Honey Crackers	New Product - Consumer	Snack Crackers	096	100	100	70	085	20	100

Figure 2.62 Scoreboard within Review

You can use operational portfolio items for review, simulating possible situations using the what-if scenario. This object can be used to represent a variation of a scenario without changing the operational data of the portfolio item, making the impact on budget, resources, and schedules clear.

4. **Create and approve budgets.**

How you create and approve budgets depends on where you've decided to do your operational project management. The approved budgets can be monitored and reviewed from PPM by ensuring they are transferred across to PPM via integration. These topics are explained in more detail in Chapter 7.

Strategic Portfolio Planning

This process focuses on performing strategic portfolio planning, which supports both financial and capacity planning. Let's walk through this process, which is illustrated in Figure 2.63.

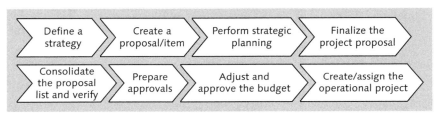

Figure 2.63 Strategic Portfolio Planning Process

1. **Define a strategy.**

See earlier step in the previous list.

2. **Create a proposal/item.**

New portfolio items get created by product developers or project managers; these new portfolio items represent the new product proposal, new service proposal, or project proposal. Basic details of the item get maintained, such as the item description, item dates, or item risk.

3. **Perform strategic planning.**

Strategic planning can be performed at the portfolio item level, initiative level, or portfolio bucket level. Note that the examples used within this chapter are done at the portfolio item level.

Within PPM, two forms of strategic planning are supported:

▸ Financial planning: To perform *financial planning*, you first enter critical success factors, such as launch costs, development costs, and net present value of the portfolio item as shown in Figure 2.64. Based on those inputs, the system calculates an EXPECTED COMMERCIAL VALUE.

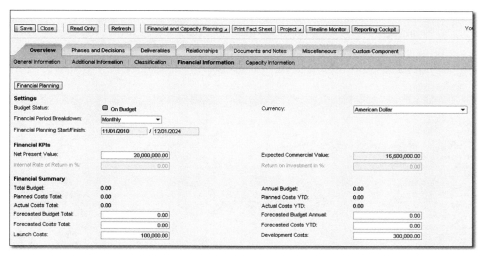

Figure 2.64 Financial Information

Then, you plan your finances, in which you use your company's predefined financial views (must be configured in PPM; you can define your own or use the SAP standard) to plan your first rough estimate of the required finances, based on financial categories and groups. Figure 2.65 shows the outcome of a financial plan, which defined the categories MATERIALS, HUMAN RESOURCES COSTS, and OTHER COSTS. The MATERIAL category is further divided into the groups EQUIPMENT, INGREDIENTS, and PACKAGING. The second category (HUMAN RESOURCES COSTS) is divided into LABEL DESIGNER, PACKAGING ENGINEER, and so on. The OTHER COSTS category includes EXTERNAL SERVICES and OVERHEADS. Note that integration from other financial systems or components (such as SAP Project System [SAP PS], Financial Accounting [FI], or other legacy systems) is possible here.

▶ Capacity planning: In contrast to financial planning, *capacity planning* allows you to plan resources required based on a specified common unit, such as people per day or ingredients per 100 pieces. The capacity planning capability provides you with the means to plan resources in an early phase of a project or product proposal. Estimates of required resources are often necessary in the context of, for example, an approval procedure, which is offered under capacity planning. Capacity planning can be executed based on a three-level deep structure made up of the combination of capacity view, capacity categories, and category groups, which are all definable in the PPM configuration based on your company's needs. Figure 2.66 shows an example of capacity planning that has been done for a new nacho chip. Within the PERSONNEL category, different roles have been identified and planned based on the unit days.

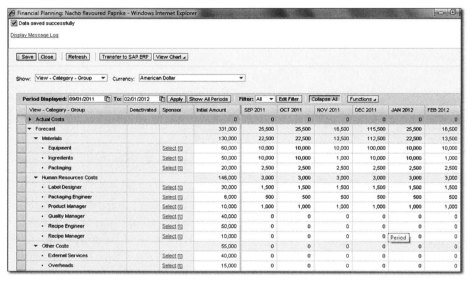

Figure 2.65 Financial Planning

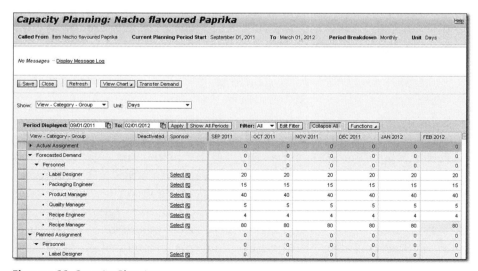

Figure 2.66 Capacity Planning

4. **Finalize the project proposal.**
   The item requester updates and reviews the portfolio item details before handing in the proposal. This process can be supported by the use of questionnaires and official documents such as a business case or other project template that includes the details required for the approval.

5. **Consolidate the proposal list and verify.**
   The portfolio board reviews all incoming proposals via a consolidated proposal list, verifies the items, and updates or removes any duplicate proposals.

6. **Prepare approvals.**
   Before the approval meeting takes place, the approved budget for each investment area is assigned, and a review is created to cluster all of the projects that need approval. These items will be used by the portfolio review board.

7. **Adjust and approve the budget.**
   The review board uses the review to prioritize and approve the project proposals. Once approved, the review board also assigns an overall budget to the project. The project manager is informed of the project approval decisions—including the budget information—and can further detail the project budget.

8. **Create/assign the operational project.**
   As soon as the project gets approved and funded, it can be turned into an operational project. Depending on which systems you're using for operational project management, the appropriate project data needs to be created. The following options are possible:

   ▶ Use PPM as the operational project system: Create the project in PPM and cost collector in SAP ERP.

   ▶ Use SAP PS as the operational project system: Create the project in SAP PS (automatically via the portfolio item or by manually linking the item and the project).

   ▶ Use an external operational project system: Use Open Project System (Open PS) and cost collection in SAP PS.

Chapter 7 explains these concepts in more detail.

Review and Control Portfolio Objects

Within this process, you can compare and prioritize portfolio items through scoring models via the review object. The process can be executed periodically (annually, bi-annually, quarterly, monthly) or on an ad hoc basis; it supports the key stakeholders when making fact-based decisions. Operational portfolio items can be used for review, however, you can also use the what-if object to work out several what-if scenarios. This object can be used to represent a variation of a scenario without changing the actual operational data of the portfolio item, so the impact on budget, resources, and schedules becomes clear. Figure 2.67 compares three product items based on their risk, budget status, probability of technical success, and so on. The input can be used to reprioritize and/or make fact-based decisions on the items involved.

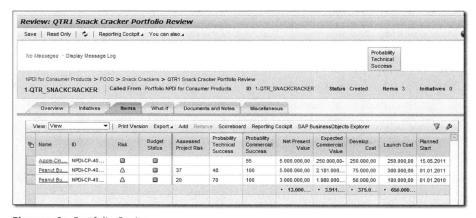

Figure 2.67 Portfolio Review

Figure 2.68 shows an example of a scoreboard that uses the NPDI RISKS risk model.

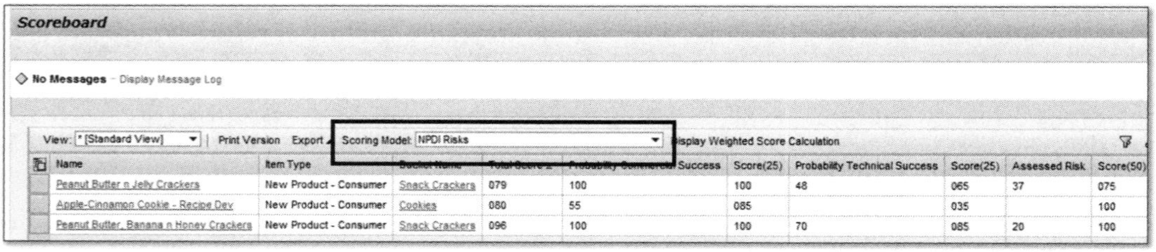

Figure 2.68 Portfolio Item Review Scoreboard

Score models provide a service used to maximize the value of a portfolio against one or more business objectives. Its results appear in a ranked list of portfolio items that can be used for making decisions in a portfolio review. This NPDI RISKS score model uses the following criteria: probability of commercial success, probability of technical success, and the assessed risk to perform the prioritization calculation based on the configured values ranges, weightings, and score, as shown in Figure 2.69. Scoring models like the NPDI RISKS model are set up in PPM's configuration.

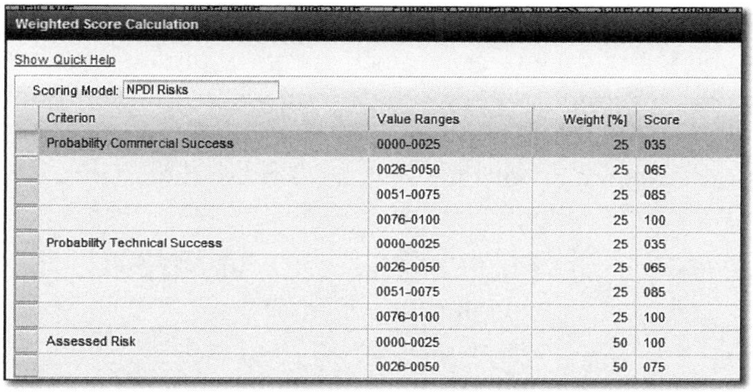

Weighted Score Calculation

Show Quick Help

Scoring Model: NPDI Risks

Criterion	Value Ranges	Weight [%]	Score
Probability Commercial Success	0000-0025	25	035
	0026-0050	25	065
	0051-0075	25	085
	0076-0100	25	100
Probability Technical Success	0000-0025	25	035
	0026-0050	25	065
	0051-0075	25	085
	0076-0100	25	100
Assessed Risk	0000-0025	50	100
	0026-0050	50	075

Figure 2.69 Scoring Model NPDI Risks

Monitor Portfolio

Portfolio monitoring is a process which should be performed continuously. On a regular basis, you should review all of your ongoing/operational projects to ensure they are on time, cover the right scope, and stay within budget. Updates to projects might be triggered by project-specific circumstances, such as a budget overrun, or be triggered centrally because of changes at the portfolio level, such as a budget cut or change of scope or portfolio strategy.

PPM offers several flexible dashboards and sophisticated analytics tools such as cockpits to drawn your attention to problem areas within your portfolio and project, so you can continuously monitor your portfolio's performance and your projects. Apart from running these reports regularly, you can also set up workflows via the Alert Management functionality to alert the stakeholders during certain circumstances or when certain thresholds have been reached, such as risk changes or budget overruns.

Collection

To perform reporting horizontally instead of vertically, you can use the PPM *collections* object. This might be useful for either reporting or management purposes, where a collection represents a set of related portfolio items with a common strategic goal. A collection can, for example, represent initiatives, a seasonal launch plan, or a brand or program. Recall that collections can only include items from the same portfolio and not from multiple portfolios but that the collection can contain items from different buckets.

Dashboards

A *dashboard* provides you with a way to get a quick overview of the requested portfolio data. It shows the requested items in a table form where icons or traffic lights represent the status of defined, detailed areas. Some example statuses that you want to track in the dashboard at portfolio item level are staffing status, risk status, budgeting status, and scheduling status.

Dashboards are available for several portfolio objects, such as the portfolios, portfolio buckets, dependencies, reviews, and portfolio items. Figure 2.70 shows an example of a dashboard for PORTFOLIO ITEMS. You can access the dashboard from several different places, allowing you to open the dashboard either for all of the items within a portfolio or for a chosen specific content. For example, the dashboard can be started based on the portfolio bucket, which then shows all of the items within the bucket. Or you can open the dashboard from within a collection, which then shows all of the items in the collection. You'll just see those items for which you have the appropriate authorizations, and you can use sorting and filtering functions when working on a large number of items.

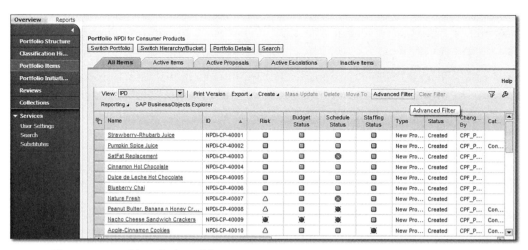

Figure 2.70 Dashboard of Portfolio Items

A *reporting cockpit* provides you with graphical and tabular representation of portfolio item information. The following graphics are available:

▶ Expected commercial value

▶ Schedule (forecasted, planned and actual)

▶ Risk reward chart

You can access the reporting cockpit from several different places, which allows you to open the cockpit either for all of the items within a portfolio or for a chosen specific content. For example, the cockpit can be started based on the portfolio bucket or from within a collection, similar to the dashboard. Because a portfolio might cover a large number of items, you can use sorting or filtering functions to filter out those items on which you want to report and drill into in more detail. (When you have the appropriate authorization to drill down into the detailed information, you can personalize the cockpit based on your individual needs.) Figure 2.71 shows an example of a cockpit where the portfolio items are visualized in the line chart based on their launch costs versus their probability of success. This information could be used to make go/no-go decisions, for example.

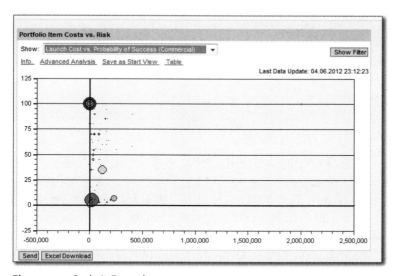

Figure 2.71 Cockpit Example

Based on your reporting requirements, the PPM administrator can set up additional charts or tables (such as portfolio, bar, Gantt, or pie charts) and allow or block drilldown capabilities and cockpit personalization options.

PPM also offers Business Context Viewer (BCV) dashboards, as shown in Figure 2.72; these provide you with fast overview and insight into the following areas:

- ▶ Planned and actual costs
- ▶ Planned and actual time
- ▶ Commitments
- ▶ Planned and actual budget
- ▶ Planned and actual revenues

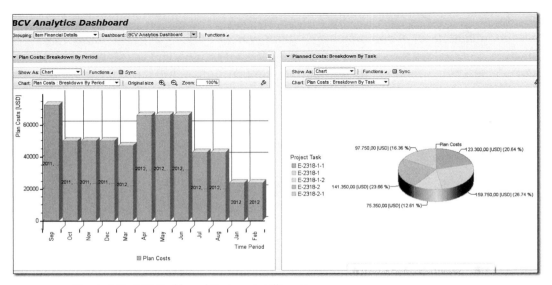

Figure 2.72 BCV Dashboard Business Intelligence

Apart from these reports available within the PPM application, you can perform advanced analytical functions by setting up SAP BusinessObjects BI and using the predefined content available from a PPM perspective. InfoCubes are available that allow you to perform analytics on costs, capacity management, capacity planning, collections, and portfolio item dependencies. These reports can be activated and used or adjusted based on your organization's requirements (although be aware that prerequisites have to be met). Chapter 10 offers more details on this topic.

2.3   Functional Execution

Functional execution is the final tier of the NPDI pyramid shown at the beginning of this chapter in Figure 2.1. Functional execution is divided into four distinct areas, which will be discussed in this section:

▶ Idea management and product development, which will be discussed in Section 2.3.1 through Section 2.3.5.

▶ Strategy sourcing and supply chain, which won't be further detailed because they are covered in the manufacturing solution map and not the SAP PLM Solution Map, and therefore fall outside the scope of this book.

▶ Prototyping and production ramp-up, which is covered in Chapter 3 when discussing product data and in Chapter 7 when describing project management (in case SAP Project Management solutions are used in combination with production). However, the production and manufacturing solutions won't be further described because they aren't included in the SAP PLM Solution Map and fall outside the scope of this book.

▶ Market launch management (Section 2.3.6), which covers the entire process of introducing a new product into the marketplace. It includes the follow-up management of the product or service in the market to ensure that the predefined business goals are achieved. The actual market launch of a product takes place after the product has been developed and often involves considerable costs for marketing activities such as advertising, sales promotions, and other efforts.

Product innovation is a starting point and should be managed as a lifecycle instead of as a one-off event. In *Living on the Fault Line,* Geoffrey A. Moore represents the innovation lifecycle as a grid, but we've adapted his lifecycle into a linear process (see Figure 2.73).

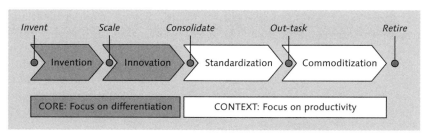

Figure 2.73 Innovation Lifecycle

The implementation of a comprehensive innovation lifecycle solution can produce the following benefits:

- Ensuring that new innovation initiatives mature to become revenue-generating products and services via an integrated solution, to speed up time to market
- Providing a knowledge-centric view on innovation and providing a collaborative working environment throughout the product development cycle
- Being able to systematically translate market and customer requirements into products and services
- Providing a seamless flow of information from product idea to product design
- Being able to continuously analyze and improve your innovation process

Let's take a look at idea management.

2.3.1 Idea Management

The innovation and requirement stage of the product development phase are covered by multiple products. SAP ERP Integrated Product and Process Engineering (iPPE) can be used to develop concepts and capture requirements. This will be discussed in more detail in Chapter 3, Section 3.1.2. Two additional products are available that can be used during the idea and concept phase of a product: code name "Edison" and SAP Product Definition, which we'll cover in an upcoming subsection. Which application is best for your organization depends on your specific requirements and additional factors, such as the product complexity, integration with product data, necessary details, and the need for collaboration between the different stakeholders.

2.3.2 Code Name "Edison"

Code name "Edison" is an application that provides functionalities to manage new product ideas. It supports requests for the submission of product ideas and provides capabilities to review these ideas by collaborating with different business stakeholders to enable purposeful innovation from strategy to execution.

You can achieve the following idea management benefits from using code name "Edison":

- **Increase growth and profitability**
  The application widens the innovation channel to increase the number of

ideas. It improves the evaluation of ideas to promote the selection of the right ideas.

▸ **Save costs**
The application supports reuse of knowledge and ideas, which saves time, and the transparency of the tool enables continuous improvements of the innovation process.

▸ **Reduce time to market**
The innovation process support and integration can accelerate idea to execution, which allows you to focus resources on the right ideas earlier on in the process.

▸ **Collaboration**
The application is easy to deploy, quick to implement, and intuitive to use.

▸ **Integration**
Optional integration is available to SAP Document Management System (SAP DMS), PPM (from 5.0 onward), and SAP NetWeaver Enterprise Search (from 7.2 onward).

The code name "Edison" process shown in Figure 2.74 is one example of how a business process can be set up. Be aware that you can adjust the process and responsible roles based on your use cases (e.g., brainstorming session setup and collaborative evaluation of ideas) and individual needs. Consider these examples of use cases and scenarios:

▸ Set up a brainstorming session for a new product idea.

▸ Search, review, and collaborate on ideas.

▸ Perform collaborative evaluations of ideas.

No master data is necessary for code name "Edison", although when you want to send and include employee data, you'll need to set that up before it can be used.

Let's walk through the idea management process, shown in Figure 2.74.

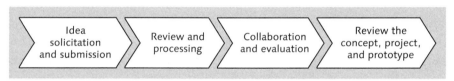

Figure 2.74 Code Name "Edison" Idea Management Process

1. **Idea solicitation and submission**

This step involves requesting idea drivers or employees (participants) for ideas via the "new ideation sessions" feature. You can set a time frame, request detailed information through questions and classifications, and have the option of adding attachments (such as videos or documents) and notifying the participants of solicitation process invites, reminders, or closures. Through the submission ideas activity, you can submit ideas based on a request, based on others' ideas, or directly without any reference. Figure 2.75 gives you an example of a request to submit an idea for an energy drink.

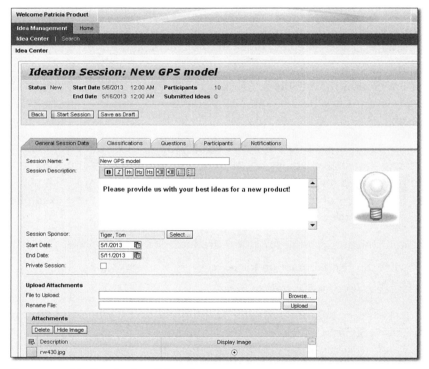

Figure 2.75 Ideation Session: Edison 1

2. **Review and processing**

During the review and processing activities, you have several options available to find the right ideas through searching, filtering, sorting, and tagging. You can also make comments about ideas.

3. **Collaboration and evaluation**

   Via collaboration tools, you can find, tag, filter, and make comments about others ideas, and you can promote the most promising ones. During the evaluation process step, you can score ideas through evaluation sessions. Figure 2.76 shows the evaluation of the energy drink ideas.

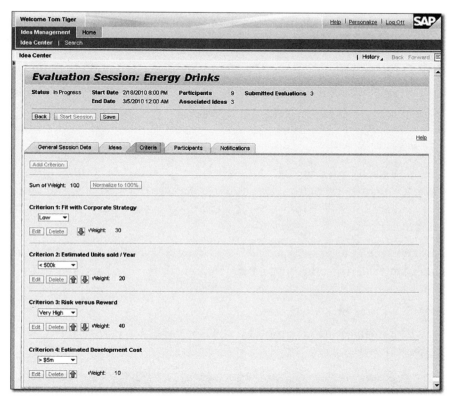

Figure 2.76 Evaluation Session Scoring

4. **Review the concept, project, and prototype**

   Different analysis capabilities are available directly in the application via the dashboard, or data can be exported to Excel. Via notifications, stakeholders can be emailed and additional documentation can be stored against the idea in the form of attachments. Integration to other relevant systems, such as PPM and SAP DMS, is available as well. Figure 2.77 shows the outcome of an evaluation session for an energy drink with a total score and score per defined area.

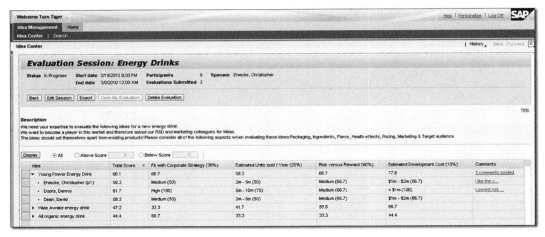

Figure 2.77 Evaluation Review

Code name "Edison" runs on SAP ERP, specifically from SAP EHP 1 for SAP NetWeaver Composition Environment (SAP NetWeaver CE) 7.10 SP4; supported web browsers are Internet Explorer 6, 7, and 8). We recommend the following optional integrations:

▶ SAP NetWeaver Enterprise Search 7.2 (based on SAP NetWeaver 7.2), which provides better performance and more comprehensive search options (including full text search)

▶ SAP DMS, which stores attachments

▶ PPM, which enables the creation of a concept based on an idea (PPM 5.0 is based on SAP NetWeaver 7.0)

> **Note**
>
> For additional details, consult the Product Availability Matrix at *http://service.sap.com/PAM*.

2.3.3   SAP Product Definition

SAP Product Definition (once known as SAP xApp Product Definition, or SAP xPD) addresses the hurdles and inefficiencies at the critical frontend of the product development process. The product gets delivered as a composite application and requires SAP NetWeaver, including the SAP NetWeaver Portal. It can be integrated to PPM, SAP ERP, SAP DMS, and SAP NetWeaver Search and Classification (TREX 7.0), which is SAP's search engine in SAP NetWeaver. SAP Product Definition 2.0 is currently the latest release and the release on which this section of the book is based; it offers smart idea management and integrated concept development for new products, services and marketing initiatives.

Simple and easy-to-use, SAP Product Definition helps you screen and rationalize new ideas, study their market potential and technical constraints, gather requirements, evaluate whether and how to efficiently produce them, and then come up with a short list of promising product concepts that match your company's strategy. The idea management process step can be fed by using relevant product information from SAP CRM, as you can see in Figure 2.78.

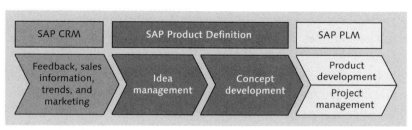

Figure 2.78 SAP Product Definition Positioning

SAP Product Definition offers several global features:

▶ Performs idea and concept classification, including relationships

▶ Uses KM as a central document repository to upload, display, and print electronically available data, such as images

▶ Performs targeted ideation where organizational teams/units can receive workflows/email notifications using the powerful authorization concept

The following benefits are associated with optimized use of SAP Product Definition:

▶ **Time to market**
You can capitalize on your best ideas by being able to focus and analyze a larger pool of ideas; through follow-up and assessment of ideas, you can improve your innovation efficiency. You can also identify constraints early, which might lead to a reduction of development bottlenecks, rework cycles, wasted effort, and errors.

▶ **Alignment of portfolio with strategic objectives**
You can develop products, services, or market initiatives that meet market needs and are in line with you company's strategy. Your approval decisions are based on comprehensive market information from multiple resources and cross-functional teams that have access to all of the necessary critical information

▶ **Mitigate R&D pipeline risk**
You can do this by being able to make go or no-go decisions earlier in the process based on equal and informed assessment of all concepts. You can even build in the flexibility to customize frontend processes based on assumed concept risk.

▶ **Single source**
You now have a single source of all "frontend" product information across functions and geographies.

▶ **Integration**
As indicated earlier, the SAP Product Definition solution can collect data from a customer relationship management system (such as SAP CRM). Data from the sales field operations, the call center, sales and trend information, and marketing input seamlessly integrate to SAP ERP and SAP PLM. It supports out-of-the-box integration to other desktop and backend systems as well.

SAP Product Definition supports the innovation and requirements management process shown in Figure 2.79.

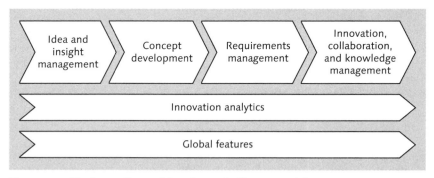

Figure 2.79 The Innovation and Requirements Management Process

The first step is idea and insight management. Let's examine it closely.

Idea Management/Insight Management Process

The following process is available for idea management. In Figure 2.80, most steps are performed by the innovation manager. The step labeled ❶ is performed by the idea submitter, and the step labeled ❷ is done by the subject matter expert (SME). Of course, you can simplify or add roles based on your specific needs.

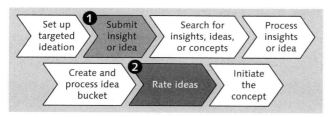

Figure 2.80 Idea Management Process

Let's walk through this process:

1. **Set up targeted ideation.**
   An idea is a business opportunity for a specific new product or service. It doesn't provide an in-depth analysis but is a suggestion presented to others for consideration. An idea can be used and transformed into a concept to further access its validity. Figure 2.81 gives you an example of the collection of an idea based on a targeted ideation. *Targeted ideation* is the process where you reach out to a group of people to request ideas for a specific campaign or initiative.

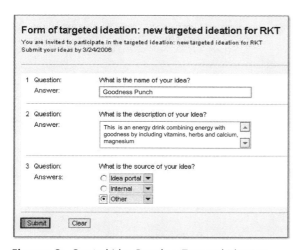

Figure 2.81 Created Idea Based on Targeted Ideation

2. **Submit an idea or insight.**

   Both internal employees and external people can submit ideas, either by logging in to the application or by using an SAP Interactive Form by Adobe or web service. Using targeted idea submission, you can also invite a group of selected people to submit ideas and answer questions about a specific idea campaign. Figure 2.82 shows an example of the targeted idea submission. The ideation process can be initiated based on a product review.

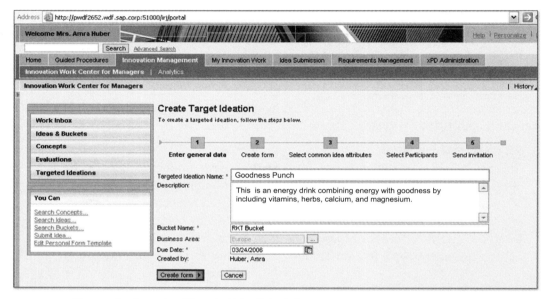

Figure 2.82 Example of Targeted Idea Submission

3. **Search for insights, ideas, or concepts.**

   To assist you as the idea owner or idea submitter, you can draw inspiration from ideas submitted in other, similar initiatives. You can use them as templates, search based on their details, and further explore or elaborate.

4. **Process insights and ideas.**

   Idea submissions and ideas can be classified by freely definable attributes, and you can attach documents. The idea owner can identify relationships between ideas and call on experts to assist in evaluating discussions by using a rating system.

5. **Create and process idea buckets.**

   Ideas can be grouped together by assigning them to idea buckets.

6. **Rate ideas.**

The idea owner can also start rating the submitted ideas to start an approval process, progress the idea into a concept via the next step, or reject the idea.

7. **Initiate the concept.**

The idea owner can progress the idea into a concept or reject the idea.

2.3.4   Concept Development

A *concept* is a draft proposal for a new product, service, radical innovation, or incremental innovation. The aim of concept development is to convert an initial rough sketch proposal into a more detailed and thorough proposal (e.g., a product or service definition). Concept development (see Figure 2.83) also enables the proposed new product or service to be formally evaluated in a phased and timely manner by SMEs to determine if the concept should progress to the next stage (e.g., project). SMEs provide predetermined deliverables that enable concepts in similar areas to be compared readily, for example, to determine which concept provides the highest benefit to the organization, perhaps through business and feasibility studies. This process streamlines and structures the development of a concept from an idea to the point at which product development can start. Figure 2.84 shows an overview of different concepts defined, which will further be explained in the next section.

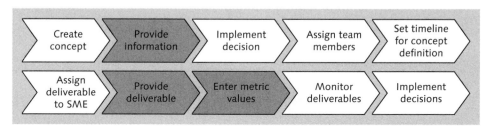

Figure 2.83 Concept Development

A *concept template* holds detailed information on the concept, such as folders for topics (e.g., finance) and subtopics (e.g., revenue and costs), attributes and KPIs/metrics, document deliverables (including templates, for example, detailed competitive analysis), and links of interest (e.g., sources of information in HTML). Figure 2.85 shows the first step of creating a concept: entering the basic data.

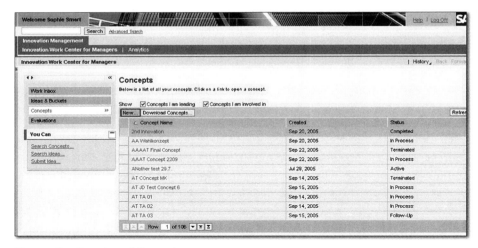

Figure 2.84 Overview of Concepts

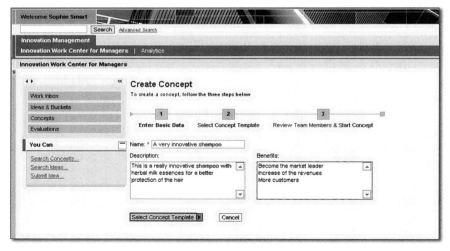

Figure 2.85 Concept Creation: Enter Basic Data

The process templates can be used to either represent a concept development process (which orchestrates work on concept content by different team members and is organized by phases and tasks) or an approval process (which organizes how a concept at a certain stage in its lifecycle is reviewed and approved by different stakeholders). Parallel and sequential approval processes are supported. Figure 2.86 shows the next step in concept creation—assigning a concept template.

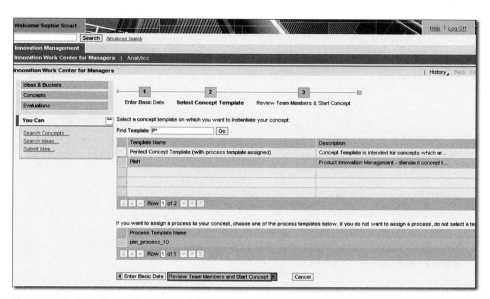

Figure 2.86 Assigning a Concept and Process Template

The deliverable dashboard tracks the progress of deliverables. All actions taken on a concept are documented, including involved decision makers, relevant decision documents, and related comments. You can upload KPIs and metrics from Excel.

During concept processing, the concept owner can update the details of a concept; define relationships between other concepts, ideas, or idea containers; start a discussion; monitor the evaluation process of the concept; and make the decision to either process the concept(s) to a project(s) or to discontinue the concept. When a concept is approved and turned into a project, the concept data can be synced and loaded into PPM as a portfolio item/project.

2.3.5   Requirements Management

You can create and/or structure requirements for an existing concept or from scratch. Standard requirements covered are any marketing, technical, legal, and system requirements you may have. These requirements can be used for comparing and benchmarking. The requirements management process is shown in Figure 2.87 and described in the following set of steps.

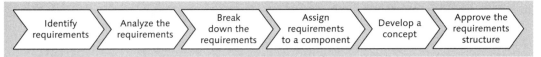

Figure 2.87 Requirements Management Process

> **Note**
>
> Requirements management is available from SAP Product Definition 2.0 SP2, which we'll cover later in this section.

1. **Identify requirements**

   You identify the requirements based on the concept and/or the idea. You can reuse existing templates or requirement structures. You can identify the members that need to be working on the concept and set up a time line. Figure 2.88 shows an example of a requirement.

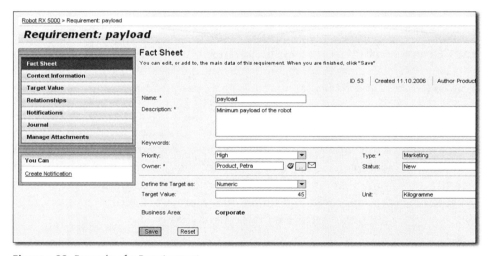

Figure 2.88 Example of a Requirement

2. **Analyze the requirements.**

   Next you can define and rate the dependencies of requirements. This step is supported by being able to use Excel to uploading and download requirements.

3. **Break down the requirements.**

   During this step, you work out the hierarchical requirements structure and look at the requirements by level. Figure 2.89 shows an example of a requirements structure where conflicts between requirements are made visible by color codings.

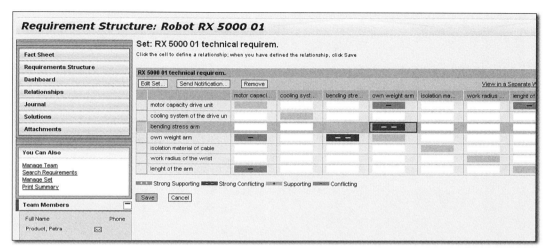

Figure 2.89 Example Relationships and Conflicts between Requirements

4. **Assign requirements to a component.**
   You can create work packages consisting of several requirements and assign them to components in your SAP ERP backend by using the generic objects interface into a project (details in Chapter 7), BOMs, the Product Design Cost Estimate (PDCE), recipes, or the iPPE requirement structure (details in Chapter 3).

5. **Develop a concept.**
   You can track your progress through target versus actual requirements via the dashboard, which allows easy navigation through work packages and assigned components.

6. **Approve the requirements structure.**
   Single or entire requirement structures can be approved. Alert functions are available for effective identification of unresolved issues.

Innovation Collaboration and Knowledge Management

Ideas and concepts can be freely classified with two levels, based on your information need; for example, you can define "Region" as a classification: level 1

(continents) and level 2 (countries). The TREX search engine can be used for finding objects and to save favorite search patterns. All documents attached to ideas,
idea buckets, concepts, requirements, and requirement structures are stored in
the central repository, also known as Knowledge Management (KM). KM facilitates discussions of ideas, idea buckets, and concepts. Figure 2.90 shows an example of such collaboration.

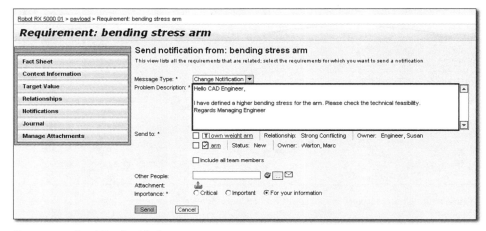

Figure 2.90 Send Email with Context

Innovation Analytics

With innovation analytics, you can continuously analyze and improve your innovation using standard delivered reports, which can organize ideas by status,
source, author, and number of concepts created from ideas supporting processes
in the conceptualizing stage.

SAP Product Definition 2.0 has tight integration with PPM, which allows you to
strategically align, monitor, and stage-gate the complete NPDI pipeline. You can
map concept templates to appropriate portfolio item types, and then assign and
upload the concepts to the strategic bucket via the bucket picker UI. You can also
use the PPM questionnaires and strategic planning capabilities, which allow you
to perform capacity and financial planning. SAP Product Definition attributes,
metrics, and classifications can be mapped with fields in PPM. SAP Product
Definition also integrates with the PPM–Project Management capabilities, where
multiple projects can be created from a concept, and a bidirectional link can be

established between the concept and its related projects, which is represented in Figure 2.91.

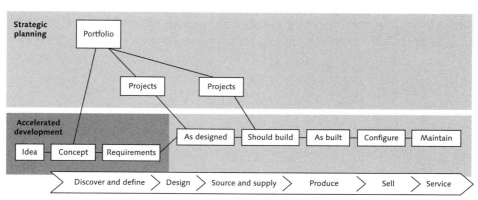

Figure 2.91 Product Definition Integrated with PPM and SAP ERP

SAP Product Definition 2.0 leverages the latest functionalities for SAP NetWeaver, allowing you to use the SAP NetWeaver Portal, the KM capabilities such as SAP DMS (see Chapter 3, Section 3.2) including the search capabilities covered via TREX 7.0 (see Chapter 10, Section 10.1.3) and the latest SAP NetWeaver BW (see Chapter 10, Section 10.3.2).

2.3.6 Market Launch Management

Market launch management covers the entire process of introducing a new product into the marketplace and includes the follow-up management of the product or service in the market to ensure that the set business goals are achieved. The actual market launch of a product takes place after the product has been developed and often involves considerable costs for marketing activities such as advertising, sales promotions, and other marketing efforts. The commercialization phase of a product ends when the product or service has reached the end of its useful life and is retired, renewed, or regenerated.

New Product Introduction

New Product Development and Introduction (NPDI) is part of market launch management and includes the process of managing all activities and resources to bring a new product to market that meets customer needs and supports business goals. New product introductions rely heavily on the processes and products that have been described in this chapter so far. Figure 2.92 shows the layers of complexity that are involved in NPDI. One complexity to be aware of is that the scope of the NPDI processes might differ based on the industry (the top row in the figure); another is the involvement of a lot of internal and external stakeholders.

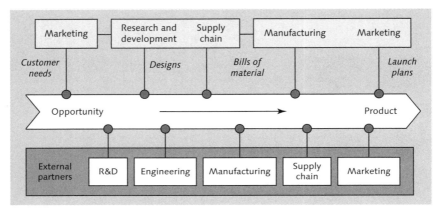

Figure 2.92 NPDI Process

Other important inputs for the market launch phase are covered within SAP Supply Chain Management (SAP SCM). Within the DEMAND AND SUPPLY PLANNING category of the SAP SCM Solution Map in Figure 2.93, DEMAND PLANNING AND FORE-CASTING, and SUPPLY NETWORK PLANNING are included; within the PROCUREMENT process category, STRATEGIC SOURCING is covered; and within the MANUFACTURING category, PRODUCTION PLANNING AND DETAILED SCHEDULING, MANUFACTURING VISI-BILITY AND EXECUTION AND COLLABORATION, and MRP BASED DETAILED SCHEDULING are included. The rest of the solution map isn't part of the scope of this book.

New product introductions require the development and implementation of a commercialization strategy and market launch plans. During the introduction stage, the primary focus is on preparation for launch (including marketing and launch plan development), product launch (release decision, market entry, and product announcement), and early user trial and product adoption. Timing of events, execution of the launch plan, and synchronization of the supply chain and demand chain are critical to the successful commercialization of the product. These activities are generally undertaken by the setup and execution of a project, which will be explained in more detail in Chapter 7.

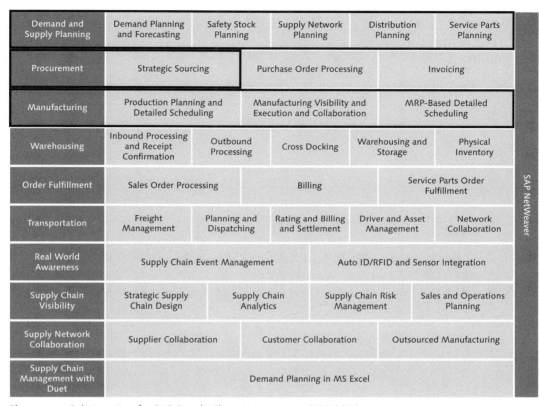

Figure 2.93 Solution Map for SAP Supply Chain Management (SAP SCM)

Post-Launch Review

Customer and market research activities are used to help measure whether the newly launched product is meeting its goals. Key goals can be categorized as customer-related, channel-related, competitor-related, or financial-related. For each, it's necessary to identify clear metrics.

After the product has reached the market, a post-launch review (or audit) is needed to assess the technical performance of the product or process versus previously defined criteria and to make appropriate adjustments as required. Such a review can also identify features of a successful implementation that can be used to improve the overall process.

During the growth stage, the primary focus is process performance assessment, product value measurement, product introduction assessment (financial), and managing the product lifecycle. This stage is marked by a rapid surge in sales and market acceptance for the good or service. It's supported by the use of the PPM–Portfolio Management solution (as described in detail in Section 2.2), which allows you to set up the measures you want to use to evaluate the success of a launch. To collect details for this measure, you might need input from other areas of your solution, such as from your operational project management system (see Chapter 7).

2.4   Summary

This chapter has covered the creative part of the product lifecycle and the solutions and applications that can help you. SAP's product portfolio assists you every step of the way, whether you require the full scope of the offered applications or want to leverage just those applications required to develop new products for your organization.

We examined the solutions available in each tier of the NPDI pyramid. The innovation strategies tier is supported by defining your product strategy via pathways and strategy maps using SAP Strategy Management.

To protect your intellectual property, ensure your product is compliant to regulations and company policies, and introduce controls to mitigate your organization's product-related risks, you should implement SAP GRC functions and processes.

The planning and management tier was covered by the management and monitoring capabilities regarding product portfolios, initiatives, and new product proposals in SAP Project and Portfolio Management (PPM). PPM can be fed by using code name "Edison" or SAP Product Definition to capture all product ideas, prioritize them, assign them to teams, and go through the appropriate collection and analysis of data to prepare for the market launch management phase; all of these are functional execution solutions, which is the last tier in the NPDI pyramid.

The chapter finished with the new product introductions process; although this process varies by customer, depending on the industry and the complexity of the innovation process, the SAP PLM together with SAP ERP components and SAP SCM solutions offer an end-to-end solution for all variations.

This chapter is just a first glance and introduction to the solutions available for SAP Product Data Management and should give you enough information and context to dive into the areas in more detail. Appendix A and Appendix B give you guidance concerning where to find additional relevant information through websites and courses.

The next chapter dives into the product master data. We'll first introduce the product structure, followed by information about SAP Document Management System (SAP DMS). Then we'll provide an overview of the product costing tools available within SAP PLM. The chapter finishes by explaining the product data via the specification database and the recipe.

Gathering, maintaining, and sharing the continuously changing product data during all the different stages a product goes through ensures that all relevant parties have the right information of the best quality at the right time to optimize success.

3 Product Data Management

The focus of this chapter is SAP Product Data Management (SAP PDM), also known as lifecycle data management. Product data is continuously shared, used, and changed by various users during the product lifecycle and is a fundamental part of an SAP PLM solution.

Successful product data management can yield the following benefits:

- ▶ Better collaboration by maintaining and exchanging data on products between both internal and external parties, thereby providing a single source of the truth
- ▶ Improved communication with the use of the latest channels, such as email, the Internet, c-folders, fax, and WebEx
- ▶ Document management, including the use of watermarks, release scenarios, and version control
- ▶ Integrated data management to prevent redundant data
- ▶ Flexible master data maintenance tools (mass updates and template use) and data enrichment via classification
- ▶ Central viewing and maintenance of all product-related data through integrated product tools, with full history of changes visible through rigorous change management
- ▶ Minimized need for changes due to early coordination with your customers and early involvement of suppliers and development partners
- ▶ Increase productivity by launching new products faster

To cover the topics important to product data management and explore the processes integral to achieving these benefits, the chapter starts by describing and comparing master data with other data, and follows with the different solutions available within SAP PLM to represent a product. The chapter then explains the integrated solutions available for product engineers to update product and product-related data. These integrated product tools such as the Integrated Product and Process Engineering (iPPE) Workbench and the product structure browser are essential when you use multiple objects to represent a product and the same people are responsible for the maintenance of this master data. These tools allow you to access and work on multiple objects simultaneously where the material/product is the central object. Currently with SAP PLM 7.01, two separate interfaces are offered: one focused on discrete industries (including product variant structure [PVS], assemblies, CAD integration, and Variant Configuration) and one focused on process industries (including formula, Specification Management, and Recipe Management). They both include common functions covering the material, BOM, document, SAP Engineering Change Management (ECM), work centers, classification, and search and navigation capabilities. In the future, SAP will seek to unify these interfaces into a single interface.

Section 3.2 describes how documents relating to a product or product component can be stored and used from SAP Document Management System (SAP DMS). Another important topic related to product data management is product costing, so Section 3.3 explains the different costing options per product phase.

The chapter finishes with Specification Management and Recipe Management in Section 3.4, where formulas and ingredients details can be modeled.

3.1   Product Master Data and Structure Management

This section will first describe the product objects and product component objects, followed by the integrated tools available for iPPE. Finally, we'll cover the information required for production, such as routings, task lists, and work centers.

3.1.1   Product Structure Management

Product-related and project-related data is needed from the first product idea, to innovation, through to production and customer delivery. This data should know no departmental boundaries. It's collected throughout all phases of the product lifecycle by the different stakeholders involved during the stages and then shared, being used and changed continuously by various users along the supply chain.

For this reason, lifecycle data management is a key part of a successful SAP PLM solution and should be considered as the foundation that is leveraged by downstream processes.

To understand SAP Product Data Management (SAP PDM) and what part master data plays in an SAP ERP system and in SAP PLM, it's important to understand the differences among organizational data, master data, and transactional data, as shown in Figure 3.1.

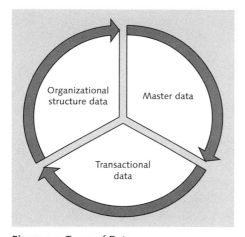

Figure 3.1 Types of Data

Through *organizational data*, you represent your organizational structure within the available organizational structure element objects. When you're implementing SAP PLM, the in-scope components will determine precisely which specific organizational elements are relevant and need to be set up for you organization. The following commonly used organizational elements of an SAP PLM system have been placed in Figure 3.2 to show you how they are connected:

▶ **Client**
 The client is the highest hierarchical level in the SAP ERP system in legal and organizational terms and in terms of data, with its own separate master records and tables. From a business point of view, the client can represent a corporate group.

- **Company code**

  The company code is the smallest organizational unit of external accounting for which a complete, self-contained bookkeeping system can be provided, such as balance sheets and profit-and-loss (P&L) statements.

- **Plant**

  The plant is an operating area or branch within a company. It's an organizational unit within logistics that subdivides an enterprise from the viewpoints of production, procurement, maintenance, and logistics operations.

- **Storage location**

  This organizational unit facilitates the differentiation of stocks of materials within a plant, so materials can be inventory managed.

- **Purchasing group**

  This represents a buyer or a group of buyers responsible for certain purchasing activities.

- **Purchasing organization**

  This is an organizational unit within logistics that subdivides the enterprise according to the purchasing requirements. It procures materials or services, negotiates conditions of purchase with vendors, and is responsible for performing transactions.

- **Sales organization**

  The sales organization is responsible for selling and distributing goods and services to customers and responsible for a customer's rights of resource. It can be used to represent regional, national, or international subdivisions of a marketplace in which products are sold.

- **Distribution channel**

  The channel is the means through which saleable materials or services reach the customer and is assigned to a sales organization.

- **Division**

  A division can represent a product group or product line, and it allows restricted price agreements and statistical analysis.

- **Sales area**

  This is a unique and allowable combination of a sales organization, distribution channel, and division assigned to each sales transaction.

- **Shipping point**

  The shipping point is responsible for the management of shipping activities.

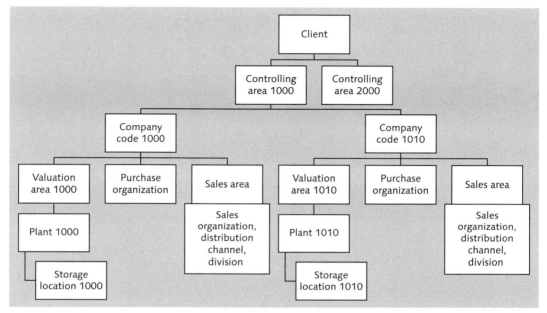

Figure 3.2 Organizational Structure

In an SAP ERP environment, *transactional data* documents the everyday events either within the business between departments or divisions, or between the business and the outside with customers or suppliers. Examples of transactions are financial postings, purchase orders, project setup, maintenance work orders, or sales orders. In SAP ERP, transactional data is related to some form of master data and organizational data.

Master data is "slow-changing" data because it doesn't change very often. In SAP ERP, master data is intended to be stored once, and replication is to be avoided (e.g., material masters and vendor masters). Within SAP PLM 7.01 and/or SAP ERP, you have to maintain different master data objects during all the stages a product goes through, which is represented in the left column of Figure 3.3. The figure maps the product lifecycle against the master data elements used. The second column shows the departments involved during product development. The last row shows the product lifecycle where, for discrete industries, CAD and BOMs are relevant and, for process industries, the specification and recipe.

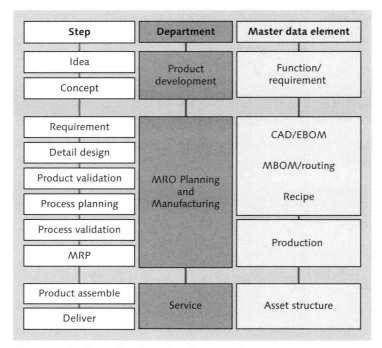

Figure 3.3 Product Lifecycle and Different Product Structures

Product Objects

Based on the master data objects used during all the stages of the lifecycle represented in Figure 3.3, Figure 3.4 gives you an overview of all the master data objects that can be used to represent a product. Each of these objects will be explained in this chapter and the next chapter in their own dedicated sections. Section 3.2 covers SAP DMS, Section 3.3 explains product costing, and Section 3.4 describes Specification Management and Recipe Management. Chapter 4 will explain classification, Variant Configuration, and sales configuration.

Material Master

The material master can be used to represent materials that a company designs, purchases, produces, stores, and sells. Each material within the company can be identified by a material number, which is created within a *material type* and an industry sector. Examples of material types that are provided as part of the SAP standard are trading good, semifinished product, and raw material. Together, the material type group's materials determine which views can be created and control several other functions (e.g., if quantities and values are updated in inventory management, if the material is procured in-house or externally, and which General Ledger [GL] accounts are updated). You can add your own material types based on your business requirements by making custom configurations.

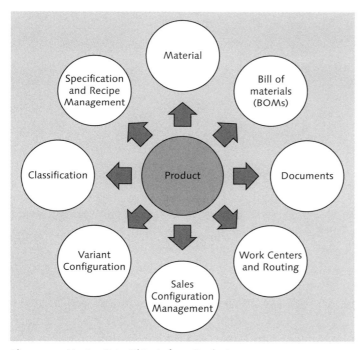

Figure 3.4 Master Data Objects for a Product

General data such as the material description and the unit of measure is valid for the entire enterprise, so this is stored at the client level (the highest level of an SAP ERP system). Apart from general data, data at other organizational levels (such as plant and storage location data) can be maintained in the *material views*, which are logically grouped together based on function. Which views are active depends on the settings in the configuration of the material type. This allows you to maintain data just for the functions in which you're planning to use the material master, such as materials requirements planning (MRP). Figure 3.5 shows an overview of all the different material views available.

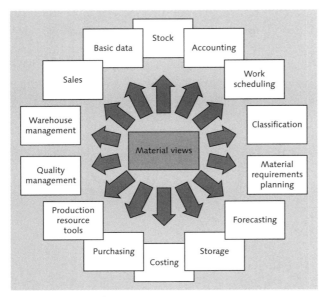

Figure 3.5 Material Master Views

Standard SAP comes with a range of standard material types, which each have the right views and fields selected. You can either use these or configure your own types by copying the closest standard material type and just making the necessary adjustments where there are differences. For all the available standard fields, you can configure the field selection, which allows you to set the field to required entry, optional (default for most fields), or to even hide them, based on your organization's needs. Apart from the standard available views, which usually cover most of your requirements, you can extend the material master with your own views and custom fields either by using classification (see Chapter 4, Section 4.1) or by enhancing the master record through standard available views for this purpose and customer exits.

Now that you understand the structure of a material and how the material type forms an important controlling mechanism, let's shift our focus to creating a material. In the initial screen of the MAINTAIN MATERIAL MASTER DATA dialog box, which can be found under menu option LOGISTICS • MATERIALS MANAGEMENT • MATERIAL MASTER • MATERIAL • CREATE or via Transaction MM01, you enter the material type and the industry sector. You may also have to define a material number, which is only required when you're allowed to externally number the material.

In the example shown in Figure 3.6, the system automatically assigns the next available number within the configured number range. In that case, there is no need to enter a number. Next, select the views relevant for your material, followed by the relevant organizational elements. In the last step, select the different material views which you want to maintain.

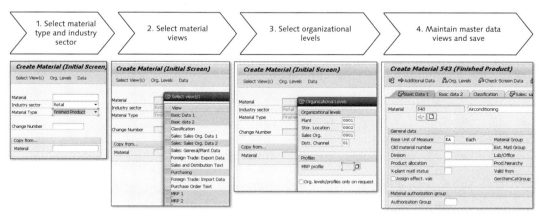

Figure 3.6 Process of Creating a Material

To simplify the process, you can maintain defaults for the industry sectors, views, and organizational levels, which is particularly useful when you're working on the same levels repeatedly. See Figure 3.7 for the process steps.

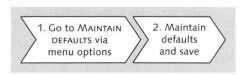

Figure 3.7 Maintain Defaults

Through the *material status,* you can control the use of a material in subsequent application components precisely. You can prevent the material from being used by locking the material or issuing a warning message when the material is being used. The status can be maintained centrally on the basic data level (client level) as shown in Figure 3.8 or can be defined plant-specifically at the work scheduling level, which is then only relevant for the specified plant. Statuses are hierarchical, and the error message will overwrite a warning.

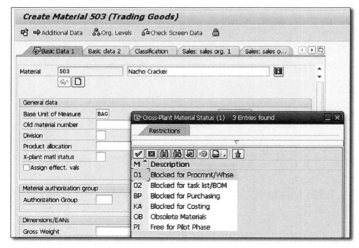

Figure 3.8 Material Status

The base *unit of measure* is used by the system to determine the smallest unit of measurement in which the material needs to be managed. This is because the system uses this base unit of measure to convert all the quantities you enter in other units of measure (alternative units of measure). Other units that are supported are the "order unit" used when ordering the material, the "sales unit" used when selling the material, or the "unit of issue" for goods issuing the material from stock. Figure 3.9 shows that for this casing, the smallest unit used is ST representing individual items. Items are contained in a CARTON, which contains 100 units, and also the PACK, which contains 3,000 units.

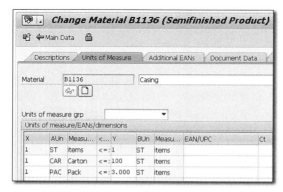

Figure 3.9 Material: Unit of Measure

When a material is no longer required, you can flag the material for deletion by setting the deletion flag in the material master record, which immediately takes effect, as shown in Figure 3.10, or by planning the deletion on a future data. This flag can be set at the client, plant, or storage location level. The flag doesn't cause the material to be deleted from the database; for that to happen, you have to archive the data through an archiving process. The archiving process results in the material being deleted from the database, but you can make sure that the data keeps being stored in an archive, when there is a need to still have the product data available, for example, due to legal requirements.

Figure 3.10 Material Flag for Deletion

Let's consider another master data object: the BOMs.

Bill of Materials

A bill of material (BOM) is a complete, formally structured list of the components that make up the master data object (e.g., a material). The list contains the material number of each component together with the description, quantity, and unit of measure.

BOM Structure

BOM data is managed in a structured form, where the header, item, and subitem are defined hierarchically, as shown in Figure 3.11.

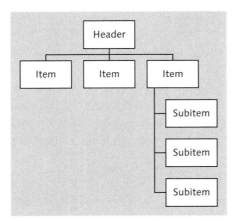

Figure 3.11 BOM Structure

The BOM header contains data that applies to the entire BOM. Figure 3.12 shows an example of the header of a BOM. Data that can be maintained at the header level are, for example, the LAB/OFFICE responsible for the product and the CAD INDICATOR, which will be set when the BOM is created or changed from a CAD system. It also contains administration information, such as who created the BOM and who made the last changes and when.

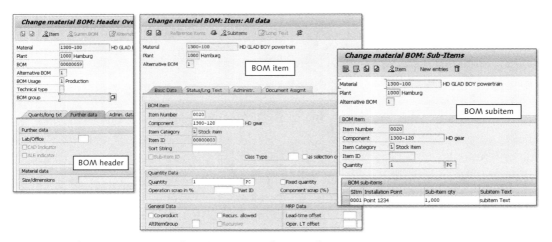

Figure 3.12 BOM Header, BOM Item, and BOM Subitem

Each BOM item contains data that only applies to a specific component of the BOM. See Figure 3.12 for an example of a BOM item. The example shown belongs to the category L, which stands for stock item. This category determines the properties and the functions of the item. It also controls several subsequent system activities, such as field selection control, default values for BOM maintenance, triggering of specific system activities, and so on. Other categories that are used often are nonstock item (N) and document item (D).

Subitems contain data on the different installation points for partial quantities of an item; see the far right example in Figure 3.12. Item data is just relevant for the assigned component; for example, the item status reflects for which areas the item is relevant and to which item category the item belongs.

BOM Level

You can create a BOM as a group BOM, so it has no reference to a specific plant. This could be useful, for example, when an engineer is working on a BOM during the design phase but doesn't know yet which plant it will be used in. It can later be converted into a plant-specific BOM by either assigning a plant to the group BOM or by creating a copy of the BOM, which produces a second BOM.

You can break down large and complex product structures into a number of related units. Each unit can be represented by a BOM, which is also referred to in SAP as a *single-level BOM*. A single-level BOM is often a collection of standardized assemblies, can represent either a complete machine or an individual part, and consists of only one level of items, so it displays the components directly needed to make the assembly or subassembly.

A group of semifinished products or parts that are assembled together and form either a finished product or a component of a finished product is known as an assembly. An *assembly* is identified by a material number and generally functions as a single unit. A product defined as an assembly, such as the DERAILLEUR GEAR SYSTEM in Figure 3.13, can in turn be used as a component in another assembly, such as in the MEN'S RACING BIKE. By doing this, your BOM becomes a *multiple-level BOM*. When you use the gear as a component, you can see that it also has a BOM because the ASSEMBLY checkbox is checked.

Phantom assemblies have their own product structure, but their assembly doesn't actually physically exist, so it's a logical grouping of materials. The components of the phantom assembly are incorporated directly in the superordinate product. The product structure of the superordinate product contains a reference to the phantom assembly. A phantom assembly can be referenced more than once in the same product structure. Changes are visible and effective immediately at all usage locations.

Material Structure: Structure List							
Material	544		Valid from	18.05.2012			
Component desc.	Men's Racing Bike						
▾ 544		Men's Racing Bike			1	EA	
▾ FRAME01		Pre-Assembled Fram and forks			1	EA	
· FORKS		Chrome forks			2	EA	
· MF01		Blue frame			1	EA	
▾ HBA		Handlebar Assembly			1	EA	
· HBAR		Handlebar			2	EA	
· GRIP		Handlebar Grip			2	EA	
▾ GEARS		Derailleur gear system			1	EA	
· GCASS		Gears Cassette			1	EA	
· PARM		Rear Arm			1	EA	

Figure 3.13 Multiple-Level BOM

Figure 3.14 gives an example of the difference between an assembly and a phantom assembly within the end product (BICYCLE). The phantom assembly SET OF WHEELS doesn't really physically exist but is just there for grouping purposes, and it contains the components FRONT WHEEL and REAR WHEEL. The front and rear wheels are immediately placed in the BICYCLE assembly. The LIGHT assembly contains the materials BULB and REFLECTOR. The light components are first assembled so the light psychically exists, and then the light is attached to the bicycle.

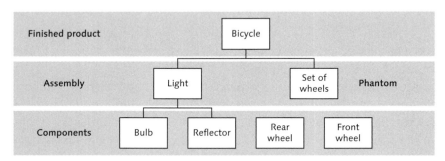

Figure 3.14 BOM with Assembly and Phantom

BOM Categories

The *BOM category* represents the different objects to be structured. The following BOM categories are defined within SAP PLM and SAP ERP (see Figure 3.15):

▸ Material BOM

▸ Sales order BOM

- WBS or project BOM
- Document BOM
- Equipment BOM
- Functional locations BOM
- Specification Management and Recipe Management BOM, which is technically a material BOM

A BOM within the process industry is referred to as a recipe or lists of ingredients, which is why it has been added as a separate category in Figure 3.15. However, in the system, technically the recipe/list of ingredients falls under the category of material BOM, because the top element is a material.

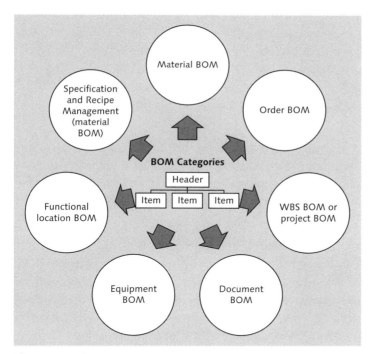

Figure 3.15 BOM Categories

In this section, we'll be discussing the material, sales order, and Work Breakdown Structure (WBS) BOMs. The document BOM is discussed in Section 3.2.2, which is focused on document management. The equipment and functional location BOMs are used in plant maintenance and will be discussed in more detail in

Chapter 5. Recipe Management is discussed in more detail later on in this chapter in Section 3.4.

Materials BOMs are used to represent the structure of products that are produced within the company. The material BOMs are used for integrated materials management and shop floor control and describes which components (discrete industry) or substances/ingredients (process industry) are necessary to produce the product. In the process industry, a BOM is also known as a recipe or list of ingredients (see Section 3.4 for more on this topic). A BOM can be single level but can become multilevel, when a component or ingredient is used with its own BOM.

The *sales order BOM* (also known as the order BOM) is used in a sales order to specify the sold product and its components. They are used by enterprises who are mainly focused on make-to-order production and who have to create a cost-effective, high-quality customer solution for each individual sales order. To support this process, SAP provides a multilevel BOM for sales order items (i.e., order BOM). The process is often iterative, where customer requirements can change or be specified more precisely at a later time, so powerful change management functions are fully integrated. This guarantees a complete history and insight into all the changes along the development process.

When you're creating a sales order BOM in a sales document (such as a sales quote or sales order), you can use an existing material BOM or other sales order BOM as a template, which saves the engineering department from having to start from scratch every time while helping them benefit from past experience.

When you're using a material BOM as a template, the materials and all the items will be copied into the order and become available in the downstream processes, such as costing, MRP, and production order processing. When viewing the BOM in the order browser, a navigation tool that you can use to view your order BOM (Transaction CSKB), it's represented as a regular BOM (order-neutral BOM). However, as soon as you make an order-specific change to the BOM, it will be visible as an order BOM. Figure 3.16 gives you an example of both scenarios.

BOM Assignment

An order BOM can be directly assigned to a sales order or can be indirectly assigned to an order, which is referred to as a detached BOM. Figure 3.17 illustrates both options.

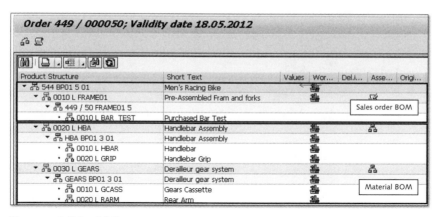

Figure 3.16 Sales BOM

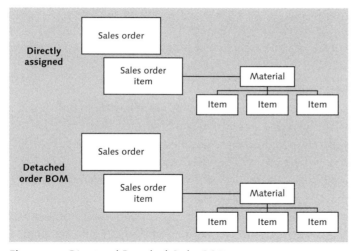

Figure 3.17 Direct and Detached Order BOM

A direct BOM can be created from within the sales document via one of the following two methods:

▸ Using the Variant Configuration function during sales order processing as well as Transaction VA01

▸ Using the BOM processing function, including Transaction CU51 (multi-level BOM) used with a configurable material; using Transactions CS61/CS62/CS63 to create, change, and display BOMs, respectively; or using the Transaction CSKB (the order browser)

When customization for products is so large that creating variants is unmanageable, you can opt to use order BOMs without Variant Configuration. After sales order creation, the BOM can be maintained through the dedicated tool—the order browser (Transaction CSKB).

> **Note**
>
> In the order browser, you process both configurable and nonconfigurable order BOMs. However, configurable order BOMs are only displayed if it's a results-oriented BOM (see Chapter 4 for more details). Detached order assemblies (explained later in this section) aren't displayed in the overview tree; however, they are visible in the sales order analysis.

If you want to create design BOMs at an early stage in the development process, assign BOMs to a sales order indirectly, and then use the CREATE BOM WITH REFERENCE TO SALES ORDER option. This can be useful in situations where the end product and its components haven't been finalized yet, but for a specific part, you *do* know that you require a component that has a long delivery time and needs to be ordered as soon as possible to fulfill the sales order.

When producing a product specifically for a customer, through a manufacturing project, you can generate a project where the number of a production lot is a Work Breakdown Structure (WBS) element from SAP Project System (SAP PS). You use this number to plan and manufacture the production lot for an assembly, and calculate the planned and actual costs for producing the assembly. The BOM that is generated as a result has a reference to a WBS element from the SAP PS, which is why they are known as *WBS BOMs* or project BOMs. If the manufacturing process of an assembly changes, you create a new production lot number and carry out the planning, production, and the planned and actual cost calculation with the new number. This enables you to determine the costs of different manufacturing processes separately and compare them to one another. This is particularly important for branches of industry which, due to continual product improvements and cost-reduction processes, have to plan and produce their finished products or semifinished parts using different BOMs, routings, or change statuses. This procedure can be applied for both finished products and important semifinished parts.

You can create a project BOM from scratch or by coping another material BOM or WBS BOM. Figure 3.18 gives an example of how you can use the BOM transfer to assign the appropriate product BOM items into the right place by transferring them into the correct project activity. The project has an accounting view and a project view relating to scheduling, which includes the activities (explained in more detail in Chapter 7).

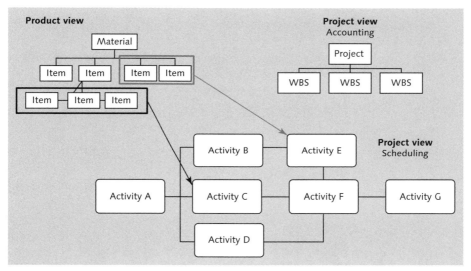

Figure 3.18 BOM-SAP PS Integration

As of SAP ERP 6.0, you can now link iPPE—explained in detail in Section 3.1.2—with SAP PS to assign material components to network activities. It provides a new option for entering and processing design and production master data, which is particularly useful for multivariant products in a single model. This allows you to create complex product structures in iPPE using abstract elements such as nodes, variants, alternatives, or relationships, and then use these later for mapping BOM data. iPPE objects are edited in iPPE Workbench Professional (Product Designer), as shown in Figure 3.19.

BOM Integration
Engineering departments can create BOMs in SAP directly or by using a CAD program and CAD program interface. The data in the material BOM forms a significant basis for various areas in SAP (e.g., in work scheduling, BOMs form the basis for the planning of operations and shop floor control; in a production order, management uses BOMs to plan the provision of parts in the sales order as an aid to entering data, in reservation and goods issue as an aid to enter data, and in product costing to calculate the material usage costs for a product).

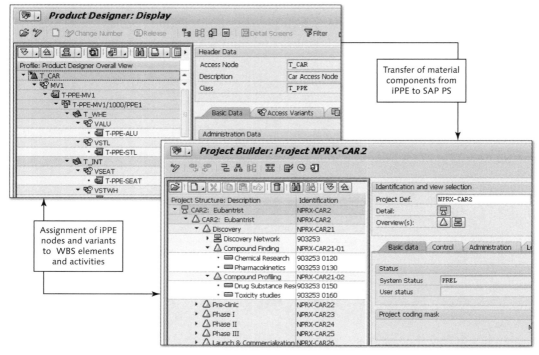

Figure 3.19 iPPE—SAP PS Integration

The use of BOM data simultaneously in several areas of a company shows the great advantage of integrated modules that are linked in such a way that they facilitate a flow of data between various work areas and allow all the users to access the current values at any time. Figure 3.20 gives an overview of all the possible BOM integration areas in which the BOM can be used, such as the sales area, the engineering technical data, plant maintenance area to represent a technical object, grouping functions via group BOMs and overall BOMs, within the production processes, and for costing purposes.

BOM Usage

The use of BOMs allows you to create a BOM specifically for the area where a BOM can be used—for example, in engineering/design, production, plant maintenance, and finance. Figure 3.21 gives you the complete overview of all the BOM usages available within SAP PLM, where UNIVERSAL usage allows you to generate a BOM that can be used by any area.

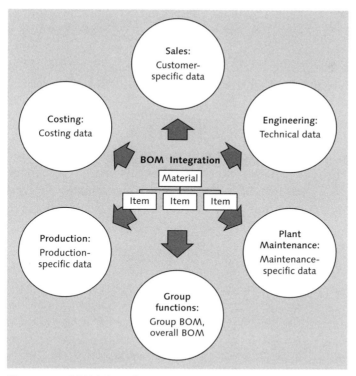

Figure 3.20 BOM Integration

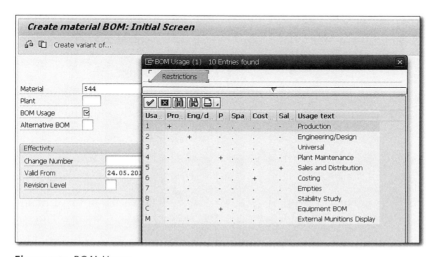

Figure 3.21 BOM Usage

The ENGINEERING/DESIGN BOM contains all the components for a product from an engineering and technical perspective. The PRODUCTION BOM is created from a production point of view and contains the process-oriented data that is required to produce the product, and COSTING BOM is the basis for automatic calculation of the material costs of a product. You can also just create one BOM for all areas by using the item status to cover all the possible differences.

Administration and Authorization

The BOM contains administrative data, such as the date the BOM was created, the name of the user who created the BOM, when it was last changed and who made the changes. When ECM is in use, you can also see which change master record governs the next validity period of the BOM. ECM is discussed in more detail in Chapter 8.

You can organize BOM processing in your company to suit the way your company is structured. Some organizations have centralized their basic master data maintenance and provide the application-specific data to the retrospective departments. To reflect those business rules, they need to be included in your organization's authorization concept. This will then provide input for defining roles and assign these roles to the right system users. For BOM maintenance, specific authorization objects are available, which are included in Table 3.1. In most SAP implementations (especially when done through the SAP-recommended ASAP methodology), authorizations are done by a separate work stream.

Function	Authorization Object
Create or change BOM	C_STUE_BER (BOM) C_STUE_WRK (plant) C_STUE_NOH (change without history)
Mass changes	C_STUE_MAS C_STUE_BER (BOM)
Archive BOM	C_STUE_BER (BOM) C_STUE_WRK (plant)
Display BOM, BOM group, and plant allocation	C_STUE_BER (BOM) C_STUE_WRK (plant)

Table 3.1 BOM Authorization Objects

Function	Authorization Object
BOM explosion, where-used list, BOM comparison	C_STUE_BER (BOM)
Display change documents	S_SCD0 (change documents)
Variable lists for BOM explosions	C_VARLIST (objects for variable lists)

Table 3.1 BOM Authorization Objects (Cont.)

BOM Validity

Two kinds of validity are relevant in our conversation about BOMs. With *time-based validity*, a BOM header and item are assigned a validity period via a valid from and to date. They determine the period at which this object is valid and when the change become effective. If you use ECM, the system determines these dates dynamically. You can assign a revision level to these validity periods. In overviews, you can display all validity periods of the BOM headers or BOM items. Under certain circumstances, the sequence of validity periods can change.

With *parameter effectivity*, if you want to use company-specific criteria (instead of dates) to determine when changes are effective, you can use parameters to define effectivity. The standard SAP system provides two effectivity types (time period and serial number range). For example, the time period effectivity type lets you react quickly to seasonal changes in the market by defining a change to a product (such as color or extras) for a specific time period. If you want to use other, company-specific effectivity conditions, you can define your own effectivity types in the SAP system through configuration.

Technical Types

The system supports two technical types of BOM to represent similar product variants and production alternatives. A *variant BOM* groups together several BOMs that describe *different* objects (e.g., products) with a high proportion of identical parts. A variant BOM describes the specific product variant for each product, with all its components and assemblies.

A *multiple BOM* groups together several BOMs that describe one object (e.g., a product) with different combinations of materials for different processing methods.

The system doesn't define the technical type until you create either an additional alternative for a BOM or a different variant for an existing BOM. If you already know which technical type you want when you create a BOM, you can define the technical type.

When you produce products that are similar, they contain several similar common parts, so they can be described by using a variant BOM. Different variants can exist by either exchanging one component with another or by changing quantities of a component. Only a simple material BOM is supported and can be used within a material BOM, document structure, equipment BOM, or functional location BOM. They are stored as a BOM group under one internal BOM number, so when you process one variant of a variant BOM, all the other variants are locked for processing.

Figure 3.22 shows how two products (blue and black bikes) are represented by using a variant BOM. The handlebar and gears are common components, but the frames are different.

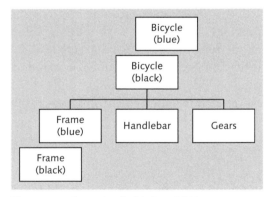

Figure 3.22 Example of a Variant BOM

BOM Reporting Options

Within SAP ERP, you have access to different reporting options from a BOM perspective, such as BOM explosion options, where-used list, BOM comparison (see Figure 3.23 for an example), and the material BOM browser.

BOM Comparison: Result (Summarized)

Primary BOM-Material BOM						Secondary BOM-Material BOM			
Material	CPF10104					**Material**	CPF10104		
Usage:	1					**Usage:**	1		
Alternative:	1					**Alternative:**	2		
Plant	0001					**Plant**	0001		
Date	25.05.2012					**Date**	25.05.2012		

O	Component number	Object description	Comp. Qty (BUn) 1	Unit	R	Difference Quantity	Comp. Qty (BUn) 2	Unit
	RMATL_47376	Vitamin C	0,994	KG		0,993	0,001	KG
	RMATL_47380	Flavoring, Cinnamon liquid	4,970	KG				
	RMATL_4748	Sugar Coating	248,509	KG		2,279	246,230	KG
	RMATL_4726	Water, Food Grade	215,810	KG		98,879	116,931	KG
	RMATL_4727	Oil, Soybean	11,771	KG		5,393	6,378	KG
	RMATL_4731	Salt, Medium-fine (unfilled)	9,417	KG		4,315	5,102	KG
	RMATL_4732	Flour, Whole-Grain	466,935	KG		213,939	252,996	KG
	RMATL_4733	Apple Pieces, Dried	23,543	KG		10,787	12,756	KG
	RMATL_4734	Baking Soda	10,202	KG		4,674	5,528	KG
	RMATL_4736	Sugar, Fine	47,086	KG		21,574	25,512	KG

Figure 3.23 BOM Report

3.1.2 Integrated Product and Process Engineering (iPPE)

Users responsible for product data, such as product engineering departments, often are also responsible for maintenance of the product documents, subcomponents, BOM data, and routing information. To allow them to update or view this data with one integrated tool, the iPPE tools have been developed. This section explains how different users can access product data based on their information needs. We'll cover the components available in the SAP Business Suite to access data (such as the product structure browser and the Engineering Workbench) and end by explaining how the SAP NetWeaver Portal can be used.

Product Structure Browser

The product structure browser is the central navigation tool within SAP PLM and is part of the core SAP ERP, where the material is the central object. From the product structure browser, you can create and maintain all these objects—for example, change or display assigned documents (such as 2D drawings, 3D models, reports, and assembly instructions), manage release information, and change statuses to plan and control all product changes throughout its entire lifecycle.

Figure 3.24 represents how the product structure browser can be used to get a graphical view of the material, including a structural representation of all assigned objects such as documents, classification, BOMs, and routings.

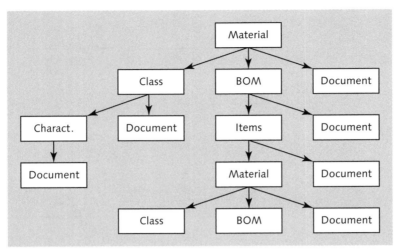

Figure 3.24 Overview of the Product Structure Browser Data Model

The product structure browser can be found under the following menu options or by using Transaction CC04:

▶ Logistics • Central Functions • Engineering • Environment • Product Structure Browser

▶ Logistics • Central Functions • Engineering Change Management • Environment • Product Structure Browser

▶ Logistics • Central Functions • Document Management • Environment • Product Structure Browser

When accessing the product structure browser, you first have to define your selection parameters in the selection screen. On the Product Structure Browser: Initial Screen shown in Figure 3.25, enter the material you want to display (or you can start with a document, equipment, or functional location) and other selection criteria, such as the selection date (defaulted to today's date), selection filters (to improve performance and limit the data that is to be returned), and specifics for the product structure depending on your hardware configuration or a certain change status (when ECM is active).

Within the product structure, you can display the original documents from a document info record (DIR), when you've activated the Engineering Client Viewer (ECL Viewer) (see Section 3.2 for more details). Figure 3.26 shows an example of a product displayed in the product browser.

Figure 3.25 Product Structure Browser Selection Screen

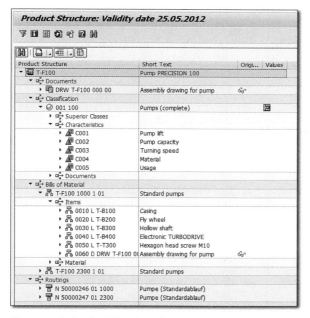

Figure 3.26 Product Structure Browser

Through the product structure browser, you can access data centrally from several logistical components. Table 3.2 shows the SAP objects available from SAP components.

SAP Component	SAP Objects
Materials Management (MM)	▶ Materials
Document Management System (SAP DMS)	▶ DIRs

Table 3.2 Accessable Objects through Product Structure Browser

SAP Component	SAP Objects
Engineering Change Management (ECH)	▶ Change master records
Production (master data)	▶ Routings ▶ Reference operation sets
Classification System (CA)	▶ Characteristics ▶ Classes
Plant Maintenance (SAP PM)	▶ Equipment ▶ Functional locations
Quality Management (QM)	▶ Inspection plans ▶ Material specifications

Table 3.2 Accessable Objects through Product Structure Browser (Cont.)

The product structure browser is more than just a viewing tool; it also allows you to change and maintain object-specific business processes. As shown in Figure 3.27, you can change objects directly, such as the change master record, recipient list for the DIR, maintenance for the SAP Plant Maintenance (SAP PM) structure (functional location and equipment data), and the object folder. The browser supports drag-and-drop capabilities. Only the material specifications and the original application file can be displayed.

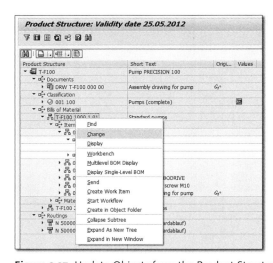

Figure 3.27 Update Objects from the Product Structure Browser

Engineering Workbench

The Engineering Workbench provides you with an integrated workbench in which you can maintain products, BOM items, and Production Planning (PP) operations with a single transaction. Through the workbench, you see these objects (BOM items and PP operations) via views, which allow you to process these master data objects together and to create, change, display, or delete objects.

The workbench contains a personalized worklist, which contains the selected objects that are temporarily copied from the database into this worklist. After you've completed all your updates to the worklist and you've saved your changes, the changes will be performed, and new objects will be created, when relevant. The workbench is part of the core SAP PLM (and SAP ERP 6) and can be found under the menu LOGISTICS • CENTER FUNCTIONS, or is directly accessible via Transaction CEWB. The Engineering Workbench can include the worklist with all the routings relevant for the material as well as the BOM headers and components, as visually represented in Figure 3.28.

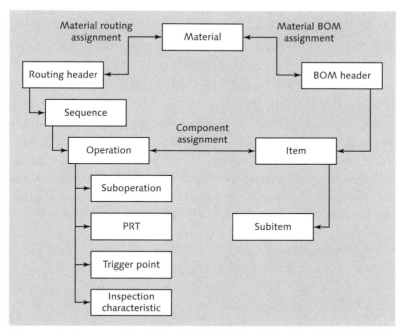

Figure 3.28 Structure of the Engineering Workbench

The following benefits are associated with using the Engineering Workbench:

▶ The workbench supports the ability to save intermediate work for you to perform complex processes that have to be done over a longer period of time.

▶ The Engineering Workbench is integrated with ECM, so it includes rigorous change management capabilities.

▶ The workbench can support simultaneous object processing, including targeted locks and releases of objects.

▶ All transactions for conventional maintenance are offered and brought together, including an extensive change management.

▶ It supports complex selection criteria for routings and BOMs, which allows you to work with the targeted information without unwanted additional information and provides a quick overview.

▶ The user-friendly workbench is easy to learn, supported by integrated graphical controls, and provides simplified printing functions, such as output in Microsoft Word.

Any items from any BOMs and various operations in a routing can be processed by different people at the same time. The system uses a locking mechanism, where the complete task list or BOM doesn't need to be locked for processing but provides targeted blocking of sequences, operations, and BOM items. As a result, other parts of the structure remain available for processing by other users, allowing simultaneous processing of the structure.

This lets users work on the same BOMs and routing data at the same time without interruptions, which is called *parallel processing*. However, as soon as you want to edit a specific BOM item or operation that is being edited by somebody else, the Engineering Workbench tells you who that person is so that you can contact him to coordinate the changes as necessary. The other user can release the BOM item or operation for you without having to interrupt his work.

Process Flow in Engineering Workbench

Let's walk through the process flow of the Engineering Workbench:

1. Set up the working area by selecting the working area or the object types to edit.

2. Select your criteria. You can select the objects of interest to you in the Engineering Workbench to give you a better overview and allow you to work

faster. The system copies the selected objects from the database to your personalized worklist.

3. Process the objects. In the next step, you start processing the objects in your worklist.

4. Save the objects. Objects that you have either changed or created in the previous step will be updated and created as soon as you save changes, which will lead to updating the database.

Figure 3.29 shows what the Engineering Workbench looks like when working on a BOM.

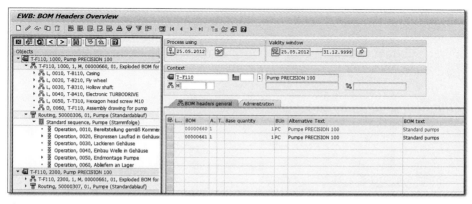

Figure 3.29 Engineering Workbench: Bill of Material Items

The Engineering Workbench is a powerful and flexible tool that most organizations can use to support more complex product master data activities such as the following:

▶ A design change has led to a component change, so all operations with the particular component need to be updated, including corresponding production resource/tool (PRT) data. The change includes checking the standard times of all inspection operations.

▶ A certain component will be fitted in a different warehouse in the future. For this reason, the issue storage location has to be changed, and the work centers for the affected operations need to be updated.

▶ When a new product is designed, the work scheduler intends to copy in one step the operations from various task lists that are already used for similar products.

A central feature in the Engineering Workbench is the integrated graphical controls, which improve navigation and user friendliness. The first control is a graphical object browser that lets you navigate easily through the worklist simply by expanding and collapsing BOM structures and task list structures as needed. It supports drag-and-drop functionality to allow you to copy BOM items. You can see assigned documents directly from within the workbench via the integrated viewer.

Integration with Engineering Change Management

You can start the Engineering Workbench with an effectivity period, which leads to a worklist that includes several change statuses of the same object. Each change status will be added in a separate line, giving you an excellent tabular overview of the object change histories. You can work on changes relating to several change numbers without having to exit the workbench in the interim, as you can see in Figure 3.30.

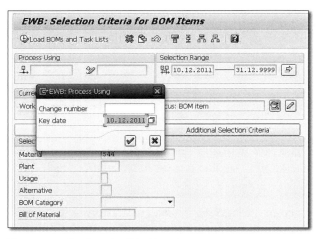

Figure 3.30 Engineering Workbench

Integrated Product Engineering (iPE)

As stated earlier, Integrated Product and Process Engineering (iPPE) is a flexible engineering tool capable of modeling product data from the early phases of product development through to later stages, free of redundancies. This component is a tool that supports all of the data for an entire product lifecycle in one integrated model. It's particularly useful when managing products with many variants and/

or products in repetitive manufacturing. This product variety results in much more complex product development and logistics processes than before.

Note that iPPE will become the standard modeling platform in the future for product development. Not all iPPE objects are available in all applications and their respective releases because iPPE is used differently in them, so check this in advance and use the Switch Framework tool to enable unavailable objects. The Switch Framework tool allows you to activate additional business processes and objects.

As shown in Figure 3.31, the tool enables modeling of the product structure in the broadest sense, including product specifications, documents, sales configuration data, costing, and the ability to show CAD drawings or access other SAP PDM legacy systems. It also includes process structures (task lists) and factory layout structures, as well as their interconnections.

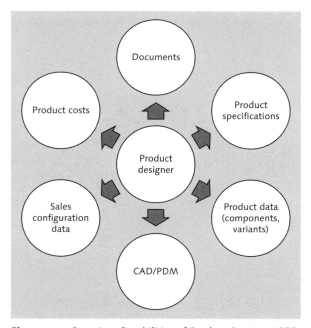

Figure 3.31 Overview Capabilities of Product Designer iPPE

The iPPE uses information from classification, Variant Configuration, and change management. During the early stages of product development, you can capture product information based on a model of requirements and gradually start to replace requirements with the actual specific product data, such as detailed BOMs and routings, which are necessary for production. This concept is represented in Figure 3.32, which distinguishes between the following product scenarios:

▶ **Request structure**
Contains product documents, requirements, specifications, and properties for the functional, conceptual, and design structure.

▶ **Functional structure**
Contains the first structure of the product, representing the conceptual ideas.

▶ **Concept and design structure**
Includes alternative concepts for individual functional structure nodes. A final decision for a concept can only be made when the product structure is released for supply chain processes.

▶ **Product and process structure**
Contains the final concepts and includes all of the specific information necessary for the PP and production modules, such as the individual BOM items and routings.

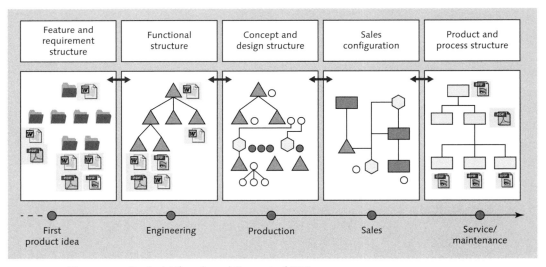

Figure 3.32 Product Lifecycle and Concept of iPPE

Full iPPE functionality supports the following three product structures, which are shown in Figure 3.33:

▶ Product Variant Structure (object type PVS) models the multivariant product.

▶ Task list and activities (object type ACT) models the process with activities and sequence.

▶ Factory layout (object type FLO) documents the line design and describes the physical structure of the production facilities.

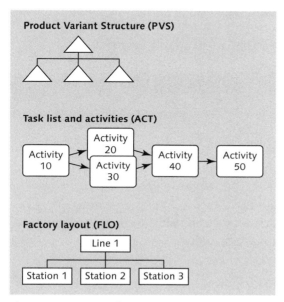

Figure 3.33 Integrated Product and Process Model

The purpose of the PVS is to create a product representing an entire group of similar products with minimal master data maintenance to avoid data redundancy. This structure forms the basis for all processes along the supply chain that use this product structure and is a highly integrated data model.

Factory Layout

The factory layout describes the physical structure of the production facilities and forms the foundation for logistics planning and execution. The top element is the line network, which is comprised of several lines. You can maintain different production rates for each of the lines, which are used to calculate the cycle time of the line. A line consists of various line segments, which in turn can be broken down into further line segments. At the lowest hierarchy level, you can use working areas to describe different labor positions. You can also define the sequence of elements for a production sequence, which enables you to model parallel and alternative lines as well. You can maintain sequence and assignment relationship via a graphical display mode. This is just a quick overview and not meant to cover all the information in this area.

Product Variant Structure

The PVS is made up of three main elements as shown in Figure 3.34 and described in the following list:

- **Access node**
  Defines the product that you want to sell or produce.

- **View nodes**
  Define logical or function groups in your product (no materials are assigned at this level).

- **Structure nodes**
  Define the components that you use to produce your product. You can define variants within a structure node, which in turn define nonvariable parts or optional parts. With selection conditions, you specify when which variants are used. During the early product development phase, a material master doesn't have to be assigned to the variants, so then they just represent ideas for variants; however, materials do have to be assigned before production starts.

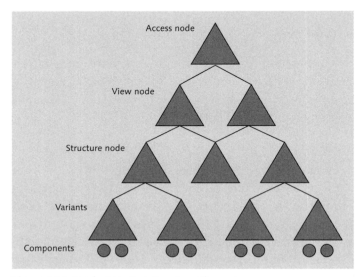

Figure 3.34 Product Variant Structure Elements

The PVS is edited in an iPPE Workbench called the product designer, which is shown in Figure 3.35.

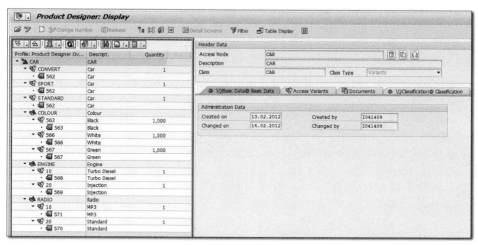

Figure 3.35 Product Designer

The product designer offers the following functions:

▶ **Loading area**
Call existing nodes to display or change them.

▶ **Navigation tree**
View the objects in the hierarchy.

▶ **Filter**
Simulate the configuration by defining multiple filters.

▶ **Navigation tree and list**
Create and change object dependencies using drag and drop (when allowed in the configuration settings).

▶ **Table view**
View all the object data in the form of a worklist.

As represented in Figure 3.36, the following basic scenarios are covered by iPPE:

▶ **APO for automotive**
iPPE is being used as a master data model for Rapid Planning Matrix (RPM). This uses the full iPPE functionality with all three structures: product variant structure (PVS), process structure (ACT), and factory layout (FLO). The master

data is maintained in SAP ERP and distributed to the SAP Supply Chain Management (SAP SCM) system (APO) via the Core Interface (CIF).

▶ **Repetitive automotive manufacturing**
The PVS of iPPE is used as the BOM. Transitional work centers and routings are used here instead of the iPPE process structure. The link between the PVS and the traditional routing is created through production versions. This scenario still has limitations.

▶ **Converter scenario**
Only the PVS is used as part of iPPE. After the product structure has reached a certain development status, it's converted to a conventional BOM. This can then be incorporated as the standard in all supply chain processes, especially in production via the converter. The BOM converter allows you to derive single or multilevel BOMs from the PVS, which can be either configurable or nonconfigurable (see Figure 3.37).

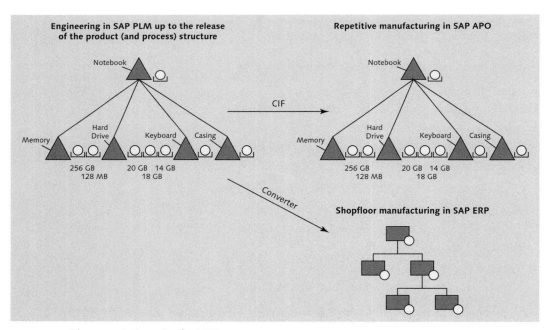

Figure 3.36 Scenarios for iPPE

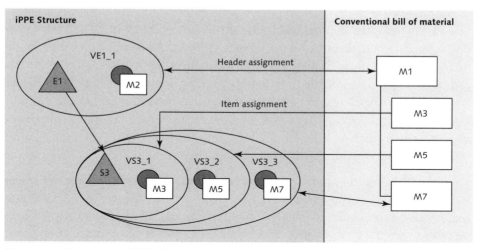

Figure 3.37 Assignment of iPPE-PVS Structure to a BOM

User Profile

To ensure that users get access to relevant structures so they can perform their work without being provided with too much additional data, you can set up a user profile to cater for a group of users. A profile for a BOM engineer will only see the product structures in the navigation area and digital mock-up (DMU) models in the integrated viewer, while an assembly planner will also see the corresponding product structures. Similarly, you can set up a profile for a factory planner to contain information around the process structures, which is explained in Figure 3.38 as well.

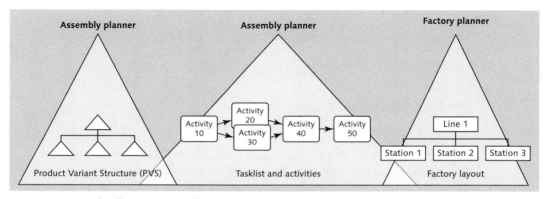

Figure 3.38 Use of Different User Profiles in the Workbench

Digital Mock-Up

You can use the DMU function to visualize new products as 3D models in the development phase throughout the whole enterprise. You can display a 3D model of an assembly and its components in the Engineering Workbench. Other areas can now use product information that used to only be accessible on paper format to the engineering/design department. All departments involved in the development project can see the 3D model of an assembly on the screen even before a prototype is available. We recommend that you reference SAP Note 945552, which regulates the availability of the DMU when using iPPE.

You can display a 3D model of an assembly and its components on the screen without opening another window while processing or displaying a BOM in the Engineering Workbench in the SAP system. You can also display individual components or several components. When you select several components, the system calculates the geometric items of the component and sends them to the viewer for display. When the components are an assembly in and of themselves, you can dismantle them and display or hide individual components.

For example, the BOM of an automobile contains the body and wheels. You can display just the wheels or just the body. When you display the body and the wheels or the whole automobile, the system calculates the geometrical positions of the components and displays them. When the body itself is an assembly, you can also dismantle it into its components (fender, doors, etc.). If the product has a multilevel BOM, you can dismantle all assemblies for the 3D models of their components. However, this requires that data from design drawings has been transferred to the SAP system. You can do this for any number of levels, and you can combine the components from any assemblies.

You can execute the following functions in 3D models:

▶ Display an individual component.
▶ Display further components.
▶ Hide individual components.
▶ Display an entire assembly.

You can also dismantle the components of assemblies to subordinate levels, such as highlighting a component and displaying multilevel BOMs. You can also use all the 3D functions of the viewer for displaying original application files such as rotating and tilting the 3D model and zooming and saving the current screen contents of a file. To use this functionality, you have to set up the integration with your CAD interface in your CAD system. The interface pulls the data for the assembly and its components, including the spatial relations of the components to each other. Contact your CAD interface provider about whether SAP's DMU viewing is supported. This information is used by the system to create a visual 3D file (such as *.JT*) out of the CAD document for each component. This file is then stored in the SAP system as an original application file of the document management system and managed by means of a DIR. You can now use the viewer that is integrated into the SAP system from Engineering Animation, Inc. (EAI) to view your 3D models of assemblies. The viewer is part of the standard SAP Graphical User Interface (SAP GUI) and is integrated into the Engineering Workbench.

The following are prerequisites for using DMU:

▶ Original application files must be in a 3D format that supports DMU (e.g., Direct Model format [*.JT*] is supported).

▶ The original application files in the SAP system are managed by DIRs, which are assigned to items in your BOM.

▶ The parameters for DMU need to be set up when you transfer data to the SAP system using the CAD interface. After you've done this, the system converts the original application files automatically and creates the DIRs and document assignments.

▶ In addition, you have made the settings for the view in Customizing for SAP DMS (menu path GENERAL DATA • DEFINE WORKSTATION APPLICATION).

New User Interface

Two users interfaces (UIs) were developed as part of SAP PLM 7.01—one tailored to the process industry and another one focused on the discrete industry, which is represented in Figure 3.39. Part of SAP's strategy for the future will be to provide a harmonized, common SAP PLM environment that covers both industries. The data model for products will still be different for discrete and process industries. Both UIs are offered through the SAP NetWeaver Business Client (NWBC), and they provide several common functions, such as searching capabilities and the sidebar. The UIs also allow you to maintain master data objects such as work centers, classic BOMs, classes and characteristics, Variant Configuration (see

Chapter 4 for more details), documents, and change management functions, as shown in the Figure 3.39.

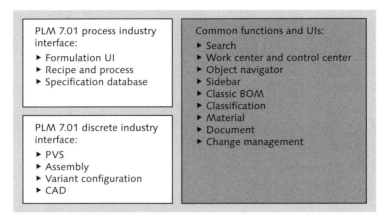

PLM 7.01 process industry interface:
- Formulation UI
- Recipe and process
- Specification database

PLM 7.01 discrete industry interface:
- PVS
- Assembly
- Variant configuration
- CAD

Common functions and UIs:
- Search
- Work center and control center
- Object navigator
- Sidebar
- Classic BOM
- Classification
- Material
- Document
- Change management

Figure 3.39 New SAP PLM User Interfaces

The process industry UI provides you with functions supporting formulas, specifications, and recipe and process data. Figure 3.40 shows an example.

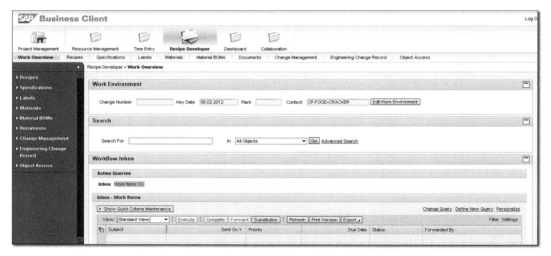

Figure 3.40 Example of Process Industry UI

The discrete industry UI gives you functions supporting the PVS, assemblies, Variant Configuration, and CAD integration. Figure 3.41 shows an example.

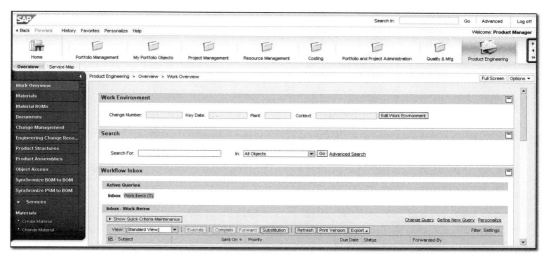

Figure 3.41 Example of Discrete Industry UI

3.1.3 Routing Management and Process Development

To conclude our product master data section, we'll explain the master data required as inputs for the process development and production process by diving into the product routings. Product routings are used directly in production orders for a material and defines the operations and the sequence in which they are carried out, so they enable you to plan the production of a product. Figure 3.42 gives an example of a simple routing for a gas tank.

In a routing you plan the following:

▶ **Which operations (production steps) need to be carried out during production and how long these production process steps will take**
This information is used during planning and scheduling activities, such as capacity requirement and cost calculations.

▶ **Where the work is to be done through assigning work centers**
This subsection will introduces you to the work centers concept in more detail.

▶ **What materials are needed for each operation**
You can assign the number of materials needed for the operation. When a stock item is requested, the requested amount will be reserved and used as input for the materials requirement planning (MRP) run. When a nonstock

item is requested, the procurement process can be started because a purchase requisition will be generated as a result.

▸ **Which quality checks need to be carried out during production**
In this area, you specify which quality checks are required within the production process. This process is described in more detail in Chapter 6.

▸ **Which PRTs are necessary during the production process**
Choose one of the following PRTs: materials, documents, equipment, tools, jigs and fixtures, drawings, and numerical control programs (which are automations of machine tools that are operated by abstractly programmed commands encoded on a storage medium).

Figure 3.42 Example Routing Gas tank

Routings have the same basic structure as the following other SAP objects:

▸ Master recipes (details in Section 3.2)

▸ Inspection plans (details in Chapter 8, Section 8.1.1)

▸ Maintenance plans (details in Chapter 5, Section 5.5)

▸ Standard networks (details in Chapter 7, Section 7.2.1)

Together, these routings are called the task list, as shown in Table 3.3. The task list types (which can be identified by the task list type directly or via the type indicator) are assigned to the different applications. The routing, rate routing, master recipe, and rough-cut planning profile are all used within the Production Planning (PP) application—the standard network is used in SAP Project System (SAP PS) (see Chapter 7 for more details)—and the Inspection Plan (see Chapter 9) is used in SAP Quality Management (QM).

Task List Type	Task List Type Indicator	Used in the Following Component
Routing	N	Production Planning—Production Orders (PP-SFC)
Reference operation set	S	Production Planning—Production Orders (PP-SFC)
Rate routing	R	Production Planning—Repetitive Manufacturing (PP-REM)
Reference rate routing	M	Production Planning—Repetitive Manufacturing (PP-REM)
Master recipe	2	PP-PI—Process Industry
Rough-cut planning profile	3	PP-Sales and Operation Planning (PP-S&OP)
Standard network	O	Project System
Inspection plan	Q	Quality Management
General task list	A	Plant Maintenance
Functional location task list	T	Plant Maintenance
Equipment task list	E	Plant Maintenance

Table 3.3 Overview of Task List Types

A work center represents a piece of machinery, a person, or a group of people where a service or a process in a plant takes place. It can contain general, scheduling, capacity, costing, and personal data, which are all collected in different tabs. Work centers are used in routings, networks, inspection plans, and orders, which are used in several SAP components, such as the maintenance orders in SAP Plant Maintenance (SAP PM), networks in SAP Project System (SAP PS), and internal orders in SAP ERP Controlling (CO). Figure 3.43 gives an example of a work center representing a machine.

Hierarchies serve to aggregate available capacities and capacity requirements in capacity planning. You can assign the work center to work center hierarchies for reporting. A work center can be assigned to multiple hierarchies and can consist of any number of levels. Figure 3.44 shows an example of a work center hierarchy.

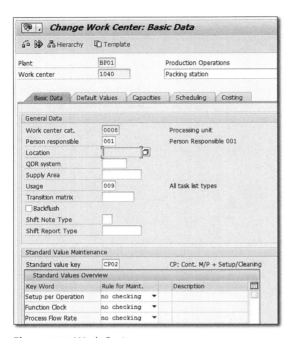

Figure 3.43 Work Center

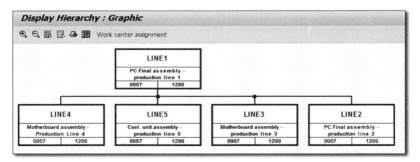

Figure 3.44 Work Center Hierarchy

3.2 Document Management

Due to the increase of digitally available data such as design drawings, photographs, and business documents, the quality and availability of these documents has become increasingly important within a business. SAP Document Management System (SAP DMS) offers functionality to support this process and, due to its integrated nature, forms an important part of the SAP PLM solution. SAP DMS is part of SAP ERP and can be found under the central functions within the logistics area. This section will provide you with the main functions and features of SAP DMS as well as the multiple frontends available to access documents. Be aware that implementing SAP DMS might require three kinds of additional hardware, which fall outside the scope of the book:

▶ **Content server**
Used for storing the original application files.

▶ **Index server**
Used for creating and managing indexes, which supports search engine integration (and can be used during full-text search, for example).

▶ **Cache server**
Enables document caching and increases access speed.

3.2.1 Benefits of Using SAP DMS

Using SAP DMS offers the following advantages:

▶ Using SAP DMS avoids unnecessary duplications of documents, provides users with a consistent approach to storing a document (original), and minimizes the workload involved in entering and updating your documents.

▶ SAP DMS provides a quick and secure document exchange platform that is accessible through different channels, such as the Internet or your intranet. This enables access to all documents immediately from any computer in the network.

▶ Powerful search capabilities give the users the ability to quickly and easily locate the specific required documents among a large pool of available documents. Accessing documents is supported for occasional users via user-friendly, web-based simplified tools, and super users can use the full scope capabilities of the tool through regular access.

▶ Documents in SAP DMS can be distributed either manually or automatically according to company-specific processes, which means you can automate the entire lifecycle of a document from document creation to document storage and from access to update. This ensures that all of the document stakeholders have access to the most up-to-date information.

► Stricter product liability laws have made document storage during the lifecycle of a product increasingly important. A company that wants to be certified for quality management (ISO 9000 to 9006) can only meet the strict quality requirements by using high-performance document management functions.

3.2.2 SAP DMS Features and Functions

Let's walk through the primary functions available in SAP DMS. The upcoming subsections will explain these features and functions in more detail.

► Maintain master data (▢)

  ► DIRs

  ► Originals

► Search for master data (▦)

  ► Via metadata

  ► Through the document browser

► Access master data (▨)

  ► SAP GUI

  ► SAP NetWeaver Portal

  ► WebDocuments

  ► SAP Easy DMS

  ► C-folders and c-projects

► Integration (▤)

  ► Object links (e.g., material, customer, quality notification, etc.)

  ► Engineering Change Management (ECM)

  ► Workflow

  ► Interfaces with external system

Master Data Maintenance

A document is a carrier of information (such as technical drawings, graphics, programs, or text) that can be stored. When complete, this information gives a full description of an object. Figure 3.45 shows an overview of the different functions that are offered when maintaining document management master data. Each function will be described in more detail in subsequent subsections.

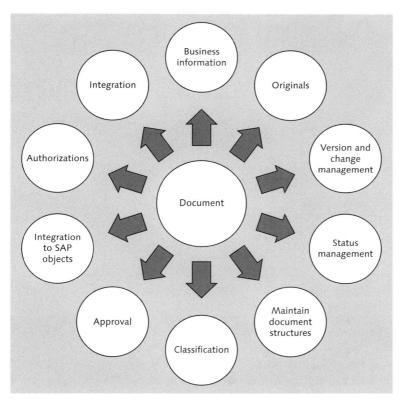

Figure 3.45 Functions for Document Info Records

Business Information

In the document management component, the DIR is the master data object that is used to store the business information of a document, together with the original file. Figure 3.46 gives you an example of a DIR.

The DIR contains the business information data (also referred to as metadata) that can be used later to search and find documents, so it's important to ensure that the data is maintained correctly and is easy to use during search functions. Table 3.4 describes which data can be maintained by tab.

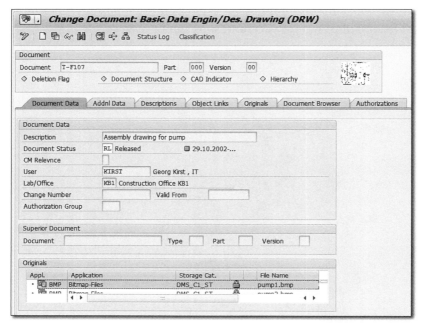

Figure 3.46 Example of Document Info Record

Tab	Used for
DOCUMENT	The DIR is uniquely identified using the document key, which is a combination of the document number, document type, document part, and document version (see Figure 3.46). The document number is assigned to your document, either manually or by the system. The document type is the central control element in SAP DMS; for example, it controls the status, the possible object links, and the screen layout. The document part serves to classify the document and can be used to subdivide the documents. You can use the document version to manage the change state of the document, so it isn't essential to use ECM for this, although using ECM is an option. It's also possible to show a thumbnail of the assigned document in this area.
DOCUMENT DATA	This tab contains general information about the document, such as the DOCUMENT STATUS, the engineering change record details, the responsible LAB/OFFICE, AUTHORIZATION GROUP, and the assigned original files.

Table 3.4 Overview of Document Info Record Tabs

Tab	Used for
ADDNL DATA	This tab allows you to define your own fields through the classification application.
DESCRIPTIONS	This tab allows you to maintain descriptions for all of the required languages.
OBJECT LINKS	This tab contains the link to other objects within SAP, such as the material, BOM, quality notification, or purchase order. See the upcoming subsection "Link to SAP Objects" for more details.
ORIGINALS	This tab contains the link to the original files.
DOCUMENT BROWSER	This tab allows you to view and maintain document hierarchies, also referred to as document BOMs.
AUTHORIZATIONS	This tab enables you to authorize users (employees) for DIRs and actions such as change and display.

Table 3.4 Overview of Document Info Record Tabs (Cont.)

Originals

The original document can be assigned to the DIR in SAP DMS. You have two options for storing the originals:

▶ Store the originals in an SAP secure storage area, which can be the SAP database, a vault, or a remote function call (RFC) archive.

▶ Use an external Knowledge Provider (KPro) and create a link to the original.

To make a file available in your SAP DMS for all of the authorized users, you can check it in. When a file is checked in, the padlock symbol next to the original is closed, as shown in Figure 3.47.

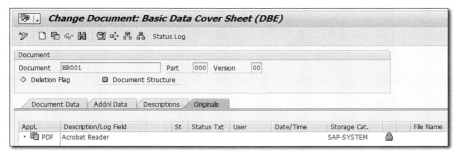

Figure 3.47 DIR: Originals

When you want to make changes to the original, you can use the CHANGE option and check the document out to a local place on your workstation. The padlock symbol will then be open. After you've made the appropriate changes, remember to check the file back in again so it becomes available for everybody else.

If you just want to copy the original—for example, to bring to a customer visit— you can use the COPY TO function. You can also reset a checkout, which can be useful when the original file has become corrupted.

Depending on the document type, you can decide whether you want to display a thumbnail and if you want the original visible as soon as the DIR is opened or to open up the original file when the user double-clicks it. To view the document as soon as the DIR is opened, install a tool called the Engineering Client Viewer (ECL Viewer). This tool is available for free through the SAP Service Marketplace and can be found under the abbreviation ECL Viewer. Here you can also check and ensure that all your file types are supported. Figure 3.48 shows an example of the direct display of a document from within the DIR.

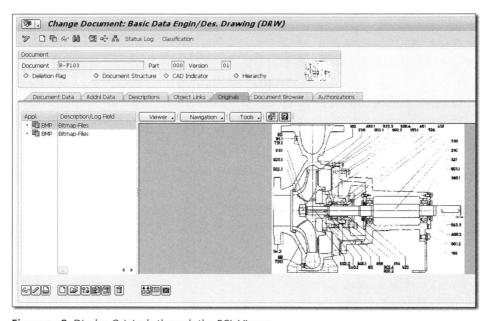

Figure 3.48 Display Originals through the ECL Viewer

Supported File Types

When implementing SAP DMS, it's important to understand which applications are being used for which types of documents within your organization. There is no restriction on the number of different file types that are supported, effectively making storing originals from just about any application possible in SAP DMS. You can choose to make the appropriate application settings so the application is supported directly in SAP DMS or convert the original files to a more commonly used extension (e.g., a neutral file format such as TIF or PDF). This process can be useful, for example, when documents need to be kept for several years, and the application in which the documents have been created is no longer available.

For Microsoft Office applications, you can use even tighter integration by setting up the Office integration; for using CAD systems, the SAP PLM interface can be used. Both these options are explained in more detail under the upcoming "Integration" subsection in Section 3.4.1.

Version and Change Management

Document versions are used to represent the different change or delivery statuses of a document. The VERSION field is part of the document key and is often referred to simply as *version*. Depending on the document type configuration settings, it can be assigned automatically by the system or maintained manually, as shown in Figure 3.49.

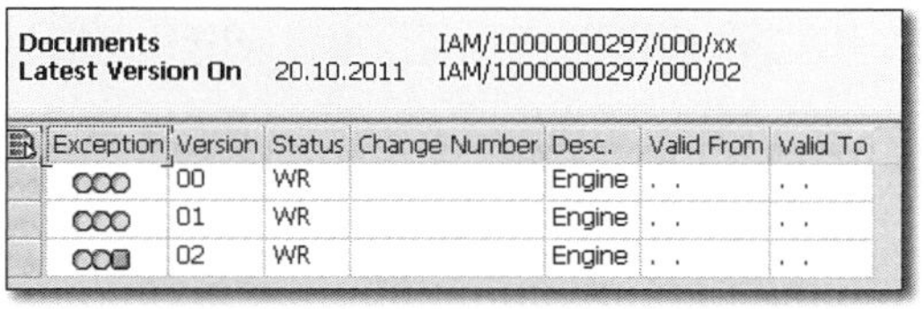

Documents IAM/10000000297/000/xx
Latest Version On 20.10.2011 IAM/10000000297/000/02

Exception	Version	Status	Change Number	Desc.	Valid From	Valid To
○○○	00	WR		Engine	. .	. .
○○○	01	WR		Engine	. .	. .
○○■	02	WR		Engine	. .	. .

Figure 3.49 Document Version

When you use ECM within the document management functions, the document version will be assigned a validity period. The version can also be linked to a particular change that may also affect other SAP objects (e.g., the BOM or routing). Figure 3.50 shows the one-to-one relationship of a document version to a chosen change number. The arrow represents the successive nature of the version. ECM is discussed in more detail in Chapter 9.

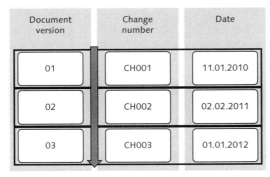

Document version	Change number	Date
01	CH001	11.01.2010
02	CH002	02.02.2011
03	CH003	01.01.2012

Figure 3.50 Versions with ECM

Status Management

Status management supports the processes of a document lifecycle by defining the different stages a document needs to go through, which can be assigned and configured based on the document type. The statuses that have been set up for your document can be graphically displayed in the DIR by choosing EXTRAS • STATUS NETWORK. In your system, the status in yellow is the current status, green indicates the possible next status, and the red indicates statuses that can't be set. Figure 3.51 shows an example of a status network. A status can be flagged as an INITIAL status, only to be used when the DIR is created. The status can prevent you from making changes to the original files, when it has been flagged as LOCKED. When you try to change an assigned original, the system checks to ensure you're authorized to perform this activity.

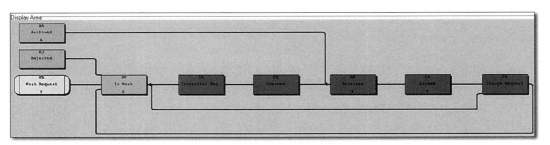

Figure 3.51 Status Network

Each change to the status of a DIR is logged in the status log (see the example in Figure 3.52) with the following details: which status was assigned, by whom, when and with which explanation, and whether the digital signature was used.

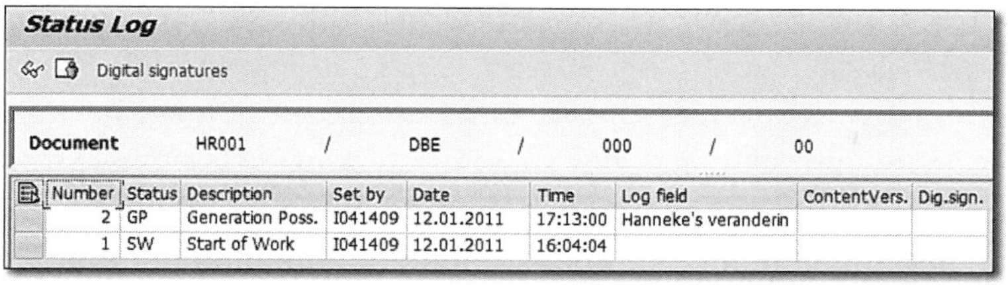

Status Log

🔏 📑 Digital signatures

Document	HR001	/	DBE	/	000	/	00

Number	Status	Description	Set by	Date	Time	Log field	ContentVers.	Dig.sign.
2	GP	Generation Poss.	I041409	12.01.2011	17:13:00	Hanneke's veranderin		
1	SW	Start of Work	I041409	12.01.2011	16:04:04			

Figure 3.52 Status Log

A status change can lead to triggering a workflow (e.g., to send an email to the document owner), to performing a function (e.g., update a field in a master data object), or to triggering a customer-specific check via a customer exit (e.g., checking a specific business rule, that all project business cases start with "PSBC").

Document BOM

You can maintain a structure (or a document hierarchy) across document types for documents that logically should be grouped together (known as a document BOM). A hierarchy can be created by assigning a superior document in the DIR via Transaction CV01N (Create DIR), Transaction CV02N (Change DIR), or Transaction CV11 (Document Structure). You can also go through SAP ERP 6 directly in the DIR via the DOCUMENT BROWSER tab, which lets you differentiate between public and private structures/folders. Figure 3.53 shows an example of a document structure, and Figure 3.54 shows the new DOCUMENT BROWSER tab.

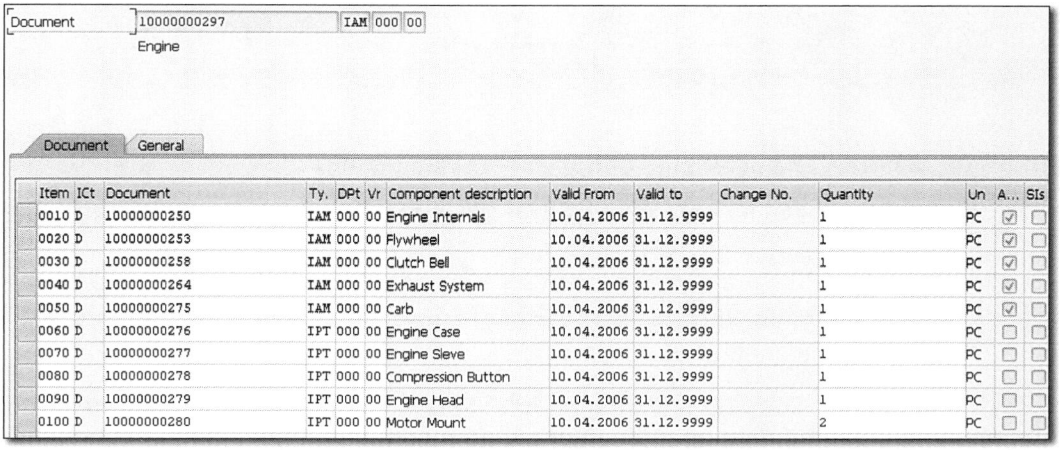

Document	10000000297		IAM	000	00
	Engine				

Document / General

Item	ICt	Document	Ty.	DPt	Vr	Component description	Valid From	Valid to	Change No.	Quantity	Un	A...	SIs
0010	D	10000000250	IAM	000	00	Engine Internals	10.04.2006	31.12.9999		1	PC	☑	☐
0020	D	10000000253	IAM	000	00	Flywheel	10.04.2006	31.12.9999		1	PC	☑	☐
0030	D	10000000258	IAM	000	00	Clutch Bell	10.04.2006	31.12.9999		1	PC	☑	☐
0040	D	10000000264	IAM	000	00	Exhaust System	10.04.2006	31.12.9999		1	PC	☑	☐
0050	D	10000000275	IAM	000	00	Carb	10.04.2006	31.12.9999		1	PC	☑	☐
0060	D	10000000276	IPT	000	00	Engine Case	10.04.2006	31.12.9999		1	PC	☐	☐
0070	D	10000000277	IPT	000	00	Engine Sleve	10.04.2006	31.12.9999		1	PC	☐	☐
0080	D	10000000278	IPT	000	00	Compression Button	10.04.2006	31.12.9999		1	PC	☐	☐
0090	D	10000000279	IPT	000	00	Engine Head	10.04.2006	31.12.9999		1	PC	☐	☐
0100	D	10000000280	IPT	000	00	Motor Mount	10.04.2006	31.12.9999		2	PC	☐	☐

Figure 3.53 Document Structure

When you want to use a folder structure in your document BOM, you can set up a document type MAP, which in turn represents a folder (see Figure 3.54). This is especially useful when you're using SAP Easy DMS (discussed in more detail in Section 3.2.4). When you're working with a CAD system, with assembly structures (examples are CATIA V5 or UG NX), you can use Transaction CDESK (CAD Desktop), which enables you to manage document structures associated with the assembly structure of the CAD application. For more about this topic, see the "Integration" subsection in Section 3.4.1.

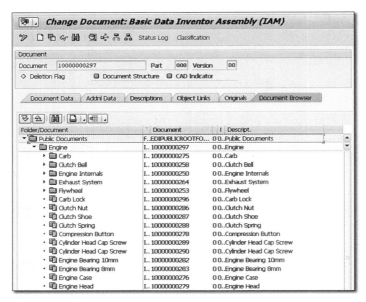

Figure 3.54 Document Browser

Maintain Characteristics of Documents via Classification

You can maintain your own defined fields in the DIR via the SAP Classification System (CA). These fields can be used as search criteria when you're trying to locate a DIR, so it's important to set it up correctly and to find a good balance between the number of fields used and master data maintenance to ensure this function can be used easily.

In short, classification is a centralized SAP function by which you can define your own specific fields as characteristics. These characteristics are grouped together via the master object called classes. The class type used and the class relevant for the classification of the document need to be assigned to the document type in configuration. Chapter 4 offers more details on classification, and Figure 3.55 shows an example of the classification data in a DIR. However, this is just an example, and with CA, the options for classifying the DIRs are endless. Chapter 4, Section 4.1, explains classification in more detail.

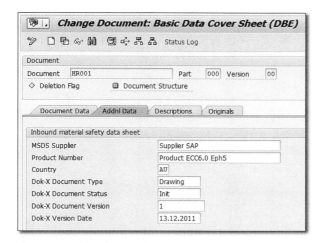

Figure 3.55 Classification Data

Approval Process

In the configuration of the document type, you assign an approval process. The approval process requires one person or a group of people to approve the DIR by documenting this via digital signature. Only after the DIR has been approved by all of the required persons can the next processing step take place. You can assign your digital signature to a DIR by changing the status. The following approval procedures are supported:

▶ **The "one pair of eyes" principle**
One authorized person must make a digital signature. After he has signed, the new status is active, the document can no longer be changed, and you can only set a predefined follow-up status.

▶ **The "more than one pair of eyes" principle**
Several authorized people must approve the DIR by a digital signature. After the first person has signed, the system recognizes that the authorization process hasn't yet been completed. Each authorized person saves the document

after he has signed. The document can't be changed. The procedure can be terminated by each person who is authorized to make a digital signature. In this case, the system resets the status that was set before the approval process started. Note that the document is in an intermediate stage during the signature process, so you should define an additional document status (e.g., Being Signed).

Figure 3.56 gives you an example of a signature sequence, which is set up in the configuration using the "more than one pair of eyes" principle.

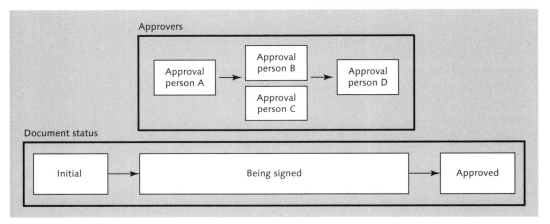

Figure 3.56 Approval

You can also link documents to other SAP objects. You can control to which other SAP objects the document can connect based on its document type. Per document type, you can configure to which SAP object the document type can be assigned. For example, if you have a document type for drawings, and a drawing can be assigned to either a material or a BOM, then these objects must be allowed to be maintained in the DIR. There are various available objects, such as the material and the trial number. Table 3.5 offers the complete list of possible object assignment options, followed by a DIR with an example of a material assignment to a document in Figure 3.57. Within a DIR, apart from the general information about the document, the document descriptions and the originals all captured within a dedicated tab, you're also able to view the linked objects by navigating to the tab OBJECT LINKS. You can see any object as defined in Table 3.5. Be aware that through configuration, you can restrict the object types based on the document type.

Objects			
Change number	Purchase requisition item	Appropriation request	Vendor
Asset master	Purchase order item	Measuring points	Material master
Claim	Equipment master	Object link	Plant material
Production resource/tool (PRT)	Subst.rep.gen.var.	Reference location	Material components
C-projects element	Substance master	Class	Charge
Document info record	Functional location	Customer	Production version
Case	General notification	Organizational unit	Patient
Packing instruction	Maintenance notification	iPPE node	Production order
iPPE variant	WBS element	QM info record	Inspection method(s)
Quality notification	QM info record SD	Equipment req. (RMS)	Process (RMS)
Service notification	BOM Header	Material BOM	BOM item
SAP EIS Master data	Trial (TMS)	Layout area	Layout module
Baseline	Configuration folder	Rental unit	Lease
Asset group	Real estate	Buildings	Room
Management contract	Network activity	Factory layout area item	

Table 3.5 Object Assignments to DIR

Authorizations

You can use SAP's well-established authorization concept, which is working with the authorization groups maintained on the DOCUMENT DATA tab. The system administrator needs to include this group in the role that is assigned to users.

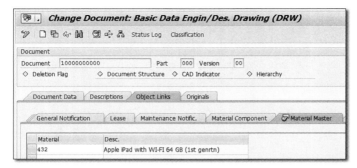

Figure 3.57 Assignment to Object Material

However, from SAP ERP 6.0 onward, it's also possible to use the AUTHORIZATION tab, which allows you to easily set and change authorizations on folders and documents directly within the SAP DMS transactions. Figure 3.58 gives you an example of how different users have different kinds of authorization, such as viewing or being able to change the DIR.

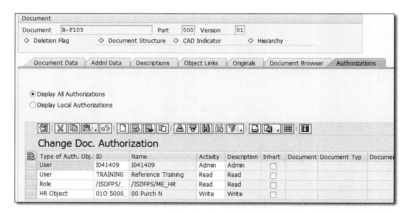

Figure 3.58 Authorizations Tab in DIR

3.2.3 Finding a Document

If you want to find a document in SAP DMS, there is a wide range of search options available to you, depending on the data that has been maintained in the DIR (see Figure 3.59). You can use the document data, classification data, the object link data, a text search, or a combination of all these options. All standard search options—such as using wildcards (find all document starting with "s", by entering "s*") and multiple search criteria—are supported. As soon as a search tab is used, the symbol "*" will be displayed in the tab. In Figure 3.59, all the search tabs have been used.

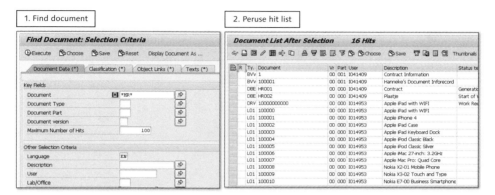

Figure 3.59 Selection and Hit List

After executing the search, SAP will present you with an overview of all the documents that comply with your search criteria. This list can be further narrowed down by using general available functions in list reports, such as filtering and sorting.

3.2.4 Access to Document Data

SAP provides the following UIs for SAP DMS, which will be explained in more detail in the following subsections:

▶ Standard UI in SAP ERP with SAP GUI
▶ SAP NetWeaver Portal
▶ WebDocuments
▶ SAP Easy Document

SAP GUI

The standard UI through the SAP GUI is powerful. As a result, this interface option is targeted at power users of the system—those users who use the solution frequently and need to use the advanced options of SAP DMS. An example of the complex SAP GUI is presented in Figure 3.60.

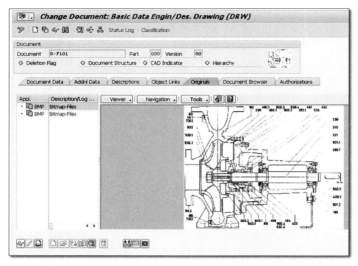

Figure 3.60 SAP GUI

SAP NetWeaver Portal

The SAP NetWeaver Portal can also be used to access document information, and it can be used for more indirect and passive access to documents via a connector. Figure 3.61 gives you an example of this.

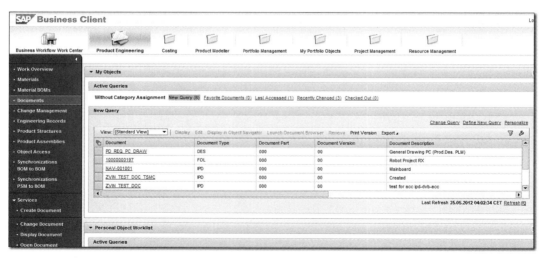

Figure 3.61 SAP NetWeaver Portal

WebDocuments

Via the WebDocuments application, which is accessible through an Internet browser, you can access document information, perform simple searches, and update DIR details, as shown in Figure 3.62. The WebDocuments application has been available since R/3 Enterprise, extension set 1.10. This application is also know under the name Docs@Web and is a Business Server Pages (BSP) application. Thumbnails are supported, so you can visualize the content of an original application file without starting the workstation application that was used to create the graphical file.

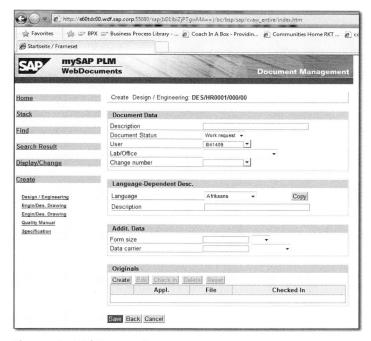

Figure 3.62 WebDocuments

SAP Easy Document Management

SAP Easy DMS is a Windows-based access to the SAP DMS. The interface makes it simple to navigate. Dialog modules help you create DIRs and assign originals in Microsoft Explorer with just basic knowledge of SAP ERP. You can use drag-and-drop functions, simple dialog boxes, and document structures through folders to differentiate between public folders available to all users and user-specific private folders. SAP Easy DMS is integrated with Microsoft products, which allows you to create new documents through Explorer, or via the Microsoft application (relevant to all Microsoft applications that can produce a document, such as Excel, Word, PowerPoint) itself. When defining a DIR, you have similar options as with DIR access through SAP GUI, and you can maintain general data, object links, and classification data. You can tailor SAP Easy DMS to your needs through personal settings for fields, thumbnail display, and filters.

From SAP Easy DMS 7.1, you can use the SAP PLM GUI authorization concept, where, after the document has been configured appropriately in the SAP ERP component, you can maintain specific document authorizations through the new GUI. Changes to the authorizations will be logged in SAP ERP and are visible through the change log of the DIR. This application also allows you to take a folder with documents offline (e.g., to assist during a customer visit). SAP Easy DMS 7.1 also supports access through the Windows Transaction Server (WTS).

This software is available free to SAP Business Suite customers and can be downloaded from the SAP Service Marketplace. The software needs to be locally installed, and Customizing is necessary in both SAP ERP and SAP Easy DMS. Figure 3.63 shows an example of creating a document in SAP Easy DMS.

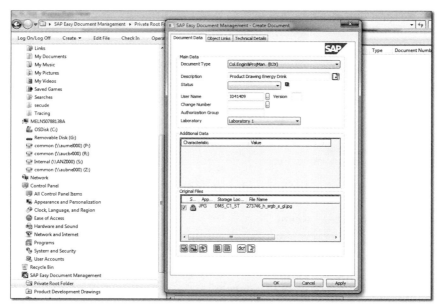

Figure 3.63 SAP Easy Document Management Example

3.2.5 Integration of External Systems to SAP PLM

SAP's status as an integrated solution is due to its integration possibilities to other applications: using classification, attaching DIRs to several SAP objects from different components, using workflow, and managing changes through ECM and SAP Office. However, apart from integrating from *within* the SAP Business Suite, you can also set up integration to externally involved systems such as Microsoft Office, CAD systems, GIS systems, product data systems, and archive solutions (see Figure 3.64).

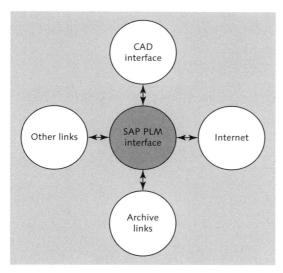

Figure 3.64 SAP PLM Interface

The integration to Microsoft Office can be set up in the configuration of SAP DMS. You can establish integration to other external systems by using the CAD SAP PLM interface, which can be used for a bidirectional exchange of data between SAP ERP and non-SAP ERP systems.

Deep integration in the SAP system provides a wide range of functions and many options for configuring your system to meet your company's specific requirements. SAP DMS can be adapted to suit the needs of different user groups and industry sectors. Figure 3.65 shows how CAD integration is established at the software component level, where a CAD plug-in and an RFC are used to integrate SAP to the CAD system, allowing the user to view the product data from SAP and CAD into a single environment.

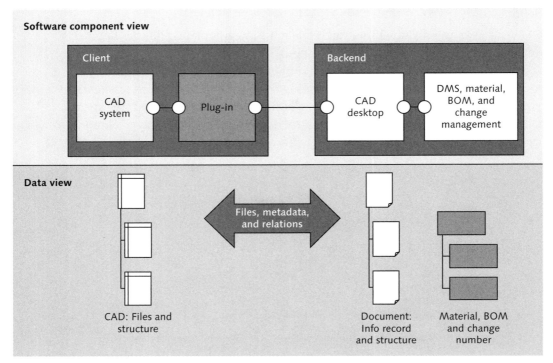

Figure 3.65 CAD Integration

Let's examine common capabilities of CAD interface and integration. Because each CAD tool is different and has its own benefits and capabilities, the following list gives you a set of typically provided capabilities offered through the SAP PLM interface so you can get a feel for the integration possibilities. However, it's by no means a complete overview of the offered integration. For more details, visit the SAP Service Marketplace (*http://service.sap.com/PLM*, go to PLM IN ERP • CAD-INTEGRATION). So let's look at the common capabilities of using SAP PLM in combination with a CAD product via the CAD interface:

► Secure storage of CAD data

► Option to update SAP document information directly from within the CAD tool by checking in and out original CAD files, adding versions, and maintaining metadata

► Maintenance of document structure and BOMs from the CAD tool when your CAD tool uses structures and relationships between models

- Use of ECM tools on stored CAD data
- Ability to add, change, or display other master data objects, such as materials and BOMs
- Non-CAD users' ability to view CAD drawings by providing a file that can be viewed without the application (e.g., a PDF file)
- Searching documents and preview thumbnails
- Multi-site CAD files management with content and cache servers

When integrating CAD and SAP PLM, you can expect the following benefits:

- When using SAP DMS to access CAD objects, you can use versioning and status management in such a way that multiple users can work simultaneously on a product, without inconsistency or loss of data.
- You can reduce redundant work steps when all authorized users have access to the CAD objects (originals) stored in a central secure storage area, in which they can follow the development processes, or make changes.
- Functions for SAP DMS, change management, BOM management, material master, classification, and workflow are supported.
- The integration provides the correct authorization options based on roles.
- You can get early access to engineering information (BOM, drawing, 3D model, etc.) throughout the organization.
- SAP provides all necessary functions for CAD integration, so no additional team data management is necessary, and the solution is supported by SAP.
- Data redundancy and synchronization aren't necessary.
- For existing SAP customers, the integration can reduce total cost of ownership (TCO) and total cost of investment (TCI) by leveraging existing SAP infrastructure and knowledge.

Transaction CDESK (CAD Desktop) provides you with a UI for managing CAD data within the SAP system. Figure 3.66 shows the transaction. These are the most important functions the CAD Desktop offers:

- Supports multiple CAD solutions
- Provides automatic document storage
- Creates DIRs for a model or drawing
- Creates a material master for a given DIR

- ▶ Automatically generates BOMs based on document structure and related materials
- ▶ Provides mass check-in/check-out of originals across multiple sites
- ▶ Uses wizards for check-in/check-out originals
- ▶ Checks status of DIR by traffic light overview
- ▶ Displays the CAD structure and BOM structure
- ▶ Exports files to c-folders and SAP Easy DMS
- ▶ Exports files to Office applications

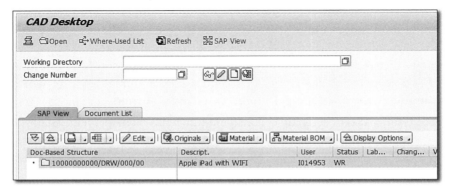

Figure 3.66 CAD Desktop

In the CAD world, the main applications use the CAD Desktop. However, this also depends on the complementary software partner. For more information, see the SAP PLM home page in the SAP Service Marketplace.

> **Note**
>
> This book covers integration in an SAP PDM context because external systems, such as CAD systems, are an important part of your end-to-end solution for the product life-cycle. However, it's just an introduction to the topic and could be easily expanded upon into its own chapter or even a dedicated book, although this is beyond the scope of this book. You can find more information on this topic on the SAP Service Marketplace (at *http://service.sap.com/PLM*, go to PLM IN ERP • CAD-INTEGRATION) or go to CAD-DESK-TOP at *http://help.sap.com*, SAP SOLUTIONS • SAP BUSINESS SUITE • SAP PRODUCT LIFECYCLE MANAGEMENT WITHIN SAP ERP CENTRAL COMPONENT • ENGLISH • PRODUCT LIFECYCLE MANAGEMENT (PLM) • CAD DESKTOP (CA-CAD). This includes information about specific CAD interfaces and development partners.

3.3   Product Costing

At different stages of the product lifecycle, it may be important to know the detailed costs for products and services—such as cost of goods manufactured (COGM) and cost of goods sold (COGS)—which pricing is used, and so on. These details will help you learn about productivity, compare several alternatives, understand where costs are coming from, influence primary cost, and evaluate inventory. It breaks down the costs for each step of the production process.

3.3.1   Business Benefits

Product costing has two benefits: you can increase revenue by maximizing profitability by product, and you can reduce operating costs and increase efficiency by reducing inventory levels and reducing development costs.

Different product costings are available to you during the different stages of a product in SAP Business Suite. Before Sales and Operation Planning (S&OP), you can use either Product Design Cost Estimate (PDCE) or Easy Cost Planning (ECP); after S&OP, you can use product costing within PP or CO. To give you insight into when to use which tool, Figure 3.67 gives you an overview of the product lifecycle, the costing tools, and the cost management activities.

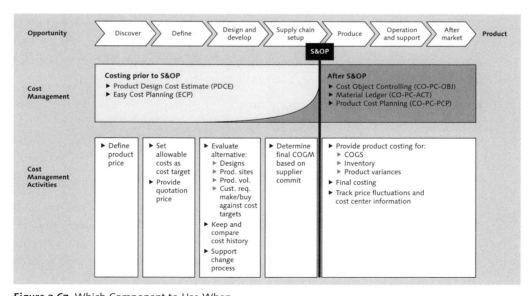

Figure 3.67 Which Component to Use When

3.3.2 Product Costing Tools

Let's explore the different product costing tools one by one in the order in which they generally are being used according to the product lifecycle stage. Which tools would be most appropriate for your organization depends on the specific business processes in which a costing needs to be created and when they take place during the product lifecycle. This is why we'll be going through them all, explaining their concept, functions, and benefits, so you can determine if they would suit your product costing business processes.

Product Design Cost Estimate

As stated previously, to perform a product costing prior to S&OP, SAP offers the Product Design Cost Estimate (PDCE) and Easy Costing Planning (ECP), as represented in Figure 3.68. First we'll focus on PDCE, which will be followed by a dedicated section on ECP. PDCE is a product costing tool that can be used to calculate the cost of a product early on in the product development stages. It can be used to perform complex costings during design, development, and the start-up phase. In contrast, ECP can be used for recurring costing requirements with tight SAP ERP process integration.

PDCE offers the following benefits:

▸ Provides a costing solution to companies making quotations before accepting work orders

▸ Gives continuous support of controlling and sales during product development

▸ Increases quality of product cost information with product maturity

▸ Enables better cost control during early engineering

▸ Provides the ability to respond to change requests

The PDCE product costing tool allows you to create targeted product costs and quotes by determining if existing products/assemblies meet requirements. If so, you can import existing cost estimates based on existing BOMs. If not, you can create a new product structure from scratch while reusing existing materials. In the next step, you can define your cost target and evaluate alternatives that are driven by, for example, design alternatives, make/buy decisions, manufacturing alternatives, and customer change requirements until the cost target has been achieved.

The following are key functionalities:

- ▶ Import BOM and routing from PP and any other logistics system.
- ▶ Import existing cost estimates from SAP ERP CO-PC.
- ▶ Complete and valuate the quantity structure.
- ▶ Perform targeted costing.
- ▶ Perform simulations.

Change Product Design Cost Estimate IM_DEM0 / 1PDCE										
Objects	Long T...	Tot Quan (loc...	RQ for CL man	Int...	Costs per TQ	Target Co...	Curr...	Targe	Target Price	Perc Pr...	Allowab...
▽ 🎛 IM_DEM0 - Demo example	Demo e...										
▽ 🎬 IM_DEM0/M											
▽ 🗗 PDCE/1/1000/IGNITION-M	Ignition...	1		0 ST	355,38	0,00 EUR	◇		400,00	30,000	280,00
▷ 🔳 1000/SPARK-COIL	Spark ...	1		0 ST	86,01	0,00 EUR	◇				
🔩 1000/1300-530	Insulat...	1		0 ST	0,22		EUR	◇			
▷ 🔳 1000/SPARK-SENSOR	Sensor	3		0 ST	146,63	0,00 EUR	◇				
🔩 1000/1300-560	Wiring h...	2		0 ST	11,00		EUR	◇			
🔩 4220/1422	Cable b...	0,050		0 H	2,80		EUR	◇			
🔩 4220/1420	Cable b...	0,667		0 15M	5,78		EUR	◇			
🔩 4220/1421	Cable b...	0,667		0 15M	11,81		EUR	◇			
➡ TEST	Openin...	10		0 MIN	30,00		EUR	◇			
🔩 4210/1422	Material...	0		0 H	0,00		EUR	◇			
🔩 4210/1420	Material...	0		0 H	0,00		EUR	◇			
🔩 4210/1421	Material...	0,333		0 15M	1,14		EUR	◇			
🔩 4210/1422	Material...	0		0 H	0,00		EUR	◇			
🔩 4210/1420	Material...	0		0 H	0,00		EUR	◇			
🔩 4210/1421	Material...	0,667		0 15M	2,29		EUR	◇			
🎚 655300	GMKZ V...				13,01		EUR				
🎚 655400	GMKZ V...				44,66		EUR				

Figure 3.68 Product Cost Estimate with PDCE

Let's turn our attention to the second product costing tool that can be used prior to S&OP: ECP.

Easy Cost Planning

ECP is a type of unit costing used for projects (WBS elements), internal orders, appropriation requests, internal service requests, and ad hoc cost estimates. If you want to plan costs without making the effort of creating a planning object in the system, you can create an ad hoc cost estimate via ECP to obtain quick results. It can be used when cost estimates of similar structure need to be created repeatedly, and costing relevant data can be derived from parameters (characteristics). ECP is also useful when a new cost model needs to be tested.

This planning method is very easy to execute because the logic and formulas of the product costing are all predefined and set in advance by a *planning form*. The planner chooses a planning form and, in the next step, has to ensure that all of the relevant cost factors are valuated and confirmed. After confirmation, the system creates a cost plan (specifically, a unit cost plan, which is explained in more detail in Section 3.3.3) automatically for you. To include overhead cost, you have to use a form with the right costing sheet and overhead key assigned so overheads get included in the product costing.

The forms used in ECP can be set up by end users. You have to define the cost-relevant factors by adding them in CA under class 051, Costing Model. Then you create your necessary forms, which include these characteristics and the used formulas in the derivation rules. From the cost plan, you're even able to enter commitments and actual costs, by using execution services, such as creating a purchase order.

ECP, which is shown in Figure 3.69, offers its users the following benefits:

▶ Quick planning
▶ Ease of use
▶ Integration of complex calculation and relationships
▶ Minimization of required input data
▶ Direct use of costing results
▶ Special knowledge of SAP transactions not required
▶ Inclusion of actual reporting

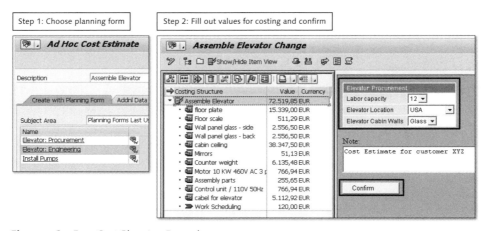

Figure 3.69 Easy Cost Planning Example

3.3.3   Product Cost Planning Features

The following section will provide you with insight into the product cost planning options available in CO after S&OP. The different costing options are Cost Object Controlling (also referred to as base planning object costing), Material Ledger (material), and product cost planning (material/BOM/routing). You can use product cost planning within the PP to do the following:

▶ Calculate the non-order-related COGM and COGS for each product unit.

▶ Establish how the costs are broken down for each product and calculate the value added for each step of the production process (concept of cost rollup).

▶ Optimize the COGM through comparison costing.

▶ Provide product cost controlling information system.

Product Lifecycle

This section provides you with insight into the product lifecycle mapped against the required detail for costing and the tools available after S&OP. This should broaden your understanding about which solutions might be relevant to your organization because you can adopt them all or in part based on your specific requirements and business processes. Figure 3.70 shows the product lifecycle after S&OP, set off against which detail of costing is necessary during the different stages. Notice that during the product idea phase, you need to create a cost estimate based on rough specifications and based on flexible and variable data. When possible, you can use existing data of a similar product, which can be changed easily.

During the specification and product design phase, more details become available by refinements to the product specifications. During the prototype stage, the first constructive data in the form of a BOM get entered to provide more specific cost estimation. After the products reach market maturity, the complete product range is costed regularly, and product costs are monitored and analyzed.

Figure 3.71 shows which costing methods are available at each stage of a product.

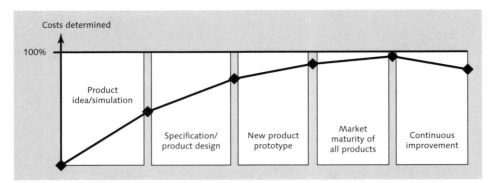

Figure 3.70 Product Lifecycle and Product Costing

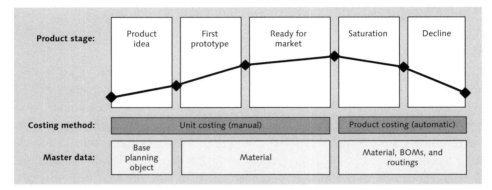

Figure 3.71 Product Lifecycle and Costing Methods

Unit Costing

Unit costing is a type of spreadsheet that, due to its integration, can use existing master data and prices in the SAP ERP system, such as activity prices from Cost Center Accounting (CCA). You can use the spreadsheet to create totals, subtotals, and formulas for mathematical operations.

With this costing method, you enter the costing items manually, and it can be performed at either single level or multiple level. This cost estimate calculates the costs without accessing BOMs and routings in PP. Multilevel unit costing is a highly flexible screen and can be used in the following scenarios:

- Creating a new product
- Creating a similar product (copy and update an existing product into a new product)
- Changing an existing product (copy the existing cost estimate and make changes to the copy)

You can access existing SAP system data through item categories, which refers to materials (M), business processes (P), internal activity (E), and external activity (F), for this purpose. Unit costing can be performed on either a base planning object (if you're planning a new product for which there isn't master data in the system yet), or on a material when the first material master data has been created (which can be found under the COST ESTIMATE WITHOUT QUANTITY STRUCTURE menu option). Figure 3.72 shows an example of unit costing done on a base planning object.

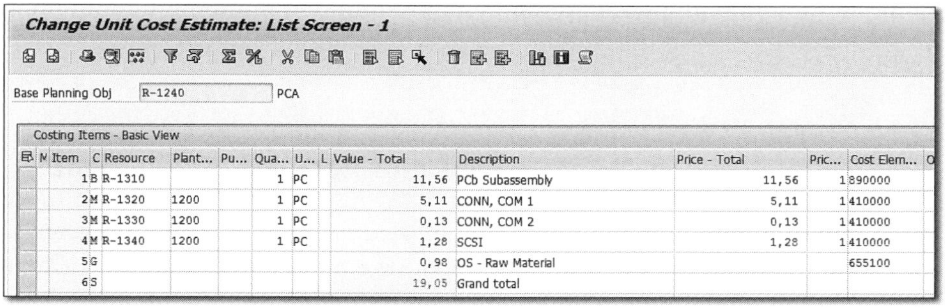
Change Unit Cost Estimate: List Screen - 1

Base Planning Obj R-1240 PCA

Costing Items - Basic View

M	Item	C	Resource	Plant...	Pu...	Qua...	U...	L	Value - Total	Description	Price - Total	Pric...	Cost Elem...	O
	1	B	R-1310			1	PC		11,56	PCb Subassembly	11,56	1	890000	
	2	M	R-1320	1200		1	PC		5,11	CONN, COM 1	5,11	1	410000	
	3	M	R-1330	1200		1	PC		0,13	CONN, COM 2	0,13	1	410000	
	4	M	R-1340	1200		1	PC		1,28	SCSI	1,28	1	410000	
	5	G							0,98	OS - Raw Material			655100	
	6	S							19,05	Grand total				

Figure 3.72 Unit Costing on Base Planning Object

Product Costing on Material

When the complete master data (BOMs and routings or master recipe) is available, you can create a material cost estimate with quantity structure—that is, a product costing—which automatically calculates the COGM and COGS from the existing data in PP (or PP-PI). Figure 3.73 shows an example.

Using the objects discussed so far for products doesn't cut it in the process industry because you're unable to model very detailed information (e.g., pH values, density, or temperatures) about an ingredient used. To do so, the Specification Management and Recipe Management functions from SAP PLM are required, which we'll look into next.

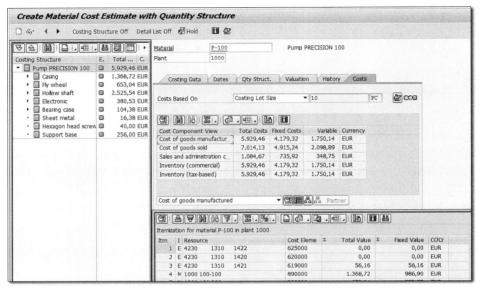

Figure 3.73 Product Costing with Quantity Structure

3.4 Specification Management and Recipe Management

Specification Management and Recipe Management were originally targeted at customers in the process industry but are now considered cross-industry solutions. They allow you to do data management in which you define your recipe and your ingredients that make up your product, and they support your product development process needs as well. By using substances, you can include more details on ingredients used, effectively adding greater detail than is available through the material master.

Three key benefits arise from using Specification Management and Recipe Management:

▶ Integrated development workbench

▶ Easy cost and nutritional calculation

▶ Complete recipe development

Figure 3.74 provides you with an overview of the functions and features of Specification Management and Recipe Management.

Figure 3.74 Specification Management and Recipe Management Process

3.4.1 Specification Management

The SAP Environment, Health, and Safety Management (SAP EHS Management) specification database is used to store very detailed product definition information for a complete business solution for environmental, health, safety, and recipe management processes. It captures detailed characteristics that uniquely describe all materials involved in manufacturing products. This includes properties and attributes about finished products, raw materials, and packaging.

The specification database is used in the following areas:

▶ Recipe Management/Product Safety

▶ Dangerous Goods Management

▶ Industrial Hygiene and Safety

▶ Waste Management

▶ Occupational Health

Integration

The specification database integrates with logistics to produce BOMs, material safety data sheets (MSDS), labels, and regulatory reports. The link between specifications and materials (detailed in Figure 3.75 and Table 3.6) provides the integration to SAP Logistics components, such as SAP Materials Management (SAP MM) for material planning, inventory management, and procurement activities.

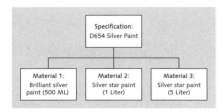

Figure 3.75 Link between Specification and Material

Possible Relationships	Specification: Material
1. One-to-one	1:1
2. One-to-many	1:M
3. Many-to-one	N:1
4. Many-to-many	N:M
5. One-to-zero	1: 0

Table 3.6 Possible Relationships between Specification and Material

In addition to the integration to SAP MM, you can use more advanced SAP Supply Chain Management (SAP SCM) functionality, such as SAP Advanced Planning & Optimization (APO), the full Batch Information Cockpit (BIC), process instruction sheet, process control interface, electronic batch record, and electronic signatures, all of which belong to the SAP SCM product suite.

Specification Data

The specification is the central data object for mapping the specification categories as shown in Table 3.7. You can use these standard categories or use them as a reference to define your own categories.

Specification Category	Possible Specification Types
Substance	Real substance, listed substance
Agent	Notice, dust, real substance
Packaging	Package
Waste code	Waste code
Dangerous goods	Specification types according to the regulation families

Table 3.7 Standard Specification Categories

The specification data is an important repository for SAP EHS Management. We'll discuss most of these categories in Chapter 6, but we'll discuss the substance category here because it's an important category used in Recipe Management. In general, the specification category groups specifications according to their usage and meaning. They are further subdivided into specification types. The specification categories are predefined—that is, you can't change them—while the standard delivered specification types can be changed or added via configuration.

The specification database is built on CA, so definition of characteristics and properties is highly flexible. (CA is described in more detail in Chapter 4, Section 4.1.) After the product development is almost complete, and time for ordering goods approaches, material masters are defined and referenced by the specifications spelled out as inputs and outputs in the formula. Specification information contains descriptions, physical characteristics, physical and technical properties, and additional information such as physical or chemical data, trade names and so on.

3.4.2 Substance Management

A *substance* represents a much more detailed view of a material or substance than is available by using the material master because physical characteristics and technical properties are described by means of classification. Early in the product creation process, developers typically work in terms of specification, without using and/or creating material masters. Figure 3.76 shows the data model of an end product (output of type Finished Goods—FERT) and its relationship with the real substances used to create it (the input substances of type raw materials—ROH), and the output specification. As you can see, the relationships are all one-to-many, which allows full flexibility.

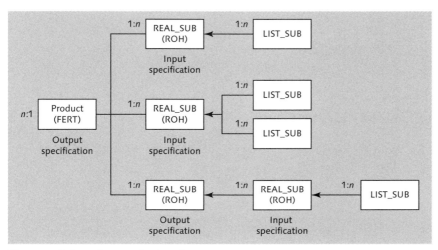

Figure 3.76 Data Concept for Specification

Table 3.8 provides an overview of the specification types, which are available within the standard category Substance, their definition, and how they are used. The last column provides an example of a substance.

Specification Type	Definition	Functionality	Example
Listed Substance (LIST_SUB)	Substance that is described in a regulatory list	Listed substances can't be assigned to materials; they can be used as reference substances.	Acetone
Listed Substance Group (LIST_GRP)	Grouping of listed substances from a logical point of view	Listed substances that have the same/referenced properties from a legal point of view.	Chromous salts
Real Substance (REAL_SUB)	Substances that are physically present in an enterprise and that correspond to a material in logistics	Real substances can be assigned to a material.	Silver paint
Real Substance Group (REAL_GRP)	Grouping of real substance from a logical point of view	Substance can be referenced to common substance properties.	Metallic paint
UN Listed Substance (LS_UN_SUB)	Legal data for Dangerous Goods Management	All legal provisions of the different regulations are assigned to a UN Listed Substance	1263 (paint)
Dangerous Goods Classification (DG_CL_SUB)	Legal rating of dangerous goods	Assigns a unique Dangerous Goods Classification to all dangerous goods.	Classification key: CL_PAI_00_99
Nutrients (NUTRIENT)	A substance that is necessary for organisms to grow and thrive and allow you to define nutrients within a product	Allows you to define the composition of nutrients.	Protein, fat, carbohydrates, fibers (general), leucine, isoleucine (amino acids), sodium, calcium (mineral), glucose, fructose, maltose, starch (sugar)

Table 3.8 Specification Types

Specification Type	Definition	Functionality	Example
Nutrient Group (NUTR_GROUP)	Group nutrients that logically belong together	Every nutrient belongs to a nutrient group to specify the nutrients for which information is to be displayed.	General nutrients, amino acids, mineral nutrients, sugar, fatty acids, vitamins, minerals, and carbohydrates
Diet (DIET)	Diet-relevant substance	You can create these substances and enter limit values. If this quantity is exceeded in a formula, you can determine that it's no longer possible to fulfill the requirements relevant to the diet.	Low-fat or low-cholesterol, milk, peanuts, vegetarian, vegan, kosher, halal
Diet Group (DIET_GROUP)	Grouping of diet-relevant substances	Every diet substance to one or multiple diet groups to relate them in terms of content.	Allergens, lifestyle diets, religious diets

Table 3.8 Specification Types (Cont.)

The substance data object is divided into header data (e.g., the substance name and status) and item data (e.g., the technical properties) as presented in Figure 3.77.

Header data includes information that is relevant for the entire substance, such as the description, category, and type. Identifiers are used to identify the substance by either entering its name (e.g., water), its assigned number (CAS 67-84-78), or its formula (H_2O). Figure 3.78 shows examples of possible identifiers for water.

Assignment of the number specification to the material (shown in Figure 3.79) triggers integration from the material master to other logistics processes and data such as material price, weight, and measurements. If the material is marked as environmentally relevant (basic data 2), and a delivery is posted for this material, SAP ERP checks if the material has been assigned to a substance for which an MSDS must be issued and, if necessary, starts the MSDS shipping. As mentioned earlier, the link between specifications and materials provides the integration to SAP Logistics components such as SAP MM for material planning, inventory management, and procurement activities, or advanced logistics planning scenarios covered by SAP SCM.

229

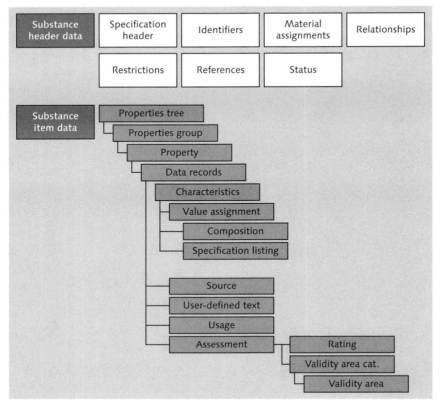

Figure 3.77 Substance Overview

S...	I...	RL	US	ID Categ.	ID Type	L	So...	Identifier
		0	1	FRM	MOLEC		7	H2O
		0	1	FRM	SUM		6	H2O
		0	1	NAM	IUPAC		4	H2O
		0	1	NAM	PROD	DE	2	Wasser, lebensmittelunbedenklich
		0	1	NAM	PROD	EN	1	Water, Food Grade
		0	1	NAM	TRIV	DE	5	Wasser
		0	1	NAM	TRIV	EN	5	Water

Real substance   SBST_4712   H2O   Water, Food Grade
08.10.2011   Water, Food Grade

Specification Header | Restrictions | Identifiers | References | Material Assignme...

Figure 3.78 Example of Identifiers for Substance Water

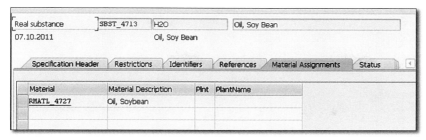

Figure 3.79 Substance Link to Material

The item data of a substance contains the details, composition, and phrase type properties. Figure 3.80 shows an example of the item details for the substance water.

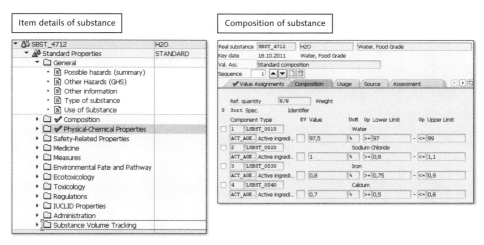

Figure 3.80 Property Tree and Composition of the Substance Water

3.4.3 Phrase Management

The next step in Specification Management and Recipe Management is phrase management, which manages and maintains your own and commercially purchased phrase libraries.

Figure 3.81 shows the structure of a phrase in the specification library, where the phrase is divided into header data and item data.

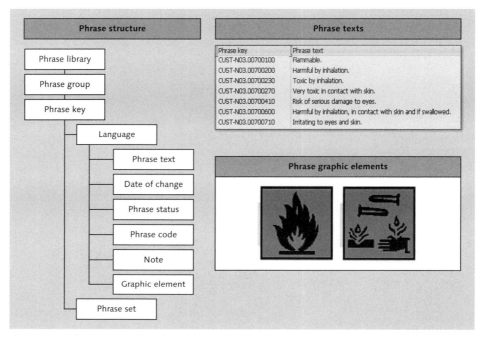

Figure 3.81 Phrase Structure

On the right hand side, notice the examples of phrases, including the graphic element which can be used as part of the phrase. You can use phrases in different kind of labels, such as nutritional labels or product labels.

3.4.4 Recipe Management

Recipe Management uses the functionality from SAP EHS Management and has been available since SAP R/3 4.6C, which included Recipe Management 1.0. The latest version is available within SAP PLM 7.02 and/or SAP ERP 6 EHP 5 and focuses on both the recipe development as well as the Recipe Management functions.

A recipe is a description of the requirements that must be met in a specific manufacturing process. A recipe comprises the material, substance, process, and resource data of a manufacturing process. Depending on the application area, the type of data ranges from a general description of the requirements to concrete procedural instructions for a specific production plant. Recipes are always independent of the dates of an order and contain no equipment control functions.

Recipes are master data of production definition and PP. Each recipe is made up of the following information, which is also represented in Figure 3.82:

▶ Recipe header data information that is relevant for the entire recipe, such as its status, validity, reference language, and related objects (e.g., projects)

▶ All the ingredients necessary as inputs to product the final product (called the output)

▶ The process that needs to be followed to produce the end product

▶ The necessary equipment and resources required during this process

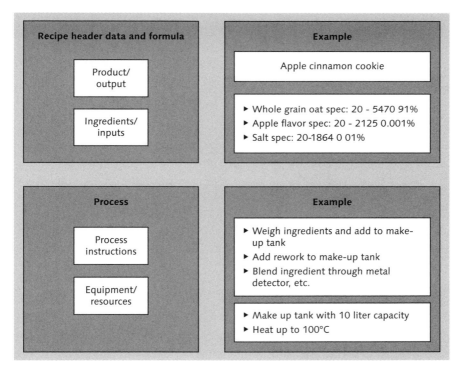

Figure 3.82 Recipe Structure

Conforming to the industry standard defined by the World Batch Forum (ISA standard S-88), the following recipe types are supported in standard SAP (and also shown in Figure 3.83):

▶ General recipe

▶ Site recipe

▶ Master recipe

▶ Control recipe

This specification defines a common, hierarchical approach for recipe information. The general and site recipe (i.e., the top two levels) are typically created and maintained during the product development process; the bottom two are using during execution by manufacturing.

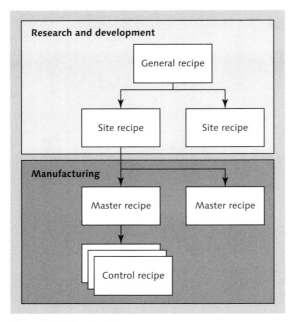

Figure 3.83 Recipe Types

The general recipe is location-independent; the site level typically contains information specific to a set of plants with common geographically needs, end requirements, or raw materials. Master level recipes are owned by PP, and control level is the process order and batch recipe.

You can use the standard available recipe types, or you can configure additional types based on your company's requirements. The recipe type determines several important things:

▶ Which objects may be linked to a recipe, such as formulas

▶ Whether or not status management is active, and which status profile is used

▶ Whether you can or must use change master records in recipe editing

▶ Which tab pages/views are active in a recipe

Change Management within Recipe Management

In Recipe Management, you have two basic options to manage changes and versioning of recipes: ECM and versioning. For each type of recipe, you must specify whether you want to use one or the other because these two options exclude each other. Through versioning, you have a simple procedure of change management (where you just define the next version), whereas with ECM, you can determine a change reason, relevant objects to change via the ECM order (such as the recipe, materials, etc.), change status, and approval process. Chapter 9 explains making changes using ECM.

Recipe Header Information

The header of a recipe contain basic data, scope of application, classifying recipes, identifiers, document links, translation, hierarchy, process model, and equipment requirements. The EQUIPMENT REQUIREMENTS tab in Figure 3.84 shows the equipment necessary for baking an apple cookie, and it also shows which tabs are available at the header level of the general recipe.

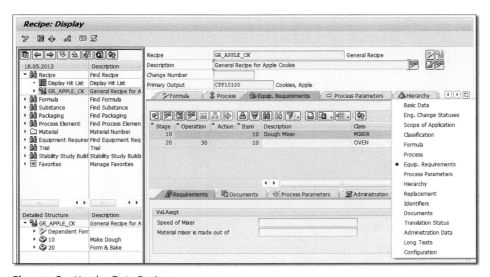

Figure 3.84 Header Data Recipe

Process Recipe Data

You use the process model master data to map the process and its activities that are required to produce one or more products. A recipe always contains just one process. A recipe process is called a "dependent" recipe, but you can also create a process without a link to a recipe, called an "independent" process. The process is the top element in the process model and is made up of the following process elements:

- Process model
- Process
- Process stage
- Process operation
- Process action

These elements have either a 1:1 or 1:*n* relationship, so a process can be split into multiple process stages and so on. This process model conforms to the ISA standard S-88. Figure 3.85 shows an example of process stages, operations, and actions that have been defined for making an apple cookie.

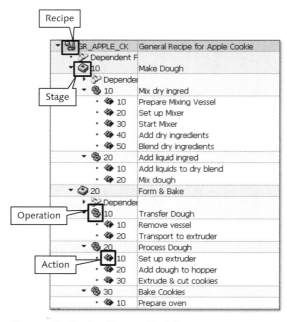

Figure 3.85 Recipe Process Model

Process Parameters

The process parameter lets you define the process in a greater dimensional detail. You can assign parameters such as temperature, density, and velocity to the appropriate process level. The PROCESS PARAMETERS tab in Figure 3.86 shows an example of a process parameter.

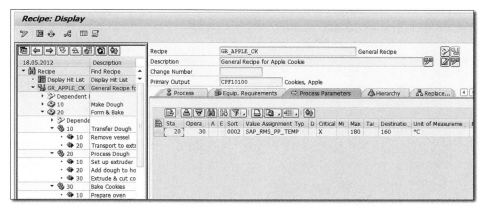

Figure 3.86 Process Parameter

Quality Inspection

At the stage and/or operation level you can require that a quality inspection be performed as part of the process activity as an in process control point. You define the standard inspection characteristics, inspection methods, and sampling procedures.

Integration

When you transform a general or site recipe to a master recipe, the planned inspection properties (inspection characteristics, inspection methods, and sampling procedures) are also transferred to the master recipe. The QM data at the *operation level* in the general or site recipe is transformed to phases; the QM data at the *stage level* is transformed to operations. Chapter 9 will discuss the QM functions and features in more detail. Figure 3.87 shows how a recipe can include quality information such as quality checks, which in this example are assigned to a recipe stage in the QM tab. The QM tab forms the integration to the QM component.

Figure 3.87 Inspection Details in a Recipe

Equipment Requirements

Within the EQUIP. REQUIREMENTS tab, you can assign which resources are used in the production process and even define more specific requirements of the equipment as shown in Figure 3.88. In Figure 3.86, shown previously, you can see the process parameters, including the oven's temperature, which for this cookie recipe was set to 180 degrees.

Figure 3.88 Recipe Equipment Requirements Example

Formula Basics

Formulas are used in general recipes, site recipes, and in your own copies of these recipe types to calculate the amount of materials/substance data that is required to produce the end product. You use the formula to assign the products manufactured in a process along with the required components and quantities to these recipes. On the other hand, plant-specific recipes and all your own copies of this recipe type are assigned the relevant production version. Formulas can be generated at the stage level, as its data is spread among the tabs HEADER, QUANTITIES, INPUT AND OUTPUT, and COMPOSITION.

Figure 3.89 shows an example of a recipe formula input and output for an apple cookie.

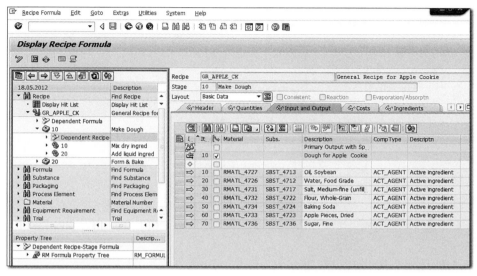

Figure 3.89 Recipe Formula

Integration of Recipe Data to Production and PP-PI Master Recipe

To produce the end product, you have to generate the right master data object within PP—called a master recipe. The system can automatically generate a master recipe (traditional SAP ERP master recipe) from a general/site recipe. In doing so, the system transforms general recipe stages to master recipe operations, and general recipe operations to master recipe phases. General recipe actions provide information for process instruction in the master recipe. Resource assignments are also determined here, which is represented in Figure 3.90.

Transformation Prerequisites

To use the transformation function, you have to ensure the right setting, and all of the master data must be present, such as material, classes, properties, resources, resource classification, master inspection characteristics, inspection methods, process instruction category, and process instruction characteristics.

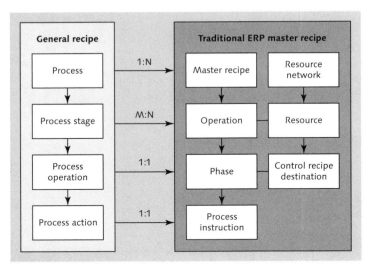

Figure 3.90 Relationship between General Recipe and Master Recipe

3.4.5 Trial Management

A trial is a product test aimed at achieving the required level of quality for a product or specification from a particular product line at the optimum cost.

Trial management, which is the next phase of Recipe Management, was introduced in the SAP ERP 5.0 release of Recipe Management. This component optimizes your product development process from the first trials and prototypes through to full production to ensure that the new recipe is generating the desired results from performance, quality, and cost perspectives, prior to producing the goods. While the functions required for trials are similar to those of production and quality assurance, a greater degree of flexibility is required for trial planning. Trial management supports carrying out a number of different trials and linking to all trial-related areas and objects, such as PPM-specific objects and SAP PS-specific objects, QM objects, PP objects such as planned or process orders, and recipes.

Master Data for Trials

The master data object is the trial, which includes information about the material, substance, process, and resource data for a procedure. Within the trial management solution, different trial scales have been identified, allowing you to have different requirements regarding your flexibility when planning trials, where the earlier phases are more flexible with less control, and the phases used to prepare production are more carefully planned and controlled. A trial can be carried out in a laboratory (where the focus is on the formula development), a pilot plant (where the focus is on the process), or in a production plant (where the focus is on confirmation, final testing, and running factory trials). Depending on your requirements, you can pick and conduct the trial phases that are relevant for your organization.

Feedback from trials is used as input for defining subsequent trials. The best result from each scale is moved forward, continuously improving the results to ensure all quality and development goals are met in the end. There is complete flexibility to copy trial results forward, even skipping intermediate steps as you move closer to production volume, or to go backward, if you need to go back to reevaluate some recipe basics. A trial can be carried out in different phases, as shown in Figure 3.91.

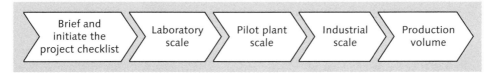

Figure 3.91 Trial Management Phases

Let's break this process down:

1. **Brief and initiate the project checklist.**
   The first step in the trial management process is conducting the project briefing and initiating the project checklist.

2. **Laboratory scale (also referred to as bench scale).**
   The main focus of this stage is on the development of the formula and the ingredients to come up with a prototype. It can take place in a lab or kitchen. QM can be used for sample management purposes. During laboratory scale trial, we assume that the materials are available "out of the cupboard"—without having to create reservations.

3. **Pilot plant scale.**
   The pilot plant scale focuses on the process and provides trial execution functions and analysis. It assumes normal line-based planning for equipment and normal MRP and uses the manufacturing planning processes. For pilot and

factory trials, material requirements will be planned and time is allotted to pre-pare the production line.

4. **Industrial scale.**
   The industrial scale focuses on confirmation, allowing you to run factory trials to further confirm and test, making sure factory equipment and factory stock is available and information flows from SAP to any required additional systems.

5. **Production volume.**
   The last step is the actual production of the product.

A trial fully integrates with PP (PP-PI) including auto-creating the master recipe, Recipe Management, and QM, such as postprocess analysis and stability studies for lab samples and in-process analysis.

3.4.6 Reporting in Recipe Management

Flexible reporting and label generation functions are available from within Recipe Management. It's integrated with other SAP lifecycle processes such as project management (PPM and SAP PS), SAP DMS, vendor/customer collaboration, QM, purchasing, planning, manufacturing, and SAP Process Control. Figure 3.92 gives an example of a label and report. Within Recipe Management, you can use a tool called Windows Word Processor Integration (WWI), but we'll go into more detail in Chapter 10.

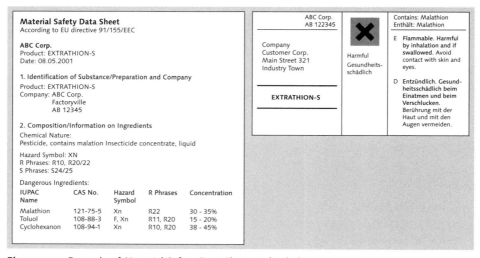

Figure 3.92 Example of Material Safety Data Sheet and Label

3.5 Summary

This chapter has introduced you to all the master data objects that can be used to represent a product such as the material, BOM, routing, document, specification, and recipe. Product costings can be created at any point in time within the product lifecycle because SAP PLM supports different costing methods depending on when costing is made and which data is available for costing at that particular time. Whether your product is a discrete product or a processed product, you should now understand how these data objects can be used to represent your product's information. When you use multiple objects to represent a product, and the same people are responsible for the maintenance of this master data, you should consider using the Integrated Product and Process Engineering (iPPE) tools such as the product structure browser, the Engineering Workbench, and the iPPE Workbench. These allow you to access and work on multiple objects simultaneously when the material is the central object.

SAP PLM 7.01 offers two separate interfaces, one focused on discrete industries (including PVS, assemblies, CAD integration, and Variant Configuration) and one focused on process industries (including formula, Specification Management, and Recipe Management). They both include common functions covering the material, BOM, document, ECM, work centers, classification, and search and navigation capabilities.

Specification Management and Recipe Management are part of SAP ERP and are specifically targeted at process industries in which a product is produced via an ingredient list or recipe (such as within the food or medical industries). Product master data and your organizational elements form the foundation of an SAP PLM solution. After you understand the objects available and which ones are relevant for your organization, you can move on to defining your processes and leveraging these building blocks during execution of the processes.

The next chapter will continue with product master data, with the specific focus on classification and variant configuration. Classification allows you to enrich product data by defining your own specific product fields. Variant Configuration enables you to easily generate all of the product variants possible from a technical and business point of view. We'll also consider the business processes available for collaboration of product master data.

Product data can be flexibly enriched with industry- and company-specific information through classification. Variant Configuration allows you to effectively and efficiently manage product variants with minimal product data maintenance. This reflects the technically and commercially feasible products. The available business processes for product data collaboration ensure that all stakeholders have access and can collaborate on the product data.

4 Product Variants, Classification, and Collaboration

Chapter 3 focused on the master data objects relevant for product data, and this chapter continues explaining classification and product variants through Variant Configuration. The SAP Classification system (CA) and Variant Configuration are two advanced product management capabilities that have been brought together in this chapter because Variant Configuration is dependent on the use of product classification. Finally, the business processes available for product collaboration are described as well. This chapter is divided primarily into three parts, which cover CA, Variant Configuration, and engineering and R&D collaboration.

CA, which we'll tackle first, allows you to enrich product data by defining your own company-specific or industry-specific product fields. The next sections focus on Variant Configuration, in which you can manage multiple variants of an "object" easily with minimal master data maintenance. The product variant is by far the most frequently used form of Variant Configuration in SAP, so it receives much coverage in this chapter. Section 4.2 offers an explanation of the concept, the scenarios, the data models for the scenario, and pricing. Section 4.3 focuses on the configuration rules or, in SAP terminology, the object dependencies. Then Section 4.4 explains the different business variants. Apart from product variants, you can also use Variant Configuration in other areas such as project systems and maintenance, as explained in Section 4.5.

The second part of this chapter focuses on the business scenarios and business processes that are available under the main process, Product Development and

Collaboration. It includes the collaboration between all the stakeholders involved along the way.

Let's begin the conversation about variant configuring by defining classification.

4.1 Classification

The SAP Classification System (CA) is a centrally available tool that can be used to classify master data and transactional data, by making it possible to define your own fields. This additional data can, in turn, be used to find the objects, report on the objects, and minimize your master data maintenance by using the Variant Configuration abilities. Because CA is a cross-application component, it can be used in most applications, such as in SAP Materials Management (SAP MM) to enrich the product master, in SAP Plant Maintenance (SAP PM) and SAP Customer Service (SAP CS) to enrich the technical objects, in SAP Environment, Health, and Safety Management (SAP EHS Management) to enrich the substance data, or in SAP Project System (SAP PS) to enrich your projects and orders.

Let's take a look at the classification features, except the Variant Configuration possibilities, which will be discussed in following sections. Figure 4.1 gives you an example of a classified material.

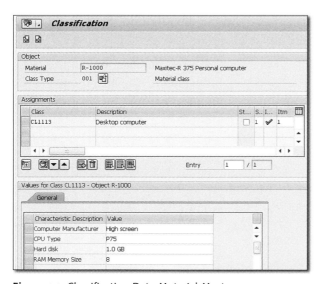

Figure 4.1 Classification Data Material Master

4.1.1 Purpose of Classification

To organize objects in a systematic way by defining your own customer specific data, the objects can either be master data (e.g., materials or vendors) or transactional data (e.g. inspection results, release procedures). This additional classification data can be used to find objects and to perform analysis on the data. CA can also be used to model product variants without creating an individual record for each possible variant by using Variant Configuration (this topic will be discussed in more detail from Section 4.2 onward). The examples shown in this first section will all be based on material classification. However, classification can also be used in the following applications/areas:

▸ **SAP Production Planning for the Process Industries (PP-PI)**
To describe the PI-PCS interface in the process control station.

▸ **Quality Management (QM)**
To describe quality results and outcomes and to produce quality certificates.

▸ **Logistics General in Batch Management (LO-BM)**
To transfer inspection values to batch classification and substance processing; the characteristics in CA are referred to as "general characteristics" in SAP PLM QM).

▸ **Logistics General in Variant Configuration (LO-VC)**
To configure complex products.

▸ **SAP Environment, Health, and Safety Management (SAP EHS Management)**
To describe the properties of substances.

▸ **SAP Production Planning – Computer Aided Process Planning (PP-CAPP)**
To determine dates, capacity requirements, and costs in formulas used for determining standard values.

▸ **SAP Materials Management (MM-PUR) in Purchasing**
To describe additional details in the release procedure for purchase requisitions of the to-be-procured articles and/or services in purchasing documents with classification.

▸ **SAP Classification System (CA)**
To describe the properties of the objects (master data objects and transactional objects), you classify and find those objects that were classified in the cross-application.

▶ **Easy Cost Planning (ECP)**
When using easy cost planning within the form characteristics are used, which need to be filled out. The values entered are used by the system to calculated costs. ECP can be performed for several SAP objects across several components, such as for a base object (PP), a product (PP), an internal order (CO), WBS element (SAP PS), internal service requests (SAP CS), appropriation request (SAP Inventory Management [SAP IM]), or generally to determine costs for a specific purpose using an ad hoc cost estimate (CO).

4.1.2   Benefits of Classification

Using CA enables you to define your own fields and field values for objects (e.g., for a material) with standard available tools without having to modify the program. The following benefits can be expected when using CA:

▶ You can personalize and enrich master data objects and transactional objects. You can include your own business logic and have the system "speak your language," and include your business-critical information without needing to enhance and change the programs. This reduces design and developmental costs, and because it's part of the standard product offering for SAP PLM (and SAP ERP), it's supported and will be maintained in future releases by SAP.

▶ As a cross-application function, CA's functions and features can be used for objects belonging to other components. So after you have CA set up, and you're considering using it in another area, you can reuse or extend existing training and documentation because the principles and methods are the same.

▶ When you choose to use the CA function for a master data object, you can use CA to find this object in every transaction where you can enter this object.

4.1.3   Classification Functions and Features

CA offers the functions and features represented in Figure 4.2, which will be explained in more detail in this section:

▶ Maintaining master data (characteristics and classes)

▶ Classifying objects

▶ Searching for classified objects

▶ Reporting

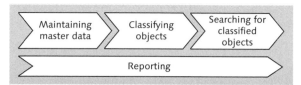

Figure 4.2 Classification Features and Functions

Maintaining Master Data

The creation of the master data is split into four separate steps:

1. Create the characteristics by performing maintenance on the specific fields or the characteristics.
2. After the fields/characteristics have been defined, you can create the class, which groups the fields together.
3. Assign the created class to the object. This provides the link to the "to be" classified master data object or transactional object.
4. Classify the object. By having the object assigned to the class, you can add values for the assigned characteristics for this specific object. The data objects and their relationships are shown in Figure 4.3.

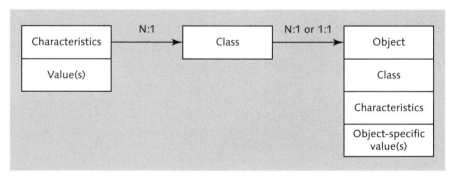

Figure 4.3 Data Model for Master Data Classification

Maintaining Characteristics

In CA, characteristics describe the properties of objects. You first need to create the characteristics centrally and then assign them to classes. You can group characteristics together by assigning them to a characteristics group, which is configurable based on your company's requirements.

When maintaining the characteristic, you need to choose its format (character, currency, numeric value, and date or time) and whether the characteristic is a required mandatory field or just optional. When classifying an object, you can define whether to assign a single value to the characteristic (just one choice—color—for car) or multiple values to the characteristic (many options—radio, speaker, leather seats, etc.—for a car). You can maintain the possible entries by specifying them individually (Figure 4.4) or entering a range (e.g., temperature needs to be between 20 and 100 degrees). You can set one of the allowed values as a default value.

Through additional data, you can assign the characteristic to a specific table/field from the SAP database. This gives you the ability to use an existing field and value from the connected object (e.g., using the material group field from the material master—Table MARA, field MATKL). Via the descriptions, you can maintain the characteristics' descriptions in all of the languages where this classification is being used. Figure 4.4 gives you an example of a character characteristic for a computer manufacturer. You can see the different data types available in the lower left and the possible values (colors) on the right.

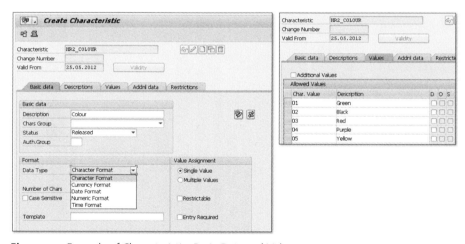

Figure 4.4 Example of Characteristic: Basic Data and Values

Table 4.1 lists the data that can be maintained by tab.

When creating a characteristic of the data type character, you can maintain possible entries by maintaining a value hierarchy. This makes it easier to select a value. Figure 4.5 shows an example of a value hierarchy for the country of origin.

Tab	Functions and Features
BASIC DATA	You can input the description, the characteristics group to which the characteristic belongs, the status of the characteristic, the authorization group, the format details such as type (character, date, time, currency), and the value assignment options to define whether valuation is a single value or if multiple answers can be entered and if the field is a required entry.
DESCRIPTIONS	You can maintain a description of this characteristic in all of the languages in which the characteristics needs to become available.
VALUES	You can define all of the possible entries, including which entry will be used as a default value. When the characteristic is of format character, this is also the place where you can set up a value hierarchy. When you want to use a database table or set up your own checking rules to make sure the value assignment is correct (by defining your checking formulas in a function module), you can activate the other value checks here.
ADDNL DATA	You can define a reference table, which needs to be used if the characteristic refers to a field in a table. A document from your Knowledge Provider (KPro) can be referenced as well, and you can define the procedure for how value assignment of the characteristic takes place (ready for input, display allowed values, etc.).
RESTRICTIONS	You can restrict the use of this characteristic to a class type.

Table 4.1 Characteristics Data per Tab

Figure 4.5 Value Hierarchy for Country of Origin

When you've defined a large number of characteristics in a class, the grouping functions allows you to group them together and represent them to the user in separate tabs, which you can name based on your own requirements. Figure 4.6 shows an example of the definition of two additional tabs—METAL PROP and OTHER.

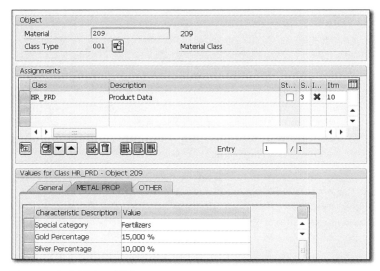

Figure 4.6 Additional Tabs

Maintaining Classes

The class is the mechanism to group the characteristics together. You can use one-to-one relationships for the class or even use a hierarchy of classes, which makes it possible to inherit characteristic data from a higher level to a lower level. A class needs to be assigned to a class type, which determines the object where this class can be used (e.g. the class type 001 is the class type used for the material master).

The left side of Figure 4.7 shows an example of a class called PBC, which is a computer component; the right side of the figure shows that this class is part of a hierarchy.

Table 4.2 gives you an overview of the data that can be maintained in each tab.

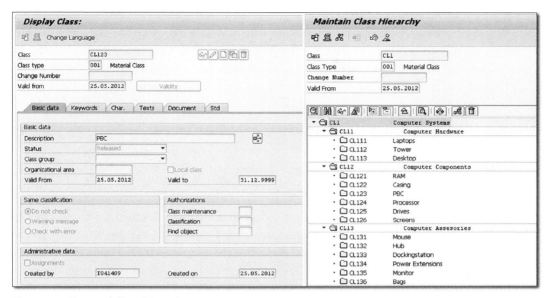

Figure 4.7 Class and Class Hierarchy

Tab	Functions and Features
BASIC DATA	This tab holds administration data, which automatically saves the user and date of when the class was created. It also contains the description, class group, authorization group, the status of the class, and validity of the class.
KEYWORDS	These strings are used for finding a class via match codes.
CHAR.	These characteristics are assigned to this class.
TEXTS	This tab holds explanatory texts for the class.
DOCUMENT	This document is linked to the class through SAP DMS. You can use the SAP document info record (DIR) to assign a document or use the object link function.
STD	This data is for DIN classes (based on German standard).
ADDITIONAL DATA	This tab has special data for Variant Configuration only, such as the class or profile.

Table 4.2 Class Data per Tab

Using Authorizations

By using authorization groups, you can restrict authorizations for class maintenance, classification (assigning an object to a class and value this), and finding
objects with the specified class. The authorization groups are assigned to the class
in the AUTHORIZATIONS area in the BASIC DATA tab; they are checked against the
user based on authorization groups. These authorization objects are available for
classification:

▶ BGRKP: Maintain class

▶ BGRKL: Classification

▶ BGRSE: Use class to find objects

The left side of Figure 4.8 shows a class and to which authorization groups this
class is assigned: CLASS MAINTENANCE, CLASSIFICATION, and FIND OBJECT are all
assigned to authorization group 001. The right-hand side of Figure 4.8 shows a
user who is assigned the role profile in which he is allowed to maintain classes
belonging to 001 to 999, to assign objects to classes belonging to groups 100 to
300, and to find objects in groups 100 to 300. So this user can only use this class
to maintain it because the other authorizations haven't been granted.

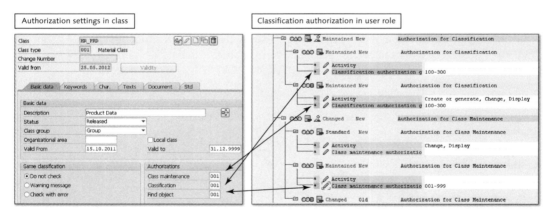

Figure 4.8 Authorization

Classifying an Object

Another feature of CA is being able to assign an object to a class and fill out the
details of that specific object, either in the maintenance transaction of that object

or via the ASSIGNMENT function offered within the CLASSIFICATION menu. Remember that you assign the object (e.g., the material) to the class for which you want to fill out the characteristics. You can assign multiple classes to an object, if required. The process of describing the object in more detail with characteristics is also known as object classification. When assigning the values to the characteristics, the system ensures that the data filled out is correct and will inform you when additional valuation is required or the data entered is accurate.

Figure 4.9 shows an example of a material that has been assigned to two different classes whose values are assigned to the different characteristics. The STATUS column with the green checkmark shows the status and indicates whether the valuation is complete, incomplete, or locked.

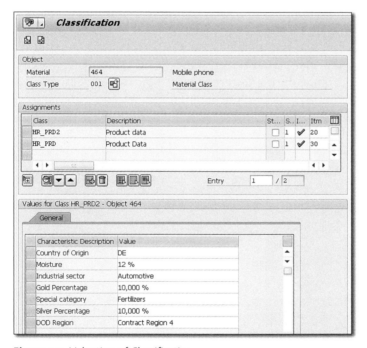

Figure 4.9 Valuation of Classification

Searching for Classified Objects

After the object has been classified, the characteristics values can be used to find the material by using the classification-specific match code.

Let's consider an example of the match code for finding a material based on classification, which takes three distinct steps, as shown in Figure 4.10:

1. **Select classification match code.**
   First you have to make sure to use the search method using classification (by pressing ⌨F4 and choosing the MATERIALS BY CLASS tab).

2. **Choose the class you want to search in.**
   As you can see in Figure 4.10, you need to select a class, which in this example, is CL111 DESKTOP COMPUTER. After the class is chosen, the characteristics assigned to this class will become available to further your selection.

3. **Value characteristics and search.**
   After you've chosen the specific characteristics, you can search for the materials. When receiving the list of the search results, you can further narrow down the results by using filtering, reselecting, or adding additional search criteria. This search function is available in the CLASSIFICATION menu, but it's also available on all the transaction screens where you can enter a material master record. For example, during the creation of a purchase order, you can directly use classification data to find the material and select a material from the search results, without the need to leave the purchase order transaction (see Figure 4.11).

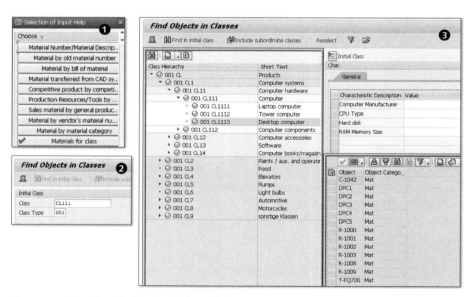

Figure 4.10 Use Classification to Find an Object

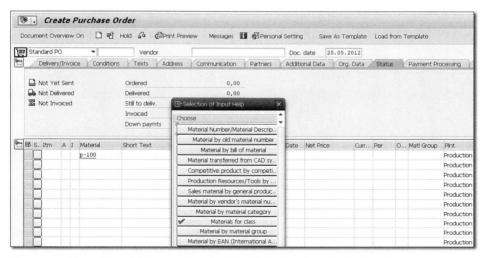

Figure 4.11 Find a Material through Classification during Purchase Order Creation

Reporting

Different standard reports are available within CA. Examples of reports include the characteristics list displayed in Figure 4.12 (an example of the standard report that is available to view characteristics), the where-used list, class list, object comparison report, and several more. They can be found under the menu option Environment. Classification data can also be available in reports within an application. An example is the equipment's overview list (Transaction IH08), where you can use classification data to find equipment and display the classification data in the list by adding classification data (Menu • Settings • Show/Hide Classification). Chapter 10 offers more information on reporting capabilities and tools that are available within SAP ERP and the SAP Business Suite.

Now you should have a good overview of how CA can be used to enrich product data by defining your own company-specific characteristics and classes. It can also be used to enrich product data with industry-specific product content. With just two additional master data objects (the class and its characteristics), you can enrich the data of a product but also enrich any other classifiable object within SAP ERP and SAP PLM. The opportunities of CA are endless, but be aware that introducing new fields via CA will add to the master data maintenance load, so finding the right balance is key.

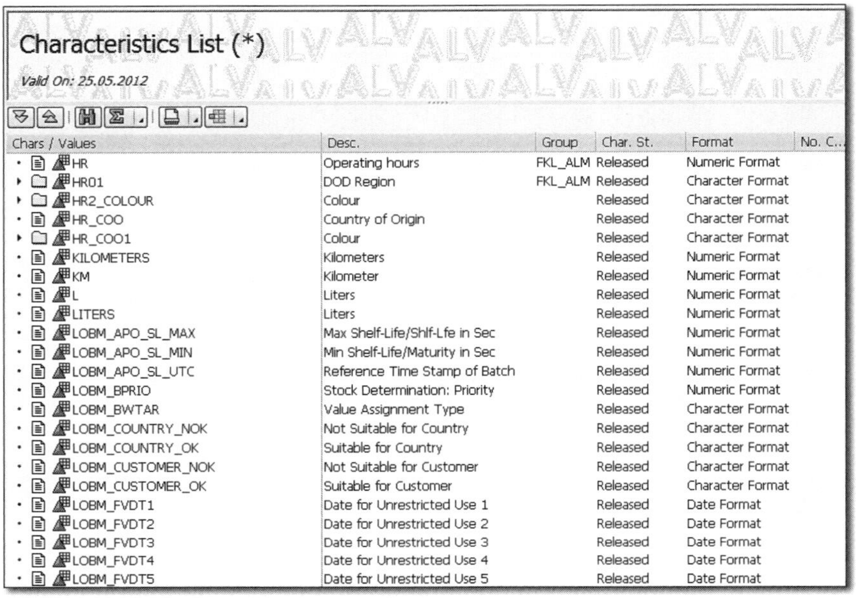

Characteristics List (*)

Valid On: 25.05.2012

Chars / Values	Desc.	Group	Char. St.	Format	No. C...
HR	Operating hours	FKL_ALM	Released	Numeric Format	
HR01	DOD Region	FKL_ALM	Released	Character Format	
HR2_COLOUR	Colour		Released	Character Format	
HR_COO	Country of Origin		Released	Character Format	
HR_COO1	Colour		Released	Character Format	
KILOMETERS	Kilometers		Released	Numeric Format	
KM	Kilometer		Released	Numeric Format	
L	Liters		Released	Numeric Format	
LITERS	Liters		Released	Numeric Format	
LOBM_APO_SL_MAX	Max Shelf-Life/Shlf-Lfe in Sec		Released	Numeric Format	
LOBM_APO_SL_MIN	Min Shelf-Life/Maturity in Sec		Released	Numeric Format	
LOBM_APO_SL_UTC	Reference Time Stamp of Batch		Released	Numeric Format	
LOBM_BPRIO	Stock Determination: Priority		Released	Numeric Format	
LOBM_BWTAR	Value Assignment Type		Released	Character Format	
LOBM_COUNTRY_NOK	Not Suitable for Country		Released	Character Format	
LOBM_COUNTRY_OK	Suitable for Country		Released	Character Format	
LOBM_CUSTOMER_NOK	Not Suitable for Customer		Released	Character Format	
LOBM_CUSTOMER_OK	Suitable for Customer		Released	Character Format	
LOBM_FVDT1	Date for Unrestricted Use 1		Released	Date Format	
LOBM_FVDT2	Date for Unrestricted Use 2		Released	Date Format	
LOBM_FVDT3	Date for Unrestricted Use 3		Released	Date Format	
LOBM_FVDT4	Date for Unrestricted Use 4		Released	Date Format	
LOBM_FVDT5	Date for Unrestricted Use 5		Released	Date Format	

Figure 4.12 Characteristics List

4.2 Variant Configuration

Configuration plays an important role in product choice. You might have already used Variant Configuration to explore your buying options or to make a purchase decision by configuring your own product online or together with a sales representative in a store. A good example of the use of Variant Configuration can be found on the BMW website, where a 3D view of a car gets updated based on your preferences about the model, engine type, and external finish. Another good example is a tailor-made suit, where endless options can determine the end product based on size, style, gender, trends, material use, and fabric used; the tailor can make a sketch to support this process.

So when you want to maintain several product variants—because they are repeatedly being produced or developed for your customer—the Variant Configuration tool can assist you. The Variant Configuration function is part of the central functions within Logistics (menu path Logistics • Central Functions • Variant Configuration); it's located here because it isn't only used for product variants but also in other components such as SAP PM, SAP PS, and SAP MM.

Successful implementation of Variant Configuration can produce the following benefits:

▶ The workload of master data maintenance activities is reduced.

▶ Storage costs are reduced.

▶ The customer gets exactly what he wants, based on his personal requirements.

▶ The configuration includes all essential restrictions of feasibility in production, so the sales department can be confident that the product quoted or sold is technically possible.

▶ It's an integrated solution, which feeds processes in the values chain from the sales or R&D engineering (e.g., materials requirements planning [MRP], production, inventory management, and procurement).

4.2.1 Why Use Variant Configuration?

Explaining and understanding the reasons for using Variant Configuration is best done through an example, so we'll be using a car example. Figure 4.13 shows the production process, and Table 4.3 shows the different product models and product options. As you can see, the car is available in three colors—white, black, and green. Another option is its body shape, again with three choices—sedan, hatchback, and sports coupe. So basically the number of variants that you can offer when restricted to these two options as the number of car options is: 3 colors × 3 bodies = 9 options.

Without using Variant Configuration, you would have to create all of the different product versions as nine different materials.

As you can see, the formula for calculating the number of possible product configurations (X) multiplies the number of possible values (V) by one another. This is the formula for calculation of possible variations: $X = V1 \times V2 \times V3$.

The example of a product variant that we will be working with in this chapter is a car—a product we are all familiar with. Table 4.3 includes the product options. You have a product with 10 product choices, including the model choice. Five product choices have three options, four with two options, and one with one option. So perform the calculation: $3 \times 3 \times 3 \times 3 \times 3 \times 2 \times 2 \times 2 \times 2 \times 1 = 3,888$ product variations for your cars.

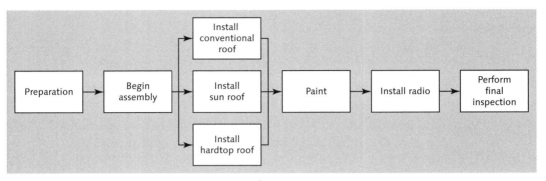

Figure 4.13 Production Process

Product	Product options
Model	▸ Standard ▸ Sports edition ▸ Convertible
Body	▸ Sedan ▸ Hatchback ▸ Sports coupe
Color	▸ Black ▸ White ▸ Green
Engine	▸ Turbo diesel ▸ Injection
Radio	▸ Standard ▸ MP3
Fuel type	▸ Diesel ▸ Unleaded gasoline
Transmission	▸ Automatic ▸ Manual ▸ Semi-automatic
Finishing paint	▸ Metallic

Table 4.3 Product BOM Options

Product	Product options
Roof	▸ Conventional
	▸ Sun roof
	▸ Hardtop
Extras	▸ Theft alarm
	▸ Cruise control

Table 4.3 Product BOM Options (Cont.)

When there aren't any configuration restrictions, this number of variations would mean that you have to set up 3,888 materials, 3,888 BOMs, and 3,888 pricing records to make all these options available for your customers without using Variant Configuration. This is a huge amount of master data maintenance. Now imagine how hard it would be to maintain all of the objects when changes need to be made! To address this problem, the Variant Configuration tool was introduced and used; it is especially recommended when product variants need to be used repeatedly.

4.2.2 Product Variants

This section will explain the data models used within Variant Configuration, the concept of a material variant, and finally the configuration profile in more detail.

Data Model or Knowledge Base

Variant Configuration supports the configuration of highly variable standard products and their allowed combinations according to individual customer requirements. To use Variant Configuration, you first need to understand the data model of Variant Configuration, which is described in the first subsection. Recall from Section 4.1 that Variant Configuration relies heavily on classification data; you might want to re-read that section to get a refresher before you continue reading.

To use Variant Configuration, at minimum, you need a configurable material, the characteristics describing the options, and a configuration profile with the appropriate class, which controls some important configuration decisions. The other objects mentioned within the model are optional based on your requirements.

When using Variant Configuration, there are two options with slightly different data models: the classic material and BOM model and the Integrated Product and Process Engineering (iPPE) model. We'll discuss the first option now and then follow that with the discussion of iPPE.

The first option is classic material and BOM, in which the data model can also be referred to as the knowledge base. Figure 4.14 gives you an overview of the data model followed by a short description of the master data objects. Within this model, the material master is the central object used to represent the product and is directly linked with the BOM, the task list (referred to as a routing, see Chapter 3, Section 3.1.1 for the distinction), and the configuration profile.

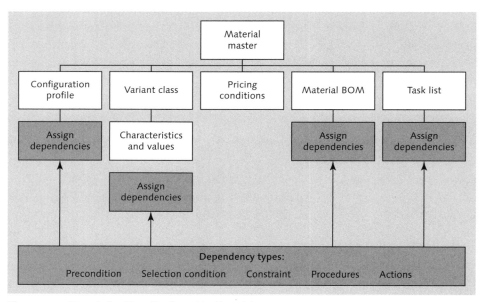

Figure 4.14 Knowledge Base Configurable Material

The knowledge base within the classic scenario consists of the following objects:

► Material master describing the product, which must have been configured as a configurable material or flagged as configurable on the BASIC DATA tab and include the classification view. The standard delivered material KMAT already has these appropriate settings. You can assign the appropriate class to the material either via the material master, CA, or the configuration profile.

- Characteristics and their values within the class type for Variant Configuration (class type 300) and class type 200 Class Node. They describe the possible product options, such as characteristic "color," with the values "Black" and "Silver."

- Configuration profile, which contains control data (explained further in the "Configuration Profile" subsection).

- Super BOM containing all possible items, that is, all standard components and all variable possible items. As soon as you include object dependencies, it can be referred to a configured BOM.

- Super task list that includes all operations, suboperations, sequences, and product resource/tools (PRTs) required to manufacture all of the possible variants.

- Pricing conditions: including all pricing data necessary for pricing all possible variants of the product.

- Object dependencies that provide the configuration rules or logic for configuration. The five different types of dependencies—selection condition (SC), procedures (P), constraints (C), actions (A), and preconditions (PC)—are described in more detail in the following section.

The second option is using Integrated Product and Process Engineering (iPPE). Within iPPE, the material remains the central object, but the iPPE structure replaces the classic BOM, which is represented as a product variant structure (PVS). The classic task list (routing) is represented in the process structure (ACT), both of which have been extensively described in Chapter 3, Section 3.1.2.

To model the different product variants, Variant Configuration is used with the configuration profile. The only difference compared to the classic scenario is that only one type of object dependency is supported through iPPE: the local selection condition. The different available object dependencies are described in more detail in the Section 4.3. Figure 4.15 represents the data model used in iPPE.

Within the data model of iPPE, where the material master remains the central object that all objects are connected to, the data model consists of the following objects:

- **Material master**
  Describes the product, which must be flagged as a configurable material.

- **Configuration profile**
  Contains the control data (further explained in the "Configuration Profile" subsection).

▶ **Object dependencies**

Provides the configuration rules or logic for configuration. Within the iPPE, only the selection condition (SC) is available, which is described in more detail in this section.

▶ **Characteristics and their values**

Within the class type for Variant Configuration (class type 300) and class type 200 Class Node, these describe the possible product options, for example characteristic "color," with the values "black" and "silver."

▶ **Pricing conditions**

Includes all pricing data necessary for pricing all of the possible variants of the product.

▶ **Product variant structure (PVS)**

Contains all possible items, that is, all standard components and all variable possible items. This is comparable to the super BOM from the classic model. As soon as you include object dependencies, it can be referred to as a configured BOM.

▶ **Process structure (ACT)**

Defines the different process steps, similar to the super task list in the classic model.

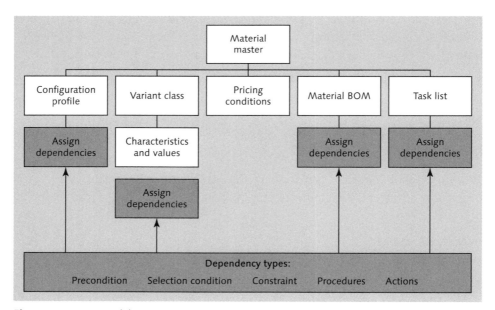

Figure 4.15 Data Model iPPE

Note that iPPE will become the standard modeling platform in the future for product development. Not all iPPE objects are available in all applications and their respective releases because iPPE is used differently in them, so check this in advance and use the Switch Framework to enable unavailable objects. The Switch Framework allows you to activate additional business processes and objects.

Because Chapter 3 has discussed most of these data elements in detail, here we'll only call attention to the new elements—the configuration profile and the object dependencies. Both elements are used in both data models, with the only exception that in the configuration profile within the iPPE model, only selection conditions can be used and no other condition types are supported. To explain the configuration profile and object dependencies, we'll use the same example from before: a configurable car with the following variant options (see Table 4.4).

Option Description	Option Values
Car Model	▶ Standard ▶ Convertible ▶ Sport
Car Body	▶ Sport ▶ Hatchback ▶ Sports coupe
Color	▶ Black ▶ White ▶ Green
Engine	▶ Turbo ▶ Injection
Radio	▶ Standard ▶ MP3 Player with 5 discs
Fuel Type	▶ Diesel ▶ Unleaded gas
Transmission	▶ Automatic ▶ Manual
Finishing	▶ Metallic

Table 4.4 Variant Options

The example should be modeled in SAP by creating a configurable material as is visible in the BASIC DATA 2 tab of the material. You need to assign the class to this material, which includes the different available car models. In this case, the car model is CLASS C_CAR1, as shown in the CLASSIFICATION pane. The CAR MODEL pane shows the characteristic values available for the model, as you can see in Figure 4.16.

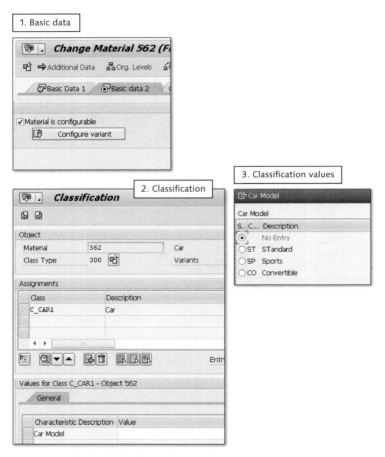

Figure 4.16 Configurable Material Car: Basic and Classification

Let's compare these two models. The top of Figure 4.17 is a screenshot of the classic scenario where the configurable item is used at the top level and the super BOM is captured, which includes all the options describing all the variants possible.

Whether or not an item is included in the sales order depends on the configuration rules that have been assigned to the item via the object dependencies. In Figure 4.17, you can see that they exist for all the items of the BOM because there is a checkmark in the column OD. When there isn't a dependency, the item will always get included.

The bottom of Figure 4.17 shows the iPPE BOM option. When you choose to go for the iPPE scenario, you create a PVS with the car at the top level and the options set up as subitems describing all the variants possible. You can also define a selection object dependency to these specific BOM items. When there isn't a dependency, the item will automatically always get included.

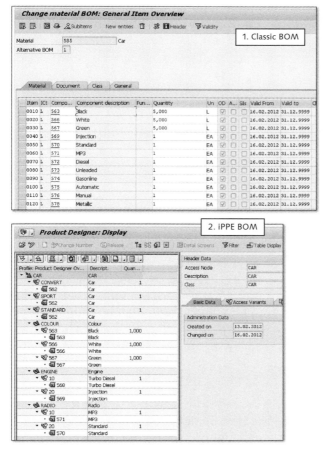

Figure 4.17 Classic and iPPE Super BOM

Material Variant

If you notice that certain variants are ordered often, you can specifically create a material for this version. It needs a reference to the configurable material and to be assigned the correct values for this version. This allows you to use this material for production purposes and warehousing functions, without the need for a sales order in advance.

Configuration Profile

The configuration profile contains fundamental settings for configuring the object to which it's assigned. In product variations, it's assigned to the material and is material-specific (i.e., has a one-to-one relationship). Because this configuration concept is used in other areas of the solution as well, you can see that it can also be set up for three other objects—the general maintenance task list, the standard network, and the model service specification—which are explained in Section 4.5.

The profile is presented and grouped with the following configuration settings as shown in Figure 4.18.

- **Basic Data**
  Here you define which class type is relevant for material configuration, which in SAP standard is always class type 300. Usually you just assign a class here without assigning values. When you do assign values, you're restricting the allowed values for the product. The Basic data tab configuration settings is the primary storage location of dependencies, which you can assign to a configurable object. Object dependencies will be explained in more detail in Section 4.3.

- **Configuration settings**
  These are important control settings for configuration. Before using the material, you need to set up which configuration scenarios or business scenario is relevant during configuration. The following are available and are explained in further detail in Section 4.4:

  - **Assemble to order (ATO)**
    The product or service is being assembled during the receipt for the sales order. The key components are kept in stock to ensure that during the receipt of the order, the product can be customized.

▶ **Make to order, individual products (MTO)**

This option can be set with the indicator SALES ORDER (SET), which basically means that the header material and the sales-specific items will be visible within the sales order and are supplied together manually. You may want to do this, for example, if the components are a set of materials that are delivered as individual parts, such as the components of a PC—keyboard, printer, monitor, and CPU—where PC is the header material.

▶ **Engineer to order with project-specific products (ETO)**

This option can be chosen by selecting the ORDER BOM option, which basically allows you to create a sales BOM specifically for the sales order item. You can have the BOM saved as a knowledge-based BOM or as a result-oriented BOM.

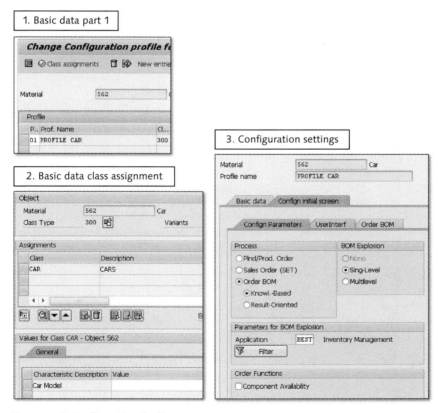

Figure 4.18 Configuration Profile

When you choose KNOWL. -BASED, a copy of the BOM will be saved with the manual changes and the object dependencies. However, when you choose RESULT-ORIENTED, a copy will be made excluding the dependencies. This saves database space, but gives you less detailed insights. Both scenarios have been represented in Figure 4.19.The original BOM and the second BOM (the suggested changes) are shown on the left-hand side. Based on these proposed changes, on the right-hand side, you see how the BOM would be saved when it was either flagged as a knowledge-based BOM or results-oriented BOM. *Results-oriented BOM* allows you to change the assigned characteristic values (not the BOM itself) through the MAINTENANCE IN THE ORDER ALLOWED radio button. If the indicator isn't set, you can only maintain order BOMs in a special function in the BOM menu.

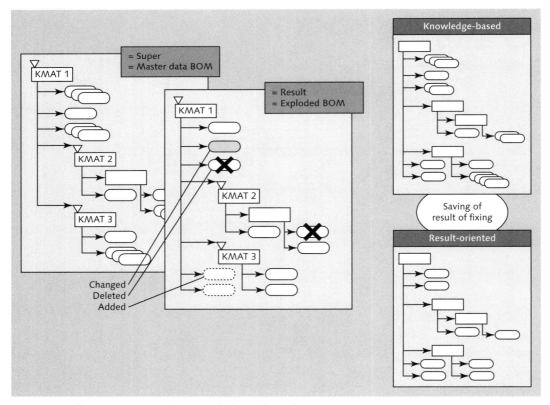

Figure 4.19 Super BOM Knowledge and Result

▸ **Automatic fixing**

When you set the indicator, AUTOMATIC FIXING lets you use the order BOM maintenance function to automatically save the order BOM for a sales order, even if no changes are made to the BOM. If this indicator isn't set, you must change the BOM for a sales order in the maintenance function to create an order BOM.

▸ **BOM explosion**

You can also set whether to allow BOM explosion during configuration and, when you do, whether you explode a single level or multiple levels.

▸ **Interface design**

You can make settings to influence how the configuration data and valuation of the characteristics are displayed via the interface as well as their relevance to printing. Figure 4.18 shows an example of a configuration profile of the material CAR, which we used earlier in the chapter, along with the profile's basic data, the class assignment (to the class CAR), the CAR MODEL fields, and the PROFILE configuration settings.

To translate your configuration rules into the data models, you need to translate these configuration rules into object dependencies.

4.3   Object Dependencies

Object dependencies can be maintained centrally and then assigned to the appropriate and relevant objects, or they can be created locally, so they are only used in this context. Although you can't name local dependencies because they are identified by a system number, you can name central dependencies through externally assigned numbers. Table 4.5 provides the different object dependency types that are available, what they do, in which master data object they can be used, and an example of the dependency type.

Object Dependency Type	Explanation	Use	Example
Pre-condition	The precondition is a dynamic control that gives you the possibility to specify which characteristics and/or values can be selected when the precondition is fulfilled. When the condition isn't met, the item won't be added. It *can* be selected but doesn't have to be.	▶ Characteristics ▶ Characteristics values	When you pick fuel type Unleaded gas for the car, the engine can be Turbo but can also be 1.8L or 2.0L.
Constraints	The constraints value assignment and consistency check in single-level and multilevel configuration. Additional reporting options for equations, variant tables, and variant functions are available.	▶ Configuration profile	This object dependency type can specify that the motor type and fuel type are compatible, or that silver, yellow, and pink can't be selected with the standard package.
Selection condition	The selection condition lets you specify which characteristics and/or values *must* be selected when the condition is fulfilled.	▶ Characteristics ▶ BOM items ▶ Operation ▶ Suboperation sequence ▶ PRT ▶ PVS	When a car with Radio MP3 is chosen, task Install Radio is included.
Procedure	The procedure allows you to derive values based on a specific circumstance (derivation of characteristic values) occurring.	▶ BOM items ▶ Task list objects ▶ Configuration profile	When the metallic paint is chosen, the painting operation takes 30 minutes longer than the standard 1 hour, so the total is 1.5 hours. When the sports model car is sold, the seats are leather.

Table 4.5 Object Dependencies

Object Dependency Type	Explanation	Use	Example
Action	The action is exactly the same as procedure, where characteristics values are derived from circumstances. In addition to procedure, however, you also have the option of overwriting and performing successive calculations.	▸ BOM items ▸ Task list objects ▸ Configuration profile ▸ Characteristics ▸ Characteristics values	When the metallic paint is chosen, the painting operation takes 30 minutes longer, than the standard hour, so it gets updated to 1.5 hours. You can update this figure by adding additional time for preparation.

Table 4.5 Object Dependencies (Cont.)

4.3.1 Syntax of Dependencies

Each of the dependency types has its own syntax rules. Preconditions, selection conditions, actions, and procedures are simple dependencies because they are Boolean expressions with a binary result (either a 0 or 1). Constraints are more complex conditions structured like a program and have a broader functional scope. Within the simple dependencies, you can use the standard syntax elements available for the variables, such as $Root (which refers to the header material), $SELF (which refers to the object itself), and $PARENT (which refers to the item immediately above the object itself). Following that, you can use mathematical functions, such as equal to (=), multiply (×), minus (–), and plus (+). You can include less than or more than commands (< >) and use operators such as AND, OR, NOT, and IF.

Figure 4.20 gives you an example of a simple dependency—the selection condition for a BOM item. The BOM item "metallic" is added in the BOM, when the configured item (in our example, the CAR) has the color BLACK.

Constraints aren't directly assigned to the object, but they are grouped together to form a dependency net, which in turn can get assigned to the configuration profile of the material. Constraints are declarative dependencies, which means that the processing sequence—or the order in which they are processed—isn't relevant to the outcome. They can be used to set a value or check the consistency of values, and they are often used to define complex multilevel product configurations as shown in Figure 4.21. As you can see, the net contains three constraints. The system only has access to and checks constraints during interactive configuration. The empty boxes are indicative of multiple layers with multiple restrictions.

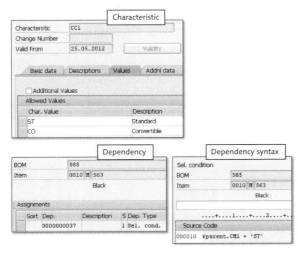

Figure 4.20 Simple Dependency Syntax

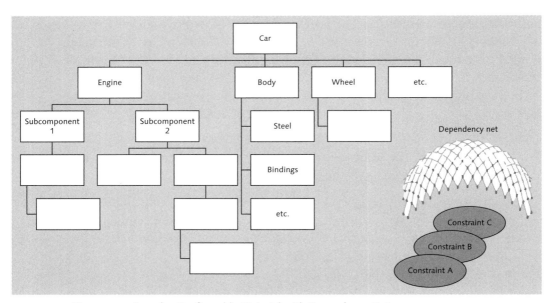

Figure 4.21 Complex Configurable Material with Dependency Net

You can use other syntax commands such as specifying an interval (command `IN`), whether a value should be specified (command `SPECIFIED`) or not (command `NON-SPECIFIED`), setting a default value (command `SET DEFAULT`), deleting a default value (`DEL DEFAULT`), and rounding (`TRUC`, `FLOOR`). These commands are included to give you an understanding of what is possible, but of course the possibilities are endless, and you need to analyze your requirements in detail and translate them to the appropriate SAP syntaxes to understand if they can be met. When the standard available syntax commands aren't sufficient to meet your requirements, you can define your own logic for calculation or consistency by defining your own business rules in an enhancement and by building this into a customer exit. A customer exit is a specific point in a standard program where customer-specific business logic can be added.

Table 4.6 gives you an overview of the user exits available in Variant Configuration, including a description of when they can be used.

User Exit	Description
Exit_SAPLCEIO_010 Exit_SAPLCEIO_011 Exit_SAPLCEIO_019	User exit for the value assignment screen
CCUX0000	Additional check on configuration
CCUX0001	Load function for configuration
CCUX0002	Specification of a class node
CCUX0800	Controls level of detail in multilevel configurations

Table 4.6 Change Fields during Sales Order Configuration

Within dependencies, you can change field values of characteristics during configuration. Table 4.7 gives you an overview of the different tables, whose field values can be changed as a result of configuration:

Table	Description
SDCOM	Structure for communication between SAP Sales and Distribution (SD) and Variant Configuration
MMCOM	Structure for communication between SAP MM and Variant Configuration

Table 4.7 Changeable Fields

Table	Description
VCSD_UPDATE	Structure for updating the sales document
STOP	BOM item fields
PLPO	Operation fields in routing
PLFH	PRT fields
PLFL	Operations sequence fields
SCREEN_DEP	Dynamic change to how characteristic is displayed

Table 4.7 Changeable Fields (Cont.)

Other field values can't be changed, but they can be read as part of a dependency. Table 4.8 offers an overview of the different tables, whose field values can be read during configuration.

Table	Description
VBAK	Header data
VBAP	Item data
VBKD	Commercial data
MAEPV	Material master fields
MAAPV	Material master fields
VEDA	Contract data
VBPA_AG	Partner: sold-to party
VBPA_WE	Partner: ship-to party
VBPA_RE	Partner: bill-to party
VBPA_RG	Partner: payer

Table 4.8 Readable Fields

4.3.2 Dependency Variant Tables

Variant tables can be used to determine the combinations of characteristics values that are possible together. For instance, consider the procedure to determine the radio based on the type of car model: the standard car contains the standard radio (with the standard CD player and 10W speakers), while the luxury model contains the fast player (with 40W speakers). Figure 4.22 shows an example of a variant table. You can create a table by choosing LOGISTICS • CENTRAL FUNCTIONS • VARIANT CONFIGURATION • TOOLS • TABLE CONTENTS • MAINTAIN.

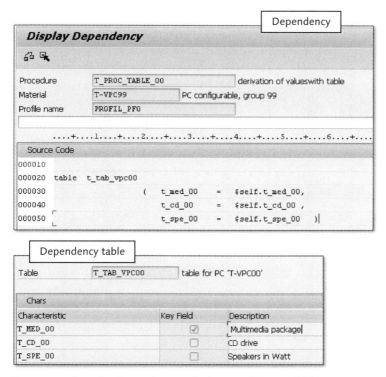

Figure 4.22 Complex Dependency with the Use of Variant Table

4.3.3 Analyze and Trace

Trace functions let you trace the internal processing steps that the system makes while processing dependencies. It provides you with information about the current configuration, overview of dependencies, explosion of all configurable items' BOMs, reporting for class nodes, and a detailed list of configuration of configurable items. The analysis tool can be called from the result screen of the configuration.

This is the processing sequence for value assignments: DEFAULTS • ACTIONS • PROCEDURES 1, CONFIGURATION PROFILE, CHARACTERISTICS, CHARACTERISTICS VALUES • ACTIONS TRIGGER BY CHANGES TO PROCEDURES • PRECONDITIONS • SELECTION CONDITIONS.

System Performance

Because the use of Variant Configuration can lead to high data volumes, it's important to understand what implications the configuration settings you've chosen will have on data volumes and growth and how to prevent system performance issues. Some general hints apply to all scenarios and hints that are specific to all dependencies:

► Reduce the number of configuration levels as much as possible.

► Keep the configuration model small and simplify where possible.

► In a task list, use alternative sequences instead of several operations with the same selection conditions.

However, going into this topic in more detail exceeds the scope of this book. More information can be found on *http://help.sap.com* under classification CROSS APPLICATION (CA)-CLASSIFICATION (CL) or via SAP training as included in Appendix A.

Master Data Process

To define a product variant, you have to perform the following steps in the system, as mentioned in Figure 4.23.

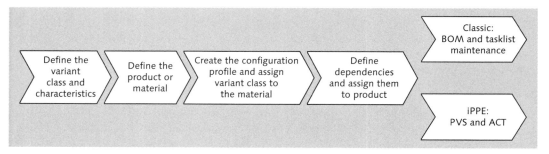

Figure 4.23 Master Data Maintenance Process Steps

1. **Define the variant class and characteristics.**
   You create the variant class belonging to the configuration class type 300 and create and assign the characteristics (options), so you can use these during configuration.

2. **Define the product or material.**
   Make sure to flag it as a configurable material.

3. **Create the configuration profile, and assign the appropriate class to the material.**
   This can be done in three different ways with the same results: either through the material master, via CA, or within the profile.

4. **Define dependencies (either local or central), and assign them to the product.**
   The next step is dependent on which scenario you choose to use:

   ▶ Classic scenario: Generate the BOM and routing next; refer to the left side of Figure 4.17.

   ▶ iPPE scenario: Start creating the PVS and the process structure next; refer to the right side of Figure 4.17.

Choosing between Classic and iPPE

In short, there's no easy answer for which scenario best fits your organization because it depends on the specifics of your situation and your priorities. You need to understand which processes are important, what functions are required, and which processes support which functions.

In comparison to classic scenarios, iPPE offers some advantages:

▶ Handles large data volumes

▶ Provides a logical structure

▶ Supports extended planning options (e.g., SAP APO)

▶ Supports collaboration scenarios (integration to c-projects) and works well with highly configurable products

▶ Supports all three technical types of BOMs (simple BOMs, variant BOMs, and multiple BOMs) in the same structure

iPPE can be seen as a platform that supports the entire lifecycle of a product, from idea to start of production to delivering and servicing it at the customer (see Figure 4.24). You can represent the requested structure, the functional structure, concept and design structure, and product and process structure (see Chapter 3, Section 3.1.2, for more details on this topic).

As Chapter 3 explains, SAP will focus on the use and further development of iPPE, but for now, not all different types of object dependencies are currently supported, which might mean you have to work with the classic scenario.

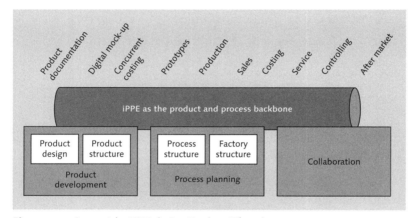

Figure 4.24 Support by iPPE during Product Lifecycle

You can perform digital mock-up (DMU) through the CAD system, which allows you to add to the CAD drawing by simply adding lines and so on to it. You can exchange data via the SAP PLM interface, which was also explained in Chapter 3. Via color nodes, you can define materials that define the color of a product or product part. It's possible to build a multilevel structure. Each level requires its own assembly node, and object dependencies aren't available for assembly nodes. You can also use phantoms. Recall from Chapter 3, Section 3.1.1, that a phantom is a BOM level that doesn't refer to a physical item but just groups mechanisms (such as "wheels" to assign all the four wheels of a car).

Product Variant Structure and Configuration

Chapter 3 introduced the iPPE and the product variant structure (PVS). To refresh your memory and to explain the PVS with the use of product configuration, we'll briefly summarize this introduction here.

As you now understand, the purpose of using PVS is to create one product structure that covers all variants and is free of data redundancy. It gives you access to product information for entire groups of similar products that can have a high degree of variability.

The PVS consists of three main elements, as shown earlier in Figure 4.24. The *top node*, or access node, describes the product that you want to sell or produce. The next level, made up of *view nodes*, describes the logical or function groups or your product; view nodes haven't been assigned materials. At the lowest level of the product structure, you have the *structure nodes*. These define the components that make up your end product. You define your variable parts at this level. Because they are variable, you have to specify the condition at which they are valid by assigning a selection condition to the structure node, which is also represented in Figure 4.25. When you don't assign a variant but instead assign a material directly, then the item is primarily a nonvariable (or non-optional) part. In the early product development stage, you might not be able to identify the specific part yet, so you don't have to fill out the material when creating a structure node. However, you need to make sure that a material reference exists before the production process can start because the parts need to be planned as a result of production planning.

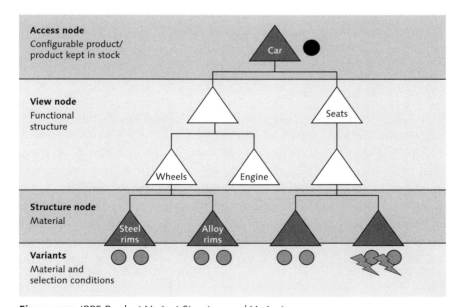

Figure 4.25 iPPE Product Variant Structure and Variants

Pricing with Product Variant

Pricing in SD is based on conditions, where objects in the configuration are described by characteristics and their assigned values. To price configurable products, you must use both the sales conditions as the characteristics values. You either directly assign the condition to the surcharge or use a procedure or action to define when the condition is valid. One-on-one assignment can be done using the user interface for configuration simulation. The standard conditions VA01 (percentage) and VA00 (absolute) can be used. For direct assignment, you have to assign the characteristic to the field condition SDKOM-VKOND and add the following object dependency to specify when the condition is relevant:

```
$SELF<reference characteristic>= 'key of condition record' if <conditions>
```

The following is an example of a surcharge, which is relevant when the extras METALLIC and ROOFTOP have been selected:

```
Example: $SELF.SURCHARGE='Surcharge_A'
If Extras eq 'METALLIC' and Extras eq 'ROOFTOP'
```

However, when you're using other applications for selling products, such as SAP Customer Relationship Management (SAP CRM) or Internet Pricing and Configurator (IPC), these methods and data models may differ. They won't be covered in this book.

Product Information Distribution

Product replication within SAP PLM enables you to distribute product information from a central SAP PLM system to other productive SAP systems via Application Link Enabling (ALE) technology, as shown on the left in Figure 4.26. Using the product replication "baseline" procedure, you can distribute products instead of the individual object and transfer this data into configuration folders in the replication workbench. (Chapter 7 has more details on this topic.) It allows you to simultaneously distribute product data to different target systems via a controlled and transparent process. During distribution, you can transfer either delta information or all data when it's an initial distribution. The sequences in which the objects are transported are important to ensuring that the data objects are available when needed, so work from the most detailed objects first, starting with classification data and object dependencies, and then on to the more granular, with creation of the materials. The object sequence has been included in Figure 4.26.

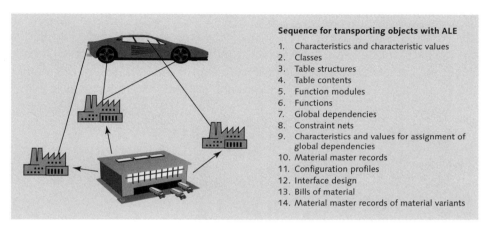

Sequence for transporting objects with ALE

1. Characteristics and characteristic values
2. Classes
3. Table structures
4. Table contents
5. Function modules
6. Functions
7. Global dependencies
8. Constraint nets
9. Characteristics and values for assignment of global dependencies
10. Material master records
11. Configuration profiles
12. Interface design
13. Bills of material
14. Material master records of material variants

Figure 4.26 Product Distribution and Sequence with ALE

4.4 Business Scenarios for Product Variants

Table 4.9 shows the seven business scenarios that are based on the settings for the process and the settings for BOM explosion and are available when you're using a configurable material.

	Process	BOM Explosion
1	Planned/production order (ATO)	No BOM
2	Planned/production order (ATO)	Single-level
3	Order BOM (MTO)	
4	Sales order (ETO) – SET	
5	Planned/ production order (ATO)	Multilevel
6	Order BOM (MTO)	
7	Sales order (ETO) – SET	

Table 4.9 Business Scenarios

We've already covered the processes (for a quick refresher on the ATO, MTO, and ETO processes, refer to the "Configuration Profile" section in Section 4.2.2), so we'll now explain the BOM explosion options.

4.4.1 One-Step Configuration (No BOM)

The no BOM explosion option can be used when the product is modeled and configured in its entirety at the product level and then sold to the customer. Because there's no need for order-specific postprocessing of the BOM and of the routing, this option is deactivated in the configuration profile. The product structure isn't relevant for sales.

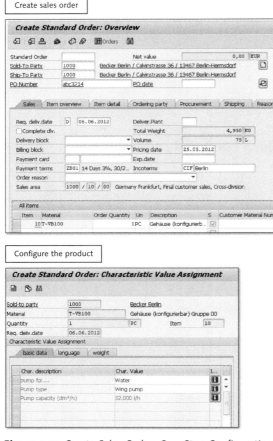

Figure 4.27 Create Sales Order: One-Step Configuration

Figure 4.27 shows an example of this scenario in which during the creation of a sales order, one-step configuration is generated (shown on the top). The bottom shows the values for the configurable material—a pump—where you can choose its category, type, and capacity. These details provide downstream processes such as the materials requirements with the right information on the number of components necessary, and you can perform an available-to-promise (ATP) check based on the lead times. The details on how this is done is a supply chain function and has not been included as part of the scope of this book.

4.4.2   Single-Level BOM Explosion/Order BOM Configuration

This kind of explosion can be used when the material BOM that results from the configuration has to be changed specifically for the customer or where the BOM has to physically exist in your system (e.g., for legal reasons). The product and the first level down from the BOM will be exploded in the sales order. When you've included configurable items within this explosion, they can be valued as well. An order BOM is the result when saving the sales order.

4.4.3   Multilevel BOM Explosion

This kind of explosion can be used for complex products where configuration has to take place at the top level of the product but also at the assembly levels/sub-item levels—even for items not relevant to sales. Characteristics values can be saved for each configurable component. All sales-relevant items will be copied into the sales order. Figure 4.28 gives you an example of a multilevel BOM explosion. On the top, you see the sales order item, which includes the configurable material as an item. The bottom shows how, during the sales order, processing values are assigned for the configurable end product and for its configurable subcomponents.

When you use this explosion in combination with the sales order BOM, you can either create and maintain the BOM directly from within the sales order (if you allowed this in the configuration profile), or you can create the sales order and do the first-level BOM explosion in the first step. In the second step, you perform the technical order processing by completing the rest of the necessary configuration at the lower levels where manual changes can be made, such as changing BOM items (such as quantities), deleting or adding items, and copying items. Subordinate material configuration can also take place (Transaction CU51).

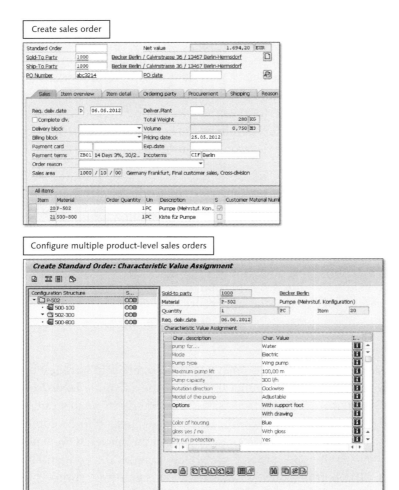

Figure 4.28 Create Sales Order with Multilevel Configuration

The previous sections have all focused on product information. First we explained the use of CA, which allows you to enrich material data with industry-specific or company-specific data. Then we continued with Variant Configuration, which, in its most-used form, uses CA information to model different product variants. However, apart from the use of Variant Configuration to model product variants, it can be more broadly used to handle variants in other areas of SAP, which we'll focus on next.

4.5   Variant Configuration Applied in Other Settings

Apart from using Variant Configuration to describe the different variations of a product, it can also be used to describe the different variations of networks (an object used in SAP PS), a maintenance task list (an object used in SAP PM), and a service specification (an object used in SAP MM). The principle works the same.

Table 4.10 gives an overview of the different standard objects available in SAP PLM that can be configured and where the actual configuration takes place. The model service specification isn't part of core SAP PLM, but it's part of SAP ERP and often used in conjunction with SAP PM or SAP CS.

Configurable Standard Object	Actual Configuration
Material master	Sales order item from SD
Configurable standard general task list	Maintenance order from either SAP PM or SAP CS
Configurable standard network	Project from SAP PS
Configurable model service specifications	Purchase order from SAP MM

Table 4.10 Configurable Objects and How They Are Configured

The following section will describe the configurable objects one by one. Because Section 4.1 to Section 4.4 already discussed product variants via the material master, this object won't be further discussed.

Configurable Standard General Task List

A configurable task includes all the operations for objects that are only slightly different. You define one single task list, which includes all the possible operations; you can configure which operations are valid through object dependencies. When no object dependency is added, the operation applies to all objects. When you use the configured task list in a maintenance order, the system will determine the correct operations based on the configured technical object, or, when the technical object hasn't been provided (or hasn't been set up as configurable object), the system will ask you to provide the classification values. Figure 4.29 shows an example of this. First you see the complete configurable task list, which includes all the operations. The next screen shows how the valuation of the relevant characteristics (pump category, mode, and type) takes place during the creation of the maintenance work order. The last screen shows that only four operations are valid and copied to the work order based on the chosen values. Another example could be two production machines of the same model, where replacement of the filter is done slightly different, but the other activities are the same.

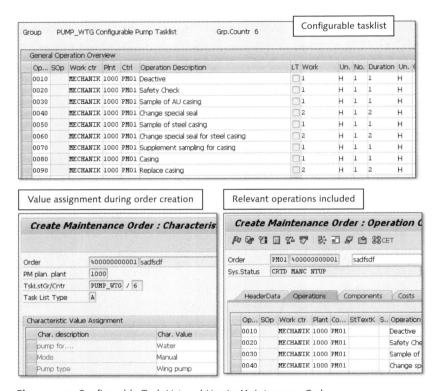

Figure 4.29 Configurable Task List and Use in Maintenance Order

Configurable Standard Network

A configurable standard network includes all of the operations for objects that are only slightly different. As with the single task list, you define one standard network, which includes all of the possible operations. Use an object dependency to configure when an operation is valid. When no object dependency is added, the operation is always valid and selected automatically. When you use the standard network in a project, the system will determine the correct operations based on the technical object, or when the technical object hasn't been provided (or isn't a configurable object), the system will ask you to provide the valid classification values.

Configurable Model Specification

A configurable model specification includes all of the services for objects that are only slightly different. You define one service model, which includes all of the possible services, where through an object dependency you can configure when an the service is valid. You assign the class type (standard type 301) to the model specification by creating a configuration profile. Set the CONFIGURATION AT THE TIME OF SERVICE SELECTION indicator in the header of the model specification. When no object dependency is added, the service applies to all objects.

When you use service model specification, the system will ask that you provide the classification values. Consider this example of how configuration in a set of model service specifications can be used: A model is created to represent the entire range of services that may be required in pipe-laying projects. Within this complete range, some services are mutually dependent or mutually exclusive. For example, the work involved in laying pipes in a new housing estate will differ from that involved in laying pipes in existing residential areas. Additionally, if cast-iron pipes are to be laid, the work involved in connecting and pressure-testing the pipes differs from that necessary if the pipes were made of steel. At the same time, various jobs may not be necessary. If the pipes were laid in remote, wooded areas, for example, some of the work involved in fencing off the job site for safety reasons—which is necessary in residential areas—would be excessive.

Now that we've discussed all the product master data in detail, the next section will explain the business processes available for the different stakeholders that are involved and need to collaborate using this master data. They all need to have access to the appropriate product information at the right time to perform the business activities they are responsible for.

4.6   Engineering and R&D Collaboration

Chapter 3 and the first half of Chapter 4 covered product master data. The next two sections will explain the business scenarios and business processes that are available for product development, product engineering, research and development (R&D), collaboration, and manufacturing collaboration. These business scenarios and processes ensure that the different business partners involved during product engineering, product R&D, process engineering, and manufacturing all have access to the appropriate product information at the right time and can manage the right access controls (authorizations).

During these scenarios and processes, the different user groups involved require a broad variety of design tools, product modeling abilities, and appropriate product methodologies. SAP PLM provides these tools by providing a central product information place, integrated to CAD system(s) and or document management system(s). The data integration and collaboration capabilities support various engineering and R&D groups to work more efficiently across disciplines within your organization. Apart from internal collaboration, it also allows you to exchange and collaborate with external parties such as suppliers, manufacturing companies, and service communities.

This section will only explain the engineering and R&D collaboration scenarios, processes, and scenario/process steps. It assumes you have a good understanding of the master data objects used for the previously described products within SAP PLM. But before diving into these business scenarios and business processes in more detail, we'll briefly explain the terms "business process" and "business scenario" according to SAP NetWeaver Business Process Management (SAP NetWeaver BPM) methodology.

Additional Resources

You can learn more about SAP NetWeaver BPM from two SAP PRESS books: *Applying Real-World BPM in an SAP Environment* by Greg Chase et al. (2011) and *Business Process Management: The SAP Roadmap* by Jim Snabe et al. (2009).

A *business process* is defined by steps that transform an input into an enriched output. It therefore is a collection of related, structured activities or tasks that produce a specific service or product that serves a particular goal. The business process is the level that aggregates essential business-oriented functions or steps to a unit that is meaningful and comprehensive to fulfill a business mission-related task. It's often visualized with a flowchart.

We'll cover the following business processes in this section:

▶ Product development
▶ Development collaboration

- Engineering collaboration
- Engineering to order (ETO)
- Engineering make to order (MTO)

The following overall business goals and objectives apply to business processes within engineering, R&D, and collaboration:

- Improve customer service by improved product quality.
- Increase speed and efficiency by reducing time-to-market and volume.
- Increase revenue by gaining market share and developing new markets.
- Lower working capital by reducing material and component obsolescence.
- Reduce operating costs and increase efficiency by reducing travel-related expense, reducing inventory levels, and reducing development costs.

The *business scenario* is a separate view on the business processes and business process variants, which can belong to different business areas and process groups. Such a business scenario describes the complete processing of one business operation, which is focused on achieving a defined business objective and is measurable through the use of key performance indicators (KPIs) that clarify the desired value and benefit. Business scenarios are always described from the point of view of one company. Although they can include the interactions and collaboration functionality with other companies, they can't include the processing in these other companies. This is why the described business scenarios will include the general business benefits as they have been reported by several SAP customers, but they are merely there as a reference. Although they have been achieved as value potentials by reference customers, they aren't guaranteed. The business process is generally a flow within a department, whereas a business scenario is a flow across multiple departments. We'll cover the following business scenarios in this section:

- New product development
- Product development
- CAD-driven design
- Process engineering
- SAP PLM data replication

4.6.1 Product Development

Product development consists of a business scenario and a business process, which we'll address in that order. The new product development business scenario is designed for all industries; it shows how different parties collaborate during the entire product lifecycle and achieve efficient management of new product development. The product development business process allows you to optimize cross-department product development, achieved by a consistent central storage of all relevant data during the entire product development process. Let's explore each further.

Business Scenario: New Product Development

SAP has developed a business scenario for new product development that is relevant and set up for all industries. It provides you with the insight on how the diverse parties involved in product development—such as engineering, marketing, customers, and product managers—work together across the entire lifecycle. In many companies, the very early stage of the new development process is an especially intuitive and dynamic phase that requires very flexible tools. The enormous number of people involved and the high volume of data that is created, structured, and managed are indicators that efficient tools and sophisticated processes are fundamental to success.

Accordingly, the SAP process for new product development has been set up around the integrated product design workbench. The strength of this process comes from the concept that all ideas, documents, structure information, early process information, and early layout information are collected and managed in one central tool along all the stages of a product life. In addition to creating a dynamic and flexible environment, it also can lead to cost savings and quality improvements.

Use of the new product development business scenario has the following benefits:

▶ All departments affected can add content easily using web interfaces.

▶ Different views on one consistent structure are supported.

▶ With the product designer, all structures required throughout the development process can be defined from the feature and requirement structure down to the final product. This results in up to 30% reduced design cycle times.

▶ Step-by-step engineering allows flexible processes where content is added according to progress.

▶ Structuring of features, requirements, functions, and concepts in the early design phases ensures quality from the beginning—and that's where the major costs of a product are defined.

▶ Structure elements of different structures can be linked or even verified against each other in controller processes.

▶ Seamless transfer between the different structures within one workbench is enabled.

▶ Results of verification processes can be stored within the structure.

▶ Variants are already supported in the concept phase to minimize subsequent work.

Let's walk through the new product development business scenario, which is shown in Figure 4.30 and described in the following list.

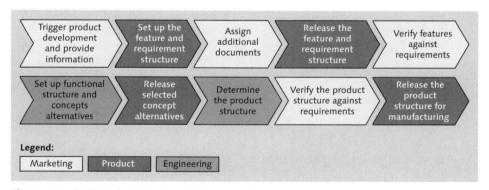

Figure 4.30 Business Scenario New Product Development

1. **Trigger product development and provide information.**
   The process is usually triggered by an external or internal customer, who will provide the responsible product managers with thousands of unstructured or only partly structured documents relating to this new product.

2. **Set up the feature and requirement structure.**
   Product management's initial task is to handle this huge amount of information in the feature and requirement structures in SAP PLM's product design workbench (or product designer). The product designer is a powerful, intuitive, flexible, and dynamic integrated workbench that is based on iPPE and can

include integration to other necessary product data environments, such as the SAP DMS or CAD system. This workbench was described in more detail in Chapter 3.

3. **Assign additional documents.**
When required, marketing can provide additional information for the development process and assign this within the product designer tool.

4. **Release the feature and requirement structure.**
After product management is finished with the setup of the required product structures in the product design workbench, the feature and requirement structure can be released so follow-up activities can take place.

5. **Verify features against requirements.**
The following step makes sure that the requirements are being met by the developed product features, which is generally done by the marketing department.

6. **Set up functional structure and concepts alternatives.**
The engineering department then works step by step on the different structures in the same working environment. Direct and seamless communication between engineering and product development is essential. The workbench can be personalized to suit the individual's needs, and occasional users can use the web interfaces.

7. **Release selected concept alternatives.**
The proposed concept alternatives can then be released by product management.

8. **Determine the product structure.**
After releasing these feature and requirement structures, and after verification by the external/internal customer, the engineering process is started via effective cooperation between product management and the engineering departments. Different product phases are supported, and the step-by-step handling of the product evolution ensures product maturity from the functional structure to the concept or design structures, through to the released product structure.

9. **Verify the product structure against requirements.**
This released product structure is checked one last time by the external or internal customer before it's finally handed over to manufacturing.

10. **Release the product structure for manufacturing.**
    The final step is releasing the product structure information to the manufacturing department.

Now that we understand the benefits of using the product development business scenario and have gone through the product development business scenario itself, we'll explore the business processes available for product development. First, we'll cover the variant for product development within discrete industries, and then we'll finish with the variant for the process industries.

Business Process: Product Development

The business process for product development allows you to optimize cross-department product development. One key element of achieving optimized product development is setting up and using a consistent central storage of all relevant data during the entire product development process, which was described in more detail in Chapter 3. This subsection will focus on the processes and process steps for product development, where there are two different variants:

- Discrete industries, which are focused on products made through manufacturing using components

- Process industries, which are focused on products made through a production process based on mixing ingredients/substances

Let's look at each of these in turn.

Product Development Process for Discrete Industries
The four steps of the discrete industries product development business process are shown in Figure 4.31 and described in the following list.

Figure 4.31 Product Development Process for Discrete Industries

1. **Set up the product structure.**
   Product development starts with the setup of the product structure, which consists of the end product and includes the necessary components and subcomponents required to manufacture the product. This can be done in

separate stages, where the focus of data collection might be slightly different (for more details, see Chapter 3, Section 3.1).

2. **Achieve functional completion.**
   After you're satisfied with the proposed end product, you can complete the concept and design structures and build your product structure with the details necessary for PP and production, so this includes the product and process structure.

3. **Achieve CAD integration and technical completion.**
   The SAP PLM interface synchronizes the product data in SAP ERP and the technical drawings in your CAD system so the latest changes are updated in both environments (for more details, see Chapter 3, Section 3.2.5). After you're satisfied, the data can be locked in and released for virtual prototyping.

4. **Export to virtual prototyping.**
   The product data is exported to CAD so you can perform a virtual prototyping. Virtual prototyping is a technique in the process of product development that involves using CAD and computer-aided engineering (CAE) software to validate a design before making a physical prototype. This is done by creating (usually 3D) computer-generated geometrical shapes (parts) and combining them into an assembly and testing different mechanical motions, fit, and function (or just aesthetic appeal). The assembly or individual parts could be opened in CAE software to simulate the behavior of the product in the real world. After this step is completed successfully, prototyping can start.

Product Development Process for Process Industry

In contrast to the discrete industries product development process, the process industry product development process describes products made through production processes based on mixing ingredients/substances. The sequence of steps is shown in Figure 4.32 and described in the following list.

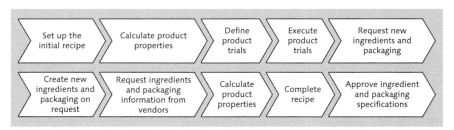

Figure 4.32 Product Development Process for the Process Industry

1. **Set up the initial recipe.**
   To start the product development process, you have to set up an initial recipe, which includes the finish product and the individual ingredients and machines required to make this product. (For more details, see Chapter 3, Section 3.4.)

2. **Calculate product properties.**
   As part of the recipe, you need to include the product properties and the proposed required formula to create the end product.

3. **Define product trials.**
   To put a new product through a trial to validate and refine the recipe, you can define one or multiple product trials.

4. **Execute product trials.**
   Execute the product trial until a satisfactory end result is achieved.

5. **Request new ingredients and packaging.**
   Any new ingredients and packaging need to be requested.

6. **Create new ingredients and packaging on request.**
   The new ingredients and packaging need to be created as master data in your SAP system.

7. **Request ingredients and packaging information from vendors.**
   To source these new ingredients and packaging, you can request costing and delivery information from vendors. This information can be requested and collected by using the collaboration scenario for a development project (as described in Chapter 7, Section 7.5) which can be integrated with SAP Supplier Relationship Management (SAP SRM). However, when you aren't using SAP Project and Portfolio Management (PPM), you can use procurement processes from SAP ERP and/or SAP SRM.

8. **Calculate product properties.**
   During trials, you need to include and keep track of the product properties and the proposed required formula to create the end product.

9. **Complete the recipe.**
   When you're satisfied with the formulated recipe and the end results of the trials (for more details, see Chapter 3, Section 3.4.5) and have finalized the formula and product properties, you can update the recipes, which can then be approved and completed.

10. **Approve ingredient and packaging specifications.**
    Ingredients and packaging specifications can be approved.

4.6.2   Development Collaboration

Development collaboration is a key capability offered through the business process for development collaboration, which engages multiple roles and communities of practice across the enterprise and the business network to drive continuous product innovation, performance, and quality.

Business Process: Development Collaboration

The development collaboration business process allows you to optimize a cross-enterprise product development with internal and external teams, including the sourcing of complex product components. You can achieve this with a consistent central storage of all relevant data during the entire collaboration process and a secure integration of external partners and suppliers. This process uses the collaboration scenario from PPM shown in Figure 4.33, so it assumes that you're using PPM for your development projects as represented in Figure 4.33. Note that this collaboration scenario is explained in more detail in Chapter 7, Section 7.5.

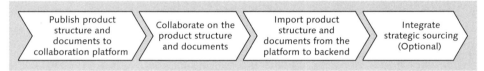

Figure 4.33 Development Collaboration Process

1. **Publish product structure and documents to collaboration platform.**
   First determine which product details and documents are relevant and necessary for the collaboration and publish them in a c-folder.

2. **Collaborate on the product structure and documents.**
   Within c-folders, you have multiple collaboration options such as discussions, notifications (emails), datasheets, and subscriptions to collaborate on the product development.

3. **Import product structure and documents from the platform to backend.**
   During the collaboration, the various stakeholders have updated the requested information; that updated information can be imported back into the backend (your SAP ERP environment).

4. **(Optional) Integrate strategic sourcing.**
   You can optionally use strategic sourcing, a function offered as part of PPM, which has been described in more detail in Chapter 7, Section 7.5.

The next section will explain the business process regarding engineering covering ETO and MTO.

4.6.3 Engineering Collaboration

Whether they are highly distributed or vertically integrated into your business, engineering and R&D groups use a number of tools and methodologies to support different product development functions. SAP solutions are focused to provide data integration and collaboration activities to support various engineering and R&D groups to work together efficiently across disciples as well as with external parties, such as suppliers, manufacturing, and service communities.

Business Process: Engineer to Order (ETO)

Each company makes products specially tailored to customers' specific requirements, which means that each sales order involves a great deal of time on design and development. The engineer to order (ETO) process, which is shown in Figure 4.34, assumes you're using SAP PS in combination with SAP SD.

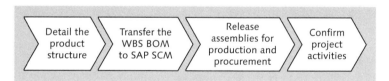

Figure 4.34 Engineer to Order Process

1. **Detail the product structure.**
   Set up a detailed product structure with the use of a project, which is a step performed within SAP PS (discussed in detail in Chapter 7, Section 7.2).

2. **Transfer the WBS BOM to SAP SCM.**
   This step assumes that SAP SCM is used to actually produce the product. If so, the product and how it's created within the project via a WBS BOM need to be transferred to SAP SCM, which won't be further discussed because it's outside the scope of this book.

3. **Release assemblies for production and procurement.**
   The assemblies required for production and procurement need to be released; however, both steps are part of SAP SCM and outside the scope of this book.

4. **Confirm project activities**

This step takes place during project execution in SAP PS, as further discussed in Chapter 7, Section 7.2.

Business Process: Make to Order (MTO)

Make-to-order (MTO) production is the process where the production order is triggered from a sales order. The MTO process, which is shown in Figure 4.35, assumes that you're using SAP PP in combination with SD.

> **Note**
>
> Although extensive coverage of PP and SD is outside the scope of this book, we've included this process to show the touch points between the product data and the MTO business process. Recall from Chapter 3 that SD and PP are used by SAP PLM (or part of SAP ERP) and use the same central master data for a product.

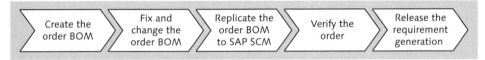

Figure 4.35 Manufacture-to-Order Process

1. **Create the order BOM.**

The first step is to set up and create a production order, which includes the order BOM. The order contains the to-be-manufactured material plus the components required to produce the item within the BOM items.

2. **Fix and change the order BOM.**

Make sure that this production order reflects the latest updates and changes. The changes to the production order and its details can be reflected in SAP Engineering Change Management (ECM), which has been described in more detail in Chapter 8.

3. **Replicate the order BOM to SAP SCM.**

After the BOM has been finalized, it needs to be replicated to the manufacturing environment, which can reside in another SAP environment such as SAP SCM. You can use the ALE replication tools within SAP PLM as described in Chapter 3.

4. **Verify the order.**

The production order will be technically verified and documented.

5. **Release the requirement generation.**

When the order is verified and released, the requirements of the components will be created so they can be sourced on time for the order to be executed within the agreed delivery time.

Business Scenario: CAD-Driven Design

This business scenario is designed for discrete industries. After the functional and conceptual structures have been set up and evaluated, the detailed design work is done in third-party mechanical (or electronic) CAD systems such as PRO/Engineer, CATIA, Unigraphics, Ideas, AutoCAD, Solidworks, or Solidedge.

The scenario shows how the creators and the internal and external consumers of design documents work together over the entire product design lifecycle, from product idea down to product delivery. The result is efficient management of the design documents and product structures without the use of information islands or silos, but instead an integrated product development environment. This provides significant value potential because current and consistent product data can be accessed by everybody early in the process, enabling simultaneous and collaborative engineering. Because data is stored only once in SAP PLM, this ensures data consistency and that everybody works on the same data (also referred to as one single version of the truth), which also leads to a simplified change process.

The CAD-driven design business scenario offers the following benefits:

▶ Advanced document search capabilities that reduce analyzing time

▶ CAD Desktop support for mass processes such as check-in, check-out, and status change of complete assemblies and the ability to compare and adjust

▶ Single source of the truth, which ensures data consistency and central storage which reduces cost for system integration

▶ Immediate availability of documents and products structures created in CAD to internal and external data consumers for further processing

▶ Support for DMU viewing, even for non-CAD users via integrated viewer

Figure 4.36 shows the CAD-driven design process business scenario.

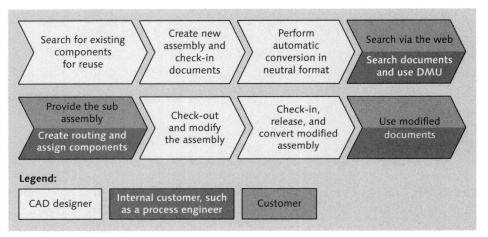

Figure 4.36 Manufacture-to-Order Process

1. **Search for existing components for reuse.**
   First the CAD designer will analyze and use advanced document search capabilities to search for existing documentation and/or components to determine if they can be reused, which would dramatically reduce design process costs. The CAD designer has access to all relevant parts of the SAP PLM solution without leaving his usual CAD environment.

2. **Create new assembly and check-in documents.**
   Based on the outcome of the previous step, an assembly gets created that includes the appropriate components. The relevant documents will be checked in to the collaboration environment. New or modified designs are checked in directly, and after release and conversion into neutral viewing files, they can be used directly by all internal and external consumers, even via an easy-to-use and navigate web browser. In the design process, new or modified parts of the product are checked in as part documents and assembly documents. As soon as part masters are created or assigned, the BOM can be derived automatically from the assembly documents.

3. **Perform automatic conversion in neutral format.**
   For concurrent and collaborative engineering, neutral viewing formats are often used instead of native CAD files because access to the CAD system is restricted to the CAD designers themselves. That's why both the conversion process and the actual viewing are integral parts of the SAP PLM solution. The

documents can be automatically converted into one or multiple neutral formats (e.g., a PDF) triggered by a status change, so they can be viewed by all relevant stakeholders along the design process. With a direct CAD interface to the SAP PLM solution, the data is stored directly in the document management vault, where it's immediately available for subsequent or parallel processes, such as release processes.

4. **In parallel:**

   ▶ **Search via the web.**
   The customer can use the web browser to view the published documents.

   ▶ **Search documents and use DMU.**
   Other internal stakeholders can use the data at an early stage; for example, process engineers can view and search the documents provided by the CAD designer and can create routings (concurrent engineering). Via the integrated viewer, they can use DMU, redlining, and measurement capabilities to provide their feedback and improve the design. Other engineers can then use the data at an early stage. External development partners can also use the design documents for their own designs, such as subassemblies (collaborative engineering).

5. **In parallel:**

   ▶ **Provide the subassembly.**
   The customer will provide the subassembly.

   ▶ **Create routing and assign components.**
   The routing will be prepared and the components will be assigned by the process engineers.

6. **Check out and modify the assembly.**
   After the customer and process engineer have completed their activities, the CAD designer will check out the documentation in SAP DMS and make the appropriate modifications to the original CAD assembly drawings.

7. **Check in, release, and convert the modified assembly.**
   After all modifications have been finalized, the documentation will once again be checked in and converted to the modified assembly. You can use mass processing via the CAD Desktop, which is essential for handling larger assemblies. All the transactions you need for this—such as check-in, check-out, and status change—are supported for either the complete assemblies or for selected parts.

The CAD Desktop also supports the comparison and adjustment of structures in a local environment, structures loaded in the CAD system, and the structure in SAP PLM.

8. **Use modified documents.**
   The customer and internal stakeholders are able to view the modified documents and provide their feedback, when required.

Integration to Engineering Change Process

Within the CAD-driven design scenario, you can use the engineering change processes to cater for any changes that might occur when executing the scenario. By using the CAD Desktop, the following functions are supported, saving time and effort:

▶ CAD designers can be notified about change tasks in their usual CAD environment.

▶ CAD drawings are an integral part of the overall change process. They can be checked out directly from the engineering change request (ECR)/engineering change order (ECO). The creation of new versions is also supported.

Business Scenario: Process Engineering

This business scenario is designed for all discrete industries. It shows how process engineers work closely together with product engineers and production planners during the ramp-up phase of a new product.

During the final phase of the product development process, in which the product structure is set up, a fast transition to production is essential for successful ramp-up and product introduction. Efficient process engineering is important at this time, which requires tight collaboration between process engineering and production. As soon as an initial version of the product structure is set up, the process engineers start to set up an initial routing. This parallel engineering reduces the time needed for new product introduction. Phased release mechanisms ensure that production is based on released data. As soon as production can be started, documents assigned to the product and process structure are provided, and even DMU viewing can be used in production orders. The result is collaborative processes during the ramp-up phase of a new product, which reduced the time to market and time to volume.

Figure 4.37 shows the process engineering business scenario, which is also described in the following list.

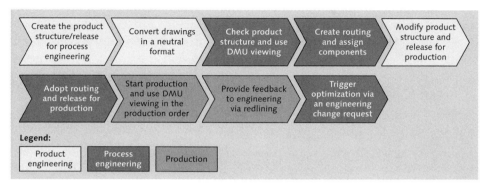

Figure 4.37 Business Scenario Process Engineering

1. **Create the product structure/release for process engineering.**
   Process engineering is supported by the Engineering Workbench, which allows the parallel processing of several BOMs and routings. The product engineer creates new assemblies for the product, checks in documents, creates document structures, and creates a BOM and releases it for process engineering. Graphical controls allow the copying of existing operations into a new routing using drag and drop. The assignment of components to specific operations in the routing is supported in the same way. These mechanisms, together with advanced mass processing capabilities—such as the replacement of a work center in hundreds of preselected operations within a few seconds—speed up the work of the process engineer.

2. **Convert drawings in a neutral format.**
   After release, all parts of the assembly are converted in viewing files in a neutral format, which can be used and viewed by non-CAD users.

3. **Check product structure and use DMU viewing.**
   Use the Engineering Workbench to check the BOM, and use DMU viewing to visualize mechanical assemblies step by step because of the tight integration of these structures.

4. **Create routing and assign components.**
   Create routing with reused and new operations, and then assign components to operations via drag and drop. Later on, the assignment of components to

specific operations allows precise procurement, especially if the production or assembly process takes several days or even weeks.

5. **Modify product structure and release for production.**
   Modify product structure based on feedback from process engineering and release BOM for production. Due to the tight integration of engineering into other business processes, a phased release concept is supported for both product and process structures. For example, the product structure can be released first for process engineering, then for product costing, and finally for MRP and production. This ensures fast but secure processes.

6. **Adopt routing and release for production.**
   This step ensures that, if required, routings are adjusted each time the product structure changes. The routing reflecting the latest product and process steps as approved by stakeholders can be released for production. This ensures the input for the production processes is correct.

7. **Start production and use DMU viewing in the production order.**
   Production is started as soon as product structures and process structures are released for production and relevant documents have been transferred into the production order. Production will have direct access to all documents needed to produce and assemble the product, which includes DMU for the product structure.

8. **Provide feedback to engineering via redlining.**
   Production can easily provide feedback if things need to optimized or changed to improve production processes. For example, the redlining capabilities of the integrated viewer allows the creation of electronic comments on the viewing files that can be sent to engineering.

9. **Trigger optimization via an engineering change request.**
   Process engineering receives documents with redlining. (Recall that the ECL Viewer allows you to document proposed BOM changes into a technical drawing by adding redlining, giving employees a means to provide feedback directly on the drawings without the tool itself.) Create the ECR to trigger optimization of product and process structure. This input can then be used by engineering to ECM. With ECM, all objects affected by a change can be modified in one controlled process. Product structures, process structures, and documents can be changed all together, resulting in a new, consistent change status of the product, which can be used for ongoing production. This means

that collaboration is supported for continuous improvement as well as for new product introduction.

The following benefits can be achieved from implementing business scenario process engineering:

▶ Reduced design cycle times because the product structures are immediately available for process engineering. Because product structures are available in an integrated environment, the information, including proposed pending changes or approval, is available to all stakeholders. This ensures up-to-date information and eliminates information islands.

▶ Accuracy in procurement of components, due to assignment of components to specific operations in the routing for advanced scheduling capabilities.

▶ Reduced engineering time to create routings by using advanced processing via graphical browsers (e.g., copying existing operations or component assignments via drag and drop, and processing multiple product and process structures supported, where only edited parts are locked to allow simultaneous processing of huge structures).

▶ Availability of DMU viewing files and product structures for process engineering and production.

▶ Advanced environment for concurrent engineering of product and process structures in one workbench.

▶ Availability of mass update processes, such as updating work centers or storage locations.

▶ Phased release of product structures supported (e.g., first process engineering then production).

Business Scenario: SAP PLM Data Replication

The SAP PLM data replication business scenario is designed for all industries. Many companies have a distributed environment out of necessity due to historical and technical reasons. In both cases, this results in the need to transfer data that describes the company's products from one source system (or several) to all target systems where this data is used for different business processes.

This scenario shows how product data can be replicated from a central engineering or R&D system to decentralized production or sales systems in a distributed environment, which is generally the case. The data that describes a simple or even complex product is frozen in a complete and consistent baseline and then distributed in a controlled process to all required target systems that use the data for production or sales purposes. The result is a secure and almost faultless replication process that can reduce effort and time required for data replication dramatically. The distribution of complete and consistent product definitions instead of the isolated distribution of single objects not only speeds up the distribution process but also reduces manual rework and errors in subsequent business processes tremendously.

The SAP PLM data replication business scenario is shown in Figure 4.38 and described in the following list.

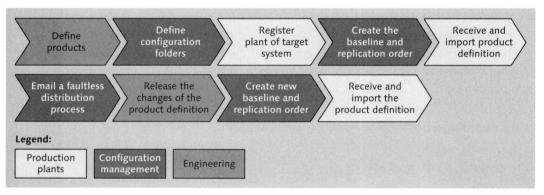

Figure 4.38 SAP PLM Data Replication Business Scenario

1. **Define products**.

   SAP PLM uses a smart and secure replication process based on the concept of configuration folders and baselines to replicate with fewer errors and faster-than-traditional replication methods such as manual replication or individual interfaces. The concept is to support the distribution of a package of all objects that can be used to describe simple or even complex products together, including the material masters (parts), BOMs, documents, classification, and Variant Configuration data. The distribution of these complete and consistent product definitions instead of the isolated distribution of single objects not only speeds up the distribution but also reduces manual rework and errors in subsequent business processes tremendously. For this kind of replication, the product has to defined by engineers or developers in the source system.

2. **Define configuration folders.**
   Then configuration folders are used to define the products that have to be distributed as well as the target system that needs these product definitions afterwards.

3. **Register plant of target system.**
   The target systems can be registered at any time, so changes in the system landscape can be supported in a very flexible way.

4. **Create the baseline and replication order.**
   Now as the replication process has to be started, a baseline is created out of the configuration folder. In the baseline, all objects are quickly collected in an automatic product structure explosion, which takes into account all relevant parts of the product definition. This product structure explosion not only ensures the completeness of the distributed package but also its consistency because the explosion is based on a defined change status. This is supported by the use of ECM capabilities in the SAP PLM solution, which are described in Chapter 8 in more detail. For the physical distribution of the data, a replication order is created and based on the ALE technology.

5. **Receive and import the product definition.**
   The entire package is exported from the source system and imported into the different target systems.

6. **Email a faultless distribution process.**
   Administration tools can be used during the process to control the export and import steps to ensure a faultless replication.

7. **Release the changes of the product definition.**
   After the initial load of the product definition in the target systems, the product is changed and further developed in the source system.

8. **Create a new baseline and replication order.**
   If the new status should be used in the target systems, the changes have to be released so a new baseline can be generated.

9. **Receive and import the product definition.**
   During this step, the distribution process includes only the modified part of the product definition, so only the delta is exported and imported, which further reduces the time needed.

The following benefits can be achieved from implementing the SAP PLM data replication business scenario:

▶ Reduced costs for system integration because central engineering system can be linked to any number of production or sales systems and tight integration of the ECM enables the definition of consistent change status

▶ Improved data accuracy because complex, configurable products can be distributed as complete and consistent packages based on a baseline

▶ Reduced time for baseline creation; all relevant parts of the product definition taken into account in automatic product structure explosion; easy assignment of target systems and users to the distribution; frequent or on request updates

▶ Production or sales processes based on predefined reproducible baselines, so less error prone in orders

▶ Reduced time for data replication, when changes are required by faultless import of complete and consistent product structures instead of manual replication

Business Process: Engineering Change Collaboration

You can collaboratively initiate and manage engineering changes with external partners to manage effective and efficient implementation of these changes, as well as to ensure the secure exchange of information with the appropriate development partners. The process is set up to improve collaboration and flexibility, and integrate with both SAP and non-SAP backend product lifecycle management systems and engineering change applications. This process assumes that you're using ECM (described in more detail in Chapter 8).

Figure 4.39 shows the engineering change collaboration process, which is described in the following list.

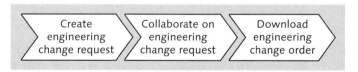

Figure 4.39 Engineering Change Collaboration Process

1. **Create an engineering change request.**
   Start by the identifying the change, which includes the affected products and other related objects, such as documents, BOMs, and routings.

2. **Collaborate on the engineering change request.**
   Before a change gets implemented, its impacts and approval by the appropriate stakeholders as set up in ECM will need to be performed. A more detailed description of how this can be done can be found in the Chapter 8, which provides an overview of ECM.

3. **Download the engineering change order.**
   The last step is to download the ECO and implement the approved changes to the appropriate objects.

This completes the engineering collaboration business scenarios and business processes, so we'll now further explore the manufacturing collaboration process category, to dive into the manufacturing-specific business scenarios and business processes.

4.7   Manufacturing Collaboration

Manufacturing collaboration focuses on the final steps required to prepare your organization for making a product. This section starts by describing the business scenario for prototyping and ramp-up, which consists of a variant for discrete industries and one for process industries. It will continue with iPPE. This topic was described from a master data perspective in Chapter 3, and it's repeated here only from a process perspective because iPPE plays an important role in manufacturing collaboration. Last, the chapter addresses interfacing capabilities, which often are supported with SAP Partner products.

4.7.1   Prototyping and Ramp-Up

Prototyping and ramp-up refers to the processes involved in experimenting or running trials on different recipe or product versions to ensure that, when finalized, an optimal product and process definition can be released to manufacturing. SAP differentiates between processes for discrete and process industries. We'll examine both of these next.

For Discrete Industries

The prototyping and ramp-up process for the discrete industries can be used when you want to run trials on different product versions through experimenting, which eventually ensures an optimal product and process definition that can be released to manufacturing when finalized. By building a prototype, you verify the developed product structure and can run the first tests with the new product, as represented in Figure 4.40 and described in the following list.

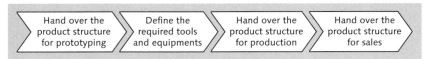

Figure 4.40 Prototyping and Ramp-Up Process for Discrete Industries

1. **Hand over the product structure for prototyping.**
   During the first step, the product structure as it was defined by the engineering departments is handed over to product development for prototyping.

2. **Define the required tools and equipment.**
   In addition to the components that are required to build/produce the trial end products, the required tools and equipment necessary for production have to be determined and assigned to the routing and potentially procured when unavailable.

3. **Hand over the product structure for production.**
   After the prototype process has been successful and a preferred product version has been defined, which might have taken multiple trials, this product structure can be frozen and handed over from product development to production. The product and process data that you process here are relevant to several logistical processes, which is why you can process specific data for different usages. The seamless transfer of product data to downstream processes optimizes the lead time for a product from development to production.

The different departments process only the data that is relevant to their respective processes, such as engineering, production, and sales and distribution. For running trials on a new product, you need to set up a pilot and a plant for this trial. Although this is just one step in the overall process, the complexity of the execution of this step can range from simply using existing production facilities, which allow you to perform product trials, or becoming a project in itself, due to the need to construct a completely new facility for product development.

4. **Hand over the product structure for sales.**
   When necessary, production will make appropriate refinements and will communicate and hand over the final product structure to the sales department to allow them to start sales processes, such as including the new product in a campaign or contacting (potential) customers.

For Process Industries

The prototyping and ramp-up process for the process industries (Figure 4.41), can be used when you want to run trials on different recipes through experimentation, which eventually ensures an optimal product and process definition that can be released to manufacturing when finalized.

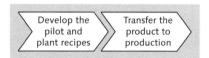

Figure 4.41 Prototyping and Ramp-Up Process for Process Industries

The process steps are described here:

1. **Develop the pilot and plant recipes.**
   The first process step for running a trial on a new recipe is setting up a pilot and a plant for this trial. Although this is just one single step in the overall process, the complexity of the execution of this step can range from the simple (using existing production facilities or laboratory to perform product trials) to the very difficult (constructing a complete new facility for product development). In the development recipe, you define the production steps in the form of stages, operations, and actions, which the system converts into operations, phases, and process instructions when it generates the master recipe. If you want quality assurance checks to take place during production, you have to define the appropriate inspection characteristics.

2. **Transfer the product to production.**
   After you're satisfied with the trial recipe and process, this new recipe and its detailed structure, including the developed production process, steps and requirements of machinery, appliances, and/or equipment are handed over from product development to production, along with process parameters (e.g., oven temperatures, pressure, etc.) in the development recipe. See Chapter 3 for more details.

4.7.2 Integrated Product and Process Engineering (iPPE)

Recall that the iPPE process allows you to document product data from early phases of the R&D process for a product resulting in the representation of the whole product lifecycle from start to finish. You start with the maintenance of the functional product structure, and you enrich as the product matures to a model with more detailed data, such as the specific components. The two business processes as described in Section 4.7.1 are relevant here. For more details on how iPPE works, the data model, and the interface possibilities, refer to Chapter 3, Section 3.1.2.

4.7.3 Interfacing

The interface process allows you to go straight from engineering and design in a CAD system to the maintenance of master data in the SAP PLM where you can also display the engineering and design documentation. It has not further been broken down into process steps. You can transfer data from Process Control Systems (PCSs) or Supervisory Control and Data Acquisition Systems (SCADA), which describe the condition or use of an object, directly to SAP PLM and/or SAP Asset Lifecycle Management. Furthermore, you can link a geographical information system (GIS) that offers you information about the geographical position of objects, an integration offered by SAP Consulting and Environment Systems Research Institute (ESRI) via the GEOgraphical Enablement of SAP ERP (GEO.e) solution offering. Other interfaces are often offered as SAP-Certified interfaces and often require SAP Partner products. Please refer to the SAP Service Marketplace quick reference SAP PLM, on the menu PLM IN ERP • CAD-INTEGRATION for more details.

4.8 Summary

This chapter introduced you to the master data objects used for product classification and for product Variant Configuration, both of which are often used in addition to the master data objects as described in Chapter 3. To collaborate on created and changed product data, the collaboration processes for engineering, R&D, and manufacturing were discussed. The chapter starts by explaining a very powerful cross-application function called the SAP Classification System (CA). Recall that CA enables you to add attributes to master data objects—such as the material master or DIR—that are specific to your organization and haven't been met by the standard available fields in these objects. CA can play an important role when setting up a product master and enriching the product master with your own company-specific data. You learned how to use this data to find objects or to reports against them. CA also plays an important role during product configuration, which was explained next.

Product configuration is a great tool to use to model similar types of products. Due to the amount of master data necessary for different variations, it's useful to start modeling it via SAP product configuration to reduce the amount of data maintenance, to prevent data redundancy, and to have one single source of the truth when it comes to product data. Because the product configuration uses CA to describe the product values, the possibilities of values and inputs are endless. Whether you decide to use the classic model or iPPE, the principle remains the same.

This chapter also taught you about the data model and the steps to set up this data model for both of these scenarios. By using object dependencies, you can include the configuration rules, such as restrictions or exclusions into the system, to ensure that the sales representative can only offer and sell a product that is valid and technically possible. The variant concept has been adopted and applied to configure other objects, such as the standard task list, the standard network, and the model specification.

Finally, this chapter explained the seven business scenarios in which the product variant can eventually be used. Then it explained how the concept for product configuration is also applied in other parts of an SAP ERP solution (e.g., within SAP PM and SAP PS). The chapter closed with an explanation of how product data maintained in different SAP systems can be distributed and used. We also introduced the business processes (department specific) and scenarios (across multiple departments) that focus on product data collaboration between stakeholders.

Both Chapter 3 and Chapter 4 have given you enough knowledge about product master data and its related required business processes and scenarios. Now, in the next chapter, it's time to move on to the SAP PLM business processes, which have been logistically grouped together based on the solution map. We'll first turn our attention to maintenance and customer service, which will focus on SAP Plant Maintenance (SAP PM) and SAP Customer Service (SAP CS).

During maintenance and operations, you'll optimize the product's performance, minimize its operational costs and expenditures, and monitor its condition.

5   Maintenance and Customer Service

This chapter will focus on stage three of the product lifecycle—the optimized asset operations and maintenance stage—which is supported by the components SAP Plant Maintenance and SAP Customer Service. This chapter will introduce you to the solutions within this stage and then describe the benefits of using them. First we'll take a look at the master data and transactional data elements before identifying supported business processes within both components.

5.1   Asset Operations and Maintenance

After you've sold your product or assets to a customer or, in the case of internal assets, you've built or bought a product or asset and started using it yourself, you've reached the asset operation and maintenance stage. This stage of a product or asset is supported by the SAP Plant Maintenance (SAP PM) and SAP Customer Service (SAP CS).

SAP PM focuses on those products or assets that are owned or leased by your company and for which you're responsible for maintenance and operations. Maintenance can be done by your own organization or by external parties. In contrast, SAP CS focuses mainly on products or assets owned or leased by a customer. The planning and execution of the maintenance and service activities on these assets are your responsibility, and, when necessary, you can charge the customer for these activities.

> **Note**
>
> Recall from the first chapter that SAP Customer Relationship Management (SAP CRM) is also offered in the SAP Business Suite, which provides support to all your customer-

facing activities. SAP CRM can also be used to supplement processes within CS. The focus of this chapter is SAP ERP, however, so only SAP PM and SAP CS are covered.

5.1.1 SAP Enterprise Asset Management

So far in this book, we've described the other stages of the asset lifecycle from the product perspective, instead of the asset perspective. Although this asset perspective is slightly different, the solutions are often similar, which makes this book a good resource for asset owners as well.

The five stages of the asset lifecycle are shown in Figure 5.1. Notice that the maintenance and operations stage is nestled between procurement and construction, and decommissioning and disposal.

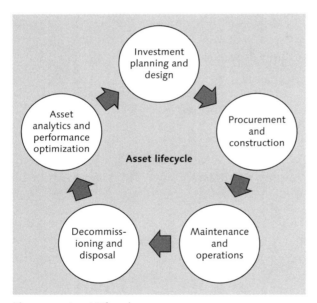

Figure 5.1 Asset Lifecycle

The asset lifecycle is supported by SAP solutions that cover all these stages, and they are offered as part of SAP Service and Asset Management, under the business scenario SAP Enterprise Asset Management (SAP EAM). SAP EAM provides you with a complete solution focused on achieving optimal asset condition and performance against the lowest costs. It allows you to improve the management of capital expenditure, reduce operational costs, optimize asset utilization, manage the internal maintenance department, and collaborate with engineering and maintenance contractors. SAP EAM supports the following elements of the assets lifecycle:

▶ Planning, building, and commissioning assets

▶ Asset visibility and performance

▶ Optimized asset operations and maintenance

▶ Operational risk management (also known as asset safety and compliance)

▶ Real estate lifecycle management

5.1.2 Maintenance Activities and Strategies

SAP PM and SAP CS processes allow you to support an asset/product during its operations and maintenance stages. SAP PM is a combination of all technical, administrative, and management tasks carried out during the life of a technical object to keep it operational or to return it to its target condition as well as delaying the reduction of the wear reserve. Maintenance activities are performed to maintain the target condition, optimize asset availability, minimize the risk of outages, and minimize maintenance costs. Activities include visual inspections, adjustments, replacements, supplements, lubrications, preserving, cleaning, and functional testing. The different types of maintenance activities you can perform fall into the following four main groups:

▶ **Failure-based maintenance**
Focuses on repairing an installation after failure to restore it to its target condition. This is also referred to as firefighting, unscheduled, reactive, or corrective maintenance.

▶ **Preventive maintenance**
Takes place after a set number of usage hours or after a set performance. The activities performed are often checks, inspections (check, measure, observe, and assess), and restoration activities; they include identifying the cause of wear and tear and deducing the consequences necessary to ensure its future use. Preventive maintenance often includes periodic replacement of spare parts.

▶ **Condition-based scheduled maintenance**
Takes place when the condition of an installation gets checked against a preset norm. As soon as the condition falls outside the norm, maintenance activities need to take place.

▸ **Improvements**

Involves tasks for improving functional safety without changing its specified function. Improvements have become the norm in recent years. Continuous improvements to systems increase the operating and functional reliability of machinery, plants, and equipment.

Other technical activities are often performed by maintenance engineers but aren't technically maintenance activities. For example, cleaning, modifications, construction, production assistance, and refurbishment can still be executed using the same processes.

SAP PM and SAP CS support different maintenance strategies for optimal assets performance, as shown in Figure 5.2. The dark boxes represent the different strategies, and the light boxes show you which activities or triggers lead you to take action and perform maintenance activities. The strategies are included based on their chronological order (from left to the right), and organizations often use a mix of strategies based on the asset group and the effect of asset failure on the organization, for example.

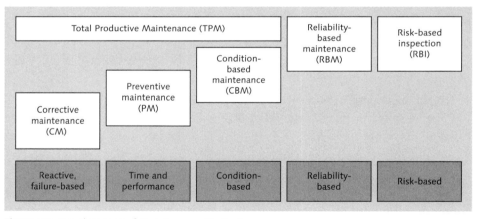

Figure 5.2 Development of Maintenance Strategies

The first three strategies (corrective maintenance, preventive maintenance, and condition-based maintenance) have been sufficiently covered under the main maintenance activities, so this section will focus on describing the other strategies.

▸ **Total productive maintenance (TPM)**

This strategy can be chosen when maintenance tasks can be largely planned and performed by machine operators. Machine operators are trained to perform many of the day-to-day tasks of simple maintenance and fault-finding. So TPM is a proactive approach that essentially is focused on identifying issues as soon as possible and planning to prevent any issues before they happen. The motto is "zero error, zero work-related accident, and zero loss." The performance of maintenance activities can be triggered based on a failure, planned event, or on the condition of an asset, which aligns with the corrective maintenance, preventive maintenance, and condition-based maintenance strategies.

▶ **Reliability-centered maintenance (RCM)**
This strategy aims to reduce costs and improve asset availability by analyzing damages, production losses, and asset cost systematically to achieve the required reliability. RCM is an analysis method that contains rules for decision making and can be linked to a risk analysis used for security-critical and environmental-critical systems. Possible functional malfunctions and their causes are determined based on the machines function.

This information is captured in an information worksheet, which largely corresponds to a Failure Mode and Effects Analysis (FMEA). A decision chart is used to check whether condition-relevant, preventive, or reactive tasks are recommend for each cause of malfunction mentioned in the information worksheet. If none of these tasks makes sense, design changes or modified operating rules are considered.

This strategy is covered by the following SAP EAM solutions:

▶ Operational maintenance through SAP PM or operational customer service through SAP CS (or additionally via SAP CRM).

▶ Reliability-centered maintenance through Reliability Centered Maintenance and Optimization (RCMO) software allowing you to create and evaluate asset strategies, which results in updating the preventive maintenance process in SAP PM and/or SAP CS. RCMO is an SAP-endorsed third-party software solution from the Certified SAP Partner Meridium, which is designed and developed within the SAP NetWeaver architecture.

▶ Failure Mode and Effects Analysis supported by SAP Quality Management (QM) (see Chapter 8 for more details).

▶ **Risk-based inspection (RBI)**
This strategy optimizes the maintenance efforts based on the risk. It focuses on the reduction of maintenance effort and minimizes the risks associated with asset operation failure (e.g., interrupting the production process). You identify and monitor risk drivers that significantly contribute to the overall risk. This

method allows you to focus your maintenance activities on the assets that form the greatest risk to your organization and thus optimize the assignment of resources with an ever-decreasing budget.

5.1.3 Benefits of SAP Maintenance and SAP Customer Service

Use of the SAP PM and SAP CS components during the maintenance and operation stage of a product will help leverage the following benefits:

- Increases asset availability
- Provides transparency of incurred maintenance and operational costs
- Documents performed tasks
- Facilitates comprehensive planning of resources
- Performs condition monitoring of technical objects
- Builds a technical history of the technical objects

The following benefits are specific to SAP CS:

- Improves customer satisfaction by retaining customers
- Provides customer support during the use of your product
- Improves profitability; that is, service brings more than sales (e.g., copiers and printers)

5.2 Service and Maintenance Structure Management

This section first covers the different available master data elements—referred to as technical objects—within SAP PM and SAP CS, such as the functional location and equipment. Then we'll summarize common functions available for these technical objects, such as categorization and data transfer. The section finishes by addressing enhancement options of technical objects with the use of SAP standard customer exits.

5.2.1 Technical Objects

Within SAP PM and SAP CS, you can record maintenance and service activities for a technical object. A technical object can be either an individual object that needs to be maintained or a more complex technical system with multiple layers and objects involved. These are the main reasons for setting up technical objects:

▶ To record and document the maintenance task
▶ To collect data over longer periods of time
▶ To enable analytics on its use and conditions

Using technical objects allows asset owners and users to determine if your technical asset provides the services in the most efficient and effective manner. The data gathered during the object's life will provide useful information on life, conditions, and operational costs, as well as insight to support investment decisions. Figure 5.3 gives you an overview of the master data objects used within SAP PM and SAP CS to represent a technical asset via the technical object. A technical object (in gray box) is the collective definition used to represent the following from a maintenance and operational perspective: an individual object, or a collection name for logically grouped technical objects.

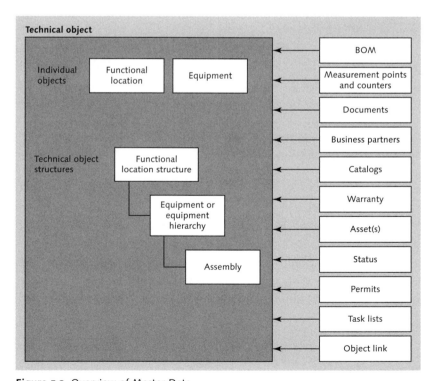

Figure 5.3 Overview of Master Data

They consist of multiple master data elements, such as multiple functional locations, equipments, BOMs, and assemblies. On the right side, note which additional master data records can be related to a technical object.

The objects used to represent a technical object within SAP PM and SAP CS are the functional locations, equipment, and assembly. Let's look at each of these.

Functional Location

A functional location represents a technical system or a part of a technical system. These are usually set up hierarchically and can be structured based on the following criteria:

- Spatial according to location (e.g., a building or plant)
- Technical according to function (e.g., gas extraction)
- Functional based on process-oriented criteria (e.g., condensation, polymerization, or pump water station)

By using functional location categories, you can define, describe, and control objects that are fundamentally different. When setting up a structure, never use organizational elements (such as cost centers and organizational units or trades) as part of the structure because they are already part of the attributes; these organizational elements can easily change over time, which would result in having to update your structure and update transactional data unnecessarily. SAP standard provides you with four categories (technical system, real estate object, linear functional locations, or customer location), which can be used directly or as a reference when defining your own.

Functional Location Hierarchy

You can use a functional location hierarchy to represent a complex system structure, which is multilevel and organized hierarchically. Examples of complex structures are the representation of a production line, an office building or production plant, or a power station or gas platform. In fact, Figure 5.4 shows an example of a process-oriented functional location structure for a production line.

> **Note**
>
> Figure 5.7, which appears later in this section, however, shows a structure that uses several other objects. Because these objects are going to be explained first, the figure is

included after their introduction so you understand the terminology used. Via the STRUCTURE indicator, you can determine the number of levels of your structure and how they are numbered. You can deviate from this numbering, as you can see in Figure 5.4 for the INLET under the MIXER.

You can create a functional location structure via the top-down approach (i.e., starting with the uppermost level), either one by one or by using list entry capabilities or even copy functions to copy an existing functional location structure either partly or completely.

A work order is the vehicle to collect costs against a functional location. It can be raised against all levels of a functional location hierarchy. During cost reporting, the cost will be automatically aggregated to the top level(s).

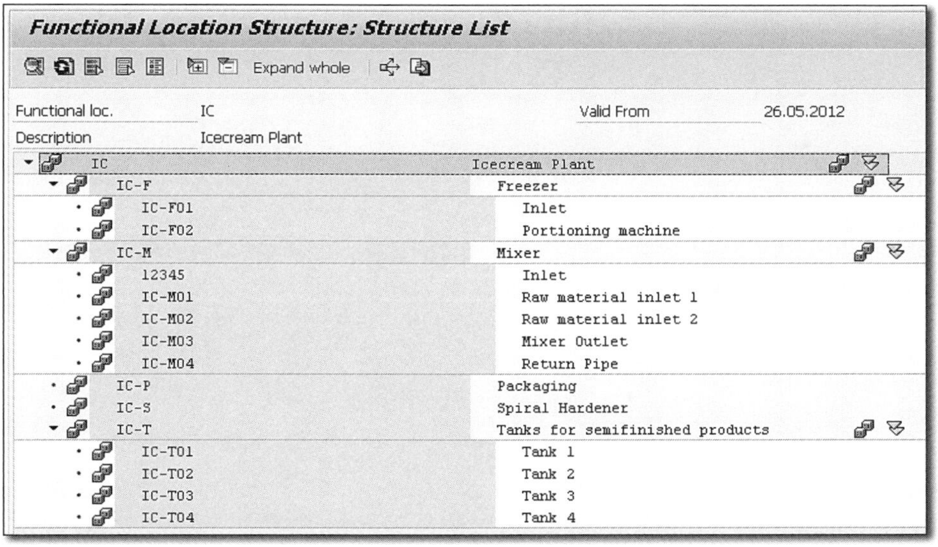

Functional Location Structure: Structure List

Functional loc.	IC	Valid From	26.05.2012
Description	Icecream Plant		

IC	Icecream Plant	
IC-F	Freezer	
IC-F01	Inlet	
IC-F02	Portioning machine	
IC-M	Mixer	
12345	Inlet	
IC-M01	Raw material inlet 1	
IC-M02	Raw material inlet 2	
IC-M03	Mixer Outlet	
IC-M04	Return Pipe	
IC-P	Packaging	
IC-S	Spiral Hardener	
IC-T	Tanks for semifinished products	
IC-T01	Tank 1	
IC-T02	Tank 2	
IC-T03	Tank 3	
IC-T04	Tank 4	

Figure 5.4 Functional Location Structure

Equipment

The equipment category defines, describes, and controls objects that are fundamentally different. An equipment can represent either an independent individual object such as a tool or a vehicle, or it can represent an object that is part of a structure. For example, within the functional location hierarchy of a production line, you can install equipment such as the engine, pumps, meters, or gears. You need to define an equipment if you want to record maintenance activities and cost at this level. The equipment installation data shows whether or not the equipment was in use within a technical system during its lifespan. A serialized equipment allows you to additionally track the equipment items that have been placed in storage.

SAP standard categories can be used or copied from when you define your own categories: categories for machines, fleet objects, product resources and tools, customer equipment, and linear equipment. The left side of Figure 5.5 gives you an example of a vehicle equipment identified by its category fleet; the right-hand side shows a serialized equipment.

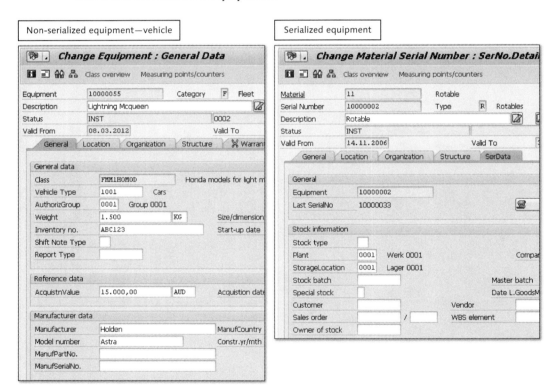

Figure 5.5 Nonserialized and Serialized Equipment

Serialized Equipment

To identify a specific individual piece of equipment and trace it within operational activities, you can consider using a serialized piece of equipment. By assigning the serial number, you're not only able to track it within the maintenance activities of this serial number, but you're also able to use warehousing functions (e.g., placing the serialized equipment in a warehouse to be refurbished). SAP PLM describes the product sold to customers; the equipment is the serial number of the product sold to a specific customer. Serialization can be done by assigning a material master with a serial number profile to the equipment, which then allows you to update the specific serial number in the equipment directly or indirectly—hence the integration to SAP Materials Management (SAP MM). The serial number profile is the control object of the serial number and includes which business operations require mandatory or optional entry of the serial number and is maintained on the plant level in the material master (either general sales plant view or plant 2 view, as described in Chapter 3, Section 3.1.1).

The serial number profile also controls how the serial number needs to be assigned (automatically or manually), which number range is allowed, and whether and how stock information in the serial number master record is checked and synchronized with the stock data from SAP MM.

The combination of the material and serial number is unique within the system. The equipment master on the right side of Figure 5.5 shows an example of a serialized equipment. It shows the assigned material and serial number combination as well as that this equipment is currently stored in a plant/storage location (0001/0001).

Complex Structures: Installation of Equipment

Within the functional location structure it's possible to install equipment, which allows you to keep a record of where the equipment items have been used throughout time. Figure 5.6 shows an example of a functional location structure of a building, which includes equipment such as the air-conditioning and lift, as well as a linear asset for this property (the airstrip). Usage information is available from a functional locations perspective (to understand which equipment was installed in which location) and from an equipment's perspective (to understand in which functional location the equipment was installed over time). Figure 5.7 gives an example of this.

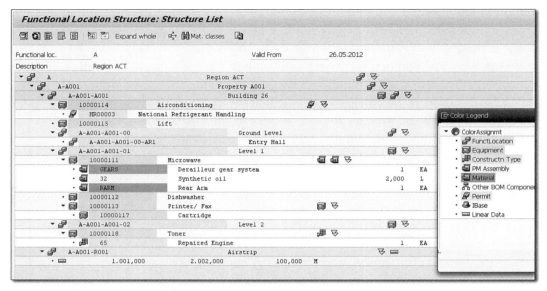

Figure 5.6 Functional Location Structure

Equipment Hierarchy

Equipment hierarchies can be used to represent the structure of a piece of equipment. This could be useful, for example, when functional locations aren't used within your organization or if you require more granular details on your equipment master.

> **Note**
>
> Equipment hierarchies cannot replace or be substituted for functional location hierarchies; keep in mind that cost reporting won't be automatically aggregated to the top level when they are occurring and collected on a lower-level object, like it does within a functional location hierarchy.

Another difference between functional locations and equipment is that the installation specifications and restrictions can't be set, as is possible in a functional location where you can set up no installation, single installations, or multiple installations. The data transfer capabilities are the same though.

Figure 5.7 shows an example of equipment hierarchy for a printer, with a sub-equipment for the toner and the cartridge.

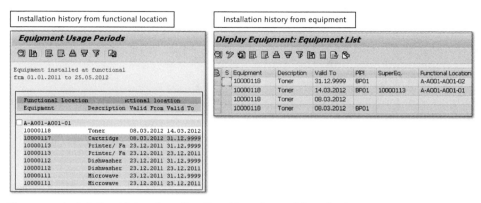

Figure 5.7 Installation History from Functional Location and from Equipment

Next, let's discuss the last component of the technical object structure—the assembly.

Assembly

During maintenance processing, you can refer to an assembly when you want to get greater detail of a particular area of the technical object affected. An assembly doesn't represent an object but an object category, similar to a material. You can assign the assembly (basically a material in SAP MM) as a reference object during order processing in the notification or work order by choosing any material from SAP MM. An example is when you create a work order for a car, and you want to specify that the air conditioning system needs attention, you can assign the equipment representing the specific car and also the air conditioning assembly, which is represented in Figure 5.8 as AIRCO.

Figure 5.8 Reference Object Assembly

This section has focused on those technical objects that can be used as reference objects during maintenance activities, which are the functional location, the equipment, and the assembly. The following section will discuss technical objects that can also be used to allow you to document detailed structure information to inform engineers or assist them when performing maintenance activities.

Bill of Materials

Within maintenance and servicing, you can use a bill of material (BOM). We'll go into more detail about using BOMs in Section 5.4.2.

Catalog and Parts Management

Catalog and part management enables you to use internal or external catalogs when planning spare parts and components. Section 5.5 has more detail about these components.

Measuring Points and Counters

A *measuring point* is a physical and/or logical location at which a particular condition is described. Examples of measuring points are measuring temperature of a building, pressure of a vessel, and rotations per minute of a wind-driven power station.

A measuring point can be flagged as a *counter*, which is a resource that enables you to represent the wear and tear of an object, the performance and consumption data of a technical object, and the reduction in its useful life. Think of a car's odometer or a property's electricity consumption meter as examples of counters.

The measuring point is used so you can record measurements in the system, such as entering a reading of 20,000 kilometers against a vehicle or entering temperature of 24 degrees against a building. The unit of measure of a measuring point-counter is defined by using a characteristic from the central SAP Classification System (CA). The measurement point can also measure quantitative condition information, for which a maintenance catalog can be set up and defined. Figure 5.9 shows an example of several measuring points defined against a vehicle; the right side of the figure shows the details of a measuring point.

Figure 5.10 shows the measurements of a measuring point over time.

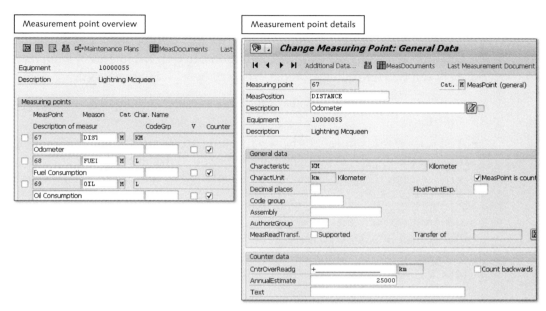

Figure 5.9 Measurement Points and Counters

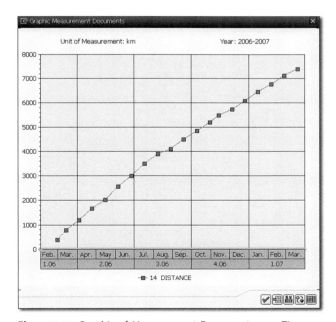

Figure 5.10 Graphic of Measurement Documents over Time

Object Links

You can use object links to represent the links that exist between various technical objects or systems, such as the connection between two pieces of equipment or between two functional locations. This can be useful in two ways:

▶ You can see the connections between various objects to identify causes of malfunctions.

▶ You can see the connections between objects to inform maintenance planning, such as which parts of a system need to be shut down either partly or entirely, or, in case of outages, which objects are affected by the outage.

Different types of links are supported, including one-way links (flow goes one direction), two-way links (flow goes multiple ways), inward and outward links, and networks of links (e.g., the water pipes in a large building are summarized in the object networks "Drinking water" and "Central heating"). The use of networks (or other object links) in combination with Linear Asset Management, allows organizations to manage linear assets and their relationships, such as a road network or electricity network. These functions were introduced in SAP ERP 6, EHP 5, and were further improved in SAP ERP 6, EHP 6, addressing important business requirements across multiple asset-intensive industries.

Figure 5.11 gives you an example of an object link.

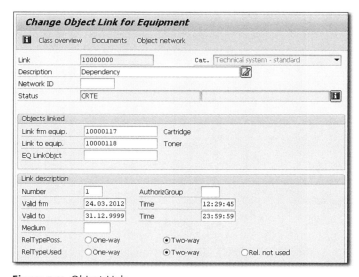

Figure 5.11 Object Link

5.2.2   Common Functions for Technical Objects

Several common master data elements are relevant for both functional locations as well as for the equipment masters. Let's examine a few of them.

Categorize and Classify Technical Objects

Alongside the functional location category and equipment category, you can use object types and object classifications to group technical objects that logically belong together. This topic is described in more detail in Section 5.4.1.

Master Data Records

The functional location and equipment technical objects both have the same standard tabs (GENERAL, LOCATION, ORGANIZATION, and STRUCTURE), which are covered in Table 5.1 in detail and are shown in Figure 5.12.

Tab	Contains Information On...
GENERAL	▸ General data is included such as the object type, weight information, and authorization. ▸ Reference data is included such as the acquisition value and date. ▸ Manufacturer's data is included such as part number, construction month, year, and serial number.
LOCATION	▸ Contains the information about where the technical object is located via the maintenance plant, location, room, and plant selection. It also includes central address data. ▸ SAP PM uses central address management, which means that the addresses in the functional location, equipment, notification, order and nonstock components are synchronized.
ORGANIZATION	▸ Account assignment is the area in which you determine the responsible cost collection objects from SAP Financial Accounting (FI) such as the responsible company code, cost center, and relating WBS elements. It's also the place where you can assign the asset number from FI. ▸ Responsibilities allow you to maintain the responsible planning plant and group, main work center and assignment to catalogs.
STRUCTURE	▸ Information is included about the hierarchical structure of the technical objects. In functional location, this is where you set up the installation specifications to allow equipment installation.

Table 5.1 Standard Tabs for Technical Objects

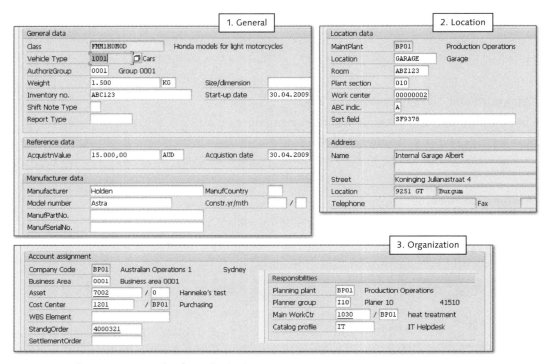

Figure 5.12 Example of Standard Tabs

Depending on the specific business requirements, you can choose per technical object category to either use them all or just use the ones that are relevant. When you want to use the standard tabs, you don't need to do anything. However when you want to influence the tabs used, tab descriptions, and the content per tab, you need to configure a view profile in the SAP PM configuration and assign this profile to the technical object category, providing you with full flexibility.

The additional tabs, which can be activated in configuration based on the category of the technical object, are described in Table 5.2. Figure 5.13 shows an example of the linear view of a functional location, including a linear reference pattern and linear attributes for pipe material, layout, and so on. The use of these specific views (tabs) is again configured through the view profile, so you can easily activate them per technical object category.

Tab	Contains Information On...
Fleet	When fleet data is activated and configured, the vehicle-specific data can be maintained, such as the registration information and the fuel type. This topic will be described in more detail in Chapter 9. Since EHP 3, you can flag both the equipment and the functional location as a vehicle—before that, it was only the equipment.
Production Resources & Tools	When a technical object is flagged as a product resource/tool (PRT), you can maintain specific data that allows you to schedule it during execution of work. A PRT is a moveable operating resource (e.g., a tool or measuring device) that can be used in SAP PM or within SAP Production Planning (PP). A PRT can be assigned to an operation in a maintenance order, where you can check its availability and change its status. It contains a usage view, so you can see when it has been used.
Warranty data	When warranty information needs to be recorded for the technical object, you can activate this by adding either a separate dedicated tab or including the information as part of an existing tab.
Vehicle data	Standard SAP delivers two separate tabs that include data specific to vehicles, such as license plate or consumption data. Chapter 9 will describe SAP Fleet Management and these two tabs: ▶ Vehicle ID & Measurement ▶ Technology
Linear Technical Object	Since SAP ERP 6, EHP 5, you can activate a technical object as a linear technical object, which allows you to maintain linear data. This may be relevant for linear objects, such as a road, railway, or a distribution network. Linear Asset Management allows you to use classification to enter dynamic segmentations against a linear asset, enabling you to describe the attributes of the asset in a flexible manner. For example, if you're responsible for a road network, then you want to know the surface and the speed limits. For George Street, a functional location is defined where the street is divided into two segments—one for asphalt and the other one for unsealed. The speed limit changes two times, from 60 MPH to 40 MPH and back to 60 MPH. Or for a sewage water pipe network, you can define the pipe material, pipe diameter used, and whether it's underground as shown in Figure 5.13.

Table 5.2 Additional Tabs: Category Based

Tab	Contains Information On...
LINEAR TECHNICAL OBJECT (Forts.)	Based on your specific requirements, you define any linear attribute via CA, which was explained in Chapter 4. Apart from linear attributes, you can define a linear asset via a linear reference pattern, such as the mileposts alongside a highway or the manholes alongside a sewage pipeline.
LOGBOOK	You can record a logbook against a technical object. The logbook business function needs to be activated (LOG_EAM_POM and LOG_EAM_POM2) in configuration through the Switch Framework.
CONFIGURATION	When the technical object is configurable, this tab can be used to assign the configurable material to the technical object.
USER DATA	Several tabs have been dedicated specifically for you to add additional information, without too much development required because the tabs are already available.

Table 5.2 Additional Tabs: Category Based (Cont.)

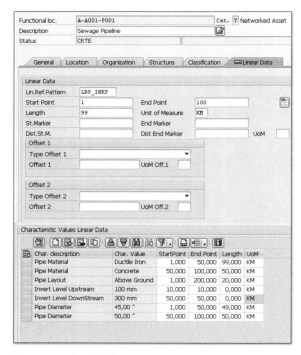

Figure 5.13 Special Views

SAP Engineering Change Management

Use ECM to record changes to your technical object structures by assigning them to your assemblies, which will be explained in more detail in Chapter 8.

Mass Update

Since EHP 2, you can perform mass updates in the list editing transaction of the equipment (Transaction IE05) and the functional locations (Transaction IL05) by going to the menu GOTO • CARRY OUT MASS CHANGE. This can be activated by the business function LOG_EAM_SIMP and by assigning the authorization object I_MASS to the users who are allowed to perform this function. Because this function can have far-reaching effects, we recommend that you only assign it to super users.

Reference Functional Location

The *reference functional location* is doesn't represent an actual location but just gets set up to assist during creation and maintenance of several similar functional locations. When used, only the location data needs to be maintained in the functional location.

Data Transfer

Data values can be transferred within a technical object structure either horizontally (where values are copied from a reference functional location) or vertically (where values from a higher functional location transfer to a lower functional location and installed equipment). Transfer happens automatically when the installation of the equipment takes place from the functional location. When you install the equipment from the equipment master itself, the system prompts you and gives you the opportunity to influence the data transfer through the function INSTALLATION WITH DATA TRANSFER. Figure 5.14 shows an example of the radio button options that allow you to choose whether the value is adopted from either the installation functional location or the equipment.

When installation happens from the functional location, you don't get a chance to influence the data transfer. All fields in the equipment that had been already filled will be unaffected; any fields that are empty will automatically be filled from the functional location.

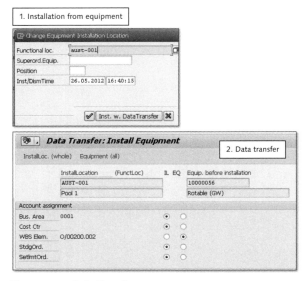

Figure 5.14 Data Transfer

Document Management

When information about technical objects exists in the form of documents (e.g., manufacturers' maintenance manuals, technical drawings, or photographs), you can use SAP Document Management System (SAP DMS). SAP DMS gives you the ability to view the documents from within the master data record and makes them available during execution of maintenance activities—in one click. You can dedicate a tab or part of a tab, so you can directly see the assigned documents in the master record, as shown in Figure 5.15. See Chapter 3 for more information on SAP DMS.

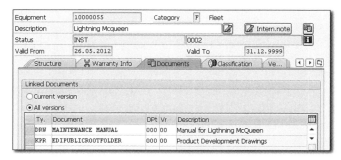

Figure 5.15 Equipment with Documents

Business Partners

You can assign various partners with different functions to a technical object. Standard SAP provides you with several partner types, including the vendor, customer, contact person, and internal partners such as the user or a work center, personnel number, job, or organizational unit. Some examples of these partner types are found in Figure 5.16.

To make a technical object relevant for customers, you have to use a partner determination procedure, which includes a partner function that is assigned to a customer. When partners are assigned to the technical object and then used in a maintenance order or service order, the partner details will be copied into the maintenance documents assigned to this object.

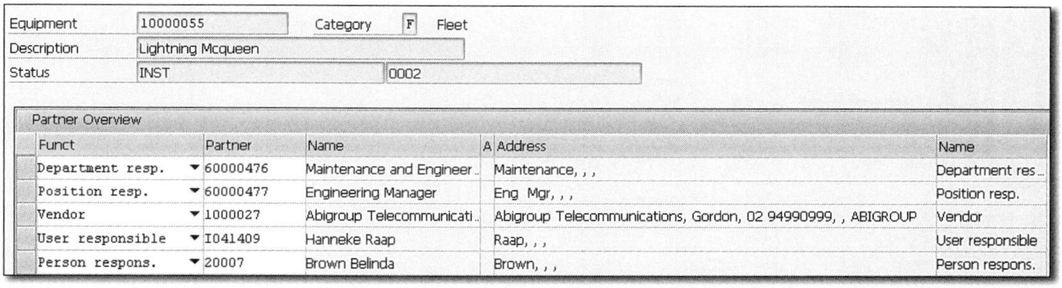

Equipment	10000055		Category	F	Fleet		
Description	Lightning Mcqueen						
Status	INST		0002				

Partner Overview					
Funct	Partner	Name	A Address		Name
Department resp.	▾ 60000476	Maintenance and Engineer.	Maintenance, , ,		Department res...
Position resp.	▾ 60000477	Engineering Manager	Eng Mgr, , ,		Position resp.
Vendor	▾ 1000027	Abigroup Telecommunicati.	Abigroup Telecommunications, Gordon, 02 94990999, , ABIGROUP		Vendor
User responsible	▾ I041409	Hanneke Raap	Raap, , ,		User responsible
Person respons.	▾ 20007	Brown Belinda	Brown, , ,		Person respons.

Figure 5.16 Business Partners

When you want to use partners and assign them to technical objects, you have to configure the partner determination procedure. The four steps of partner determination are shown in Figure 5.17. During the first step, the system finds the partner determination procedure based on the technical object category. The procedure includes a list of the relevant partner functions. A specific partner function is assigned to one partner type.

The partner determination procedure is a grouping mechanism to specify the partner functions that are allowed for a particular object and determine which partner functions are possible during business transactions. The partner function defines a partner's rights, obligations, responsibilities, and tasks during the processing of a business transaction. You can use the standard partner types that are supported or set up and use others when necessary via user exit ICSV0008.

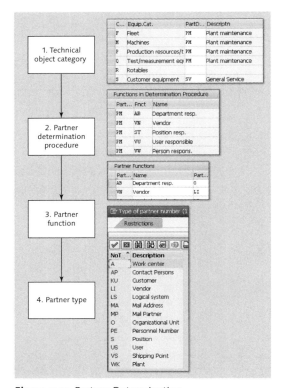

Figure 5.17 Partner Determination

Business Partner Customer

The business partner customer deserves its own section because the customer is the main stakeholder within the SAP CS processes. The master data object used within SAP CS and others parts of the solution (e.g., SAP SD) to describe the patterns who buy from your organization is the *customer master*. This master data record structure (see Figure 5.18) consists of three distinct areas: general data, company code data, and sales and distribution data.

In terms of the customer structure, *general data* contains information that is relevant for the entire system, such as the company name, address, and general phone number. The *company code data* is only relevant to the specified company code and its financial accounting. It includes information on the account management and insurance data. Finally, *sales and distribution data* is only relevant for the specified sales area. The sales area is a combination of the sales organization, distribution channel, and division. It includes, for example, pricing data, delivery priority, and shipping conditions.

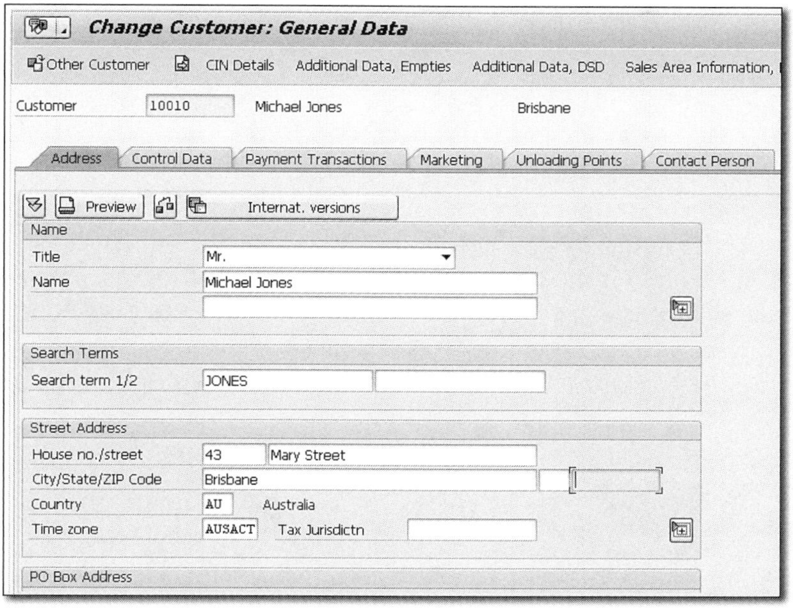

Figure 5.18 Customer Structure

Maintenance Catalogs

By using catalogs, you can collect, enter, and analyze information relating to a notification such as the object part, the damage, and the cause of a breakdown in a standardized and error-free manner. Catalogs are either technical object-specific (where the catalog profile is connected to the master data) or notification type-specific. When both are available, the system will use the most detailed catalog, which is the one of the technical object.

In previous versions of SAP ERP, catalogs could only be configured; however, they can now also be maintained as master data (via Transactions QS41 and QS42), which is why it's important to understand how this is done. The catalog codes used can be analyzed within the Plant Maintenance Information System (PMIS) (see Chapter 10 for more details). When creating a catalog code, you have to assign it to a catalog category such as tasks, cause, defect, or object part, and then create a code group used for grouping the catalogs, as you can see in Figure 5.19.

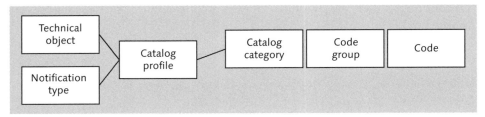

Figure 5.19 Catalog Profile

Figure 5.20 gives you an example of the setup of a catalog profile for the IT Help Desk to support software-related issues as represented in the left-hand table. Codes have been created for the CATALOG CATEGORIES CODING, DAMAGE, DEFECTS TYPES, and so on, which have been grouped in the CODE GROUP SOFTWARE. On the right, you can see how the catalog codes 01 REFERRED TO TRAINING MANUAL and 02 REQUESTED REMOTE ACCESS can be chosen when entering activities.

Catalog Profile for IT Help Desk

Catalog category	Code Group	Code
D Coding	SOFTWARE	01 Operating mistake 02 Software bug
C Damage	SOFTWARE	01 Software bug 02 Hardware bug
9 Defect types	SOFTWARE	01 End-user error 02 training issue
B Object Part	SOFTWARE	01 Desktop 02 Terminal
5 Causes	SOFTWARE	01 End-user error 02 training issue
2 Tasks	SOFTWARE	01 Referred to training manual 02 Remote access request
A Activities	SOFTWARE	01 Referred to training manual 02 Remote access request

Result in Activities for IT Help Desk

No.	Code gr...	Ac...	Activity code text	Activity text
1	SOFTWARE	01	Referred to training man...	

Catalog Selection

▼ Activity PM Activities (PM)
  ▶ PM1   Maintenance Activities
▼ SOFTWARE Software
  • ▶ 01   Referred to training manual
  • ▶ 02   Requested remote access

Figure 5.20 Example of Catalog

Warranty

A warranty represents a binding commitment to a customer by which services are provided either partly or fully during a specific period of time or lifetime of an individual technical object. When defining a warranty against a technical object, you have to specify whether you're the warranty receiver (i.e., the inbound vendor warranty) or the guarantor (where the warranty outbound is provided by you to the customer). After you understand which warranties are applicable to your technical objects, you can make the warranty information available in the master data through the view profile, as shown in Figure 5.21. On the top, you see an equipment master, to which a master warranty is assigned. On the bottom, you can see that this warranty is valid within a time frame or within the first 40,000 kilometers.

> **Note**
>
> Most of the screenshots captured within this book have been based on the metric system. However, it is also possible to use the imperial system using miles and miles per hour instead. SAP supports both systems with their own sets of units of measure. Generally speaking, you decide per business object which system will be used.

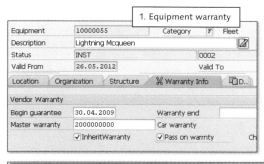

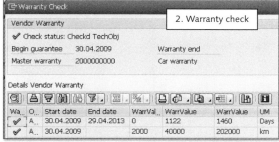

Figure 5.21 Warranty in Technical Object

When you just want to know whether a technical object is under warranty, you can fill out the start and end date. If you want to specify exactly which services are provided under warranty or what the conditions of a valid warranty are, use a master warranty. The master warranty can be set up and assigned to several technical objects. By using a warranty check, you can see if the object still complies with the warranty conditions (see Figure 5.22). A master warranty is structured with a header, items, and counters; each area will be briefly explained in the next section. Figure 5.22 shows an example of a warranty for cars; the first screen shows the header and the items. The second screen shows the counters of the warranty, which are based on time and kilometers.

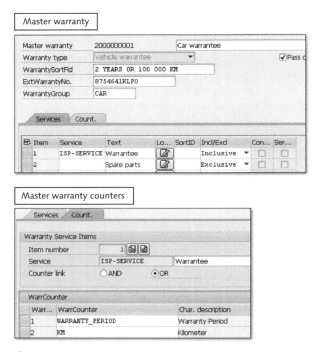

Figure 5.22 Master Warranty Structure

A master warranty contains the following data:

▶ **Header**
The header contains the warranty type, the description, and optionally the classification data.

▶ **Items**
The items contain the services that are included or excluded under the warranty. To describe the services, you can either use the service master or the material master from SAP MM, or you can describe them via a description.

▶ **Counter**

For each warranty item, you can specify the validity criteria of the warranty. This can be a period of time or can be a performance counter of a technical object. Counters can be set up with AND or OR links, which means that both the conditions need to be met or only one of the conditions must be met, respectively.

SAP ERP Financials Asset Accounting

Within the technical object, you can define an asset number, which is the master data element in SAP ERP Financials Asset Accounting (FI–AA). It represents the asset from a financial perspective and includes information about the asset value, asset life, and asset depreciation. You can activate the integration between FI-AA and SAP PM in the configuration, where you define various mapping rules. You can establish direct synchronization (where an asset is created automatically when a piece of equipment is created or when fields are updated directly), or you can set up indirect synchronization (where a workflow is triggered when one of the master records is changed). Figure 5.23 shows an equipment master and its assigned asset master and asset values.

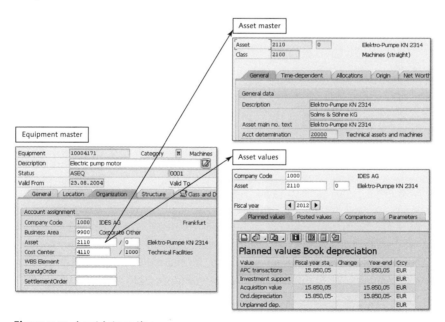

Figure 5.23 Asset Integration

Status Management of the Technical Object

Through status management, you can determine if a technical object is available for a certain business operation. The status of a technical object is defined by two types of statuses: the system status and the user status (optional).

The system status is set automatically by the system based on activities performed in SAP, and this can't be changed. It determines whether or not a particular business transaction can be performed. For example, when a piece of equipment is deactivated, it can't be used in a maintenance plan.

To add your own business logic to status management, define your own statuses by setting them up via a status profile. This also allows you to include the sequence of statuses and to set up which business transactions are allowed and denied when a certain user status is assigned to an object. Figure 5.24 shows the equipment status with the SYSTEM STATUS on the left side and the user status of the equipment (STATUS WITH STATUS NO.) on the right side.

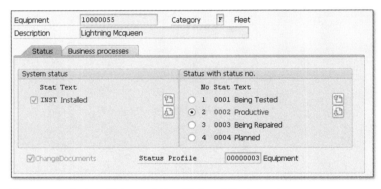

Figure 5.24 System Status and User Status of Equipment

Permits

You can set up and use permits to ensure that special activities, instructions, or approval steps are being undertaken, either before orders are executed or before orders are closed. Permits can be assigned to each individual work order directly or to the technical object, so that each time a maintenance activity takes place, the permit data is available in the order, as shown in Figure 5.25.

Permits can be case by case, or you can set up their use through Work Clearance Management (WCM), which will be described in Section 5.6.4.

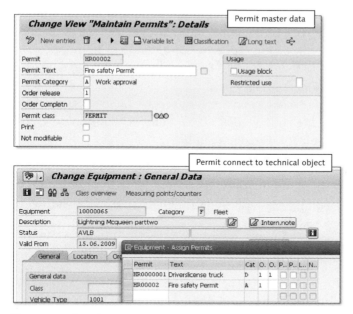

Figure 5.25 Permit

There are two kinds of permits:

► **Technical permit**
These include safety precautions for the employees and surroundings of a job, such as providing ear protection for employees, safeguarding a work area, providing a flame-proof zone, or granting a work clearance certificate. When a permit is assigned to a technical object and a work order is generated for the lower level, the permit will still be proposed.

► **Process-oriented permit**
These are determined automatically based on a field in the order header, and they can be used to influence the release. You could, for example, set up an additional approval permit when the planned value of a work order is above a threshold of $10,000. Automatic determination is done based on the classification of the permit.

SAP CRM Integration

A bidirectional replication process allows you to upload and download customer equipment data from SAP CS into SAP CRM, where it's created as an installed base. The replication ensures that data is synchronized, independent of where changes were made to keep data consistent across both environments. Replication consists of three different loading options: the initial load (required when transferring data for the first time), the permanent load (for ongoing data exchange), and the delta load (focuses on transfer of all the changes, called deltas). Replication to activate equipment data transfer is a process that needs to be set up within SAP CRM and, once set up, is undertaken by the SAP CRM middleware. You'll perform the following steps, listed here in brief:

1. Harmonize the product hierarchy settings, and make sure that the business partners and the materials used are available in SAP CRM.

2. Make settings for the equipment replication (this is a step that needs to be undertaken within the SAP CRM system).

3. Optionally, activate and flexibly enhance the data transfer process and validation in SAP CRM by implementing the BAdI `CRM_EQUI_LOAD`.

4. For the additional uploads to work properly, activate the appropriate adopter objects (for general equipment, the `EQUI_CONFIG`, or for serial numbers, the `SERNR_CONFIG`).

Installation Base

An installation can be used to display and manage products in a hierarchy with multiple levels and to document the installation on the customer side. You can assign related equipment, materials, serial numbers, and documents to a shared installation as components. An installation can, for example, represent an airplane, with all service-relevant components. Or it can comprise the two wings that will be integrated into the installation when production is complete. Usually the installation is used to generate a structure from a production or sales order. It's a multilevel representation of components.

The advantages of using an installation are that you can insert and remove components from the installation as time progresses, and you don't need to use an equipment master to do this. The disadvantages are that the installation isn't an object that is considered part of the technical objects within SAP PM or SAP CS because the link to maintenance processing has not been realized. Neither are the mapping of equipment hierarchies and the documentation of changes using change documents currently possible. Figure 5.26 shows an example of an installed base, where this customer installation includes a material, multiple pieces of equipment, and functional locations.

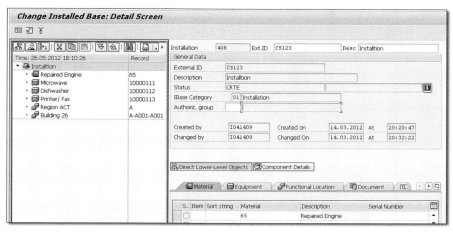

Figure 5.26 Example of installed Base

Alternative Labeling

You can change the label of the functional location through the alternative labeling function. Two scenarios are supported. The first is the renumbering of the functional location number that results in the primary key being changed, which could be used when a mistake has been made during creation. In the other scenario, you maintain a second label alongside your original label. This would allow you to keep a record of the manufacturer or customer numbering alongside your own numbering logic. You can switch from your own label to the alternative label through the user profile. To use alternative labeling, you must activate this in configuration. Be cautious and test comprehensively because turning on alternative labeling can cause performance issues.

5.2.3   Enhancing Technical Objects

Business Application Programming Interfaces (BAPIs) are standardized, stable interfaces (methods) that enable you to access SAP objects and thereby represent an important option for integrating the SAP system with external systems. An example of a BAPI for the creation of equipment is BAPI_EQM_CREATE.

Customer exits allow customers to add customer-specific functions to the SAP standard applications within the SAP enhancement concept. Customer exits themselves don't have any functions but are program exits that enable you to include user-defined programs. The two main advantages to using customer exits are that they have no effect on the SAP standard source text, and they aren't affected by software updates. Enhancement code represents potential customer requirements that aren't met in the standard system. They are possible in the SAP standard and can be arranged for customers with customer-specific logic. Upward compatibility is ensured, meaning that the call of an enhancement from the standard software and the validity of the call interface will remain in the future releases.

Now that you understand the different types of technical objects within SAP PM and SAP CS, we'll go into the main documents used when performing transaction in these areas, in which technical objects can be referenced.

5.3   Main Transactional Objects

Before we go into the SAP PM and SAP CS processes, let's look at an overview of the object information and the different transactional documents used within SAP PM and SAP CS so you understand their purpose and which data they can contain. This section will end by explaining the visualization and publication possibilities within maintenance processing, where the use of SAP Interactive Forms by Adobe is explained.

5.3.1   Object Information

As soon as you assign a technical object to one of the maintenance or services documents, you have the option to view a summary of its history either automatically or by clicking on the available L icon. The object information provides you with the last active maintenance notifications and the last active order, the link to a maintenance plan, and the classification data of the technical object. Object information also enables you to search for replacement equipment; when doing so, the system will automatically copy the search parameters from the original equipment to the search for the replacement equipment. Additional functions are available such as viewing of the entire technical object structure, going to the maintenance plan, and viewing related documents. Figure 5.27 shows an example of the object information for a piece of equipment, showing you the last notifications and orders and the classification details.

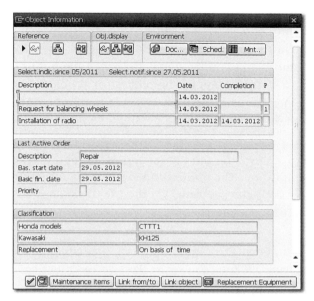

Figure 5.27 Object Information

5.3.2 Maintenance Notification

The maintenance or customer service notification is a document for collecting maintenance or service requests, malfunctions, or maintenance activities. The main controlling element of a notification—which defines, for example, whether it's a customer-specific notification or which numbering is used, and controls several other things as well—is the notification category. SAP standard delivers three different maintenance notification categories (malfunction, activity request, and maintenance request) and, for SAP CS categories, delivers problem, activity, and service request. They can be used directly or used as a reference to define your own.

Based on your company's requirements and based on the different roles that can add, change, or display notifications, you can set up which areas are relevant and visible for a notification category. You can choose to use the basic order view for casual users (via Transaction IQS21) and the extended view for key user (Transactions IW21 and IW24).

A notification structure has the following components:

▶ **Header**
This contains information that is relevant to the entire notification. The notification category is an important controlling mechanism and determines, for example, if it's a maintenance notification or an SAP CS notification. The notification header contains the information on by whom and when the notification was created and reported, a description of the request or problem, the technical object affected, the location data, the priority of the notification, the start and end date, the time of the breakdown, and possibly the downtime of the technical object involved.

You can activate the recording of the name and time stamp each time a person updates the long text of a notification. The notification is the main document to collect the technical data causing the problem. Via the use of catalogs and the PMIS, you can perform statistical analysis.

▶ **Item**
In the notification item, you can enter the damage location, the nature of the damage, and the cause of the damage. You can use the damage and cause code catalogs, which contain values for these entries. The catalogs can be dependent on the technical object or can be assigned to the notification category.

▶ **Activities**
In the ACTIVITIES area, you can enter the different activities performed as a result of the notification. They can be recorded either at the header level or specifically for the notification item. Use an activities catalog with predefined entries.

▶ **Tasks**
In the TASK area, you can enter the different tasks performed as a result of the notification. They can be recorded either at the header level or specifically for the notification item. You can use a task catalog with predefined entries.

▶ **Action box**
The action box can be used to perform follow-up or supplementary functions, which can be set up specifically based on the notification type. The follow-up can include an email to notify someone of the action that needs to be taken, which uses workflow.

After the follow-up function has been successfully executed, the system documents this by adding the details to the notification header as a task or activity.

Some examples of standard available follow-up activities and functions include the following:

- ▶ Generating a repair order
- ▶ Using the solution database (when maintained, the solution database can be used to find possible solutions based on the symptoms)
- ▶ Creating an internal note
- ▶ Logging a phone call

Figure 5.28 gives an example of a notification.

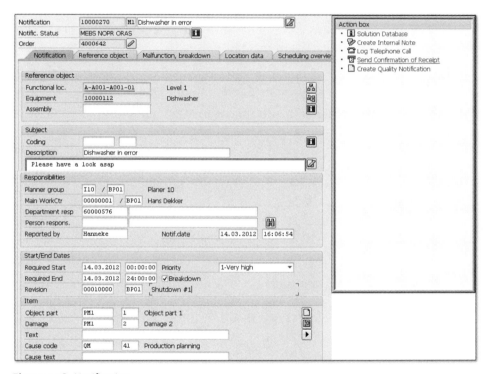

Figure 5.28 Notification

Because a notification can be raised in most organizations by basically anyone who has found a problem or wants to request a maintenance job for a technical object, the creation of the notification needs to be as simple as possible. SAP offers several different ways to generate one:

▶ The SAP GUI, simple or extended transaction.

▶ Via the Internet by using a simple Internet form or SAP Interactive Form by Adobe (which can be made available offline or online). This option gives you the advantage that no SAP user and SAP experience is necessary to perform this function. When you make this available for a wide audience, you might want to consider an additional approval for the request or malfunction report. Before you can use this option, an Internet scenario needs to be configured in Customizing via IMG • Cross application Component • Notification • Notification Processing • Define Scenarios.

▶ Via the SAP NetWeaver Portal (when used within your organization).

When using SAP CS, you can also use the customer interaction center or extend the processes by using functions from SAP CRM.

5.3.3 Maintenance or Customer Service Work Order

The *maintenance work order* is the document used within SAP PM to collect all maintenance costs relating to the individual work order. Within SAP CS this is called a service order, which includes in addition the customer details and the billing information. The service order can be generated as a result of a customer quotation, customer inquiry, or sales order. The focus of this chapter is order processing, so these additional documents won't be described in more detail, however, they have a very similar structure to the service order. Their content can easily be copied into a service order when the customer decides to accept the offer from the inquiry or quotation.

The order type is the main controlling element in SAP PM and SAP CS. Standard SAP delivers orders for breakdown, corrective, preventive, investments, and refurbishment. The service order and the repair order are delivered within SAP CS, which will be discussed in the next section. You can use the standard order types directly or as a reference when defining your own.

Work Order Structure

The structure of the order includes the following components:

▶ **Header**
The header of a work order contains information that is relevant to the entire work order presented through the first dedicated tab. It will copy the relevant

data from the notification to the work order, such as the reference object and the short description. The header contains the start and end date of the work and the priority. Since EHP 2, you can change the calendar used within an order; the default is the work center calendar.

▶ **Customer and service product**
In addition to the data just described, a service order contains the link to the customer, which is referred to as the sold-to party. You can use a service product to describe the different services provided to the customer.

▶ **Object list**
The object list contains all of the links to additional objects, such as additional assigned notifications, effected technical objects, and the used task lists. You can include a list of technical objects that are assigned to this work order. The object list is presented as the OBJECTS tab. These objects can be the following:

  ▶ Functional locations

  ▶ Pieces of equipment

  ▶ Assemblies

  ▶ Materials

  ▶ Material and serial numbers

This has the advantage that the data entry requirement is reduced, and order processing is facilitated considerably. Another advantage is the reduction in paper used as a result. No cost update takes place for objects in the object list. You can't perform an evaluation for the reference object that you have directly specified in the maintenance item in the PMIS.

▶ **Operations**
Operations contains the overview of the activities that need to be carried out and available through the OPERATIONS tab.

▶ **Settlement rule**
Because a work order is just a temporary cost collector, the requesting cost collector needs to be charged with actual costs confirmed on the order. This process is done by settlement of the work order, which credits the work order to the amount of zero and debits the cost collector entered in the settlement rule of the work order. Operational work orders usually settle to the requesting cost center (e.g., production), investment orders to the asset or asset under construction (AUC), project-specific work orders to WBS elements or network

activities, and refurbishment orders directly to stock material. The settlement rule can be accessed through the SETTLEMENT RULE icon.

► **Costs**

In the COSTS tab within the work order, you can find the estimated costs (which can only be maintained before order release, because as soon as the order is released, they will only be displayed), the planned costs, and the actual costs. Planned costs are automatically determined by the system based on your planned resources, which can be internal or external work centers, procurement activities, or planned materials. The actual cost of a work order gets updated as a result of actual cost being booked against the order; this can happen by time recording, purchase activities, or materials movements.

Based on your company's requirements and the different roles that can add, change, or display work orders, you can set up which areas are relevant and visible for the work order type. You can choose to use the basic order view for casual users and the extended view for key users. An example of a maintenance work order with extended view is displayed in Figure 5.29. As you can see, the extended view includes the HEADERDATA, OPERATIONS, COSTS, and OBJECTS work order tabs.

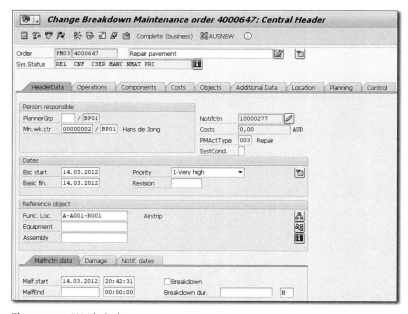

Figure 5.29 Work Order

As you can see in Figure 5.30, the maintenance operation differentiates between *work time* and *activity duration*. You can, for example, split the eight hours of work to two people, which leads to an activity duration of four hours. It's also possible that the actual work an operation takes is less than the duration because of waiting times (e.g., machine shut down time or paint drying). To assign appropriate resources to the maintenance order operations, the following options are available to you:

▶ Use of SAP PM and/or capacity planning either with or without SAP ERP Human Capital Management (SAP ERP HCM) integration, which is described in more detail in Section 5.6.1—a combination SAP PM for smaller tasks and SAP Project System (SAP PS) for larger maintenance jobs.

▶ Use of mobile scenarios (such as Work Manager, Service Manager, Rounds Manager, and Inventory Manager); see Chapter 9 for more details.

▶ Use of SAP Multiresource Scheduling, an SAP product that exceeds the scope of this book (visit the SAP website or SAP Service Marketplace for more details).

▶ Any other external scheduling tools (such as the third-party Primavera, Microsoft Project, etc.) can be integrated via the SAP NetWeaver Process Integration (SAP NetWeaver PI) tools.

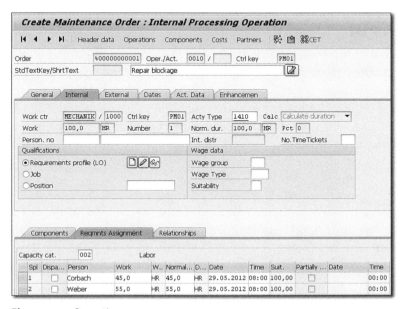

Figure 5.30 Operation

> **Note**
>
> You can use SAP Enterprise Project Connection to exchange data between SAP Project Management software and external project management tools.

Communicate Order Details to Workforce

Several options to communicate the orders to your workforce are available:

► Paper-based forms (via output determination)

> **Note**
>
> Since EHP 2, as soon as you change an operation after printing has taken place, the system status Modified After Printing (MPRT) will be assigned automatically.

► Email directly from the system

► Text message to a mobile device, which is called paging

► Send to mobile device via mobile apps Work Manager and Service Manager

► Mobile services and SAP CRM, which supports the whole service lifecycle (utilized specifically for service notifications, service orders, and sales orders)

Orders and Suborders

When you want to group several work orders together and report on them both individually and overall, you can use a work order with several suborders. The overall order represents the overhaul, for example, and the suborders are generated based on the different individual jobs that are required. It's a very restrictive piece of functionality, which is why most customers choose to use a project-oriented approach over this function.

Time Zone Support

When you've activated the business function (LOG_EAM_TZS_1), your work orders can reside in multiple time zones, enabling planners and maintenance technicians to operate in different time zones. Figure 5.31 shows an example of the TIME ZONE panel showing which time zone an order belongs to in the maintenance order.

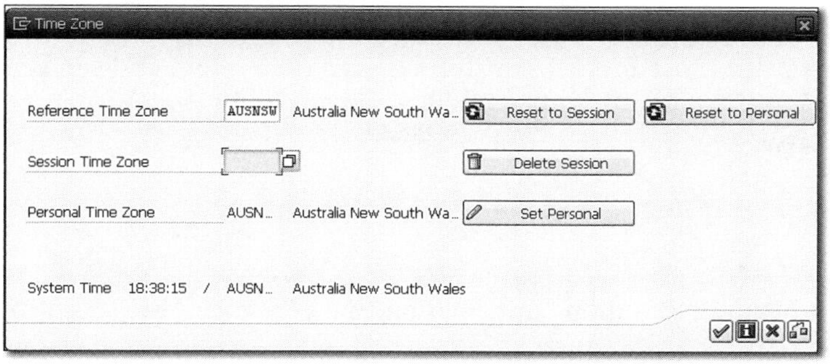

Figure 5.31 Time Zone

Billing a Service Order or Return/Repair Order

SAP CS supports two billing methods: billing based on the effort (also referred to as time and materials billing) and billing based on a fixed price. These two methods are represented in Figure 5.32.

The effort-based billing is usually performed in two steps; first you generate a billing request, which includes all the billing-relevant items, and then you generate a billing document. For fixed-price billing, you just need the billing document.

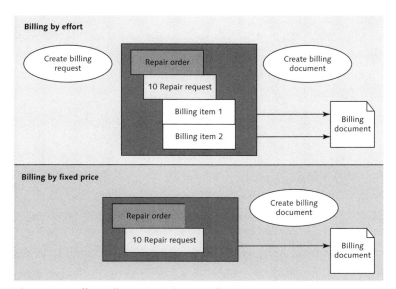

Figure 5.32 Effort Billing or Fixed-Price Billing

5.3.4 Customer Repair Order

The customer repair order is used when a customer has a faulty item and sends it back to have it repaired or simply to return the item. Figure 5.33 shows its structure and an example.

The structure of the order includes the following components:

- **Order header**
  The header of a work order contains information that is relevant to the entire return or repair order and is presented through the first dedicated tab. The header contains the customer details and references the purchase order number and the start and end date of the work.

- **Order item repair**
  The order item repair contains the item that the customer would like to have repaired or returned. It includes information about the service product, serviceable material, sales order stock, costs, status, and so on.

  A repair item is assigned a repair procedure within the configuration. The procedure contains information about the phase of the repair, which is defined as a stage such as registration, initiation of repair, execution, and finalizing. The stages are assigned to actions, which represent the activities undertaken. The following are standard available actions:

  - Return: The Return action allows you to include information about the returned item requested to be repaired, such as the material number and the return reason.

  - Dispatch Loan Item: During the repair of the customer equipment, you can provide loan equipment to the customer.

  - Exchange Part: An exchange part can be identified and sent to the customer.

  - Perform Repair: This action triggers the repair activity, enabling your service technicians to start the repair process. It can be accompanied by a service order.

  - Outbound Delivery: Representing the movement of a delivery of an item, such as the loan or the repaired item back to the customer.

  - Credit Memo Request: This allows you to generate a credit memo, which is a financial document used when a customer is reimbursed for the irreparable goods.

▷ Pick up replacement: This is the activity in which the loan item is picked up from the customer.

▷ Scrap the goods: This action documents that the item couldn't be repaired anymore but will instead be scrapped.

▷ Debit Memo Request: This financial document is used to record resource-related billing activities, which allow you to invoice based on actual time spent and actual material used.

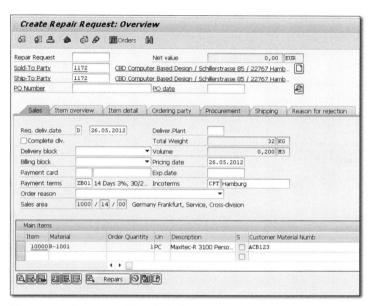

Figure 5.33 Returns and Repair Order

5.3.5 Measurement Documents

When a measuring point or counter is created for a technical object, you can record its performance and/or measurement into SAP by entering a measurement document. A measuring document contains the date the measuring was done, the results of the measuring, and the related measuring point. The technician can also include additional information, such as a short description with explanation. Since EHP 3, you can also enter measurement documents during order processing. You can also assign a processing status to the measurement document, which can indicate the need for a follow-up action based on the measurement value and whether this action has taken place or is still to be undertaken.

Measurement Readings

You can enter measurement documents into SAP PM or SAP CS in a number of different ways. You can record them manually directly in SAP via the GUI or SAP NetWeaver Portal, via individual data entry, or by using the several mass entry updates that are available. You can also record measuring documents via the Internet, which uses the Internet Application Component (IAC). To automatically record measurements (e.g., measurements can done during a production process, through a Supervisory Control and Data Acquisition System [SCADA] system), you can utilize the SAP PM–Process Control System (PCS) interface.

Figure 5.34 shows an example of a collective entry of measurements for a single piece of equipment; on the top, you enter the specific equipment number, and on the bottom, you see that the measurements DISTANCE, FUEL, and OIL have been defined as measurement points for this vehicle.

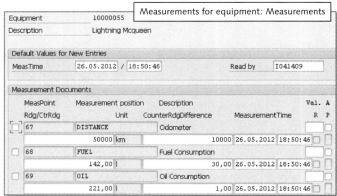

Figure 5.34 Collective Measurements for Equipment

Perform Reading via Mobile Device

Mobility is becoming increasingly important for SAP PM and SAP CS scenarios because it allows a paperless execution of maintenance tasks and makes it possible to process maintenance tasks anywhere, anytime. Within the SAP Mobile Platform, you can support two main scenarios:

▶ The online scenario, where the technician has direct access to the live SAP PM system (also referred to as the backend) onsite.

▶ The offline scenario, where you aren't connected to the backend system, which can be required when the location where the technician is working doesn't have any connectivity option. This can be the case, for example, when jobs need to be carried out at a customer site, out in the field, in remote locations, or underground.

Several different devices are supported, including mobile phones, PDAs, and tablets, as shown in Figure 5.35. The mobile scenarios can be supported by Radio Frequency Identification (RFID) readers or barcode reading devices to identify the technical object. We'll cover mobility in more detail in Chapter 9.

Figure 5.35 Collective Measurements for Equipment

5.3.6 Maintenance Plan

The maintenance plan is the object used within the preventive or condition-based maintenance scenario and represents the maintenance schedule and maintenance activities.

The structure of the maintenance plan can be broken down into the following components:

- **Maintenance plan header**
  This contains information that is relevant to the entire maintenance plan. The specific inputs might vary based on the maintenance category chosen.

  - MAINTENANCE PLAN CYCLE: This contains the interval after which a task becomes due. For time-based cycles, this can be, for example, every 3 months; for performance-based cycles, it can be, for example, every 6,000 miles.

  - MAINTENANCE PLAN SCHEDULING PARAMETERS: This contains the detailed time scheduling settings, (e.g., the system behaviors to the next call data, when a call object was performed earlier or later than planned, which calendar is used for determining available dates, the call horizon, etc.). The call horizon determines when a call for the plan gets created in relation to the cycle of a year. This can be done either immediately (0%), on the planned date (100%), or during a period before the call date (80%, meaning after 80% of a year has passed), which gives you time to arrange your required resources to execute the work.

  - MAINTENANCE PLAN ADDITIONAL DATA: This tab contains the maintenance plan category. The category determines which call object the maintenance plan will create when maintenance is due. There are several call objects and standard categories available: maintenance notification, maintenance order, service entry sheet, and service notification with or without outline agreements.

- **Maintenance item**
  In the maintenance item, you specify which preventive maintenance tasks need to be performed regularly at a specific technical object or group of object. Each maintenance plan always contains at least one maintenance item.

  - Reference objects: This area contains the technical object to which the maintenance plan is related.

  - Object list item: The object list item contains a list of technical objects that are assigned to this particular maintenance item. With an object list, you can create logical groups of similar or interlinked technical objects that can then be linked with a group of maintenance activities. The scenario is particularly useful when you're performing small preventive maintenance tasks that don't require you to collect the maintenance cost or evaluate activities for all the technical objects specifically. An example could be general visual inspections where, instead of creating an order for each object, you create one order with all objects in the object list. Once called, the object list will be copied into the call object (such as `noti` or `workorder`).

▷ Item location: The item location contains the location data of the plan and the account assignment data.

▷ Task list (optional): You can add a maintenance task list to the maintenance plan (Section Preventive Maintenance has more details). This is optional. When no task list is assigned to the maintenance plan, the short description of the plan will be used as operational data in the call object, which will provide no planned cost.

An example of a maintenance plan is shown in Figure 5.36.

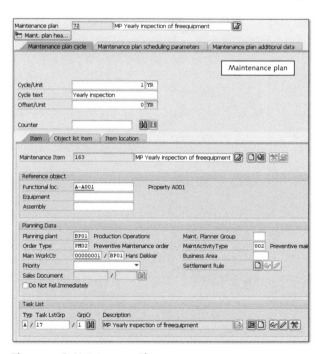

Figure 5.36 Maintenance Plan

5.3.7 Maintenance Strategy

The maintenance strategy can be used when recording maintenance activities to distinguish which tasks are relevant based on the maintenance package due. The strategy is used within the strategy-based maintenance plan and within the task list.

The structure of a maintenance strategy is composed of two pieces:

▸ **Maintenance strategy header**
The strategy header contains data that is relevant for the entire strategy. It includes the Scheduling indicator (which flags the strategy as performance- or time-based), the Strategy unit, and the scheduling parameters (such as Call Horizon and Shift Factors). Which specific scheduling parameters are active depends on the Scheduling Indicator.

▸ **Maintenance strategy packages**
The maintenance packages contain the different maintenance intervals and their relationship to each other.

Figure 5.37 shows an example of a strategy header and strategy packages.

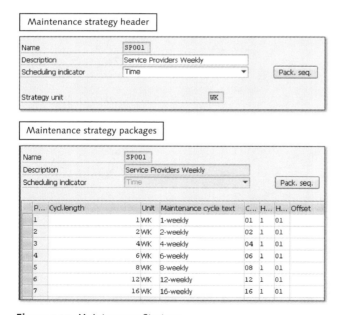

Figure 5.37 Maintenance Strategy

5.3.8 Maintenance Task List

The maintenance task list has the same structure as the task list described in Chapter 3, so we won't spend much time on it here. The only difference is that when you want to record activities based on a maintenance strategy, you can assign the strategy to the task list header. After you've assigned it, you can assign the task list operations to the maintenance packages. Figure 5.38 shows the maintenance task list header, operations, and assignment of operations.

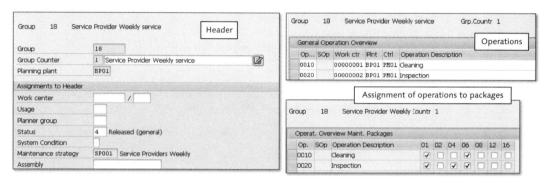

Figure 5.38 Strategy Task List Example

5.3.9 Service Contracts

The service contract is used within SAP CS to specific a long-term agreement with a customer that includes services. In a service contract, you define an SAP CS agreement by stating the period of the contract, the services included, the price agreements and billing information, and which technical objects are covered.

The structure of service contracts can be broken down into the following parts:

▶ **Order header**
  The header of the contract contains information that is relevant for the entire document, including the following:

  ▷ Customer data

  ▷ Contract data (e.g., start and end dates)

  ▷ Pricing and billing data (e.g., a payment plan on a monthly basis)

▶ **Order items**

This section contains information relevant only to the service order item, including the following:

▷ Services provided

▷ Conditions

▷ Billing plans

▷ Price agreements

▷ Assigned technical objects

Figure 5.39 shows an example of a service contract for Hershey's, Inc.

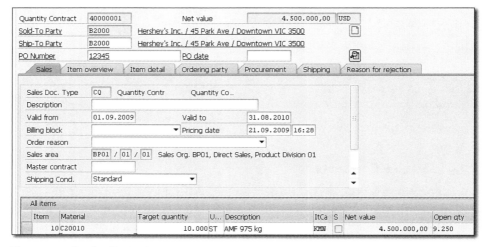

Figure 5.39 Service Contract

5.3.10 Visualization and Publication

To process and automate asset-related or product-related documents for technical publications, training materials, manufacturing assembly, and repair instructions, you can chose to use SAP Interactive Forms by Adobe. Adobe Forms can bridge the paper-to-digital divide by helping organizations that rely heavily on paper forms leverage the versatility, consistency, and accessibility of these electronic forms; they can be used by organizations in any industry to extend the power of SAP and other software in automated form and document-based processes. The interactive document can be processed either online or offline, depending on your requirements. Because SAP Interactive Forms by Adobe are intuitive and easy to use, they accommodate all types of users both within and beyond the firewall.

Figure 5.40 shows an example of an SAP Interactive Form used during vehicle inspections. The easy-to-use Adobe LiveCycle Designer is integrated within the SAP developer environment to rapidly develop customized and personalized papers such as forms and documents.

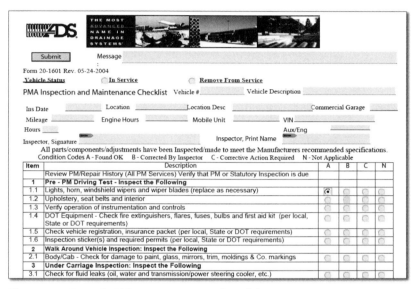

Figure 5.40 Example SAP Interactive Forms by Adobe

5.3.11 Logbook or Shift Reports

The logbook provides asset operations personnel with an easy-to-use tool to log defects and operational data. The shift note and report allow you to collect information from a specific shift to inform the next shift of what has happened during the previous shift.

Logbook

The *logbook* provides personnel who are operating the assets (such as maintenance engineers and technicians) with an easy-to-use tool to log defects and operational data during execution of daily maintenance tasks. It can possibly replace existing paper-based logbooks. The logbook originated as an aerospace and defense industry solution for logging the daily line maintenance tasks when maintaining aircrafts and supporting the Maintenance, Repair, and Overhaul (MRO). There the logbook was used to record both defects encountered during aircraft flights and the actions taken to correct them and could include additional information such as flight data, the names of the crew members, flight parameters, payload data, fuelling data, flight hours, and cycles operated. By using the logbook as an input, the engineer can release the aircraft back to service when satisfied that the defects have been corrected.

Because other industries also use logbooks for similar purpose, the logbook has been made available as a general function in SAP PLM (and SAP ERP). You can activate the logbook business function by the activation of business functions LOG_EAM_POM and LOG_EAM_POM2 in the Switch Framework (note that additional prerequisites apply) and additional configuration settings are required.

The following data can be captured in the logbook:

▶ **Capture defects and follow-up documents from the defect, or defer defects**
The defect found gets logged as a log notification in the logbook. This notification can be used to trigger follow-up processes such as a corrective maintenance process, where a notification and maintenance order get created to perform the repair.

▶ **Monitor defects**
Captured defects can be monitored and analyzed in real time by maintenance engineers. They are able to analyze the defect, include repair instructions, plan operations, and reserve spare parts to fix the defects.

▶ **Capture operational data**
You can capture operational data against the technical object as necessary. Operational data is collected by using measurement documents and by logging additional fields against these technical objects. Accurate daily logging of current counter readings will improve preventive maintenance planning.

▶ **Complete maintenance activities**
After the repair has been executed, the maintenance technician can capture the maintenance execution information within a maintenance order. When components have been replaced either serialized or nonserialized, the dismantling of the faulty part and installation of the new part can be documented as well. Apart from the installation information, all general maintenance confirmation

activities, such as defect information, time recording, and so on can be documented, which can include the use of digital signatures.

▸ **Defer defects**
Quality engineers and maintenance technicians can defer a defect to a more suitable time slot. This business decision is recorded within the defect and becomes immediately visible to other users such as maintenance planners.

▸ **Certify complete maintenance activities**
As part of the confirmation processes, after maintenance technicians have entered the maintenance execution information, this information can be verified and digitally certified for correctness and completeness. Once you certify the logbook, you're no longer able to make any further changes to the log, all log entries have been completed correctly, and the asset can be re-released for service. Certification is done via digital signatures, which document the user's first and last name, time stamps, and comments to ensure traceability. Additional identification software can be used when required.

A logbook can be created within SAP PM automatically (Transaction LBK1) as a folder assigned to the technical object. In its details, the logbook uses objects (such as notifications, orders, materials, and measurements) from SAP PM in a hierarchical structure, which must be chosen within the SAP PM configuration.

Figure 5.41 shows the structure of the logbook. The top element of the logbook is the logbook folder, which is connected to the technical object and used to collect all log entries. Within this folder, you can include log entries, which are either operational log entries in the form of measurement documents or defects in the form of notifications.

Shift Note

Via the shift report, you can collect information from a specific shift to inform the next shift of what has happened during the previous shift. A shift note can include brief comments for events or special occurrences. They can be created either for a specific work center or a technical object. The shift note was a function offered within PP but has recently been added to SAP PM. You can either extend the use of one of your notifications by including the shift note in it, or you can define a shift note specifically to record shift notes. The menu path for shift notes can be found under LOGISTICS • CENTRAL FUNCTIONS • SHIFT NOTES AND REPORTS. Figure 5.42 shows an example of a technical object shift note.

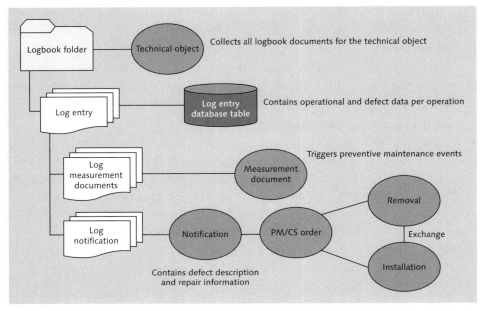

Figure 5.41 Logbook

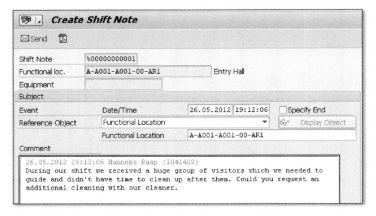

Figure 5.42 Shift Note

Shift Report

A shift report such as the one shown in Figure 5.43 can be generated either for a specific work center or a technical object; it contains a summarization of everything that has happened during a given period. You can either look up a shift report in the system, or you can generate a PDF document (delivered within the standard), which contains several sections. Shift reports can be stored in the Knowledge Provider (KPro) or SAP DMS.

The following sections are delivered within SAP standard and can be activated in the configuration: cover sheet, shift notes, completion confirmations, goods movements, maintenance notifications, maintenance orders, and work clearance documents.

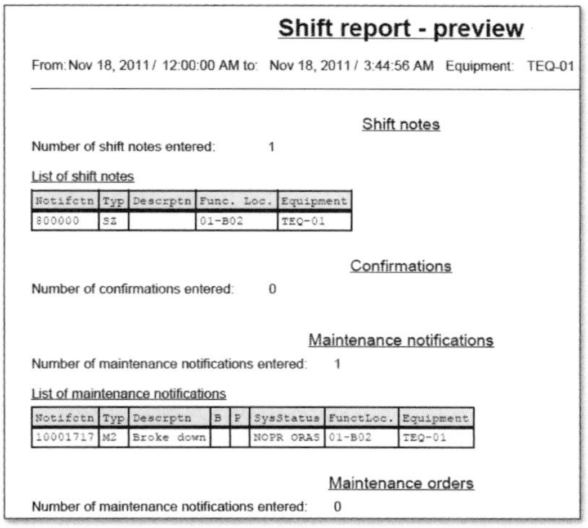

Shift report - preview

From: Nov 18, 2011 / 12:00:00 AM to: Nov 18, 2011 / 3:44:56 AM Equipment: TEQ-01

Shift notes

Number of shift notes entered: 1

List of shift notes

Notifctn	Typ	Descrptn	Func. Loc.	Equipment
800000	SZ		01-B02	TEQ-01

Confirmations

Number of confirmations entered: 0

Maintenance notifications

Number of maintenance notifications entered: 1

List of maintenance notifications

Notifctn	Typ	Descrptn	B	P	SysStatus	FunctLoc.	Equipment
10001717	M2	Broke down			NOPR ORAS	01-B02	TEQ-01

Maintenance orders

Number of maintenance notifications entered: 0

Figure 5.43 Shift Report

Section 5.3 has given you an overview of the main transactional objects used within both SAP PM and SAP CS, explaining the most commonly used objects such as object information, notification, work order and repair order, measurement document, maintenance plan, and service contract. Less common are the visualization and publication, as well as the logbook and shift note objects, because these are relatively recent additions. The next section will cover configuration management and explain how you can use the master data collected for a technical object structure to verify its configuration.

5.4 Configuration Management

Configuration management allows you to manage the actual configuration of technical objects. After you've mapped your company's maintainable items to

SAP PM technical objects, the next step is to use the categorization and classification system to further describe your technical objects. You can use the BOM to specify the individual components of a technical object, which is either specific to the technical object or not, in which case you can assign a general material BOM, also referred to as an indirect assignment. The actual technical object configuration can be used to check whether all the elements of the structure have been maintained according to a manufacturer, supplier, or your organization's recommended configuration.

This recommended configuration—or the allowed configuration—contains the business rules regarding validity. This allows you to validate whether or not your actual configuration complies with the recommended one. In case of noncompliance, a warning can be issued or even stricter measures can be enforced so that the technical object isn't being allowed back into operation. Finally, we'll explore the options of spare parts management and maintenance catalogs, which can be used to support maintenance processes.

5.4.1 Categorize and Classify Technical Objects

The category is also an important control object, where settings such as the activation of change documents are activated. Alongside the functional location category and equipment category, you can use object types and object classification to group logically similar technical objects. The functional location category and equipment category are two independent configuration tables, where the object type (which specifies the technical object type) is a shared field available in both the functional location and equipment master record. As shown in Figure 5.44, the equipment category FLEET is used, and the object type CAR, chosen from the OBJECT TYPE dropdown list, has been assigned.

As described in Chapter 3, you'll define your own fields or characteristics through classification. The functional location can be classified by using class type 003 FUNCTIONAL LOCATION, and the equipment uses class type 002 EQUIPMENT. You can access classification details in the technical object by dedicating a tab or by accessing it via the menu GOTO • CLASS OVERVIEW in the master record, of which Figure 5.45 is an example.

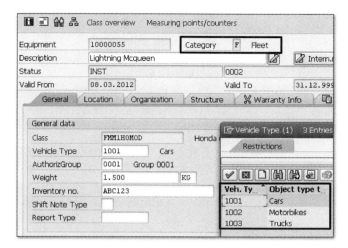

Figure 5.44 Category and Object Type

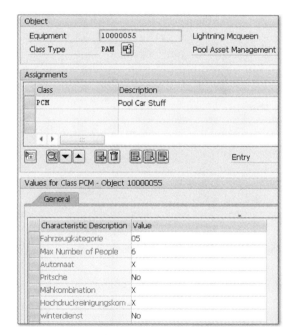

Figure 5.45 Classification

5.4.2 Use Bill of Materials

Within SAP PM and SAP CS, you can use a BOM for two different purposes:

- Structuring the technical object
- Planning spare parts either in the order or in the task list

You can choose to create a specific equipment or functional location BOM directly or use indirect assignment by assigning the material BOM to the technical object master record using the CONSTRUCTION TYPE field (available on the STRUCTURE tab for this purpose). Indirect assignment can be very useful when you have several similar pieces of equipment or functional locations. You can create a material and a material BOM once and assign this BOM to multiple equipment masters and/or functional locations masters. Return to Chapter 3 for more details on BOMs.

5.4.3 Verify Configuration

Part of setting up your technical object structure is performing a configuration check. This function allows you to verify your actual technical object structure configuration against an approved target configuration. This step in the master data maintenance process is optional, although several industries require this step before allowing use of the technical object.

Like the logbook, configuration control originated as an aerospace and defense industry solution. The process is used within the aviation industry to check whether the actual plane conforms to the expected structure, which needs to be verified before a plane is allowed to take off.

When you want to use configuration control, you need to use Integrated Product and Process Engineering (iPPE) to define the target structure via the master part list (MPL), which is assigned to the technical object in SAP PM via the function identifier. After this has been activated for the technical object category, you can carry out your maintenance activities as normal in SAP PM and the configuration check at any time within the iPPE. They are connected to one another via the configuration details in the actual configuration via the FID function.

On the left side of Figure 5.46, you see the actual configuration of an airplane; right below it, you see how the target structure has been set up in a MPL. After you perform the configuration check, the system will show you on the left-hand side of the workbench the results of the check, where every airport item will be checked against the MPL. Problems will be highlighted by yellow (triangle) or red (circle). This particular check has raised two warnings and one error. For the error, we investigate further and find that this spot allows two parts; however, no part has been detected.

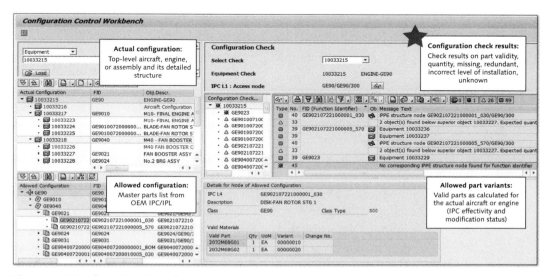

Figure 5.46 Configuration Control

Using the iPPE Workbench, you can verify your *actual configuration*, which is done by comparing the "actual" technical structure, including functional locations, equipment, and materials, to an "expected" structure defined through the MPL. Part of configuration management includes the ability to maintain spare parts and maintenance catalogs to plan and use during maintenance preparation, scheduling, or execution.

5.4.4 Spare Parts Management and Maintenance Catalogs

In this section, we'll explore the options of spare parts management and maintenance catalogs, which can be used to support maintenance processes. Catalog and parts management enables you to use internal or external catalogs when planning spare parts and components on your work order as well as having a predefined list available of catalog items during execution of your work order to assist in picking parts that are unplanned items. Within SAP ERP, you can set up and use materials, via the following options:

1. Use material masters from within SAP MM, where they can be represented as either stock items or as nonstock items (known as consumables). We'll describe these in more detail in the discussion of the breakdown maintenance business process in Section 5.5.5.

2. Use BOMs representing the spare parts, as described in Section 5.4.2.

3. Use a separate product from the SAP portfolio called spare parts management.

4. Use spare parts catalogs (which are either set up internally by your own organization or vendor-provided catalogs), as discussed next.

Catalog and parts management enables you to use internal or external catalogs when planning spare parts and components. You can either set up your own defined catalogs, or you can load catalogs provided by third-party suppliers. After they've been loaded, you can use catalogs during your work order planning stage to pick a component from the catalog within the COMPONENTS tab by punching out to the catalog. After you've picked the appropriate part, it will translate it to your SAP component. It will translate the vendor part into either a company part (which can be a stock or nonstock part), or it can be added as a description item. Of course, price details can be copied as part of this procedure. Figure 5.47 shows an example of a catalog where first you punch out on to the catalog by choosing the CATALOG icon. When multiple catalogs are available, you need to pick the appropriate one and browse the catalog until you find the spare part, which is copied when selected. This last step often consists of multiple smaller steps that vary depending on the specific catalog, but the concept is the same.

The technology used for setting up catalogs is the Open Catalog Interface (OCI), which originated within the SAP Supplier Relationship Management (SAP SRM) offerings and has been incorporated into SAP ERP. Before you can use catalogs, you'll need to configure its use settings in the IMG under MAINTENANCE AND CUSTOMER SERVICE SETTINGS. To find out more details on the specific catalog products available, please consult the SAP Service Marketplace.

> **Note**
>
> Catalogs are also used within a notification to code the problem, causes, and so on. These are known as *maintenance catalogs* and are described in more detail in Section 5.2.2; just be careful not to confuse them.

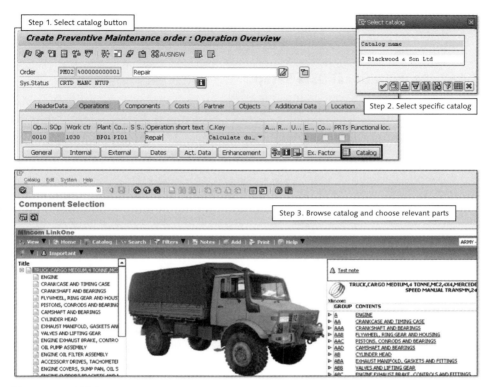

Figure 5.47 Catalog

5.5 Main Maintenance and Customer Service Processes

Let's examine the main business processes that are supported within SAP PM and SAP CS. Apart from maintenance cost budgeting, they are all part of SAP ERP 6. The processes can be done in both SAP PM and SAP CS, with the exception of the returns and repairs, which are only customer-specific. The takeover and handover process requires the use of SAP NetWeaver Portal.

Whether or not a process is relevant for your organization is often determined during the scoping phase of an implementation project. The business process can be further designed, detailed, and configured based on a blueprint, which is the design document and phase as defined by SAP's ASAP project methodology. To accelerate blueprint and implementation activities, SAP offers best practices,

Rapid Deployment Solutions, and services, which provide standardized, prepackaged, fixed-scope and fixed-price solutions that reduce risk and cost.

5.5.1 Organizational Data Setup

Before you can perform any master data maintenance or service processing, you have to set up the organizational structure supporting these processes within the SAP Configuration Guide and within the master data elements. Figure 5.48 displays the process for the setup of the organization structure.

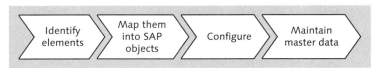

Figure 5.48 Set Up Organizational Data

Let's walk through the organizational data setup process:

1. **Identify elements.**
   First you need to identify all the maintenance and customer service organizational elements that are relevant for your organization. During this step, you identify both the maintenance-specific organizational elements (such as maintenance sites and planning sites, the different work crews, and the use of contractors and maintenance planners) as well as determine the specific assets that your organization is responsible for in either maintenance activities (SAP PM) or servicing activities (SAP CS).

2. **Map them into SAP objects.**
   After you've identified these elements and entities, you need to map them to the appropriate object. (Please refer to Chapter 3, Section 3.1.1, for details about which organizational elements are available and which master data elements are available.)

3. **Configure.**
   The configuration through Customizing of the selected element (e.g., a maintenance planning plant) occurs at this time.

4. **Maintain master data.**
   When master data elements have been chosen to represent the organizational data, such as a work center, they need to be created through the master data maintenance process, which is described in more detail in the next section.

5.5.2 Technical Objects

Figure 5.49 shows the process for setting up the master data.

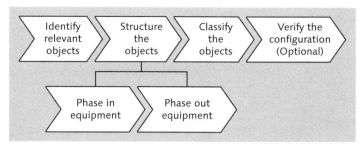

Figure 5.49 Master Data Maintenance

Let's walk through the master data maintenance process:

1. **Identify relevant objects.**
   First identify which objects are relevant to maintenance or are relevant from an SAP EAM perspective—for example, the different production lines within a manufacturing facility; the networks (power, water, gas, or telecom) that provide services; the company's real estate portfolio with all the owned properties, land, and buildings, and the relevant systems inside; and the company's fleet, such as vehicles, ships, and airplanes. Basically the entire asset portfolio of the organization for which you're responsible from an SAP PM and SAP EAM perspective must be identified.

2. **Structure the objects.**
   Understand how the relevant objects will be translated into the master data element available. When pieces of equipment are identified as part of the structure, you can use the PHASE IN EQUIPMENT subprocess (see Figure 5.50) to add equipment with all the additional master data elements such as documents, measurement points, task lists, and so on. The PHASE OUT EQUIPMENT subprocess (see Figure 5.51) is the business process where a piece of equipment is being removed from operation. Apart from deactivating the master data, any outstanding notifications and orders need to be reviewed and closed, and the equipment must be deactivated or removed from maintenance plans. Only after all these activities have taken place can you archive the master data from your system. The exchange function allows you to phase out one piece of equipment and replace it with another, so this is the combination of the two subprocesses.

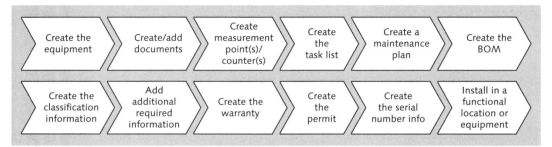

Figure 5.50 Phase In Equipment

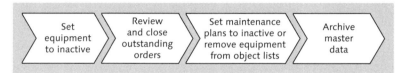

Figure 5.51 Phase Out Equipment

To install or dismantle a piece of equipment, you can use either the master data object (i.e., the functional location or the equipment) to perform this task, or you can use the install, exchange, and dismantle transaction (Transaction IE4N), which can be found in the PLANT MAINTENANCE MANAGEMENT OF TECHNICAL OBJECTS menu as a submenu called CONFIGURATION CONTROL. The advantage of using this transaction is that apart from the change in master data as a result, the material movements and any notification data are also captured here. You can set up user-specific defaults to simplify the data entry.

3. **Classify the objects.**
   Make sure the technical object can be assigned to the appropriate categories, including the optional additional information necessary via classification.

4. **Verify the configuration.**
   Within the CONFIGURATION CONTROL function, you can verify your actual configuration of a technical object structure against an approved target configuration, as described in more detail in Section 5.4.

5.5.3   Handover and Takeover

In capital-intensive industries, technical objects such as airplanes, turbines, and serialized components and their configurations are tracked and monitored carefully over their entire lifecycle. This ensures safety and compliance with legal requirements and industry standards. During different stages in their lifecycle (e.g., during sales or repair work), the technical objects are handed over to various business partners. When the business partners receive the technical object, work on the configuration, and report back to the owner the changes to the configuration, they usually build a detailed structure of the technical object in their IT system with all the applicable maintenance requirements for the technical object and its components.

Because the handover and takeover scenario is available through the SAP NetWeaver Portal, using the portal is a prerequisite to use this scenario. It's executed using a central user interface and has the following advantages:

- Less time needed to set up the data
- Reduction of the amount of errors
- Simplified transfer of data of complex technical object structures during handover and takeover
- Improved transparency of progress and status of transfer at any time during the handover or takeover
- Electronic data transfer via Extensible Markup Language (XML)
- Accelerated process of creating and updating object structures for both the asset owner and for the subcontractor
- Reduced complexity on the operational level by automatic update functionality and mass maintenance functions

The functions for handover and takeover of technical objects can be used to support this process because they allow you to construct the data for new, used, or repairable technical objects efficiently and to exchange the technical object structure between different systems. The takeover and handover functions are available to help asset owners transfer complex technical objects to subcontractors for service or repair work by facilitating and accelerating a time-consuming and complex process that runs across system boundaries.

Handover and takeover has been available since EHP 3; to use it, you need to activate the business function LOG_EAM_TOHO and use the SAP NetWeaver Portal as well as SAP NetWeaver Folders Management. The process is represented in Figure 5.52, in which the asset owner carries out the process steps marked ❶, and the subcontractor performs the process steps marked ❷.

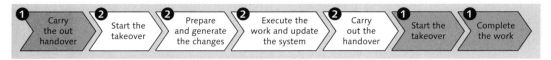

Figure 5.52 Process Handover and Takeover

Let's examine the handover and takeover process steps individually:

1. **Carry out the handover.**
   The asset owner loads the profile and loads the existing objects (configuration). These objects are converted into an XML file and the file is saved, which leads to a record in SAP NetWeaver Folders Management.

   As soon as the subcontractor starts the takeover, the asset owner will notice that the maintenance plans are stopped, any outstanding notification and order are changed to the In Process status, and the system status for technical objects is updated, so it's clearly the subcontractor.

2. **Start the takeover.**
   The subcontractor loads the profile, loads the XML file, and copies the structure. Functional locations, equipment, equipment BOMs, measuring points, and counters are supported; materials and MPLs aren't supported.

3. **Prepare and generate the changes.**
   The subcontractor performs a consistency check and performs changes.

4. **Execute the work and update the system.**
   The subcontractor performs the work on the structure and updates the information of the objects

5. **Carry out the handover.**
   The subcontractor loads the profile, converts the structure to an XML file, and sends the XML file back to the asset owner.

6. **Start the takeover.**
   The asset owner receives the XML file, including the profile, and copies changes to the existing structures, such as changes to an equipment or the creation of new equipment. Remember to perform a consistency check first! Figure 5.53 shows an example of a takeover.

7. **Complete the work.**
   The asset owner can close outstanding notifications from within the phase-in table and create and schedule new maintenance plans.

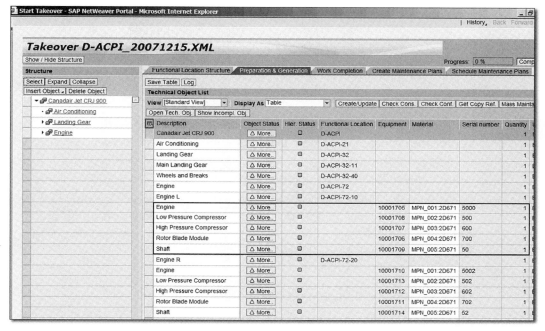

Figure 5.53 Takeover: Asset Owner Receives Updates

5.5.4 Maintenance Cost Budgeting

Let's now shift our attention to how maintenance activities can be budgeted using SAP ERP 6. This section describes budgeting options from a maintenance perspective; however, budgeting is usually a business activity taking place in multiple areas within a business, so it can't be viewed this simplistically. The following section will provide you with the most commonly used budgeting scenarios in maintenance but can't possibly cover all possible budget solutions. Which budgeting and planning tool is right for your organization should be approached from this broader perspective and is often determined by the finance workstream.

To perform budgeting activities related to maintenance work, you have several options:

1. Use the budgeting capabilities within SAP PM, which can be found via the menu path: PLANT MAINTENANCE • MAINTENANCE PROCESSING • ORDER • BUDGETING.

Here you can define a budget per maintenance order. This isn't a widely use maintenance budgeting option because most companies define their maintenance budget at a higher level and won't budget at the individual order level. This is why this option hasn't been further described.

2. Use SAP PS with the standard integration capabilities to SAP PM. You set up a project structure, which reflects how you want to manage your maintenance budget. This budgeting option is briefly explained in the following section.

3. Use the maintenance cost budgeting tool. The MCB tool requires SAP NetWeaver Business Warehouse (SAP NetWeaver BW). This option will also be briefly introduced in the next section.

4. You can also choose to use SAP Business Planning and Consolidation (SAP BPC), which is part of the SAP BusinessObjects product offerings and is an enterprise planning tool. This option isn't part of the scope of this book and won't be explained in more detail.

Maintenance Cost Budgeting Using SAP Project System

When using SAP PS as your dedicated budgeting tool, you need to set up a project structure that reflects the different levels at which you want to manage your maintenance budget. The next step is to track and trace the planned and actual costs through the project and to assign each maintenance order that is generated to the appropriate WBS element. This assignment can either be done manually or automatically by defaulting a WBS element from the technical object's master data, as is represented in Figure 5.54.

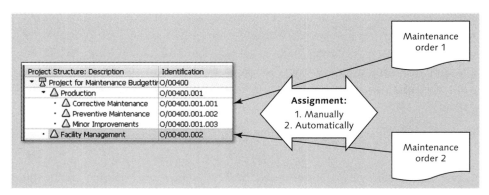

Figure 5.54 Maintenance Budgeting with SAP PS

You have to assign a WBS element in the organizational data of the technical object. After this assignment has been done (and configuration has been set up correctly), you can see the aggregated planned and actuals from the maintenance orders in the budgeting tools in SAP PS.

Next, you can use the standard available budgeting tools from SAP PS to assign the original budgets and following supplements. For more details on how this works, see Chapter 7.

Maintenance Cost Budgeting Using MCB

Maintenance Cost Budgeting (MCB) is a web-based tool used to build a maintenance budget based on data from an SAP ERP system. Maintenance cost budgeting uses two important components from the SAP Business Suite:

▶ The data from the SAP PM component

▶ The planning and budgeting capabilities performed through SAP NetWeaver BW

The following activities can be performed in maintenance cost budgeting:

▶ Define and initiate the budget planning process.

▶ Plan the budget on appropriate levels, based on the desired budget strategy.

▶ Approve or reject budget proposals.

▶ Trigger workflow.

▶ Perform reporting.

The business processes that include these activities are shown in Figure 5.55 and will be briefly explained in the following section, which will be followed with the explanation of the two budget methods supported in maintenance cost budgeting: history-based budgeting using historic maintenance costs to propose a budget, and zero-based budgeting, which uses the planned preventive maintenance costs to create a proposal.

Figure 5.55 shows the maintenance cost budgeting process for building a maintenance budget.

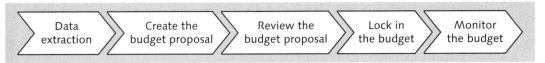

Figure 5.55 Maintenance Cost Budgeting Process

Let's walk through it now:

1. **Data extraction.**
   The information necessary for the chosen budgeting method needs to be extracted from the SAP ERP environment into the SAP NetWeaver BW–Business Planning and Simulation (BPS) system. For history-based budgeting, this is the actual cost of the maintenance orders. For zero-based budgeting, this is the planned future costs, from maintenance plans and task lists. We'll go into these two types of budgeting shortly.

2. **Create the budget proposal.**
   The system will generate a budget proposal based on the budget method chosen. This proposal can be adopted 1:1, or it can be changed either by applying an increase/decrease percentage or by manually overwriting the proposal, allowing full flexibility. Figure 5.56 shows an example of a budget proposal that has been generated using the zero-based budgeting method. The screenshot shows the budget proposal figure the system proposes per functional location and equipment.

3. **Review the budget proposal.**
   The manager who receives the budget proposal can either approve or reject the proposal.

4. **Lock in the budget.**
   After a budget has been approved, it will be locked in; the budget can be retracted into the SAP ERP system.

5. **Monitor the budget.**
   After the budget has been set, you can monitor its use by reviewing planned costs, actual costs, planned commitments, and actual commitments. Figure 5.57 shows two reports delivered as part of standard maintenance cost budgeting: the TOTAL BUDGET PROPOSAL (the breakdown of the budget proposal per budget category) and the BUDGET SPECIFICATION (the actual budget assigned again per budget category).

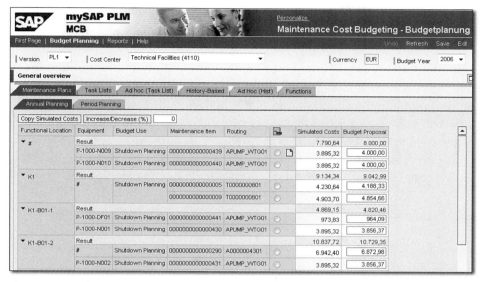

Figure 5.56 Budget Proposal

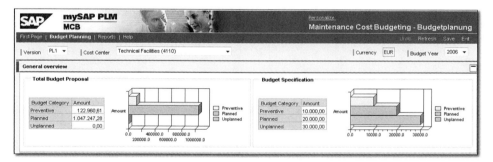

Figure 5.57 Monitor Budget

The following primary benefits can be gained from using the MCB tool:

▶ Standardized and automated budget process

▶ Reduction in budget preparation time because data extraction from the back-end system happens automatically

▶ Better data integrity than budgeting based on spreadsheets

▶ Better transparency of the budget planning process and budget monitoring, where budget changes are tracked and controlled through status management

▶ A user-friendly frontend, which is accessible from anywhere

▶ Flexible and accurate reporting that enables budget monitoring

Budgeting Methods and Categories

Maintenance cost budgeting supports two ways of budgeting: the history-based budgeting method and zero-based budgeting method. History-based budgeting uses SAP PM order history in the actual cost to create a budget proposal. The zero-based budgeting method, which is used by most organizations, uses the future expected planned cost (also called simulated planned costs) to calculate a budget proposal. Figure 5.58 compares the two budgeting methods.

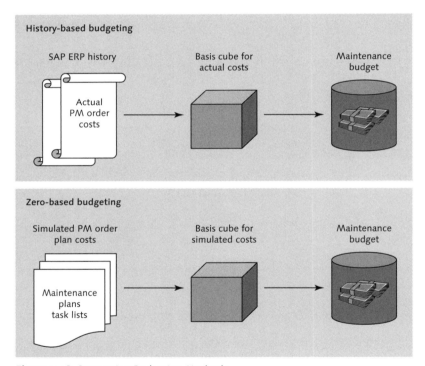

Figure 5.58 Supporting Budgeting Methods

Planning budgets only on the level of a budget method are useful primarily as a first, rough calculation. For a more detailed budget planning, you can distribute your budget to budget categories. In the standard software, the following three categories are supported, as shown in Figure 5.59, and all are linked to the two budgeting methods:

- Preventive maintenance costs (e.g., SAP PM maintenance plan items)
- Planned/corrective maintenance costs (e.g., SAP PM: PM task lists)
- Unplanned/corrective maintenance costs (e.g., SAP PM: PM orders) not covered by the previous two categories

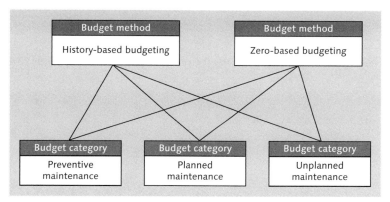

Figure 5.59 Budget Methods and Categories

In addition to using the budget category, you can plan and group budgets along a second, more maintenance business-driven means with the *budget use* feature. SAP won't deliver predefined budget uses, however, when budget categories aren't sufficient to cover your individual business needs, you can define your own. Examples of budget uses are engineering modifications and shutdowns.

You can restrict both budget use and budget category according to planning scenarios. SAP provides the following planning scenarios with preconfigured standard entries:

- The history-based scenario is based on history, and the budget categories are combined in one overall planning scenario. This scenario can create records with the budget categories PREVENTIVE, PLANNED, or UNPLANNED.
- The maintenance plan scenario is zero-based and can only create records with budget use PREVENTIVE.
- The task list scenario is zero-based and can only create records with budget use PLANNED.
- The ad hoc (plan) scenario is zero-based and can create records with budget categories PLANNED or UNPLANNED.

Maintenance Cost Budgeting Roles

To perform the different functions within the budgeting process, the following roles are provided with the standard software:

▶ **MCB administrator**
Provides maintenance cost budgeting Customizing or configuration.

▶ **Maintenance manager (existing SAP ERP role)**
Defines, triggers, monitors, and closes the budget planning process.

▶ **Maintenance budget planner (or maintenance planner; existing SAP ERP role)**
Plans the budget for an organizational area.

▶ **Maintenance engineer (existing SAP ERP role)**
Ensures completeness and correctness of operative master data.

▶ **BW operator**
Provides SAP NetWeaver BW–BPS data basis.

Status and Tracking System

The SAP NetWeaver BW–BPS Status and Tracking System (STS) provides an automatically triggered supervision of the planning round's progress. STS helps you monitor the processing progress within the different planning tasks of your company. The system keeps a record of the iterations, which run through a specific planning task in practice (requisition note bottom-up, resource assignment top-down) and brings together the planning objects created in the planning environment with the employees who edit the actual planning tasks with these objects. STS is a web-based application exclusively designed for execution in a web browser. Through traffic lights, you can get a quick view on the progress and status of the activities and send email to involved employees. As a result, you can execute the work where the system supports you wherever you are—without any special installations on your PC. On the other hand, you customize (configure) subplans and the planning sessions belonging to them in the SAP NetWeaver BW system.

The planning process in the STS is divided into the following elements:

▶ **Subplan**
This is a specific business subarea of business planning (e.g., profit planning, balance sheet planning, cost center planning).

▶ **Planning session**
This single program is run from the iterative planning process that aims for a better adjustment of deviating plan values with every iteration (e.g., requisition note vs. resource assignment, sales key figures vs. sales targets). A planning session is used in STS for the versioning of the different planning cycles so that the approximation process is documented in the system and can be understood. A particular subtask can change status times (e.g., New, For Approval, Rejected, For Approval, or Approved) several times within a planning session. A planning session is completed when all the subtasks it contains have the Approved status.

▶ **Organizational hierarchy**
This part of the hierarchical organizational structure of your company describes the employees involved in the planning process and their corporate relations. Every hierarchy node represents a person responsible for a specific subplan within the planning process. At the same time, the hierarchy serves as a guiding line for the approval process of a subplan and for performing status-dependent notification management.

5.5.5 Breakdown Maintenance

Breakdown maintenance is a form of corrective maintenance, which basically means that maintenance actions are carried out to restore a defective item to a specified condition. Breakdown maintenance is simply "run to failure"; it allows no intervention in plant operation, and plant maintenance only happens when forced by breakdown. The process of breakdown maintenance is shown in Figure 5.60. The first two steps are boxed because they can be done together as one step when this is configured.

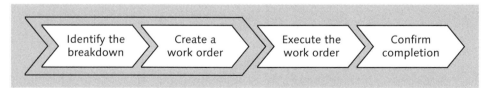

Figure 5.60 Breakdown Maintenance Process

Let's walk through it now:

1. **Identify the breakdown.**
   As soon as a breakdown has been identified, you can use a breakdown notification to enter it into the system. The notification holds the detailed data of the breakdown (e.g., the effected object, person reporting the breakdown, the malfunction details through codes, a description, and the priority of the notification). To speed up the process, you can create a notification and a work order together, when this has been activated through configuration.

2. **Create a work order.**
   To record activities, use spare parts, and collect cost against a breakdown, you need to set up a work order. The activities required can be done by internal employees, which will be assigned to the work order operation through a work center as Figure 5.61 shows.

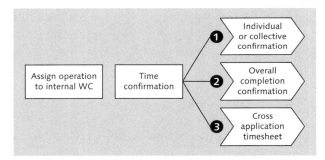

Figure 5.61 Internal Work Order Creation

It's also possible to have the maintenance operations either partly or completely performed externally. Performing operations externally can be done through three different scenarios; the first two scenarios include integration to procurement, and the last one is a more indirect approach:

▶ Set up an external work center. The link between the bought services and the performed services will be made indirectly, by assigning both the external work center and the procurement document (either a purchase order or contract) to the same cost center. This can be very useful when you want to include the contracts in your capacity planning or when there is no need to send an individual purchase order

▶ The operation is flagged as externally processed and will lead to the generation of a purchase requisition. The activities required are just described via a short text. No master records (such as a service master) are used to describe what needs to be done as opposed to the next scenario does, making it harder to analyze. For example, the operation "Monthly Service" is ordered via this text, instead of setting up a service master "1003 Monthly Service" to be reused. This scenario uses the CONTROL KEY PM02, which is a field available in the work order operation.

▶ The operation is flagged as externally processed and will lead to the generation of a purchase requisition. The activities required are described via the operation text, and service master records describe what needs to be done in detail. One advantage is the ability to analyze activities performed against this service. The other advantage of this scenario is that you can include a contingency amount by specifying an amount for unplanned services. You could say, for example, that a maintenance service costs $1,000 to fix and then allow an additional $100 for travel. This scenario can be done by using the CONTROL KEY PM03. (Note that the CONTROL KEY is a field available at the operation level, controlling how the operation is executed.)

Figure 5.62 reflects these three external options.

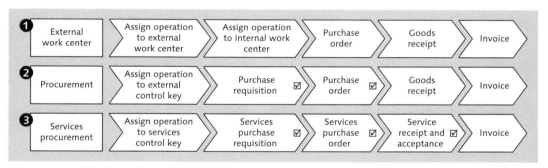

Figure 5.62 External Work Order Creation

Because it's a breakdown and requires immediate attention, you usually create the work order and release it immediately. The release of the work order ensures that assigned work order forms can be printed or emailed, that confirmations can take place, and that used spare parts can be recorded against the work order via goods movement in SAP MM.

3. **Execute the work order.**
   During execution of the work order, the activities to fix the breakdown need to be carried out by the assigned work crews as defined in the previous step.

4. **Confirm completion.**

This is the most important step. During completion confirmation, you carry out the administrative activities such as time recording, technical data collection, usage of spare parts recording, and work order closure.

Let's examine the areas involved during completion.

Confirmation of Internal Activities

The activities performed by internal or external work centers can be booked as time against the order using one of the following confirmation options (refer to Figure 5.61):

▶ **Perform time confirmation**
Within SAP PM, record your time either individually or collectively for maintenance operations.

▶ **Perform an overall confirmation**
Use a special transaction in SAP PM to record your time, technical details, measurements, services performed, and technical confirmation of both the notification and the work order.

▶ **Use a cross-application time sheet**
Confirm work orders and confirm activities performed for other application areas, such as project activities against either a WBS element or a network activity, or either book time as absence of leave or meeting as set up within the SAP ERP HCM solution, or book time against QM activities.

The time confirmation will change the status of the operation to either Partially Confirmed or Final Confirmation based on your entry. You can also choose to use digital signatures, which allow you to digitally sign operations during the time confirmation process. This function is available since EHP 2 and needs to be activated via business function `LOG_EAM_TZS_1`. You can use digital signatures either with or without the use of an external security product, which is supported in SAP NetWeaver through Secure Store and Forward (SSF).

Confirmation of External Activities

When externals were involved, the procurement activities (such as the goods receipt, service receipt, acceptance, and invoice receipt) will trigger the actual cost to be booked against the work order because the work order is used in the purchase order as an account assignment. The technical completion of a work order isn't dependent on these activities being finished, and they can be done when required.

Confirmation of Spare Parts

If materials are used during execution of the work order, and you use SAP Inventory Management (SAP IM), you can book them against your work order via a material movement in SAP IM (or directly via the overall confirmation transaction). Nonstock items can be ordered and booked to your work order via a procurement processes.

Technical Data Collection

Record the technical data collected during execution, such as entering the damage codes, cause codes, activities, and tasks for the notification. It can also include entering measurement documents for assigning measuring points related to the technical object.

Update Technical Structure

During execution, if your work has led to a change in the technical object structure, you have to update the master data so that these are reflected in its master record.

Technical Completion of the Work

You can close the work order and the notification together or separately. The *technical completion* of a work order leads to a change in status to Technical Completion, which gives you limited ability to change the order; this is also the time when a settlement rule must be created. Technically confirming the notification sets the notification to Notification Completed status, which leads to locking the notification for changing and to updating the reference time and date for response time calculation. The settlement rule of a work order needs to be created at the time of technical completion to make sure that the next and last phase of a maintenance order (which is the settlement and business completion) can be performed. This is usually a step undertaken by the controlling and record measurement documents.

Business Completion

To close a work order, it needs to be entirely settled because a work order is just a temporary placeholder to collect costs; the requesting party should be receiving the costs. Settlement can be performed to the allowed receiving cost objects, as configured in the order type. Figure 5.63 shows an example of a settlement rule, where costs are settled to cost center 1102. The cost occurred on the work order will be transferred to this cost center. The settlement rule has two entries: one used for periodic settlement (such as during month end) and one for full settlement, used after an order is completed. Settling the order will result in crediting the total balance of the order to reduce its total costs to zero, and debiting this amount to the receiver. So if the maintenance work order in the example would have incurred a total cost of $1,000 USD, the work order would be debited with $1,000, and the cost center would be credited with this amount. The settlement of the cost to the cost receiver is often done by the finance and controlling department and can be performed automatically. After the work order is settled, it can be closed, as is being done in the second screen in Figure 5.63.

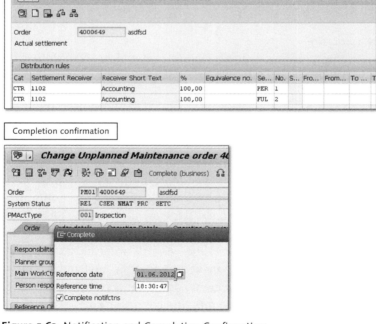

Figure 5.63 Notification and Completion Confirmation

5.5.6 Emergency Maintenance

The emergency maintenance variant is a form of corrective maintenance business process, which basically means that maintenance actions are carried out to restore a defective item to a specified condition. The emergency variant is used to record activities performed after the event has happened and the issue has been solved. Figure 5.64 shows the business process for emergency maintenance.

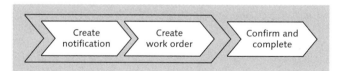

Figure 5.64 Emergency Maintenance Process

The process flow of emergency maintenance is very similar to the breakdown maintenance flow, with the only exception that the work order execution isn't part of the flow because the work already has been performed. The steps to identify the emergency and create the work order can either be done as two individual steps or together in a single step, as shown in Figure 5.64. To differentiate between breakdown and emergency activities, you can configure two separate notification types or use specific maintenance catalogs. To record the activities, the administration of the work execution process still needs to take place, so you can confirm activities. For a detailed description of the steps, refer to Section 5.5.5.

5.5.7 Corrective Maintenance

Like emergency maintenance, the corrective maintenance variant is a form of the corrective maintenance business process (see Figure 5.65). Here, as well, you must carry out maintenance actions to restore a defective item.

Figure 5.65 Corrective Maintenance Process

The process flow of corrective maintenance is the exact same as for breakdown maintenance, except that another step—planning and control work order—has been added. This is because for corrective maintenance, the work doesn't have the same urgency as breakdown or emergency work, so resources such as work centers and materials can be planned in advance of work order execution. This information provides input for you to perform capacity leveling and planning for the involved work centers to ensure they can keep up with the demand and that work is evenly spread over the work periods. This also allows you to perform material availability checks to make sure the required spare parts planned on the order are available on time for the work to commence.

Apart from the other functions mentioned during the breakdown scenario, the release of the work order now also affects and triggers reservations for planned inventory-managed spare parts, the creation of purchase requisitions, and the creation of required capacities. The same applies for technical completion, which, besides the effects mentioned during breakdown, now also closes open reservations, open capacities, and open purchase requisitions.

5.5.8 Inspection

The inspection is a form of the corrective maintenance business process where, instead of performing maintenance activities, you perform an inspection; this basically means that as part of the activities, you measure and record the measurement results. For example, you might carry out a temperature check of a machine, which you record as 90 degrees. You can set up inspections by assigning a measuring point to an operation via the PRT assignments. Figure 5.66 shows several work order operations linked to technical objects.

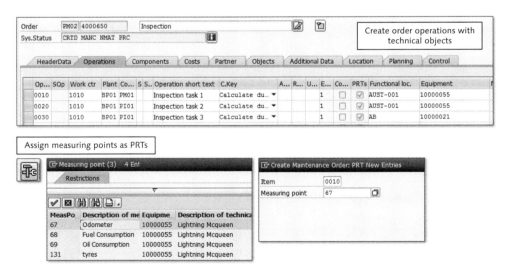

Figure 5.66 Inspection Maintenance

A measurement point can be assigned by selecting the PRT ASSIGNMENT icon, and choosing the PRT type MEASUREMENT POINTS, which allows you to assign the relevant measurement points. Since EHP 3, you can use the inspection process by activating the business function LOG_EAM_CI_3.

5.5.9 Preventive Maintenance

Preventive maintenance is undertaken by organizations to maintain or inspect the condition of technical objects on a regular basis to prevent unexpected breakdowns and minimize maintenance costs. As shown in Table 5.3, organizations choose preventive maintenance as a maintenance strategy for many reasons.

Reasons	Explanation
Legal requirements	Legislation or industry standard may stipulate regular inspections and maintenance activities.
Quality assurance	The quality of a product may depend on the condition of the production facility.
Reduction in frequency of malfunctions	Malfunctions can be contained by keeping the production facility continuously available.
Environmental protection requirements	Effective preventive maintenance can contribute to prevention of breakdowns that may lead to environmental impacts.
Manufacturers' recommendations	Manufacturers may recommend certain procedures for ensuring optimal system use.
Improved utilization control of capacities	Workshops can be used more consistently through effective balance between corrective and preventive tasks.
Decrease in maintenance costs	Finding the optimum intensity level for corrective and preventive maintenance costs can minimize the overall cost of SAP PM.

Table 5.3 Reasons to Perform Preventive Maintenance

Figure 5.67 gives you an overview of the types of maintenance, types of maintenance plans, and maintenance plan categories that are supported.

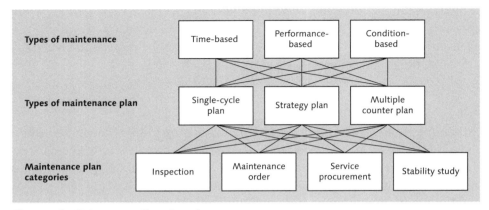

Figure 5.67 Maintenance Plans Overview

To understand these units, consider a few examples of preventive maintenance plans:

▶ The annual inspection of fire extinguishers per fire prevention regulations

▶ The maintenance regime of a compressor whereby a minor inspection needs to take place after 1,000 operating hours, filters need to be replaced and after 3,000 hours, and a major refurbishment needs to be performed every 6,000 hours

▶ The inspection of air-conditioning units when a building's temperature rises above 28 degrees Celcius

▶ Vehicle maintenance plans in which after every 6,000 miles or each year, a minor inspection has to take place, and a major inspection after every 40,000 miles or every five years

The first is an example of maintenance based on time, where the same inspection is needed every time, so a single cycle plan can be set up. In the second example, the performance of the compressor is used, which is measured in operating hours. Different activities take place during each interval. This can be translated in SAP as a performance-based strategy plan. The third example is based on an exception to occur: as soon as the threshold of 28 degrees Celcius or higher is reached, maintenance is due. This is a condition-based plan. The SAP PM—PCS interface can be used to get data on the current condition of a technical object from another system (e.g., PCS, SCADA, Budget Control System, etc.). The last example looks at both the odometer and the time and is translated into a multiple counter plan.

The process of preventive maintenance is shown in Figure 5.68.

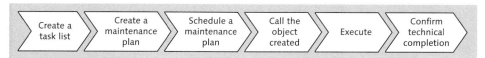

Figure 5.68 Process Preventive Maintenance

Let's walk through it:

1. **Create a task list.**
   The creation of a task list is an optional step during the preventive maintenance processes. The task list can be used to describe the details of the operations to be carried out when maintenance is due. When you're using planning to set up a strategy plan, you have to assign the task list header to the relevant maintenance strategy and the operations to the specific maintenance package.

2. **Create a maintenance plan.**
   You can create a maintenance plan for a specific technical object, which will automatically create call objects such as a maintenance order or notification. When you're creating a maintenance plan, you have to assign the type of maintenance, the type of plan you're using, and the maintenance plan category.

3. **Schedule a maintenance plan.**
   Through scheduling, you regularly check if maintenance of a planned maintenance activity is nearly due, and based on the settings in the plan, the system will create the specified maintenance call object. This activity is usually done automatically by the system on a periodic basis—daily, for example. When setting up a maintenance plan, you have to set the correct start details for scheduling, so the system can use these details during the run, which is referred to as deadline monitoring.

4. **Call the object created.**
   When the call object is created during the scheduling activities, your maintenance planners or maintenance crews can pick it up and plan the activities as mentioned before, through the planning activities mentioned in the breakdown maintenance scenario from execution of the work order.

5. **Execute.**
The planned maintenance activities are performed by the maintenance technicians as assigned to the operations. During execution, they generally keep track of time spent and which spare parts they used.

6. **Confirm technical completion.**
The process is finalized by work order confirmation and technical completion, as described during the breakdown process execution of the work order. When billing of the activities is required (only relevant and available for a customer service order), this can be an additional step that needs to be performed.

5.5.10 Project-Oriented Maintenance

Maintenance activities are becoming major and more complex, requiring significant resources and time to execute. You can manage them via an integrated scenario where both SAP PM and SAP Project Management are used. Examples of project-oriented maintenance activities include major shutdowns, overhauls, modifications, major repairs, or investment activities, such as refurbishments. They usually take a considerable amount of effort to plan, prepare, and execute, and are often high in cost. To help manage these challenges, you can use SAP PS.

From an SAP PM perspective, two separate scenarios are supported:

▶ Standard SAP PM/SAP PS scenario

▶ Maintenance Event Builder

The first scenario's main focus is on controlling cost, whereas the second is more focused on controlling time.

Standard PM-PS Scenario

Figure 5.69 shows the standard SAP PM–SAP PS process steps.

Figure 5.69 Standard SAP PM–SAP PS Scenario

Let's walk through the steps here:

1. **Create the project.**
   A project structure is created for the project to be executed. Usually there are different project types set up within SAP Project Management. From a maintenance perspective, you can set up a project as an operational project (where costs are expensed to the project) or as a capital or investment project (where the activities lead to a change of value of a financial assets). For more details on this topic, see Chapter 7.

2. **Create the maintenance orders.**
   Maintenance orders are created and assigned to the relevant project. This can be done manually or automatically. When you just want to budget control and control costs from the project, it's sufficient to assign only a WBS element to the work order. By doing so, the order planning data, such as the planned cost, is condensed to the WBS elements. If you also want to control start times and end times from the project's perspective, you need to assign both the WBS and the project network.

3. **Perform scheduling and costing.**
   During this phase, the maintenance activities are being executed. The planned and actual costs can be monitored through project reporting. Interfaces to external project planning tools (e.g., to Primavera) can be established.

4. **Monitor and execute.**
   You can monitor the current situation through the SAP Project Management perspective. For example, this allows you to monitor the consumption of your budget or to set up a budget availability check to prevent spending more money than budgeted for.

5. **Complete and settle.**
   When the work is finished and all tasks have been completed, you can set the work orders and project to Technical Completed, and controlling activities such as order settlement and project settlement can take place. You can use reporting within SAP PS to evaluate overall costs, materials consumed, time, and progress to inform you about a project.

Process of Maintenance Event Builder

The Maintenance Event Builder (MEB) is an intuitive and easy-to-use tool in which you bundle maintenance requirements into work packages. The work packages are set up as revisions. The MEB has been available since EHP 2 and can be activated by the function LOG_EAM_POM. Let's explore the maintenance event building scenario as represented in Figure 5.70 and described next.

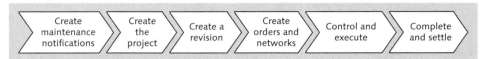

Figure 5.70 Maintenance Event Builder Scenario

1. **Create maintenance notifications.**
   During the first step, you generate or collect the outstanding notifications. You can use and assign a hierarchical task list to the notification, which can be picked up when the maintenance orders get generated.

2. **Create the project.**
   A project gets created and assigned for SAP Project Management activities, such as deadline control, cost control, and budgeting purposes.

3. **Create a revision.**
   A revision is set up for the purpose of grouping the maintenance requirements and linking them efficiently to the project.

4. **Create orders and networks.**
   Based on the provided input, such as notifications with assigned task lists, you can generate orders and networks automatically.

5. **Control and execute.**
   Execute the work and monitor the individual work orders via both SAP PM and SAP Project Management monitoring capabilities for the complete project.

6. **Complete and settle.**
   After the work has been finished, work orders, projects, and business can be technically completed and settled.

Figure 5.71 shows the MEB, which can be used to perform all the steps mentioned in the process. The top part of the MEB shows the notification list, which provides you with an overview of the selected notifications; the bottom part gives you access to the revisions.

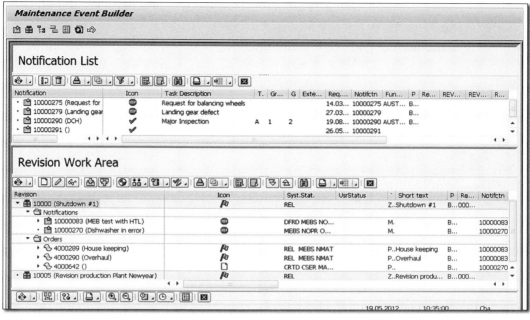

Figure 5.71 Maintenance Event Builder

5.5.11 Returns and Repairs

The returns and repairs process occurs when customers send you their products either for repair work or as a return, as shown in Figure 5.72.

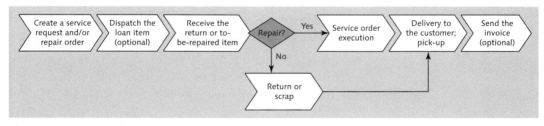

Figure 5.72 Return and Repair Process

Let's walk through the steps:

1. **Create a service request and/or repair order.**
   The process starts with a customer request to repair a defective serviceable

item. You can either start this process by the creation of a service notification for the requested repair or start with a service order directly.

2. **(Optional) Dispatch the loan item.**
On request or as an additional service offered to the customer, you can send a loan equipment/item to him, which can be used while his own equipment is being repaired.

3. **Receive the returned or to-be-repaired item.**
When you receive the serviceable item from the customer, you can receipt it against the service order. During this movement, the stock will be flagged as customer-specific stock.

4. **Perform a technical check.**
During a technical check, a technician decides, based on directions given by the customer, if the item should be repaired or if it isn't worth repairing:

▶ Repaired: This is the main process based on the technical check outcome to repair the item.

- Service order execution: When the item is repaired, the service order will be generated and executed to repair the item.

- Delivery to the customer: After the repair is performed, the repaired item will be returned to the customer. The loan equipment can be picked up. You can send the customer a quotation based on the planned repairable activities, if required.

▶ Not repaired: This is the process where the outcome of the technical check is to not repair the item.

- Delivery to the customer: You can return the item to the customer resulting in the delivery (see the arrow in the figure).

- Scrap the item: Instead of sending the item back to the customer, the item is disposed of for the customer by scrapping it and notifying the customer with supporting documents.

5. **Send the invoice.**
When the customer is being invoiced for the services performed, you can send him an invoice per the business requirements (times/materials or fixed price). See Section 5.4.3 for more details on invoicing.

5.5.12 Reporting and Analysis

Within both the components, several available reports or list functions let you select and display the necessary details based on your requirements. You can look at transactional data, such as a list of notifications or work orders, but you can also look at the master data reports. Figure 5.73 shows a simple list display of work orders alongside a multilevel list of notifications

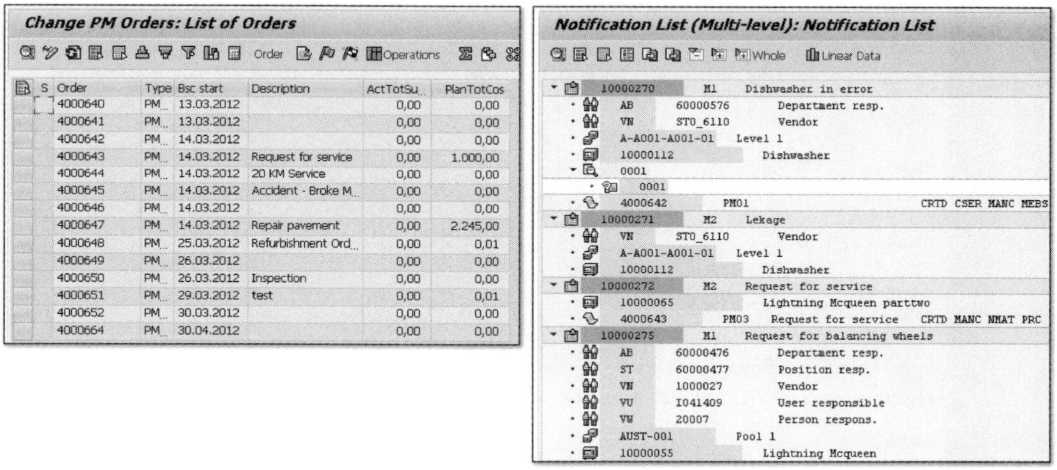

Figure 5.73 Standard Reports

Both components use the Logistics Information System (LIS) to perform statistical queries. Several standard reports can be run, of which the damage analyses, the object class analysis, and the breakdown analysis have been represented in Figure 5.74. We'll discuss the LIS and other reporting options in more detail in Chapter 10.

SAP also offers a Rapid Deployment Service in this area, which is basically a deal for fixed-price, fixed-scope services and products. The Service is called Asset Analytics. For more details, visit the SAP Service Marketplace and navigate to SAP EAM (*http://service.sap.com/rds*).

Individual Object: Damage Analysis: Basic List

Switch drilldown... Top N...

No. of Notification type: 2

Notification type	Damage	DmgeCause	Activities
Total	2	1	2
Maintenance Request	2	1	1
Activity Report	0	0	1

Object Class Analysis: Drilldown

Switch drilldown... Top N...

No. of Manufacturer: 3

Manufacturer	NotifCreat	BrkdnReptd	OrdsCrtd	TotalPlnndCosts	Total act.costs	Int. wage costs
Total	12	1	15	3.245,02 AUD	0,00 AUD	0,00 AUD
	5	0	7	3.245,02 AUD	0,00 AUD	0,00 AUD
Holden	5	0	7	0,00 AUD	0,00 AUD	0,00 AUD
Miele	2	1	1	0,00 AUD	0,00 AUD	0,00 AUD

Breakdown Analysis: Drilldown

Switch drilldown... Top N...

No. of Functional Location: 2

Functional Location	ActBreakdn	MnTmToRepair	MnTmBetRepair	TimeBetweenRep	Time To Repair
Total	2	387,025 H	8.208,650 H	16.417,300 H	774,050 H
	1	6,067 H	16.402,933 H	16.402,933 H	6,067 H
LPG	1	767,983 H	14,367 H	14,367 H	767,983 H

Figure 5.74 SAP Plant Maintenance LIS Reports

5.6 Supplementary Maintenance and Customer Service Processes

Let's examine the supplementary business processes that are supported within SAP PM and SAP CS, which are all delivered and are part of SAP ERP 6. These processes are captured as supplementary because they supplement the core processes as described within Section 5.5. Many organizations, however, see them as fundamental to performing maintenance activities and service activities and categorize them as a part of their main processes.

Whether a process is relevant for your organization is often determined during the scoping phase of an implementation project. These supplementary business processes can be further designed, detailed, and configured based on a blueprint, which is the design document and phase defined by SAP's ASAP project methodology. To accelerate blueprint and implementation activities, SAP offers best practices, Rapid Deployment Solutions, and services, which provide standardized prepackaged fixed-scope, fixed-price solutions to reduce risk and cost.

5.6.1 Capacity Requirements Planning

Through capacity planning, you can spread the work load of all the requirements on your work centers evenly based on their available capacity.

Capacity planning is a two-step process, as shown in Figure 5.75 and described in the list following.

Figure 5.75 Capacity Planning Process

1. **Capacity evaluation**
   During this step, you determine and compare the available capacity with the required capacity. Figure 5.76 shows the capacity planning board; the top half shows the capacity of work center MECHANIC (the white areas show available capacity), and the bottom shows the work orders that haven't been assigned yet.

2. **Capacity leveling**
   During capacity leveling, you try to make sure that the capacity of the work center is optimally used by preventing both overloads and underuse. During this step, you assign and select the appropriate resources for the work. When your work centers have connections to employees in the SAP ERP HCM part of the system, you can plan at individual person levels.

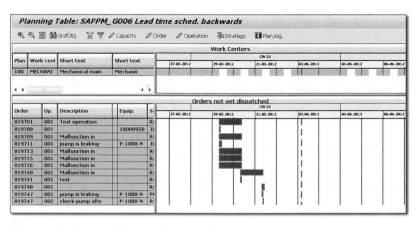

Figure 5.76 Capacity Planning Plan Board

5.6.2   Refurbishment of Spare Parts

To carry out refurbishment to valuable components that have returned to the warehouse in a faulty condition, you can use the refurbishment process. Refurbishment is an internal process and therefore is only available within SAP PM. These faulty items can be repeatedly and economically restored to a fully serviceable condition and rotate through the system—which is why they are often referred to as rotables. A rotable in the refurbishment process is a serialized material and can optionally include an equipment number. This process improves the visibility of defective components and is closely integrated with SAP MM.

Prerequisites for the Refurbishment Process

Within SAP MM, the inventory management for tracking refurbished parts and subcontracting procurement of the service "refurbishment" functions are used when done by an external company (as opposed to in-house). Within SAP IM, you have to set up a material with the activation of condition-based movements by a condition type, which represents the different conditions a material can be in.

Two scenarios are supported to handle refurbishment using a material or a serialized material:

▶ Using an internal subcontractor

▶ Using an external subcontractor

> **Note**
>
> This external subcontractor scenario is available since EHP 3 and needs to be activated by business function LOG_EAM_ROTSUB.

Let's first consider the internal subcontracting process, as shown in Figure 5.77 and described next.

Figure 5.77 Internal Subcontracting Process

1. **Refurbishment order**

   Create the refurbishment order and specify in the order header the effected rotable, its current state (e.g., "To be repaired"), and the state after refurbishment (e.g., "Refurbished"). You can use either the general transaction for order creation and select the refurbishment order type, or use the transaction created specifically for refurbishment (Transaction IW81). Figure 5.78 shows in its header that the MATERIAL 165 is being refurbished. In the REFURBISHMENT section, you see that the valuation type will change from To Be Refurbished (TBR) to REPAIRED.

Figure 5.78 Refurbishment Order

2. **Material withdrawal**

   Because the rotable or the to-be-refurbished item is inventory-managed, it needs to be booked from the warehouse—called a storage location in SAP ERP—to the refurbishment order, which can be done by using the transaction goods receipt for refurbishment order (Transaction IW8W).

3. **Refurbishment**

   During this step, the technician executes the tasks necessary to refurbish the item. Hours can be recorded against the order, and spare parts can be used and consumed against the order.

4. **Return**

   After the refurbishment is complete, the item can be booked into stock.

5. **Technical completion**

   When all the work is complete, the order can be set to Technical Completion status.

Next let's walk through the external subcontracting process, as shown in Figure 5.79 and described in the following list.

Figure 5.79 External Subcontracting Process

1. **Create the refurbishment order.**

   Create the refurbishment order and specify in the order header the effected rotable, its current state (e.g., To be repaired), and the state after refurbishment (e.g., Refurbished). In comparison to the internal subcontracting order, here the operation is executed by an external subcontractor, and the to-be-refurbished parts need to be delivered to him.

2. **Generate the purchase requisition.**

   The external operations will lead to the automatic generation of purchase requisitions. These can either be approved first or directly turned into a subcontracting purchase order.

3. **Create the purchase order.**

   The subcontracting purchase order handles the commitment to the contractor for execution of the work and performing the follow-up material movements, such as sending the spare parts to the subcontractor and receiving it back. This can also be integrated to the MRP processes.

4. **Deliver to the subcontractor.**

   The to-be-refurbished part needs to be delivered to the subcontractor.

5. **Repair.**

   The subcontractor refurbishes the part and will charge his activities through the procurement process (by goods receipt and/or service entry) to the work order.

6. **Return.**

The subcontractor sends the rotable back to you, and you'll receive it into your storage location with the new condition (e.g., Repaired).

7. **Confirm technical completion.**

When all the work is complete, the order can be set to the Technical Completion status.

5.6.3 Pool Asset Management

Pool Asset Management (PAM) supports the internal rental process of a group of assets (called a pool). It allows you to track your company's need for these pool assets, who has borrowed a specific asset, when it was returned, and how the use will be charged to the user. Typical examples of pools of assets managed via PAM are vehicles, laptops, and projectors. PAM is available as of EHP 3; you need to activate the business function LOG_EAM_PAM before you can use it.

The PAM process is shown in Figure 5.80.

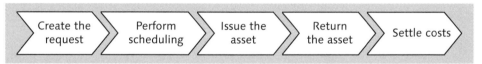

Figure 5.80 Pool Asset Management Process

Let's walk through it now:

1. **Create the request.**

The person who requires the use of a pool asset can generate a request to the pool manager. She can specify when she needs the asset and the specific details of the asset (e.g., the number of anticipated passengers in the car, whether it needs to have an automatic or a manual transmission, and the time and date of use). To record the request, the notification document within SAP PM is used, which should be configured to have the PAM details activated. Figure 5.81 and Figure 5.82 show you an example of a request, including the details of requested pool asset.

2. **Perform scheduling.**

   The pool manager can see all the requirements within the pool. Through the planning board, you can reserve a specific asset for the requested time frame and send the requester a confirmation of this reservation. You can also include the details needed for collection, such as the pickup location or instructions.

3. **Issue the asset.**

   When the requester collects the asset, this can be recorded in the system. Any additional information needed for cost collection can be recorded, such as the odometer reading of the vehicle at the time of collection.

4. **Return the asset.**

   When the requester returns the asset, this again can be recorded in the system, including additional information needed for cost collection.

5. **Settle costs.**

   Based on the rental conditions, you can charge the cost of the rental period to the asset requester. This process is done through settlement to the chosen cost object, which, for example, can be the requester department's cost center or the project code and WBS element for which the requester works.

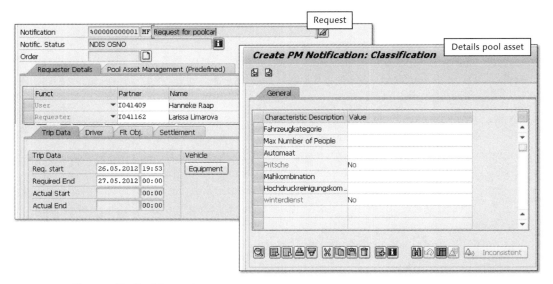

Figure 5.81 Pool Request

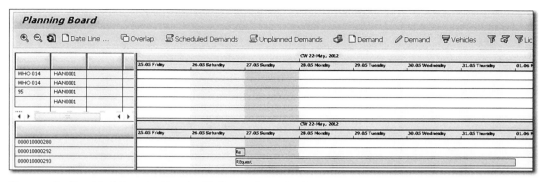

Figure 5.82 Graphical Planning Board with Demands per Pool

5.6.4 Work Clearance Management

Work Clearance Management (WCM) can be implemented when inspections, repairs, or other maintenance or service work for a technical object may only be carried out when a measure or multiple measures have been implemented to ensure safety. These safety measures include lockout/tagout (for isolation or mechanically separating objects during tasks), fire protection, and radiation protection. It helps to ensure safe and secure working conditions for your technicians and comply with safety and environmental requirements by standardizing processes for tracking safety and health-related measures. It's relevant when your technicians work in hazardous environments with safety and health risks, when maintenance activities need to be performed, and when technical objects are operational. WCM can be used based on the following:

▸ Type of task

▸ Technical requirements of the equipment

▸ Qualification of staff

▸ Organizational form of the maintenance department

Figure 5.83 shows the typical order process, including the WCM steps, to implement safety measures. The steps marked ❶ are done from either SAP PM or SAP CS, using the functionality described in previous process flows, including work orders. All the other steps belong specifically to WCM, together providing an integrated solution. The WCM steps can also be performed as stand-alone steps, if there is no need to collect order information, but asset-specific safety measures need to be documented.

Figure 5.83 Order Processing with WCM

Let's walk through the steps:

1. **Create the order.**
   You create a work order in either SAP PM or SAP CS, or, in case of preventive maintenance, the work order can be generated automatically by the system.

2. **Create WCM documents.**
   Work clearance details are determined by the technical objects assigned to the work order, triggering the creation of a WCM application document.

3. **Approve the WCM application.**
   The WCM application optionally can include an approval step (only relevant in the enhanced model) before the work can be performed.

4. **Perform tagging.**
   The technical objects and their environment need to be prepared for the upcoming work. Preparation might include activities such as tagging the object so others can easily see that it will be worked on shortly and the isolating the work environment by fences or other isolation methods. The isolated work area might include further restrictions for maintenance technicians, such as the use of appropriate safety equipment (e.g., wearing helmets, gloves, and glasses).

5. **Release and execute the order.**
   During this step, the work is released and can be performed.

6. **Normalize the WCM application.**
   After the work has finished, you can undo the lockout, untag the technical objects, and restore the working environment back to normal.

7. **Complete the WCM application.**
   After the WCM application has been normalized, the WCM application needs to be completed.

8. **Complete the work.**
   During the last step, you technically complete the work, which can only be done after the application has been closed. When the application isn't closed, the system assumes that the work is still being performed.

5.6.5 Warranty Claim Processing

The Warranty Claim Processing component has been developed to fulfill the needs of product manufacturers and product importers, as well as for vendors of complex products and their suppliers. By using Warranty Claim Processing, you can handle a large number of warranty claims comfortably and, where possible, process them automatically. Manual processing is only necessary for claims that produce negative results in the automatic checks.

In many companies, Warranty Claim Processing is a time-consuming and costly process because of the warranty restrictions (based on time or use of the object), the necessary authorization processes, and the comprehensive check mechanisms in the warranty claim. Additionally, the number of incoming warranty claims has increased.

Warranty Claim Processing is a cross-application component that is completely integrated into the SAP solution, from master data management (using master data objects from MM, SD, CS, PM) and pricing (SD) through checking master warranties and creating measurement documents (CS, PM), to posting FI documents (FI-CO), and evaluating the warranty data (SAP NetWeaver BW). It can be accessed via PLANT MAINTENANCE • TECHNICAL OBJECTS, via CUSTOMER SERVICE • TECHNICAL OBJECTS, or via LOGISTICS GENERAL • ENGINEERING.

Warranty Claim Processing offers the following functions:

▶ Storage of master data for warranty claim processing

▶ Data management and interface between claimant and reimburser

▶ Checks for automatic processing of warranty claims

▶ Automatic pricing and revenue account determination with posting of documents in SAP ERP Financials.

▶ Numerous actions that cover the most common warranty claim processing procedures

Figure 5.84 illustrates the warranty claim process.

Figure 5.84 Warranty Claim Processing

Let's walk through it now.

1. **Maintain the warranty master data.**
   Enter a warranty against a technical object, which can be a piece of equipment (serialized or not) or a functional location.

2. **Perform the warranty check.**
   During order processing (or from within the master data), you can execute a warranty check, which gives you information concerning whether or not the technical object is still under warranty.

3. **Enter the warranty claim.**
   During warranty claim, you enter a warranty against a technical object (functional location, equipment, or installed base) based on a customer or vendor request.

4. **Process the warranty claim.**
   During this step, the system handles the warranty claim based on your business rules. When the warranty data is complete and details are verified, the system can automatically handle financial follow-up documents such as credit notes. Other processing functions can include the following:
   - Processing with precrediting/postcrediting
   - Processing with authorized goodwill
   - Processing with parts to be returned
   - Processing with claim split
   - Processing with recalls/technical campaigns

5. **Follow-up on exceptions.**
   When an exception occurs, the claim needs to be manually followed up. The processes discussed in the following subsections are supported.

5.6.6   Lean Scenario

Lean maintenance is an alternative to the breakdown maintenance process, which automates some processing steps. It's especially suited to non-capital-intensive companies interested in fast, simple processing. It provides a simple, web-based entry of problem notifications, where no specialized knowledge or training is required. The follow-up order gets generated automatically via background processing. After this, the work order is picked up and executed as normal; the person who opened the problem is assumed to close it after completion.

The lean maintenance scenario has been offered as of EHP 2 and can be activated via business function LOG_EAM_SIMP.

Figure 5.85 shows the lean maintenance processes in which the system automatically creates the order.

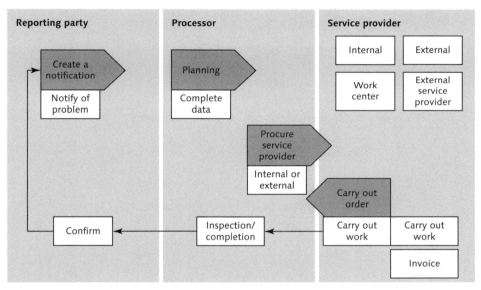

Figure 5.85 The Lean Maintenance Process

Technical additions are leveraged from the SAP NetWeaver BW platform. They include the use of Business Workflows, Smart Forms, and service-oriented architecture (SOA) bundles. Simplifying the user experience has been addressed by the introduction of two things:

▶ The latest SAP EAM portal content (delivered via basic maintenance processing and the maintenance planner, maintenance supervisor, and maintenance technician roles)

▶ A simplified screen layout for the work order

Table 5.4 offers an overview of the SOA services offered, organized by asset configuration enterprise services and maintenance processing enterprise services.

Service Bundle	Services
Maintenance processing enterprise services	▶ Activate Maintenance Plan ▶ Check Maintenance Plan Creation ▶ Check Maintenance Plan Update ▶ Create Maintenance Plan ▶ Deactivate Maintenance Plan ▶ Find Maintenance Plan by Elements ▶ Find Maintenance Plan Item by Elements ▶ Read Maintenance Plan ▶ Read Maintenance Plan Schedule Line ▶ Reset Maintenance Plan Delete Indicator ▶ Set Maintenance Plan Delete Indicator ▶ Update Maintenance Plan ▶ Find Maintenance Task List Simple by Elements ▶ Read Maintenance Task List ▶ Check Maintenance Confirmation Creation ▶ Find Maintenance Confirmation Simple by Elements ▶ Read Maintenance Confirmation ▶ Reset Maintenance Order Delete Indicator ▶ Set Maintenance Order Delete Indicator ▶ Simulate Maintenance Order Scheduling ▶ Create Measuring Device ▶ Find Material by Elements
Asset configuration enterprise services	▶ Find Installation Point by Installation Point Template ▶ Read Maintenance Plan ▶ Create Maintenance Plan ▶ Update Maintenance Plan ▶ Find Maintenance Plan by Elements ▶ Read Maintenance Task List ▶ Find Subordinate Maintenance Task List by Maintenance Task List ▶ Find Top-Level Maintenance Task List by Maintenance Task List ▶ Find Parent Maintenance Task List by Maintenance Task List ▶ Find Maintenance Task List Simple by Elements ▶ Find Subordinate Individual Material by Individual Material

Table 5.4 SAP EAM Service Bundle and Services

5.6.7 Mobile Scenarios

Via mobile applications, you can execute maintenance work orders and service orders on a mobile device, such as a PDA, iPad, iPhone, or laptop. We'll go into more detail on mobility in Chapter 9.

5.7 Summary

This chapter has given you an overview of the functions and features that SAP CS and SAP PM offer during the maintenance and operating stages of a product. The chapter first introduced SAP EAM and detailed the benefits, supported maintenance activities, and strategies. We then focused on the master data in both areas referred to as technical objects, detailing objects such as the functional location and the equipment. The common functions available for technical objects were explained—categorization, classification, change management, data transfer, document management, business partners, status, permits, and SAP CRM integration and enhancement options.

We also gave an overview of the objects used when performing a transaction in SAP PM or SAP CS. You saw the structure and purpose of object information, notifications, work orders, repair orders, measurement documents, maintenance plans and strategies, service contracts, visualizations and publications, and logbook and shift reports.

In our discussion of configuration management, you learned how technical objects can be further categorized with the use of object types and how the BOM can be used for both spare part planning as well as structuring of the object. You can use the verification process to verify the actual technical object structure against an expected structure. Last, the section covered spare parts management, which included information about how they can be grouped and accessed using catalogs.

This chapter also focused on the main business processes, covering the organizational set up, master data maintenance (including handover and takeover), maintenance cost budgeting, corrective maintenance process (including its variations, breakdown and emergency), inspections, preventive maintenance, project-oriented maintenance, and returns and repairs. We also covered reporting and analysis.

The last section of the chapter focused on the supplementary business processes, such as the capacity requirements planning processes, performing refurbishments, using PAM for loaning assets, providing a safe working environment with work clearance maintenance, performing warranty claim processing with the lean scenario for simplified processes, and using mobile devices in the field to improve and shorten paper-based processes.

Ensure your products comply with the latest regulations and conform to industry best practices through a holistic solution that covers the entire lifecycle of a product, gives insights about its contents, and includes labeling and datasheets for the product itself.

6 Product Compliance

In Chapter 2, we began to discuss product compliance and how SAP Governance, Risk, and Compliance (SAP GRC) can help you ensure product compliance. But product compliance is more than just making sure that you record your products and legislation information; as you can see in Figure 6.1, a growing number of laws and regulations require that you keep a record of which specific materials or ingredients were used in self-produced or purchased end products. All of the processes needed to support those product compliance activities are supported by SAP Product Compliance and SAP Environment, Health, and Safety Management (SAP EHS Management) offerings.

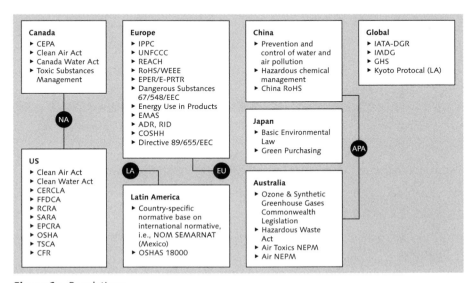

Figure 6.1 Regulations

External pressure to ensure product safety and compliance is on the rise, and manufacturing companies are increasingly being held accountable for the environmental and safety performanceof their products. As a result, product compliance is becoming a core business activity. The introduction of new and more complex product laws such as Registration, Evaluation, and Authorization of Chemicals (REACH) and Restriction of Hazardous Substances (RoHS, or Directive 2002/95/EC) has led to more detailed product information, often reflected on product labels. REACH is a new EU regulatory framework for chemicals; RoHS originated in the European Union and restricts the use of specific hazardous materials found in electrical and electronic products. All applicable products in the EU market after July 1, 2006, must pass RoHS compliance.

Consumers are spreading social pressure fostered by other organizations, including Greenpeace and the World Wildlife Foundation (WWF), to produce and consume products in a sustainable and green way, effectively keeping the impact on the environment to a minimum.

On the whole, product compliance focuses on managing the full scope of global regulatory requirements, integrated with all business processes associated with internal, customer, and supplier compliance management and reporting. SAP GRC has already been covered in Chapter 2, so this chapter will focus on SAP EHS Management, the use of SAP Audit Management to perform product-related audits, and the Operational Risk Management process, focusing on compliance regarding workers safety by a proactive risk-based approach. We'll start by explaining how product compliance and REACH are supported and then describe parts of product safety and stewardship used for product compliance.

Product compliance touches all the business processes in which internal stakeholders, customers, and suppliers perform activities related to products. Product compliance processes seek to improve regulatory compliance by achieving the following:

- Secured and compliant operations
- Improved auditability of information and actions
- Reduced risk of fines and penalties
- Reduced risk by permanent compliance tracking with internal and external regulations

Similarly, they seek to increase transparency and accountability, with the following results in mind:

▸ Improved transparency and reliable auditability of activities

▸ Establishment of one source of the truth

▸ Improvement of regulatory compliance

▸ Standardization of processes and tools, which improves SAP EHS Management performance and reduces costs

▸ Reduced operating cost and increasing efficiency by reducing inventory levels

▸ Improved brand value and corporate reputation by sustainable operations

Let's walk through the solutions that SAP Product Compliance offers.

The solution overview of SAP Product Compliance consists of the four end-to-end sustainability processes shown in Figure 6.2. These processes provide a complete set of solutions to manage sustainability programs across your organization:

▸ **Operational Risk Management**
This includes the key processes that create a comprehensive solution for management of operational risks. Based on a continuous improvement model, risk assessment can be performed proactively and incidents recorded to learn from them.

▸ **Embedded product compliance**
This end-to-end process focuses on all aspects of product safety from "cradle to grave" (described in detail in Section 6.3).

▸ **SAP Energy and Environmental Resource Management**
This focuses on reducing energy use as well as maintaining compliance with environmental requirements. (This topic falls outside the scope of this book.)

▸ **Sustainability reporting and analytics**
This provides a comprehensive view of all sustainability reporting and helps to drive strategic initiatives. (This topic falls outside the scope of this book.)

Operational Risk Management is both relevant from a product perspective and for managing a safe work environment for maintenance and service workers—which is why we've included it here. The solution is an integrated closed-loop process, which mainly uses SAP EHS Management functionality, but the outcomes of risk assessments and safety measures can be used as input for maintenance or service activities.

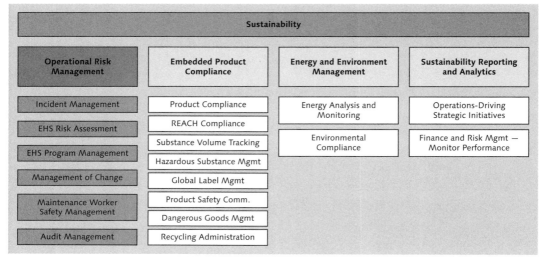

Figure 6.2 Overview of SAP Solutions for Sustainability

Although it once stood on its own, SAP REACH Compliance has been folded into SAP EHS Management. Within SAP PLM, SAP EHS Management forms part of SAP's sustainability offering, as shown in the solution map in Figure 6.2. SAP EHS Management forms one generic platform to support all environment, health, and safety processes and contemporary challenges.

Embedded into SAP ERP, SAP Product Compliance consists of the end-to-end processes and the functions shown in Figure 6.3. Embedded product compliance provides you with the ability to do the following:

▶ Manage your product's environment, health, and safety master data effectively and efficiently.

▶ Communicate critical SAP EHS Management data within the supply chain.

▶ Provide evaluation tools to check product compliance within the product development process.

▶ Integrate product compliance and safety controls within existing processes to mitigate business risk.

▶ Embed product compliance within procurement, SAP Quality Management (QM), order management, SAP Extended Warehouse Management (SAP EWM), and SAP Transportation Management (TM).

▶ Provide reporting capabilities to support compliance, safety, and end-of-life information to customers, authorities, or other stakeholders.

In this chapter, we'll dedicate subsections to the embedded product compliance functions. Section 6.1 will cover product compliance and REACH compliance, and Section 6.2 will cover all the other functions, which are all part of SAP EHS Management. The chapter will finish with coverage of SAP Audit Management, a new component introduced in SAP ERP to plan and execute audits.

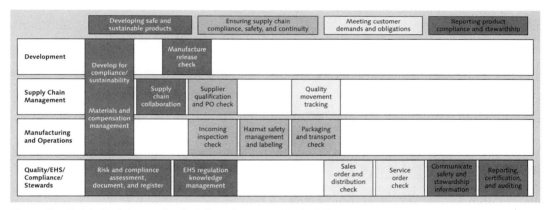

Figure 6.3 End-to-End Process Product Compliance per Product Stage

So why does it make sense for SAP Product Compliance to be an embedded solution? Because the product information is used through the entire logistic value chain, the compliant data that is used throughout your organization needs to be reflected in all the processes and process steps where it's used. Figure 6.4 shows the most important touch points of this data regarding other components within SAP ERP, such as the following:

▶ SAP Logistics General (LO), such as material master data maintenance and business partner details

▶ SAP Materials Management (SAP MM) for procurement and SAP Inventory Management (SAP MM–IM) activities

▶ SAP Sales and Distribution (SD) for selling of your products to customers

- SAP Logistics Execution (LE) for SAP EWM

- SAP Plant Maintenance (SAP PM) for maintenance master data and processes data such as safety measures, corrective actions, and standard operating procedures

- SAP EHS Operational Risk Management to perform product-related risk assessments and implement measures and controls to mitigate these risks; it includes providing safety measures to maintenance planners and engineers performing work on these products, which will be discussed from a product and asset perspective in Section 6.3

- SAP ERP Human Capital Management (SAP ERP HCM) for organization structure management to hold employees, organizational structures and exposure groups, and training and certification data

	Material Management		Inventory Management		Plant Maintenance		Human Capital Management
LO	Logistics General— Material Master	MM	Inventory management— Stocks	PM	PM notification, safety measures, corrective actions	HCM	Organizational Management — person, organizational unit, exposure group
MM	Materials Management — Purchasing	LE	Logistics execution— warehouse management	PM	Standard operating procedures	HCM	Personal Protective Equipment (PPE) and training and certifications
SD	Specification management, substance volume tracking, risk assessment	EHS	HIS risk assessment				
BP	Business partner						

Figure 6.4 Integration

Manufacturers from all different types of industries need to prove the safety of their substances, products, and respective uses according to relevant product legislation, such as REACH, or to provide proof of compliance with environmental directives, such as RoHS, Joint Industry Guide for the electrotechnical industry (JIG), and Global Automotive Declarable Substance List (GADSL).

Within SAP Product Compliance, two main end-to-end processes are supported: *product compliance* and *REACH compliance*. They are part of the SAP Business Suite's SAP EHS offering and support both the process industry and the discrete industry meeting the respective directives and regulations.

Technically, SAP Product Compliance and REACH Compliance are comprised of two subcomponents:

▶ **Portal application**
This Java WebDynpro application integrated in the SAP NetWeaver Portal communicates with the SAP ERP database.

▶ **SAP ERP**
SAP EHS Management as a prerequisite means that the same data basis is used, thus avoiding the storage of redundant data.

These core SAP product and REACH compliance processes are supported by three general functions: task management and BOM transfer, worklist management, and data exchange.

Task Management

Task management enables you to coordinate activities between the various parties involved in executing compliance checks by using tasks. You can set up tasks either automatically or manually and assign them to one or more people. The system can generate tasks automatically in the following processing situations, after they have been configured:

▶ Bill of material to bill of services transfer (BOM–BOS transfer)

▶ Product compliance checks and REACH compliance checks

▶ Data imports and exports (see the information about the data exchange function of product compliance in Table 6.2)

▶ Content provider integration

The automatic creation of tasks is based on the system messages generated during the processing of the program. Task management can then be used to process, execute, delegate, monitor, and document the tasks. Figure 6.5 shows an example of task management where a task is being created and assigned to a vendor. Tasks can have different statuses, and they are updated during execution. Worklist management allows the automated processing of tasks.

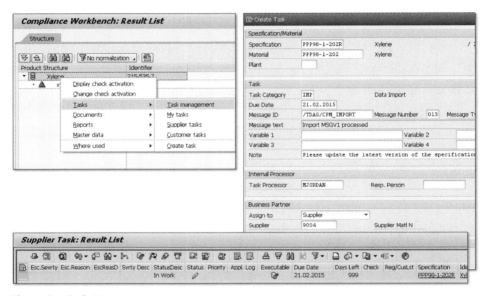

Figure 6.5 Task Management

Bill of Material Transfer

This function enables you to import material master data and BOM data into a specification structure. You can choose SAP systems or external product data management systems to transfer materials that you manufactured or materials that were manufactured by a supplier, which must be set up in the system configuration. The following application scenarios are supported:

▶ Creation of a new specification structure

▶ Update of an existing specification structure

▶ Automatic BOM transfer when the BOM is changed.

The system does the following with automatic transfer:

1. Creates the individual specifications and links them bidirectionally with the material master data record to preserve the structure of the BOM.

2. For each product or product part that is supplied, creates a supplier-specific external specification.

3. For each product or product part that is produced in different plants, creates a plant-specific specification.

4. If PERFORM CHECKS is selected, performs the standard checks automatically. The result of the BOM transfer is displayed in a log list, and a task of the type BOM is generated in task management.

Worklist Management

Worklist management collects open tasks from task management and allows automated background processing. You can use this function to monitor specification changes in advance of product compliance and REACH compliance checks. By monitoring changes in the database, worklist management determines new check requirements and identifies documents and declarations that need updating to ensure and proactively monitor product changes and the necessary product compliance checks.

To trigger the follow-up steps, monitor the changes made in Specification Management using the change documents that are generated each time a change is made in the specification database. Table 6.1 explains which changes lead to the generation of items in the worklist, based on the worklist type. Figure 6.6 shows an example of a worklist.

Worklist Type	Evaluation of the Following Changes
Check worklist	▶ Changes to legal content—legal information on pure substances and pure substance groups ▶ Changes to the assignment of declarable substances
Declaration worklist	▶ Changes to revised entries ▶ Changes to the assignment of declarable substances ▶ Changes to identifiers
Check worklist *and* declaration worklist	▶ Creation of a specification ▶ Changes to weight properties ▶ Changes to compliance properties ▶ Changes to the product structure (composition)

Table 6.1 Events That Trigger Worklist Item

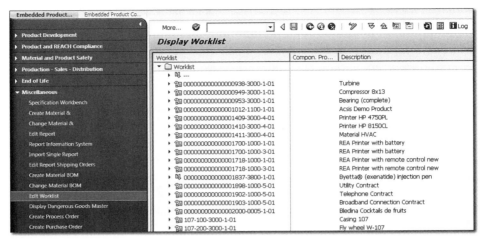

Figure 6.6 Worklist

Data Exchange

Using the data exchange function, you can exchange data electronically with customers and suppliers. Data exchange is supported in the formats listed in Table 6.2.

Format	Explanation
Import and export of IMDS files	Enables exchange of files based on the International Material Data System (IMDS)
Import and export of data in AIAG format	Enables exchange of files in Compliance Connect data format as defined by the Automotive Industry Action Group (AIAG)
Import and export of data in CfP XML format	Import and export data based on the CfP XML format
Exchange of WWI documents	Import and exports documents based on SAP's Windows Word Processor Integration (WWI) tool
Import of data in IEEE format	Import data in IEEE format, a format which is used in the electrical and electronic industry
Import of IPC 1752	Ability to exchange data in the IPC 1752 format (international standard)

Table 6.2 Supported Data Exchange Formats

Format	Explanation
PDF	Ability to exchange product data via PDF format
Export of data as output variants	Ability to export specification data to Microsoft Excel via an output variant.
Customer-specific import and export interfaces	Ability to define your own specific formats for exchanging data with other systems

Table 6.2 Supported Data Exchange Formats (Cont.)

Both the product compliance and REACH processes lean heavily on the data provided by SAP EHS Management because they use this data as the backend when performing all their process steps.

The Product Compliance Process

The process supported for product compliance is shown in Figure 6.7 and described in the list following.

Figure 6.7 Product Compliance Process

1. **Specification management**
   You manage the necessary specification data by creating a specification for each product using the BOM transfer. The specification describes the environmental properties of a product and is used as a basis for all compliance checks.

2. **Worklist management**
   You use worklist management to monitor the changes made in Specification Management. It triggers the relevant follow-up steps after specifications have been changed.

3. **Compliance check**
   You perform compliance checks either automatically or manually, of which a number are being delivered with the standard system. If required, you can define additional checks. Figure 6.8 shows the COMPLIANCE WORKBENCH.

4. **Supplier communication**

If necessary, you request and import additional data from suppliers. This data is needed to complete the specification data for materials that are produced by an external supplier. To organize the communication with suppliers, you can use campaigns.

5. **Compliance analyses and reports**

You can analyze the results of compliance checks to internally display the compliance status of a product at different levels. You can also document the check results in reports to inform authorities and customers of the compliance status. A number of compliance analyses and reports are delivered with the standard system. If required, you can define additional analyses and reports.

6. **Data export to customers**

To provide compliance data to your customers, you can use the electronic data exchange function. Interfaces for different exchange formats are delivered with the standard system (e.g., the AIAG and IMDS).

Figure 6.8 Compliance Workbench

REACH Compliance Process

The process supported by SAP REACH compliance is shown in Figure 6.9 and described in the list following.

1. **Material assessment**

Determine the REACH relevance of materials using the material assessment. During this process, the system determines the materials that are relevant for the REACH regulation and how the materials are affected by it. The process consists of the following subprocesses:

- Rough material assessment
- Precise material assessment
- Real substance assessment
- Substance composition maintenance

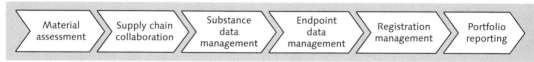

Figure 6.9 Reach Compliance Process

2. **Supply chain collaboration**
   You manage the data that is required on the material level to determine the use of substances. In conjunction with collecting the relevant data, maintaining good communication with your customers and suppliers is important for the REACH process of collating use information and the corresponding exposure scenarios. To request information on uses of materials from your customers or from suppliers, you can use campaigns.

3. **Substance data management**
   You manage the REACH-relevant data on the substance level. The information on uses provided by the system after a successful aggregation of material data is automatically transferred to the substances you need to register. To organize the registration, you need additional data that can be maintained in substance management.

4. **Endpoint data management**
   To register a substance for your legal entity with the European Chemicals Agency (ECHA), you must provide information on the effects of the substance on human health and the environment. That means that you have to provide data on the physiochemical behavior, toxicology, and ecotoxicology. This data is called endpoint data and is maintained in the International Uniform Chemical Information Database (IUCLID), which is used to capture, store, maintain, and exchange data on intrinsic and hazardous properties of chemical substances. SAP Product Compliance and REACH Compliance also allows you to add further administrative data (e.g., costs). The data in SAP Product Compliance, REACH Compliance, and IUCLID are matched using a synchronization

process. In addition, SAP Product Compliance and REACH Compliance provide an overview of the coverage status of your endpoint substances.

5. **Registration management**

   You start and monitor the registration of a substance for each legal entity. registration management supports you in organizing your registrations for each legal entity. These processes comprise the collaboration in a Substance Information Exchange Forum (SIEF) and with the European Chemicals Agency (ECHA), the completion of endpoints, and the submission of the IUCLID 5 dossier.

6. **Portfolio reporting**

   You can export REACH compliance data for reporting purposes. Figure 6.10 gives an example of a dashboard for REACH COMPLIANCE.

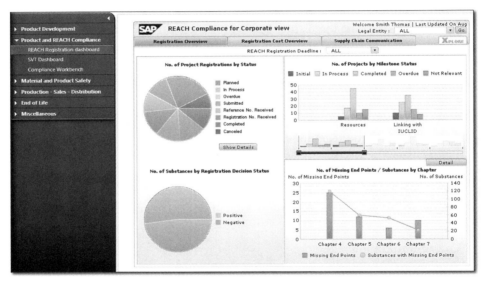

Figure 6.10 REACH Dashboard

Beyond the activities you have to undertake in SAP GRC, you also have to collect and ensure product compliance in the operational steps during production and manufacturing or trading activities. These activities, such as different functionalities; environmental, occupational and product safety processes; regulatory compliance; and corporate responsibility are supported by SAP EHS Management.

The following section provides you with a functional overview of SAP EHS Management and a focused look at product-relevant areas.

6.1 SAP Environment, Health, and Safety Management

SAP EHS Management enables you to maintain the product data necessary for product compliance and product safety. The product master data is used when executing operational activities because it's embedding corporate policies, compliance, and environmental, health, and safety information within your business processes for human resources, logistics, production, and finance.

Figure 6.11 gives you an overview of SAP EHS Management, detailing how its subcomponents are grouped together in the three main business areas or main pillars, which are tightly integrated and at times overlap. It supports the following:

▸ **Health and safety**
Provides an enterprise-wide platform to ensure the safety and well-being of employees and communities and includes the following:

  ▸ Hazardous Substance Management: Includes observing national regulations, defining how to manage hazardous substances onsite, and determining how to protect employees from harm. It includes analytic tools such as hazardous materials logs.

  ▸ Dangerous Goods Management: Allows you to manage dangerous materials labeling and movements under the dangerous goods regulations, which is a UN regulation and applicable worldwide (note that in the United States, these are known as hazardous materials and hazardous materials regulations).

  ▸ Incident management and accident management: Manages incidents and accidents supported by workflow capability and root cause analysis. It can be integrated with HR scenarios and data, such as organizational elements, personal records, and time management, and includes a powerful cockpit.

  ▸ Preventive and occupational medicine: Preventive health and occupational medicine ensures well-being of employees and increases productivity through fewer incidents and absences.

▶ **Product safety and stewardship**

Delivers safe products and includes all of the activities necessary to ensure product compliance and to know which products and product components or ingredients are used where and when, during the processes. This not only focuses on your organization's data—such as your own material safety data sheets (MSDS)—but also includes collection of data from suppliers or data that needs to be supplied to customers, such as the following:

- ▶ Substance management and SAP MM
- ▶ MSDS and Hazardous Substance Management
- ▶ SAP Product Compliance reporting
- ▶ Customer and supplier communication
- ▶ Compliance for ingredients
- ▶ Dangerous Goods Management
- ▶ SAP Supply Chain Collaboration
- ▶ Support for legal processes

You'll notice an overlap of areas with health and safety.

▶ **Environmental performance**

Tracks and traces all the resources you consume and ensures you dispose of it in an appropriate way, with even the possibility of using recycling management. You can trace your waste footprint by examining the following:

- ▶ Air emissions: Prevent air pollution, conserve resource use, and comply with emission regulations.
- ▶ Resource consumption: Monitor resource consumption.
- ▶ Water emissions: Prevent water pollution, conserve water use, and comply with regulations.
- ▶ Work permit management: Request a permit and execute certain activities that interrupt normal tasks.
- ▶ Waste and recycling: Minimize waste in compliant manner.

Our main focus will be the product safety and stewardship pillar. First, we'll briefly refresh your understanding of the general master data objects in SAP EHS Management and the connection to product compliance, followed with the subareas Global Label Management, substance volume tracking (SVT), report management, and Dangerous Goods Management, which all have been highlighted in in Figure 6.11.

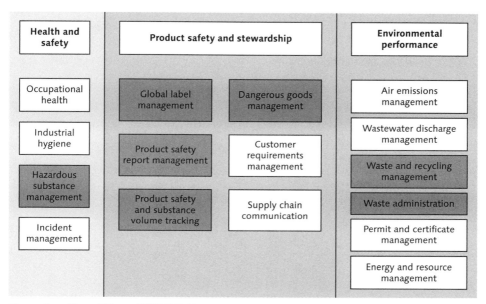

Figure 6.11 Three Pillars of SAP EHS Management

Next, we'll focus on the Hazardous Substance Management from the health and safety pillar. Dangerous Goods Management and Hazardous Substance Management are often confused with one another, so it's important to become familiar with both of them and understand how they align with your business activities and definitions. Finally, we'll go into SAP Waste and Recycling, a subarea from the environmental performance pillar. The other areas aren't part of the scope of this book, so they won't be described in more detail. For more information on these topics, please refer to SAP websites listed for this chapter in Appendix B.

6.1.1 Basic Master Data in SAP EHS Management

To use any of the functions offered through SAP EHS Management, you first need to set up the BASIC DATA AND TOOLS area. This area is highly integrated to other areas of SAP ERP, and you must have the following other components and sub-components set up to use it:

▶ SAP Engineering Change Management (ECM)

▶ SAP Document Management System (SAP DMS)

- SAP Classification System (CA)
- Material master in SAP Materials Management (SAP MM)
- SAP Sales and Distribution (SD)

Briefly recall the discussion of the specification database from Chapter 3, and refer to Figure 6.12 to see how the SAP EHS Management master data is all captured in the specification database. This section will just focus on the new areas that have not been addressed so far.

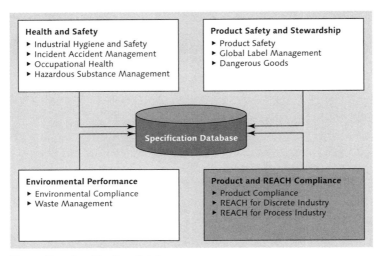

Figure 6.12 Specification Database

You can create specification data; edit SAP EHS Management reports (such as MSDS, labels, and standard operating procedures); import and export specifications, phrases, MSDS, and other documents; and manage them after import just like all other SAP EHS Management data and reports.

Figure 6.13 gives you a brief overview of the specification database to refresh your memory. As you can see, a specification is a data record, which includes identifiers; a key; the assignment to a material; status and restrictions; relationships and properties; and composition information; which heavily uses CA. The specification database supports different specification types, such as real substances, packaging materials, agents representing hazards, and dangerous goods classifications.

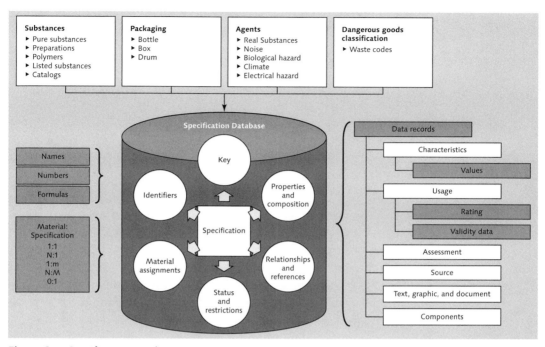

Figure 6.13 Specification Database Overview

6.1.2 Global Label Management

When you're selling products you've produced or products produced by suppliers, you might need to describe the product contents and the product properties on a product label or product packaging. These product labels include goods receipt labels, article labels, hazardous substance labels, danger labels, transportation labels, handling instructions, safety information, and other labels tailored to suit your customers' needs. Depending on the possible destinations, the labels must be created in several languages and show graphics such as hazard symbols, usage symbols, and company logos. The layout and content of labels can also be dependent on the jurisdiction for which the labels are destined, which means you have to observe numerous laws and regulations worldwide.

For all of this, you can use Global Label Management within SAP EHS Management. Although it was grouped under the product safety pillar in Figure 6.11 and can be found in SAP EHS Management under menu option PRODUCT SAFETY, other areas within SAP EHS Management also heavily rely on its functions, including

Dangerous Goods Management and Hazardous Substance Management, which is why it's also available in their menus. The following labeling scenarios are available to you in the standard system:

- Make-to-stock
- Make-to-order
- Delivery
- Goods receipt
- Generic
- Sample

The labeling scenarios are based on the integration to other processes in SAP ERP. For example, goods receipt, make-to-stock production, make-to-order production, and delivery labeling scenarios allow the system to create legally compliant labels automatically and print the required number of labels when you need them. If you wish, you can number the labels with serial numbers and with the use of a partner product You can also control automatic labeling directly in the production line.

Global Label Management is a completely integrated labeling concept in SAP that can lead to the following:

- Minimized data maintenance
- Regulatory compliance output of hazardous and dangerous goods data
- Support for multilingual output and exotic character sets
- Use of a centralized labeling cockpit
- Versioning/archiving/tracking of labeling history
- Easy extension
- Intranet and internet integration

Let's walk through the process for Global Label Management, which is represented in Figure 6.14.

Figure 6.14 Process for Global Label Management

1. **Edit label data in the material master.**

   In the material master, you enter material-dependent data and texts for labeling and the packaging hierarchy. The hierarchy can include a primary container, box, outer box, and pallet with shrink film, for example.

2. **Edit specifications.**

   In specifications, you enter all environmentally relevant data and other data for substances (pure substances, preparations, mixtures, and residual substances), products, agents, packaging, and wastes. This data includes information for identification, material assignments, compositions, and properties. From the specification data, the system puts together the content for the labels that is required according to regulations.

3. **Edit phrases.**

   You enter texts that have a standard character in the form of phrases. These texts include safety and risk information. You enter the phrases in the specifications and on the LABELING tab page in the material master.

4. **Edit label stock.**

   You define the properties of the label stocks. Each label requires a special label stock depending on its size, color design, or need for weather resistance or seawater resistance. The properties of label stocks also depend on the printers used, for example, if special label printers or printers with continuous form paper or cut sheet feed are used.

5. **Edit customer-specific labels.**

   If your customers have special labeling requirements, you can create customer-specific labels. If the customer is known in a process, such as in make-to-order production or delivery, the system creates the customer-specific label automatically.

6. **Edit label templates.**

   You use a label template to design the layout of the labels. You can print specification data, data from the material master and other SAP components, and graphics on the labels. Text modules such as headings can be integrated in the labels, independent of the language, using phrases.

7. **Print labels.**

   The system generates labels like other SAP EHS Management reports (such as MSDS and standard operating procedures) from report templates (label templates) and stores the generated labels in the SAP EHS Management report database. You can assign versions to the stored labels and use and print them for information purposes. The system can be configured so that the labels will be automatically printed during goods receipt handling, sales order processing, production order processing, and delivery processing in SAP ERP.

Figure 6.15 shows an example of a product label. When printing labels from a process, the system determines the label template according to label determination logic and generates and prints the labels from scratch each time. You can extend label printing to other business processes.

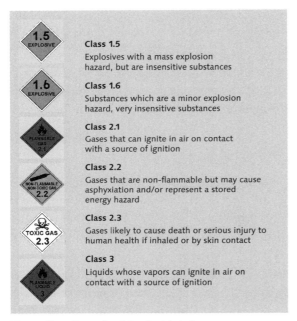

Figure 6.15 Example of Product Label

6.1.3 SAP Product Safety Component

If you produce and sell hazardous substances in your company, you must protect people and the environment from the hazards these substances pose. You also have to observe numerous laws and regulations on hazardous substances worldwide. The SAP Product Safety component helps you to handle hazardous substances safely, bring them safely to the market, and comply with all relevant regulations automatically. Hazardous Substance Management (EHS-HSM) also supports you with managing hazardous substances, with the following distinction:

- SAP Product Safety supports companies that *produce* hazardous substances.
- Hazardous Substance Management supports companies that *use* hazardous substances.

SAP Product Safety is part of SAP EHS Management and, apart from using the BASIC DATA AND TOOLS area, also uses the following:

- Report management supports you with the required work steps for SAP EHS Management reports from generation to final release. For data archiving purposes, you can save reports you no longer require with the Historical status and call them at any time.
- Released reports are available for report shipping. Report shipping controls the processes involved from creating a report shipping order all the way to saving it. As well as allowing you to ship reports such as MSDS automatically, it lets you set up automatic subsequent shipping for updated reports. These are then shipped automatically if, for example, the data for specifications or phrases that is output on the reports was changed.
- The report information system enables you to search and display existing reports with the Released and Historical statuses.
- Substance volume tracking (SVT) enables you to track certain substances within the logistic processes (more details on SVT are given a bit later in the "Substance Volume Tracking" subsection.
- BOM transfer supports you with creating the composition of a specification from the BOMs for a material.
- Global Label Management supports you with entering all data for labels and then using this data to determine suitable labels in various labeling scenarios and printing them as described previously.

Let's explore a few of these tools further.

Report Management

Via report management, you can be guided through the individual work steps required to manage reports from report generation to report release. The generated reports contain all specification-related data and phrases for a particular language and usage. Figure 6.16 shows a report generated in Microsoft Word containing all specification details of the product industry cleaner. All other current parameters are generated later when the report is shipped. You can use user exits to control the parameter values determined by the SAP system during the process, and you can overwrite them manually in report management if necessary.

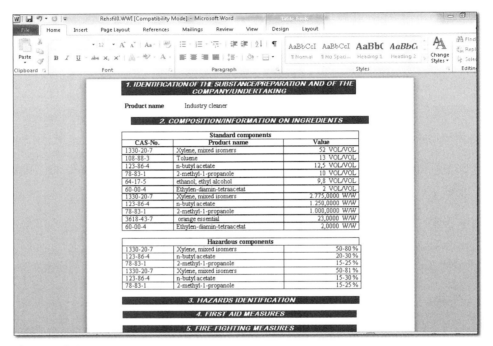

Figure 6.16 Report

The following are important report management features:

► **Versioning**
Version numbers are assigned to reports to determine if a report was changed in a way that is relevant or not to its predecessor. In updated reports, the changed specification data is displayed in a different color, thereby providing an instant overview of all relevant changes.

► **Creating worklists automatically**
The SAP system ensures that when changes are made to specification or phrase data, new report requests are created automatically for the reports affected by these changes.

▶ **Linking into word**

You can compare any two reports and display the differences between them in report management using a link between your system and a suitable display application (such as Microsoft Word or Adobe File Utilities).

▶ **Integrating inbound reports**

You can manage imported reports, including inbound reports that weren't generated in an SAP system but originate from an external system. You can display inbound reports in report management in any format, provided the corresponding application is installed on your frontend.

Substance Volume Tracking

In many countries, regulations state that you must register with the authorities the maximum quantities of certain hazardous substances that you plan to purchase, import, produce, sell, or export within a certain period above a certain quantity of chemicals. Substance volume tracking (SVT) helps you to comply with the relevant regulations by recording the quantities of substances to be tracked that you purchase, import, produce, sell, or export. By comparing the recorded quantities with the limit values, the system can warn you before a limit value is exceeded; if a limit value *is* exceeded, the system can also block the respective business process.

Figure 6.17 shows the process for SVT, which is explained in more detail following.

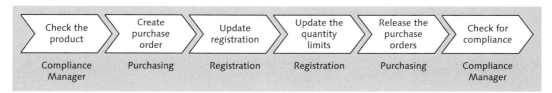

Figure 6.17 Process Substance Volume Tracking

1. **Check the product.**

Before you can use SVT, you have to ensure that the master data is set up correctly. You have to set up a material and specification and assign the registered allowed quantities for the registered company for tracking purposes (see Figure 6.18 for an example). After this has been set up correctly, the system will determine which quantities are tracked.

Figure 6.18 Specification with SVT Create Purchase Order

2. **Create purchase order.**

   As soon as you're using the specification, for example in a purchase order, the system can check the quantity online against the quantity limits, and depending on what you've set up, the system will respond appropriately. You can, for example, send a follow-up email to the person responsible for registration, who can then decide if a higher quantity needs to be registered.

3. **Update the registration.**

   As soon as the limit quantity has been reached, you can block the purchase order from further processing or warn the purchase order processer, to let him know that the limits have been reached.

4. **Update the quantity limits.**

   The compliance officer can request a higher volume or decide against this and block the purchase order from further processing.

5. **Release the purchase order.**

   After the higher volumes have been registered and approved, the purchase order can be released for further processing.

6. **Check for compliance.**

   At any point in time, reports can be produced with up-to-date information on the substances and the volumes handled so far, allowing you to monitor the planned against actual figures. Figure 6.19 shows the use of a corporate dashboard for SVT.

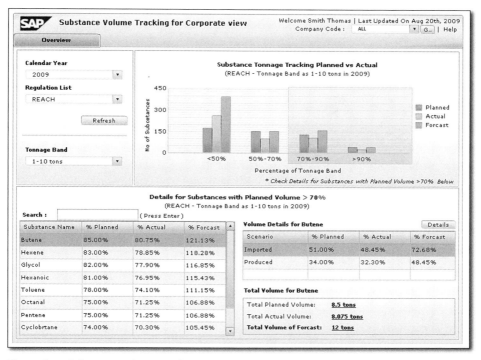

Figure 6.19 Substance Volume Tracking Monitoring

6.1.4 Dangerous Goods Management

Dangerous goods are the substances or objects that pose a risk to public safety, to the life and health of humans and animals, and to property, due to their nature, properties, or state. The difference between dangerous goods and hazardous substances is that they are classified differently; in fact, most countries contain two separate laws that govern them.

Dangerous goods are defined by their direct risk to public safety to life and health of employees. Examples of dangerous goods are corrosive, flammable, gaseous, spontaneously combustible, toxic, or water-reactive substances, such as fuels and oils, gases, paints, explosives, bitumen, tar, poison and pesticides, ammonium nitrate and acids, and radioactive materials.

Meanwhile, the term *hazardous substance* describes any substance that, because of its chemical, physical, or biological properties, can cause harm to people, property, or the environment. These are defined by their direct health effects on people, both immediately and in the long term, and are classified according to the hazard they present, including but not limited to dangerous goods, combustible liquids, and hazardous substances. Reconsider the examples of dangerous goods, and you'll notice that all these goods are also hazardous, which is often the case in which both regulations apply.

The term dangerous goods is used everywhere (through the common resource of ICAO, IATA, and the IMDG Code, which all take direction from the UN Committee of Experts and the UN Recommendation on the Transport of Dangerous Goods) except for the United States. In the United States, the regulation published by the U.S. Department of Transportation uses the term "Hazardous Materials," and these regulations are referred to as the "Hazardous Materials Regulations." So note that a hazardous material becomes a dangerous good in SAP terms, not a hazardous substance.

Dangerous Goods Management manages the storage, transportation, movement, delivery, compliance, and reporting of dangerous goods. Note that the Dangerous Goods Management component maps the legal regulations for *packaged* goods in the system but not those for unpackaged (bulk/tank) goods. Another difference is that Dangerous Goods Management is used when transporting dangerous goods, whereas Hazardous Substance Management focuses on managing the hazards when handling a product. Of course, in reality, these terms often coincide, whenever a dangerous good is also a hazardous good.

Master Data

Within Dangerous Goods Management, you use data from the material master, a real substance specification master, and its properties via dangerous goods classification, as shown in Figure 6.20. The dangerous goods master is an enhancement for the material master that contains the data required to perform dangerous goods checks and to generate dangerous goods documents according to the respective dangerous goods regulations.

Let's walk through the steps involved in Dangerous Goods Management.

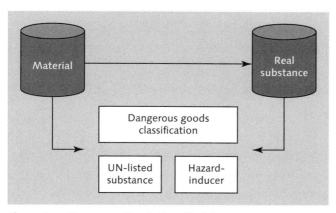

Figure 6.20 Dangerous Goods Data Model

Dangerous Goods Management Process

Figure 6.21 shows the process of Dangerous Goods Management. The first three steps of the process for Dangerous Goods Management are all related to master data maintenance. Within Dangerous Goods Management, you use data from the material master, ECM, and phrase management, where the last three steps are transactions. All these steps will be explained in more detail in this section.

Figure 6.21 Process for Dangerous Goods Management

1. **Edit dangerous goods specification.**
   To create a specification that is unlisted, you can use the specification type UN-listed substance (LS_UN_SUB). For listed goods, you use the value assignment specification type DG_CL_SUB (dangerous goods classification). You define the identification number for the specification by creating an identifier of identification category NUM and of identification type UN, ID, or NA. You must specify whether a collective number is used and whether transport is permitted. Figure 6.22 shows an example.

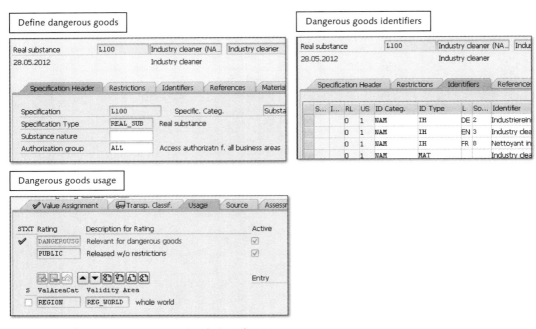

Figure 6.22 Dangerous Goods Specification

2. **Classify dangerous goods.**

   You edit the dangerous goods data, or in other words, the risk classification, packaging code approval, and transport approval. You define an identifier for the specification, for example, of identification category NAM and enter a descriptive text such as "Dangerous goods classification for varnish". You call the property tree that contains the value assignment type DANGEROUS GOODS CLASSIFICATION, as shown in Figure 6.23.

   Next you assign the specification of the specification type real substance to the dangerous goods classification in the REFERENCES tab and assign the material to this specification as well (see Figure 6.24).

   An environmentally relevant material must be assigned to a real substance that requires a MSDS if automatic MSDS shipping is to be set up. To enable the transfer of dangerous goods data from the specification database to the dangerous goods master, the assignment of the material to the dangerous goods classification must be unique. Data isn't transferred if you assign two dangerous goods classifications to a material via two different real substances.

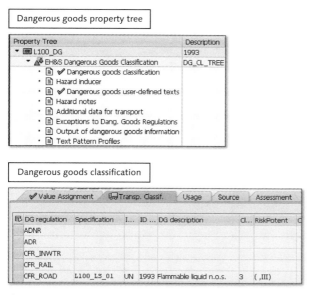

Figure 6.23 Dangerous Goods Classification

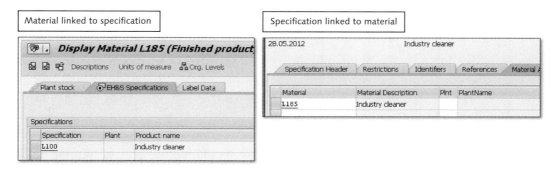

Figure 6.24 Link between Specification and Material

3. **Edit the dangerous goods master.**

The dangerous goods master is an enhancement for the material master, and it contains the data required to perform dangerous goods checks and generate dangerous goods documents according to the respective dangerous goods regulations. Figure 6.25 shows how the material is linked to a road-specific regulation and the further assignment to the dangerous goods classes as defined within the regulation. For the dangerous goods checks and when creating dangerous goods documents, you must ensure that the correct dangerous goods regulation is applied for each phase of a dangerous goods transport. Within the master data, you can use the Release Product status for a product released at the product definition stage in accordance with dangerous goods regulations. At a later stage in the logistics processing chain, the system simply checks this indicator setting, which makes the dangerous goods checks much faster.

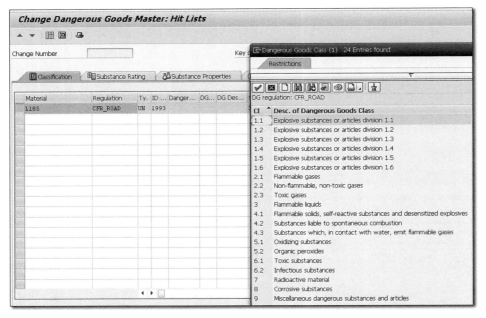

Figure 6.25 Dangerous Goods Master

4. **Perform dangerous goods checks.**

You can use the dangerous goods check to check sales and distribution documents against dangerous goods regulations from SD such as sales orders and shipping documents. Dangerous goods checks can be performed automatically or on request when creating and processing SD documents. By doing so, you avoid sending out deliveries or shipments that don't comply with the appropriate dangerous goods regulations.

When activated, the DANGEROUS GOODS CHECK button appears on the SD documents. You can use this button to start dangerous goods checks as required—for example, to check an intermediate stage in the document. You make corresponding settings in Customizing to specify which checks are to be performed at which stage and how documents are to be processed further, by the implementation of a user exit. The results of dangerous goods checks (positive and negative) are recorded in a log that you can consult immediately. Figure 6.26 shows an example of a failed check.

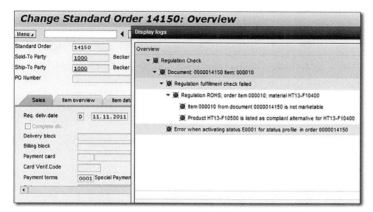

Figure 6.26 Failed Dangerous Goods Check during Sales Order

5. **Populate dangerous goods documents.**

   You use this function to create transport documents for dangerous goods and output them automatically or manually using SAPscript forms. You can tailor these forms to fit your requirements. Two SAPscript forms supporting the output of dangerous goods data are delivered with the dangerous goods documents component:

   ▶ RVDELNOTE creates a delivery note.

   ▶ SD_PACKING_LIST creates a packing list.

   To output a delivery note or packing list with dangerous goods data, you assign the delivery to an output (LD00 is standard). You define a communication method with which the output is to be produced, and depending on the processing time you specify for the output, the delivery note is output automatically, or you must trigger it yourself. You can send dangerous goods data in electronic form for a delivery or a shipment. The data with which the form is filled is obtained using the printing program from the corresponding dangerous goods master records and the delivery document. The process described here has been included in Figure 6.27, which shows the system steps involved in printing a dangerous goods document.

Figure 6.27 Printing a Dangerous Goods Document

If you compare dangerous goods regulations, you'll find that dangerous goods information varies in form and content according to the regulation that applies. The different regulations require dangerous goods-relevant information to appear on transport documents in a different sequence and with varying contents. Using text patterns allows you to print dangerous goods information on a delivery note and in the IDocs for delivery and transportation in a manner that fulfills the requirements of the respective dangerous goods regulations. The varying requirements for transport documents in different regulations affect the following details:

▸ Type of information (such as class, packing group)

▸ Sequence of information

▸ Additional text

▸ Additional information, such as flash point

6. **Generate and print transport emergency cards.**
TRansport EMergency Cards (tremcards) are written instructions for operators of vehicles, such as the captain of a ship or a rail conductor. The purpose of these cards is primarily to inform the transporters on the necessary actions to be taken in case of an emergency, and secondarily so that police, firefighters, and other emergency services can prevent accidents. They contain specific instructions for actions to be taken to prevent or minimize hazards. Examples of tremcards are the ADR tremcard (road transport) and the ADNR tremcard (inland waterway transport). In the United States, instead of using a tremcard, a MSDS or emergency response guide is often used.

The standard tremcard includes the following information:

▸ Load (UN number, etc.)

▸ Properties of the goods in the load

▸ Nature of danger

▸ Personal protective equipment

▸ General actions to be taken by the driver

- Additional and/or special actions to be taken by the driver
- Fire (information for the driver in case of fire)
- First aid
- Additional information (such as telephone number for inquiries)

Generating tremcards requires inputs from Specification Management, phrase management, the specification information system, report definition, report management, report shipping, and report information system.

6.1.5 Hazardous Substance Management

If you use hazardous substances in your company, you must protect both your employees and the environment from the hazards that these substances can cause during the handling of these materials. As stated at the beginning of this section, "hazardous substance" is a collective term used to describe any substance that, because of its chemical, physical, or biological properties, can cause harm to people, property, or the environment. They are classified according to the hazard they present, including but not limited to dangerous goods, combustible liquids, and hazardous substances. You also have to observe numerous rules and regulations worldwide. You can use the Hazardous Substance Management business process to help you handle hazardous substances safely and comply with all laws and regulations worldwide, as is represented in Figure 6.28.

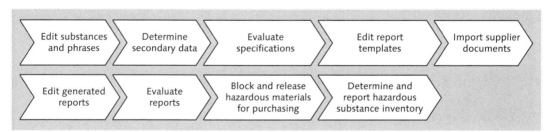

Figure 6.28 Hazardous Material Process

Let's walk through the process:

1. **Edit substances and phrases.**
   In the specifications, you enter all relevant data for the substances. For hazardous substances, it's important to assign the substance to the regulatory lists so

the system can include details of the substance on the MSDS, standard operating procedures, and hazardous substance labels.

Under the master data for hazardous substance, you can access and maintain work areas and agents, and you have access to necessary reports. The work area is the basic organizational unit in the Industrial Hygiene and Safety component, and, with work area management, you have maximum flexibility when specifying the work areas and work area patterns. For example, you can define work areas in terms of processes, installations, person groups, or tasks. You link the work area to your higher-level enterprise structure by assigning the work area to a plant.

The specific or potential negative effect of a chemical, physical, biological, or other nature on the health or well-being of persons in a company is represented in the specification database as an *agent* (or, alternatively, as a hazard). Examples of agents are UV radiation, lifting loads, mechanical hazards caused by lack of a safety barrier, and butyl alcohol. You can edit agents in and assess risks and create hazardous substance inventories as part of Hazardous Substance Management, which can be found under the AGENTS menu option. Figure 6.29 shows an example of a hazardous specification of the substance xylene.

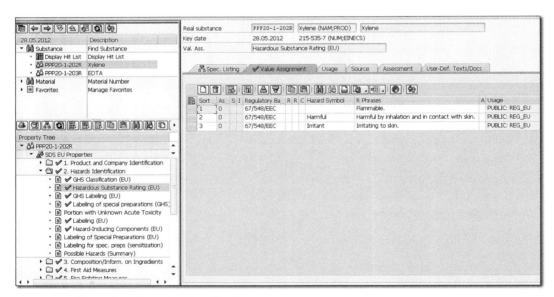

Figure 6.29 Hazardous Specification

2. **Determine secondary data.**

Specification data is sometimes interdependent, meaning that it's possible that properties can be derived from other properties. For this purpose, define rule sets and the relevant mapping tables using the supplementary application SAP EHS Expert, and derive secondary data for the specification data with these rule sets and mapping tables. You can also license rules from providers.

3. **Evaluate specifications.**

You search for specifications and their data using various criteria. You can prepare and display the data in different ways and transfer it to Excel spreadsheets for further evaluation. You can edit SAP EHS Management reports (such as MSDS, labels, and standard operating procedures) in report definition, release them in report management, dispatch them using report shipping, and then search for and display them using the report information system. You can import MSDS and other documents from your vendors and manage them like all other SAP EHS Management reports.

4. **Edit report templates.**

Using report templates, you structure the layout of SAP EHS Management reports—that is, of documents such as MSDS or labels. You can edit hazardous substance data and other data for the substances that occur in your company in Specification Management, and search for and display it using the specification information system.

5. **Import supplier documents.**

If required, you can import documents that you receive from suppliers, such as MSDS. You can scan these documents and assign them to the relevant hazardous substances. If your supplier transmits the documents electronically, you can import them into your report database automatically. You can import documents from suppliers manually as of SAP R/3 Enterprise PLM Extension 2.00.

6. **Edit generated reports.**

You can assign versions to generated and imported SAP EHS Management reports and submit them to a status-controlled release workflow. Reports that are no longer current can be set to Historical status and archived.

7. **Evaluate reports.**

You search for generated and imported SAP EHS Management reports using various criteria. You can send the reports manually to internal or external recipients. Using the SAP GUI for HTML or the SAP EHS Management web interface, you can make the reports accessible for external users.

8. **Block and release hazardous materials for purchasing.**
   You can place a purchase block on new materials, so they can only be used after you've rated and released them for purchasing.

9. **Determine and report hazardous substance inventory.**
   You assign the hazardous substances to one or more work areas. By means of the assignment of the substance to a material and thus to logistics, the system automatically determines consumption data and stock data and assigns this data to the individual work areas. This allows you to document comprehensively the use of hazardous substances in the various work areas.

   With this information, the system automatically compiles an up-to-the-minute hazardous substance inventory, allowing you to comply with the relevant laws. As of SAP R/3 Enterprise PLM Extension 2.00, you can create the reports prescribed by the U.S. Superfund Amendments and Reauthorization Act (SARA). In these reports, companies must list hazardous substances that belong to specific hazard categories and whose quantities exceed prescribed threshold levels onsite. SAP Supply Chain Management (SAP SCM) system and SAP EWM functions support you with the storage of hazardous substances.

   In the putaway checks, you can then also activate hazardous substance checks, allowing the system to put away and position hazardous substances in the warehouse on its own according to the properties of the hazardous substances. You create the hazardous substance data required for this in the hazardous substance master in the SCM system or you distribute it via Application Link Enabling (ALE) from an SAP ERP system to the SAP SCM system. In the SAP ERP system, you can fill the hazardous substance master from Specification Management.

6.1.6 SAP Waste and Recycling

Waste is a substance or object that is no longer useful for the rest of the business process, with the result that the enterprise wants to or has to dispose of the waste. SAP Waste and Recycling centralizes waste management. It integrates relevant business processes while improving visibility, logistics, service management, reporting, and compliance. In enterprises, substances and products are accumulated that can no longer be used during production and must be disposed of as waste. In this sense, disposal means either the recycling (recovery) or the disposal (dumping) of waste; in many countries, these disposal processes are regulated through laws and regulations. During the disposal processes, you consume resources (e.g., personnel, storage, containers, vehicles, etc.), and costs arise for the actual disposal of waste that depends on the quantity and level of risk of the waste and on the situation in the disposal market. Waste management (which is part of SAP EHS Management) handles waste disposal processes, complying with national and international regulations and laws that are relevant for generation, transport, and disposal. It also allows you to distribute costs proportionally among the departments within the enterprise that generated the waste.

In many cases, waste generators or waste disposers must also take into account the regulations and laws governing hazardous substances and dangerous goods, industrial hygiene and safety, and occupational health, alongside waste law. If this is the case in your enterprise, you should be using SAP EHS Management, specifically the following functions:

- Basic Data and Tools (EHS-BD)
- SAP Product Safety (EHS-SAF)
- Dangerous Goods Management (EHS-DGP)
- ECM
- CA

The use of the following SAP components and their integration objects (e.g., cost centers, materials, vendors, contracts, and storage locations) are optional; they depend on which specific requirements are needed or not:

- SAP DMS
- SAP MM
- SAP EWM
- Batch management
- SAP ERP Controlling (CO)/SAP Financial Accounting (FI)

Before we dive into the waste management business process, let's first define a few important waste management terms:

- **Waste generation**
  Combination of a waste generator with a waste, such as a point of waste generation production process.

- ▶ **Waste disposal**
  Combination of a waste disposer with a waste.

- ▶ **Waste transport**
  Combination of a waste transporter with a waste.

- ▶ **Authorities**
  Identifies the waste management business partner.

- ▶ **Disposal channel**
  Combination of waste generation and waste disposal; the waste generation and waste disposal have to contain the same waste. In a disposal channel, you specify that a waste disposer can dispose of a particular waste that has been generated by a particular waste generator.

Figure 6.30 shows the waste management process.

Figure 6.30 Waste Management Process

Let's walk through the process:

1. **Maintain basic and master data.**
   You can, among other things, enter all the data that is required for describing waste (e.g. from a logistics, physical-chemical, or legal point of view). You also enter the waste catalogs and waste codes, which are important for describing waste from a legal point of view.

   The following master data objects are used to describe waste, as shown in Figure 6.31:

   - ▶ Specification and phrase: In Basic Data and Tools in SAP EHS Management, you can set up phrases representing the waste catalogs and a specification to represent the waste code. You can also include details such as physical chemical properties, waste-relevant and waste law data, safety data, transport-relevant data, and toxicological data.

   - ▶ Material: In SAP MM, you create a material where you store the logistics data required. SAP recommends that you create your own materials for wastes, even if an existing material becomes a waste due to a shortfall batch or its shelf-life date expiring.

▶ Waste code: In Dangerous Goods Management in SAP EHS Management, you can create a master record used for describing waste. If the wastes are dangerous goods, enter the required dangerous goods data in the Dangerous Goods Management component. Dangerous goods processing for waste is carried out in the same way as for other materials.

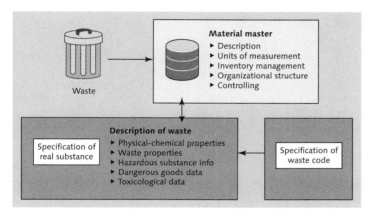

Figure 6.31 Waste Master Data Model

Figure 6.32 shows an example of all these master data elements, describing the waste from a cleaner product. The first row shows the material and the assignment to the specification, and the second row shows the specification and the waste code.

You use the SAP EHS Management master data to enter all the master data that is required for the disposal of wastes to be processed correctly. You can, among other things, enter all the data for waste generators such as points of generation, waste disposers, waste transporters, authorities, and waste approvals. Furthermore, you can link waste generators, waste transporters, and waste disposers to wastes and specify possible disposal channels. This enables you to document which wastes are generated by which waste generators, and which wastes can be disposed of or transported by which waste disposers and waste transporters, respectively. The data in waste generations, waste disposals, and waste transports is automatically transferred to some places in waste management and used for checks.

Figure 6.33 shows the waste generators referring to how the waste was created; the second pane shows the purchase order used to dispose of the waste through an appropriate waste disposal company.

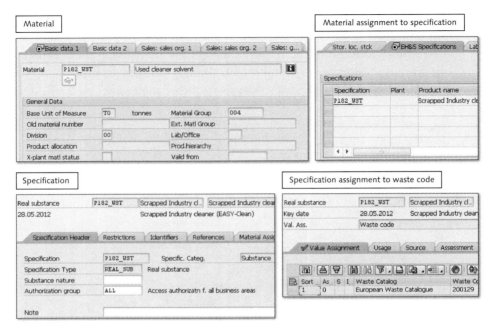

Figure 6.32 Material and Waste Code Example

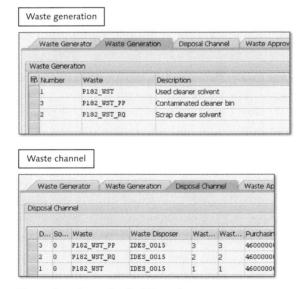

Figure 6.33 Example of a Waste Generator

2. **Edit waste approval.**

A waste approval is a document prescribed by law or defined within an enterprise relating to the permissibility of the planned disposal of certain wastes. In Germany, the waste approval directive (NachwV) stipulates the waste approvals for hazardous waste and describes, for example, the maximum quantity of waste belonging to a certain waste code that can be generated and disposed of over a specified time period. You can enter the following data, for example, for a waste approval (see Figure 6.33):

- Waste management business partners involved
- Waste codes to which the waste approval applies
- Licensed waste quantity
- Processing status of the waste approval, which allows you to release a waste approval

3. **Perform waste disposal.**

In waste management (from its dedicated menu folder), you can enter waste quantities and trigger further disposal processing. Links to numerous SAP components are available for this. The following activities are available to you in disposal processing:

- Post waste to SAP MM–IM
- Post waste to storage bins in SAP EWM (LE Logistics Execution)
- Trigger purchase orders for disposal in the SAP Purchasing component (SAP MM procurement and/or SAP SRM)
- Specify account assignment objects for distributing costs proportionally among the departments that generated the waste in the CO component (FI–CO)

Using waste management in combination with SAP MM functions, such as SAP IM or Purchasing, allows you, for example, to post waste directly to SAP MM–IM from waste management and trigger purchase orders for disposal. The exact details that need to be captured in the disposal document and the following process steps depend on how you decide to implement it and which other parts of SAP ERP are used. The process will always start with the disposal document, which can be created directly or can be entered through an entry tool available for disposal processing. For the entry documents from which at least one follow-on document of this type has been produced, the system creates a follow-on document record in which it automatically assigns the follow-on documents to the entry document. As a result, the processing steps and dependencies are specified and documented.

4. **Monitor disposal document return.**

   In the waste management area, you can create, print, and manage various disposal documents, such as German waste manifests or US hazardous waste manifests. At the same time, you can also monitor the return leg of the disposal document. When you create disposal documents, various checks ensure that only permitted data is entered; certain data is taken directly from the waste management basic data and master data. In Customizing for waste management, you can specify for each disposal document type separately which checks are to be carried out. Figure 6.34 shows an example of a disposal document created for used cleaner solvent.

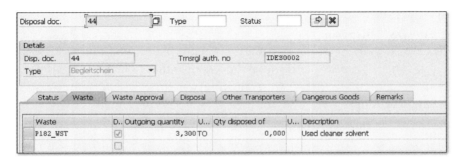

Figure 6.34 Disposal Document

On the screens for displaying and editing disposal documents, the system displays all the disposal documents in an overview tree, separated by the disposal document type. For each disposal document type, disposal documents with the same status are displayed in the lower-level nodes. This arrangement makes it easier for you to edit data because disposal documents for which the same editing steps must be carried out are combined in a worklist, as you can see in Figure 6.35.

In Customizing for waste management, you can specify the tab pages, screen areas, and fields that are available on the screens for displaying and editing disposal documents. In addition, you can specify the ready-for-input status of individual fields, which could depend on the status of a disposal document. This means that you can ensure, for example, that certain data is no longer changed after a disposal document has been printed. You can therefore also use the SAP disposal documents component to record information about disposal documents.

Furthermore, there is a print preview function available as well as functions with which you can detect quantity variances and monitor the disposal document return leg that is stipulated by certain laws and regulations.

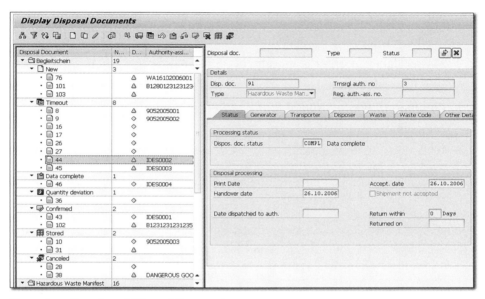

Figure 6.35 Overview of Disposal Documents

5. **Perform waste disposal analysis.**

You can create various reports based on the information captured in the previous business process steps, such as waste lifecycle analyses to enable you to gain insight into the origins of waste and the further process steps taken to dispose of this waste appropriately. You can use Customizing to flexibly adapt the waste management interface to suit your needs. You can thus hide fields, screens, and functions that you don't require and also add new ones.

6.1.7 SAP Recycling Administration

RECYCLING ADMINISTRATION can be found under the SALES AND DISTRIBUTION menu under BILLING. When using it, the following subcomponents can be used within the three main areas:

- ▶ Master data waste logistics
  - ▷ Container management
  - ▷ SAP Fleet Management
  - ▷ Human resources
  - ▷ Routes
  - ▷ Properties and clean objects
- ▶ Disposition routes and resources
  - ▷ Master data and order management
- ▶ Waste disposal services
  - ▷ Commercial waste disposal
  - ▷ Municipal waste disposal
  - ▷ Hazardous waste disposal
  - ▷ Cleaning and winter service
  - ▷ Loose and bulk waste

> **Note**
>
> This section is just a short introduction to what is possible with SAP Recycling Adminis-
> tration. For more information, see the SAP websites listed for this chapter in Appendix B.

The process supported for SAP Recycling Administration is represented in Figure
6.36.

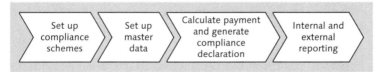

Figure 6.36 SAP Recycling Administration

Let's walk through the SAP Recycling Administration process:

1. **Set up compliance schemes.**
   Set up a declaration scheme (also known as a stewardship program) with the
   partner to whom you'll submit the declaration. In this step, the system finds all
   the sold items with the SAP Recycling Administration article called packing
   master data details for packaging weights. An SAP Recycling Administration

article is a material that is used as the main object in declaration administration on the basis of the contract between your organization and the recycling partner. The SAP Recycling Administration solution package contains templates for more than 50 different compliance schemes worldwide (you can find more details on these templates and how to load them easily through a wizard tool via SAP Note 1515357).

2. **Set up master data.**
   The REA article and the packaging material data need to be set up to support processing, which is usually performed by a master data management specialist.

3. **Calculate payment and generate compliance declaration.**
   Based on the master data maintained, you can calculate payment and generate a compliance declaration like the one shown in Figure 6.37.

4. **Internal and external reporting.**
   Several reporting and analysis functions are available, both in the standard SAP ERP as well as by activation of SAP Business Content in business analytics tools (for more on this topic, please refer to Chapter 10).

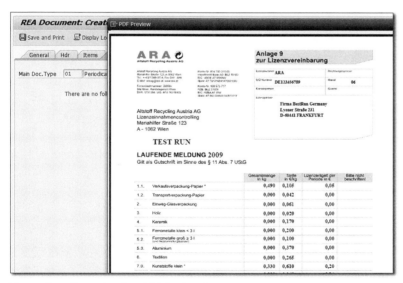

Figure 6.37 Example of an REA Declaration

Section 6.2 has taken you through the different parts of SAP Product Safety covering product compliance, which include basic master data, Global Label Management, SAP Product Safety, and Dangerous Goods Management. SAP

Product Safety supports companies that *produce* hazardous substances, whereas the SAP EHS Management subarea Hazardous Substance Management supports companies that *use* hazardous substances. If you use hazardous substances in your company, you must protect both your employees and the environment from these potential hazards.

In addition, we looked at dangerous goods, which are substances classified as dangerous because they pose an immediate risk to people and the environment. They need to be labeled accordingly—often by a diamond signal—and often require special care and labeling when *transported*. Recall that multiple rules and regulations apply; these often distinguish between a hazardous substance and a dangerous good (or hazardous material in the United States).

Last we looked into SAP Waste and Recycling, allowing you to dispose of waste in a controlled manner, which is a function of environmental performance.

6.2   Operational Risk Management

Another part of the sustainability solution offering is the end-to-end process Operational Risk Management. It's important from an SAP PLM perspective because you may want to manage product-related and asset-related risks. (Note that this process requires SAP ERP 6, EPH 6.)

Although this process can also be used to manage injuries and environmental incidents, this section will mainly focus on the product- and asset-related incidents. Risk assessments can take place regarding a product or asset, where a team of cross-department specialists documents the identified risk, its impact, and likelihood via a matrix and the monitoring and control mechanism.

Operational Risk Management also provides you with a subprocess called worker safety, through which you manage and relate worker safety information to maintenance and service activities to provide a safer working environment for your employees. SAP Audit Management is another part of this solution, which was will be described in Section 6.4.

But first let's explore the concept of Operational Risk Management further. This is one of the four end-to-end processes that provide a complete set of solutions to manage sustainability programs across your organization. Operational risk management provides the key process to manage operational risks based on a continuous improvement model, where risk assessment is performed proactively and incidents can be recorded in order to learn from them.

Operational Risk Management has the following primary objectives:

- To manage and learn from incidents and safety observations to build a proactive safety culture
- To identify operational risks and hazards, and to implement and communicate effective controls
- To develop and execute required safety programs
- To reduce risks caused by operational changes using risk assessment and approval processes
- To communicate risk information to maintenance workers and manage safe work permits
- To maintain compliance to regulatory and management system requirements and drive continuous improvement

To accomplish these objectives, Operational Risk Management includes a comprehensive risk management process. It uses the continuous improvement model that links planning, doing, and checking to perform proactive risk assessment as well as learning from past incidents.

Figure 6.38 shows the end-to-end process covering Operational Risk Management. Several different areas within the solution are identified by the first row, such as incident management and SAP EHS risk assessment, and the first column shows the departments involved when executing the process steps. As you can see, the identification and management of a risk is dependent on the specific type of risk, how it was identified, and within which area of the organization and system it will be monitored and controlled. To map this correctly within the process flow, this has resulted in many relationships between the activities, which can be done in parallel and are bidirectional. So instead of explaining the process step by step, we'll explain the different areas.

In Operational Risk Management, where the key integration points ensure that a common data model enhances communication and action with respect to reducing risks. Closed-loop action tracking ensures that agreed actions are really completed. Simple forms for incident recording and change requests ensure that all workers can contribute to safer operations.

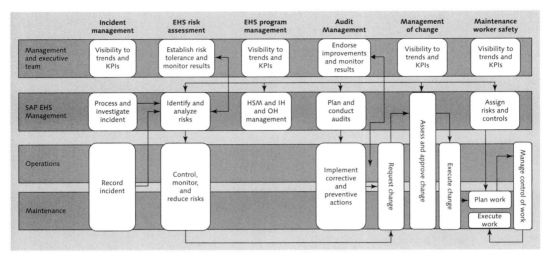

Figure 6.38 End-to-End Operational Risk Management Process

Let's explore those facets of Operational Risk Management, beginning with incident management and moving to maintenance workers safety.

6.2.1 Incident Management

The objective of incident management is to learn from close calls and safety observations to build a proactive safety culture. Its main functions include the following:

▶ Fast-entry incident recording to foster a proactive safety culture

▶ Managing injuries and medical treatments, environmental responses, and asset failures

▶ Managing incident investigation processes, root cause analysis, and lessons learned

▶ Performing closed-loop action management with SAP ERP integration

▶ Monitoring incident data and trends to identify opportunities for incident prevention

Though organizations strive for no injuries and no impact to the environment, incidents do occur. SAP EHS incident management allows you to manage the incident resulting in an injury, environmental damage, asset damage, or other consequences. Leading companies also use incidents as an opportunity for improvement. By conducting a thorough investigation and root cause analysis, they identify failures in their management system and take preventive action to reduce the likelihood of similar incidents in the future. Companies that are building a safety culture also track very small incidents—perhaps where no damage at all has occurred—referred to as "near misses," "close calls," or "safety observations." They encourage all employees to report these issues and incident details to get better insight into trends that can be acted on to prevent incidents.

Let's walk through the major components of incident management, as shown in Figure 6.39.

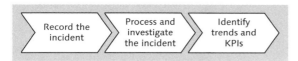

Figure 6.39 Incident Management Process

1. **Record the incident.**

   The recording of an incident within SAP EHS Management (see Figure 6.40) can be done via multiple channels, such as providing an SAP Interactive Form by Adobe on the intranet, optimizing the mobile application with voice recordings and photographs, or directly in the system via the SAP NetWeaver Portal or SAP GUI. Figure 6.40 shows the creation of an incident through the SAP NetWeaver Portal, which guides you through incident creation step by step.

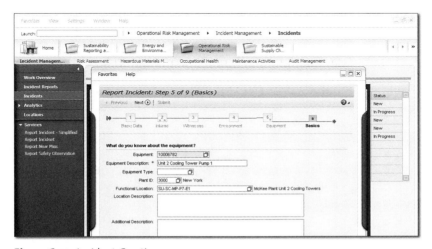

Figure 6.40 Incident Creation

2. **Process and investigate the incident.**

An incident in SAP EHS Management is basically the generation of a notification document (described in more detail in Chapter 5, Section 5.3.2) with the only distinction being that it belongs to SAP EHS Management (by its category) and can only be created with the notification types as configured within SAP EHS Management. Because the notification and the further processing possibilities work similarly, it provides you with a detailed business processes for specialists to manage the actual incident further. Finally, by integrating a closed-loop action system within SAP ERP, corrective and preventive actions can be tracked from creation to completion, which has been described in more detail later in this chapter.

3. **Identify trends and KPIs.**

By analyzing and monitoring incidents to identify trends and KPIs, you can get insight into how your organization is doing based on its goals. Figure 6.41 shows an example of a HEALTH AND SAFETY dashboard where the SAP EHS Management KPIs defined by this organization are graphically represented for the year (using supplementary SAP reporting tools; see Chapter 10, Section 10.3 for more details).

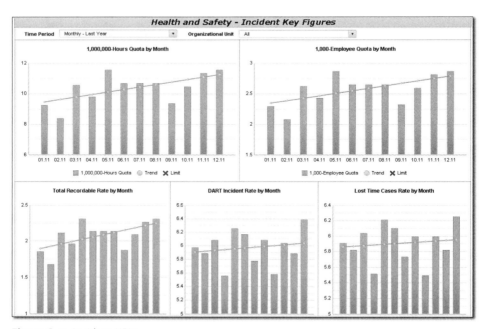

Figure 6.41 Incident KPIs

6.2.2 SAP EHS Risk Assessment

The risk assessment process enables you to identify and reduce risks and hazards and put controls and monitoring measures in place. The main functions of risk assessment include the following:

▶ Identifying and analyzing risks using risk and controls matrix, job hazard analysis, and other analysis methods

▶ Managing measurement amounts and comparing to occupational exposure limits

▶ Communicating risks and controls to workers

▶ Managing closed-loop action/tasks with SAP ERP integration

▶ Gaining visibility into top risks and evaluating control effectiveness

Regulations in many countries prescribe certain programs and procedures that must be followed for risk management, but industry-leading companies know that compliance with those programs and procedures by itself isn't sufficient to prevent all incidents. This has led them to the introduction of proactive risk assessment processes, which go beyond the scope of compliance.

These competitive organizations also found that operational risks are often interrelated because they run across multiple processes and affect multiple parts of the organization. Therefore, they must be managed holistically—that is, in such a way that the responsibility for safety is shared between all employees from your organization. Whether they are SAP EHS experts, operational workers, service and maintenance engineers, or the management and executive team, everyone is responsible for recording incidents, using appropriate risk controls, implementing corrective actions, recognizing operational changes, and reviewing whether the implemented changes have been effective in reducing risk. The workforce should have clear, complete instructions about the hazards and the controls they should be using to minimize harm.

Now that we've covered what risk assessment can accomplish, let's walk through the steps to achieve it. Figure 6.42 shows the three main steps, with are further broken down into substeps.

1. **Identify the operational risk.**
   During the first risk management step, you administer the basic data of the assessment, which contains the assessment type (either health, safety, job hazard, or environmental), description, the assessment team members, any

regulations, and assessment reason information. You can configure and use extensive catalogs to standardize this process and facilitate speedy risk data collection and entry. Assessment types can be used directly or as part of a template to create your own in the configuration. Our focus here will be based on a safety risk assessment because this type is relevant for SAP PLM. Figure 6.43 shows a risk assessment for a piece of equipment (a cooling tower). The other types won't be discussed because they are outside the scope of this book.

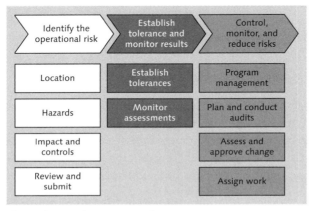

Figure 6.42 Risk Assessment Process

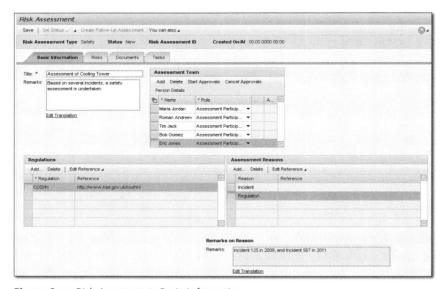

Figure 6.43 Risk Assessment: Basic Information

With this data inputted, you next follow the sequence of the risk management process, as shown in Figure 6.44. First identify the location of the risk. During this step, you can actually use master data from the technical object structure from SAP Plant Maintenance (SAP PM) or SAP Customer Service (SAP CS). Notice how two pieces of equipment can be assigned to the same risk assessment in Figure 6.44.

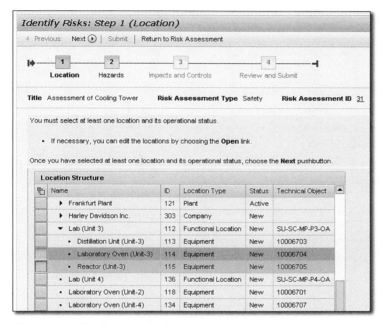

Figure 6.44 Identification of Risk Location

In the following steps, you identify the hazards and the relevant impacts and controls, as shown in Figure 6.45 and Figure 6.46, respectively. During these steps, you can use predefined catalogs to standardize this process and improve risk data collection and entry.

If a catalog entry you want to assign isn't available in the catalog, you can create a request for this new entry, which will be sent to the system administrator. Figure 6.45 shows the catalog options for HAZARDS, which are grouped in categories, such as BIOLOGICAL and CHEMICAL. The BIOLOGICAL category has been assigned with four hazards defined and the last two chosen. Above these specific hazards, beside the SELECT ALL and DESELECT ALL buttons, you see the REQUEST HAZARD button for when a new entry needs to be requested.

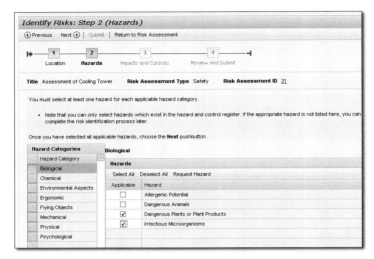

Figure 6.45 Identify Risks: Hazards

Figure 6.46 Identify Risk: Impacts and Controls

The last step in this dialog box sequence is to review and submit the information (see Figure 6.47).

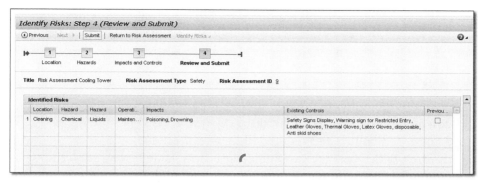

Figure 6.47 Review and Submit Step

After the risk identification has been completed, the following step is the performance of the actual assessments of the identified risks. Based on the type of assessment, you can configure the order and the steps of the assessment. The left side of Figure 6.48 shows the standard available assessment steps for an equipment-specific risk assessment. In this example, during the inherent risk determination, the level of the risk is found to be HIGH (note the RISK section on the right), based on a risk matrix that consists of the risk likelihood and severity of the risk. These matrixes and their values can be configured based on your own business rules.

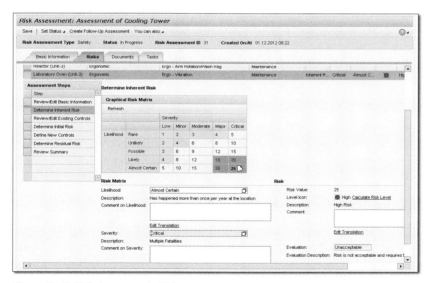

Figure 6.48 Risk Assessment: Risks

2. **Establish tolerances and monitor the result.**
Management communicates the organization's objectives regarding risk tolerance and provides the resources for risk reduction and operational improvements. During this step, you establish the risk tolerances and monitor the
results of risk assessments. When changes to a risk matrix are required, a
change request to the administrator needs to be sent.

3. **Control, monitor, and reduce risks.**
To control, monitor, and reduce risk, you can conduct one of the following
processes, which will be listed and described in the following subsections:

   ► Perform program management

   ► Plan and conduct audits

   ► Assess and approve change

   ► Assign work

6.2.3   SAP EHS Program Management

SAP EHS Management programs can be managed to ensure worker safety during
high-risk work within operations (such as maintenance activities) or customer
service activities on electrical products/assets (such as electricity poles or stations). You can identify the possible risks, and through safety measures, you can
ensure that the risks you've identified are being controlled and that you're meeting regulatory and company requirements. SAP EHS program management, in
which programs can be set up and managed, consists of three areas: Hazardous
Substance Management, Industrial Hygiene and Safety, and occupational health
management.

The programs can be created and monitored via the respective SAP EHS Management area, which includes different available reporting capabilities that can provide you with insights into trends and KPIs. However, details of these processes
aren't discussed further here because they are outside the scope of this book.

6.2.4   Management of Change

Through the management of change, you can make sure that the ever-changing
operations environment is supported through a change management process,
which ensures that these changes are managed in a way that reduces the risks. A
change can be initiated during a risk assessment or as a result of an audit. A good

example of a change is selecting a corrective action in the form of a maintenance request directly from the incident, so the maintenance department can check the problem and find an appropriate solution. Because the maintenance request is created from the incident, you can see the maintenance request, its follow-up activities, and its status changes within the incident.

Another next step after an incident occurs is performing a risk assessment. Any changes proposed through either a risk assessment or as a result of an audit can be managed and recorded by going through the steps shown in Figure 6.49 and described following the figure.

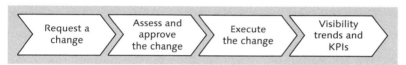

Figure 6.49 Change Management Process

The incident allows you to generate a maintenance notification, a service notification, a quality notification, or a general notification. Figure 6.50 shows an example of how a maintenance request ("The pump is leaking again") is created from within the incident.

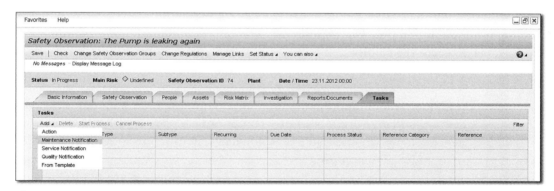

Figure 6.50 Creating a Maintenance Request from an Incident

1. **Request a change.**
   A change request can be captured in the change request master, where you can include the details of the change, the requester, and so on. Figure 6.50 and Figure 6.51 show you an example of how a request for change (in this case, a maintenance request) is created from within the incident.

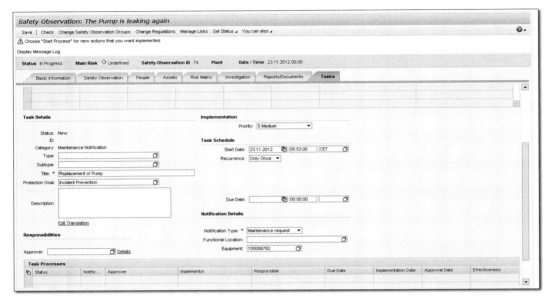

Figure 6.51 Assigning Details to a Maintenance Request

2. **Assess and approve the change.**
   The next step makes sure the change is received by the appropriate employee(s) who will assess the requested change and add additional details. When required, the change can go through an approval step.

3. **Execute the change.**
   After the change is approved, it can be executed and implemented. Other business processes can be triggered depending on the size and impact of the change (e.g., the creation of project management steps, such as creation of a business case, an initiative proposal, a program or project plan, or, when it's a maintenance activity, the creation of a maintenance notification or work order).

4. **Visibility trends and KPIs.**
   A change can be proposed, assessed, and implemented after approval. The implemented changes can be tracked against set response profiles to ensure they were handled within the set time frames.

6.2.5   Maintenance Workers Safety

The maintenance workers safety solution allows you to communicate relevant risks and safety measures to the maintenance engineer about the maintenance tasks, the locations, and the job in general. The main functions of maintenance workers safety include the following:

- Document risks and controls relevant to maintenance tasks, locations, and people.
- Create safety measure lists to manage tools, approvals, and safety instructions.
- Manage safe work permit processes to control hazardous energy and maintain safe working conditions.
- Provide instructions on the job card to clearly communicate directly to the workers.

Because they perform a variety of tasks (and often in urgent breakdown situations), maintenance workers experience some of the highest risks in the field. Some examples of dangerous maintenance activities are working with electricity, working in confined spaces, or welding. Managing maintenance work requires specific safety-related business processes, including the management of safe work permit processes.

For these workers, it's essential that risk and control information relevant to their exact task is available to them at that exact time. This function is provided through the integration between SAP EHS Management and SAP Enterprise Asset Management (SAP EAM). It allows you to communicate the safety-relevant information captured by the SAP EHS experts who performed that asset's risk assessment to the maintenance planner, who then provides the information to the workers on their work order via the job card.

A second related solution provides additional support for maintenance worker safety: Work Clearance Management (WCM). WCM supports the very detailed requirements of the control of hazardous energy procedure, sometimes called lock-out/tag-out. It supports the tagging and untagging of equipment to ensure that electricity and other energy sources have been isolated before the work takes place. It also supports complex review and approval processes required by this procedure. This process was described in detail in Chapter 5, Section 5.6.4.

So let's go through the maintenance workers safety process as shown in Figure 6.52 and described next.

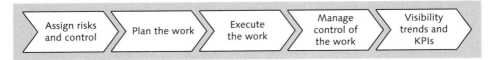

Figure 6.52 Maintenance Workers Safety Process

1. **Assign risks and control.**

   During the creation of the work order, the relevant risks and controls will be proposed based on the specific maintenance tasks, locations, and employees determined during the risk assessment in SAP EHS Management.

2. **Plan the work.**

   When the technical object is chosen (or the location or person), the safety data from the safety plan is copied into the work order and placed into a dedicated SAFETY PLAN tab. During the planning of the work, the maintenance planner can choose which safety measures to apply to this work order on a case-by-case basis. He is also able to add any additional risks and safety measures, when required. The planned (or applied) safety measures are visible on the left side of Figure 6.53; the identified risk and the proposed safety plan measures based on the safety risk assessment are shown on the right side.

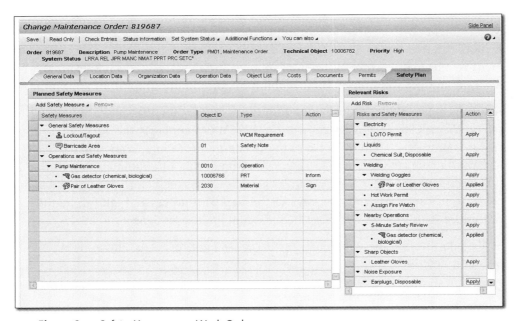

Figure 6.53 Safety Measures on Work Order

3. **Execute the work.**

   After the planner has applied the safety measures to the maintenance work order, the information gets included in the work order header and can be printed onto the form, along with any safety symbols (see Figure 6.54), whether it's supplied via paper or electronically as a PDF or through a mobile channel (e.g., the mobile app).

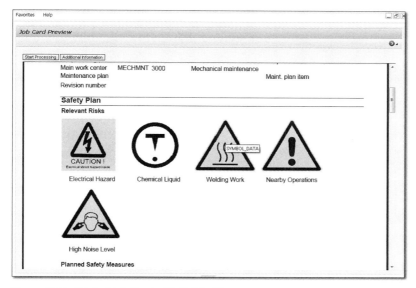

Figure 6.54 Printed Job Card with Safety Measures

4. **Manage control of the work.**

   After the maintenance work execution has taken place, the risk assessment can be finalized by assessing the residue of the risk, closing the assessment, and (when required) requesting a follow-up activity.

5. **Visibility trends and KPIs.**

   To get a complete view of the risks and easily determine the areas of highest concern, management reviews the increasing trend for safety observations by using dashboards that include information on the top risks. This enables management to prioritize activities to ensure risk reduction to the level of the organization's established objectives. Management needs visibility into trends and KPIs across all of these subprocesses to ensure that safety is being managed according to the organization's objectives and risk tolerance. Figure 6.55 shows an example of a risk dashboard, which has been generated via SAP

BusinessObjects business intelligence (BI) tools and will be explained in more detail in Chapter 10.

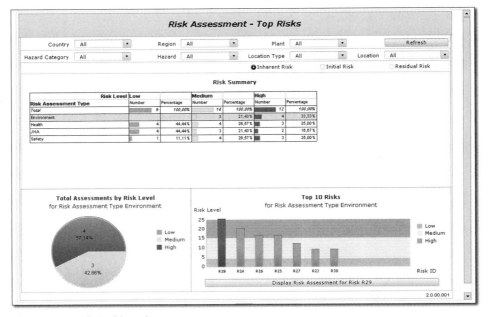

Figure 6.55 Risk Dashboard

To ensure that your components, end products, and processes comply with the relevant regulation, you can systematically perform audits to determine and check compliance based on predefined criteria at set times. SAP Audit Management allows you to audit any object; however, we'll look at it from a product perspective.

6.3 SAP Audit Management

An *audit* is a systematic examination used to determine to what extent an object meets previously specified criteria. Audits are usually performed using question lists that represent the criteria.

SAP Audit Management helps companies comply with legal requirements or industry standards. It supports all phases of auditing, from the planning of a comprehensive audit program and of the individual audits, through the definition of the audit criteria or question lists, to the actual auditing process and the assessment of the audit object in the audit report. SAP Audit Management also supports you in defining and monitoring corrective and preventive actions that were based on the findings. It's an effective tool for the evaluation of all audit data.

SAP Audit Management is a very versatile cross-application component that can support all different audit types (such as supplier audits, internal audits, and environmental audits) and other kind of assessments, examinations, inspections, or revisions. SAP Audit Management provides company-wide, real-time access to consistent information at any time, in any language, and from any location. All programs are object-oriented and modular, and most enhancements can be made without modification. Security, protection, and archiving of audit data can be secured through system administration.

SAP Audit Management is suitable for a variety of audit usages and relevant standards, and you can easily combine audits where this is possible. Forms of usage are audit, revision, inspection, and examination. The following list provides some examples of supported uses according to standards:

- Quality Management, ISO 9000, is a family of standards developed by the International Organization for Standardization (ISO), which provides guidance and tools for companies and organizations who want to ensure that their products and services consistently meet customer requirements, and that quality is consistently improved. It includes audit management, where organizations must perform internal audits to check how its quality management system is working. An organization may decide to invite an independent organization to perform the audit to verify that it's in conformity to the standard or conduct the audit themselves. Audits can be related to systems, processes, or products, as well as FMEA.

- Environmental management, ISO 14000, is another family of standards from ISO that provides practical tools for companies and organizations looking to identify and control their environmental impact and constantly improve their environmental performance.

- Safety and security management, ISO 19000, is a family of standards for geographic information, including concepts, principles of quality, quality assessment, specifications, and metadata standards. ISO 19011 provides guidance on auditing management systems, the principles of auditing, management of an audit program, and the evaluation of competence of the individuals involved in the audit process.

▶ Hygiene Good Manufacturing Practice (GMP) is a production and testing practice that helps to ensure a quality product. Many countries have legislations covering GMP procedures and guidelines specifically for pharmaceutical and medical device companies to safeguard the health of the patient as well as produce good quality medicine, medical devices, or active pharmaceutical products.

▶ Internal Controls, Financials, and Risk Management (Base II) is an international standard for banking laws and regulations issued by the Basel Committee on Banking Supervision. It won't be discussed further because it falls outside the scope of this book

Effective use of SAP Audit Management can bring about the following benefits:

▶ Official documents and private notes can be attached to the data objects used in SAP Audit Management, which can be printed or sent. For each phase of the auditing process, you can specify your partners and communicate with them.

▶ Interfaces to external tools are possible, such as Microsoft Project for the project management of an extensive audit program and Microsoft Excel (via XML) for question lists, extended data analysis, and report templates that can be defined with Smart Forms.

▶ The DOWNLOAD/UPLOAD VIA XML option enables you to easily conduct audits on any mobile device.

▶ Graphical analysis of audit data enables benchmarking, Pareto, and trend analysis.

▶ The component is easy to learn and use; most aspects are self-explanatory.

SAP Audit Management is available in all SAP solutions based on SAP NetWeaver. In fact, the SAP Audit Management component was originally developed for mySAP CRM (Customer Relationship Management, version 3.0 and up), was transferred to the SAP NetWeaver platform in 2005, and is now available in all SAP solutions based on SAP NetWeaver (e.g. SAP ERP 6.0 and SAP PLM 7.02).

SAP Audit Management is a cross-application function found under CROSS APPLICATION COMPONENTS. The core competency of TechniData, acquired by SAP in 2010, was in the SAP EHS Management space and offered the SAP Audit Management software as an add-on for older SAP releases on a project basis.

Now that we've covered the purpose of an audit and multiple types of audits and benefits of SAP Audit Management, we'll go into the master data elements that are available in SAP Audit Management, such as the audit plan, question list, audit, and actions.

6.3.1 SAP Audit Management Master Data Objects

The following objects, which are referred to in the system and documentation as audit components, are used within SAP Audit Management:

- Audit plan
- Question list
- Audit
- Corrective and preventive actions

These objects and their relationships are as represented in Figure 6.56.

Figure 6.56 SAP Audit Management Data

Let's explore each of these SAP Audit Management master data objects in further detail.

Audit Plan

The *audit plan* is used to keep an overview of your audits and have them organized in a logical fashion. (In ISO 19011, this is called an Audit program.) In the audit plan, you define the schema (e.g., in the form of an annual schedule), taking into consideration the scope, object, and date of the audits. An audit plan can contain several subordinate audit plans and links to audits.

Figure 6.57 shows how you can group audits together in a hierarchical structure according to organizational criteria (e.g., annually). You can use the interface to connect to Microsoft Project, to export your audit plan, and to reimport the audits after you've redefined your work packages. You can also create *unplanned audits*, which means creating audits without relating them to audit plans.

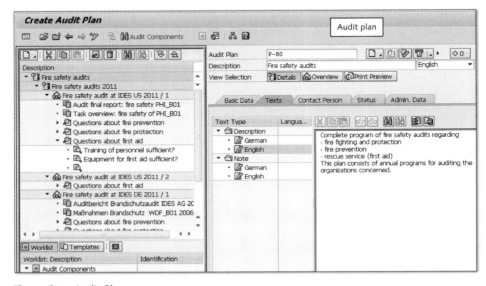

Figure 6.57 Audit Plan

Question List

A *question list* (also referred to as audit criteria) is usually required to execute an audit, and it stores the criteria to which the audit objects are assessed. A question list can be created as an independent master data object with the purpose to reuse its contents. After you perform an audit, you copy this question list into the audit, which makes it part of the audit. This, however, is optional; you can also create the question list specifically for a particular audit. Question lists contain the expertise of the auditor regarding the audit area he is responsible for.

SAP can't deliver any preconfigured question lists for particular regulated areas due to licensing law restrictions. However, question lists can be maintained manually or uploaded from Excel files into the system via a standard XML interface.

The question list has two structural components. At the header level, along with the hierarchy profiles, you can define the number of hierarchy levels that exist and the formatting mask, whether questions can be assigned at all levels or only at the lowest level, and the levels at which valuations can be performed. At the item level, you can then enter a priority, a weighting, and a valuation proposal for the items to be evaluated. The valuation profile is assigned to all the questions that need to be answered, and the profile controls the valuation of the relevant items. The system contains a series of ready-to-use profiles—for example, a qualitative valuation with steps (Good, Satisfactory, or Poor) or quantitative (percent fulfillment). However, you can freely configure your own profiles. Figure 6.58 gives an example of a question list. For combined audits, you can include more than one question list in an audit and relocate the questions.

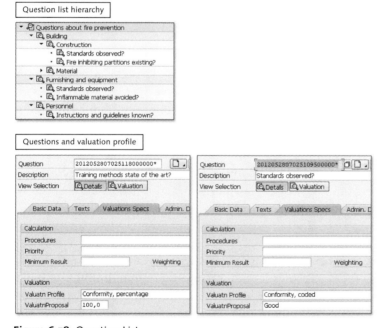

Figure 6.58 Question List

Audit

The audit (recall that this is called the audit plan within the ISO 19011) describes the audit type and the audit triggers, as well as the audit object. The definition of audit objects makes it possible to analyze similar audits to determine best practices or trends. The structure of an audit consists of the following elements:

- **Audit plan**
  This is an optional element for reoccurring audits.

- **Audit**
  This is the object that is being audited, such as the product or process, the audit team, the audit type and cause, deadlines, texts, valuation rule, result, or status.

- **Audit question list**
  The question and/or question list gets assigned to the audit. As soon as you use a question list or create a question list or additional questions, these all are specific to the audit and contain both the question list header and items.

- **Actions**
  This is related to audit questions, which contain follow-up actions, such as an additional audit, or preventive, corrective, or improvement actions.

Audits can be performed with reference to organizations, enterprise areas, products, and vendors. If an audit object is described using data elements for the system repository—for example, by the combination vendor and material—the information related to these data elements is available, which is an advantage of integration.

However, it's also possible to define your audit object freely. The audit object is also used for the recording of the execution of the audit by assigning audit question lists and entering the valuation of the questions in this list. Figure 6.59 shows an example of a fire-safety revision audit.

The actual execution of an audit can be triggered in two ways:

- **By an obligation to collect information on the part of the partners involved**
  This procedure is supported by the Audit Monitor (Transaction PLM_AUDIT-MONITOR), where every system user can generate individual worklists. All partners are responsible for collecting information about their individual task using this worklist.

- **By an obligation to provide information on the part of the person responsible for the audit**
  This procedure is supported by the notification function, which allows the audit planner to define a worklist and to send email invitations for participation

to the partners concerned. The audit planner can also set up the system so it regularly updates the worklist and automatically sends such invitations.

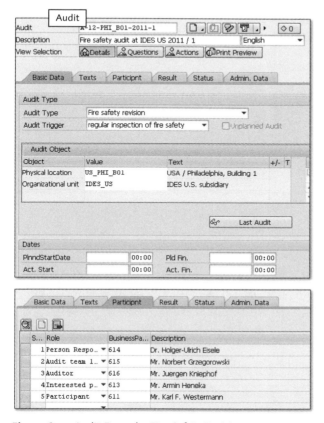

Figure 6.59 Audit Example: Fire-Safety Revision

Follow-Up Actions

During auditing, you can determine follow-up activities based on the results of an audit, including actions to determine the necessity of a subsequent audit, or corrective, preventive, and improvement actions. You can assign persons responsible, monitor the subsequent steps, and verify the effectiveness of all actions by recording and reporting on the progress data via the Audit Monitor. Figure 6.60 gives you an example of a corrective action, where a training course has been identified.

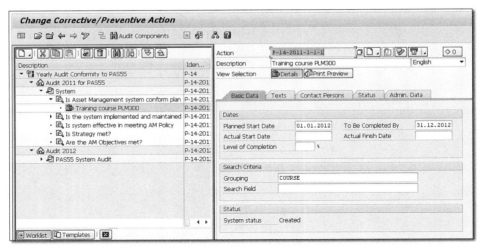

Figure 6.60 Action

6.3.2 The Audit Process

A typical audit process can include the phases and tasks represented in Figure 6.61. You can consider an audit to be a process with a beginning and an end, or in part a cyclical sequence triggered periodically, as the arrow represents.

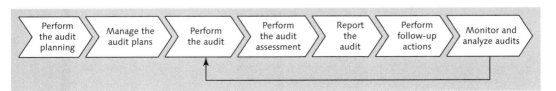

Figure 6.61 SAP Audit Management Process

Let's walk through the process:

1. **Perform the audit planning.**
   During the audit planning stage, you prepare the necessary question lists and audit criteria, depending on relevant standards, regulations, or rules of the auditable area. You can set up an audit plan and define the periodic schedule, taking into consideration the scope, the audit object, and the dates of the audits.

2. **Manage the audit plans.**

   When the audit is part of a program, the audit plan and any relevant audit sub-plans need to be set up accordingly in the system. The subplans should contain information about the plan, a general description, and a validity period. This is often the case for obligatory audits, in which case it's recommended to use the audit program. The audit program allows you to plan the type, scope, and frequency of audits, as well as the resource requirements. You can create an audit program by hierarchically structuring audit plans, which also allows you to combine certain types of audits. From a business perspective, it makes sense to group together, for example, an environment audit and health and safety audit.

3. **Perform the audit.**

   During this stage, you're collecting evidence and recording the findings. Prepare the individual audits by determining the question lists, identifying the partners involved, and preparing the required documents. This step involves the following actions: releasing the audit in the system, inviting the participants, providing the documents, and examining the audit object with regard to the criteria or performing interviews with the auditee.

   Although SAP Audit Management is designed for online, paperless application, SAP supports exporting and importing of audit data and audit question lists to allow for *offline and mobile auditing* via a standard XML interface. The XML file can then be transferred to an Excel file and loaded on the auditor's laptop so the audit can be performed based on this data. After returning to the office, the auditor can upload the file via the standard XML interface into SAP Audit Management, where the process can be completed.

4. **Perform the audit assessment.**

   Based on the evidence entered in the previous step, the questions are valuated and based on the question configuration settings (set up according to your business rules), so the system will rate and automatically grade your audit object. Because you're grading the audit object, this stage is sometimes referred to as grade audit or grade object. The overall assessment and grading for the audit object is determined on the basis of the valuations of all items that have actually been assessed. To consolidate the valuations across several hierarchy levels of the question list, the degrees of fulfillment or deviation from each hierarchy level are used for calculation in the standard SAP system. The valuation on the supreme hierarchy level is then used to grade the audit object using a rating profile. In the rating profile, you determine the degrees of fulfillment that must be achieved for separate grades. However, you can also program your own valuation algorithms if required without modifying standard programs (a BAPI is available).

5. **Report the audit.**
This phase begins with the creation of the audit report, which contains all important administrative data related to the audit, including comments, results, and the corrective/preventive actions that have been determined. The audit report is an official document that is signed by the lead auditor and the head of the audited area. Parts of the audit report are usually confidential and can, therefore, not be viewed by all users. SAP Audit Management addresses this by providing the following reports, which can be used and added to:

▶ Overview of the whole audit program or of selected groups of audits

▶ Overview of all or of selected groups of audit questions and results

▶ Overview of all or of selected groups of findings and actions

▶ Analysis of audit results and actions (Pareto, trend, benchmark)

▶ Feedback of audit results to audit planning

The audit report is created in several steps. In the first step, all data relevant to the audit is made available internally. In the second step, this data is made available in the desired form using Smart Forms and is displayed on the screen. In a third step, you can then print the data, save it as a PDF document, or email it to all business partners. To document this step in the system, the status of the audit will be updated after you've printed the audit report.

After the assessment, you can create a preliminary audit report, which can be used to discuss the findings, the corrective actions, and the overall result of the audit. The audit can then be signed (physically or using a digital signature), created, and distributed. The signature is represented by a status of the audit. If the signature itself must be documented and verified, you can scan the signed report into the system and attach it to the audit.

6. **Perform follow-up actions.**
If, during an audit, the auditors detect that there are inadmissible deviations, dangers, or potential for improvement, they can note their findings and make recommendations, determine the need for a subsequent audit, or create corrective or preventive actions for the relevant items of the audit question list.

When recording the action, the partners responsible for execution (as well as planned and actual execution dates and statuses) are recorded. To ensure that the actions get executed, the following methods can be used to trigger the actions:

▶ Audit Monitor: Shows every system user his individual worklist of actions that are to be processed and in which the user is involved in any partner role.

▶ Notification function: Allows the auditor to send email reminders to partners involved.

▶ Periodically scheduled background job: Automatically sends the reminders to involved partners of an action in advance or if a deadline has elapsed.

External partners have access to all required and authorized information and to all action-processing functions—that they are authorized to use—via the Internet and the web interface (web-enabled collaboration). If, instead of the basic and easy-to-use function for managing actions that is available with SAP Audit Management, you want to use more detailed processing functions, you can consider using processes within SAP Quality Management (QM) (see Chapter 8) or functions from SAP CRM.

7. **Monitor and analyze audits.**
The last step of SAP Audit Management focuses on monitoring the outstanding actions and finalizing the audit report, which was described in the report audit and within the audit is reflected by the Signed and Approved status (or the Rejected status if that is the outcome), which allows you to close the audit.

The audit process is supported by two separate SAP transactions: the audit cockpit (Transaction PLM_AUDIT) and the Audit Monitor (Transaction PLM_AUDIT-MONITOR). These transactions can be found in the CROSS-APPLICATION COMPONENTS menu or by entering them directly. We'll discuss these transactions next.

Audit Cockpit

The *audit cockpit* is a powerful transaction providing you with an overall view of audits because it gives you access to all the audit-relevant objects. Figure 6.62 shows an example of the audit cockpit and shows the three main areas:

▶ **Structure tree**
Lets you view and access the audit and its related objects, which are presented

to you hierarchically. After you've selected the object you want to work on in the structure tree, the details of the object become visible on the detail screen.

▶ **Detail screen**
Gives you access to the detailed information on the object chosen in the tree. In display mode, you can only see the details; in change mode, you can also see the change data.

▶ **Worklist/template area**
Gives you access to your personalized worklist, to the objects you've worked on recently, and to predefined templates (when set up), which you can use when creating your own audits.

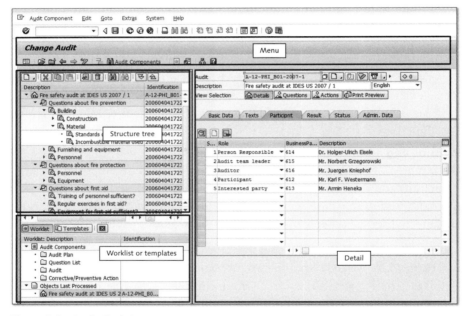

Figure 6.62 Audit Cockpit

Audit Monitor

The *Audit Monitor* is mainly used to monitor audits and actions on the basis of status or date, and to evaluate audit results (see Figure 6.63). However, this transaction provides you with various selection criteria—such as the status, partners involved or identification characteristics—to find audit plans, audits, actions, question lists, or even by the freely definable audit object.

The *audit evaluation* provides different search possibilities for all audit components on the basis of various search criteria. In the audit evaluation, you can, for example, determine the number of outstanding corrective or preventive actions, display all audits or question lists, and determine which audit plans exist for a certain time period. The audit evaluation accesses all data that was created in the system in the context of SAP Audit Management.

Apart from the reports available with the provided standard transactions in SAP ERP, SAP also provides ready-made reports in SAP NetWeaver Business Warehouse (BW) 7.0. The following is an example of the currently available ready-made reports; of course, report content is continuously evolving and may change between the time of writing and the date of publication:

▶ Overview of the audits

▶ Audits and their results (here you can drill down to the audit question level)

▶ Audits and their state of completion (here you can drill down to the action level)

▶ Audit objects and their assessments

▶ Partners responsible for audits and actions

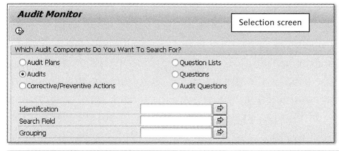

Figure 6.63 Audit Monitor

6.4 Summary

The increasing number of laws and industry standards has made product compliance an SAP PLM topic that deserves the full attention of companies developing and producing products. SAP offers integrated and embedded product compliance via a holistic solution that covers the entire lifecycle of a product from product idea, to development, to delivery, and eventually disposal of the product.

Based on detailed product data, you can gain insights in product compliance via dashboards. The SAP Environment, Health, and Safety Management (SAP EHS Management) component of SAP ERP provides functions to cover product labeling, Hazardous Substance Management, Dangerous Goods Management, and SAP Waste and Recycling.

This chapter walked through the Operational Risk Management process, allowing you to manage product and asset risks through a closed-loop process, which includes worker safety. Operational Risk Management is an important integration between SAP EHS Management and SAP PM/SAP CS.

Performing regular audits regarding the product information and product-specific processes is another important area that ensures product compliance. Finally, you saw how product audits can be planned, performed, and monitored by using SAP Audit Management, a cross-application component.

The next chapter focuses on the design, source, and creation phases of a product, especially when these phases are done through a project-based methodology. We'll first provide an overview of the different SAP solutions in this space and then go into the SAP ERP components Project Systems (SAP PS) and Investment Management followed by the Project and Portfolio Management (PPM) solution, which includes project collaboration. We'll also cover the integration tools available to external project management.

Ensuring that projects are done on time, are accomplished within the budget, and achieve the set goals is critical to the success of an organization. SAP's project management tools give you the insights required to ensure informed decision making and provide an overall view across the lifecycle of a project. It ensures that you understand the project pipeline and align your resources appropriately.

7   Project Management

The focus of this chapter is project management. During any stage within the product lifecycle, SAP's project management solutions can be used to manage a specific outcome. A project can be used to simply represent a single stage such as a marketing campaign or can be used to build a product specifically for a customer, starting with a customer quote and ending with delivery of the product.

To cover the topics important to project management, first we'll introduce the project management topic in general. Section 7.1 will provide you with a brief overview of the SAP products available for projects management, including SAP Project System (SAP PS), SAP Project and Portfolio Management (PPM), and SAP Investment Management. We'll also include some guidance on when to use which solution.

Section 7.2 goes through a project lifecycle in SAP PS from project initiation to planning, approval and budgeting, execution and monitoring, and closing a project.

Section 7.3 explains the data model and the business scenario in SAP Investment Management and includes a subsection where a comparison is made between SAP IM and PPM to help you understand their differences and make an informed decision.

Section 7.4 and Section 7.5 focus on PPM; Section 7.4.1 explains the data model and goes through a project lifecycle from setup to planning, integration, managing resources, visibility, execute and track, and project closure within PPM.

Section 7.5 discusses project collaboration (which used to be done by c-projects, and now has been absorbed within the PPM product).

The chapter finishes with how SAP's solutions can be integrated to other project management applications by using PPM centrally and using the integration tools such as Open Project System (Open PS) and the SAP Enterprise Project Connection tool.

A project is an undertaking that is conducted by a company that has a unique result. In general, projects are influenced by the following conditions and constraints:

▶ They are generally complex, unique, and involve a high degree of risk.

▶ They have precise goals agreed upon by the project team, the project stakeholders, the internal and external customers, and the project sponsors.

▶ They are limited in duration and are cost- and capacity-intensive.

▶ They are subject to certain quality requirements.

▶ They are mostly of strategic importance for the company carrying them out.

Because they are usually undertaken by employees from several different departments, the subsequent project management business processes can be quite complex, but high-quality results are often expected. Projects are often cost-intensive, time-consuming, and of strategic importance to the organization, so it's important to manage progress well and minimize the risk of project failure. Any changes to project resources, whether to project time lines, project resources such as employees or materials, or project costs, often affect the other areas. For example, if the delivery of raw materials is delayed several weeks, this will impact the project time line and time frames of production line use. These characteristics of a project have been summarized in Figure 7.1.

Motivations for undertaking projects range from investment or capital projects, research and development (R&D), marketing campaigns, make-to-order projects, service delivery, and routine and extended maintenance such as overhauls, shutdowns, turnarounds, and refurbishments. Project hierarchies are often used to allocate and evaluate budgets, track progress, and define responsibilities. As you've seen in Chapter 2, Figure 2.2, program and project management process is part of the continuous product and service innovation business process. This process is supported by multiple SAP products, so let's take a look at which products are available and when to use which one.

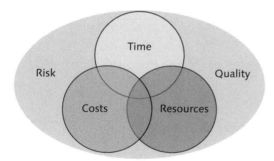

Figure 7.1 Projects Characteristics

7.1 SAP Project Management Solutions

This section covers two of SAP's solutions for project management: SAP Project Systems (SAP PS), which is a component of SAP ERP, and the project management capabilities of SAP Project and Portfolio Management (PPM). Recall that the Portfolio Management capabilities of PPM have already been described in Chapter 2; we won't spend much time on it here. SAP Investment Management, which is also an SAP ERP component, is used quite regularly in combination with SAP PS, so we'll explore it briefly. Finally, we'll consider how to determine whether to use SAP Investment Management or PPM for strategic planning (or possibly both) by comparing the two solutions based on the functions and features offered.

7.1.1 SAP Project System

SAP PS is a highly integrated component and integrates to other areas within SAP ERP such as logistics for procurement and inventory management; accounting for determining costs, overheads, and budgeting purposes; and human resources for skills information, personnel details, and time management, for example. With SAP PS, you can set up project structures flexibly, and you can plan and monitor all the required resources through planning dates, costs, revenues, budgets, resources and materials, production resources, and so on, for these projects and project parts. Figure 7.2 shows a project lifecycle from initiation to project closure, including how the project details will expand over time. It's an important overview figure because the phases will be used as subheadings in Section 7.2, and the project elements Work Breakdown Structure (WBS) and networks will be detailed further.

Figure 7.2 Overview of SAP PS

7.1.2 SAP Project and Portfolio Management

Alongside SAP PS, SAP Project and Portfolio Management (PPM) allows additional functions for achieving efficient portfolio and project management capabilities as shown later in Figure 7.37. PPM offers functionality for three distinct levels: the foundation of the PPM "house" is the operational level, the middle level is the project management area, and the roof represents the portfolio level. Before going into how these areas are related, we'll briefly describe these three distinct areas.

▶ **Operational level**

The operational level is a shared responsibility between both PPM and the SAP ERP. Depending on the amount of integration required from SAP ERP, more or fewer functions can be performed in either part of the solution. Especially for projects that don't require tight integration with SAP ERP, more of the execution can take place in PPM. Depending on which system you set up as your operational project management system, different scenarios are supported. We'll cover these in more detail as we explore project planning in Section 7.4.3.

It's important to understand that PPM won't replace the financial capabilities of SAP ERP; that is why, for the collection of project costs and the assignment and changes to the project budget, it relies on the SAP ERP system.

▶ **Project level**

The main benefit of using the project management capabilities is that by having one central place for all your project information, you can uniformly monitor all your enterprise projects through dashboards and other analytical capabilities, which allows you to perform system-wide, uniform resource planning for all projects. This is why the project level of the solution is referred to as the engine room of PPM because it forms the beating heart of the solution. It also gives you the ability to set up projects via an easy-to-use, flexible, web-based tool. The project management capability of the PPM solution was previously known under the name c-projects (short for collaboration projects). It can be used and supports integration scenarios with c-folders (collaboration folders) to share project documentation or deliverables, and it integrates very well with SAP PS. However, apart from the integration to SAP PS, it can be used in combination with other project management tools and systems feeding information to it, such as SAP PS and c-projects, but also other non-SAP project management solutions such as Microsoft Project or Primavera.

▶ **Portfolio level**
Another function of PPM is Resource and Portfolio Management, previously known as Resources and Portfolio Management with the abbreviations xRPM or RPM. It allows you to strategically manage entire projects or product and services portfolios. The PPM–Portfolio Management capabilities and overall resource management were explained in Chapter 2.

Definition Refresher

▶ Portfolio management: Identifying, evaluating, and managing the "family" of products (the portfolio) that a company offers and maintains. A portfolio is either a range of products or services offered by an organization or the investments held by an organization. Portfolios can be set up based on organizational, functional, or regional criteria (or a combination of these).

▶ Resource management: Managing the required resources to successfully manage and execute business initiatives and projects. A resource within PPM is either the required employees within a certain time frame managed through capacity planning or the required budget within a certain time frame managed through financial planning.

The last three sections of this chapter (Section 7.4 to Section 7.6) explain the project management capabilities of PPM and the integration scenarios possible. It includes dedicated coverage of the project collaboration tools in Section 7.5 and the integration to other project management applications in Section 7.6.

7.1.3 SAP Investment Management

The SAP Investment Management component, which is part of SAP ERP, provides you with functions to support the planning, investment, and financing processes for investments. Investments are measures and expenditures that often must be approved by several members of the company because of their importance or volume, such as the following examples:

▶ Capital investments, such as the acquisition of fixed assets as the result of house production or purchase

▶ Investments in R&D

▶ Projects that fall primarily under overhead, such as continuing education of employees or establishing new markets

▶ Maintenance programs

Figure 7.3 gives an overview of the investment cycle phases, starting generally speaking with the planning phase, where within IM you can capture different investment ideas in an appropriation request.

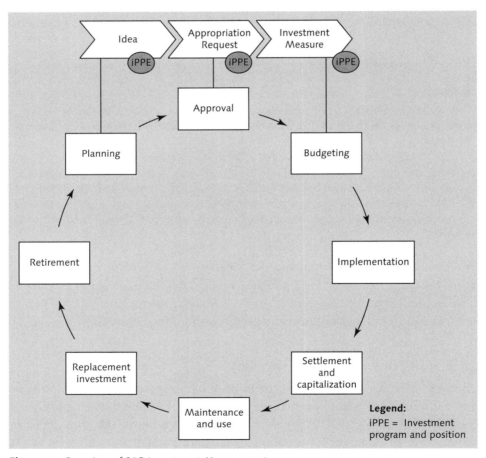

Figure 7.3 Overview of SAP Investment Management

An idea captured in an appropriation request can further progress after it's approved into an investment measure, at which time, a budget can be assigned. This investment measure gets implemented; once complete, settlement and capitalization takes place. The investment flows on into the maintenance and use phase until it's due for either replacement and retirement or reinvestment, which kicks off the planning process phase again. During planning, approval, and budgeting, your entire investments portfolio gets managed by setting up and assigning an investment program and investment positions to appropriate documents.

Section 7.3 will explain some of the functions and business processes offered by SAP Investment Management and includes a comparison table to help you decide when to use SAP Investment Management and/or PPM because their processes are similar and might even overlap occasionally.

7.1.4 Determining Which Project Management Solution to Use When

Because both PPM and SAP PS offer project management capabilities, the question arises of when to use which solution. The answer to this question depends on your organization's specific requirements and the integration between your strategic solutions and your operational project management system. Based on the assumption that you use PPM to oversee and monitor the entire project portfolio, you have basically three options, which have been represented in Figure 7.4:

▶ Use SAP PS as your operational project management system.

▶ Use PPM as your operational project management system.

▶ Use non-SAP systems as your operational project management system.

In Figure 7.4, the rows with the system information shows you the minimal setup regarding project information, which can either be a single object or the entire project structure. If you choose SAP PS as your operational project management system, the project structure needs to be set up in SAP PS, and you can either set up a single project element or a project structure within PPM. An example here could be the operational project in SAP PS, where the project and the project phases are available in PPM for reporting purposes. The arrows show you the flow of information.

When you choose PPM as your operational project management system, you must set up a cost collector within SAP ERP for the financial information, which can be done via a project (or via another cost collection object within SAP Financial Accounting (FI)/SAP ERP Controlling (CO) such as an internal order or cost center). The same applies when you use an external project management system as your operational project system.

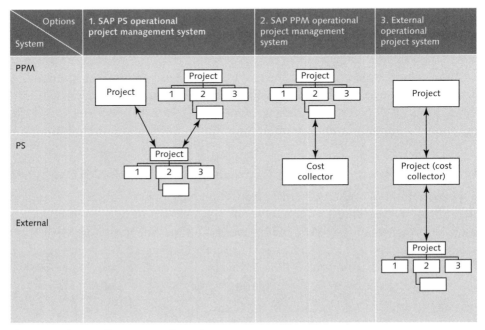

Figure 7.4 Project Management Scenarios

Let's look at when which scenario, generally speaking, has preference over the other.

If you need very tight integration to other areas within SAP ERP, it's generally a better choice to use SAP PS as your operational project management system. SAP PS has the ability to integrate tightly to purchasing, manufacturing, supply chain, plant maintenance, and financial areas—for example, in the case of investment projects, where you need to set up assets under construction, fixed assets, and work in progress (WIP) reporting. Using SAP PS as your operational project management system means that you maintain the project and its entire structure in SAP PS. The detailed cost planning, budgeting, and execution are being done within SAP PS as well. Generally this is the case for investment projects, manufacturing projects, and large maintenance projects. However, you can still use the overall tracking and monitoring reports within PPM, both from a portfolio and from a project perspective, which can be achieved by the replication of the SAP PS project structure into PPM.

For projects that don't need this tight integration, we recommend that you use PPM as the operational project management system. The project and its structure in this scenario is maintained and monitored within PPM. Cost planning, budgeting, and execution are tracked and monitored within PPM. You use SAP ERP merely as a budgeting and cost collection tool, and you just need a cost collector to book actuals against. This is why PPM is often used for IT projects, product development projects, and innovation projects.

SAP's Project Management solutions should be able to support any of your project lifecycles; however, when there is a need within your organization to use external project management system(s), all you need to do is set up a single project element in both PPM and SAP PS, which then allows you to monitor and track your entire project collection. The integration scenarios will be explained in more detail in Section 7.6.

Now that you have an understanding of SAP solutions in project management space, this chapter will continue to explain SAP PS in more detail in the next section.

7.2   Project and Resource Management with SAP ERP

The SAP PS component is shared by SAP ERP and SAP PLM. It's a very well integrated component into other areas of SAP ERP as well such as procurement, SAP Production Planning (PP), materials requirements planning (MRP), and SAP Financial Accounting (FI). SAP PS has earned a place in both the FINANCIAL and LOGISTICS menus.

When you're setting up a project in SAP PS, you can set it up in a way that the project has to go through different phases or stages, as you can see in Figure 7.5, and it offers functionality for all these stages. As the project matures, the amount of detail kept about a project grows, as you can see in the WBS and NETWORK columns.

SAP PS doesn't have its own dedicated organizational structure elements, but it uses the organizational units defined in the finance or logistics areas. Figure 7.5

gives you an overview of the different project structure elements, including the relevant organizational data. The project structure elements start with the project definition at the project header level, followed with the WBS elements, the network, and the network activities. The figure includes an overview of the different types of activities with their relevant organizational data:

- ▶ Internal activities
- ▶ External activities
- ▶ General cost activities
- ▶ Material components

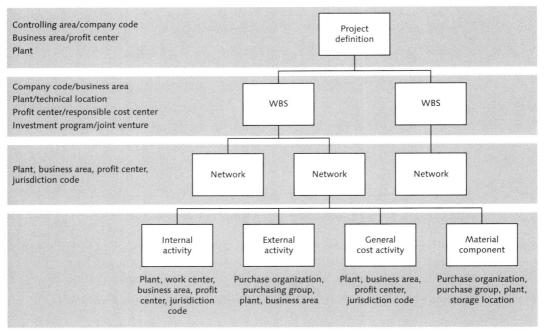

Figure 7.5 Project Structure

The following sections will go through the set up and creation of these elements per project phase and will explain each of these project elements in more detail, during the phase where it's most likely to be used or introduced.

As we walk through those project phases—project initiation, project planning, project approval and budgeting, project execution and monitoring, and project closing—be aware that the set up and use of phases is flexible, and the details during the phases might differ based on the purpose of the project. Consider, for example, that a sales project might need a quotation during the concept stage, whereas for an investment project, this phase might include writing a business case with a high-level cost plan. Also the scale of a project might influence the stages and the amount of details necessary. Large-scale projects such as the construction of a production facility might be going through an extensive approval process; as time progresses, you might close out parts of the project and release the next stage by setting up a complex project structure accordingly. Small-scale projects such as organizing a trade fair might not need an approval at all (or a very minimal approval) and might include a very simple project structure.

7.2.1 Project Initiation

When setting up a project in SAP PS, you first start with the project definition. A *project definition* includes information relevant to the entire project, such as the project type and the controlling area in which the project is being done. Most organizations distinguish between at least two types of projects:

▶ Externally financed projects, such as customer projects or service delivery projects

▶ Internally financed projects, such as overhead cost projects, maintenance projects, or capital investment projects

In the configuration, you can set up your own project types and the project type controls using several important settings (e.g., the project numbering and the ability to use networks, activities, and release procedures). SAP PS provides you with project master data, which gives you the following two main elements to structure a project:

▶ Work Breakdown Structure (WBS)

▶ Networks and activities

The WBS organizes a project in a hierarchy and maps the project's structure. The *WBS elements* are usually set up by phases (such as preparation, execution, etc.), functions (product development, marketing, engineering), assets (building, production line, or installation), or a combination of these.

A WBS element can be set up as a controlling object, which you can use to plan and monitor costs, revenues, payments, budgets, and dates. This is the reason the WBS structure of a project is sometimes referred to as the accounting view or financial view of the project.

Activities represent the work packages or the things that need to be done. They can be even further detailed in *activity elements*, if required. The network and activities represent the individual project activities or work packages that need to take place, including their logical relationships (e.g., Activity 2 can't start until Activity 1 is completed)— also referred to as the *flow* of a project. They are used for the basis of planning, analyzing, controlling, and monitoring. Multiple networks can be generated for a project. The network is used to group the activities together logically and can be seen as the header object, where your activities are your items belonging to this header. This is the same, for example, as for the maintenance order header and the maintenance order operations. Because activities can only be created within a network, you'll need at least one network to use activities in a project.

Networks and activities are assigned to WBS elements, which are then used to aggregate the dates and costs defined in the individual activities to be totaled up at the WBS level, making aggregated evaluation possible. The use of networks and activities is optional, but they have to be implemented if you want to leverage the integration to logistics. Figure 7.6 shows how the financial view of a project and the activities are assigned to each other and how a single project can integrate several different networks.

To explain this concept and provide you a better understanding of when to use which project elements, let's use a simple project—building a garden shed—as an example. To monitor and build the garden shed, the following project phases have been identified, along with their subordinate activities:

▶ Project preparation (prep.)
  ▹ Make technical drawing.
  ▹ Request building permit.
▶ Building and construction (B&C)
  ▹ Procure building materials.
  ▹ Build foundation.
  ▹ Build garden shed.

► Evaluation (eval.)

  ► Create reports.

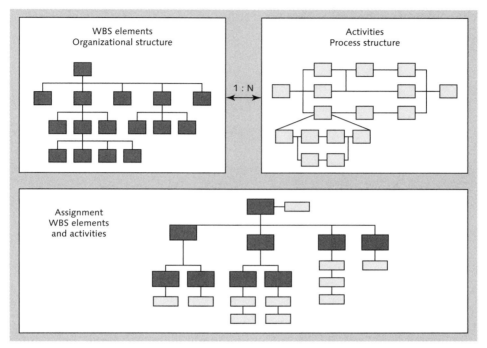

Figure 7.6 Master Data in SAP PS

Assigning the activities to the WBS shows the aggregated view at this level and the total view at the project level. To plan some contingency into the cost plan, we'll set up an activity called Contingency. Figure 7.7 shows you how this example is set up as a project in the SAP Project Builder. The SAP Project Builder gives you access to nearly all project structure elements. The screen is split up into three main areas: the project structure (top left), the work list/templates with the last 20 projects you've been working on (last 5 prior to SAP ERP EPH 3) (bottom left), and the details or overview screen for the selected object in the project structure (right). This layout is very similar to the Integrated Product and Process Engineering (iPPE) and/or specification database layout.

Figure 7.8 shows you this exact same example with just the project's WBS elements view and the project network view. From the SAP Project Builder, you can easily navigate to the project planning board, which shows you the Gantt chart of the project, in which you can save your changes via intermediate saving (requires SAP ERP EHP 3 or above). Recently, SAP has also introduced the option to maintain project information in multiple languages and also to maintain project authorizations using the access control list (ACL).

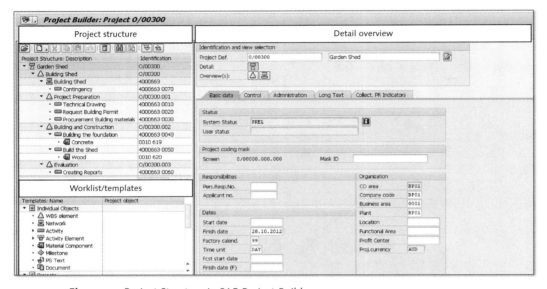

Figure 7.7 Project Structure in SAP Project Builder

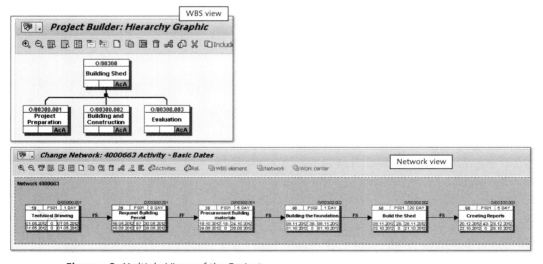

Figure 7.8 Multiple Views of the Project

The *milestone* is another object used within SAP PS that you'll assign to a WBS element or to an activity. The milestone can be used to document important project events. Creating a milestone can be done for the following purposes:

▶ Perform milestone billing (to invoice based on milestones reached within the project)

▶ Perform analysis (such as milestone trend analysis to identify project delays or progress analysis to monitor project progress value determination based on earned value analysis)

▶ Triggering event (e.g., to send an email or release the next activities)

▶ Information (to document an event)

So you can set up a project that adequately includes all the required project structure elements, SAP PS offers you several accelerated project creation options (beyond simply creating the project from scratch). You can, for example, use part of a previously performed project as a reference to copy from or you can set up a template project specifically for this purpose, which can be used repeatedly. This book doesn't intend to explain all these possibilities in detail because its focus is on providing you with an overall overview, but you can find more details on project management courses and other resources in Appendix A and Appendix B.

7.2.2 Project Planning: Initial and Detailed Planning

During the planning phase of a project, you can plan the resources that are required for project execution. This stage of the project often results in a cost plan and a project schedule. Take the following resources into consideration:

▶ The required money or funds necessary to execute the project and the planned revenues through customer payments

▶ The required project documents (such as a project charter and a project scope) and the use of project standards or methodology

▶ The required time to plan and execute the project

▶ The required human resources (e.g., internal personnel or external contractors)

▶ Materials necessary (e.g., the raw or semifinished materials needed to build the end product), either inventory managed or directly sourced from vendors

▶ The tools and equipment required to perform the activities

The planning of these different types of resources will be explained in more detail in dedicated subsections. A lot of organizations start with an initial rough cost project plan and schedule and then continue to add more detail to the project as the project matures. So keep in mind that the use of the planning options described here can differ depending on the project stage, the project complexity, and its scale, scope, and maturity.

Cost Planning

To plan costs for a project, SAP PS supports two different cost planning methods: network costing and manual costing.

You'll use *network costing* when you perform cost planning automatically by using network activities to provide the planned cost of the activity. In addition to using activities to collect planned cost, you can also assign orders (e.g., maintenance orders or internal orders) to networks or WBS elements so that the planned cost will be available both on the individual order and on the project. This can be very useful, for example, when a maintenance project is being used for budgeting purposes. Of course, to use network costing, the WBS element or the network activity must be set up as an account assignment object first.

In *manual costing*, you manually plan the costs by entering costing data for the WBS elements. You can use one of the following four manual cost planning options:

- ▸ **Overall planning**
  Costs are entered on the WBS elements manually, where they can be either entered overall, or they can be broken down by fiscal year if required.

- ▸ **Detailed planning of primary costs and activity inputs**
  The cost planning is done at the WBS level on cost elements and periods.

- ▸ **Unit costing**
  Using a scheme, you can enter quantities for materials, internal activities, external activities, variable items, and so on, which results in a cost element-based planning.

- ▸ **Easy Cost Planning (ECP)**
  This very easy and user-friendly method can be used with the accelerator of a planning form to provide quantities for the characteristics in the form, which the system automatically translates into cost-element-based planning. ECP is

often used as a way to create a preliminary cost plan for a project, which later in the project is replaced by a quantity structure of networks and activities.

Figure 7.9 shows an example of an ECP, where on the right side you see the form with the characteristics. The inputs in the characteristics, for example, PROJECT SIZE: SMALL, determine the basis for the automatically generated cost plan, which is visible on the left-hand side. ECP was introduced in release R/3 4.6C for WBS elements and its use has extended to networks since SAP ERP 6.0 EHP 3. You can use Execution Services during ECP to enter commitment and actual data relating to planned costs.

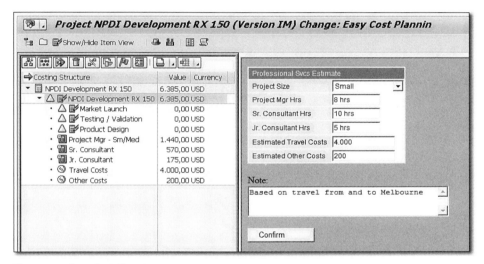

Figure 7.9 Easy Cost Planning

There isn't really a one-size-fits-all answer to which cost plan method is recommended. Often, organizations use multiple cost planning methods—for example, they'll use ECP for a preliminary cost plan and a detailed cost plan during detailed planning. So let's examine the benefits of each of the cost plan methods.

The network costing method is the most integrated cost planning method, which uses rates and prices captured in other SAP components. For example, for internal activities, the rate of the work center is maintained in SAP ERP Controlling (CO) and used and multiplied by the work unit to determine the planned costs. For external activities, the pricing details from SAP Materials Management (SAP MM) can be used; for example, a vendor contract includes the price or the information record (both also provide you details about the delivery times of the procured item). The other big advantage of using network costing is that when you postpone or move your networks and activities, your cost plan moves automatically with it.

In contrast, manual cost plans have to be updated manually when you postpone or move your project or part of a project. Of course, manual cost planning might still be the preferred planning method for your organization, due to its user friendliness (ECP) or because the cost plan is done at a very high level, based on rough estimates.

Figure 7.10 shows you the result of a cost plan based on the network costing method, which was the method used for the creation of the example garden shed. When you use network costing, your costing will usually be saved automatically to the plan version 0.

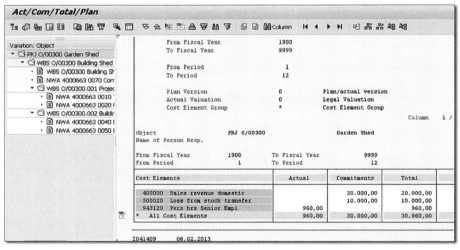

Figure 7.10 Cost Plan via Network Costing

In Figure 7.10, you see that the cost plan is generated in PLAN VERSION 0. A *plan version* is used to store your planned and actual cost against the project and is controlling-area specific. Plan version 0 gets created automatically when you plan costs in a project for the first time, and the current planning always takes place in version 000. During planning and execution, changes to the project happen constantly, so you can use additional planning versions, in which you can store planning data, make a snapshot of a version, or use this version to compare against future states of the project. It might also be useful to make additional plans to compare alternatives, such as best-case and worst-case plan versions. If you want to create a new plan version for your project cost planning, you can copy an existing plan version into one of the defined plan versions (as configured within your organization). Several standard reports within SAP PS allow you to compare plan versions.

Revenue Planning

To plan revenues in your project, SAP PS offers you the following three options, as represented in Figure 7.11:

- Manual revenue planning (either structure-oriented or on the basis of revenue elements and periods)
- Revenue planning using SAP PS billing plans, which is revenue element- and period-specific
- Revenue planning using SAP Sales and Distribution (SD) documents, such as a sales order or quotation, which is also revenue element- and period-based

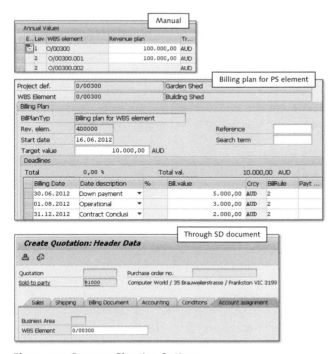

Figure 7.11 Revenue Planning Options

The revenue planning using SD documents method is one way to plan revenues into your project. You can, for example, agree on an overall price with the customer, which will be partially paid depending on milestones defined in the project plan. You could say that the first payment of 40% is done after the design phase has been signed off and completed, the next 35% after the construction has taken place, and the last 25% upon final delivery. This needs to be reflected in a sales order with a billing plan, where the billing items will be determined based on the activity milestones from the project. By assigning them this way, the status change of the confirmation becomes the trigger (unlocking billing plan items) to allow billing. Figure 7.12 shows you an example of a sales order with a milestone-based billing plan, where you see that the milestones from SAP PS are used to determine the invoicing percentage.

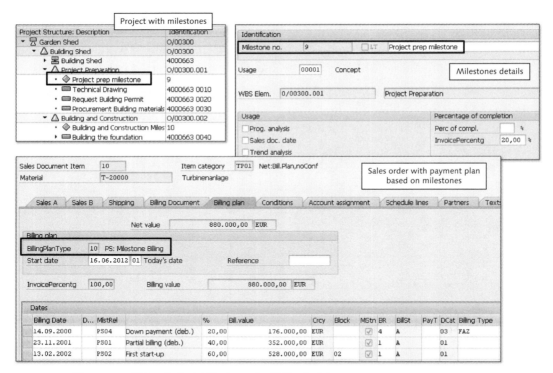

Figure 7.12 Using Project Milestones for Billing in Sales

In the SAP Project Builder, you have access to the Sales Price function, which allows you to determine a sales price based on the project cost plan. This function works in combination with ECP. To generate a sales price based on other types of cost plans, you have to use the specific sales price transactions. Figure 7.13 shows an example on the left of the cost per the cost plan and on the right of the transfer percentage and the sales price. To use this sales pricing function, you need to configure a Dynamic Item Procedure profile (DIP profile), which determines which plan or actual project values will be used and translated to which saleable item and against which terms. The sales price that is determined can be used within sales documents—such as in a customer inquiry or a customer quotation—but it can also be used directly by copying it into the billing plan within SAP PS. This might be useful when the SD component hasn't been set up.

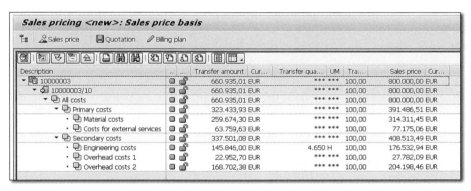

Figure 7.13 Sales Pricing Based on the Project Cost Plan

Time Planning

Of course another important resource that must be planned for during a project is time. Several approaches can be taken: one is the bottom-down approach (starting with the overall time frame and translating this to the stages), and another is the bottom-up approach (in which you plan at the most detailed level, and the dates get translated to the higher related project elements). Next we'll discuss the following two supported planning project time lines:

▶ **Projects with activities**
Generally used for projects, where integration to logistics is necessary, and detailed planning and execution is required.

▶ **Projects without activities**
Generally used for financial-focused projects, where integration to logistics isn't necessary.

Organizations often use both, although within SAP PLM, the first is more common.

Projects with Activities

In projects where activities are used, the dates are determined automatically by performing scheduling with the appropriate scheduling settings. The scheduling parameters need to be set up in the configuration, or you can use the predefined scheduling scenarios. These scheduling parameters can be changed and influenced in the project planning board.

Networks are always scheduled forwards and backwards. With forward scheduling, the system calculates the earliest start and finish dates; with backward scheduling, the system determines the latest possible start and finish dates. The difference between the earliest and latest dates is called the *float*. When the float is positive, the activity is considered to be noncritical, giving you some flexibility in planning. When the float is zero or negative, the activity is part of the critical path and needs to be executed on time and monitored well because any delay will have an impact on follow-on dependent activities. After the dates of the network activities are finalized, you can perform scheduling, which will extrapolate the dates from the network activities to the WBS elements.

Project without Activities

For projects without activities, you can plan dates manually in WBS elements. You can use SAP Project Builder to update the dates in the detailed screen of the WBS elements. Another option is to use the project planning board, which gives you the project time planning capabilities using a Gantt chart, in which you can update dates by dragging and dropping them in a time line. SAP PS provides you with several options to accelerate the time and effort required to perform time planning. You can, for example, use the date extrapolated function, which copies dates from lower to higher level WBSs and vice versa; this function can be followed up by a consistency check.

An important tool during project time planning for understanding the impacts of changes on time lines is the project planning board.

Project Planning Board

The project planning board enables you to plan and change project dates and update project elements in an integrated manner by using the integrated Gantt chart. You access the project structure and use sorting, filtering, hiding, and grouping functions to select just the objects of the project that are relevant to you. You can also update the detailed information by right-clicking to bring up all of the options available for displaying and changing the element.

Through the planning board, you can plan and update the following elements:

- Project definition
- WBS elements
- Activities
- Relationships
- Materials
- Milestones
- Basic dates
- SAP PS texts
- Documents

Figure 7.14 gives you an example project planning board. As shown here, the default view of the project planning board is generally the scheduling overview, which gives insight into the project elements on a time line.

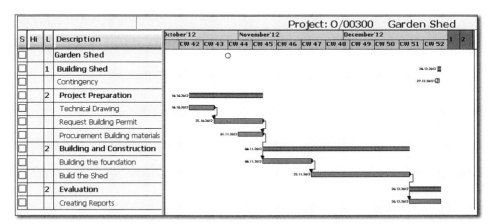

Figure 7.14 Project Planning Board

Apart from this default view, the project planning board supports the following views as well:

▸ **Capacity overview**
Provides you insight into the capacity load on the work centers that are assigned to the project activities; shows utilization using colored bars; and displays overloads in red and available capacity in green.

▸ **Materials overview**
Provides you an overview of when the planned components assigned to the activities are required.

▸ **Cost and revenues overview**
Provides you with an overview of the cost and revenues that are planned and actually occurred on the project.

▸ **Maintenance orders overview**
Provides you with a view of all the maintenance orders assigned to the project activities.

Figure 7.15 shows you the planning board with the project scheduling view, as well as the material component view.

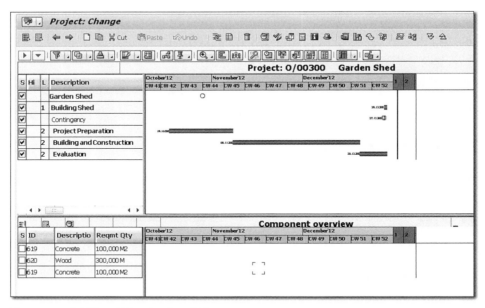

Figure 7.15 Additional Planning Board Views

Human Resource Planning

To plan the people required to execute the project, you can either use internal personnel or external personnel, in which SAP distinguishes between external resources and external services. Figure 7.16 gives you an overview of these three activity types, including their most commonly used follow-up activities, which are performed during execution.

Several steps can be optional; for example, when you want to hire a contractor to make the technical drawing for your project, and you already have a contract in place, you can skip the RFQ, quotation, and vendor selections steps. The activities and their follow-up flow are based on the same principles as the maintenance work order operations or internal order operations and their follow-up flow. Recall that the process steps in Figure 7.16 were described in Chapter 5, Section 5.5.5, which included the same figure and explained the use of control keys. SAP PS uses the exact same principles, but instead of the SAP Plant Maintenance (SAP PM) control keys PM01 to PM03, it uses the control keys specific to SAP PS, which are PS01 to PS03.

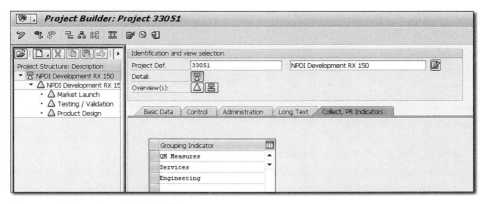

Figure 7.16 Overview of Activity Types

SAP PS distinguishes between the following types of activities:

▶ **Internally assigned activities**
These are performed by a work center. The work center represents a person, a group of persons, a machine, or a group of machines (see Chapter 3 for more details). To plan work across resources, you have to assign the work center to the activity and then add the amount of work that is required to perform this

activity. The system will use the data from the activity and the work center to determine the activity's planned costs and the capacity requirements on the work center. Capacity planning and leveling can be used to evenly distribute the amount of work across your different work centers. This capacity scheduling and leveling process is the same as the maintenance capacity planning, which has been described in more detail in Chapter 5. Figure 7.17 shows you an example of an internal activity, in which a work center is assigned as well as the internal CONTROL KEY (PS01).

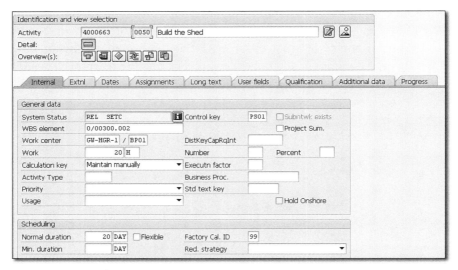

Figure 7.17 Internal Activity

▶ **Externally processed activities**
These are carried out by a third party, such as a vendor or contractor. By creating the activity as an external activity, it will trigger the procurement process by generating a purchase requisition, which can be picked up by the procurement department. Figure 7.18 shows you an external activity, as recognizable via the external control key and the procurement details, such as the vendor, contract, and purchase requisition number.

As of EHP 3, apart from either creating a purchase requisition per project or per project element, you can also use the purchase requisition grouping indicator as a mechanism to generate purchase requisitions, which needs to be set up at the project definition level. Figure 7.18 also includes an example of the grouping indicators defined for a building project.

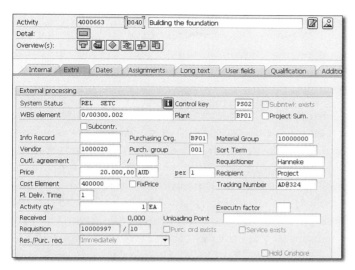

Figure 7.18 External Activity

You can use master data from procurement directly in the activity—for example, assigning the info record that contains delivery dates and price information—which provides valuable inputs for planning and costing of the activity.

▶ **Service processed activities**
These are also carried out by a third party, but this activity type additionally allows you to use service specifications and service limits. The service master is a master data record for services, which helps you aggregate statistical information on consumption. The service limit can be used to introduce a certain amount of flexibility during the execution of the procured service without having to change or update the purchase order.

This could be very useful, for example, in a scenario where you don't know the precise cost of a service. Let's say that you or your procurement department agree with the vendor that he will charge a fixed amount ($500) for execution of a maintenance activity, plus up to $55 for additional spare parts used. Similar to the previous activity, the service activity will also trigger the procurement process by generating a purchase requisition.

Material Planning

The materials planned in a project form an important integration point between SAP PS and other logistics components within your organization, such as SD, PP, and SAP MM for procurement, MRP, and SAP Inventory Management (MM–IM). When you're running a customer-specific project and have sold a product to a customer via SD, you can use this material to set up project structures automatically and assign materials and their requirements by date and quantity to the appropriate project structure element.

When you're assigning a material to a project network, either via SD or otherwise, you have to assign it either as a non-stock item or stock item. The non-stock item will be directly procured and consumed by the project and will trigger a procurement process through a purchase requisition, where the stock item will go through inventory and lead to a reservation. Different stock types—for example, warehouse stock, project stock, and sales order stock—can be supported through MM–IM. Figure 7.19 shows you the material flows within SAP ERP or SAP PLM environments without including any approvals—though when you're using SAP Supplier Relationship Management (SAP SRM), for example, additional steps such as the SAP SRM shopping cart might be included

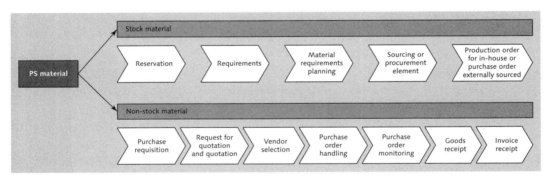

Figure 7.19 Material Flow

The materials planned and required in the project will, in turn, form important input for the MRP in SAP MM. During the MRP run, you can determine whether the material will be sourced through an in-house production process or procured externally via a procurement process. The left side of Figure 7.20 shows you a non-stock item as determined through the ITEM CATEGORY field value N for non-stock, which includes the purchase requisition and vendor details procurement data. The right side of Figure 7.20 shows you the reservation examples in the system and the stock item with the value L for stock item, from *Lager*, the German word for "stock."

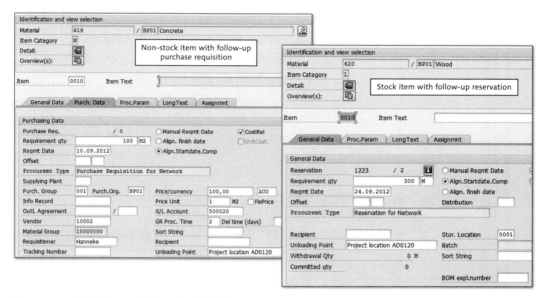

Figure 7.20 Materials and Follow-Up Activities

BOM Transfer

The BOM transfer function gives you to ability to quickly and easily assign material components belonging to one or multiple BOMs to the appropriate project activities. This function is very useful in engineering projects, where BOMs get changed and updated frequently. The automatic transfer can take place by assigning the REFERENCE POINT field to both the material components and the project activity. However, this isn't a requirement of using the BOM transfer function; it just allows you to make the assignments manually.

7.2.3   Project Approval and Budgeting

During the planning phase of a project, it's important to plan your costs as accurately as possible because they will form the basis for the project approval and budgeting phase of the project. In the approval phase of a project, the project actually receives funds that get allocated to the project in the form of a budget; that budget is approved and assigned by the decision-making committee (often a management team or steering committee). The budget is the approved cost framework for the project; in comparison to the earlier cost plans, the approved budget is binding. The project manager can assign the approved budget to the project in the form of "an original budget," which, based on your configuration settings, is either assigned as an overall value or is assigned per fiscal year. Figure 7.21 is an example of the original budget assigned for the garden shed project.

You can either set up a budget directly in SAP PS or use integration scenarios with other SAP solutions to distribute the budget from. Within SAP ERP, you can distribute a budget from SAP Investment Management to a project, when this has been configured correctly. You're also able to use additional SAP solutions for budgeting and planning tools, such as SAP Business Planning and Consolidation (SAP BPC) or non-SAP budgeting tools used within your organization.

The project manager can further distribute and allocate the budget to lower-level WBS elements, which can be monitored during project execution. You can optionally use the budget release function, which allows you to make funds available at various points within the fiscal year.

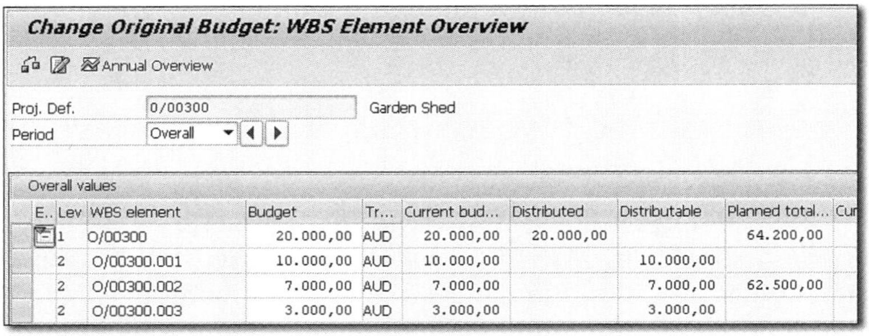

Figure 7.21 Project Original Budget

After it has been set up, the original budget can be locked or frozen by using user statuses, which then forces you to use the budget update functions when a change to the budget takes place. Changes can be supplements, returns, and transfers. Through the change logs for budgeting, it's always possible to track by whom and when changes to the budget have taken place.

During project execution, various activities lead to a either a commitment or a posting of actual cost, and use up the available funds. Actual costs are either booked directly onto the project or indirectly via the use of orders or through financial processes, such as allocation of overheads. You can see the budget consumption in the funds overview. This is a passive availability control because overspending won't be automatically actioned by the system.

However, within the SAP PS configuration, you can also set up an active availability control for the controlling area and project profile, which allows you to calculate and check the budget at the time of consumption. When the thresholds defined are breached (say, 95% of the budget is consumed), you can trigger a system reaction such as a warning message to the user and an automatic email to the project manager informing him of the situation.

Releasing is a mandatory step, so before you can confirm actuals onto your project, you must release either the entire project or part of the project. Figure 7.22 gives you an example of this project release step. You can just use the standard available statuses, or you can define your own user statuses. You can track and trace statuses within the project and can use them as selection criteria during execution of project reports.

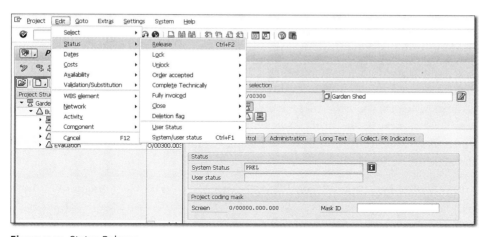

Figure 7.22 Status Release

7.2.4 Execution and Monitoring

During the execution phase of a project, the activities and processes that were planned at the beginning of the project are actually performed. So during the execution of the project, you'll collect the actual data around the resources used:

time, money, internal and external employees, and materials. Information for actuals for the following is collected:

- Start and end dates
- Costs for execution of activities, whether done internally or externally
- Consumption of materials, either stock or non-stock
- Incoming revenues and payments
- Budget consumption

Next we'll describe how these actuals are collected.

Confirmation of Time and Dates

There are two ways to collect this information during project execution: manually at the WBS level or through activities.

When you're using a project without activities, actual dates and the status of the WBS element can be set manually in the WBS elements during the execution phase. Of course, before you can enter actual dates, the WBS elements must be released, either in parts or as the entire project. Entering actuals can be done in the graphical planning board.

The other time and date collection option is through activities. When internal employees work on a project, they can confirm their activities and hours by entering confirmations on these activities. When you and your team enter confirmation documents, the processing status of activities and activity elements gets updated automatically, and the actual dates, actual cost, actual labor, and status of the activity are updated.

You can enter confirmations against activities and activity elements in the following different ways:

- Directly in SAP PS (multiple transactions are available, such as individual confirmation, collective confirmations, and pool confirmations; see Figure 7.23 for an example of collective time recording)
- Through cross-application time sheets (CATS)
- Using the Project Information System
- Via the Internet or the intranet

- Offline scenarios, such as through the Mobile Time and Travel app
- Palm Pilot/Open PS or CATS notebook interface, in which you can perform execution activities on a smartphone or notebook device in on offline capacity to later sync back into your live environment
- Plant Data Collection (PDC), in which you can use the confirmation data of external systems and transfer it to SAP PS via the PDC data transfer (requires configuration settings for the PDC interface in SAP PS)

Be aware that many options are available for entering confirmations against activities and activity elements, and you should choose the ones that are most appropriate for your organization. The most commonly used time recording option is CATS because this time recording allows you to enter times against objects from multiple components, such as SAP PS elements (WBS elements and networks), SAP PM orders, internal orders, HR activity types, and so on. CATS time recording uses the employee number from SAP ERP Human Capital Management (SAP ERP HCM) to record activities and then sends the entries to the manager for approval. Once approved, the cost will be reflected on the chosen activity. CATS is the preferred way of time recording when you're using both SAP PS and PPM. It requires integration with SAP ERP HCM where SAP ERP HCM can be used either minimally (scenario with HR mini master) or in full scope. We won't spend any more time on the different confirmation options, but they can be found on SAP Help.

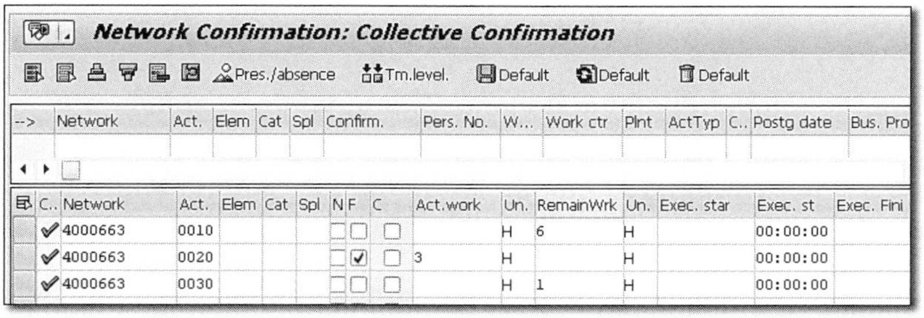

Figure 7.23 Time Confirmation

Confirmation of External Activities

Actual times and costs are recorded and booked based on the procurement process. Most organizations choose to have the actuals flow through to the project at the time of goods receipt and service acceptance (which can also be entered through CATS apart from the procurement process). And if an unplanned variance is identified during invoice receipt, this variance is approved (or rejected) and booked during invoice receipt. However, it's also possible to have the goods receipt or service acceptance unvaluated, which will lead to having the actuals booked to the project at the time of invoice receipt.

Within SAP PS, Transaction PROMAN has been developed to monitor and document all of the project-related procurement activities. Figure 7.24 shows you an example of Transaction PROMAN, where you can see the component CONCRETE and its details based on the chosen project element BUILDING THE FOUNDATION. It can be used to update and monitor procurement activities, such as goods receipts, goods issues, transfers, and so on. Since EHP 3, three improvements have been implemented in the COMPONENTS area:

▶ Dragging and dropping components to activities

▶ Activating separate tabs for tracking data

▶ Adding customer-specific data

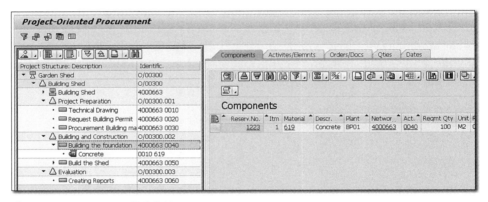

Figure 7.24 Transaction PROMAN

Confirmation of Materials

Recall that two kinds of materials must be budgeted and tracked: stock and non-stock materials.

You can issue stock materials to the project by using a materials movement, which issues the materials from stock to the project. This can be done as a planned movement, which is based on a reservation created during the project planning phase (see the example for WOOD in Figure 7.25) or as an unplanned movement, where materials are issued without any prior planning steps.

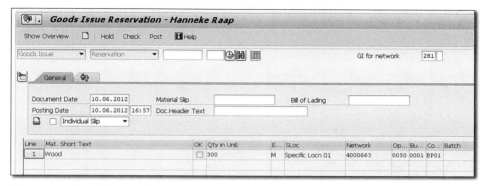

Figure 7.25 Goods Issue to Project

The actuals of the consumption of non-stock materials are booked against the project through the procurement process. They will either become visible at the time of good receipt when it's a valuated goods receipt, or at the time of invoice receipt when the goods receipt is unvaluated.

Using Execution Services from within Easy Cost Planning

Another means of performing confirmations is the use of Execution Services within ECP. When you've used ECP as a costing method and set up and configured the use of Execution Services, you can enter commitments and actual costs via the Execution Services. The user will need the appropriate authorization to do so. The following postings are possible:

▶ Internal activity allocation

▶ Direct process allocation

▶ Reservations for materials

▶ Goods issues for materials

▶ Purchase requisitions for materials, external activities, and variable items

▶ Purchase orders

Progress Tracking

You can use the progress analysis workbenches to track the progress of your project, of which Figure 7.26 is an example. This used to be done based on the project components and procurement orders, in which progress tracking was helpful for monitoring critical components in the project closely, and SAP PS and purchase order data from SAP MM was used to track events. However, in EHP 3, progress tracking for WBS elements and project activities was introduced via the progress analysis workbenches; they are accessible via Transactions WBSXPD and NTWXPD.

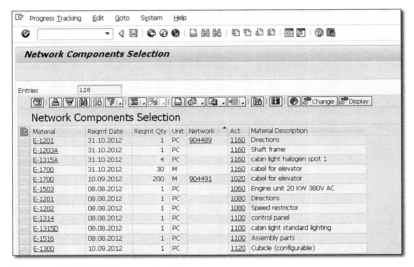

Figure 7.26 SAP PS Progress Tracking

SAP Cash Management

SAP Cash Management is a subcomponent of SAP Financial Supply Chain Management (FSCM). Its main purpose is to monitor cash flows and to safeguard that you have sufficient liquidity to cover your payment commitments. SAP Cash Management is integrated with a range of other SAP components, including SAP PS. When money is spent directly on the project (direct booking) or indirectly by using other processes (e.g., through production processes or procurement), actual cash needs to be paid to vendors. Additionally, when the project is a customer project, the project must have a way to receive payments from customers. With SAP Cash Management you can monitor and track actual incoming and outgoing payment data as a result of actual costs and revenues, which provides you with a liquidity forecast.

SAP Claims Management

When you're executing a project, you might experience circumstances that influence the project and result in increased cost or the late delivery of parts of the project or the entire project. If this occurs, you can use the SAP Claims Management process to document the variances and determine the appropriate follow-up activities such as claiming costs from a vendor, starting a change request process, or requesting additional resources. You can enter claims directly in the system or via the Internet through a form. Several reports are provided for you to monitor claims in the Project Information System. Figure 7.27 shows an example of a claims overview list that is monitoring a late delivery.

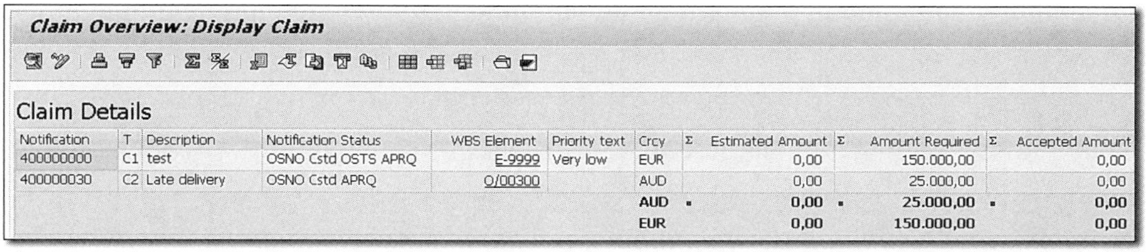

Claim Overview: Display Claim

Claim Details

Notification	T	Description	Notification Status	WBS Element	Priority text	Crcy	Σ	Estimated Amount	Σ	Amount Required	Σ	Accepted Amount
400000000	C1	test	OSNO Cstd OSTS APRQ	E-9999	Very low	EUR		0,00		150.000,00		0,00
400000030	C2	Late delivery	OSNO Cstd APRQ	O/00300		AUD		0,00		25.000,00		0,00
						AUD	•	0,00	•	25.000,00	•	0,00
						EUR		0,00		150.000,00		0,00

Figure 7.27 Overview of Claims

Project Reporting and Monitoring

The Project Information System provides you with structure, claim, financial, progress, resources, and materials reports using the menu sequence PROJECTS • INFORMATION SYSTEM. These reports, such as the standard available financial report found for the garden shed shown in Figure 7.28, offer a comprehensive means of tracking and monitoring the progress of a project. Apart from reporting, specific reports also allow you to perform activities, such as confirmations.

One of the most frequently used reports within SAP PS is the structure overview report available through Transaction CN41. This complex report's inclusion of many functions made it rather challenging to navigate, so it has been supplemented by the introduction Report CN41N. Although the functions offered are slightly less comprehensive, it's easier to use.

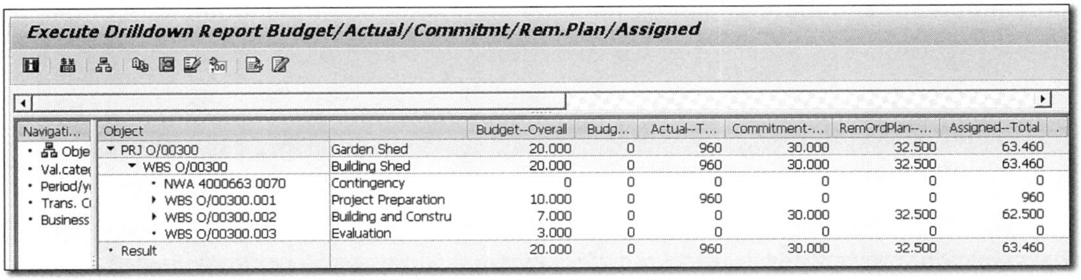

Figure 7.28 Budget Report

Figure 7.29 shows the both reports—CN41 and CN41N.

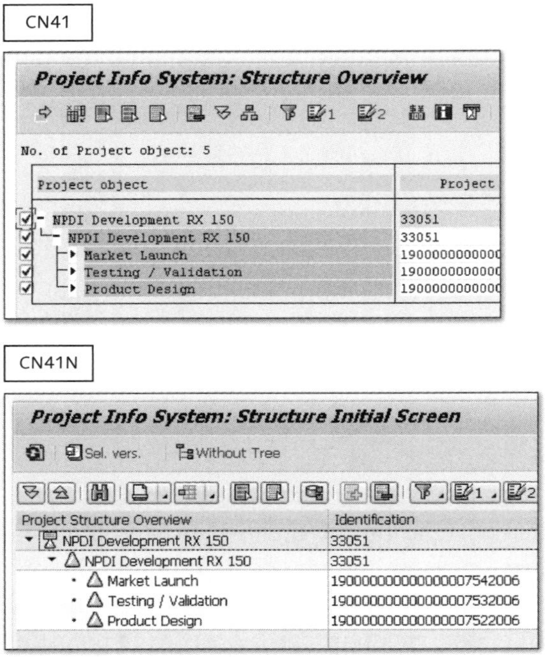

Figure 7.29 SAP PS Structure Display

Within SAP, you can use statistical key figures to provide actionable information on non-monetary data, such as the number of employees, number of machines, capacity usage, and market information. For example, when you have collected the cleaning cost, an activity/expense is charged monthly and collected on a general cost center. You decide to reallocate these costs from the general cost center to the department-specific cost centers based on the number of employees per department; you can do this via the action based on this statistical key figure ("Number of employees"). You can assign the statistical key figures to WBS elements, networks, activities, and activity elements, and, as of EHP 3, you can update them directly in the SAP Project Builder via an additional tab instead of using the older change transactions.

7.2.5 Closing

The last phase within a project is project closure. Before you can close a project, you have to prepare the project data and ensure the costs are settled. Settling the cost is a mandatory step for business completion because a project is a temporary cost collector during the project time line, but when closed, it should be zero. Period-end activities such as adding overheads, calculating project interest, and performing cost forecasts might be required, which are often conducted by members of the financial department, who can use the Schedule Manager to guide them through the steps required.

Period-End Closing

During period-end closing, you need to carry out several activities based on details of the steps you chose during the project planning, budgeting, and execution phases of your project. Closing is when and where you might need to calculate overheard costs, calculate project interests, perform a cost forecast, or create a progress or results analysis. (Note that as of EHP 3, you can manually update remaining work in the forecast workbench.) Results analysis carries out a period valuation of the project results, which includes calculating data such as stock values, cost of sales, and reserves. Settlement is one of the last steps before the project can be closed, which is explained in the next subsection. Figure 7.30 gives you an overview of the different activities performed during period-end closing. Our main focus is on SAP PS, so we'll cover the steps specifically relevant in SAP PS, which are settlement, project closing, and project reporting. Because the period-end closing process is performed at the end of each period (often monthly), it's a reoccurring cyclical process. Certain steps are set up as a schedule job, performed automatically by the system in the background.

You can use the different individual transactions to perform these period-end tasks; however, you can also use the Schedule Manager, which is a user-friendly tool in which you can plan and edit all period-end closing tasks by dragging them into a calendar. The tool can be found under the following menu path: SAP PROJECT SYSTEM • FINANCIALS • PERIOD-END CLOSING • SCHEDULE MANAGER. It isn't just focused on period-end closing for SAP PS, so it can be used by the financial department to include tasks from other financial components such as SAP ERP Financials Asset Accounting (FI–AA). More details on this tool can be found in Appendix A.

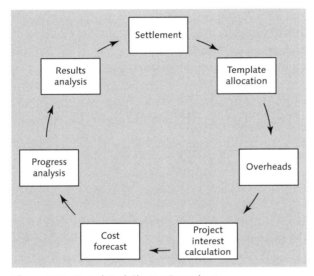

Figure 7.30 Period-End Closing Procedures

Project Settlement

Project settlement allows you to allocate the costs and revenues from the project, which is seen as a temporary cost collector and holder, to one or more *permanent cost receivers*. A receiver can be one of the following:

▶ General Ledger (GL) account, which is an object from FI

▶ Fixed asset, which is an object from FI–AA

▶ Order, cost center, or profitability segment (all objects for cost accounting)

▶ WBS element, network, or activity from another project

The cost and revenue receivers often depend on the nature of the project. For example, an investment project is usually settled to an asset under construction

(AUC) periodically, and when the project is finished, it is settled to the final fixed asset. Meanwhile, an operational project is usually settled to the requesting cost center(s) of the project, and a customer project can be settled to a profitability segment. Within the configuration and during project setup, only settlement receivers are available to you, which are allowed for your project type; the system can default the settlement rule. Settlement can include a mixture of settlement receivers (e.g., where the capital part of the project cost incurred gets settled to an AUC and eventually to a fixed asset, and operational costs get settled to a cost center. When the balance on your project is zero, which means all of the costs and revenues have been settled, you can close your project.

Project Closing

When all work on parts of an entire project has been completed, you can flag this with technical completion, which can be done either via time confirmation or through status management within the SAP Project Builder. This status change will close out any outstanding reservations and purchase requisitions, and it will effectively keep you from confirming any new hours or booking new costs against the project, although costs can still be booked. When the project balance is zero—indicating that all the project costs have been settled to its final receiver—then the project status can be set as Business Completed status. This completes the project. When necessary, you can revoke the status change.

Project Reporting

The reports within SAP PS can be used to summarize project financials such as budget, plan, actual, and variances information. Reporting also allows you to view and provide input for project closure state; see the "Project Reporting and Monitoring" subsection under Section 7.2.4 for more details.

7.3   SAP Investment Management within SAP ERP

SAP Investment Management provides you with functions to support the planning, investment, and financing processes for investments. These could include—but aren't limited to—the following:

▶ Capital investments, such as the acquisition of fixed assets as the result of-house production or purchase

▶ Investments in R&D

▶ Projects that fall primarily under overhead, such as continuing education of employees or establishing new markets

▶ Maintenance programs

Usually, investments are measures and expenditures that must be approved by several members of the company because of their importance or volume.

The functions and business processes supported through SAP Investment Management and SAP PPM–Portfolio Management are similar and might even overlap occasionally. Both solutions offer valuable business functions to manage your investment portfolio, and both have earned their place within the SAP PLM solution portfolio. Which solution suits the need of your organization depends on the detailed business requirements and what you're trying to achieve. Section 7.3.3 offers some guidance in making this decision by providing a comparison between SAP Investment Management and SAP PPM–Portfolio Management. First, we'll give an overview of SAP Investment Management by explaining the data model it uses, followed with the business scenario it supports. The last section will conclude with the previously mentioned comparison of SAP Investment Management and PPM–Portfolio Management.

7.3.1   SAP Investment Management Data Model

SAP Investment Management is a highly integrated solution and SAP ERP component that has been around for a long time as part of SAP ERP Financials. It includes only two specific SAP Investment Management master data objects:

▶ **The investment program**
This represents your company's investment program and provides you with a hierarchical structure to manage and monitor your investments. You set up your investment program based on your own company program types. An investment program is made up of the project and its investment program positions. All investment programs together provide you with a complete overview of the planned company investments. Your investment tasks—which can be executed either through an order (such as an internal order or maintenance order) or via a project—need to be assigned to the investment program items, if you want to use SAP Investment Management to monitor them and to distribute budgets to the approved investment measures. Figure 7.31 shows

you an example of an investment program set up for a fictitious bike production company.

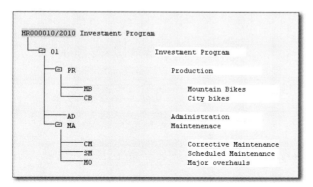

Figure 7.31 Investment Program and Positions

▶ **An appropriation request**

This is used to represent an investment idea after it has been approved to generate an investment measure from. An investment measure can be an internal order or a project. The appropriation request type is an important controlling object; it controls the investment measures you can use and the number range of the appropriation request. You can choose to either use the standard types delivered within SAP Investment Management or configure your own either from scratch or via copying. Figure 7.32 shows you an example of an appropriation request created for a major overhaul, which has been assigned to the investment program on the left side.

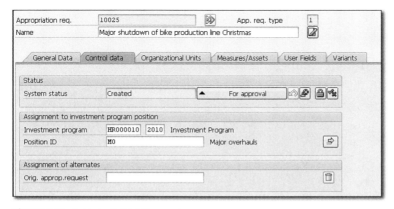

Figure 7.32 Appropriation Request

After the appropriation request has been approved, it can be turned into an investment measure, which is either an order or a project. Figure 7.33 shows you the basic lifecycle of an investment measure like this one. When you use SAP Investment Management, you can start planning and budgeting at the program level. After a measure is approved (via the appropriation request), part of the budgets assigned to the program can be allocated (or distributed) to the newly created order or project.

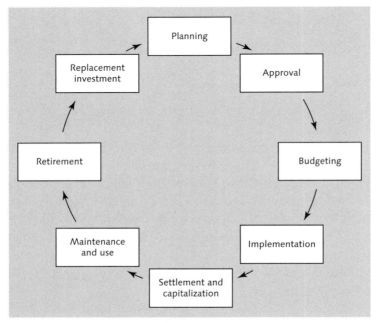

Figure 7.33 Lifecycle of an Investment Measure

7.3.2 SAP Investment Management Business Scenario

Let's walk through the SAP Investment Management business scenario and the business process steps. SAP Investment Management is often the starting place to initiate an investment and obtain approval, and it isn't where the investment measure execution takes place. Execution of an investment measure is usually done by other operational SAP ERP components (e.g., through a project in SAP PS, via a maintenance order in SAP PM, via a customer service order in SAP Customer Service [SAP CS], or via an internal order in CO). Because of this, SAP Investment Management is a highly integrated solution.

The business scenario represented in Figure 7.34 is the most commonly used business scenario in SAP Investment Management; the detailed process steps and roles can be combined or extended as necessary based on your company's requirements through configuration. The business scenario is based on the assumption that the investment measure (because this is the focus for this chapter) is a project and that the project will be settled periodically to an AUC and at completion to a fixed asset. However the steps described here have been made more generic so they can be applied to other types of investment measures and other settlement receivers.

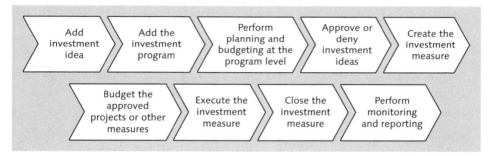

Figure 7.34 SAP Investment Management Process

Let's take a look at each step:

1. **Add investment idea.**
   The first step in the SAP Investment Management business scenario is to collect and add your investment ideas to the SAP Investment Management appropriation request. The appropriation request can include details such as the investment scale, reason, period, and priority. You can assign it to the appropriate organizational elements and can include one or several cost plans (based on different investment scenarios).

2. **Add the investment program.**
   The investment ideas and—once approved—the investment measures are going to be assigned to and monitored by the appropriate investment program.

3. **Perform planning and budgeting at the program level.**
   Planning and budgeting takes place at the program level. After this stage come the follow-on stages of investment measure (such as a project or a maintenance order) based on its lifecycle as represented in Figure 7.35 (we'll explain this in more detail soon).

4. **Approve or deny investment ideas.**
   After all the details of the investment idea from within the appropriation request have been completed, the idea can go through the official approval procedure where it's either accepted and approved or declined.

5. **Create the investment measure.**
   One of the most important activities is to set up the investment measure to execute the idea. An investment measure can be set up as a project, a maintenance order, or an internal order, depending on how you set up and use your system. You can then distribute the approved budget from the investment program to the investment measures (such as to a project, a maintenance order, or an internal order).

6. **Budget the approved projects or other measures.**
   The approved appropriation request can be turned into an investment measure. After the measure has been created, you can allocate budget from the program level to the project (or other measure) by using the budget distribution.

7. **Execute the investment measure.**
   Several follow-up activities can take place after the investment measure has been set up. For example, within this scenario, procurement activities take place, several steps within FI–AA are taken to decommission old assets and replace assets, information is updated in SAP PM to perform SAP Asset Lifecycle Management, and several controlling and settlement measures take place.

8. **Close the investment measure.**
   After the measure has taken place, actuals costs are collected, and the measure can be closed through the process chosen. It's during closure that activities such as settlement of the project to the investment asset takes place, replaced assets get decommissioned, and so on.

9. **Perform monitoring and reporting.**
   During execution and after closing a measure, you can use reporting possibilities within SAP Investment Management to report holistically and give you insight into how the programs are going. This will give you an understanding of whether the objectives set for the measures are being met.

This business process and these steps include the flow of the money, starting from the appropriation request, distributing the budget to the investment measure in the investment project, until periodic settlement to AUC and final settlement to the asset, as shown in Figure 7.35. When an internal order or maintenance order is used as the investment measure, it can be directly capitalized within the fixed asset register, or you can settle the order to the cost center.

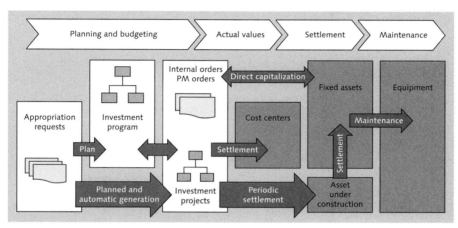

Figure 7.35 SAP Investment Management with Money Flow

To oversee and report on the information captured within SAP Investment Management, you can make use of several reports available either in the component itself (see the standard SAP Investment Management report in Figure 7.36), in the FI systems, or from additional business analytic tools whose standard content you can leverage. See Chapter 10 for more on this topic.

InvProgPosition		Plan Prog.--O...	Budg.Prog.--...	Difference--O...	Plan Prog.--2...
HR000010/2010	Investment Program	80.000	100.000	20.000-	0
01	Investment Program	80.000	100.000	20.000-	0
PR	Production	50.000	60.000	10.000-	0
AD	Administration	20.000	20.000	0	0
MA	Maintenenace	10.000	20.000	10.000-	0

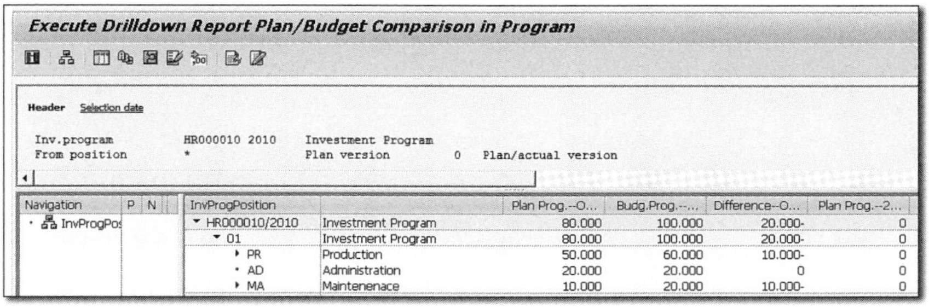

Figure 7.36 SAP Investment Management Report

7.3.3 When to Use SAP Investment Management or PPM–Portfolio Management

The functions and business processes supported through SAP Investment Management and PPM–Portfolio Management are similar and might even overlap occasionally. Both applications have pros and cons, so you should choose the application that suits your organization's needs based on the detailed business requirements and what you're trying to achieve. You might even find that there is a need within your organization to use both applications.

To inform your decision about which solution to use, consider Table 7.1. All the relevant different functions are listed in the first column, followed with the columns for SAP Investment Management and PPM–Portfolio Management to indicate whether the function is included or not.

Function	SAP Investment Management	PPM–Portfolio Management
Investment structure/portfolio structure	Yes	Yes
Additional structure	No	Yes
What-if scenarios	No	Yes
Web access	No	Yes
Additional licenses	No	Yes, depending on the contract
Budget distribution	Yes	No
User-friendly and intuitive	Less	More
Financial planning	Yes	Yes
Resource planning (internal and external employees)	No	Yes
Dashboards	No	Yes
Landscape extension	No	Depends; see Section 7.6.1

Table 7.1 Comparison of SAP Investment Management and PPM–Portfolio Management

Now that we've gone through the SAP Investment Management application, let's continue on with the project management capabilities of PPM.

7.4 Project Management in PPM

PPM is an application used for Portfolio Management, Project Management, and scheduling processes as shown in Figure 7.37. Chapter 2 covered the Portfolio Management capabilities of PPM, so the following section will cover PPM–Project Management and project scheduling.

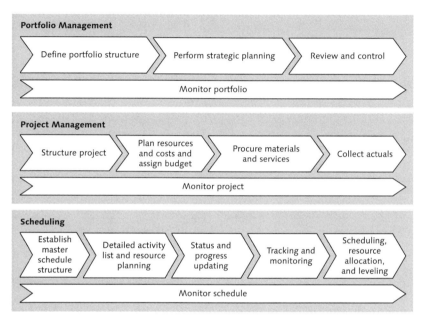

Figure 7.37 PPM Processes

Project team members are often spread across various locations, both internal and external to the organization, involving multiple communication channels (such as email, web meetings, phones, etc.) and cover information formats ranging from Word documents to complex 3D drawings. SAP PPM is able to support this complex project collaboration and supports multiple channels. The Project Management capabilities of PPM allow you to manage projects by doing the following:

▶ Clearly defining deliverables during a project

▶ Clearly defining roles and responsibilities, and creating ownership and accountability for project team members

▶ Using commitment management of all parties involved to complete their tasks and agreement of goals

- Collaborating among project team members in the project context
- Using a method with clear stage gates (templates, quality gates, handover, and milestones)
- Supporting multiple project management methods (e.g., ASAP, Prince2, and quality management methods such as Six Sigma)
- Using a project type that can be directly used for improvement projects

The Project Management functions in PPM used to be called c-projects. PPM can be used for both strategic and operational project management. It's a web-based application accessible through either a simple web browser or via the SAP NetWeaver Portal. This means it's especially suitable to use for IT, development, and service projects because it's intuitive to use, doesn't require extensive training, and doesn't require tight integration (which investment projects usually do). SAP PPM integrates well to SAP ERP 6.0, specifically to FI, HCM, and SAP PS.

Use of PPM offers the following benefits:

- A single source of truth to provide company-wide transparency of all projects
- Right information, right people, right systems, right time, and right decisions
- Modern, easy-to-use solution accessible via a web browser
- One unified solution for planning, consolidation, and financial reporting for SAP and non-SAP data (such as with Microsoft Project)
- Effective use of resources via enterprise resource planning and tracking
- Leverages existing data of all operational sources (including FI–CO, SAP PS, HCM, and CATS)
- Alignment of capital and operational spend and strategic intent
- Effective stage/gate control for projects
- Auditable planning and budgeting process
- Early identification of opportunities, bottlenecks, and risks
- Improved visibility and management of the portfolio
- Link between business case and actual spend
- Agile process of reviewing and adapting the portfolio
- Governance through comprehensive authorization and project history
- Collaboration with internal/external stake holders through c-folders

7.4.1 Data Model for Projects

Next we'll introduce the different project elements used in PPM–Project Management, which also have been represented in Figure 7.38.

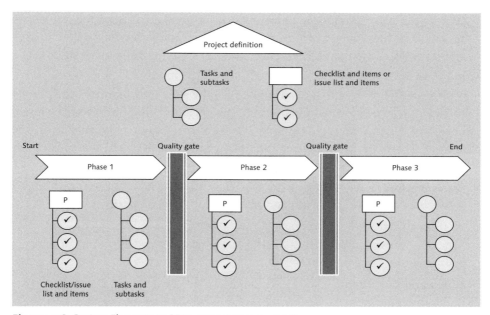

Figure 7.38 Project Elements in PPM–Project Management

▶ **Project definition**
Uniquely identifies the project.

▶ **Phase**
Used to structure the project in individual time segments, which usually will be executed successively.

▶ **Approval**
Used to assign an approval process to the completion of a project phases. Decision makers approve or reject the phase, which provides the quality gate between various phases.

▶ **Checklist**
Lists the things that need to happen during a project or an individual project phase. Checklist items can be used to monitor progress because you can flag items as relevant (optional or mandatory), and they can be set up in such a way

that they have to be completed before you can approve them or go to the next phase.

▶ **Tasks**
The individual activities that need to take place during the project. Information such as the task description and duration can be maintained. They are either assigned to the project or the project phase. Tasks can be related to one another by setting them in sequence, and tasks can be made up of subtasks.

▶ **Role**
A position in a project that needs to be filled by a business partner. The project role can include information about the qualifications that the resource should have and when and for how long the resource should be available on the project. The role also has a cost rate or revenue rate assigned that is used for project costing.

▶ **Qualification**
A specific capability or permission to carry out a specific task.

▶ **Business partner**
A person, organization, group of people, or group of organizations in which a company has a business interest.

▶ **Notes and documents**
Can be assigned to all of the preceding project elements (phase, checklist, etc.). Three options are supported for the SAP Document Management System (SAP DMS) integration:

- ▶ Use PPM–DMS.

- ▶ Use a document info record (DIR) from SAP DMS or multiple SAP DMS systems. Within PPM, you can use object links to assign SAP ERP items (e.g., a purchase order) to a PPM item (e.g., task, phase, checklist).

- ▶ PPM–Project Management and PPM–Portfolio Management integration for web-based exchange of materials, documents, and BOM with partners

▶ **Project version**
Used for the following two purposes:

- ▶ The *snapshot version* can be used to save a snapshot of a project at a certain point of time, which can't be changed. These are often used for analyzing and reporting purposes and are taken at preset times (e.g., creating a version during project forecasting, planned/actual costs before start and during execution, version for the approved plan, and versions for estimates).

▶ A *simulation version* can be used to simulate and test a proposed project change before implementing it to understand the effects certain changes will have on an operational project by comparing several simulations. You can save simulations and call them again later. If the changes produce the desired result, you can reconcile the simulation with another simulation or with the operational project.

These project elements ensure that you can manage and monitor the entire project lifecycle from start to finish. Figure 7.39 shows you the process steps starting with the creating of a project to project closure. Each step will be described in its own dedicated subsection from project setup to closure. The project planning stage of a project includes the details of the integration between PPM and SAP ERP in detail.

Figure 7.39 Project Management Process

7.4.2 Create Project

During the first step in managing a project, you have to create and set up the project structure. You can use the project proposal (when captured in PPM by an initiative) as a predecessor step and include the documentation and approval steps. You can either start a new project from scratch or use a template to minimize the capacity required to create and structure the project and also to mandate a company standard. A project template will then pre-fill phases, tasks, and checklist items. This method is used in the example in Figure 7.40, where because a template is used, a complete project structure is directly created based on the template's project structure elements.

Templates can be created for projects, tasks, checklists, and control plans. At the project definition level, you include data that is valid for the entire project, such as the project type and responsible person. The phases represent the successive phases of a project, tasks, activities, and so on.

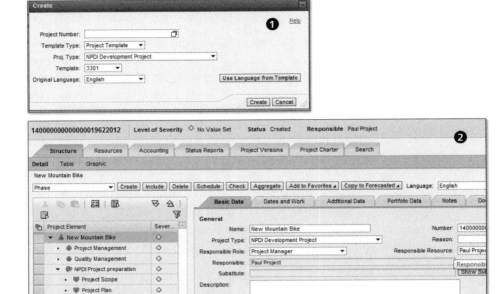

Figure 7.40 Create Project

Portfolio Assignment

To monitor the created project from a Portfolio Management perspective, you must assign the project to its corresponding portfolio item. Figure 7.41 shows you an example of this assignment. The assigned portfolio item belongs to a portfolio and portfolio bucket. You can assign the portfolio item to a project via one of the following three options. The first two options can be used when PPM is the operational project management system, while the last option is only relevant when a different application is chosen (e.g., SAP PS or Microsoft Project).

1. Start with the project in the PORTFOLIO DATA tab, or start from the PORTFOLIO ITEM and go to the MANAGE RELATED OBJECTS tab. The system will guide you through the assignment steps; for example, when assigning the portfolio data in the PPM project in the PORTFOLIO DATA tab, you first choose the relevant portfolio, then the bucket belonging to the portfolio, followed by the item. In

this tab, you can also delete an assignment. You can relate the project and or portfolio item to a business initiative via menu option MANAGE RELATED OBJECTS.

2. As soon as you *create* a portfolio item, you can have the project generated automatically by setting the AUTOMATICALLY CREATE A PROJECT indicator. This needs to have been configured because a project type needs to have been assigned to the PORTFOLIO ITEM type.

3. As soon as you *save* the portfolio item, you can have the project generated automatically by setting the AUTOMATICALLY CREATE A PROJECT indicator. This needs to have been configured because a project type needs to have been assigned to the PORTFOLIO ITEM type.

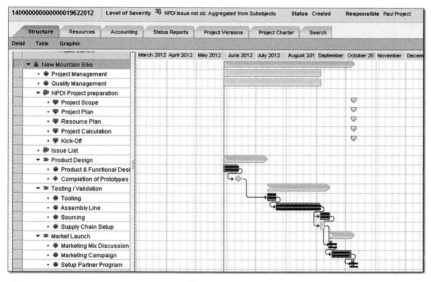

Figure 7.41 Assign a Project to a Portfolio

Create and Assign Documents (Optional)

Optionally, you can create and assign project documents to any project element. The "Project Documentation" subsection in Section 7.4.3 describes the different available options for doing so. Through project documentation, you can send out project status reports (which can be based on a company standard template) during set times to inform stakeholders about the project, which can be used for a project evaluation.

Organize Collaboration with Partners (Optional)

Another optional step is to set up project collaboration with an external partner such as a project manager or an external product developer. We'll discuss the details of how to set this up shortly.

Project Scheduling

You can schedule projects in PPM by one of the following two methods:

► **Top-down scheduling**
The system uses the dates entered in the project definition and the duration of the phases to plan the underlying elements accordingly.

► **Bottom-up scheduling**
The duration of the phases is determined from the assigned tasks and their relationships.

Rescheduling happens with each change, as long as the project hasn't been released. Independent of the chosen scheduling option, during scheduling both top-down and bottom-up scheduling will be run to determine time-critical tasks. After release, rescheduling only happens when triggered manually. Time-critical tasks will be highlighted in red or shaded within the project schedule, as you can see in the example displayed in Figure 7.42.

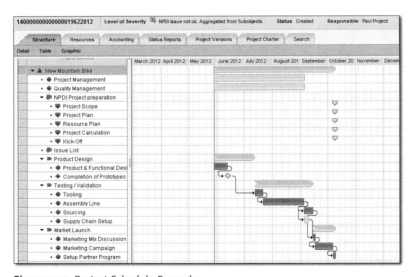

Figure 7.42 Project Schedule Example

Approvals and Status Management

After you're satisfied with the project structure and you want to start with the first phase of the project, you have to release the project. Releasing the project definition will also automatically release the first phase of the project. As soon as a phase is released, the system allows you to enter confirmations for assigned tasks and activities. During the course of the project, the subsequent phase can only be released when the current phase has been completed.

To cater to exceptional circumstances, you're also allowed to release tasks, checklists, or checklist items individually, when their parent phases haven't been released, so you can confirm actuals against them. For example, maybe ordering a necessary part has a delivery time of six months, so this needs to be procured as soon as possible. The premature release of this task can be done and will be documented.

Tasks and Checklist

Via tasks and subtasks, you can set up individual activities or tasks that need to take place during the project. These can, in turn, be assigned to a project role; after the role has been assigned to a specific person, this person can perform this task and confirm progress on the tasks. When a person is assigned to multiple tasks across projects, then his worklist will become visible in the confirmation functions to make confirmation easier (although this requires configuration). When a task has been completed, a notification/email can be sent to inform someone of this change (e.g., the project leader).

A checklist consists of a list of things that need to happen during a project or an individual project phase. They can be set up so that they have to be completed before you can approve them or go to the next phase.

7.4.3 Plan Project

During the planning of a project, you'll need to plan your financial resources in the form of costs and revenues and plan the required roles to conduct a project and its defined activities. This is often referred to as resource planning and includes the planned project deliverables per activities in the form of project documentation, often standardized per project type. This section describes how these resources can be planned within a project.

Financial Integration

In the financial management area in PPM, you have the option of forecasting financial data for the portfolio items and portfolio buckets in a very early phase of your projects. If your project planning makes detailed plan data available later, it should be possible to use and evaluate this financial data in PPM, so this can be used for decision-making purposes. For monitoring and controlling purposes, you also need insight into the actual costs incurred and the outstanding commitments. To get this detailed information into PPM, you can use the FI–CO interface, which includes the following items:

▶ Planned costs
▶ Planned times
▶ Planned revenues
▶ Budget
▶ Commitments
▶ Actual costs
▶ Actual revenues

You can set up the financial interface to run the required programs in the background during regular intervals so that updates are performed automatically without the need to engage an IT support resource, although regular monitoring is recommended. Multiple scenarios are supported, but the two most commonly used scenarios introduced earlier in Section 7.1 are explained in more detail and are included in Figure 7.43:

▶ Operational project management in SAP PS
▶ Operational project management in PPM

The cost integration between PPM and SAP ERP Financials give you four different cost controlling scenarios, which are shown in Figure 7.44:

▶ Internal order at a project level
▶ Internal order(s) per project element
▶ WBS element per PPM project role
▶ WBS element per PPM project element

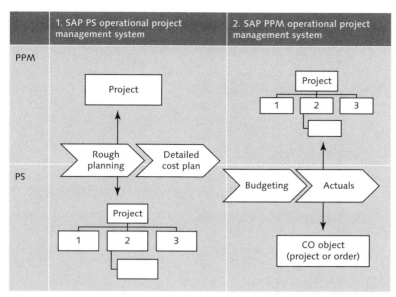

Figure 7.43 FI–CO Integration

The link can either be established automatically by the system or be set manually. Note the exception linking a project element to an internal order; this always needs to be done manually because automatic assignment is not supported.

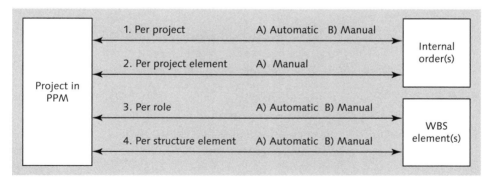

Figure 7.44 Cost Integration Controlling Scenarios

Using Operational Project Management in SAP PS

Recall that large projects—such as construction projects, maintenance projects, or large R&D projects—often require more extensive integration than other types of projects need (e.g., the fixed asset register, PP, and SAP MM). In these cases, the operational project management is best performed through SAP PS. The detailed cost planning and revenue planning is done in SAP PS, and more importantly for the integration, the project and its elements are used as account assignment object. In this scenario, SAP PS is used as the primary system for detailed cost planning, revenue planning, budgeting, and assigning accounts for documents of other applications, which result in commitments, actual costs, and actual revenues.

To use SAP PS for operational project management, follow these steps:

1. Early on in the project initiation phase, use PPM to set up the appropriate portfolio items, critical success factors, and rough planning of required funds.

2. Create the detailed project in SAP PS. The project structure, tasks, and activities will be created in SAP PS, due to the nature of the fixed integrations to other areas such as SAP MM for procurement and MM–IM, PP, SAP PM, SAP CS, SAP Investment Management, and FI–CO.

3. As a next step, the following two options are available:

    ▶ When you want to use PPM as the operational project management system that monitors all your projects, you have to convert the SAP PS project into a PPM project and include the structure, scheduling data, and resource data. This step is independent and not related to the FI–CO integration; once done, the FI–CO integration can be used to transfer the detailed accounting data.

    ▶ Customers who are only interested in the accounting data of the project can use the FI–CO integration without uploading the detailed project data, where the interface passes the data below through to the portfolio items.

4. Perform the execution and operational project management activities within the SAP PS perspective.

5. Perform portfolio monitoring from a PPM perspective and monitor the project via the details by which you've loaded the project and its structure into PPM (depends on the choice of step 3). So it's either at the entire project level or at the project and activity level.

Using Operational Project Management in PPM

When you're using PPM as the main system for operational project management, this integration scenario is relevant for you. Typically this scenario is relevant for the execution of smaller projects that don't need the extensive integration that other projects need (e.g., the fixed asset register, PP, and SAP MM). This is often the case for IT projects, development projects, and services projects.

Follow these steps to use PPM for operational project management:

1. Start with rough financial planning on the portfolio item, and later generate a more detailed financial plan at the project and activities level.

2. Link the relevant controlling object to the item, which can be either a project structure or an internal order from CO.

3. Transfer planned costs and capacity requirements to the chosen controlling object, which is used for automatic cost and revenue planning.

4. As required, adjust plan data in the backend and perform budgeting.

5. Capture the project costs during project execution in two areas:

   ▶ Internal costs for resources: These apply to your project, depending on whether you use internal resources. The resource can start with the tasks and confirm them, after the phase has been released. CATS confirmations are booked and will be visible on the controlling object through the interface.

   ▶ Other costs: Other actual costs (e.g., through procurement or MM–IM) or overheads/revenues booked against the controlling object will also flow to the PPM project.

6. Perform project and portfolio management from PPM's perspective.

Now that you understand the financial integration possibilities, let's explore the integration of PPM to SAP ERP HCM. This should provide you with the understanding of how you can use and upload the data from your SAP ERP HCM system and use the employee records to plan and allocate resources to your project tasks within PPM capacity planning.

Human Resource Management Integration

The main purpose of the integration is to provide the PPM system with the correct information to perform resource planning without the need to enter master data objects multiple times. The HR employee records from within your SAP ERP HCM systems will be used and transferred into a business partner in your PPM environment, which can include capacity details of the resource. The interface can be used both for the initial upload of the resources as well as for uploading ongoing changes.

Figure 7.45 gives an overview of the following objects that can be transferred from SAP ERP HCM to PPM:

1. Employee data (e.g., person)
2. Organizational structure data (e.g., structure, jobs, position, and organizational units)
3. Qualifications (e.g., qualification and qualification group)

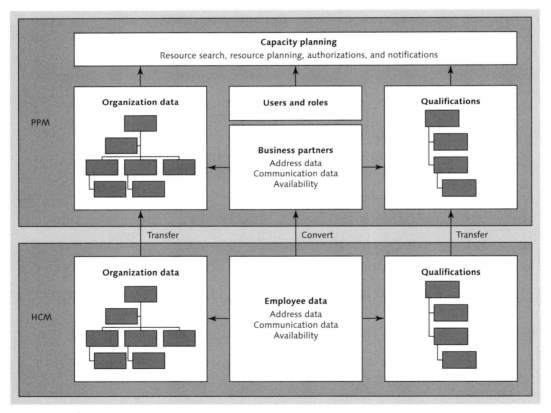

Figure 7.45 SAP ERP HCM Integration

Apart from the resource (the PPM term) or the employee (the SAP ERP HCM term) data, the organizational structure and qualification details can also be transferred via the interface so it will become available within PPM. Organizational data might be important during the search for resources or the assignment of a resource manager during resource management. The purpose of using SAP ERP HCM qualifications is to allow you to assign a specific requirement or qualification against a role. The assignment of the qualification can then be used by the resource planner as a search criterion to locate a suitable resource with the specified qualification. An example of this concept is the assignment of the qualification "PMO-certified" to the role of project manager. When you're looking for a project manager, the system will propose project managers who have this certification

Project Documentation

During a project, several documents can be delivered or worked on as part of a project task or as part of a quality gate. You can manage your documents against both the portfolio-specific items (portfolio, bucket, review, collection, item, initiative, or decision point) as well as against a project element (project definition, phase, task, checklist, etc.). Project documentation can include but isn't limited to product specifications, checklists, technical drawings via CAD, photos, performance data, and documents such as project charters, business cases, and blueprints.

PPM offers the following four document management options:

▸ Document management from PPM–Project Management

▸ Document management function from the collaboration scenario (see Section 7.5)

▸ SAP DMS from SAP ERP

▸ External document management system

Let's explore these document management options and SAP's recommendations on when to use each one. SAP recommends that you manage your documents with SAP DMS in the following cases:

▸ You want to exchange your documents between SAP DMS and SAP Project Management.

▸ You're already using SAP DMS and require access to the existing SAP DMS documents.

▸ You want to map your project structure via the SAP DMS document structure.

▸ You want to classify your documents.

In all other cases, SAP recommends that you use the document management function embedded in PPM that works together with the use of the SAP NetWeaver Portal, and can be used with or without c-folders.

Using the Document Function within PPM

Within PPM, you can assign a document to any project element by using the document function on the DOCUMENTS tab. Here you can specify project templates, update documents with version control, check-in and check-out capabilities, set up a folder structure, and provide information on who is able to access, update, or simply display documents via the authorization function. You can also configure status management by setting up a status profile in the configuration of PPM. Figure 7.46 gives you an example of an assigned document via this method.

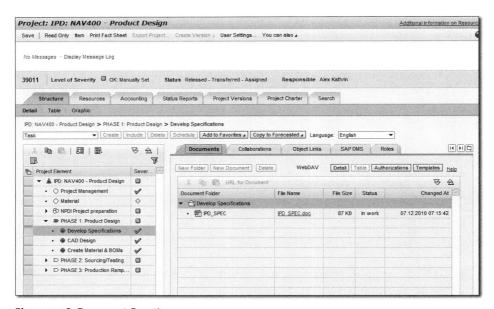

Figure 7.46 Document Function

Knowledge Management and Provider

Available through the SAP NetWeaver Portal, Knowledge Management (KM) supports you in structuring information and making it available to the correct audience. In contrast, Knowledge Provider (KPro) is the technology infrastructure through which documents are stored centrally in content servers; that is, it's a repository for your documents.

For more information about these topics, see the SAP NetWeaver section of the SAP Help Portal. The options available for your organization depend on the configuration settings for the assigned project type.

The Web-based Distributed Authoring and Versioning (WebDAV) interface enables you to connect PPM with Microsoft Windows Explorer, which allows you to navigate, edit documents, and upload documents via a mass upload.

Using Project Collaboration via C-Projects and C-Folders

By using project collaboration, you set up a structured environment (via collaboration rooms and folders) to exchange information in a web-based environment, including establishing the appropriate authorizations and carrying out web-based conferences. This enables virtual teams to communicate, collaborate, and exchange information whether these are staffed with internal employees from different locations across the globe or with external partners. In the past, c-folders and c-projects were offered as separate solutions alongside Resource and Portfolio Management (xRPM), however both solutions are now part of PPM. Figure 7.47 gives you an example of a project folder, which includes a public folder with subfolders per product phase. The user is working in the subfolder As DESIGNED, which includes three visible materials (MILK, SPECULAAS COOKIE, and DOUGH) and a recipe (SPECULAAS COOKIE BOM). We'll explore the project collaboration topic further in Section 7.5.

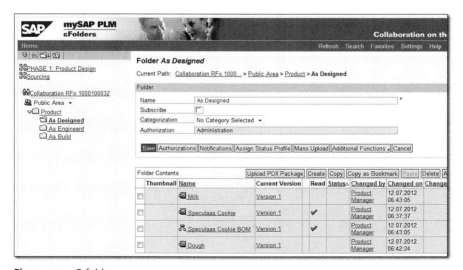

Figure 7.47 C-folder

SAP DMS

You can either create a link to the document info records (DIRs) in the backend or exchange documents from the SAP ERP system to PPM via remote function calls (RFCs). (Figure 7.49, later in this chapter, shows you how the SAP DMS tab is visible in this PPM project task.) This might be useful when documents need to become available in the collaboration scenario or when you want to use functions from SAP DMS in SAP ERP, such as document classification. Before this scenario can be used, several configuration settings are necessary in both PPM and in the SAP backend. The integration requires the use of a plug-in in the backend (available from 4.7 Enterprise), so you need to check the prerequisites and compatibility requirements on the SAP Service Marketplace.

External Document Management System

By using the SAP NetWeaver technology, you can integrate to any other non-SAP document management system, such as OpenText or Microsoft SharePoint. Please check the SAP Service Marketplace to find out whether or not your document management solution is or isn't supported by an SAP Certified interface.

Project Documentation Process

SAP defines the project documentation process as shown in Figure 7.48.

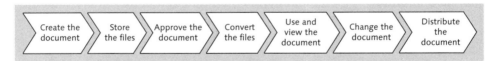

Figure 7.48 Project Documentation Process

Let's walk through it:

1. **Create the document.**
   The first step in project documentation process is to create the document and the container (e.g., the DIR) to which it belongs.

2. **Store the files.**
   The document needs to be stored on a centrally available location.

3. **(Optional) Approve the document.**
   Depending on the company's procedures, the document may or may not need approval/review by a senior employee.

4. **Convert the files.**
   When required, original files can be converted into a more neutral format, which is accessible be a larger user group.

5. **Use and view the document.**
   Once available, the document can be used and viewed by those users with the appropriate access.

6. **Change the document.**
   The document can be changed; this may include the creation of a new project version.

7. **Distribute the document.**
   Finally, the document can be distributed to the appropriate stakeholders.

Object Links

An object link is a connection of a business object, which exists in various systems, to a PPM object—for example, the assignment of a maintenance order or purchase order to a project task. You can assign any project element (project definition, phase, checklist or checklist item, task, subtask, control plan, or project role) from within PPM to an object in SAP ERP via an object link. This connection lets you perform combined evaluations but isn't a data exchange. The advantage is that you can report on a budget assigned to this object, and you can update this object via an additional web GUI (if you have the appropriate authorization and this is configured).

The following object links are possible in the indicated components:

▶ WBS element – SAP PS

▶ Network – SAP PS

▶ Internal order – FI–CO

▶ Plant maintenance order (since release SAP ERP 5.0) – SAP PM

▶ Sales order (since SAP ERP 5.0) – SD

▶ Purchase order or purchase contract (since SAP ERP 5.0) – SAP MM/SAP SRM

▶ Material (since SAP ERP 5.0) – SAP MM; see Figure 7.49 for an example of an object link to a material

▶ Master inspection characteristics – SAP Quality Management (QM)

▶ Control plan – QM

▶ Fault probability analysis and impact analysis – QM

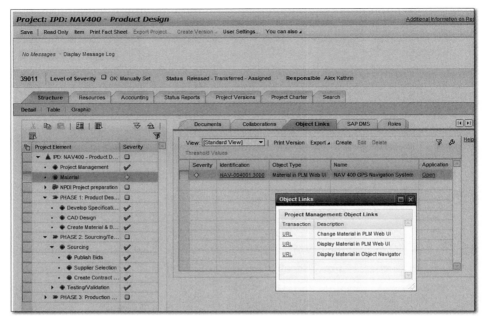

Figure 7.49 Object Link to Material

7.4.4 Manage Resources

PPM offers comprehensive resource management, which gives you the ability to plan internal employees or external contractors to fulfill project tasks and checklist items. The assignment can also be used in Alert Management to notify an employee (recipient) of specific circumstances, which will be explained in more detail in Section 7.4.6. PPM–Project Management provides you with three different sourcing scenarios for assigning resources to a project:

▶ **Project lead**
Resourcing is done at the project level by the project lead or a dedicated resource manager. The administration and resource management authorizations are required.

▶ **Resource manager via authorization**
The staffing manager or candidate manager can use the fast entry screen and

assign staff roles. The staffing manager and candidate manager authorizations are used.

▶ **Resource manager via responsible organization**
The roles are staffed using the extended staffing process via the fast entry screen.

Integration to Capacity Planning in PPM

If you want to integrate resource planning from PPM–Project Management with capacity requirements planning in PPM, you have to assign role functions defined within PPM–Portfolio Management to roles defined within PPM–Project Management. This assignment makes sure that the PPM–Project Management roles information gets aggregated within PPM capacity requirements planning in a role function. A role function in this context provides you with a grouping mechanism; some common examples of role functions are project management, product development, or quality management.

Prerequisite for Resource Management

Before you can assign resources, they must exist in the PPM–Project Management solution. A resource in PPM can represent either an internal employee or an external resource hired from outside your company. A resource is represented in PPM as a business partner of the type employee (BUP003) and the role resource (WFM001). You can create a business partner using one of the following three options:

▶ Manually in PPM via the RESOURCES ADMINISTRATOR menu

▶ In the SAP Menu via the BP Maintain Business Partner transaction (use business partner role employee with BUP003 and role resource WFM001 when using a cost/revenue rate)

▶ By uploading them from another SAP environment via the SAP HCM ERP integration, as discussed in Section 7.4.6.

After the resources have been set up as business partners, you can allow the resource administrator to update detailed information, such as availability periods, location assignments, and active or inactive periods via the ADMINISTRATION menu. Use Transaction PPPM to assign qualifications to a resource, and use Transaction OOQA to update the qualification catalog. The administrator can also set up resource pools, which group resources together in a pool so they can be managed by one or multiple dedicated resource managers, who can analyze the capacity utilization and their assignment to project roles.

A resource or person can be assigned to a task via the role this person plays (see Figure 7.50). The use of the tasks in resource management is optional; the advantage it offers is that the assigned tasks will be proposed during task confirmation.

Figure 7.50 Data Model for Assignment of Resource

Resource Management Process

Figure 7.51 shows the steps that are required for resource management, which enables you to assign an employee to a project task(s) or checklist item(s). Note that the process and the steps for resource management are the same for all three supported scenarios. The only difference is where and in which screen resource management is performed because this depends on the chosen scenario.

When resourcing is done at the project level by the project lead or by a dedicated resource manager, it can be done directly in the project on the RESOURCES tab; a cross-project resourcing view isn't possible. The resources view gives you access to the following two overviews at the project level:

▶ **Staffing overview**
Shows you the project roles and their assigned resources.

▶ **Resources overview**
Shows you the resources and to which project roles they have been assigned.

When staffing and resourcing is done centrally via a resource manager with the appropriate authorization or via organizational responsibility, then the fast entry screen is used, which the resource manager uses to manage the pool of resources for which he is responsible. The fast entry screen is accessible via menu option RESOURCE MANAGEMENT, which then gives you access to the same two overviews (staffing and resources), only for your own resource pool, giving you a cross-project view of your resources and roles. Strategic resource planning can be done at the portfolio or program level with capacity planning, which has been described in more detail in Chapter 2. If you want to integrate resource planning from PPM–Project Management with capacity requirements planning in PPM, you have to assign role functions to roles. A role function is a generic description of the function of a role; project management, product development, or quality management are commonly used role functions.

Let's walk through each step in the resource management process, as shown in Figure 7.51.

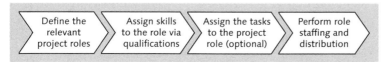

Figure 7.51 Resource Management Process

1. **Define the relevant project roles.**

   Roles are required either to determine a resource requirement or to assign a responsible user. They are project-specific definitions of the resource demand and requirements. Figure 7.52 shows you an example of several roles defined for this project: the project manager, design engineer, testing engineer, marketing, and product manager.

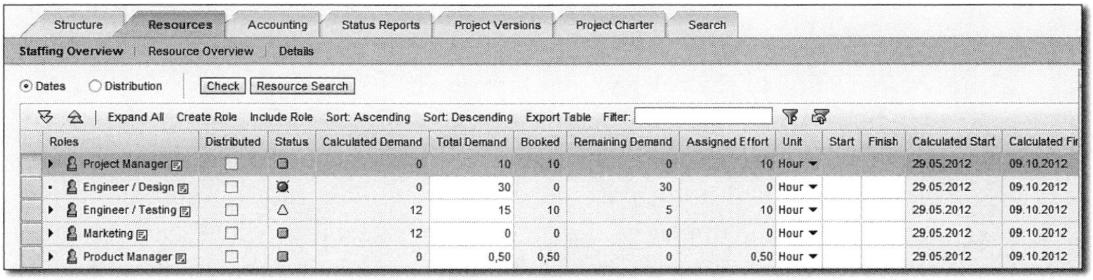

Roles	Distributed	Status	Calculated Demand	Total Demand	Booked	Remaining Demand	Assigned Effort	Unit	Start	Finish	Calculated Start	Calculated Fi
▶ 👤 Project Manager ☑	☐	☐	0	10	10	0	10	Hour ▾			29.05.2012	09.10.2012
· 👤 Engineer / Design ☑	☐	☒	0	30	0	30	0	Hour ▾			29.05.2012	09.10.2012
▶ 👤 Engineer / Testing ☑	☐	△	12	15	10	5	10	Hour ▾			29.05.2012	09.10.2012
▶ 👤 Marketing ☑	☐	☐	12	0	0	0	0	Hour ▾			29.05.2012	09.10.2012
▶ 👤 Product Manager ☑	☐	☐	0	0,50	0,50	0	0,50	Hour ▾			29.05.2012	09.10.2012

Figure 7.52 Example of Project Roles

Before you can assign roles in a project, you need to have set up the role type in configuration and assigned the required role types to the project type in configuration. Figure 7.53 shows an example of a project role, including the demand details and the time frame. The specifics that need to be maintained during project role creation depend on the setup and assigned role type. Required capacity can be included either in a table or in graphic form (available since version 4.5). Via the graphic form, requirements are compared with staffing, reservations, and posted required capacity.

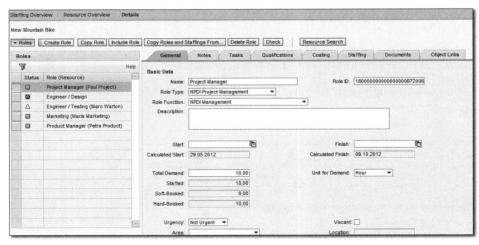

Figure 7.53 Details of Role

Note that instead of creating your own roles from scratch, you can also choose to include a role from the repository and make adjustments when necessary. When you've used a template during the creation of the project, it's possible that the roles and their requirements have already been set up for you. If that is the case, then you can use these roles and requirements and just make the necessary changes, if required.

2. **Assign skills to the role via qualifications.**

    If you want to use and assign qualifications to a role, you have to activate it for the project type. You'll use the qualifications catalog to assign qualifications and the required proficiency. By assigning qualifications to the role, you can use this information later on in resource management, when you'll be searching for suitable resources by qualification. Figure 7.54 shows which qualification requirements have been assigned to the role PROJECT MANAGER, such as BUDGETING, CREDIT and RISK MANAGEMENT, and FINANCIAL ACUMEN. You can either manually maintain the qualification catalog in PPM or upload the catalog data from SAP ERP HCM via the standard integration scenario.

3. **(Optional) Assign the tasks to the project role.**

    Next you can assign project tasks and checklist item to the defined project role. The advantage of assigning tasks to a role is that the assigned person will see the tasks being proposed during confirmation. Figure 7.55 shows you the tasks assigned to the ENGINEER/DESIGN role.

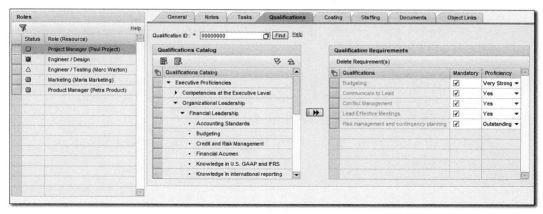

Figure 7.54 Role with Qualifications

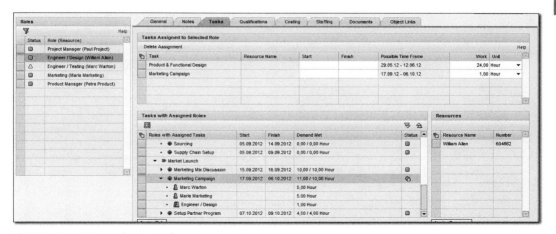

Figure 7.55 Assign Tasks to a Role

4. **Perform role staffing and distribution.**

   Staffing is the determination and assignment of suitable resource(s) to a project role. After you've finalized staffing, you can distribute the workload needed appropriately to the assigned resources within the individual periods such as days, weeks, or months. Staffing and distribution can be done either from the project itself or centrally across multiple projects, depending on the chosen scenario, as discussed in the introduction.

Both the staffing overview and the resource overview give you quick insight into the resource management status of the project using status color codes in the system (see Figure 7.56):

▶ Red: Staffed

▶ Yellow: Staffed, but not fully distributed to the assigned resources

▶ Green: Fully assigned and distributed

▶ Green with yellow circle: Overstaffed (more capacity is assigned to a role than was planned)

Roles	Distributed	Status	Calculated Demand	Total Demand	Booked	Remaining Demand	Assigned Effort	Unit	Start	Finish	Calculated Start	Calculated Finish
Project Manager	☐	▣	0	10	10	0	10	Hour ▾			29.05.2012	09.10.2012
Paul Project	☐	△	10				10	Hour ▾			29.05.2012	09.10.2012
Engineer / Design	☐	▣	25	30	30	0	30	Hour ▾			29.05.2012	09.10.2012
Product & Functional Design		▣	24			0	24	Hour ▾			29.05.2012	12.06.2012
Marketing Campaign		⊙	10			1-	1	Hour ▾			17.09.2012	06.10.2012
William Allen	☐	△	30				30	Hour ▾			29.05.2012	09.10.2012
Michelle Reekie												
Engineer / Testing	☐	△	12	15	10	5	10	Hour ▾			29.05.2012	09.10.2012
Marc Warton	☐	△	15				10	Hour ▾			29.05.2012	09.10.2012
Marketing Mix Discussion		▣	10			0	5	Hour ▾			15.09.2012	16.09.2012
Marketing Campaign		⊙	10			1-	5	Hour ▾			17.09.2012	06.10.2012
Setup Partner Program		▣	4			0	2	Hour ▾			07.10.2012	09.10.2012
Marketing	☐	▣	12	0	0	0	0	Hour ▾			29.05.2012	09.10.2012
Maria Marketing	☐	▣	0				0	Hour ▾			29.05.2012	09.10.2012
Marketing Mix Discussion		▣	10			0	5	Hour ▾			15.09.2012	16.09.2012

Figure 7.56 Overview Role, Task, and Assigned Resource

PPM–Project Management supports the following types of staffings:

▶ Hardbooking: Confirmed staffing

▶ Softbooking: Not yet confirmed staffing

▶ Candidate: Staffing proposal

A role can be staffed directly, which was done for the role project manager in Figure 7.56. A softbooking (for which you still need final confirmation) is useful, for example, when the resource, his manager, or the customer needs to approve the staffing. Candidates can be useful when you want to designate a resource based on the resource manager's preference, manager's preference, or customer's preference, which has occurred for the second role ENGINEER/DESIGN. During the staffing process, you can contact either the resource or his direct line manager by sending him an email with the request. We'll cover this process in more detail in the following section.

When you're searching for suitable resources, you can use the SAP Workforce Management searching capabilities, where you can use selection criteria such as availability, capacity, and location information, as shown in Figure 7.57.

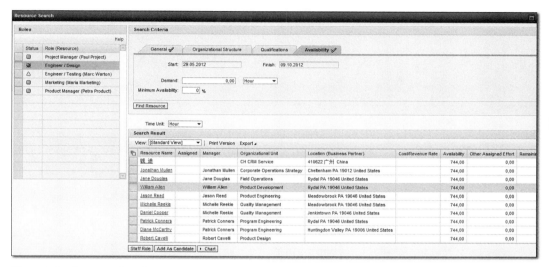

Figure 7.57 Resource Search

After you assign the found resource, you can then choose to do one of the following:

▶ **Staff the role directly with the resource.**
You can hardbook the resource (when the resource is definitely confirmed), or make a softbooking (assign resource, but wait for final confirmation). During this step, you can also contact the found resource or his manager via email or phone to brief them about the upcoming work, when required. As soon as the confirmation is in, you can change the softbooking to a hardbooking.

▶ **Propose the found resource(s) as a candidate..**
Again, you can use the emailing capabilities to contact the resource or the line manager of the resource to inform or speak to them about this upcoming work.

Both staffing choices are represented in Figure 7.58.

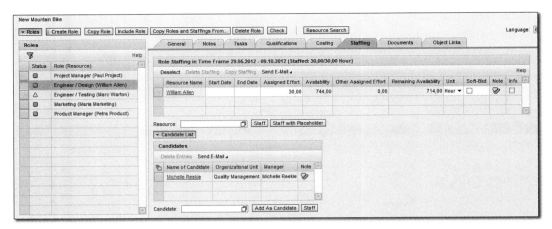

Figure 7.58 Staffing

The resource can only work on and confirm the tasks assign to him when they have been released.

7.4.5 Manage Visibility

You can monitor project execution by using the dashboards (also known as cockpits) set up for your organization.

Project Dashboard

When you open a project in PPM, you can use threat management to quickly get an overview of your project's status via the configured severity levels. These are either determined automatically or are assigned manually against a project and its elements, and they become visible by the SEVERITY indicator icon next to the project item. An example of this has been included in Figure 7.59.

Threat management is a requirement for an object that is checked in the evaluation. If the object meets the requirement, the system displays the icon of the severity that is assigned to the threshold value in the evaluation. In the project, you can see that a green indicator means that the project element is still on time, the yellow indicator appears if the date for a project element passed up to one week ago, or the red indicator appears if the date for a project element passed more than one week ago.

Within the PPM configuration, you assign a severity level, including an icon representing this level to a threshold value. Threshold values are evaluated by severity from the top down, and the system displays the severity and its assigned icon if the threshold value condition is fulfilled. This allows you to set up your own threshold values and severities with formulas based on your specific business requirements.

Severity violations are aggregated up the project structure, where the aggregated value of a project element is the highest severity of the subordinate elements or of the corresponding project element itself. However, when a severity is set manually, this will take precedence over one set automatically.

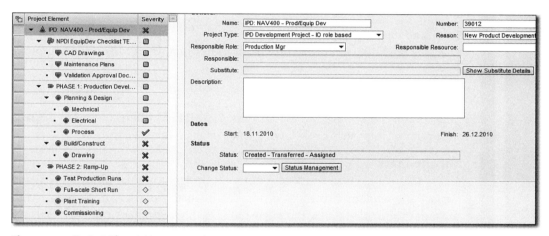

Figure 7.59 Project Threat Management.

Decision Flow Management

Decision Flow Management (DFM) supports the process of integrating the strategic PPM–Portfolio Management with the operational PPM–Project Management by the bidirectional synchronization of dates, status, authorizations, and other project attributes between linked project objects within the initiative/item/ project management and project accounting grouping.

Synchronization can be done horizontally or vertically. Horizontal synchronizes attributes between the different areas or applications used, such as PPM–Portfolio Management, PPM–Project Management, or SAP PS. This means that when you change an object in one area, the same changes are carried out in the corresponding object in another area. In contrast, vertical synchronizes attributes of objects within a single area; when you change an object in, for example, PPM–Portfolio Management, the same changes are carried out in a related object within the same area.

The key business enabler in DFM is the *initiative*, which provides program management capabilities for both PPM–Portfolio Management and PPM–Project Management. DFM also offers additional services:

▸ **Metrics**
Enables the configuration of attributes that can be measured in both initiatives and items.

▸ **Time line monitor**
Provides portfolio and project time line views in a Gantt-type visualization.

Cross-Project Visibility

Because projects often depend on each other, SAP PPM offers a number of cross-project relationships via the following inter-project link scenarios:

▸ **Mirrored task**
A task that is linked to a task of a different project (original task). The existing project (dependent project) must take the dates of the original task into account in the fixed dates; the mirrored task inherits dates of the original. Figure 7.60 explains this concept graphically.

▸ **Subproject**
A project that is represented as a task in a different project (master project). The link between the project and the subproject is a rather loose link, which is established through the use of alerts. Alerts make sure that the other project or subproject gets notified when changes occur. Figure 7.60 shows where the master project includes a task for the subproject.

▸ **Program**
Project of the category "program" to which other projects or programs are assigned. It's used to map complex project structures, as is represented in Figure 7.61.

When using these inter-project scenarios, you can use the multiple project monitor within the PPM dashboard.

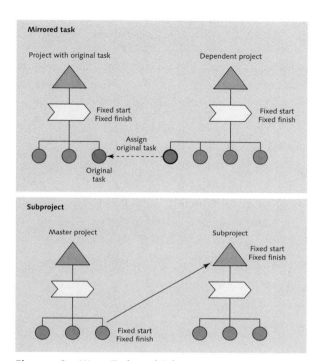

Figure 7.60 Mirror Tasks and Subprojects

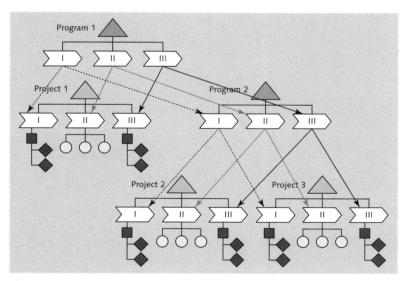

Figure 7.61 Program

7.4.6 Execute and Track

You're only able to plan and cost resources in PPM–Project Management. To plan other costs, such as material costs, you have to use a FI–CO controlling object, such as an internal order or a project WBS element. This is supported by the standard cost integration from PPM to SAP ERP as was explained in Section 7.4.5.

Confirmation of Tasks and Checklist Items

When confirming tasks, you can enter the actual data (e.g., the actual start and end date and work carried out), percentage complete, and remaining work, when required. When you've assigned a resource to the task, directly or via a role during resource management, the user can navigate directly to the confirmation of these tasks because they will be loaded as a worklist during task confirmation.

When confirming the checklist; you can record items as OK, Not OK, or Not relevant; when finished, you can set the status as Completed.

Confirmations and CATS Integration

The advantage of using CATS for confirmation is that the actual costs of the activities will also directly be booked to the used controlling objects, which were chosen as part of the cost integration scenario. When you've assigned a resource to the task, directly or via a role during resource management, the user can navigate directly to the confirmation of these tasks because they will be imported automatically in the worklist. Figure 7.62 shows an example of using CATS for worklist confirmation.

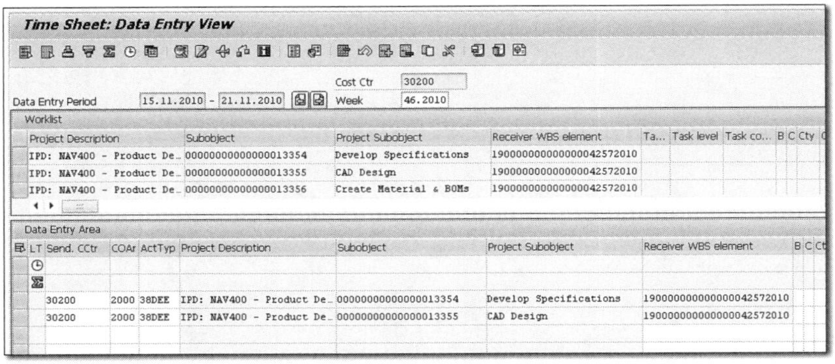

Figure 7.62 CATS with Worklist

When you're confirming task and checklist items, you can configure and confirm additional statuses via status management. You need to configure these before you can use them.

Confirmation of Completion of Phase

The user responsible for a phase can trigger an approval procedure as part of the completion of the phase, after all the project tasks and checklist items have been completed. This user prepares this approval procedure in two steps:

1. Determine the decision makers.
2. Prepare the approval document.

The decision makers can then decide to approve or reject the phase. If a phase isn't approved, the phase and project will be stopped and terminated as a result.

Alert Management

You can also use Alert Management to notify responsible users automatically by email when certain exceptions have occurred or when certain threshold values have been reached. You can also use Alert Management to generate a link between multiple projects. Because of this link, shifts in one project can have a direct impact on other projects (by using mirrored tasks) or an indirect impact by notifying at least the user responsible by email.

Status Reports

The project lead can regularly create project status reports with information about the current status of the project and send them to the relevant project stakeholders.

7.4.7 Close Project

The project phases are being executed one after the other and—when necessary—approved at the end of the phase until the last phase is reached and closed. After all the tasks and checklist items have been completed, you can complete a project phase. Closing and approving the last phase will set the project to Completed and close out any confirmations. An approval process can be used as part of the completion of a project phase, which can be triggered by the user responsible for the phase. The responsible user can send out the link to the approval step to the relevant decision makers and draft an approval document, which includes the relevant information for the decision makers. This ensures that the planned targets and goals of the phase have been reached and the deliverables have been completed. When a phase isn't approved, the phase and the project are stopped as a result.

7.5 Project Collaboration

Collaboration within PPM offers you a web-based collaboration platform to support intercompany teamwork as a virtual team across different locations. The team can consist of employees performing activities from different company locations and external partners—for example, an original equipment manufacturer (OEM) or other partners within the supply chain. Via collaboration, you can exchange information such as project plans, product data or project documents, and project structures to the virtual team over the web. It's a great tool to use during Product Innovation Management (PIM). Collaboration means exchanging information, communicating, and coordinating activities.

Collaboration is both part of the PPM solution offering and used within SAP SRM for collaboration. It offers users the following benefits:

▶ A single source of truth and less manual work results in fewer errors, misunderstandings and communication problems.

▶ A virtual team workspace allows you to set up fewer face-to-face meetings and less travel than classical collaboration and reduces time to market.

▶ Data is more reliable and structured, and every team member always has access to the latest data via the central vault (with redlining, markups, datasheets, and secure storage areas).

▶ Both internal and external team members have access to product data in a secure and economic way. Authorizations can be managed at the object level, and sensitive project information is protected against unwanted access.

▶ Status management controls data flow effectively and provides the next team member with the appropriate next step info.

▶ The needs for classic communication such as email, phone, fax, and employee meetings is reduced, and synchronous communication is improved.

Collaboration consists of two applications:

▶ Collaboration folders (c-folders) for design collaboration

▶ Collaboration projects (c-projects) for Project Management

Let's examine each of these.

7.5.1 Collaboration Folders

C-folders is a web-based cooperation platform that allows you to easily exchange project and product data with project members, including external partners such as engineering and design partners, suppliers, manufacturers, and customers. You can exchange information in a structured manner on a material, a BOM, document, and datasheets (which include product requirements, iPPE objects, or even your own customer-defined structures), as represented in Figure 7.63. You can also transfer 2D and 3D drawings when you're using the CAD Desktop. As part of collaboration, c-folders can be used in combination with the PPM–Project Management capabilities, with SAP SRM, or as a standalone solution (accessible via an Internet browser). You can set up authorizations to make sure that just the data that is required to perform the tasks are available. C-folders is typically set up outside of the enterprise firewall and accessed via a web browser through the SAP Web Application service (version 4.7 or higher) to prevent users accessing the productive systems within the firewalls. C-folders allows direct integration with the Windows Explorer, allowing you to upload and download folder structures.

Three scenarios are supported in c-folders:

▶ **Collaborative scenario**
Creation and management of engineering and design data in a public area (see in Figure 7.64 how a c-folder is created from within a project and how this can be accessed via the web).

▶ **Competitive scenario**
Creation and management of engineering and design data using separate, partner-specific areas requesting and evaluating quotations and data from suppliers and other partners.

▶ **Standard scenario**
Mainly available for you to use in the first two scenarios; use the templates to copy from.

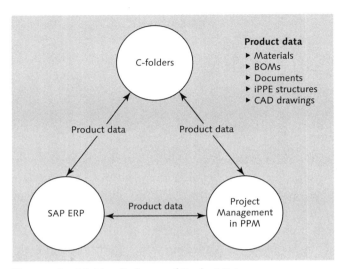

Figure 7.63 C-folders Exchange of Product Data

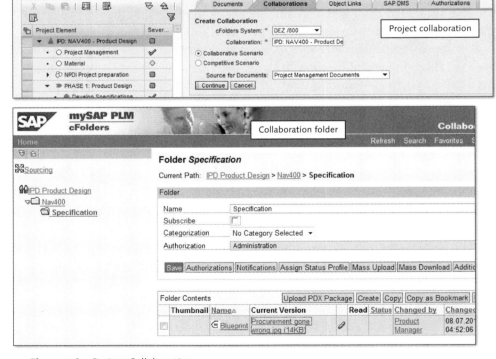

Figure 7.64 Project Collaboration

Because the processes used within c-folders are usually very customer-specific and can't really be generalized across the board, we've described the functions offered in detail in Table 7.2.

Function	Description
Structured collaboration	You can collaborate via a structured approach on the objects in the bullet list. All these objects, with the exception of the generic objects, can be transferred between c-folders and an SAP ERP or SAP PLM environment. They are described in more detail in Chapter 3. ▶ **Folders** These are used to structure collaborations and are containers in which objects are saved. You can add folders to a structure and subdivide a project in several levels to get a better overview of data and to set up authorizations per folder. When setting up a folder structure, you can use preset templates to ensure uniformity and consistency. ▶ **Materials** These objects represent items or products that are produced, used, traded, or consumed. ▶ **BOMs** This object contains a product and its subcomponents. Its structure is used for sales, production, maintenance, and so on. ▶ **Engineering change numbers** When you use SAP Engineering Change Management (ECM) to manage changes, the engineering change number or the engineering change request/order (which is one object, just a different status) can be included when making changes to materials, BOMs, or documents. ▶ **Documents and templates** These objects carry information used by a user or used to exchange information between systems. You can use templates to create documents (e.g., a template for meeting minutes or for presentations). The prerequisite for this is that when you set up the working environment for authors you've created templates and assigned these templates to the folder. ▶ **Datasheet** An object that describes product requirements in a structured way by using classification.

Table 7.2 C-Folder Functions

Function	Description
Structured collaboration (Cont.)	▶ **Technical assets** Ability to exchange information on technical assets, containing details on your functional locations or equipment, especially when a material was the basis of this. ▶ **Manufacturer part numbers** Material number as is listed by manufacturer or supplier. ▶ **Product variant structures (PVSs)/iPPE objects** An object used to set up different variants of a product. An iPPE node and variant nodes are used during product developments and can contain requirements, products, or product items. ▶ **CAD Desktop** When you're using a CAD system for your 2D or 3D drawings and are using the CAD Desktop, the information on used materials and BOMs can be transferred to c-folders via this transaction, via Easy DMS, or via the Microsoft integration. ▶ **Customer-defined (generic) objects** An object that has been defined to be used to cater for customer-specific objects.
Communication	The following functions allow you to collaborate with your team: ▶ **Discussions** An online discussion forum. ▶ **Notification** A short message within an email that can include status management for process control. You can set it up in such a way that the system collects all your email notifications and sends them together in one mail during a set time (e.g., daily or weekly). ▶ **Datasheet** Contains the product requirements, which are included in a structured versioned document with specifications based on classification data (classes and characteristics). Within the competitive scenario, the datasheets are used to receive structured proposals from vendors and to perform a simple comparison of quotations from multiple vendors. ▶ **Notes** Used to create long text. When using them, you need to be clear on the differences between discussions and notifications

Table 7.2 C-Folder Functions (Cont.)

Function	Description
Communication (Cont.)	▸ **Bookmarks** Quick links to pages on the Internet or intranet, or to objects within the folders, such as documents, materials, or links to other c-folders. ▸ **Subscribe** Subscribe to c-folder elements, which inform you of changes made to this element.
Transfer	By using c-folders in combination with PPM–Project Management and SAP ERP, you can transfer (import and export) product data from these environments to each other, as represented in Figure 7.63. To allow you to check the differences, the system will show you a result screen of what will be imported so you can compare two versions of a material BOM before you transfer it. The export of data from c-projects is also supported, which might be useful when an external partner wants to save and use the information from c-folders as input for its own systems. This is supported according to the IPC-2571 standard, which results in a PDX or CSV file/format.
Authorization/SAP Access Control	A sophisticated authorization concept for SAP Access Control can be used where, at the folder or individual item level, one of the following access roles is assigned per user. Several standard roles are provided, which can be used or copied and adjusted. There are four kinds of access: ▸ Read: User can read the content. ▸ Write: User can read and change the object. ▸ Administration: User can read, write, and assign authorizations. ▸ None: No access to the object.
Comparing BOMs	Via BOM comparison (including multilevel), you can compare different versions of a BOM.
Redlining and measuring	When using CAD (2D or 3D) drawings in your SAP DMS and also the Engineering Client Viewer (ECL Viewer), you can use visualization, measuring, and redlining functions.
Searching	Local (searching within a folder) and global search options (searching across all folders) are supported. Additionally, the SAP NetWeaver Search and Classification (TREX) search engine can be used.

Table 7.2 C-Folder Functions (Cont.)

Function	Description
Large volumes	If large external files are used, an external FTP service can be set up to enable faster exchange of data.
Integration	**Document management protocol** By using the WebDAV interface, you can work directly on documents that are stored on remote servers from different geographic locations. You can open the file directly from the server and make your changes. When you save the document, it's updated directly on the server. You can create, copy, move, or delete documents, which includes locking and version control (status management as releasing a document) mechanisms to support working in groups, and prevent unwanted overwriting of documents. You can find out more on this topic in SAP Help, under SAP NETWEAVER • ENTERPRISE KNOWLEDGE MANAGEMENT. **Procurement** Via the competitive scenario, you can request and evaluate quotations from different partners and/or suppliers. The competitive scenario starts with the setup of a public area with the project and product specifications. Based on this public area, the project and product data can be made available for the areas specific to the different bidders. This allows you to choose which specific project and product information you want to receive information on from the supplier. You can, for example, request all product data from the first supplier and just ask for information on several subcomponents from a second supplier. This is enabled by the setup of c-folders as a container for technical specifications in the SAP Bidding Engine. C-folders collaboration can be generated within the SAP Bidding Engine (SAP SRM 3.0 and C-folders 2.00 SP7 or C-folders 3.0). Collaboration also integrates with SAP SRM: You can create a shopping cart in an SAP SRM system for collaboration in the competitive scenario via the detail screen of the collaboration. You receive an external reference to the shopping cart in the SAP SRM system. Apart from this reference, no data is saved in c-folders. The shopping cart in the SAP SRM system contains a reference to the c-folders collaboration, which allows bidirectional navigation.

Table 7.2 C-Folder Functions (Cont.)

Function	Description
Integration (Cont.)	Several prerequisites have to be met to use SAP SRM integration: you must be using the competitive scenario with the correct authorization, a valid product category ID must have been maintained against your user, and your system administrator must have made certain system settings. (For more details, see the configuration guide for c-folders on the SAP Service Marketplace.)

Table 7.2 C-Folder Functions (Cont.)

Figure 7.65 shows you how a collaboration partner (in this example, Chris Robertsen) uses an Internet browser to access all four collaborations he has been involved in.

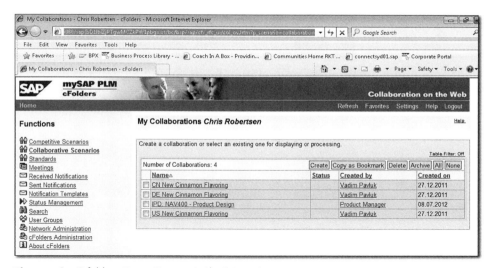

Figure 7.65 C-folders Home Screen via the Internet

7.5.2 Collaboration in Projects

By using collaboration in projects you can easily exchange project and product data with your involved project members, including external partners. You can use collaboration by setting up a collaboration room (c-room). The c-room can be set up for any project element, for example, for the entire project (at the project definition level), for a project phase for checklist and checklist items, and for tasks. It includes functions to manage project templates, and it enables project communication and coordination. When you want to exchange documents, c-projects uses the functions from c-folders; this is why they are often used and implemented together. The current release of PPM includes both collaboration scenarios (c-projects and c-folders) as well as the PPM–Portfolio Management and PPM–Project Management capabilities. The SAP Business Content available for reporting tools is quite substantial in this area. Please refer to Chapter 10 for more information on this topic.

7.6 Other Project Management Applications

Before we go into the details of how to integrate to other applications, first we'll briefly describe the system architecture for PPM. This allows you to understand the different components required to set up and use PPM.

Because this book has a functional focus, Figure 7.66 shows you a simplified view of a landscape for PPM with the required and optional components, which will be explained briefly in this section. The section will finish with links so you can find more detailed information, such as the link to the master guide for PPM, which includes a more comprehensive technical landscape.

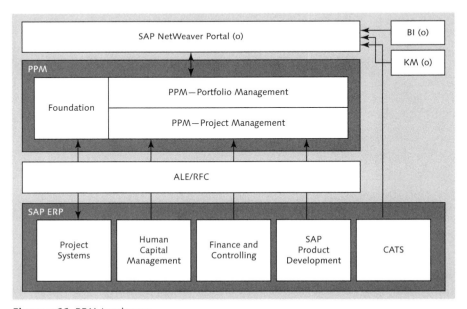

Figure 7.66 PPM Landscape

The following elements are important to run PPM:

- **PPM core**

  This includes the SAP NetWeaver Application Server, both for ABAP and Java, and the SAP PPM add-on component (CPRxRPM), in which you make the configuration settings for PPM and the SAP Business Suite Foundation.

- **User interface for PPM**

  You can either access the PPM system via the Java screens or the SAP NetWeaver Portal. When using the portal, you can utilize the business package for PPM, which includes the role-based sets of Java and the ABAP-based iViews. If you want to use KM to support content management and collaboration (which is also an optional component), the SAP NetWeaver Portal is mandatory.

- **SAP BusinessObjects Business Intelligence**

  This optional component can be used for enhanced, cross-portfolio reporting and analytics. For PPM, predefined content such as data sources or InfoCubes are available.

- **Integration**

  Recall that you can integrate PPM with various other SAP components, such as FI and CO, SAP ERP HCM, product development, and SAP PS through RFC or Application Link Enabling (ALE). To use external project management applications such as Microsoft Project Client or Server, you can either use Open PS or the SAP Enterprise Project Connection, which we'll cover further later in this section.

If you would like more information on the technical requirements and setup, the following links might be worthwhile:

- Installation guides: *http://service.sap.com/instguides* • INSTALLATION & UPGRADE GUIDES • SAP BUSINESS SUITE APPLICATIONS • SAP PLM • PPM 5.0.

- PPM Help files: *http://help.sap.com/ppm*

- The Portal content for SAP Business Suite Foundation applications within the Business Package for Common Parts 1.5 contains the Business Context Viewer (BCV); see Chapter 10, Section 10.2.4 for more information.

7.6.1 PPM as a Central Tool

When you're using additional applications for project management—such as Microsoft Project and/or SAP PS—and you've chosen PPM to be the central tool for monitoring and controlling these projects, you can upload the project from the other tools into PPM by using the download and upload project data action. The following possible applications are supported:

- SAP PS (Release 4.6C or higher)
- SAP c-projects (Release 3.1 or higher)
- Microsoft Project Client (Version 2002 or higher)
- Microsoft Project Server (Version 2003)

As you can see in Figure 7.67, you can upload or download four different types of data:

- Item data (including actual start and end dates)
- Task data (including actual start and end dates)
- Roles and resource data (resource assignment to tasks)
- Roles and resource assignment (resource data with requirements and staffing)

Technically, the project structure is mapped as a c-project structure when you upload it. You'll need to configure mapping details (including the physical connection, object links, and mapping rules) in PPM. Before the actual uploading is done, first execute a test run to ensure the upload can be performed without any warnings and/or error messages. You can upload data as often as you require.

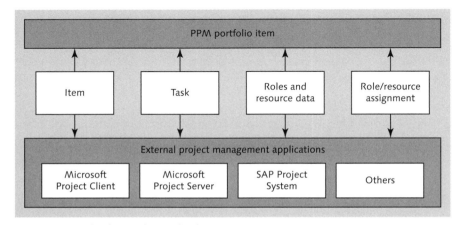

Figure 7.67 Uploading and Downloading Data

Downloading project data from PPM to external project management applications is also possible, which can only happen once for a specific project. The only exception to this rule is for Microsoft Project Client, to which you can download project details as often as required. When downloading to another PPM application or to SAP PS, you have to specify a template, which then will be used to generate the project. Before using download capabilities, you must have configured PPM for this function.

7.6.2   Open PS

Open PS is a tool available to exchange project data from SAP PS with other project management systems or personnel organizers. It's specifically tailored to share data between SAP PS (release 4.5 and higher) and Microsoft Project, from version 2000 and higher. However, Open PS can also be used as a basis to develop interfaces to any other external project management system or personnel organizers.

Open PS is offered as an independent solution, is installed locally on your PC, and is available as an add-on. It's developed based on the PS-EPS interface (Interface to External Project Software) that uses standardized BAPI technology. You can exchange the following project business objects via Open PS:

▶ Project definitions

▶ WBS elements

▶ Networks

After you've installed Open PS, you can use the interfacing option through several buttons that become available within Microsoft Project, which allows you to perform data exchange. Open PS supports the following actions:

▶ Create projects either from SAP PS or from Microsoft Project.

▶ Synchronize project structure data.

▶ Update actual costs or dates.

▶ Access resource information.

More detailed information can be found on the SAP Service Marketplace via the quick link PS.

7.6.3   SAP Enterprise Project Connection

SAP Enterprise Project Connection, which is shown in Figure 7.68, allows you to integrate SAP Project Management and the execution level covered either with SAP PS or PPM–Project Management to other applications (e.g., Microsoft Project or Primavera). For asset- and project-intensive businesses who want to execute projects more successfully, SAP Enterprise Project Connection helps with reducing project schedule and cost variances through automating the synchronization of project information within context.

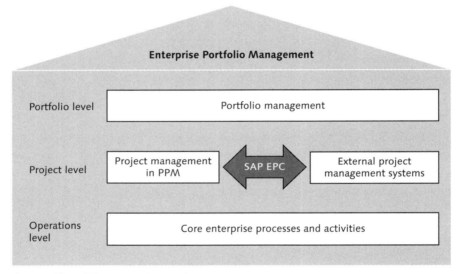

Figure 7.68 SAP Enterprise Project Connection

SAP Enterprise Project Connection is an automated "in-context" bi-directional interface. This provides out-of-the-box integration to ensure a faster, more cost-effective way to perform project and portfolio management centrally based on the latest information from SAP modules such as project management (SAP PS or PPM) and maintenance data (SAP PM/SAP CS). Adaptors are available for Primavera, Microsoft Project, and other project management tools. SAP Enterprise Project Connection uses the service-oriented architecture powered by SAP NetWeaver. SAP Enterprise Project Connection addresses some common challenges experienced by static and non-integration data exchange within project management, such as the manual entry of project data impacts accuracy, completeness, and timeliness. And the lack of automation and integration can cause multiple sources of the truth, inefficiency, delayed visibility in projects and schedule cost variance, and insufficient insight into resource availability and utilization.

The key benefits of SAP Enterprise Project Connection include the following:

▶ Enables complete and timely information in context

▶ Provides a single source of the truth from one environment, offering a holistic view of the project portfolio across multiple project systems

▶ Leverages previous investments within project management

▶ Includes critical data, such as costs, materials, assets, and resources, in SAP ERP

▶ Leverages the built-in "best practice" project management methodologies

▶ Eliminates double data entry and data entry errors, which improves productivity and reliability of available data

▶ Lowers TCO through the elimination of manual inefficiencies and reduction in maintenance overheads

▶ Enables efficient planning of resources from a single platform

▶ Ensures accurate reports that are available in a timely manner

Within the cross-application components, under menu option SAP ENTERPRISE PROJECT CONNECTION, you can find three available transactions:

▶ **Transfer projects**
   The transfer project integration is designed around engineering and construction operations, capital projects, or other types of project where organizations have significant investments in Primavera either from a product perspective or a resource knowledge perspective. Figure 7.69 shows you how a project can be transferred from SAP PS to Primavera by performing the following steps:

   ▹ Initiate a project within SAP PS.

   ▹ Use SAP Enterprise Project Connection to transfer project data from SAP.

   ▹ Use a third-party tool to schedule the projects.

   ▹ Transfer the data third-party tool to SAP.

   ▹ Use SAP PS to control the project.

   Any changes can be transferred again if required.

▶ **Transfer PM orders**
The transfer of SAP PM orders is designed to assist with heavy maintenance, repair, and overhaul (MRO) planning and scheduling as well as plant/facility turnaround or shutdown. Orders are added to different Primavera P6 projects based on SAP PM order revision codes and priorities.

▶ **Display transfer results**
This allows you to view the results of the transferred information, which enables you to follow up when warnings or messages are being generated during the transfer process.

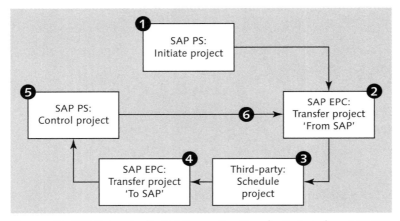

Figure 7.69 SAP Enterprise Project Connection Transfer Projects from SAP PS to Primavera

SAP Enterprise Project Connection uses the following five concepts to effectively structure the integration:

▶ **Object correspondence**
The high-level mapping between systems is visible through the object correspondence diagram at an object level. For example, the work order header and operations of an SAP PM order are mapped to start milestone activities and activities with labor resource assignments objects in Primavera P6.

▶ **System of record**
This identifies the system that owns the object and is identified on the object correspondence. Ownership can be important when establishing business rules and system behavior. For SAP Enterprise Project Connection, the system of record for most objects is SAP ERP.

▶ **Object identity**
This determines whether an object exists already in the target system to identify whether it needs to be created if unavailable, or just updated if already available. To determine object identity, objects use key attributes that have the same values in both systems.

▶ **Field-level mapping**
Field-level-mapping identifies the fields of an object (data set) that SAP Enterprise Project Connection will modify during data transfer.

▶ **Business rules**
These identify how and when to modify the target system.

Figure 7.70 shows you the architecture of how SAP PS projects and the Primavera P6 attributes are mapped. More details can be found in the Operation Guide and the User Guide for SAP Enterprise Project Connection, which are available on *http://help.sap.com/epc20* or on the SAP Service Marketplace, quick link INST-GUIDES • CROSS APPLICATION TOOLS • SAP ENTERPRISE PROJECT CONNECTION.

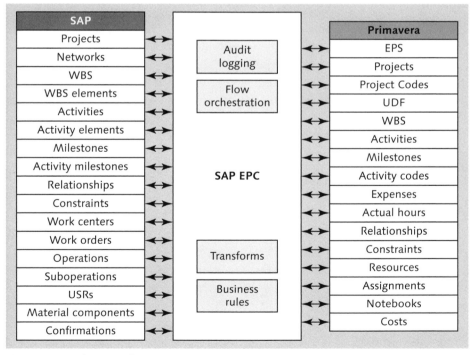

Figure 7.70 Architecture for Projects

7.7 Summary

By now, you should have a good understanding of the different applications within the SAP product portfolio for managing your projects, including their functions and features. SAP PS—the application from within SAP ERP—has been around for a while; it seamlessly works together with other areas such as your financial and controlling setup, including SAP Investment Management, SAP DMS, procurement processes and materials planning, and MM–IM processes. SAP Project and Portfolio Management (PPM) is a somewhat younger application, which is web-enabled, is intuitive to use, and provides a number of exciting dashboards and reporting cockpits to enable a quick insight into the status of your projects and the portfolio to which they are assigned.

This chapter also demonstrated how a fundamental part of successful project management is making sure you have the right means to collaborate within the team, within and outside company firewalls; this is known as project collaboration. The chapter has concluded with the integration of SAP tools to other project management environments.

The chapter has offered you a high-level perspective of these available products, their functions and features, the benefits their implementation can bring, and when they are recommended. It provided the appropriate vocabulary and links to find additional information on a topic you might want to explore in more detail and to enable informed decision making on when to use which component or at least have a good discussion about it. Be aware that this chapter is just an introduction to project management and SAP's products in this space, and this topic could have been easily been expanded on. See the appendices for courses and additional resources.

Now that you understand how projects relating to product development and product engineering are supported by SAP PS and SAP Investment Management and through PPM, we'll focus in the next chapter on two additional processes within the main process of product development and collaboration: SAP Quality Management (QM) and SAP Engineering Change Management (ECM). QM plays an important role during all of the different phases of a product's lifecycle to ensure and improve product quality by planning, performing, and recording quality checks and results along the way. In turn, the ECM component manages changes to a product and/or its documentation, which need to be formalized and managed.

The closed-loop processing within SAP Quality Management enables you to ensure and continuously improve product quality by assessing the product at any given step in the logistics supply chain. By doing so, you can understand and prove whether your products conform to relevant product regulations, industry standards, and/or company quality standards. Any change proposed to product data, either as part of quality management or initiated by any department within the organization, can be captured and formalized via the change process offered within Engineering Change Management.

8 Product Quality and Product Change Management

This chapter focuses on two processes within the main process of product development and collaboration: SAP Quality Management (QM) and SAP Engineering Change Management (ECM). QM plays an important role during all the different phases of a product's lifecycle to ensure and improve product quality by planning, performing, and recording quality checks and results along the way. In turn, the ECM component manages changes to a product and/or its documentation, which need to be formalized and managed. The change record collects the performed impact analysis and the approval of the change, together with the impacted products and additional objects, including the validity of the change (the window when the change is valid). So both QM and ECM are used across the product's lifecycle, which is why they are grouped together in this chapter.

This first part of this chapter is focused on QM from a product's or SAP PLM perspective and will address the big picture of how QM fits into an integrated solution covering all steps of the product lifecycle. It includes the following product quality management topics:

▶ Product quality master data, which is divided further into SAP Logistics General (LO) master data, inspection planning master data, and quality planning basic master data

▶ Quality engineering, which is divided into the following areas:

  ▶ Closed-loop inspection planning: The first step of the Quality Engineering process, followed by the activities Failure Mode and Effects Analysis (FMEA), control plan, and inspection plan.

  ▶ Quality engineering business process: Focuses on the continued Quality engineering business process, including defining a development project, managing master data and inspection data, performing stability studies, and maintaining a quality manual.

▶ Quality assurance and control, which will be introduced at a high level because it isn't part of the SAP PLM solution map, but forms such an important part of QM in general. After your quality processes are in place, you must strive to maintain and improve the attained level of quality. Quality control involves inspections at all stages of the supply chain of a product, continuous monitoring, and intervening quickly to deal with unexpected events.

▶ Quality improvement, which will explain the quality improvement process, with a particular focus on the complaints handling, defect prevention, and analyzing processes available within QM

The second section of this chapter will discuss product change management, which focuses on the definition and efficient management of engineering changes to ensure that product data conforms to the latest changes, approved by the appropriate stakeholders and the right stakeholders are notified of any last minute changes. It's divided into two separate sections:

▶ Change master data, which will introduce the master data objects used within ECM: change master, engineering change request (ECR), and engineering change order (ECO).

▶ Business scenario change and configuration management, which will describe the business scenario in detail.

Let's begin with product quality management. Remember that although the focus of this chapter is QM from a product's perspective, the processes are often also relevant for assuring quality of assets or the quality of processes.

8.1   Product Quality Management

SAP Quality Management (QM) is the wide-ranging solution that supports the company throughout the product lifecycle and along the supply chain. It offers a wide range of functions and business processes, which are fully integrated into SAP PLM and SAP ERP, focused on assuring and managing the quality of products and assets. Accordingly, QM can be found in the SAP PLM solution map under the main process product development and collaboration, and as part of the SAP ERP solution map under the main process corporate services (both shown in Chapter 1, Figure 1.8). It includes the prevention of quality-related problems and offers continuous process improvement abilities through collaboration and sustained quality control.

This chapter covers QM from an SAP PLM or product's perspective, where quality engineering and quality improvements are part of the ramp-up to production stage, in the end-to-end integrated product development business processes, shown in Figure 8.1.

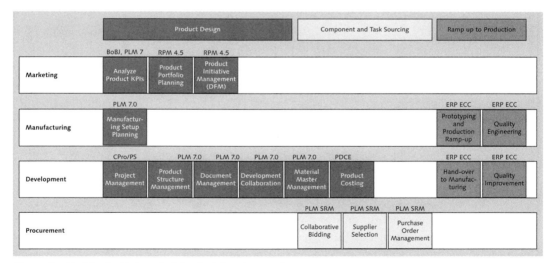

Figure 8.1 End-to-End Integrated Product Development

Which activities QM includes and how quality assurance is performed differs enormously based on the individuals you speak to, which department they work in, the industry they belong to, and the focus of their quality management activities. QM in SAP offers wide-ranging business processes and functions to ensure your products and their ingredients or subcomponents conform to your quality standards, whether they are regulatory, based on industry standards—such as the industry-sector VDA (Federation of the German Motor Industry), FDA (U.S. Food and Drug Administration, and GMP (Good Manufacturing Practices)—or based on internal quality standards.

The QM processes within SAP support the entire product lifecycle from conception to disposal during all parts of the logistics supply chain. QM provides a completely integrated quality management solution based on the *total quality management* (TQM) approach, which is an integrative approach for continuously improving product and process quality. TQM includes making sure that the interactions of the processes are supported by an electronic data processing (EDP) system. SAP ERP 6 and SAP PLM 7.02 even take this approach one step further due to the adoption of the closed-loop inspection process based on the automotive standards.

QM is characterized by increasing demands on performance, availability, and profitability. The constant optimization of the processes has led to permanent optimization of the software, which in turn has led to changing product names and the use of different terms. The QM component has progressed from area- and module-oriented thinking to the consideration of the entire process and complete lifecycle of a product as well as cross-system lifecycles. So QM in the broader sense focuses on the entirety of all QM-relevant processes for a product (quality planning, quality certificate, quality notification, quality control, test equipment management, and stability study).

The entire lifecycle of a product can be captured by combining the relevant functional areas of SAP ERP, as discussed in Chapter 3. The QM application component is integrated in and offered through SAP ERP, SAP PLM, and SAP Business Suite. For more details, see Chapter 1.

But before diving into the detailed business processes, first let's consider QM's big picture, which has been captured in Table 8.1, so you can get a good understanding of what SAP QM does and doesn't provide.

SAP PLM-Specific Business Processes				Other Areas
Master data ▶ Quality certificates ▶ Batch management	Quality engineering ▶ Control plan ▶ FMEA analysis ▶ Inspection plan ▶ New Product Development and Introduction (NPDI) project	Quality assurance and control ▶ Quality inspections ▶ Mobile quality inspections	Quality improvement ▶ Quality notifications ▶ Complaint handling	Quality standard Vendor evaluations Calibration of test equipment

Table 8.1 Quality Management Big Picture

So the QM activities that are in the scope of this book are the processes and activities put in place to ensure that the quality of end products, ingredients, and subcomponents used to produce the end product conform to the quality standards. Note that for further detail, Appendix A and Appendix B include additional information sources per chapter.

In this chapter, Section 8.1.2 covers product quality master data—the master data elements, which are either part of QM or are used during the execution of QM processes.

Section 8.1.3 addresses the quality engineering process, which includes closed-loop inspection planning and the QM engineering steps (such as the project setup, master data setup, performing of stability study and setup, or updating a quality manual) during early product development. Quality engineering focuses on the incorporation of the appropriate quality during the entire product development process. Quality engineering can have a very high impact on other logistics supply chain business processes within an enterprise because quality is crucial for most industries, is part of the integrated value chain, and has a strong influence on costs. Figure 8.2 represents a generalized logistic value chain where the diamonds represent quality gates that can be implemented and must be passed before the product can move on to the next step.

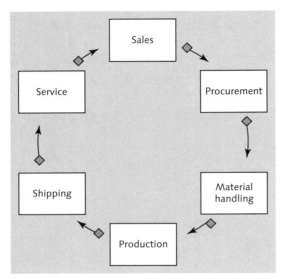

Figure 8.2 Logistics Value Chain with Included Quality Gates

It's important to have the correct quality planning strategies, processes, tools, and mechanisms in place during the early stages of product design and development. Quality engineering provides the functions and tools to incorporate these quality aspects throughout the entire product development process, which is why it plays such a fundamental role during New Product Development and Introduction (NPDI). The goal of quality engineering is to promote "quality by design" rather than "quality by test." The solution gives employees role-based access to the information they need, which puts them in control of quality management through the global exchange of key information. Support for collaborative and mobile business promotes the exchange of information with external sources, which will be included in Section 8.1.3.

Section 8.1.4 will introduce you to quality assurance and control business processes at a high level. Recall that although it isn't part of the SAP PLM Solution Map, quality assurance and control forms an important part of QM. The section will describe general logistics quality assurance activities, such as requesting and checking quality certificates from vendors and/or suppliers at time of goods receipt of a purchase order. As soon as the goods are receipted at your storage location (such as a warehouse), the certificate is checked and electronically stored as part of quality assurance. Another quality assurance activity—and the main activity which QM supports—is the setup and performance of quality inspections as part of the logistics supply chain. The quality inspection process includes the setup of the master data relevant for quality inspection, quality planning, the quality trigger (an event, such as a goods receipt, goods issue, or customer complaint), the sample information, the inspection itself, the recording of the results, and the validation of the results, followed by a usage decision and any follow-up activities. Often batch management is used to provide full traceability of the used ingredients or components. These processes will be described in Section 8.1.4.

Last, the quality improvement process will also be discussed in detail in Section 8.1.4 in which the recording, handling, and analyzing of quality problems will be explained.

Let's briefly consider three other supplementary areas often conducted with QM: maintaining the quality standard, performing vendor evaluations, and calibrating test equipment.

QM can, for example, simply mean that the quality management processes are documented according to the *quality standard* (e.g., the ISO standard). This can be achieved by the activation and use of the SAP Document Management System (SAP DMS), which allows you to structure your documents in the required way as the standard prescribes. The creation or updating of the quality manual in the SAP environment is part of the quality engineering process, where often just a document management solution can cover this requirement.

Another activity often performed within QM is the *vendor evaluation*. You can perform an evaluation based on the vendor's performance during agreed contracts and purchase orders. Examples of performance measures are the amount of times the goods were delivered on time, within the tolerances agreed, and so on; these metrics are often set up during the procurement business process.

The *calibration of test equipment* process can be conducted via QM to support the complete calibration process in accordance with ISO 10012 and other standards. The standard integration between SAP Plant Maintenance (SAP PM) and QM is used when the maintenance order is created (either manually or based on a preventive maintenance plan to provide an equipment calibration order on a regular basis) and also results in the creation of an inspection lot with the referenced equipment, based on the referenced equipment in the maintenance order (and the maintenance plan). The inspection lot follows the process as described in Section 8.1.4. The lot includes the calibration instruction and the comparison of a measurement instrument of unverified accuracy to a standard instrument of

a measurement instrument of unverified accuracy to a standard instrument of known accuracy to detect any deviation from the accuracy specification. It enables results recording, which can lead to automatically adjusting the status of the equipment depending on the inspection result.

A good example of the integration between SAP PM and QM is the use of an inspection to determine whether further maintenance activities are required. For an example of this process, consider a grain grower company, which decides based on the inspection results whether to perform further maintenance activities after the inspection of a silo.

In particular, the QM solution offers the following benefits:

▶ Provides a single quality management solution for all company processes, providing you with a single source of truth and access to the most current quality information at any time

▶ Serves as a full Laboratory Information Management System (LIMS)

▶ Helps recognize risks and defects at an early stage and helps to avoid them

▶ Enables your employees to perform a variety of tasks quickly and efficiently to support their central role

▶ Provides a consistent and transparent closed-loop quality management solution for all company processes in which you can automate the information flow and process steps by using workflow

▶ Serves as a tightly integrated component into the supply chain, which can be used and started during execution of processes such as production and procurement

▶ Supports assignment to objects from other components, such as customer masters, vendor masters, batches, purchase orders, and production orders

▶ Ensures compliance with industry standards and legal requirements (for example, the VDA, FDA, and GMP)

▶ Complies with quality management standards such as ISO 9004, DIN EN ISO 9001:2008 and QS9000 and DIN EN ISO:9001:2008 QM System Requirements; the QS 9000 Quality standard developed by General Motors, Chrysler, and Ford; and the ISO 9004:2009 Managing for the Sustained Success of an Organization — A Quality Management Approach

▶ Increases revenue by improving customer retention and loyalty, improves order fill rate, and maximizes profitability by customers

▶ Reduces operating costs and increases efficiency by improving asset and maintenance management, improving the procurement process, lowering communications expenses, re-deploying labor to higher value-added activities, reducing costs of goods sold (COGS), and reducing product returns

▶ Improves customer service and customer satisfaction by providing better service levels, using complaint management and tracking, improving product and service quality, improving quality and accuracy, and strengthening market competitiveness

▶ Includes comprehensive quality management functions, such as tools for planning support (e.g., inspection plans) and process improvements (e.g., monitoring processes and implementing corrective tasks in notifications) and systematic root cause analysis

▶ Provides a central role for employees, with the ability to perform a variety of tasks quickly and efficiently

Supplementary Quality Management Areas

The following supplementary QM functions are often covered under the quality assurance and quality control process:

▶ **Test equipment interfacing**
A standardized interface (QM-IDI) for connecting measuring subsystems and for external control of inspection operations on the shop floor level. RS232 interfaces, keyboard wedges, serial interfaces, or file transfer methods can be connected for simple measurement systems, or additional partner products are available that can provide interfaces.

▶ **Statistical process control (SPC)**
The application of statistical techniques to control a process. This is used interchangeably with statistical quality control (SQC). Six Sigma approaches are supported for analyzing measured values and non-conformance data, such as the use of various quality control charts, Western Electric rules, capability indicators (cap), Pareto analysis, trend analysis, and exception analysis. An interface to external tools for statistical analysis is provided (QM-STI) to allow you, for

example, to verify a significance test. Additionally, SAP Manufacturing Integration and Intelligence (SAP MII) can be used as a frontend to visualize quality data from QM and execute SPC.

▶ **Laboratory Information Management System (LIMS)**
Facilitates the testing of samples that routinely pass through an analytical lab. The complete routine is managed from sample log-in and testing until final reporting. The inspection results can be organized into specific report formats to meet regulatory requirements. The trend of shifting from isolated data islands to global information is followed due to its tight integration in the supply chain components, which offers functions for inventory control, batch tracking, as well as problem handling and management of corrective action and preventive action (CAPA).

▶ **GAAP compliance (according to ISO 9000)**
Good Clinical Practice/Good Laboratory Practice/Good Manufacturing Practice (GCP/GLP/GMP) includes guidelines for enterprises that are regulated by the FDA. SAP ERP provides all the functions necessary to fulfill such requirements. For example, it supports FDA document control (corresponding to 21 CFR Part 11), digital signature, audit trial, batch traceability, and electronic batch record (EBR). SAP's development and service organizations are certified according to ISO 9000.

▶ **Quality costs**
Includes the cost associated with inspecting a product to ensure it meets the internal or external customer's needs and requirements. It includes the costs associated with providing poor quality products or services. There are four categories of costs:

  ▶ Internal failure costs: Costs associated with defects found before the customer receives the product or service.

  ▶ External failure costs: Costs due to defects found after the customer receives the product or service.

  ▶ Appraisal costs: Costs incurred to determine the degree of conformance to quality requirements.

  ▶ Prevention costs: Costs incurred to keep failure and appraisal costs to a minimum.

Quality Management Integration

Depending on the scope of your QM activities, you might need to use other supporting components, including the following:

- **Logistics supply chain**
  To cover all the functional areas available in logistics, for example, SAP Sales and Distribution (SD), Procurement (offered as part of SAP Materials Management [SAP MM] and SAP Supplier Relationship Management [SAP SRM]), Inventory Management, Warehouse Management, Manufacturing, Logistics execution, and so on.

- **SAP Document Management System (SAP DMS)**
  To store quality documents such as manuals, procedures, or quality certificates (see Chapter 3).

- **SAP Engineering Change Management (ECM)**
  To control the change process for quality documents, inspection plans and so on. This topic will be explained in more detail in Section 8.2.

- **SAP Classification System (CA)**
  To set up quality catalogs for recording results and for using within batch management. CA was described in detail in Chapter 3.

- **SAP Audit Management**
  To use the audit processes, including plans, questionnaires, and so on.

- **SAP ERP Financial Accounting (FI) and SAP ERP Controlling (CO)**
  To perform activities within FI–CO, such as analyzing quality cost, setting up labor rates and overhead rates, and so on.

- **Other central tools**
  To perform other specific tasks, other central tools are available, including workflow, analytic tools, and so on.

Let's begin by exploring product quality master data—those master data elements that are either part of QM or used during the execution of QM processes.

8.1.1   Product Quality Master Data

This section describes and introduces the most important master data objects used within QM. They are grouped together in the following three areas:

▶ **Logistics master data**
The data that is used and referenced within QM, such as material, customer, vendor, and batches; Q-info records for procurement; and sales and quality certificates.

▶ **Inspection planning master data**
The master data used to perform quality inspection planning, such as the inspection plan, reference operation sets, material specification, routings and task lists, and master recipe (the process is described in Section 8.1.3).

▶ **Quality planning basic master data**
The master data that belongs to the QM component such as the catalog, set, master inspection characteristics, inspection methods, sample, sampling procedure, sample scheme, dynamic modification rule, sample drawing procedure, work center, and production resource/tool (PRT).

Let's consider each type in turn.

Logistic General Master Data

Figure 8.3 provides an overview of the QM master data objects within the logistics.

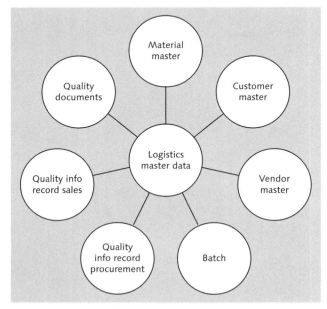

Figure 8.3 Logistics Master Data

Material Master

Recall from Chapter 3, Section 3.1.1, that the material master describes the product. The QM-specific data is maintained at the plant level, via a dedicated QUALITY MANAGEMENT tab shown in Figure 8.4. This is where you define the quality assurance data for the material/plant combination, such as the required quality system used to produce the goods, the inspection duration, or certificate requirements. You use the inspection setup data (which can be reached through the INSP. SETUP button) to define if and when inspection needs to take place.

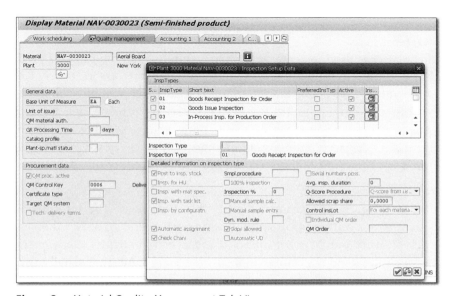

Figure 8.4 Material Quality Management Tab View

The INSPECTION TYPE field defines for which logistics processes quality inspection is to take place. For example, inspection type 01 GOODS RECEIPT INSPECTION FOR ORDER defines that *goods receipt inspection* for a purchase order will be triggered at the time the goods are receipted. Inspection type 03 IN-PROCESS INSP. FOR PRODUCTION ORDER triggers *in-process inspection* when the production order is released. For each inspection type, you can maintain detailed information, such as how results recording needs to be processed, the sample determination and dynamic modification, the quality order for the inspection lot, and the quality score calculation. (We'll define these terms later.) You can define the inspection requirements, select the inspection task list to be used with the inspection instructions, confirm a material specification, or, based on the configuration (such as sales order configuration or product order configuration), confirm a recipe, an end product, or the parts thereof.

Customer Master

The customer master is used to represent the customer to whom you can sell products and/or services; it controls how business transactions are recorded and posted to the customer (for more details, see Chapter 5, Section 5.2.2). Quality inspections and quality documents such as a quality certificate can be carried out and generated based on the combination of material and customer master data.

Vendor Master

The vendor master is used to represent vendors from whom you can buy products and/or services; it controls how business transactions are recorded and posted to the vendor. A vendor master record contains information such as the vendor's name, address, bank details, the procurement currency, and account control data (such as the number of the General Ledger [GL] reconciliation account for the vendor account, payment methods, and terms of payment set up with the vendor). The vendor master record consists of three specific data views:

- ▸ **General data**
  This data (see Figure 8.5) is maintained at the client level. The information maintained here is central information (valid for everyone who uses the vendor), such as every purchase organization and every company code. General data includes the vendor's name, address, and communication details (language, email address, telephone number, etc.).

- ▸ **Purchasing data**
  This data is maintained at the purchasing organization level, which means that when you've defined multiple purchase organizations, multiple views can be generated. For example, the procurement currency, the payment terms, and the partner roles are maintained at this level. The data in this area are used as defaults when the vendor is used in a procurement document, such as a request for quotation, purchase order, or invoice.

- ▸ **Financial data**
  This data is maintained at the company code level. Again, multiple views can exist when multiple company codes exist. Company code data includes the reconciliation account number and payment terms, for example. The vendor master is also known within FI as the creditor.

These views allow you to maintain the data performed by different groups—for example, the general data and purchasing data are maintained by the procurement department, whereas the financial data are maintained by the finance department. Centralized maintenance is also supported. Based on a quality inspection and the recorded results, it might be necessary to block the vendor either entirely or in part, for quotations, purchase orders, and/or goods receipt. Because entering the vendor is mandatory within these procurement documents, the block will prevent the user from using this vendor and will notify the user that a block is activated.

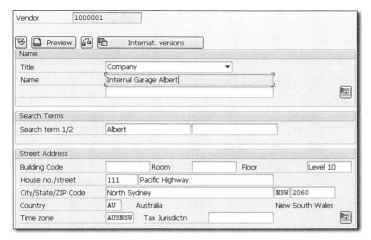

Figure 8.5 Vendor Master General Data

Batches and Batch Management for Traceability

In various industries—but especially in the process industry—you're required to track and trace specific groups of products and/or ingredients used throughout the logistics value chain, if products vary in quality or originate from different production runs. This requirement can be fulfilled by the use of batch management, a central function offered under SAP Logistics.

A *batch* is a general master data object that represents the whole or partial quantity of a certain material or product that has been produced according to the same recipe and represents one homogenous unit with unique attributes and/or assays. It's found under LOGISTICS • CENTRAL FUNCTIONS. Because the batch is a master data element, which is so often used within quality engineering and QM especially in SAP PLM, it has been included as an object.

The various compelling reasons to use batches include the following:

- **Legal requirements**
  For example, the guidelines set out by GMP or the regulation of hazardous materials.

- **Defect tracing, callback activities, and regression requirements**
  For identification, usage, and monitoring purposes; to allow the tracking and tracing of a specific group of materials through the logistics value chain (such as MRP, SD, and SAP Production Planning [PP]).

- **Production or procedural requirements**
  For example, the settlement of material quantities on the basis of different batch specifications.

A batch, an example of which is shown in Figure 8.6, provides the means to identify and classify specific groups of materials, allowing you to track and trace its use and whereabouts within the logistic supply chain. Bottom-up as well as top-down analyses are offered to show the flow of goods either starting with the end product and the used raw materials or starting at the raw materials and visualizing which final product it ends up in. Moreover, process data can be stored in an order record and in an optical archive (electronic batch record [EBR]). Within QM, you can perform a quality inspection for a batch, for example, during the receipt of a batch of raw materials. The inspection results and usage decision can be passed on from QM to the batch characteristics for follow-on functions such as batch determination, certificate creation, batch-specific pricing, and batch posting to either restricted or unrestricted stock. Apart from using batch management to identify a group of materials, you can also track individual materials to show the lifecycle and traceability by using a material-specific serial number.

Quality Information Record Procurement

Through the quality information record (Q-info) as shown in Figure 8.7, you can create quality information for the combination of vendor master and material master to document the details of a quality assurance agreement made with the vendor if quality documents are required or if a vendor release is required for this material. During procurement, the system checks whether a Q-info record is required and available for the combination of material and vendor, whether goods receipt or source inspections (supply relationships can be staged) are required, and whether any blocks are active.

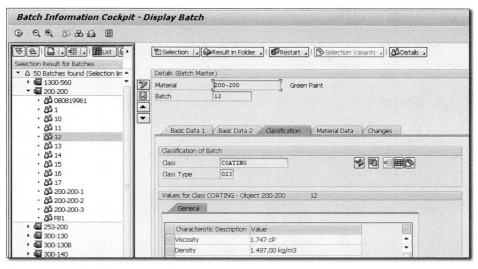

Figure 8.6 Batch Information Cockpit

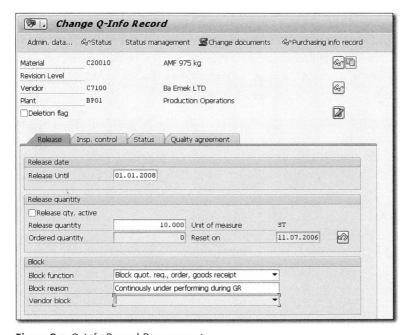

Figure 8.7 Q-Info Record Procurement

Quality Information Record Sales

Through the Q-info record, you can create quality information for the combination of customer master with the material master and include whether or not you have to provide quality documents to the customer during material delivery. By setting up the appropriate data in both QM and SD, you can make sure that the QM component automatically creates an inspection lot for the delivery items that must be inspected when a delivery is created for this specific product or material. The delivery can only be released for the goods issue posting after the inspection has been performed and the usage decision has been recorded. During this process, quality certificates can be issued based on data from sales (such as customer or sales order), QM (such as inspection specifications and results), and procurement information (such as batch information).

Quality Certificates and Documents

A *quality certificate* guarantees that specific manufacturing procedures or practices have been followed, an inspection based on regulations or other agreements has been conducted, and the results have been recorded. *Quality documents* can be created for a product or an asset and used to capture the agreed-upon technical delivery terms and quality assurance agreements with either vendors or customers. You can save these documents in SAP DMS and assign them to the appropriate transactions in the operational area within logistics, such as during a goods receipt from vendor or during a delivery to a customer.

You can monitor the receipt of a quality certificate during goods receipt, which can be accompanied by a workflow message to ensure that the document is received and stored against the appropriate material/purchase order as an electronic file and emails the relevant quality engineer. Internet services are available, so your customer has access to the quality certificates you supply.

Table 8.2 provides an overview of the standard delivered quality documents, including the area they belong to, their document type, and to which master data object they need to be assigned. Some examples are a certificate of conformity, a works test certificate, or a certificate of analysis. You can use these standard delivered quality documents or extend/define your own. More information on SAP DMS can be found in Chapter 3, Section 3.2.

Area	Document	Document Type	Assigned To
Procurement	Quality assurance agreements	Q01	Q-info record vendor
	Technical delivery terms	Q02	Vendor master and additional data material master
Sales	Quality assurance agreements	Q03	Q-info record customer
	Quality specification	Q04	Material via Q-info record

Table 8.2 Standard Delivered Quality Documents

Inspection Planning Master Data

This section briefly goes through the master data used to perform quality inspection planning (described in Section 8.1.2) because most of the master data objects have already been covered in previous parts of the book. Figure 8.8 provides an overview of these QM master data objects.

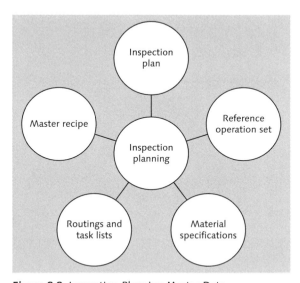

Figure 8.8 Inspection Planning Master Data

Inspection Plan

Inspection plans describe how (reoccurring) quality inspections need to be performed for either a single material or multiple materials. You can create inspection plans for different inspections, such as preliminary series, goods receipt, goods issue, stock transfer, or repetitive manufacturing.

Simply put, the inspection plan is the template or form you use when performing an inspection; it details how, when, and where to perform an inspection on which material. It includes the material (or other objects, such as an asset) to be inspected, the individual inspection steps via a task list, the relevant inspection characteristics, and any PRTs (such as required test equipment). The structure of an inspection plan is very similar to a maintenance plan; it consists of a header, operation, and inspection characteristics.

You can set up an approval process for the inspection plan, which is often used within the process industry. The task list has been described in more detail in Chapter 3, Section 3.1.3, where the type indicator "Q" makes the task list QM-specific. Figure 8.9 shows an example of an inspection plan, which includes the inspection characteristics.

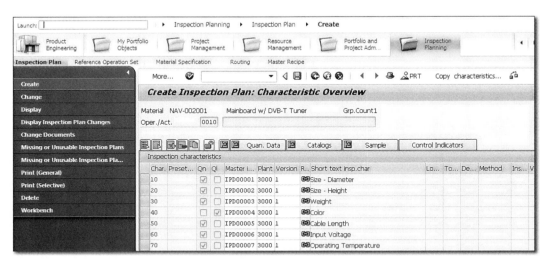

Figure 8.9 Quality Plan: Characteristics Overview

Reference Operation Set

A *reference operation set* is a type of task list (or routing) to be used as a template reference or to copy from, which is very useful when certain inspections are recurring. You can also copy an existing quality inspection plan. For more details on this topic, see Chapter 3, Section 3.1.3.

Material Specification

In QM, you can inspect either based on an inspection plan or (with certain limitations) based on *material specifications* that are valid on a company-wide. Within the material specification, you assign the material to the inspection characteristics and update them with specific inspection instructions as required. This enables you to simplify inspection planning by doing it at the client level, and it includes the integration into the product structure (Transaction CC04). When an inspection lot is created, the system copies the master inspection characteristics from both the inspection plan and material specification into it. The inspection specifications from the material specification take priority over the inspection specifications in the inspection plan.

Routing

The *routing menu* gives you access to the various types of routings and task lists, such as standard routings used within PP, the SAP PM task list, the reference operations sets, and so on. For production routing, recipes, and SAP PM or SAP Customer Service (SAP CS) task lists, the quality master data is maintained along with prediction routing information, which adds the quality characteristics to the preexisting production header/operations. Apart from planning the quality operations, the routing menu gives enables you to use inspection characteristics in the existing routing or task lists and identify the objects for which an inspection is to take place and how this inspection is to be performed. In the routing or task list, you assign the inspection characteristics for the operations for which the inspection is to be carried out. You use the master inspection characteristics that are created as master records in QM. The system distinguishes between *qualitative inspection characteristics* (e.g., the color of the product) and *quantitative inspection characteristics* (e.g., the density of a material). For more details on routings, see Chapter 3, Section 3.1.3.

SAP Plant Maintenance Task List

The SAP PM task list, described in detail in Chapter 5, Section 5.3.8, is primarily used within QM when the equipment must be tested or calibrated. This process can be triggered by using the standard integration between QM and SAP PM, which automatically creates an inspection lot with the relevant equipment during the creation or release of the maintenance order (either manually created or via a maintenance plan). During recording of the results into the inspection lot, the system can change the status of the technical object being calibrated.

Master Recipe

The master recipe is the last object covered by inspection planning. It refers to the master recipe as used within the process industry (described in detail in Chapter 3, Section 3.4.4). Figure 8.10 shows the task list elements header and operations (shaded), which were described in Chapter 3 in Section 3.1.3 in more detail. By using the characteristics, the QM-specific data (white) are assigned to the operations. These characteristics include details on the tolerances, sample procedure, result recording, and quality method.

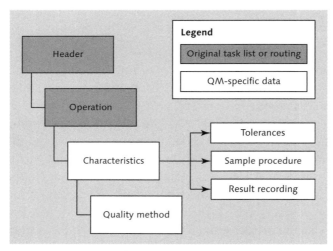

Figure 8.10 Structure of Master Recipe and Assigned QM Data

Quality Planning Basic Master Data

Quality planning basic master data covers master data that is required for quality planning and belongs within the QM component specifically, as shown in Figure 8.11. Because some master data objects have already been covered in previous parts of the book, we'll only add a short description where necessary here.

Several objects use status management, so you can flag it as work in progress by assigning the Being Created status, which ensures it can't be used until it's been finalized and set to the Released status, at which time it becomes available. Engineering change management can be activated as well, which allows you to track all changes in a change log.

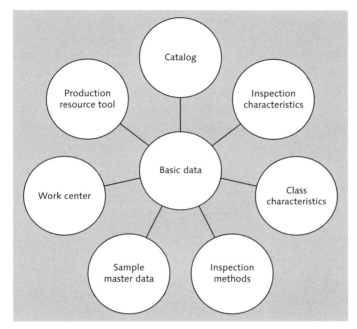

Figure 8.11 Overview of General QM Data

Let's explore each of these quality planning basic master data types.

Catalog

Catalogs enable you to maintain, manage, collect, and standardize information consistently to easily record and evaluate qualitative data by defining code groups and codes per catalog type. Catalogs in QM are used for many different purposes, such as providing a list of allowed values when recording qualitative results, defect codes, defect causes, defect locations, and usage decisions. QM offers multiple optimized maintenance functions (e.g., transfer transaction, copy functions, or transporting mechanisms, which are outside the scope of this book). More details on the quality planning basic master data catalog can be found in Chapter 5, Section 5.2.2, which discusses the same principle regarding maintenance catalogs.

Set

By defining a set, you set up and combine several catalog code groups and codes (also known as *set codes*) to make data entry easier. This means you can either extend or restrict possible entry options, preventing incorrect data entry during result recording. You can use it by assigning the set to the relevant inspection characteristic. The characteristic attribute catalog type and the usage decision catalog type also contain a valuation for each code, which defines whether the valuation leads to either acceptance or rejection. When rejected, the valuation includes the defect codes. You can also assign whether follow-up actions are automatically triggered. Figure 8.12 shows an example of a *catalog set*, which includes the usage decisions, valuation, and follow-up action email used during the goods receipting process.

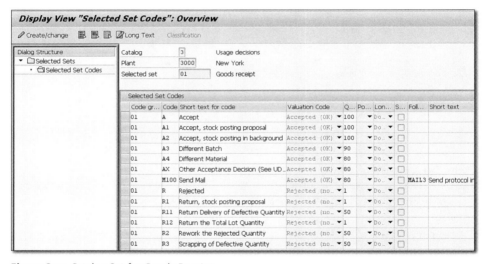

Figure 8.12 Catalog Set for Goods Receipt

Master Inspection Characteristics

A plant-specific *master inspection characteristic* or simply *inspection characteristic* describes the inspection criteria for materials, parts, and products. You can assign qualifications to a master inspection characteristic to ensure the person performing the inspection has the appropriate skills. They help to simplify and standardize data entry and terminology used so you can perform evaluations. You use them in inspection plans, material specifications, and certificate profiles. Master inspection characteristics can be put into two categories:

▶ **Quantitative**

Based on objective measurements, for which you can set up a target value and tolerance limits (see Figure 8.13).

▶ **Qualitative**

Based on subjective measurements, where you use inspection catalogs to record results that are either valuated as pass or not pass (see Figure 8.14).

When creating a master inspection characteristic, you can use data from Variant Configuration by assigning a specification determination rule (available since EHP 5 for SAP ERP).

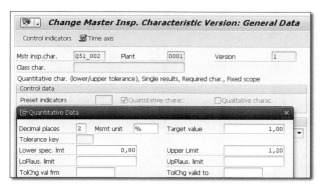

Figure 8.13 Quantitative Master Inspection Characteristic

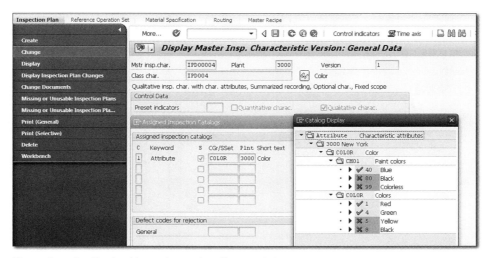

Figure 8.14 Qualitative Master Inspection Characteristic

Class Characteristics

With CA, you can set up classes and characteristics used within QM. Return to Chapter 4 for more details on these.

Inspection Methods

An *inspection method* defines how the inspection is to be carried out by defining different procedures for an inspection characteristic. It's plant-specific to simplify and standardize inspection planning. Like the master inspection characteristic, you can assign qualifications to ensure the person performing the inspection has the appropriate skills. You can also assign an SAP DMS document such as a QM instruction in a Microsoft Word document or a supporting technical drawing. You can assign multiple inspection methods to a master inspection characteristic.

When the master inspection characteristic is added into a specific task list, you decide on the specific inspection method that results in a 1:1 relationship. Direct assignment of catalogs is called *method-independent assignment*, and indirect assignment of catalogs via inspection methods is called *method-dependent assignment*. For material specifications, only method-dependent assignment can be used. Method-dependent assignment has priority over method-independent assignment. Figure 8.15 shows the assignment of multiple inspection methods (including wrong examples to show multiple methods) to an inspection characteristic.

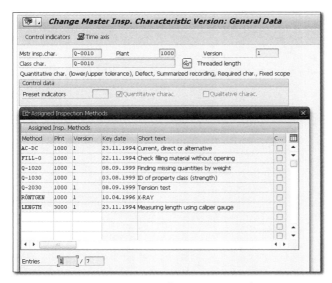

Figure 8.15 Master Inspection Characteristics with Inspection Methods

Sample Master Data

Sample master data consist of four things: the sampling procedure, sampling scheme, dynamic modification rule, and sample drawing procedure.

The *sampling procedure*, which is either assigned to the inspection characteristic of the inspection plan or to the material in the QM view, determines how the sample is taken and its sample size via sampling type for example, 100%, a percentage, or a fixed lot. The valuation mode in the procedure includes the rules for the sample's (or characteristic's) acceptance or rejection.

Figure 8.16 shows an example of the sampling procedure. The procedure can depend of the lot size of the to-be-inspected goods, which is a requirement in industries using ISO 2859 and 3951 and which allows the use of sampling schemes (see the next section). However, the procedure can be lot size-independent as well. The sampling type defines how the sample is determined, whereas the valuation mode defines rules for acceptance and rejection. Further information might be required based on the input provided (e.g., the use of inspection points, which are outside the scope of this book).

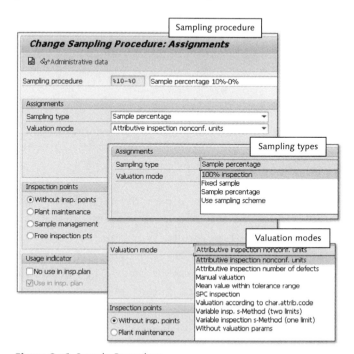

Figure 8.16 Sample Procedure

A *sample scheme* consists of a collection of sampling plans that determine the sample size based on a specific inspection lot size quantity (quantity of the population) and define the criteria for determining whether and how a sample is accepted or rejected. Figure 8.17 provides an example of a sample scheme and sample plan. These sampling plans comply with international standards, such as ISO 2859 and ISO 3951, and they can—apart from the inspection severity—also include the acceptable quality levels (AQL). Further information might be required based on the input provided—for example, the acceptability constant, referred to as the K-FACTOR, the acceptance number C, or the rejection number B, which are outside the scope of this book. (For further information on this topic, see SAP Help via menu SAP ERP • SAP ERP CENTRAL COMPONENT • LOGISTICS • QUALITY MANAGEMENT • QUALITY PLANNING • BASIC DATA.)

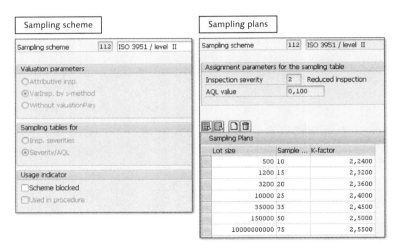

Figure 8.17 Sampling Scheme

To reduce the costs of quality inspection, you can use the dynamic modification rule, which will automatically reduce the size of quality samples or even skip inspections based on the previous inspection results. When quality results are below standard, you can also increase the number of inspections. These business rules are captured in the dynamic modification rule in stages. You define the number of accepted inspections to be performed before an inspection stage change can occur, which leads to an upgrade in a stage with less inspection. The stage also captures the number of rejections, which will lead to downgrading to a stage with a higher number of inspections.

Figure 8.18 shows an example of the dynamic modification rule and its stages. Let's briefly look at STAGE 3 (NORMAL), of which the stage change details are included in the figure. STAGE 3 (NORMAL) will upgrade to STAGE 2 (REDUCED) after 10 successful inspections, but it will be downgraded to STAGE 4 (INCREASED) after just 1 failed inspection. You generally only use the rule in combination with both sampling procedure and sampling scheme.

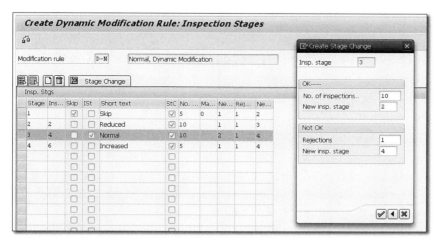

Figure 8.18 Dynamic Modification Rule Stages

Via this master data object, you define your strategy for creating and drawing physical samples, including specific instructions on how to create these samples. Together with the information in the inspection plan, the system determines how to calculate the physical sample sizes and to create physical-sample records when an inspection lot is created. In the sample drawing procedure, you specify the following: which categories of physical samples must be drawn, how many physical samples must be drawn, the size of each physical sample, and whether the drawing of physical samples must be confirmed.

Work Center

Work centers were discussed in Chapter 3, Section 3.1.3. Please be aware that the work center capacity planning isn't available in QM.

Production Resource/Tool

A *production resource/tool* (PRT) is a type of equipment that is used as an operating resource during production processes or maintenance activities. A PRT can be used to simply consult such as a technical drawing or to perform checks or make changes to settings influencing product sizes, structures, or efficiency. (Recall that equipment was discussed in Chapter 5, Section 5.3.1.) Apart from the use of the maintenance equipment master (which is generally used for high-value tools, such as gauges, measuring devices, cranes, scaffolds, or high-quality tools), you can also use stock materials (via SAP MM), documents (from SAP DMS, such as sketches, technical drawings, or instructions), and small tools define in QM (a cut-down version of the equipment master for lower value tools). After a PRT is set up, you can ensure it's available at the planned operational activities by using the availability checks. Another benefit is the ability to collect wear and tear information, which can be used as input for performance- or condition-based maintenance activities.

8.1.2 Quality Engineering

Quality engineering is focused on incorporating quality into the entire product development process. The quality engineering business processes ensure that the quality of your products is correct from product idea through product delivery and into service at the customer's site — that is, from cradle to grave.

The quality engineering process often starts with the setup of a project, which can include defined deliverables, quality gates, and stability studies. (Note that we discussed defined deliverables and quality gates in Chapter 7 for Project Management and stability studies in Chapter 3.) After these initial stages, you continue quality engineering by closed-loop inspection planning, which is the focus of this section. Closed-loop inspection planning enables you to perform FMEA, set up a control plan, and set up the inspection planning details. This process includes efficient supplier management, maintenance of quality-related documents, and Recipe Management when required.

Closed-loop inspection planning is an integrated inspection planning process for goods receipt inspection and inspection during production. It's an iterative process in which changes can be initiated from any activity in the loop, and provides functions and features to understand the effect of the change on the other objects (the closed-loop). It starts in the very beginning of the product development process for a new product, providing an Advanced Product Quality Planning (APQP) process.

The business goal of closed-loop inspection planning is to perform according to the international standard ISO/TS 16949, which is an especially important standard within the automotive industry.

Two related concepts that are important to quality engineering are FMEA and control plans; these both play a role in the closed-loop inspection planning process, so we'll cover them briefly before returning to the closed-loop inspection planning sequence. These are relatively new concepts (SAP ERP 5.0 EHPs 3–5), and their steps fulfill important requirements for several industries. However, they aren't required to perform quality engineering activities and to set up an inspection planning process or complaints processes.

Failure Mode and Effects Analysis

FMEA is an analysis performed by a team of experts from multiple departments to analyze potential failures or defects of product, process, asset, or service by the severity and likelihood of the possible failure. It's often used in product development, systems engineering, reliability engineering, and operations management. Each potential cause must be considered for its effect and risk on the product or process; the team tries to eliminate the possible risk by defining detection and prevention actions as early as possible.

Successful execution of a product FMEA can help a team eliminate or reduce product weaknesses by identifying potential failure modes based both on past experiences with similar products and on common failure mechanism logic. This information enables the team to redesign the product or its components with minimum effort and resources when required, resulting in reduced development time and costs.

A *product FMEA* should be performed during the product design process, and a *process FMEA* should be done before starting a new process. FMEAs are often used for root cause analysis in Six Sigma projects to perform a risk assessment and/or product review during product development and for operational quality control and planning.

Before starting an FMEA, you must ensure that the following prerequisites have been met:

- The business functions `OPS_QM_EXTENSIONS` (delivered from SAP ERP 5 EHP 3 and higher) and `OPS_QM_EXTENSION_2` (EHP 5 and higher) must be switched on in the Switch Framework.

- The business partners for the team members involved in executing the FMEA have been recorded in the system.

- The possible required FMEA types and the required valuation profiles have been configured.

- (Optional) The use of FMEA codes, which standardizes and provides more analytical options, is highly recommended but optional. You can define codes for the function, prerequisites, failures, causes, effects, and actions.

- (Optional) Linking the FMEA characteristics to the QM master inspection characteristics provides you with the opportunity to create inspection planning in an accelerated way.

Let's transition to how to perform FMEA to eliminate or reduce product weaknesses.

Performing FMEA

FMEA is offered within the QUALITY PLANNING menu of the QM component. Two transactions are offered:

- **Transaction QM_FMEA**
  The FMEA Cockpit transaction gives you access to create and change an FMEA.

- **Transaction QM_FMEAMONITOR**
  The FMEA Monitor transaction gives you access and the ability to monitor outstanding actions.

As Figure 8.19 shows, the FMEA cockpit gives you access to all of the FMEA objects used. It consists of a navigation area (which allows you to navigate to the object you want to work on), a work area (which gives you access to the detailed information of an object), a worklist area (which gives you access to your worklist, including previous FMEAs and templates), and a hierarchy view (which gives you access to the assigned network of FMEAs and, when not required, can be switched off). The cockpit also allows you to set up your own personal defaults, which will be loaded every time you open the cockpit.

The FMEA transactions offered are technically the same as the Audit Management transactions, which were described in Chapter 6, Section 6.4. The FMEA process offered within QM complies with the ISO TS16949 automotive industry standard and lets you perform FMEA as part of the comprehensive inspection planning process.

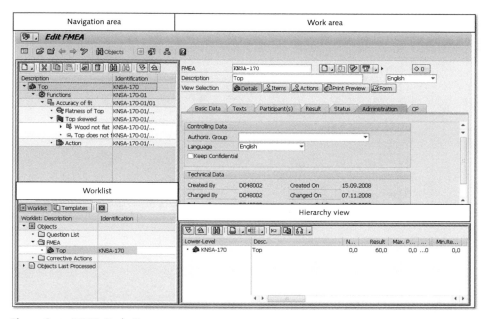

Figure 8.19 FMEA Cockpit

Master Data in FMEA

The left side of Figure 8.20 shows the structure of the FMEA objects and their icons. The FMEA objects and the detection and preventive actions are specific to FMEA, and all of the other objects (function list, functions, defects, etc.) are generic elements. The right side of this figure gives an example of an FMEA performed for a product. This section will briefly introduce these objects.

The following FMEA objects will appear in an analysis:

► **FMEA**

The FMEA object consists of the overall information, such as the analyzed product (or other object, such as a process or asset), the involved team, and when the analysis was performed. It will contain the detailed analysis performed, which contains the elements provided in the rest of this list.

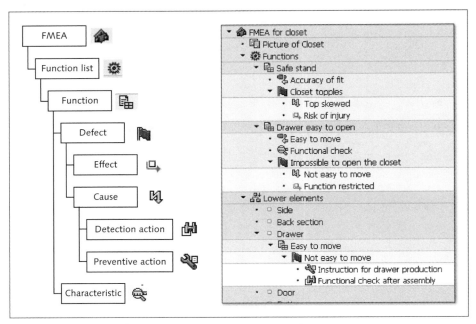

Figure 8.20 Structure of FMEA

▶ **Function list and functions**
Contains the identified product functions or elements (or the identified process elements in case of a process-related FMEA).

▶ **Defects**
Provides the information on the potential failures relating to the specific product function (or process function).

▶ **Effect**
Contains the possible defect causes.

▶ **Cause**
Describes the reason for the defect or what triggers the defect.

▶ **Action**
Assigned to a cause, which contain the action description, the person responsible, dates, the processing status, and the valuation of the probability of detection or probability of occurrence. An action is always either a *detection action*, which identifies possible defects before the product is delivered to customers, or a *preventive action*, which prevents defects from occurring.

▶ Functions, failure types, failure causes, and effects can be described either by text or a configured code. FMEA is integrated into the quality notification, allowing you to copy preventive and detection actions, failure codes, and cause codes from the notification onto the FMEA function, failure, and cause by right-clicking on this object. A FMEA function can be linked to a characteristic.

Note that FMEAs can be connected to each other in a network. Because they represent a complex product via a hierarchy or part of a network, asset, or process, the entire effect chain of a failure can, in that case, be tracked based on FMEAs done at different levels on the functional dependencies. Figure 8.21 shows that the FMEA for a closet includes lower-level elements covering the side, back, and drawers of the closet. As you can imagine, the FMEA structure can become quite complex, so at any point when required, you can perform an FMEA consistency check to ensure your data is correct and consistent by right-clicking and choosing the CONSISTENCY CHECK option or the CHECK AND UPDATE option shown in Figure 8.21. Right-clicking also brings you to the NOTIFICATION ANALYSIS option that allows you to access any notifications concerning your FMEA object.

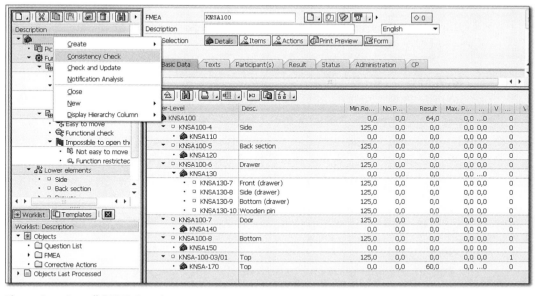

Figure 8.21 Overall FMEA Functions

▶ **Question list (optional)**

Using question lists during planning and execution of the FMEA is optional and can be assigned by copying a template question list into the FMEA at the header level or by creating the question list within the FMEA directly. For example, you can use it to evaluate conformity to specified regulations or to provide a checklist for preparation. You can copy one or more question lists to an FMEA. When you do this, each item that is copied from a question list is given a reference to the original question list item. You can then change the copied items, mark or delete questions that aren't relevant, and add additional questions. An authorization group (display, change) is stored in the question list. Documents can be assigned to a question list. For more details on question lists, see Chapter 6, Section 6.4.

The integration of the functions in SAP ERP allows objects from other processes (such as materials, BOMs, quality notifications, or task lists) to be linked to FMEAs and control plans directly. Apart from the execution of an FMEA for a product, as this section is focused on, it can also be used to analyze a process or process step, a service, or an asset, which is dependent on the FMEA type you've assigned (and configured in your system).

With this understanding of the FMEA prerequisites and master data, let's study the FMEA process.

FMEA Process

The process can be broken down into four basic steps, as shown in Figure 8.22.

Figure 8.22 FMEA Process

Let's walk through the steps of the FMEA process:

1. **Set up FMEA.**

   Prepare the data necessary to plan the FMEA. First, you generate the top level of the FMEA and assign the product (or process) you're about to analyze. You also decide whether or not to use additional subordinate FMEAs for product elements and their relationships.

Recall that the example described the end product (closet) but also contained the FMEAs for the product elements (closet side, closet back, and closet drawers). You also assign the participants who will be involved during the FMEA.

You can choose to either create an FMEA from scratch or use the CREATE WITH TEMPLATE function to copy an existing FMEA, either with or without the assigned actions, as represented in Figure 8.23.

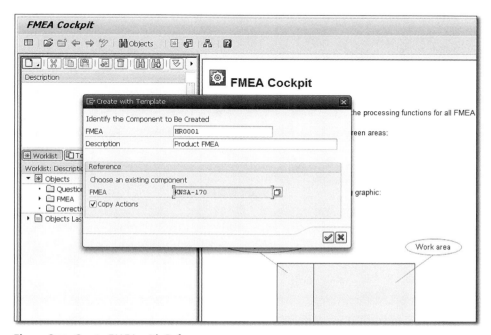

Figure 8.23 Create FMEA with Reference

Figure 8.24 shows the central FMEA for a coat closet with included lower elements for the side and back sections, and so on. You can display the networks or relationships that were created by selecting the hierarchy view. Depending on the component or list item that you select, the hierarchy view represents a structure network, a function network, or a defect network. You can display a table-based overview of the list items that were created by choosing FORM-BASED ENTRY, which is an action available in the VIEW SELECTION, as you can see in the FMEA details of Figure 8.24.

Figure 8.24 Product-Related FMEA

2. **Perform function analysis.**

   Identify with the assigned team the different product functions. Predefined catalogs can be used for this purpose, and ideally this step is directly done within the FMEA cockpit. You could, for example, project the contents of the cockpit within a meeting room so the FMEA participants can see the identified functions being documented by a central administrator. The FMEA function, failures, preventive and detection actions, and causes allow you to assign a specific quality notification element, such as a notification task, a defect, or a cause. This is done by right-clicking on CREATE • FROM NOTIFICATION OBJECT, loading the notification, selecting the required elements, and copying them into the FMEA. Figure 8.25 shows an example of this.

3. **Perform defect analysis.**

   As a team, you perform a *defect analysis*, in which you determine all the different defects of the products specifically related to the previously determined functions. You can create one or more defects for a specific function. You can also create one or more causes or effects for a specific defect. For each potential failure (or defect), you calculate the RPN by evaluating the damage effect of the failure and weighing it with the evaluation of the probability that the failure will actually cause a problem.

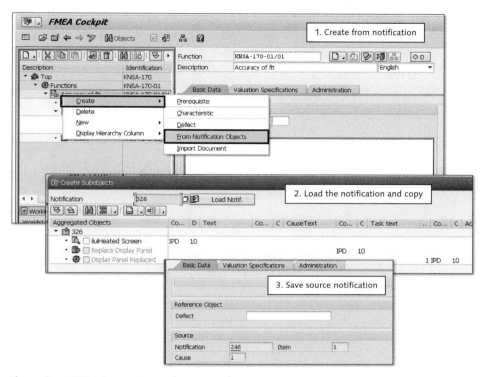

Figure 8.25 FMEA Integration with QM Notification

Even if you don't have any actions, you can still assign an occurrence probability to the cause. Otherwise, the risk valuation takes place using the preventive actions that you can specify for the cause. You can also still specify detection actions for a cause. These specify the probability of detection. The system uses the valuation procedure stored in every new valuation within an FMEA to calculate the RPN.

The RPN is calculated by multiplying the effect severity by the cause occurrence by the detection action. In Figure 8.26, the RPN for the defect = 8 × 4 × 2 = 64.

4. **Perform action and risk analysis.**

   If you can identify actions that prevent failures from occurring, you assign them to the causes as preventive actions that contain information about the probability of occurrence. Detection actions are used to identify potential failures identified and also include probability of occurrence. When no actions have been identified, you can assign the occurrence probability directly to the cause to allow risk valuation to take place. Otherwise, the risk valuation takes place using the preventive actions that you can specify for the cause. You can also still specify detection actions for a cause. These specify the probability of detection. You can display a table-based overview of the actions that were created via the overview of actions.

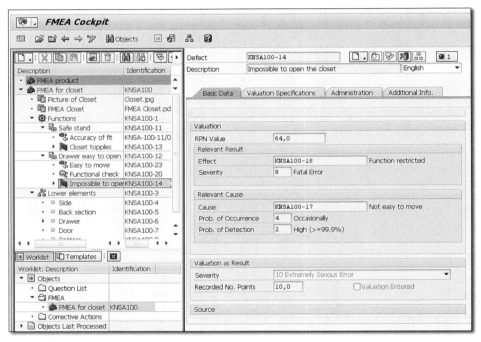

Figure 8.26 Defect with RPN Valuation

Using a Digital Signature

You can configure the use of a digital signature when creating a preventive or detection action. A *digital signature* provides a means to fulfill compliance requirements, which is especially important within the process industry to document the approval of a preventive or detection action. The digital signature can also be set up at the top level of the FMEA to validate the outcomes of the FMEA. You can configure a single signature, where just one person needs to sign, or a multiple-signature strategy, where several persons are required to sign. You can either use the system statuses against the FMEA object to track the provided signatures or the digital signature log; both will become available through the FMEA cockpit (Transaction QM_FMEA). Figure 8.27 shows an example of the active SIGNATURE button on the FMEA RESULT tab and the use of a system status SIGNATURE PROVIDED on the STATUS tab, both of which indicate the approval.

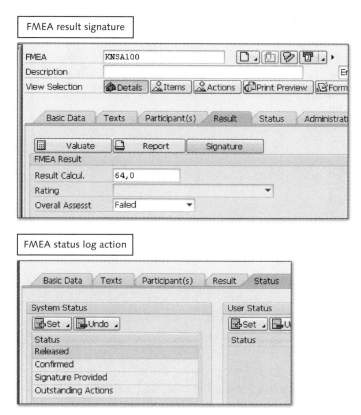

Figure 8.27 Signatures FMEA Results and Actions

Printing FMEA Results

You can output the data of the analysis in an FMEA form. SAP standard provides two forms according to QS9000 and VDA 96 (recall that this is the German automotive standard), which result in a PDF form. This form can be printed, previewed, and assigned as an attachment to the analysis, or it can be sent to all business partners involved in the execution of the FMEA. You can choose to use this standard form as-is or use it as a starting point to define your own forms. Figure 8.28 shows an example of a standard FMEA form.

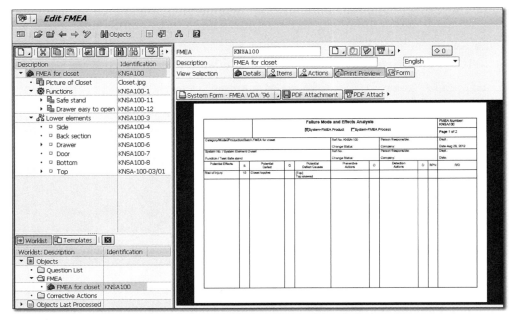

Figure 8.28 FMEA Form

Integration to Control Plan

You'll soon learn to create a control plan. This will become visible in the CP tab of the original FMEA, as Figure 8.29 shows. These characteristics are then copied to a control plan, which contains an overview of all relevant inspections for a product, process, or individual components. With the control plan, you can plan and visualize all relevant inspections for a final product and all its components. As you'll see shortly, the control plan connects all information from the related objects and is a basis for detailed inspection planning for each step (in-process control, goods-receipt inspections, etc.).

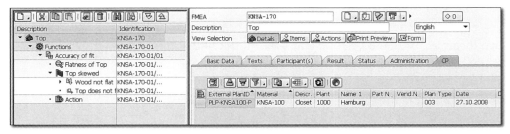

Figure 8.29 FMEA Assigned to a Control Plan

Control Plan

A *control plan* is the description of the entire technical or functional system — usually a newly designed product — that is being monitored or checked for possible risks and defects. Fundamentally, the control plan describes all of the actions that need to be performed in each phase of the process, which includes the inspections during goods receipts, goods issues, and during production with the required specifications, tolerance values, process parameters, control methods, and action plans in case non-conformities occurs.

The business goal for the setup of a control plan is to plan and visualize all relevant inspection for the final product and all its components. A control plan connects all information for the related objects.

When SAP Project and Portfolio Management (PPM) is used as a project management tool for new product developments, you can create the control plan directly from within PPM, as long as this has been set up via object links and the SAP ERP transaction has been web-enabled. The control plan can be used later as input to create the inspection plan or routing for operational use. PPM also offers the efficient project-status reporting to ensure that you can view project progress at all times.

Such control plans are used for APQP projects. APQP is a framework of procedures and techniques used to develop products used within the automotive industry or high-tech industries to produce a product quality plan that will support development of a product or service that will satisfy the customer. Advanced Product Quality Planning (AQPQ) is similar to the concept of Design for Six Sigma (DFSS). AQPQ is specifically used by General Motors, Ford, Chrysler, and their suppliers. They combine elements of routings with inspection plans. For more information about PPM, please refer to Chapter 7, Section 7.4 to Section 7.6.

Control Plan Types

The ISO TS 16949 automotive industry standard requires the maintenance of a control plan according to a fixed schema. For this reason, you can set up several types of control plans to represent the planning phase (e.g., prototype, prelaunch, and production). Due to its integration with operational business processes such as complaint management, in-process controls, and so on, the control plan can also be used to improve a product or process in a productive environment. Any problems during production or any customer complaints are checked against the defect avoidance measures (preventive actions) that were previously determined in the FMEA and/or control plan and may result in adjustments. This is accomplished by having direct access to the FMEA and control plan of a problem during notification processing; we'll cover this topic in more detail in Section 8.1.3.

Control Plan Process

This section describes the typical process steps in a control plan, as represented in Figure 8.30.

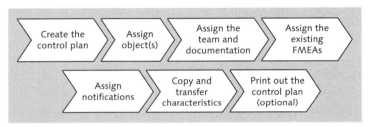

Figure 8.30 Set Up the Control Plan Process

Let's walk through the steps in this process:

1. **Create the control plan.**
   Create the control plan for the distinct process, product, and phase (development, serial production, etc.). The control plan type determines the planning phase, which can be, for example, PRELAUNCH, PRODUCTION, or PROTOTYPE. Figure 8.31 shows the CREATE CONTROL PLAN screen and the basic data when creating a control plan.

2. **Assign object(s).**
   Assign the relevant product components, such as the material, the BOM, and any quality inspection results (QIR)—or, in the case of a control plan for a process, the process steps. Based on the details entered in the control plan items and the process data, the structure of the control plan gets built automatically on the control plan STRUCT. (structure) tab shown in Figure 8.32, where a distinction is made among the processes for goods receipts, production, and goods issues controls. You can optionally extend this view to include information on the Q-info record, quality notifications, FMEA details, and documents.

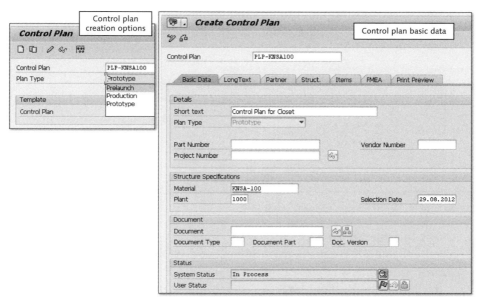

Figure 8.31 Create Control Plan

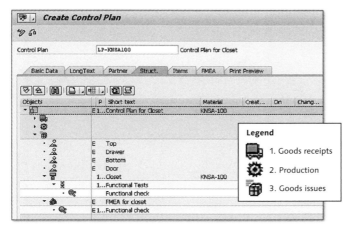

Figure 8.32 Control Plan Product and Process Structure with Legend

3. **Assign the team and documents.**

Within the next two steps, you assign the team responsible for the setup of the control plan, which can be done by assigning partners (via partner role BUP003 Employee). Figure 8.33 shows that different employees have been identified as AUDIT TEAM LEAD, audit APPROVER, RISK MANAGER, and PERSON RESPONSIBLE. Any relevant documents can also be assigned to the plan.

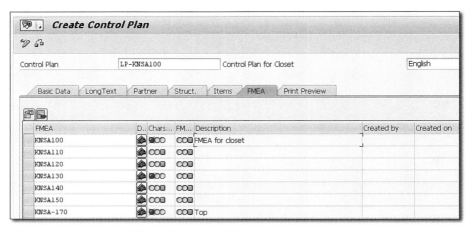

Figure 8.33 Assign the Team to the Control Plan

4. **Assign the existing FMEAs.**
   Because the FMEA is usually performed first, this FMEA can be assigned to the control plan. That way you can transfer the inspection characteristics defined in the FMEA, copy them into the control plan, and perform any follow-up inspection plans. Figure 8.34 shows an example of all the FMEAs assigned to the control plan.

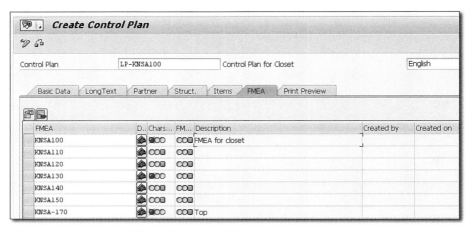

Figure 8.34 Assign the FMEA to the Control Plan

5. **Assign notifications.**
   Within the control plan structure, you can assign existing notifications to the processes, such as assigning outstanding production problems, vendor complaints, or customer complaints.

6. **Copy and transfer characteristics.**

Transfer any relevant characteristics from FMEA or other sources into the control plan. This, in turn, can be used as inputs to the operational inspection plans (see Section 8.1.2 for more details) and/or routings. Figure 8.35 provides an example where FMEA characteristics are copied across into a GOODS RECEIPT INSPECTION plan.

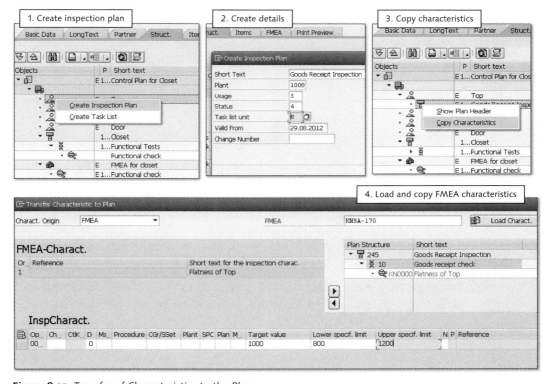

Figure 8.35 Transfer of Characteristics to the Plan

7. **(Optional) Print out the control plan.**

The last step within the control plan is printing out the control plan. SAP delivers a printout according to the QS9000 standard, as shown in Figure 8.36.

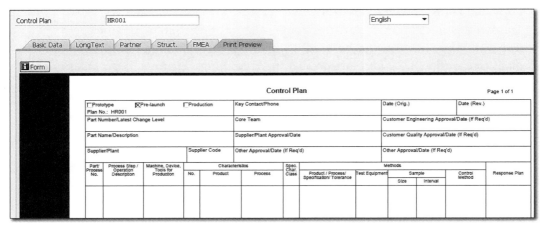

Figure 8.36 Printing the Control Plan

These benefits can be gained from using closed-loop inspection planning with FMEA, the control plan, and the inspection plan:

▶ Provides the basis for closed-loop inspection planning and is compliant with ISO/TCS 16949

▶ Allows you to assign process information or master data objects (e.g., assign a document from SAP DMS, a QM notification, or a material) due to the integrated solution with access to other areas within SAP ERP

▶ Reuses existing master data such as materials, operational routings, inspection plans, catalogs, characteristics, and defects, which prevents additional master data maintenance activities

▶ Provides an easy-to-use user interface that visualizes existing information from one central place

▶ Enables you to make customer-specific adjustments via Business Add-In (BAdI) technology by reusing Audit Management

Closed-Loop Inspection Planning Process

Now that we've covered the FMEA and control plans, let's explore the loop inspection planning process shown in Figure 8.37.

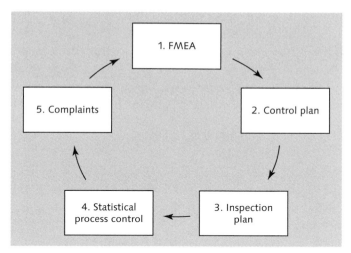

Figure 8.37 Closed-Loop Inspection Planning Process

Steps 1 and 2: FMEA and Control Plan

Generally speaking, the closed-loop inspection planning process starts with performing an FMEA, often followed by a control plan. Both objects allow you to prevent production defects at an early stage during product development, in particular for new developments, which aim to reduce quality costs. After the control plan is set up, this can be used to set up the inspection plan, as outlined earlier in Section 8.1.2.

Steps 3 and 4: Inspection Plan and Statistical Process Control

Because the setup of the inspection plan is one of the process steps in the quality engineering process (covered later in this section), the process will include additional activities during NPDI, such as the setup of a project, master data creation, stability studies, and quality manual updates. During inspection planning or execution, you can use statistical methods to monitor or control a process to check that the product is meeting specifications by using control charts or other means of statistical process control (SPC). These will be described in Section 8.1.4.

Step 5: Complaints

After the start of production, a closed loop (in terms of a continuous improvement process) is created by ensuring that each incoming product complaint is recorded and checked against the initially identified FMEA defects and their related specified preventive or detection actions (as described earlier in this section). The result of the complaint could lead to changing the FMEA, the control plan, and the operational inspection plans. Further along the logistics value chain, continuous improvements to the product or process might impact some or all objects in this iterative process. The loop finishes with the complaints process, including activities to improve the quality of a product, which will be described in more detail in Section 8.1.4.

Quality Engineering Process

The quality engineering process (represented in Figure 8.38) starts with the closed-loop inspection planning recently described. Let's look into the subsequent steps in the quality engineering process.

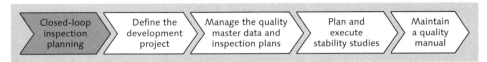

Figure 8.38 Quality Engineering Process

1. **Define the development project.**

   Efficient project management is one of the cornerstones of successful product development. You should have an established process around product development projects to ensure that the planned product will fulfill the requested requirements and that the product will be delivered to the customer (either internal or external) on time and within budget.

   Quality management during product development starts with defining the deliverables and quality gates, which includes inspection planning, efficiently managing suppliers, and the setting up quality-related documents. In several industries (mainly process industries), this process includes the performance of stability studies.

   There are different ways to ensure quality at the beginning of the product lifecycle. An example used within the automotive industry from the ISO TS 16949 is APQP. As described earlier, APQP is a phase-based approach for development projects. The project management capabilities described in Chapter 7 give you insights into which features and functions within project management you'll need to activate and implement to support such an integrated approach in your company. In particular, we highly recommend the use of PPM–Project Management because the setup of different phases and quality gates, the setup of checklists and tasks, and the ability to plan required resources are particularly useful.

Another benefit is the out-of-the-box integration to QM (as discussed in Chapter 7, Section 7.4.3, in the "Object Links" subsection), where you can assign a QM objects, such as the quality plan to a project. Figure 8.39 provides an example of a product development project set up in PPM, which defines the different phases and the expected deliverables and quality gates.

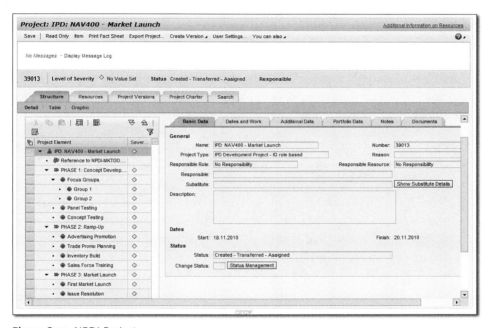

Figure 8.39 NPDI Project

With the use of PPM, you can also run Six Sigma projects, where you first define the project goal and key figures, measure all influencing factors, analyze the results, improve the process, and control the effectiveness of your measures to enhance quality and save costs within your company. PPM helps you to manage the overall process and consolidates all of the different tools and systems used for this investigation. Of course, there are other phase-based approaches with various functions and key figures. SAP PLM 7.02 and PPM offer a highly flexible solution for the entire development process, from conception of planning and quality checks, through to the start of production. Quality engineering is integrated in all of these steps.

According to APQP, the *Production Part Approval Process* (PPAP) can also be part of a product development project. PPAP is a successive procedure which ensures that predefined specifications for developed parts or products are observed and, therefore, allows production to start without any problems. This scenario is also supported with the use of PPM–Project Management in combination with QM, where by the use of the collaboration scenario (c-folders/c-projects), you can easily exchange quality-relevant documents with internal and external partners, which provides input to efficiently set up the QM master data and process data.

2. **Manage the quality master data and inspection plans.**
   In general, quality planning consists of all the activities required to ensure the product's quality and provides the basis for effective quality assurance and control. It's a continuous iterative process managed by multiple departments and requiring a high degree of collaboration. Usually, multiple departments are involved (e.g., procurement, production, and quality engineering). You need to set up the appropriate product data as discussed in Chapter 3, including the product quality planning master data (described in Section 8.1.2). The setup of the inspection plan is especially fundamental because this forms the basics required for performing quality inspections. It can also include the creation of FMEA and control plans, when required. The following two areas are often important and included during the management of quality master data and inspection plan setup:

   ▸ SAP Supplier Relationship Management (SAP SRM): In some cases, you have to coordinate specifications and inspection plans with suppliers and customers. You can do this using the collaboration function from PPM, for example, which lets you exchange documents relevant to quality, such as quality assurance agreements or test reports. Also, you have to define supplier relationships in terms of shipment agreements, approved delivery quantities, inbound certificate processing, and model inspections. This information must be built into inspection plans and supplier information records with defined status schemes. These functions are all available within SAP ERP Procurement, which is offered in the SAP MM area and covers the procurement basics. SAP SRM offers multiple products specific to industries and contract lifecycle management and also extensive procurement functions, such as the ability to publish bids on the Internet to make them publically available or just available to a chosen vendor group.

▶ Recipe Management: Recipe Management enables you to manage your product and process development in the process industry from the initial idea through to implementation in manufacturing and integration in the supply chain. Tight integration between Recipe Management and QM ensures that quality aspects are being considered right from the start. Within the recipe, you can include the relevant inspection characteristics as well as trials and trial-specific stability studies, which assist during developing a new formulation or recipe. Refer to Chapter 3, Section 3.4.4.

3. **Plan and execute stability studies.**
Stability studies give you a means of testing and evaluating products during various stages of the product lifecycle so you can determine how products or product batches will hold up under controlled environmental conditions over predefined periods of time. For example, you can use a stability study to investigate a product's shelf life based on conditions such as temperature, moisture, atmospheric pressure, and brightness. Stability studies during product development are also often used to determine the ideal product composition and/or to determine the most suitable product packaging. They allow you to meet legal requirements, such as GMP. Stability studies are not only suitable for use in process industries (e.g., chemicals, pharmaceuticals, cosmetics, and foods), but they can also be conducted in specific areas of discrete manufacturing (e.g., to test the stability of paints in the automotive supplier industry).

The stability study is a main process offered and found directly in the QM component menu, which offers functions for the following four main areas:

▶ Basic master data: Includes the creation and management of basic master data used during a stability study, such as materials, batches, and BOMs.

▶ Stability study: Includes the functions to create, change, and display the stability study, either in header information or the individual tasks, such as physical sample creation.

▶ Planning: Includes the planning (test schedule, inspection strategies), execution (inspection specifications), and inspection characteristics and catalog information.

▶ Performing a stability test: Offers you the ability to access inspection lots and record results, defects, and usage decisions, including detailed sample information such as the storage conditions.

The stability study process, which is included in Figure 8.40, is generally performed in three stages: creating the study, planning, and conducting tests, which are identified in the figure by different shades of gray. Please note that this process is a generalized process flow, which can be flexibly changed and adjusted to meet your specific business requirements.

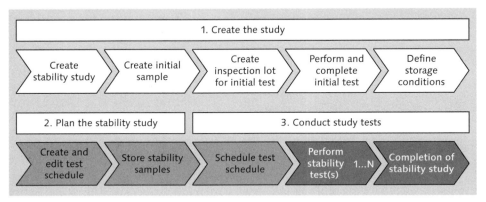

Figure 8.40 Stability Study Process

The first stage is the creation of the stability study, which is represented in QM as a specific type of notification. Three types of notifications are available for a stability study:

▸ QS: For a material-specific stability study, where you optionally can assign a product BOM.

▸ QR: For a stability study without a material.

▸ QT: For a stability study trial.

All of the required process steps during stability study creation—such as creating the initial sample, creating the inspection lot, defining the storage conditions, and removing stability samples for storage—are made available in the create stability study transaction via the ACTION BOX. As soon as you execute it, it's recorded in the notification as an activity and is also tracked as a status change against the header of the notification. This ensures you're fully informed of where the stability study is at any given time. These activity statuses are delivered as user statuses (which can be adjusted based on your needs in configuration), and they can include rules to guide you throughout the process, such as that an activity can only be performed after the previous one has been completed. Figure 8.41 shows the creation of a stability study's storage conditions for storage temperature.

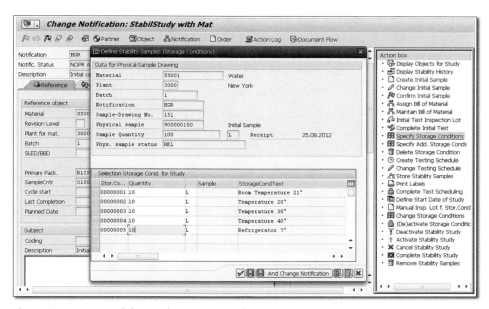

Figure 8.41 Create Stability Study: Storage Conditions

The second stage focuses on the steps required to plan the stability test. You identify the physical samples (drawn from the initial sample), what needs to be checked, under which environmental conditions (known as storage conditions in QM), and when to conduct tests. All of this information is captured in the test schedule. The stability study can run over multiple weeks, months, or years, and you can use the deadline monitoring functions to ensure activities are planned accordingly. The test schedule basically uses the maintenance plan object and functions, so see Chapter 5, Section 5.3.6 for more details. Figure 8.42 shows the creation of a testing schedule using a strategy and inspection type.

The action option Display Objects for Study in the Action box provides an overview of all the objects that were created as a result of the stability study, which complies with an important GMP requirement. Figure 8.43 shows an example of the document flow for a stability study.

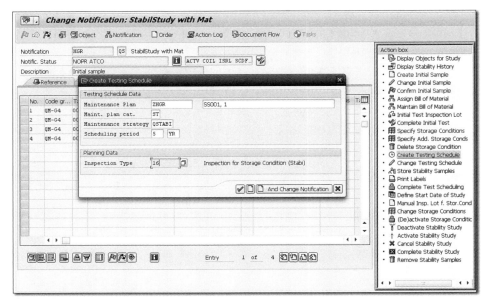

Figure 8.42 Create Test Schedule

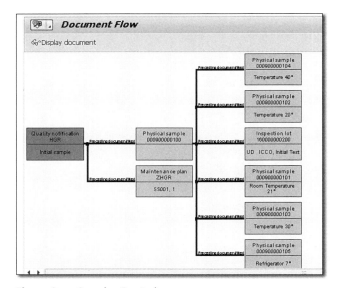

Figure 8.43 Samples Created

During the last stage of the stability study process, you conduct the defined stability test. The inspection lots created during test scheduling are used for recording the inspection results, any defects, and usage decisions. Figure 8.44 shows an overview of the inspection lots, which were created as a result of our stability study schedule.

This stage can be repeated as often as required. At any point during the stability study, you can decide to either completely or partially stop or start the study. For example, you can stop the study for one or multiple storage conditions and decide whether to keep the samples in storage or discharge the samples. After a stability test is set to Completed status, it's finished and can't be reactivated.

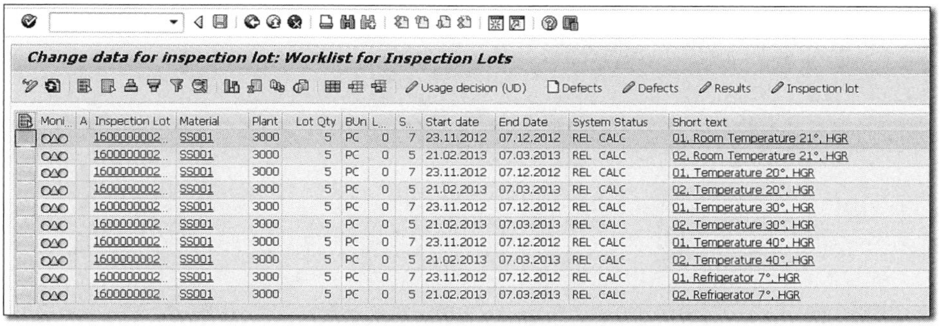

Moni...	A	Inspection Lot	Material	Plant	Lot Qty	BUn	L...	S...	Start date	End Date	System Status	Short text
○△○		1600000002...	SS001	3000	5	PC	0	7	23.11.2012	07.12.2012	REL CALC	01, Room Temperature 21°, HGR
○△○		1600000002...	SS001	3000	5	PC	0	5	21.02.2013	07.03.2013	REL CALC	02, Room Temperature 21°, HGR
○△○		1600000002...	SS001	3000	5	PC	0	7	23.11.2012	07.12.2012	REL CALC	01, Temperature 20°, HGR
○△○		1600000002...	SS001	3000	5	PC	0	5	21.02.2013	07.03.2013	REL CALC	02, Temperature 20°, HGR
○△○		1600000002...	SS001	3000	5	PC	0	7	23.11.2012	07.12.2012	REL CALC	01, Temperature 30°, HGR
○△○		1600000002...	SS001	3000	5	PC	0	5	21.02.2013	07.03.2013	REL CALC	02, Temperature 30°, HGR
○△○		1600000002...	SS001	3000	5	PC	0	7	23.11.2012	07.12.2012	REL CALC	01, Temperature 40°, HGR
○△○		1600000002...	SS001	3000	5	PC	0	5	21.02.2013	07.03.2013	REL CALC	02, Temperature 40°, HGR
○△○		1600000002...	SS001	3000	5	PC	0	7	23.11.2012	07.12.2012	REL CALC	01, Refrigerator 7°, HGR
○△○		1600000002...	SS001	3000	5	PC	0	5	21.02.2013	07.03.2013	REL CALC	02, Refrigerator 7°, HGR

Figure 8.44 Worklist of Inspection Lots

SAP NetWeaver Business Warehouse (SAP NetWeaver BW) provides flexible reports to analyze stability tests. For more details, see Chapter 9.

With the introduction of trial management as part of Recipe Management (see Chapter 3 for details), you can now manage trial-related stability studies in QM as well. The basis for this is the stability study building block (shown in Figure 8.45), which includes information about the study in the header. Examples of this header information include the notification type used, where SAP delivers the QT type, and details on the initial sample, storage conditions, and the product hierarchy assignment. This planning building block is accessible via both Recipe Management (Transaction RMWB) or through QM (Transaction QST09). Stability planning can be accelerated with reusable modules. A critical success factor during product development in process industries is the planning, execution, and evaluation of laboratory trials. In parallel, companies are required to conduct stability studies with samples taken from different trials and to carry out quality inspections.

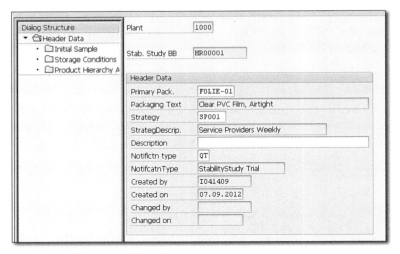

Figure 8.45 Planning Building Block

4. **Maintain a quality manual.**

   More and more companies have decided to introduce a quality management system as a result of world market requirements and a desire to improve security in product liability processes. At the same time, they use the quality management system as a tool for analyzing and improving their business processes. Various industry standards, such as DIN ISO 9000:2002, require companies to establish and maintain a process-oriented quality manual. Within this manual, quality goals and processes for ensuring consistent quality management within the enterprise must be defined, documented, and distributed to employees. Different hierarchy levels can be provided, starting from a high-level description down to detailed operational procedures, graphics, process flow diagrams, or organizational charts. You can also include other quality management documentation—standard operational procedures, quality certificates, and quality manuals—and store that documentation with SAP DMS.

The discussion of the quality engineering process brings us at the end of the quality engineering topic; the process ties the closed-loop inspection planning process to earlier discussed quality objects. The process starts off with the closed-loop inspection process—a continuous process that includes product FMEAs, product control and inspection plans, and the management of product-related complaints, which can, in turn, trigger changes. It's continuous with the NPDI project, management of master data relating to quality, and the maintenance of the quality manual. Optionally, the engineering process can include stability studies and trials, allowing you to test and evaluate a product at any stage under controlled environmental conditions and over predefined periods of time to determine its shelf life, for example.

The next logical QM activity is the quality assurance and control, which enables you to maintain and improve the attained level of product quality. Quality assurance and control involves inspections at all stages of a product's lifecycle, its continuous monitoring, and quick intervention to deal with unexpected events.

8.1.3 Quality Assurance and Control

Quality assurance and control is a process already covered in the SAP SAP ERP Solution Map as part of the main process QM (inside the process category corporate services). This is why quality assurance and control isn't officially part of the SAP PLM Solution Map. But because it forms such an important part of product quality assurance, we'll address the business process at a high level.

Quality Assurance and Control Business Process

After your quality processes are in place, you must strive to maintain and improve the attained level of quality. Quality control involves inspections at all stages, continuous monitoring, and intervening quickly to deal with unexpected events. Quality assurance and control checks can be performed during any step within the logistics value chain with the goal of ensuring that the quality of a product conforms to the necessary quality standards.

The following examples are quality checks that can be implemented as part of quality assurance measures within the logistics processes. The results of the compliance to these quality assurance measures can be used as input for vendor evaluation.

▶ At time of goods receipt, the warehouse clerk checks two things: the shelf expiration date of the incoming cans of tomatoes against the remaining shelf-life as recorded in the material master, and the European Article Number (EAN).

▶ The warehouse clerk checks compliance with shipping instructions as agreed to with the vendor; these can be recorded in the purchase order. A check can be made during goods receipt to determine whether the instructions were followed. This also enables the marketability of the goods to be checked and complaints made, if necessary. The results of this check can be included in the vendor evaluation.

► Check underdelivery/overdelivery tolerances for raw materials, such as the milk ordered to produce a batch of fruit yogurt.

These checks don't require the QM *quality inspection process*, which is defined as the measuring, examining, testing, and gauging of one or more characteristics of a product or service (or asset) and comparing the results with specified requirements to determine whether conformity is achieved for each characteristic. Basically, all of the quality inspection process steps can be divided into four distinct phases: the trigger, the request for an inspection, the inspection itself, and any follow-up activities, as shown in Figure 8.46.

Usually the closed-loop inspection planning is the predecessor process, which includes the setup of the required data, as was described in detail in Section 8.1.2. Some industries don't use the FMEA or the control plan, so either an inspection plan or a material specification is the first step of their quality engineering process.

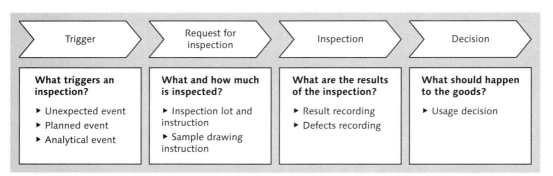

Figure 8.46 Quality Inspection Process

Let's walk through the process steps:

1. **Trigger**
   You can inspect products of various origins, such as raw products delivered through a purchase order or in-process goods used during product manufacturing. The inspection process starts with the *trigger* caused by an *event*. The possible events are shown in Table 8.3.

Event Type	Specific Event	Example
Planned	Goods receipt (goods movement)	The goods receipt of a purchase order of raw materials (meat) automatically triggers the inspection process where 100% of the material needs to be checked. A skilled quality engineer checks the meat by classifying different carcasses by size, volume of muscular tissue, fat layers, color, and so on.
		When Procurement decides to include a new product (let's say, a new laptop), the following are checked extensively in the first shipment: the laptop specifications, the ordered accessories, visual damages, warranty certificate, and completeness. Following receipt, these are checked again, although less comprehensively.
	Goods transfer (goods movement)	A quality engineer checks the consistency of iron ore after it has been mined and reaches the port by train. Positive results lead to direct shipment; negative results lead to mixing the iron ore to the consistency requested by the customer.
	Goods issue (goods movement)	During the issue of ingredients (dairy products) to the production line, the milk is checked for the presence of harmful bacteria, the correct temperature, and so on.
	Product delivery to customer	Before a car is delivered to the dealership based on a custom order, during a final check, the quality engineer ensures that the car is configured and works as requested—for example, the sunroof is built in, seats are leather, the air conditioning is climate controlled, the correct satellite radio is installed, and the correct winter gear is provided.
	Create or release of maintenance/ service order	When a water meter is replaced with a new one at a property, the quality engineer needs to calibrate it. During creating or releasing a maintenance or service order, the system automatically creates an inspection lot for the relevant technical object (either functional location or equipment). The inspection characteristics need to have been assigned to the used task list and, during the order type configuration, an inspection type needs to have been assigned.

Table 8.3 Events That Can Trigger an Inspection

Event Type	Specific Event	Example
Planned (Cont.)	Production order with an in-process control during the production of product	A prerequisite of using this is the inclusion of the inspection details in the recipe or the routing. During the production of cookies, the production process is checked by recording whether the cooking temperature is within the range of 180 – 200 degrees. Also every 1,000th cookie is checked in a lab for the right consistency, the right flavor and shape, and the correct packaging.
	Customer/sales order	Every hundredth sales order for an Apple iPhone gets checked for correct color and measurements (length, width, and depth).
	Batch management	When cheeses reach the age of six months in the warehouse, a sample is taken and checked for the number of bacteria.
	Deadline monitoring	Planned inspections are performed when plan requirements are fulfilled. Consider an inspection order that is created every week (time-based plan) or an inspection order created every 100 operating hours (performance-based plan). See Chapter 5, Section 5.3.6 for more details.
	Manual	A warehouse clerk can see that incoming goods have been damaged during transport and performs a quality check.
Unplanned	Customer complaint	A customer calls the call center to file a complaint about the failure of a digital camera he bought, triggering a quality investigation.
	Product error	After a coffeemaker has been launched into the market and sold to several customers, the buttons to choose between black coffee and cappuccino seem to fade away.
Analytical	Threshold value breach within the information system	The number of complaints against a sales organization/product combination exceeds 10 per month.

Table 8.3 Events That Can Trigger an Inspection (Cont.)

2. **Request for inspection**

   Based on the trigger, the inspection request gets created by the creation of an inspection lot, which basically is a request to a plant to carry out a quality inspection for the material (or the technical object, when it's a maintenance request). The inspection lot, such as the example shown in Figure 8.47, consists of the information about what, where, and how the inspection is done; the origin of the lot; the scope and size of the inspection (a mandatory step determined automatically via sample determination); and who execute it. This information is based on the master data either from the material or from the inspection plan.

Figure 8.47 Inspection Lot

   Sample management allows you to plan and automatically generate samples (physical samples, pooled samples, and/or reserve samples) at goods receipt or in production. You can create individual sample master records for all kinds of sample types (e.g., goods receipt samples, environmental samples, and competitor samples).

3. **Inspection**

   The QM controller executes the inspection, records the results and the defects, and determines whether or not the inspected product fulfills the quality requirements. You can use difference means to record results, such as manual methods (catalogs, tolerance ranges, sampling plan via S-Method) or by using SPC control charts, graphics, or process capability indexes.

Figure 8.48 provides an example of a result recording an inspection lot worklist, which is available via Transaction QE51N. Figure 8.49 shows a result recording through the portal, where this includes the identification of a defect. Results recording can be done directly via the SAP GUI, the portal, the web, or mobile devices. Follow-up actions include batch classification and quality scoring.

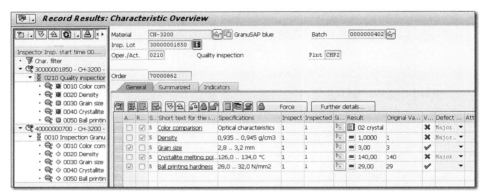

Figure 8.48 Results Recording

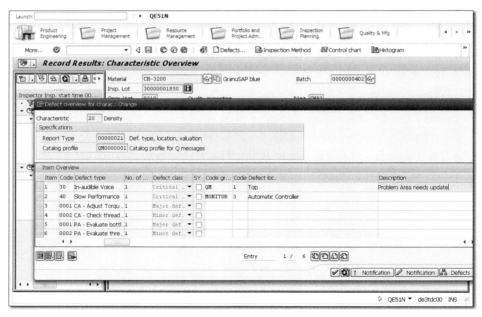

Figure 8.49 Results Recording with Defect

4. Decision

After the results have been recorded, a usage decision such as the one shown in Figure 8.50 is made for the inspection lot. The usage decision is captured via the use of the usage decision catalog type (type 3), in which you can store decisions that completely accept the lot, accept the lot under restrictions, or reject the lot. The usage decision can lead to an automatic stock posting, where, for example, the stock is posted from quality stock to unrestricted stock during acceptance, or you can send the stock back to the vendor or scrap the stock during rejection. Note that this needs to be configured in QM.

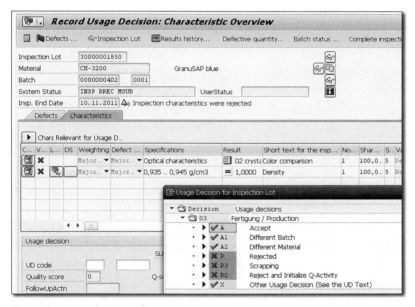

Figure 8.50 Results Recording Usage Decision

Certificate of Analysis

You can create a *quality certificate,* which is related to an inspection lot, a batch, or a delivery, and use it to document that the product meets the quality requirements. QM supports the creation of all types of certificates that may be sent to customers, such as those suggested by European standard EN 10204. Form, contents, recipients, language, and the delivery form of a certificate are automatically selected depending on material, customer, or other criteria. Outgoing certificates are usually created at delivery time, and the inspection results on the certificate can be automatically transferred to a goods receipt inspection lot or manually to another inspection lot type. Structured and textual certificate data can be transmitted to the recipient via a quality data interchange (QDI).

Quality certificates for delivery or batches enable customers to obtain a quality certificate for goods delivered over the Internet. The customer can either retrieve a certificate that is created instantly or access one that is stored using SAP ArchiveLink. Incoming certificates—which are delivered together with supplied material during goods receipt—are also supported. Exchanging quality certificate data offers easy access to the quality data in certificates, in which the certificate is sent to the target system in electronic form. For more detailed information on this topic, please refer to the sources provided in Appendix A and Appendix B.

This section focused on the quality assurance process, starting with an event that triggers the inspection process, followed by the request to perform an inspection, conduct the inspection, record the inspection results (including the creation of the accompanying quality certificates), and consequently make a decision as a result of the inspection. It provides valuable context into how this process provides inputs to start improving product or process quality via a continuous quality improvement process, which is the main focus of the next section.

8.1.4 Quality Improvement

Quality improvement records quality problems and includes problem solving by systematically determining their cause, solution follow-up and actions. The quality notification process is available to document problems of any type for this purpose—especially problems related to poor quality of a product, such as processing complaints against suppliers and complaints from customers. It can also be used for processing an internal company problem relating to processes and products and for handling positive events, such as proposals for improvement.

The *notification* is the document used to capture these events. The document is used within several different components within SAP (e.g., within SAP PM to record a malfunction or within PS to capture a claim). General notifications can subsequently be converted to notifications of another type. The structure of a notification has been described in detail in Chapter 5, Section 5.3.2, so we won't get detailed here. Instead we'll discuss the quality improvement process in detail, as included in Figure 8.51.

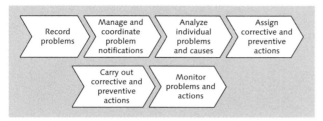

Figure 8.51 Quality Improvement Process

Let's walk through the process:

1. **Record problems.**

   Via the notification, you can record and process different types of problems, such as problems resulting from poor-quality goods or services received from a vendor or delivered to a customer. The notification type defines the type of problem and the included reference object. SAP delivers notification types for a vendor error with purchase order item or material document (type F1), a customer complaint based on a sales order number (type F2), an internal problem with a production order number (type F3), and for an error relating to a material based on a material document number. You can use these standard problem types or set up or extend them with additional types. Figure 8.52 shows an example of a vendor notification created via the SAP NetWeaver Business Client (NWBC).

   When the person who records the problem sends a written complaint, you can attach this document using either SAP DMS or object link capabilities. The notification can be created directly via the SAP system, but SAP offers several Internet services (Transaction QISR) as well, so your problem reporters can create the notification via the web. You can use the simplified general notification when the notification creator isn't familiar with the system and just wants an easy way to report a problem.

   The various notifications are managed by one or more coordinators who have the necessary subject knowledge and organizational expertise. The coordinator can receive an email with a newly created notification when workflow is active, or he can regularly check the notification list for newly created problems and start the coordination activities (such as converting the original notification category, if necessary, to a more suitable notification category, and adding information such as the reference objects, problem details, priority, time frames, and persons involved).

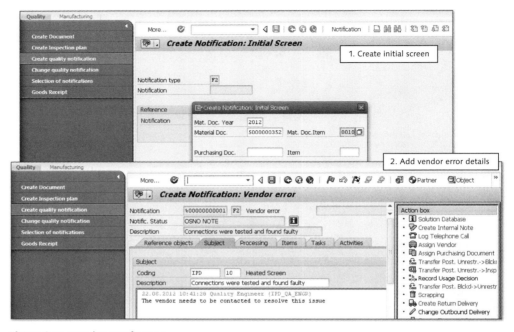

Figure 8.52 Vendor Notification

Worth special mention are the newly introduced functions and buttons CHECK CONTROL PLAN and CHECK FMEA ANALYSIS, which you can include as actions in the ACTION BOX shown in Figure 8.53. They allow you to access the control plan and the FMEA directly from within the notification screen with the material automatically defaulted as a reference object. This provides an important part of the closed-loop inspection process.

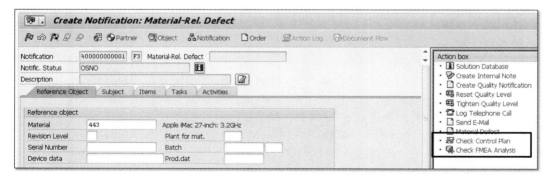

Figure 8.53 Notification with Action Box to FMEA and Control Plan

During notification processing and inspection processing, you can be alerted about similar or related problems, helping you to prevent a repetition. This can be activated for the following master data objects: material, customer, supplier, material-customer, material-vendor, batch, and batch item.

When you want to receive notifications from either vendors or customers directly and exchange data with them on CAPA taken, you might want to consider implementing the Quality Collaboration scenario. The Quality Collaboration scenario is offered as part of SAP Supply Network Collaboration (SAP SNC 7.0) and comes with two new notification types: Q8 supplier-created notifications and Q9-customer created notifications. It requires the activation of business function OPS_QM_EXTENSION_2.

2. **Manage and coordinate problem notifications.**
The quality coordinator defines the problem details, the individual defects, the defect causes (when known), and a priority (which often includes response times such as medium priority to be solved within a week, high priority to be solved within a day, and very high priority to be solved within an hour), and then dispatches the notification to suitable experts by assigning them follow-up tasks and activities.

He also determines if it's necessary to react to the incoming notifications immediately with *immediate tasks* even before the problems can be subjected to a detailed analysis. These tasks are assigned to the notification header as opposed to *corrective tasks*, which are created as part of the defect at the notification item level. When certain prerequisites are met, the system can also predefine follow-up tasks and activities, which might be useful when you want to standardize an approach for a specific type of problem. SAP offers personalized worklists that are relevant to you so you can just focus on the outstanding notifications or task. Figure 8.54 is an example of a quality notification list.

3. **Analyze individual problems and causes.**
The coordinator generally requires the assistance of a technical specialist to weigh in on the product's defects. The expert investigates the problem, detects the causes, suggests a solution, and records his findings in the notification to enable standardization and reporting. When set up, the expert can use the solution database, which can assist in finding an appropriate solution based on the symptoms of the problem. Figure 8.55 is an example of a solution database used by a technical specialist.

Figure 8.54 Quality Notification List

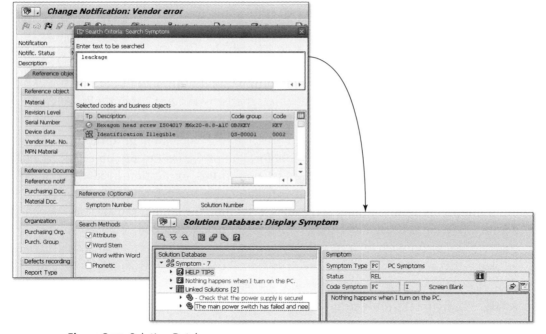

Figure 8.55 Solution Database

4. **Assign corrective and preventive actions.**

After finalizing the defects and their causes, the technical specialist will typically consult the people responsible for the defect causes to cooperate with
them in defining CAPAs and assign the partners responsible for processing
these tasks. Each action is documented in the notification. The statuses of the
tasks are controlled, and the deadlines are monitored. When a more detailed

work order is required as part of these follow-up activities, you can do so by creating a QM work order. The work order allows you to plan the work, plan the parts, and plan the required resources such as employees and required measuring devices. Because the work order is a cost collector, it allows you to collect any costs during the work order by confirming hours, use of parts (stock or non-stock items via SAP MM), or procurement activities. The QM order is very similar in structure and approach to the maintenance work order or the project activities, with the exception that capacity planning for QM work centers isn't available.

5. **Carry out corrective and preventive actions.**
   Within your personalized worklist (such as the one shown in Figure 8.56), you can see the outstanding CAPAs assigned to you or your department. Corrective tasks must be processed in a series of traceable steps. For example, the automotive industry uses the 8D process, in which all eight steps are required to solve a problem and must be documented.

   To achieve this, you can use the system status against the tasks provided, which are Released, Completed, and Successful, and then extend them with the additional statuses required by defining them as user statuses and including them as part of the sequence of tasks.

Change list of tasks: List of Notifications

Exce..	Task Status	Code group	Task code text	Task text
	TSCO	QM-S2	Correction in the Warehouse	Inspection of delivered screws
	TSRL	QM-S2	Correction in the Warehouse	Sort the long screws from short
	TSRL	QM-G2	Return Delivery	Send the delivery back to vend...
	TSCO TSSC			Lagerbestand überprüfen
	TSCO TSSC	QM-S2	Correction in the Warehouse	Trocken lagern
	TSOS	PC	Send Technician	
	TSOS	PC	Send Spare Part	
	TSOS	PC	Send Technician	
	TSOS	PC	Send Spare Part	
	TSOS	PC	Send Repair Instructions	
	TSOS	PC	Send Technician	
	TSOS	PC	Send Spare Part	

Figure 8.56 Notification Tasks

6. **Monitor problems and actions.**
   After all the outstanding CAPAs have been processed and completed, and the solution has been approved by the problem initiator, communication to other interested parties may be required, after which the notification can be com-

pleted. The quality coordinator might update any additional technical information during completion, such as the causes of the problem and recorded
defects, as well as the end date and malfunction time. Coordinators can monitor the stock of outstanding notifications using several available worklists.

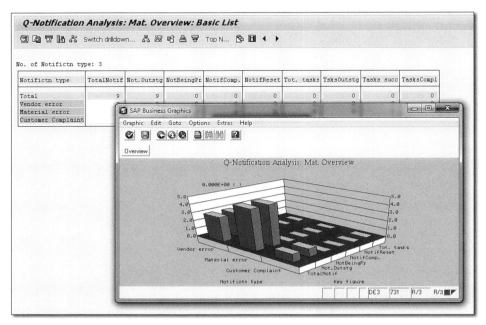

Figure 8.57 QMIS Report

Quality managers will want to evaluate notification data. To do this, they can
use the Quality Management Information System (QMIS), which allows you to
perform the following QM analytics:

▶ Compare the frequency of similar notifications and defects for different
reference objects (e.g., with reference to different materials, vendors, or
customers) to infer the main problem sources. Figure 8.57 shows an example of the frequencies of a specific problem category.

▶ Analyze the recorded defects and monitor the correction of these problems
by checking that the CAPAs have been followed up within the established
time frames.

▶ Evaluate the problem data. You can, for example, perform a Pareto analysis
of the most frequent defect types and defect causes, or perform a Pareto

analysis of the materials and business partners most frequently affected by problems to find main problems and starting points for improvements.

▷ Perform exception analyses, which identify apparent exceptional situations related to the problem and thereby provide impetuses for defect prevention and improvement tasks.

Apart from using the QMIS, you can use additional reporting tools, such as SAP NetWeaver BW or SAP BusinessObjects BI, or both, which can be used with the activation of QM-specific content. Notification data can be analyzed with SAP BusinessObjects BI, in which advanced evaluation tools are available to quality managers. Chapter 9 discusses this in more detail.

Quality improvement was the last topic to be discussed as part of product quality management. We'll continue with product change management within the respective ECM component and explore its master data objects and business scenario for product changes.

8.2   Product Change Management

Product change management represents the definition and efficient management of engineering changes to ensure that your product data is up to date (i.e., representing the latest changes) and that product quality in all phases of the product lifecycle is met. Product change management is addressed by the SAP PLM component Engineering Change Management (ECM) (also available within SAP ERP). It includes all types of changes (e.g., form, fit, and function) with processes and procedures that manage how changes are proposed, reviewed, approved, and incorporated into a product and its associated data items. Change control is a part of an overall configuration management methodology and uses review and release processes to enforce compliance with company change policies.

Figure 8.58 shows the end-to-end process for continuous product change and transformation. This process provides the means to proactively manage all product changes before product information is handed over to supply chain operations (manufacturing, procurement, service/maintenance, recalls, etc.) along with workflows and full visibility of impact when changes are initiated from supply chain operations. It shows in the four different columns the four main processes with their business owner:

▶ **Change initiation**
Owned by all business owners or lines of business (LOB).

▶ **Change investigation**
Owned by engineering and research and development (R&D).

▶ **Change audit and approval**
Owned by all LOBs.

▶ **Change implementation**
Again, owned by all LOBs.

The rows include the individual LOBs.

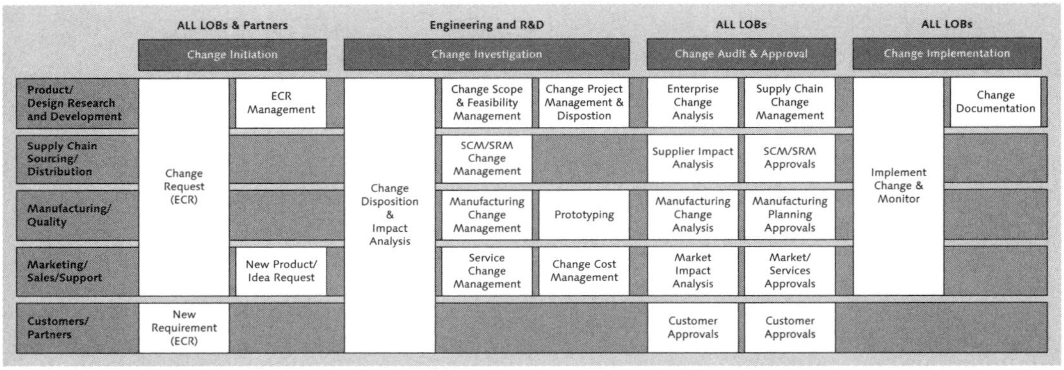

	ALL LOBs & Partners		Engineering and R&D		ALL LOBs		ALL LOBs	
	Change Initiation		Change Investigation		Change Audit & Approval		Change Implementation	
Product/ Design Research and Development	Change Request (ECR)	ECR Management	Change Disposition & Impact Analysis	Change Scope & Feasibility Management	Change Project Management & Dispostion	Enterprise Change Analysis	Supply Chain Change Management	Implement Change & Monitor	Change Documentation
Supply Chain Sourcing/ Distribution				SCM/SRM Change Management		Supplier Impact Analysis	SCM/SRM Approvals		
Manufacturing/ Quality				Manufacturing Change Management	Prototyping	Manufacturing Change Analysis	Manufacturing Planning Approvals		
Marketing/ Sales/Support		New Product/ Idea Request		Service Change Management	Change Cost Management	Market Impact Analysis	Market/ Services Approvals		
Customers/ Partners	New Requirement (ECR)					Customer Approvals	Customer Approvals		

Figure 8.58 End-to-End Process of Continuous Product Change and Transformation

The following business goals and objectives can be achieved by implementing ECM:

▶ Results in increased customer satisfaction, service, and delivery with last-minute changes by reducing product errors, constantly improving product quality, and capturing product changes easily and quickly.

▶ Satisfies the requirement to document and monitor the change process by including the change history of the affected object with a "before" and "after" status to ensure consistency of products. It includes the ability to specify that changes are only effective under defined conditions (via effectivity parameters) and the ability to group changes that belong together.

▶ Integrates to the logistics value chain where changes can automatically be performed to a sales order, MRP settings, or product details based on a release key.

- Ensures that all people affected by the changes—including data consumers—are involved in the change process. The change process can be flexibly configured to cater for specific business requirements, which can optionally use workflow-driven tasks. ECM is a centerpiece of the SAP PLM solution.

- Increases speed and efficiency by reducing time-to-market and volume. Some organizations see up to a 50% reduction in the change cycle time because change notifications are checked quickly (to trigger the appropriate follow-up activities such as approvals via workflow), and data consumers can be involved in the approval process.

- Increases transparency and accountability for the secure and reproducible change process for the package of all objects affected by the change, which provides a single source of truth. Parallel processing of changes is possible due to optimal use of change packages.

- Reduces operating costs and increases efficiency by reducing product returns, reducing rework required on production orders, and providing seamless, rule-based transfer of product structure changes to operative production order via order change management (OCM). Data accuracy improves because changes can be easily controlled, monitored, and viewed via SAP DMS integration, which includes providing feedback directly in context, for example, by using redlining.

- Reduces time to volume due to the phased release of the ECO to subsequent areas.

8.2.1 Master Data Objects Used for ECM

The main objects used within ECM are the *engineering change record* (ECR) and the *engineering change order* (ECO). But before we describe those, we need to quickly address the difference between validity by time or by parameters.

Validity Parameters

Both these objects are used to capture the change information; they can be either created with a validity time frame or with an effectivity type. An *effectivity type* determines the valid conditions under which object changes are valid. Standard SAP delivers the effectivity type SERNR (serial number), allowing you to make the change relevant to a certain range of serial numbers. This is done by assigning the parameters material number of parameter type S (single value) and serial number of parameter type O (open interval) to it. So when you assign effectivity type SERNR, you must include the relevant material number and the serial number start and end numbers of the range affected by the change. You can freely define your own relevant effectivity type and assign your own defined parameters based on fields within SAP (some common examples are the definition of a product model range, customer, or a combination of the two).

You can process the following objects with reference to a change number whose validity is defined by an effectivity type:

- BOMs
- Routings
- Characteristics
- Characteristics of class
- Classification

Change Record

Figure 8.59 and Figure 8.60 show the structure of a change record, which consists of the change record itself, plus an independent object management record that is generated per assigned object. The change record header holds the reason for the change, the change validity dates and parameters, the possible affected objects (via object types), and the specific affected objects via objects. You can assign any relevant documents to the change record, and you can classify the change record via CA. Based on the change type, you can configure and restrict which specific objects can be assigned. The change record can be assigned to capture changes for the following type of objects:

- Product data, such as materials, BOMs, routing, iPPE product variant structure (PVS), and process structure and supporting documents. Revisions can be used as part of the change process when updating material, BOM, and routings information.
- Variant configuration data such as the configuration profile, object dependencies, variant tables, and other CA data.
- Recipe development and Recipe Management.
- SAP Environment, Health, and Safety Management (SAP EHS Management) data, such as specifications, phrases, dangerous goods, and labeling.

For complex product changes, you can set up and use a hierarchy of change masters, which includes a leading change master with different change packages.

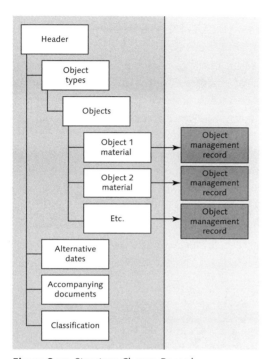

Figure 8.59 Structure Change Record

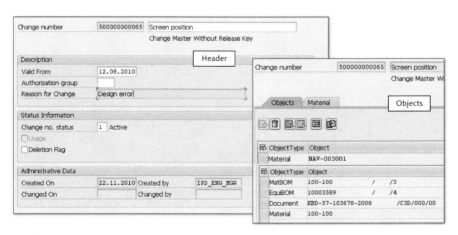

Figure 8.60 Change Record

Engineering Change Request and Engineering Change Order

When you require a process for change management to cater to multiple departments with a clear request stage and change stage, then you should implement the engineering change request and order (ECR/ECO). When using the ECR/ECO objects, you can use the standard available workflows (which allow people to receive email notification when they are required to perform an activity, such as approving the request) and the approval of changes either with or without the use of digital signatures. Technically, the ECR is the same record as the change record, created via the same transactions and using the same structure. The only difference is that the ECR requires the use and assignment of the change type. The change type is tightly integrated with the follow-up processes, workflow, and status management. Figure 8.61 shows the initial creation screen of an ECR, which shows an extensive list of the change types that have been configured within this environment.

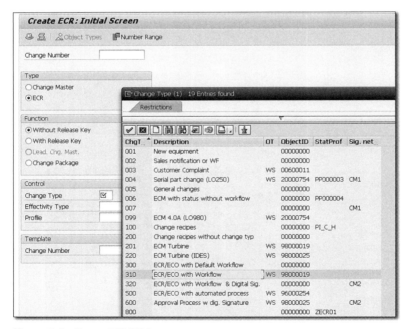

Figure 8.61 Create ECR/ECO

The ECR/ECO are represented in SAP as one object. The flow of the change record and change order are represented in Figure 8.62, which is further explained in this section. You start the change process by generating an ECR. After you've added and checked the affected objects, it can be approved, and the request gets converted into an ECO. During the check of the affected object, which is done via the created object change masters who are automatically created per assigned object (same as for the change request), you can choose one of the following three options:

▸ **Change possible**
Choose when the object can be changed.

▸ **Change unnecessary**
Choose when no changes are required to this added object.

▸ **Change impossible**
Means that the object affected can't be changed, and the object will be blocked and won't allow change, even when the request is approved

Only after this status has been reached can the affected objects be changed. After the changes to all the objects have been completed, the ECO can be completed and released. The system statuses the ECR/ECO and the object change master need to go through have also been included in Figure 8.62. As system statuses, these can't be changed, but they can be supplemented with your own user statuses.

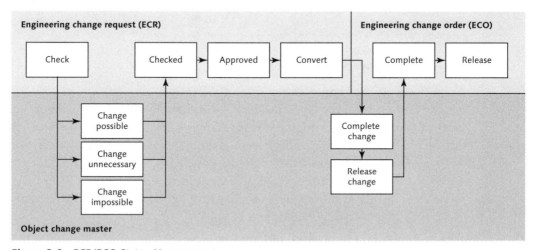

Figure 8.62 ECR/ECO Status Management

8.2.2 Business Scenario for Change and Configuration Management

This following business scenario for change and configuration management is designed for all industries. It results in efficient management of engineering changes for the extended enterprise, which potentially provides significant value—especially in the areas of reduced cycle times and increased customer satisfaction. It shows how engineers and central configuration management work together with the customer (either external or internal) who requires a change, to allow changes to product master data. Note that the business scenario shown in Figure 8.63 uses the ECR/ECO as the object for change, but a cut-down version of the scenario could be implemented (all but the workflow, approval, and digital signature steps) when using the change master.

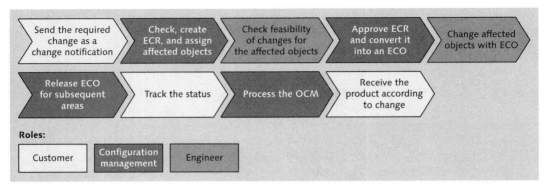

Figure 8.63 Business Scenario Change and Configuration Management

Let's walk through each of these steps:

1. **Send the required change as a change notification.**
   On the first optional level, you need an object that is used to report all kinds of issues that might lead to an engineering change. The object change notification can be used for this purpose; it's designed for external or occasional users who seek an easy way to report issues on the web. After the external partners or internal colleagues report an issue, it's changed to a change request notification, when it relates to a request for changing a product or its related master data, such as BOMs, documents, and so on.

2. **Check, create ECR, and assign affected objects.**
   The change notification is then routed by workflow to the responsible configuration management agent, who uses the change notification to check the issue

and to decide on appropriate follow-up activities. If the decision is made that an engineering change is necessary, an ECR is created and linked to the change notification. The ECR includes the link to the affected objects. You can use the integrated product structure browser to drag and drop the affected objects into the ECR, as shown in Figure 8.64.

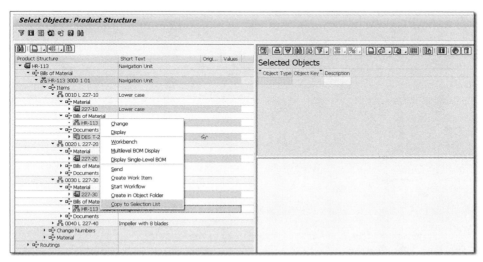

Figure 8.64 Select Objects from the Product Structure

3. **Check feasibility of changes for the affected objects.**

   Now that the internal change process for the selected objects has started, the workflow of the feasibility study is routed to the responsible person(s) and/or departments who perform the study, see Figure 8.65, step 1. A feasibility study is performed to check whether the affected objects can be changed; if the result is positive, they are flagged CHANGE POSSIBLE in the relating object management records (see Figure 8.65, step 2).

4. **Approve the ECR and convert it into an ECO.**

   The internal change process is started by the use of the workflow, which allows all the approvers to receive an item automatically. The workflow item can be used to approve the change and, when setup, the approval can be accompanied with a digital signature such as the one shown at the bottom of Figure 8.66. SAP ECM supports digital signatures at both the change header level as well as at the object management record level.

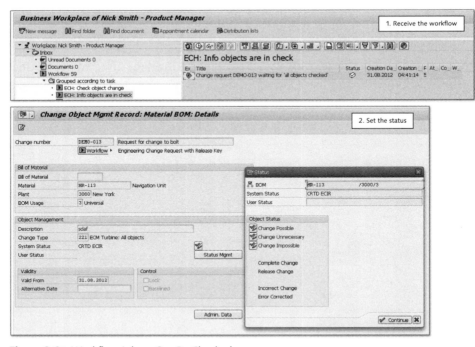

Figure 8.65 Workflow Inbox: Can Be Checked

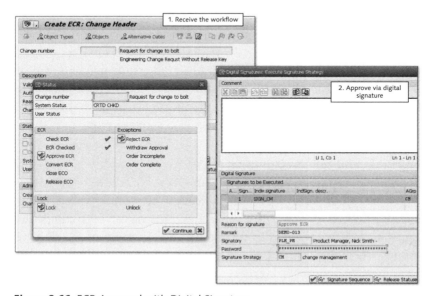

Figure 8.66 ECR Approval with Digital Signature

5. **Change the affected objects with ECO.**

   Make the appropriate changes to the affected object either from the ECO or by updating the object and including the change number, as shown in the BOM item update in Figure 8.67. You can also see that the change number is recorded against the changed BOM item, which is done for most changed objects via a change order, with the exception of CA.

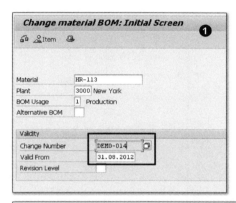

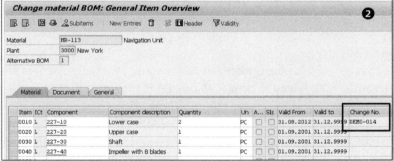

Figure 8.67 Change Object with ECR

6. **Release the ECO for subsequent areas.**

   You can release changes to any subsequent areas affected, such as maintenance or costing.

7. **Track the status.**

   Via the change order, you can always get the latest view of the status of the change and further process any organizational change management steps if required. When all changes are done and executed, the change request can be closed as Figure 8.68 shows. The recently introduced Transaction CCUNDO lets you undo any changes implemented via ECM so you can backtrack and undo changes for some objects if you have the appropriate authorization (object C_AENR_BGR, activity 85).

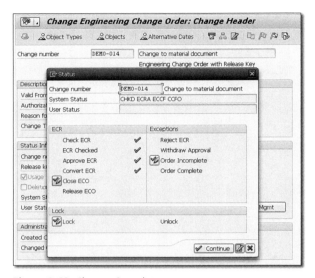

Figure 8.68 Change Complete

8. **Process the OCM.**
When your change includes the updates of outstanding production orders and any customer orders, you need to use OCM functions to update the production BOMs, sales order BOMs, and routings within these documents, which can be either started from the initiator, sales order, or production order offered with the Transactions COCM (Initiating Object Records) and COCM1 (Procurement Element Change Records) within production.

9. **Receive the product according to change.**
The customer will receive an update of the approved changes and will receive the product as promised.

8.3   Summary

This chapter introduced you to the QM master data objects, which are important during processes relevant for ensuring product quality. First the logistics general master data were introduced, including the material, customer, vendor, batches,

Q-info record for sales and procurement, and quality certificates and quality documents. Next, the inspection planning master data was explained, covering the inspection plan, reference operation set, material specification, routing and task list, and master recipe. Finally, we discussed the quality planning master data elements, including the catalog, set, master inspection characteristics, class characteristics, inspection methods, sample master data, work centers, and PRT.

We continued with the business processes within QM, starting with quality engineering. First the Failure Mode and Effect Analysis (FMEA) and the setup of a control plan where described, which are both important business processes to eliminate or reduce product weaknesses and set up appropriate actions and controls. We then continued with how the FMEA and control plan are part of the closed-loop inspection planning processes, which ensures product quality from product idea, through to product development into operational quality control via inspection planning and complaint management.

Furthermore, the quality engineering process includes product development via a product development project with the appropriate quality gates and the execution of stability studies. This chapter also briefly touched on quality assurance and control, before going into the recording of any problems via the quality improvement process.

Finally, the chapter closed with ECM, where the change master or the engineering change request and order can be used to capture and manage the processes and steps involved when a product needs to be changed.

The next chapter introduces you to two topics that supplement SAP PLM. First we look into SAP Fleet Management and explore its three main supported fleet management areas. We'll consider the second topic, mobility, from two perspectives—the platforms available today and SAP's future direction to provide a single SAP Mobile Platform. We examine the different available mobile apps through which your business users can perform business activities such as recording a safety issue or entering a time sheet from a mobile device.

SAP Fleet Management provides a holistic solution to support all of the stages relevant to your company's transportation means. The SAP Mobile Platform extends the use of your business applications to mobile devices, giving employees access to important information anywhere, anytime, and from any device.

9   Relevant SAP PLM Additions

In this chapter, we'll offer an overview of two important topics—SAP Fleet Management and SAP Mobile Platform—that supplement the SAP Product Lifecycle Management (SAP PLM) components and aid in achieving product-related business goals. We'll cover the entire SAP Fleet Management solution, which allows you to manage your company's vehicle fleet, as well as discuss the SAP PLM-specific master data and processes. Then we'll address SAP Mobile Platform from an SAP PLM perspective, which, as one of SAP's main focus areas, promises to be an exciting topic. The acquisition of Sybase and Syclo—both companies with decades of experience with mobile solutions and SAP integration—has led to the substantial growth and improvement of the product portfolio in this area.

9.1   SAP Fleet Management

In general, *fleet management* is the management of a company's vehicle fleet, which covers all kinds of ground, air, and sea travel. As a solution, SAP Fleet Management includes a range of functions, such as vehicle financing, vehicle maintenance, vehicle telematics (tracking and diagnostics), driver management, speed management, fuel management, and safety management.

Note that SAP Fleet Management isn't a component or specific area of SAP PLM but is a solution that leverages functions from several components. Based on your requirements, you can choose which of these are relevant for you. For example, a transportation company with a mixture of owned and contracted trucks can implement the entire scope of the solution, while a utility company with only company-owned vehicles can just choose the administration and incident management capabilities.

Partial or complete implementation of SAP Fleet Management can produce the following benefits:

▸ Ensure highest safety for drivers, passengers, and vehicles.

▸ Track and trace vehicles.

▸ Optimize the use of vehicles.

▸ Remove or minimize the risks associated with vehicle investment.

▸ Improve efficiency and productivity by keeping vehicle utilization at optimal levels and maintaining low maintenance and operation costs.

▸ Reduce overall transportation and staff costs.

▸ Provide 100% compliance with government legislation.

▸ Reduce total costs by identifying and analyzing costs by d0istance traveled per car model, which informs the business on total cost of ownership (TCO) per car model.

▸ Identify and analyze costs.

▸ Offer decision support for repair or disposal.

▸ Support contract negotiations (lease or buy, discounts versus repair costs, etc.).

▸ Provide predictive maintenance with high availability for assets.

So where does SAP Fleet Management fit into the SAP Business Suite and SAP PLM? It leverages features and functions from several areas within the SAP Business Suite.

SAP Fleet Management leverages the following SAP PLM components:

▸ SAP Plant Maintenance (SAP PM)

▸ SAP Document Management System (SAP DMS)

▸ SAP Environmental, Health, and Safety Management (SAP EHS Management)

Other SAP ERP components that can be used include the following:

▸ SAP ERP Financial Accounting (FI) (especially the fixed-asset accounting sub-area)

▸ SAP ERP Controlling (CO)

- SAP Materials Management (SAP MM)
- SAP ERP Human Capital Management (SAP ERP HCM)

Fleet analytics are provided via the following:

- SAP PM standard reports, such as incident analysis, consumption analysis and so on.
- SAP NetWeaver BW
- SAP BusinessObjects BI, for which multiple queries and data sources have been specifically developed for SAP Fleet Management, such as the fleet attributes, query for liters fuel per 100 kilometers, cost per distance, and query for asset value at current depreciated price versus maintenance costs

SAP Fleet Management also leverages these resources outside SAP ERP and SAP PLM:

- SAP Customer Relationship Management (SAP CRM)
- SAP Supply Chain Management (SAP SCM)
- SAP Supply Chain Event Management
- SAP Transportation Management (TM)
- SAP Supplier Relationship Management (SAP SRM)

Technical additions leveraged from the SAP NetWeaver BW platform include workflows, Smart Forms, the latest SAP Enterprise Asset Management (SAP EAM) portal content, and service-oriented architecture (SOA) bundles (covered in Chapter 5, Section 5.6.6).

Analytics can be done via several SAP standard reports as delivered within SAP PLM and SAP ERP. However, SAP also delivers standard content for both SAP NetWeaver BW and SAP BusinessObjects BI. Figure 9.1 charts the SAP Fleet Management solution, using shading to offer insight into which features and functions are covered within SAP PLM, partly within SAP PLM, or outside SAP PLM. The inner ring illustrates where those tasks fall in relation to the main structural areas of SAP Fleet Management: administration, maintenance, and operations.

Let's begin our exploration of the SAP Fleet Management functionalities by addressing the functions that are covered by the administration structural area.

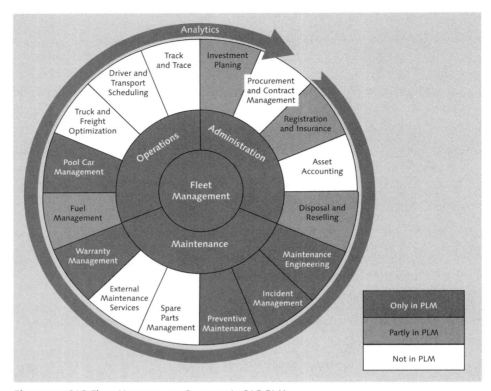

Figure 9.1 SAP Fleet Management Coverage in SAP PLM

9.1.1 Administration

The following functions fall under the administration structural area of SAP Fleet Management.

Investment Planning

Depending on the chosen financial investment planning solution, you can use the financial investment planning capabilities for fleets in SAP Strategy Management, SAP Project and Portfolio Management (PPM), SAP Investment Management, and SAP Project System (SAP PS) (as described in Chapter 2 and Chapter 7) from an SAP PLM perspective.

Apart from these SAP PLM solutions, other SAP products are often used for financial investment planning, which belong to FI—for example, SAP Business

Planning and Consolidation (SAP BPC) or SAP Strategic Enterprise Management (SAP SEM), which are outside the scope of this book.

Procurement and Contract Management

Procurement and contract management activities can be managed outside of SAP PLM, with the SAP MM Procurement standalone or in combination with SAP SRM. The following are the main procurement and contract management processes:

▶ Sourcing (plan, manage, qualify, negotiate, and create contracts)

▶ Procurement (request, order and receive goods or services, and settle costs)

▶ Analyzing supplier performance management and global spending analysis

▶ Demand aggregation strategy and planning and procurement strategy planning

▶ Supplier management with the ability to preselect suppliers, qualify suppliers, and, negotiate and award suppliers

▶ Contract-integrated document editing using Microsoft Office with SAP SRM contract management

▶ Spare part planning and buying (often using SAP Advanced Planning & Optimization [APO] for advanced planning capabilities)

Registration and Insurance

The fleet model in Figure 9.2 shows the master data elements (light), the transactional data (dark), and the analytics used by SAP Fleet Management. The arrows show how they are linked together; the supplementary areas or other areas aren't directly connected because they aren't directly linked to the vehicle. The elements are basically split into three separate areas:

▶ **Financial master data**
The financial fixed asset register is used from SAP FI–CO. We'll discuss the integration between assets and equipment further in the "SAP ERP Financials Asset Accounting" section.

▶ **Maintenance master data — technical vehicle details**
The equipment master specific for a fleet can be used, together with measurement points and measurement documents. Within the vehicle equipment, you can assign registrations using SAP DMS or by simply using the object link

function. See Section 9.1.3, which describes maintenance engineering master data in more detail.

▶ **Supplementary used master data**
Depending on the scope of your SAP Fleet Management solution, you'll need to use or create additional master data. Some examples have been included, such as the responsible cost center or profit center from CO, relevant payroll information relating to the use of a company car in SAP Payroll, or sales information regarding a contract or sales order in SAP Sales and Distribution (SD).

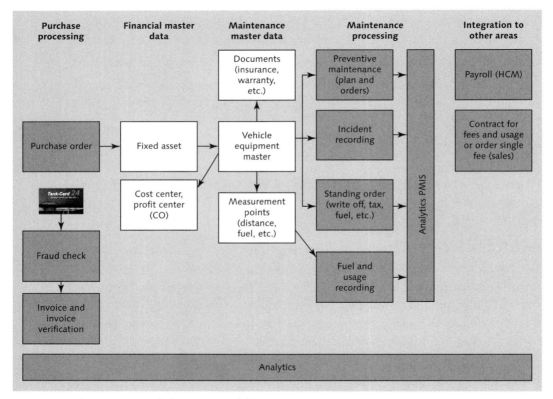

Figure 9.2 Typical Fleet Data Model

Maintenance Processing

A *cost collector* is required to capture all expenses and costs relevant for a specific vehicle to determine the TCO. Because costs can't directly be captured against the equipment vehicle master record, a *maintenance order* is created for this purpose.

To collect costs incurred from the vehicle's commissioning to its decommissioning, you'll create a work order for the duration of the expected life of a vehicle and assign it to the vehicle. This concept is called a *standing SAP Plant Maintenance order* and is often used to collect all the planned (or more static/upfront) costs, such as vehicle registration, insurance costs, and fuel. After the work order is released, it can be used for cost planning or cost collection. Often this happens through the procurement process or via financial invoices assigned to the order. See Chapter 5, Section 5.6.5, for more details on this process.

To perform consumption analytics as part of fuel entry, you must enter the required measurements either through the dedicated fuel entry transaction (Transaction IFCU, which lets you also set up tolerances) or via the general measurement document collection transactions (such as Transaction IK11), as described in Chapter 5, Section 5.6.6.

To differentiate and capture *unplanned costs,* such as unplanned maintenance activities or accidents/incidents, you can use the standard corrective maintenance process, which starts with a maintenance notification and is followed by the order, and so on. When you want to use the vehicle-specific object information in the header of the work order (this will be shown later in Figure 9.14), you might want to set up a specific order type for this. *Preventive maintenance costs* are collected by using the preventive maintenance process, which ensures that all vehicle-related costs flow through the maintenance component so you can collect and report from it.

You can use the information captured through the standing order, corrective maintenance processing, and preventive maintenance processing to make informed investment decisions about replacing or repairing a vehicle or group of vehicles; this is offered by an Enterprise Service Repository (ESR) within SAP NetWeaver called repair versus replace. When you decide that replacing is required, the analytics help decide to either lease vehicles or buy and manage them in-house. Analytics are also available in the Plant Maintenance Information System (PMIS) and the SAP BusinessObjects BI reports available for replace or repair decision making.

Equipment Master

The following are prerequisites to using SAP PM technical objects for SAP Fleet Management:

▶ Configuration to set up of a vehicle-specific equipment category and the required vehicle types (including the view profiles and fuel types)

▶ Setup of the classification for the measurements recorded against the vehicle (master data)

The following are optional:

▶ Configuration for the usage types, oil types, engine types, and the settings required to perform consumption calculations for all data kept about the vehicle

▶ Warranties information

You can create the fleet object in SAP PM as an equipment master via Transaction IE31 (Create Vehicle transaction), which directly requests the vehicle category and the vehicle type. Technically, these are the same fields as the equipment category and the object type as described in Chapter 5, Section 5.5.1. The fleet-specific information is maintained in two additional tabs. VEHICLE ID/MEASMNTS contains the common vehicle attributes, such as the vehicle type and license plate (see Figure 9.3). VEHICLE TECHNOLOGY contains the technical details of the vehicle, such as the vehicle's make, model, engine details, fuel type split into primary fuel and secondary fuel, and other lubricants like oil used (see Figure 9.4).

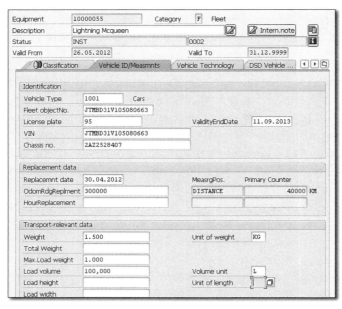

Figure 9.3 Vehicle ID/Measurements Tab

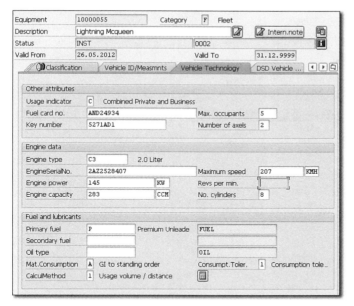

Figure 9.4 Vehicle Technology Tab

The FUEL AND LUBRICANTS area of the VEHICLE TECHNOLOGY tab provides you access to the consumption details of the vehicle (accessible via the calculator button), of which Figure 9.5 is an example. Based on the calculation method assigned, the system will automatically calculate a short consumption (the past three months) and long-term consumption (the past year). Consumption can be set up and defined based on your own requirements, but one of the following two options are often set up:

▶ **Fuel usage over distance**
The liters of fuel used per 100 kilometers or number of gallons used per mile is calculated. This method requires that you collect fuel and odometer readings.

▶ **Fuel usage over time**
The amount of fuel used is divided over time—that is, liter per hour or gallon per hour. This method requires that you collect the fuel and the operating hours.

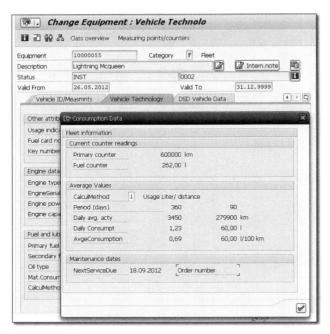

Figure 9.5 Consumption

Measurement Points

To calculate the consumption, you need to capture information on the vehicles' fuel use, distance traveled, or operating hours. This can be done by the setup of a measurement point, as was discussed in Chapter 5, Section 5.3.5. The only difference is that for it to be picked up and used by the formula defined in configuration for consumption, you must also assign the measurement position used within the formula (which is configured in Customizing) to the measurement point, as shown in Figure 9.6. To record vehicle consumption data, you can choose to either use the standard transactions available for capturing measurement documents (such as Transaction IK11) or use the fleet-specific transaction for vehicle consumption (Transaction IFCU). Using Transaction IFCU allows you to check tolerances and to consume fuel from internal fuel depots or as identified within SAP as gas stations.

SAP PM also offers the ability to run a vehicle report (Transaction IE36) or use the change vehicle report to update a group of vehicles (Transaction IE37). It provides all the necessary selection criteria. Figure 9.7 shows an example of the selection and list display.

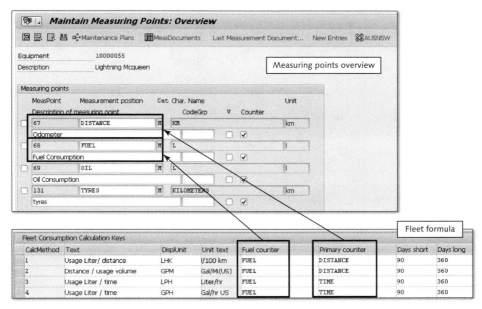

Figure 9.6 Measuring Points and Assignment to Consumption

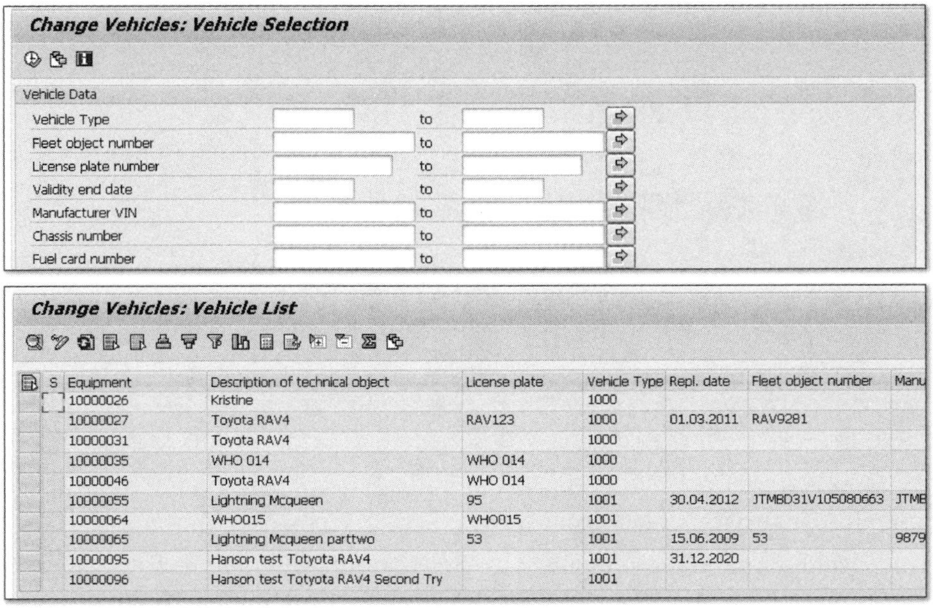

Figure 9.7 List Display for Vehicles

Assigning Documents

You can use SAP DMS to store electronic documents for the vehicle, such as its car insurance or registration (see Figure 9.8).

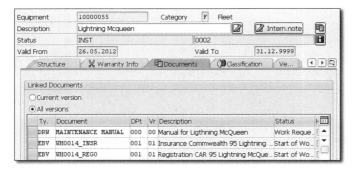

Figure 9.8 Vehicle with Assigned Documents

When you don't use SAP DMS, use another external document management system, or want to reference documents available through a website, you can use the object link function (shown in Figure 9.9), which is available in the vehicle master through the OBJECT LINKS button. Using this function leads to the hyperlinks (or, as SAP calls them, object links) that become available against the vehicle master.

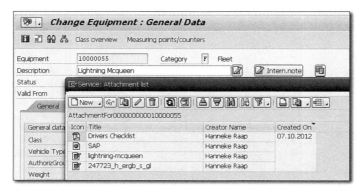

Figure 9.9 Equipment Object Link

SAP ERP Financials Asset Accounting

The integration from the equipment (or functional location) to the fixed asset register is the same as described in Chapter 5, Section 5.3.5. But let's briefly reexamine SAP ERP Financials Asset Accounting (FI–AA) because within SAP Fleet

Management, the relationship between the vehicle master record and the financial asset is often 1:1, allowing you to use extensive synchronization.

Fixed Asset Register

Apart from the assignment of the fixed asset in the ORGANIZATION tab (which contains the asset values and depreciation details), you can also assign other DF structure data. This FI structure data is shown in Figure 9.10, where the arrows show you how they are linked. The equipment or functional location belongs by its assignment to the plant, to a specific company code, a controlling area, and a business area. Furthermore, within the record you assign the cost center that is responsible for the vehicle and assign the fixed asset belonging to the vehicle. The cost center can be part of a cost center hierarchy and/or part of a cost center group, both of which are used within CO. The fixed asset within FI belongs to a specific asset class and can be assigned to an asset group. Within this area, you can also assign the standing work order, which is used in the fleet data model to capture the reoccurring costs.

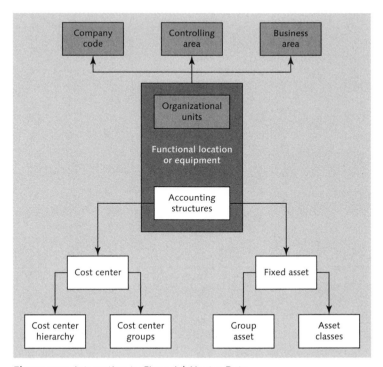

Figure 9.10 Integration to Financial Master Data

Figure 9.11 shows an example of assigning an equipment asset to an account.

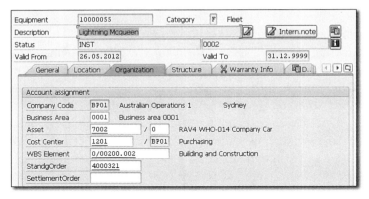

Figure 9.11 Equipment Assignment to Financial Data

When you have the authorization to do so, you can double-click on the financial asset record to get access to the financial assets, asset values, depreciation details, and useful life information (see Figure 9.12).

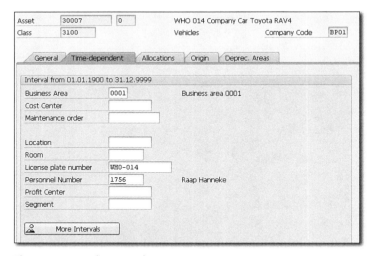

Figure 9.12 Fixed Asset Values

Synchronization

To ensure that the correct equipment is assigned to the asset, you can set up automatic synchronization, which can be activated for the combination of asset class with equipment category or asset class equipment category with object type.

You can set it up and activate it from the assets perspective, which, after an asset is created or edited, will look at the synchronization rules and behave accordingly. The other option is to activate it from the equipment's perspective, which after the equipment is created or changed, looks at the synchronization rules and performs its action. The following synchronizations can be set up either during the create action or when changing the master record:

▶ **Direct synchronization after saving**
When the asset master record is created, the system automatically creates and assigns an equipment record in the asset master record and automatically synchronizes relevant fields (e.g., company code) using the assigned equipment category and object type (when configured—this isn't required), or vice versa. As soon as an equipment master is created, an asset record is created, assigned, and synched with the asset class assigned to the equipment category.

▶ **Direct synchronization plus workflow**
The system synchronizes the master data and also triggers a workflow to a responsible person to notify them of and allow them to check the changes made.

▶ **Saving triggers a workflow**
Master data isn't synchronized; instead, a workflow is triggered, allowing the responsible person to be informed of the changes and then make adjustments, when required.

▶ **No synchronization**
No synchronization takes place. The master data needs to be created independently and manually assigned to one another.

Let's use an example of synchronization to reinforce the concept. Say you assign asset class 3100 (Vehicles) to equipment category F (Fleet) and choose SAVING TRIGGERS A WORKFLOW for creating equipment and DIRECT SYNCHRONIZATION AFTER SAVING for changing equipment under EDIT ASSET MASTER RECORD. The system will just create a master data shell, which still needs to be enriched by a master data specialist.

When you create an asset in asset class 3100 with cost center 1000, the system first starts a workflow event because you made the setting SAVING TRIGGERS A WORKFLOW for creating equipment. If you've set up a suitable workflow, and this is executed, the system automatically creates an equipment master record in category M (also with cost center 1000). The system enters the number of the asset in the equipment master record. In addition, it enters the direct synchronization after saving the setting as the synchronization mode. If you change the cost center in the asset master record to 4110 later, the system directly synchronizes the equipment master record—that is, the cost center is changed to 4110 there as well because the synchronization mode Direct synchronization after saving was set.

Customers implementing the SAP Fleet Management solution often use direct synchronization because the relationship between the asset class and the equipment category and object type is often one-to-one. The unique assignment in both directions ensures that the system is always able to determine the right asset class and the right equipment category (and object type). That is, you shouldn't assign the same combination of equipment category and object type to more than one asset class. Otherwise, when you create the equipment master record, direct synchronization won't be possible because the system can't uniquely determine the asset class.

Several existing fleet customers even take the integration one step further, where the procurement process based on an item with a material uses the goods receipt processes to automatically create the equipment master via reference equipment. This also creates the appropriate measurement points, and an asset master is created based on the equipment category. This method requires minimal adjustment based on a customer exit.

When multiple equipment masters are assigned to the same asset, SAP cautions against using direct synchronization; instead, use the workflow option for better control of which changes lead to which updates.

Most customers who use this synchronization find that the number of fields available to be synchronized is limited. This is because the asset master allows you to record certain time-dependent data, such as the cost center, as you can see in Figure 9.13. You can make changes to time-dependent data that may not actually take effect until a future date. In equipment master data, on the other hand, changes to master data are immediately effective on the day the change is made; changes effective in the future aren't supported. For this reason, the synchronization reflects only data valid on the given day. Remember that direct synchronization means that each time there is a change to the assigned master record, this results in the transfers of all attributes relevant to the synchronization. For more information, on sample workflows provided by SAP for synchronization, refer to SAP Note 370884 and related notes.

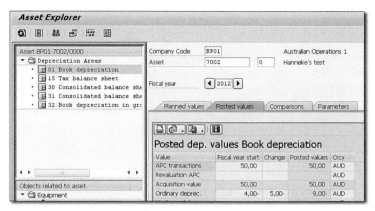

Figure 9.13 Asset Time-Dependent Data

Disposal and Reselling

The last function that falls under administration is the disposal and reselling of a vehicle. At the end of the vehicle's useful life, you can either decide to dispose of it by eselling it or by throwing it out. You can capture this by changing the status of the equipment to Deactivate and notifying the accounting department either via automatically triggered workflow or the manual process steps. You can capture whether the equipment was sold or disposed of via a user status. When you decide to throw out the vehicle, you can use SAP Waste and Recycling as described in Chapter 6, Section 6.1.6.

Fleet managers often want insight in the revenue of the sale of the vehicle so they can include this value as part of the TCO of their fleet. The sale of the vehicle can be captured via a sales order process in SD or SAP CRM, where you can offer your vehicle for sale and then create a sales order with sales price information, a delivery, and a customer invoice. However, if this isn't an active process (or not a core business activity), you can simply record the revenue using a financial journal or an invoice. Whichever solution you use to make the revenue visible on the vehicle, you have to book the revenue toward the standing work order covered in the administration structural area.

9.1.2 Maintenance

The following functions fall under the maintenance structural area of SAP Fleet Management.

Maintenance Engineering

By using SAP PM or SAP Customer Service (SAP CS), you can capture and record the information required to apply engineering concepts to the optimization of equipment, procedures, and departmental budgets to achieve better vehicle maintainability, reliability, and availability. The upcoming topics give with fleet specifics, which, together with Chapter 5, should provide you with the entire maintenance engineering solution. We'll continue with incident management.

Incident Management

You can use the corrective process described in Chapter 5, Section 5.5.7 to capture vehicle incidents. To distinguish fleet incidents from other corrective maintenance activities, often specific fleet notification type(s) are configured with their own specific layouts and their own specific content via catalogs. A dedicated notification type for the fleet also allows you to use the fleet-specific reference object, which can be made available within both the notification and the maintenance order header, shown in Figure 9.14.

Figure 9.14 Notification Reference object Fleet

Preventive Maintenance

You can use the preventive maintenance process described in Chapter 5, Section 5.5.9, for the fleet-specific preventive maintenance process. To capture the more complex maintenance regimes used within the automotive industry, often the multiple counter plan is used in combination with the cycle set sequence. This combination is very similar to the strategy plan, in which you can distinguish different activities to be performed. The only difference is that the multiple counter plan is able to look at two separate counters or triggers as opposite to just the one from the strategy plan and works sequential and gets reset after each service. For example, this allows you to capture the strategy to perform a small service every year or every 12,500 miles and a large service every three years or after 37,000 miles (or 12,500 miles from the last small service).

Spare Parts Management

You can use the spare parts process described in Chapter 5, Section 5.5.4 for fleet-specific spare parts. In addition to this process, the comprehensive processes offered through SAP SCM, APO services, spare part planning, and logistics can be adopted (which was included in Chapter 2, Figure 2.93).

External Maintenance Services

The external maintenance services process described in Chapter 5, Section 5.3.5 can be used for external maintenance services, such as performing a car service or exchanging a tire.

Warranty Management

Warranty can be used for warranty services, such a servicing the car within the warranty period or replacing a spare part.

9.1.3 Operations

The last structural area of SAP Fleet Management is operations. Let's examine each functionality.

Fuel Management

Fuel management consists of two separate areas:

▸ **Consumption data**
Information on the latest odometer and the amount of fuel pumped at the station.

▸ **Costs**
The amount paid for the fuel. This can be an internal charge, when the fuel is consumed from an internal gas station or an external charge, when the fuel is consumed from an external gas station. The internal charge happens because SAP uses the Inventory Management (IM–MM) capabilities and books the stock—the amount of fuel tanked—against the standing work order. When externally bought, the fuel costs need to be booked against the work order by a procurement process (SAP SRM or SAP MM) or a financial booking (FI–CO).

Often both steps can be done by uploading data received from fuel companies via an interface automatically into the system.

Pool Car Management

A group of vehicles are collected in a *pool*. Pool asset management (PAM) is a business process within SAP Fleet Management that is adopted from the SAP PM and SAP CS area. It supports the internal rental process of a group of assets or, specifically within fleet management, a pool. The process was described briefly in Chapter 5, Section 5.6.3, but we'll expand upon that coverage here by providing some SAP Fleet Management context and screenshots.

From an SAP Fleet Management perspective, PAM allows you to set up a group of vehicles and lend it for a limited amount of time to your employees. In a nutshell, those employees request a vehicle, selecting specifications via the request form; the pool scheduler assigns the most appropriate available vehicle. On the start day of the loan period, the requester picks up the vehicle, at which time details such as the odometer reading can be registered. After the loan period, the requester returns the vehicle, and the odometer reading is registered again. Based on the loan period, the cost of use can be charged to the requester via a cost center or project (e.g., the department's cost center or the NPDI project number P-1001).

Of course, before you can use the PAM process, you have to set up the pool. The pool of cars (see Figure 9.15) is represented by a functional location (top element); the cars themselves are represented within the system as equipment/vehicle masters (lower levels) installed within the pool functional location.

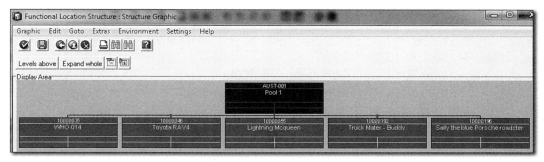

Figure 9.15 Vehicle Pool

Let's walk through the PAM process with a focus on the vehicle-specific content (see Figure 9.16).

Figure 9.16 Process of Pool Asset Management

1. **Create the request.**

   The person who requires the use of a pool asset (or an administrator) can generate a request to make her requirements known to the pool manager. She can specify when she needs the vehicle by using the from and to dates and time, and she can specify details about the desired vehicle (e.g., the number of possible passengers or transmission type).

   You'll use the notification document within SAP PM to record the request; that notification document should be configured to have the PAM details activated. Figure 9.17 shows an example of a request made by Jocelyn Dart for a vehicle to be used in September; on the right side are the details of the requested vehicle, such as an automatic transmission and a passenger minimum of one person.

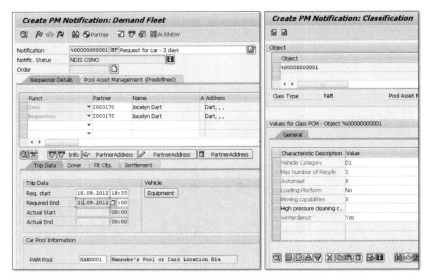

Figure 9.17 Create Request

2. **Perform scheduling.**

   The pool manager sees all the vehicles managed within the pool in the top half of the planning board, followed by all the vehicle requests in the bottom screen, as shown in Figure 9.18. The requests and assignments have different colors so the planner can see the status immediately when the planning board is displayed. The standard planning board uses white for outstanding requests, yellow for assigned requests, and gray for finished requests.

   From within the graphical planning board, the pool manager can reserve a vehicle for the requested time frame by dragging the request to the available vehicle. Then an automatic workflow can be emailed to the requester with the confirmation of this reservation and the details needed for collection (e.g., the pickup location or other accommodating instructions). Figure 9.19 shows an example of this express workflow message.

3. **Issue the asset.**

   When the requester comes and collects the vehicle, the hand-off and any additional information needed for cost collection can be recorded. When you use the actual driven miles or kilometers, you need to record the odometer reading of the vehicle at the time of collection for the system to calculate the rate per distance. This can be done by right-clicking the reservation and the vehicle issue, as shown in Figure 9.20.

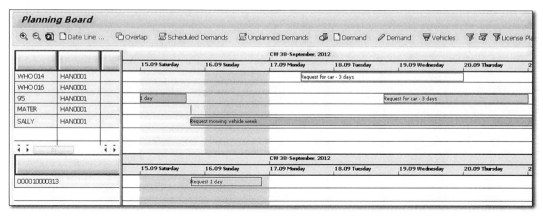

Figure 9.18 Graphical Planning Board

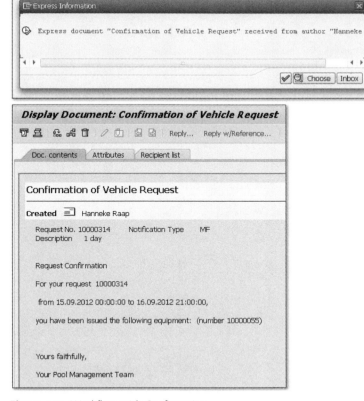

Figure 9.19 Workflow with Confirmation

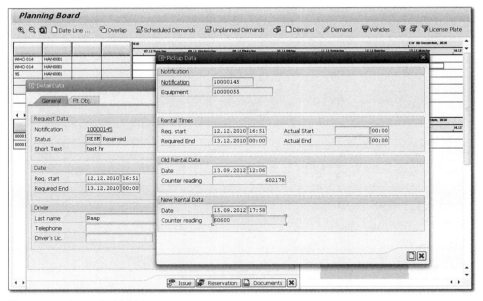

Figure 9.20 Issue the Vehicle

4. **Return the asset.**

When the requester returns the vehicle, this again can be recorded in the system, including additional information needed for cost collection (see Figure 9.21).

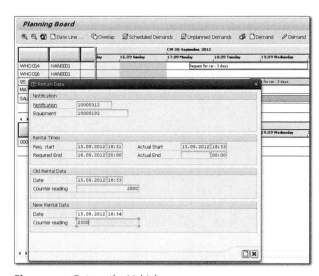

Figure 9.21 Return the Vehicle

5. **Settle the cost.**

Based on the rental conditions, you can charge the cost of the rental period to the asset requester. This process is done through settlement to the chosen cost object, such as the requester department's cost center or the project code and WBS element, for which the requester works. Figure 9.22 shows an example of the settlement process steps, by which the cost center is charged based on the distance driven during the rental period and the rates configured.

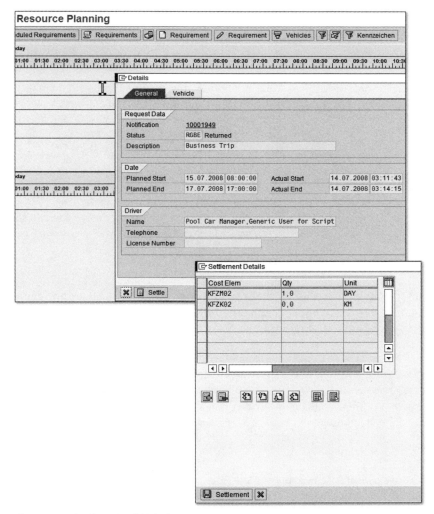

Figure 9.22 Settlement of Vehicle Use

Driver and Transport Scheduling

The assignment of the driver to the vehicle can be done using one of the standard methods in SAP PM or SAP CS shown in Table 9.1.

Method	Details
Assign the driver to the equipment master using a partner role representing the driver.	You need to add the role driver in configuration, where you can choose how the role is defined (e.g., using the user name or employee number). The driver allocation isn't done with a time frame, which might cause problems when drivers switch vehicles frequently and you have to support the handling of infringements notices.
Set up functional locations with drivers, and install and dismantle the vehicles to the drivers.	This method requires additional master data maintenance efforts; however, assignment is done with a time frame. Performing install and dismantling equipment within a technical structure was described in detail in Chapter 5, Section 5.5.2.
Use the ADDITIONAL tab in combination with the user exit to add the driver and time frame.	Apart from these standard methods, you can also use the ADDITIONAL tab and user exit ITOB0003 to add driver details and a time frame, but this method requires both configuration and the adjustment of the user exits.

Table 9.1 Driver Assignment Methods in SAP PM/SAP CS

Another possibility is driver assignment from other non-PLM SAP components, as described in Table 9.2. Choose which one would be most appropriate for your SAP Fleet Management solution based on your scope and your specific customer requirements.

Component	Function	Prerequisites and Restrictions
FI asset register	Within the time frame-specific information of the asset, you can assign a personnel number.	Standard functionality requires the use of Financial Fixed Asset, where the used asset class has the option of entering the personnel number.

Table 9.2 Driver Assignment Methods outside SAP PLM

Component	Function	Prerequisites and Restrictions
SAP ERP HCM	You can assign an asset to the personnel number via either infotype 0032 (Internal Data) or via infotype 0040 (Objects on Loan).	Requires the use of SAP ERP HCM personnel management, including the setup of the infotypes mentioned. Figure 9.23 shows an example of infotype 0032 (Internal Data).
SAP ERP HCM	Assign the asset to your personnel number via the Portal via Employee Self Service	Requires the use of HR, the SAP NetWeaver Portal, and the Employee Self-Service (ESS) scenario.
SAP SCM	Assign a vehicle to the driver and to logistics information such as deliveries, transportation routes, partners, and so on.	This can be done in the following solutions, among others: ▸ SD ▸ SAP Direct Store Delivery (SAP DSD) ▸ TM within APO ▸ SAP Event Management

Table 9.2 Driver Assignment Methods outside SAP PLM (Cont.)

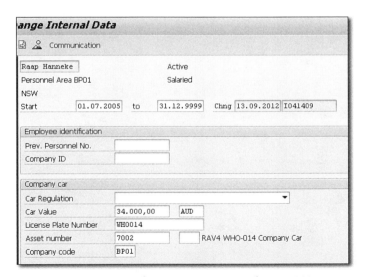

Figure 9.23 Assignment of Company Car Using Infotype 0032

Transport scheduling is a business process outside the SAP PLM scope, but again is part of SAP SCM, which is described in the next section.

Transport Scheduling and Truck and Freight Optimization

The truck and freight optimization business process isn't part of the SAP PLM scope, but it's part of the SAP SCM Solution Map (which was included in Chapter 2, Figure 2.93), and more details can be found in the following process categories, among others:

▶ **Order fulfillment**
This category covers sales processes including delivery and transportation, and SAP DSD via SD.

▶ **Transportation and real world awareness**
This category (specifically the Transportation Planning and Vehicle Scheduling [TP/VS] function and workbench in combination with SAP Event Management) enables you to schedule vehicles for upcoming logistical events during different stages from beginning to end. For example, it shows the sales order and the different delivery stages it goes through and assists you in determining the most optimal assignment of vehicles and carriers based on demand and costs. The TP/VS workbench is part of APO. Figure 9.24 shows an example of the transportation cockpit from APO, which allows you to schedule vehicles for the different logistical processes.

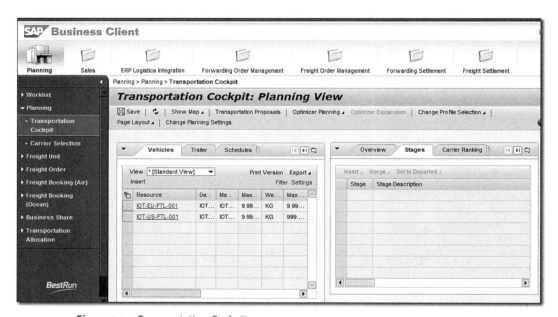

Figure 9.24 Transportation Cockpit

Track and Trace

Track and trace fleet operations is another business process that isn't part of the SAP PLM scope, but is part of SAP SCM Solution Map. To track and trace a specific vehicle against an event, you can use TM in combination with SAP Event Management. TM and SAP Event Management are offered as part of APO; specifically, the TP/VS function and workbench can be used together with SAP Event Management to track events from beginning to end.

So by now you should have a good understanding of how SAP PLM supports the three main areas of SAP Fleet Management. First we discussed vehicle administration—the investment, procurement, registration, and insurance of the vehicles, including the links between the vehicle and the financial asset register within FI–AA. Next we looked at the maintenance structural area, where we discussed processes covering maintenance engineering, incident management, preventive maintenance, spare parts management, the use of external services, and warranty management. These processes specifically explained how the standard maintenance processes have been enriched by including SAP Fleet Management specifics, such as the object information for the vehicle and the fleet-specific consumption measurements. The last structural area we dove into was operations, which uncovered the operational side of SAP Fleet Management—fuel and pool management, both of which belong to the SAP PLM solution offering. We also briefly covered the subareas in APO, TM, and SAP Event Management, which included the ability to perform driver and transport scheduling, transport scheduling, and tracking and tracing.

Now let's shift gears from SAP Fleet Management, which is used to send your products throughout the world, to SAP Mobile Platform, which is used to give your team access to information all over the world.

9.2 SAP Mobile Platform

SAP Mobile Platform is currently one of the main focus areas within SAP as it seeks to keep users connected using various platforms. The acquisition of Sybase and Syclo, both companies with decades of experience with mobile solutions and integration to SAP, has led to the substantial growth and improvement of SAP's product portfolio in this space.

This section covers SAP Mobile Platform from an SAP PLM perspective. Before going into the product portfolio and explaining the platform and the applications, let's consider the wide-ranging benefits that mobile solutions can offer.

Mobilizing business applications such as work order processing, purchase order approvals, or time and activity recording ensures that there are no delays in completing those critical tasks, among the following other benefits:

▶ Speeds up the decision-making process

▶ Leverages a convenient and familiar email inbox

▶ Provides direct interaction and integration with existing backend solutions

▶ Increases ROI on wireless email and business solutions

▶ Extends reach of business apps and workflows

▶ Supports heterogeneous devices through a single platform

▶ Enforces enterprise-class security

▶ Simplifies deployment

▶ Provides easy-to-learn and easy-to-use web apps

▶ Supports an intuitive, action-driven workflow based on a natural progression of work

▶ Displays only relevant info and actions

▶ Validates data capture; enforces all rules on the device

▶ Captures status, time, location, and other work-related data automatically

▶ Provides similar user experiences across platforms

It's probably not a surprise to you that the use of mobile devices—which range from a mobile phone, to smartphones (Apple iPhone, RIM's BlackBerry, Samsung's Galaxy), to tablets (Apple iPad, Samsung Galaxy Tab) and other devices such as eReaders (Amazon Kindle or Kindle Fire)—has grown explosively in the past decade. According to the Media (R)evolution report "Global Mobile Trends" from March 2012, 87% of the world's population has a mobile phone. In 2011, the number of smartphone shipments surpassed the number of PC shipments, according to the IDC report "Worldwide Smart Connected Device Shipments 2010–2016." The prognoses for the next five years are that the number of smartphone shipments will continue to grow to over a billion.

SAP has identified mobility as one of the five main market categories, along with cloud, analytics, business applications, and database and technology. Its mobile vision is to provide your organization with an unwired enterprise where mobile devices are the new frontend to business applications (see Chapter 1, Figure 1.1) giving your employees and other business partners access to company data anytime and anywhere. This holistic mobile strategy isn't just connecting employees to SAP solutions such as SAP PLM and/or SAP ERP, but also connects complete business networks and value chains via mobile devices and allows you to connect to custom applications, as shown in Figure 9.25.

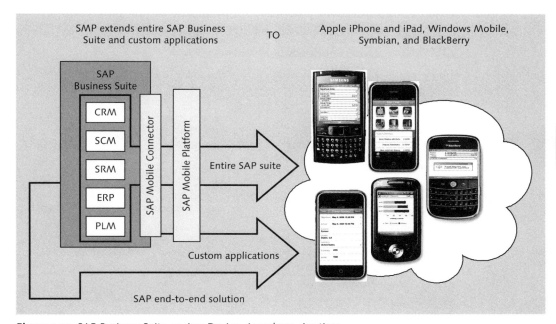

Figure 9.25 SAP Business Suite on Any Device, Anywhere, Anytime

9.2.1 SAP Mobile Product Portfolio

Figure 9.26 gives you an overview of the SAP Mobile product portfolio with one unified platform: an end-to-end solution strategy that addresses current mobile market trends with a comprehensive solution for end-to-end supportability, administration, and security for different types of devices.

Let's look at this mobile portfolio more closely. The overall solution is basically divided into two different areas (see Figure 9.26):

▶ **Mobile applications**

These can be categorized as apps for business to employee (B2E), business to business (B2B), and business to consumer (B2C). Section 9.2.2 will introduce SAP apps that are currently available, along with important links to find more information, as this industry is changing rapidly.

▶ **Mobile platforms**

SAP currently offers three different *mobile platforms*: Sybase Unwired Platform from Sybase 2.2, Agentry from Syclo, and SAP Mobiliser 5.1. The reason for offering three separate platforms is due to the recent acquisition of both Sybase and Syclo.

The Sybase Unwired Platform can be divided into the following areas:

▷ **Mobile enterprise application platform (MEAP)**

Offered via Sybase Unwired Platform, Syclo Agentry, and SAP Mobiliser 5.1.

▷ **Mobile Device Management (MDM)**

Offered via SAP Afaria (a former Sybase product), and includes features for device security, data security, identify management, and messaging.

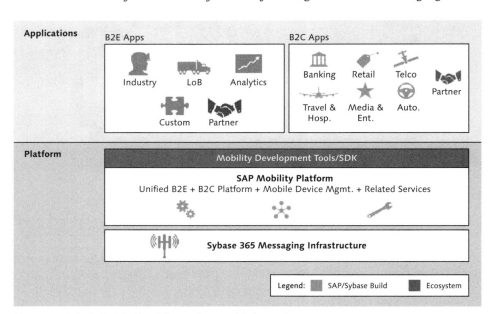

Figure 9.26 SAP Mobile Portfolio: End-to-End Solution Strategy

▶ **Mobile Consumer Application Platform (MCAP)**
Available via Sybase 365 mCommerce products; it offers B2C applications for mobile operators, financial institutions, and enterprise mobile messaging and mobile commerce services that help reach the world with one connection. It provides mobile messaging interoperability, end-to-end mobile commerce solutions, innovative mCRM, and mobile marketing services. Providing end-to-end mobile banking, mobile payments, and mobile money solutions for developed and emerging markets, Sybase 365 processes more than 1.8 billion messages per day, reaching 900 operators and 5.5 billion subscribers around the world.

▶ **Enterprise Content Platform**
Sends information such as documents and configuration settings to members and devices such as SAP Box. Mobile applications can also retrieve application settings for automated application configuration, which is known as one-touch configuration.

Three platforms are offered by SAP at the time of writing, but SAP is moving in the direction of one unified SAP Mobile Platform. Existing customers will be able to upgrade their current platform to the new platform.

To provide you with a functional understanding of what the platform allows you to do, Figure 9.27 shows the four function areas (connection, consume, create, and control) of the Sybase Unwired Platform. The platform manages the entire application lifecycle from deployment (tooling) to provisioning management and updating. Although the platform will be unified into one in the near future into the SAP Mobile Platform, these four main areas will most likely still be offered.

▶ **Connect**
This area allows you to connect to your SAP applications, other enterprise databases, or software applications. Sybase Unwired Platform provides integration into backend systems using SAP-certified connectors and open standard connectors. It provides the ability to cache data, giving mobile users the flexibility to work either offline or online.

▶ **Create**
This area, offered via the Eclipse environment, lets you develop your own mobile applications via a web-based application environment (using HTML5, JavaScript, or CSS). It lets you seamlessly use/reuse industry standard web development tools and provides a software development kit (SDK).

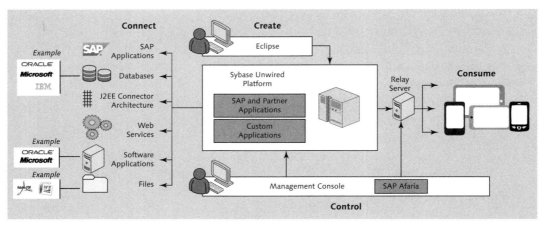

Figure 9.27 Sybase Unwired Platform

▸ **Consume**

Use the mobile applications on any device. The cross-platform architecture is consistent across key mobile platforms, including Apple iOS, Google Android, BlackBerry OS, and Microsoft Mobile. This architecture allows the following:

- ▸ Integration and use of native device capabilities, such as using GPS to provide location details, using the camera to take pictures, or using sensors to read barcodes

- ▸ Ability to use personal information management capabilities such as accessing your calendars with appointments, meetings, birthdays, and other events; accessing contact persons and their addresses; and using reminders

- ▸ Ability to email or fax from the device

The applications can be push-enabled, meaning that the device can inform the mobile users of a new incoming task, activity, or report.

▸ **Control**

The control functions are offered via the management console in SAP Afaria. Through data encryption, data partitioning, transport encryption, and authentication security options, you can manage, secure, and protect all your critical enterprise data stored and consumed via mobile applications and devices. It takes the complexity out of supporting your mobile workforce because it allows you to take control and have insight into a large number and wide range of devices and apps. You can use apps provided by SAP and SAP partners or develop your own web apps via the create function. It provides the ability to remotely back up and delete data on the device in the event that a device is lost or stolen. The help desk can easily deliver fixes, upgrades, refreshes, and usage analytics to mobile users.

As you can see in the future roadmap in Figure 9.28, SAP's future direction is to first unify Sybase Unwired Platform and Agentry into SAP Mobile Platform (SMP) 3.0 Enterprise, upgrade Mobilizer to SMP 3.0 Consumer, and develop an SAP Mobile Platform (SMP 3.0) for use in the cloud. Next, SMP 3.0 Enterprise and Consumer will be unified into SMP 3.5 alongside the SMP Cloud. Finally, the two remaining platforms would merge and be offered as one: SMP 4.0. From SMP 4.0 onward, both cloud and on-premise platforms are supported.

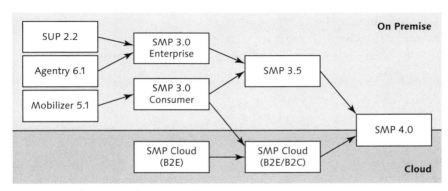

Figure 9.28 Platform Unification Roadmap

Mobilizing internal business processes is a significant first step toward creating a truly mobile environment. With mobility, you can extend beyond your organization and out to your customers, partners, suppliers, and anyone in your ecosystem using any device. Within a few years, SAP anticipates that we'll be in the midst of what Yankee Group describes as an "anywhere revolution," in which everyone is constantly connected to everything that matters to them.

The SAP Mobile Platform (currently Sybase Unwired Platform/Syclo/Mobiliser) effectively allows any SAP application to be adapted to this model, making your potential upside vast. The flexible and open infrastructure of the future SMP allows you to strategically respond as your device type and data source needs change in a timely manner. As enterprise data needs change due to acquisitions, system refreshes, or mobile device technology changes, you can use one consistent development platform to easily adapt to these changes. You can confidently develop mobile solutions for today's business with the knowledge that you can quickly and strategically adapt to the complex and changing world around you. SMP allows you to *create* compelling mobile applications by *connecting* to any SAP or non-SAP data source and applications and allows your user to *consume* the mobile applications from the device of their choice. With SMP, you can *control* mobile devices with full confidence. Figure 9.29 supports the vision by giving you an insight into the architecture of the SAP Mobile Platform. The architecture is separated into the following main areas:

- SAP Mobile Platform, which can be further broken into presentation frameworks, application services, and foundation services. It includes the ability to develop applications. The SAP development tools allow you to generate apps based on native or hybrid container technology; third-party app development tools can be used to develop apps based on HTML5 and SMS technology.

- SAP applications, partner applications, and custom applications

- SAP Afaria, which includes your SAP app catalog, the application management capabilities, and device management

- SAP Store, where you can buy or sample new applications or services

- SAP Services, which provides implementation services; Rapid Deployment Solutions (RDS), which are repeatable services with a predefined scope to allow fast implementation, often with a fixed price; strategic services; or managed mobility.

Always a powerful message is the fact that SAP itself also uses the Sybase Unwired Platform. At the time of publication, its employees use around 22,000 BlackBerrys, 17,800 iPads, 11,000 iPhones, and 1,000 Samsung Galaxy phones and tablets. It offers more than 40 different mobile applications and has globally implemented the Bring Your Own Device (BYOD) policy, which allows employees to use their personal devices on the SAP network as long as their mandatory security settings comply with SAP Afaria.

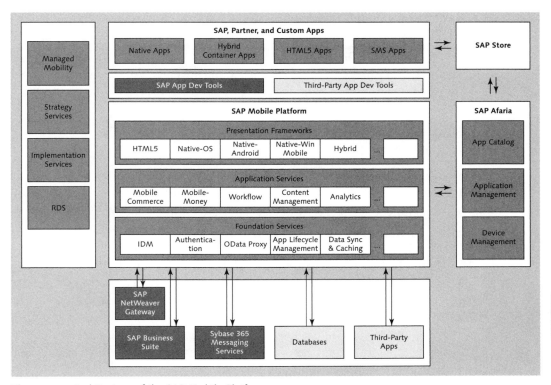

Figure 9.29 Architecture of the SAP Mobile Platform

9.2.2 SAP PLM Mobile Applications

Application management enables you to use prebuilt application and templates, develop your own applications inside an easy development environment, and leverage a vibrant ecosystem, including SAP and its partners. The open platform allows you to use SAP apps, use SAP partner apps, build and develop your own apps, or combine these options. This section describes the SAP PLM-specific apps and the productivity apps SAP offers.

Currently, the apps that SAP offers are either grouped by their target group or line of business (LOB). Both grouping mechanisms are briefly explained to provide you with enough context to navigate through the SAP sources such as the SAP Service Marketplace and *www.sap.com*. The apps that SAP offers are grouped into the following categories based on their target user group:

▶ Business-to-employee (B2E) apps are targeted at employee user groups; they allow employees to perform their day-to-day activities (e.g., filling out timesheets or travel expenses).

▶ Business-to-business (B2B) are targeted at the businesses with whom you trade; they allow these partners to perform business activities (e.g., performing payments).

▶ Business-to-consumer (B2C) are targeted at your customers; they allow them to reach out to you (e.g., reviewing their orders and status details).

In this section, we'll cover the apps offered by SAP through Syclo (previously offered by Syclo in the SMART product range), starting with the benefits, followed by a functional overview of each app, and ending with the integration possibilities to native applications. The section will continue with the apps for entering a quality issue and an SAP EHS safety issue, and will conclude with one example of apps in other areas, such as the timesheet app from SAP ERP HCM. Table 9.3 shows the B2E apps per LOB, in which the SAP PLM-relevant apps have been marked with an asterisk. If you're looking for more information on a specific SAP app within SAP resources, note that they are often grouped according to the LOB in which they are used or by the specific industry. In addition, the analytical apps category groups reporting apps based on the reporting tools, as will be discussed in the next chapter.

LOB	Applications
Strategy Management	▶ SAP Strategy Management
Sales and Service	▶ SAP CRM Sales
	▶ SAP Customer Briefing
	▶ SAP Customers and Contacts
	▶ SAP Customer Financial Factsheet
	▶ SAP ERP Order Status
	▶ SAP ERP Customer Order Entry
	▶ SAP Material Availability
	▶ SAP Sales On Demand
	▶ SAP Sales Order Notification
	▶ Sybase Mobile Sales and Workflow

Table 9.3 Overview of the B2E Apps per Line of Business

LOB	Applications
SAP through Syclo	▶ SAP Work Manager by Syclo* ▶ SAP Work Manager by Syclo for utilities* ▶ SAP Rounds Manager by Syclo* ▶ SAP Inventory Manager by Syclo* ▶ SAP Service Manager by Syclo*
SAP SCM and Manufacturing	▶ SAP Cart Approval ▶ SAP ERP Quality Issue *
SAP EHS Management	▶ SAP EHS Safety Issue*
SAP ERP HCM	▶ SAP Employee Lookup ▶ SAP Interview Assistant ▶ SAP Manager Insight ▶ SAP HR Approvals ▶ SAP Leave Request ▶ SAP Timesheet ▶ SAP Learning Assistance ▶ SAP Travel Expense Approval ▶ SAP Travel Expense Report ▶ SAP Travel Receipt Capture
Finance and Risk	▶ SAP GRC Access Approver ▶ SAP Payment Approvals ▶ SAP Travel Expense Approval ▶ SAP Travel Receipt Capture ▶ SAP Real Spend
SAP Employees	▶ SAP Now ▶ SAP Box ▶ SAP ValueVU ▶ SAP Streamwork ▶ CRM@SAP

Table 9.3 Overview of the B2E Apps per Line of Business (Cont.)

So first we'll dive into the apps offered by SAP through Syclo (remember, these were previously offered by Syclo in the SMART product range).

9.2.3 B2E Apps for SAP by Syclo

Five of the apps offered within the SAP PLM space were previously found under the Syclo name SMART, so a lot of information is available about the benefits they offer users:

▸ **High reliability and scalability (100% availability in and out of wireless coverage)**
Your maintenance engineers have constant access to the assets data and their work-related activities, whether they are online or offline. They are scalable to thousands of users and large data sets, with fast synchronization times, efficient use of networks and server resources, and support for server clusters and load balancing.

▸ **Great usability**
The platform allows you to provide the user with a consistent user experience because you can include unique features and controls within the native applications.

▸ **Single set of business logic**
There's no need to cross-compile application code for every platform or set up separate development environments and skill sets. Configuration is easy, and supporting the app and making modifications are easy as well.

▸ **Proven and functional**
There's no need for pilot projects because the applications are already proven and live at multiple reference customers sites, where the preceding benefits were accomplished.

▸ **100% configurable**
The mobile apps are totally configuration with tailored screens, workflow, business logic, validation, synchronization, communications, and integration.

▸ **Easy to learn and administer**
The technology can be quickly adopted by your IT team.

▸ **Broad device support**
You can provide the best device to each member of your workforce and easily add new devices as they become available.

Let's look at a few specific B2E apps.

SAP Work Manager by Syclo

SAP Work Manager by Syclo lets you quickly dispatch work orders and notifications to your mobile employees. The app gives users real-time access to asset history and details such as asset installation, removal, maintenance, inspection, and repair processes, and it allows users to start, hold, transfer, create, and complete work orders right on the mobile device.

The focus of this app is on SAP EAM, providing you with the ability to perform work orders, do time and attendance entries via cross-application time sheets (CATS), create notifications on the spot, and enter measurement documents. Because it's developed on the Agentry platform, it's flexible and can be modified to support processes that overlap into field service functions.

This application is designed primarily for complex, long-cycle, and project-based work where service level agreements (SLAs) and entitlements aren't an emphasis (such as non-customer-facing construction and maintenance jobs). The app is often implemented and well received in asset-intensive industries such as mining, oil and gas upstream/midstream, and power generation/transmission.

SAP Work Manager by Syclo (see Figure 9.30) provides the ability to perform the following functions:

▶ Start, hold, transfer, complete/non-complete, and edit work orders and notifications.

▶ Record labor, parts, notes, measurement documents, and failure information.

▶ Create field work orders and notifications.

▶ Access operations, asset, safety, and history information.

▶ View pending work orders.

▶ Capture signatures.

The following functions are available in SAP Work Manager by Syclo for CATS time and attendance recording:

▶ View and edit daily time.

▶ Record non-work order time, belonging to labor type OT, and overtime pay scale.

▶ View and filter pay periods.

▶ Use pop-up calendars and automatic start/stop calculator.

▶ View daily summary of time.

▶ View and edit attendance.

Figure 9.30 Notifications on SAP Work Manager by Syclo

SAP Work Order Manager

SAP Work Order Manager for SAP ERP lets you quickly dispatch work orders and notifications to your mobile employees. The app gives them real-time access to asset history and details, and allows them to start, hold, transfer, create, and complete work orders right on the mobile device. This co-innovated product has been implemented at customers such as National Grid, First Energy, US Sugar, Baker Hughes, Axtel, PG&E, RheinEnergie, AstraZeneca, and BP.

Apart from the functions for work order processing and time and attendance recording, additional functions are available specifically tailored at the SAP Industry Solution for Utilities (ISU) users, such as performing inspections, surveys, meter management, meter operations, operator rounds, SAP CRM orders, and crew reporting.

SAP Work Order Management provides you with the following functions:

▶ Perform inspections and surveys.

▶ Perform meter management and meter operations (specific to ISU).

▶ Make operator rounds.

▶ Use SAP Mobile Asset Management (SAP MAM) or Mobile Asset Management for Utilities.

▶ Have access to asset information, including details such as its location, the previous incidents and work orders, and used spares.

▶ Record working times against work orders and attendances for general activities, such as meetings or leave.

▶ Record measurement documents against a technical object, either as a planned activity within a work order or as an unplanned activity.

▶ Set up guided workflows, which enable you to alert a stakeholder about a work management activity or outcome.

▶ Collect work order information in real time, which provides you with up-to-date and reliable information both for the work orders and the technical assets effected.

▶ Capture all mobile device touches within SAP ERP.

▶ Create notifications directly from the field.

▶ Support both the SAP PM and SAP CS work management processes.

SAP Service Manager by Syclo

SAP Service Manager by Syclo automates field service processes more typical of short cycle, after-market, and customer-facing jobs in which SLAs and entitlements are important. This application is better suited to the operations side of companies (e.g., power distribution companies, home repair, office equipment repair, and commercial facilities management). It's a flexible solution that can be modified to support processes in emergency response services and other segments where rapid response is critical. The SAP Service Manager by Syclo, which is shown for the Apple iPad in Figure 9.31, is focused on field service and delivers the following:

▶ Service orders

▶ Customer data

- ▸ Territory data
- ▸ Entitlements
- ▸ Vehicle inventory

Figure 9.31 Work Order Manager Screenshot for an iPad

SAP Rounds Manager by Syclo

The SAP Rounds Manager is designed primarily for meter and measurements readings on the road or in the plant; it's flexible and can be modified to support more complex inspection processes or specialized inspection processes such as SAP EHS and fire and safety inspections. The SAP Rounds Manager by Syclo focuses on condition monitoring of technical objects and includes the following functions:

- ▸ Quickly perform inspection rounds, including recording readings in the form of measurement documents and recording observations.
- ▸ Automatically alert users when measurements are outside the set safety limits, which can include enforcing an action.

- ▶ Download and filter measurement points using flexible filters and sorting based on multiple criteria.
- ▶ View measurement history.
- ▶ Create notifications on the spot.

SAP Inventory Manager by Syclo

SAP Inventory Manager by Syclo automates inventory handling tasks in the warehouse, onboard the fleet, or in remote field locations. It's designed primarily for discrete parts, tools, and materials, but you can modify it to support retail items, bulk items, and so forth. The SAP Inventory Manager by Syclo app is used to perform mobile goods movements via the SAP MM functional area, which includes SAP Inventory Management (MM–IM). The app is able to do the following functions:

- ▶ Cycle counts
- ▶ Goods issues
- ▶ Stock transfers
- ▶ Goods receipts
- ▶ Physical counts (planned and ad hoc)
- ▶ Material information views
- ▶ Serialized inventory
- ▶ Material issues, material transfers, and material receipts adding, editing, and clearing
- ▶ Material reservations
- ▶ Material reversals

For product demos or additional information, check out Syclo's YouTube channel at *http://www.youtube.com/user/syclomobile*.

Integration

This section shows you how the Syclo apps can integrate with other applications you use within your organization to give you a feel for additional use cases. We'll explain three integration examples:

▶ SAP Work Manager by Syclo integrated with Google Maps (a Geographical Information System)

▶ SAP Work Manager by Syclo integrated with SAP Visual Enterprise and SAP BusinessObjects Analysis

▶ SAP Work Manager by Syclo integrated with SAP Visual Enterprise for work instruction

These examples show how the Syclo apps, in combination with another application of SAP, can make a positive difference in doing business as usual and enriching the user experience by quickly providing data. Figure 9.32 shows the maintenance engineer on Google maps and all the outstanding work activities.

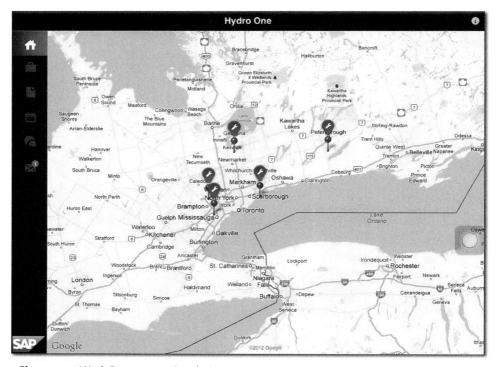

Figure 9.32 Work Requests on Google Maps

Figure 9.33 shows SAP Work Manager by Syclo in combination with the SAP Visual Enterprise and SAP BusinessObjects Analysis. Through the app, a maintenance engineer can visually see the installation, the work order history on the asset "Technical Hub Equipment," the performance history, and analytics.

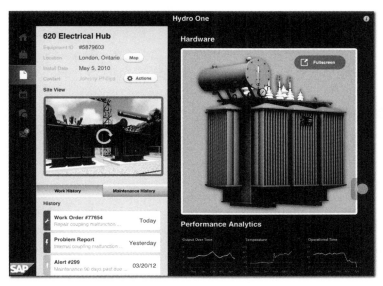

Figure 9.33 Work Order Management with Site View and Analytics

Figure 9.34 shows SAP Work Manager by Syclo in combination with the SAP Visual Enterprise, where a maintenance engineer can visually see the steps on the mobile device, which guide him step by step through the activities required.

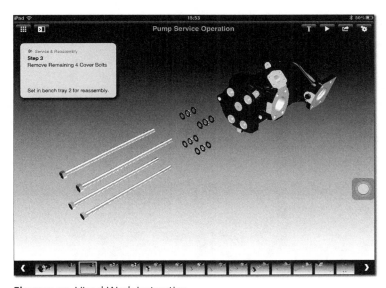

Figure 9.34 Visual Work Instruction

9.2.4   B2E Apps by SAP

The following section describes the B2E apps developed by SAP that are targeted at employee user groups specifically within the SAP PLM space and allow employees to perform their day-to-day activities. We'll look at the Quality Issue app, which is relevant for quality management (Chapter 8); the SAP EHS safety issue, which is relevant for SAP EHS Management (Chapter 6); and finally close with the Timesheet app, which is often relevant across specific areas such as maintenance, quality management, and project management activities.

Quality Issue

The SAP EHS Quality Issue mobile app lets you log quality issues as soon as they're detected. The issue logger can assign codes for object or issue, enter a detailed description, attach photos, and assign a priority directly from a mobile device.

Figure 9.35 shows what this app looks like on an Apple iPhone; in the figure, the SUBJECT CODE, ISSUE CODE, DETAILED ISSUE DESCRIPTION, PHOTO, REFERENCE OBJECT, and PRIORITY fields are completed for an issue with a PC mouse.

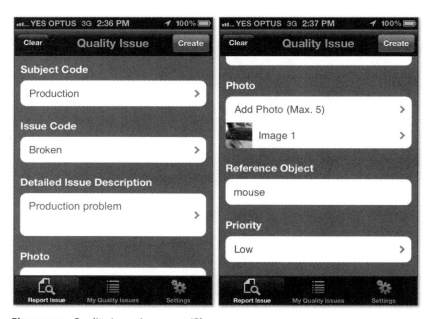

Figure 9.35 Quality Issue App on an iPhone

SAP EHS Safety Issue

The SAP EHS Safety Issue mobile app allows you to enter a safety issue via a mobile device. This app lets you take photos or videos, describe the problem in detail or verbally record an issue description instead of typing, and include the location where the issue is located, as shown in Figure 9.36.

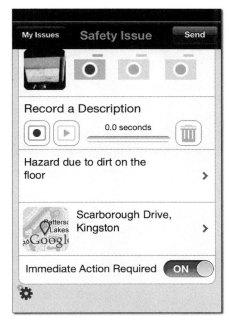

Figure 9.36 SAP EHS Safety Issue App

Timesheet App

The SAP Timesheet mobile app from SAP ERP HCM allows your employees to save time spent on recording work hours by creating, reviewing, and submitting time entries from a mobile device. Figure 9.37 shows in the first screen the user's calendar color-coded based on fully, partially, or non-activities recorded. Here, March 17th was only partially confirmed; if you click on the date, you see that two hours are booked against consulting and another three to productive. The next screen shows how a new time entry is done for five hours for a customer visit during office hours.

Figure 9.37 SAP Timesheet App on an iPhone

9.2.5 Analytics Apps

Apart from the B2E and B2C apps, the last type of available apps are the business analytics apps, which provide you with the means to look at reports and analytics from a mobile device:

▶ SAP BusinessObjects Experience

▶ SAP BusinessObjects Explorer

▶ SAP BusinessObjects Mobile

▶ SAP Business by Design Dashboard

▶ SAP Business One

Chapter 10 will provide you with a better understanding on reporting and the different SAP capabilities in this area and the history of how this area has grown and evolved over time. It will also introduce you to the other processes covered under product insights and analytics, which explains 3D Visual Enterprise and searching capabilities. For more information on the SAP business analytics apps, visit the SAP page *http://www.sap.com/solutions/technology/enterprise-mobility*.

9.3   Summary

This chapter has focused on two areas that aren't core to SAP PLM but often offer substantial benefits to manage within the same environment and leveraging of the integrated nature of SAP PLM and the SAP ERP core component capabilities. SAP Fleet Management can be leveraged to support SAP Enterprise Asset Management (SAP EAM) for your company's transportation means from procuring the fleet, maintaining and operating your fleet, to optimizing planning capabilities and finally disposing of the fleet and starting the cycle again using a single source of truth. This chapter has given you an overview of SAP's solutions in the SAP PLM area for SAP Fleet Management, which provides a holistic solution supporting all of the stages of your company's transportation needs.

Within SAP PLM, several business users and roles need to work outside of the office on different devices while still being able to perform business activities instead of only working onsite in an office environment with access to their organization network. For example, the maintenance and operating crew want to use mobile devices to receive their assigned work, execute the activities, and record their time, spare parts used, and technical findings to replace their existing paper-based, error-prone work order. A product developer might, for example, want to collaborate with a manufacturer and bring along the product specifications on his tablet; when in the field, a quality engineer should be able to log a quality issue using his mobile phone. This business need was focused on in the second section on the SAP Mobile Platform. This allows you to extend the use of your business application to mobile devices so employees have access anywhere, anytime, and from any device to the relevant business data.

You gain access to business information such as outstanding notifications, work orders, and the related asset information via different apps from Syclo, Sybase, or SAP, such as SAP Work Manager by Syclo or the SAP Quality Issue app.

The next chapter introduces product intelligence and gives you an overview of the solutions for product-centric content that are offered within SAP PLM 7.02 and the SAP Business Suite.

Insight and analytics is a cross-business process that allows you to get insight into product information from across the business in a timely manner to support the decision-making process and to adjust your product strategy.

10   Product Insight and Analytics

Product intelligence is one of the main processes within the SAP PLM foundation, and it represents the capability to access product-centric content and context from your organization. It supports various different stakeholders, such as product development and product management activities, by informing them about product sourcing information, manufacturing numbers, supply chain and sales figures, and much more.

This chapter gives you an overview of the product intelligence solutions for product-centric content that are offered within SAP PLM 7.02 and the SAP Business Suite. It includes enterprise and Internet web services and real-world diagnostics. This chapter is merely an introduction with, where possible, real-world examples to give you a good sense of what is available and feasible; it aims to provide you with enough information to know how and where to find out more details. Your specific reporting and analytic requirements will determine which solutions are relevant for your organization.

Because the product insight and analytics process category belongs to business intelligence category, we'll briefly define "business intelligence" to ensure a common understanding of the definition. So what is business intelligence? According to Gartner, *business intelligence* is a catch-all term that includes the "applications, infrastructure, and tools, and best practices that enable access to and analysis of information to improve and optimize decisions and performance." It's an iterative, user-centered process that includes accessing and exploring information, analyzing this information, and developing insights and understanding that lead to improved and informed decision making that focuses on a range of users both internally and externally through any enterprise. So this chapter will cover product insight and analysis, addressing the business intelligence processes with a focus on products.

The first section of this chapter provides the business processes available within the SAP PLM Solution Map for product intelligence, which are the SAP Visual Enterprise, reporting, query, and analyzing, SAP NetWeaver Enterprise Search, and business object search. The business processes reporting, querying, and analyzing will provide an overview of SAP's entire product portfolio and introduce standard reports in SAP PLM, SAP NetWeaver BW and SAP BusinessObjects BI. It includes the history and background information on these analytic solutions because product names and acronyms used in the past overlap with acronyms used today, so we aim to get on the same page and clear up any confusion.

Section 10.2, which covers standard reporting, will introduce you to all of the available reporting and insight capabilities on product information available in SAP PLM 7.02 (within the SAP Business Suite) by providing information on SAP ERP standard reports, Windows Word Processor Integration (WWI) from SAP Environment, Health, and Safety Management (SAP EHS Management), the Logistics Information System (LIS) and the Business Context Viewer (BCV).

Last, Section 10.3 elaborates on the comprehensive reporting ability through SAP NetWeaver BW and the SAP BusinessObjects BI solutions, such as its platform, dashboarding tools such as Xcelsius, the Microsoft integration tools, and the SAP BusinessObjects Explorer.

So let's begin with the product intelligence process.

10.1 Product Intelligence Business Processes

Product intelligence is one of the main processes within the SAP PLM foundation; it represents the capability to access product-centric content and context from your organization. It supports various stakeholders during product development and management activities to make informed decisions on any product-relevant strategies and focuses. Product-centric content is sourced from across the SAP Business Suite, through enterprise and Internet web services, and real-world diagnostics.

Figure 10.1 shows the four main processes that together create the product intelligence sequence.

Figure 10.1 Product Intelligence Processes

The processes are listed here as well:

- SAP Visual Enterprise
- Reporting, query, and analysis
- Enabling SAP NetWeaver Enterprise Search
- Providing business object search

We'll spend the rest of this section detailing these processes, first explaining SAP Visual Enterprise, then focusing on the reporting, query, and analysis process and providing an overview and introduction to the different SAP solutions covering this area, which are standard reporting in SAP ERP, SAP NetWeaver BW, and SAP BusinessObjects. The section finishes with the search capabilities from SAP PLM, covering both SAP NetWeaver Enterprise Search and business object search available through SAP NetWeaver.

10.1.1 SAP 3D Visual Enterprise

The SAP 3D Visual Enterprise lets you see into and across your enterprise by integrating visualization and business data. This allows you to have the right up-to-date product (or asset) information available in the right document or application, delivered at the right time.

The recent acquisition (March, 2012) of Right Hemisphere provides SAP customers with intuitive product and asset navigation capabilities to all of its associated data in a single unified environment, bringing the following benefits:

- Combine business information with visual content.
- Enhance product collaboration, which reduces training time and improves process knowledge.
- Accelerate processes to reduce time to market.

► Increase asset and product productivity.

► Improve information quality across all lines of business (LOBs).

The SAP Visual Enterprise Viewer provides up-to-date, real-time walk-throughs on any size product or asset model, and extends collaboration capabilities to CAD, 2D, and 3D documents and media types in a single platform. For example, visual manufacturing solutions provide easy-to-understand, step-by-step manufacturing procedures with accurate BOMs, multiple configurations and affectivity, and integration with manufacturing execution systems. Additionally, visual support and service applications provide easy generation and automation updating of technical publications and training materials. Figure 10.2 shows an example of how a service technician is guided through a step-by-step maintenance task list.

Figure 10.2 Step-by-Step 3D Maintenance Task List

Visual sales and marketing provides 3D or illustrated parts catalogs as well as hyperreal product inventory. Figure 10.3 gives you an example of an airplane from Adobe Flex. The SAP Visual Enterprise Viewer enables importing of more than 45 industry standard formats directly into business-user documents; this means that product information and other visual content can be produced, stored, and transferred in a number of formats.

Figure 10.3 Custom 3D Configuration of an Airplane

SAP 3D Visual Enterprise software consists of three core products:

▶ **SAP 3D Visual Enterprise Generator**
This application serves as a processing engine that translates nearly any 3D CAD file into a lightweight file format used in downstream processes. It performs the heavy work of transforming massive engineering design files into ultra-lightweight visualizations of data. To support downstream processes such as engineering, manufacturing, and maintenance, the application combines business data with visual information such as high-resolution images, dynamically creating complex graphics, media files, or documents.

▶ **SAP 3D Visual Enterprise Author**
This end-user application creates animated procedures, 3D embedded documents and high-definition imagery. It helps you produce extremely large, high performance, 3D models that either stand alone or can be integrated with other applications. It creates streaming files that allow you to quickly examine multiple configurations at once and explore massive models for entire airplanes, ships, or manufacturing plants.

▶ **SAP Visual Enterprise Viewer**
This free, lightweight, powerful, easy-to-use end-user tool views and interacts with the authored and published content. It makes visual content available to

743

everyone who could benefit from viewing, publishing, and reusing 2D and 3D visual information to complete their own tasks, independent of the device used because this viewer has no hardware requirements.

10.1.2 Reporting, Querying, and Analyzing

The process reporting, querying, and analyzing belongs to the business intelligence process category, which focuses an iterative user-centered processes that include accessing and exploring information, analyzing this information, and developing insights and understanding that lead to improved and informed decision making focused on a range of users both internally and externally through any enterprise. SAP PLM runs on the SAP NetWeaver platform, which provides users with different applications and tools; allows them to design, deploy, and execute lists, reports, and queries; and formats them or makes them available to a wider audience through, for example, the intranet or Internet. Generally, the following benefits are achieved by implementing this business process, although you should be aware that they may vary slightly based on the specific technology and/or tool chosen:

▶ Empower business users in a user-oriented and flexible way.

▶ Design queries in an easy and intuitive way and use them as the basis for a user-oriented presentation of information and effective analysis.

▶ Design presentation-quality, print-optimized formatted reports.

▶ Use SAP Business Content (BI Content), including ready-to use content based on SAP's experience through other implementations in this space.

▶ Provide personalized access to information to support quick and efficient decision making.

▶ Convert reports and web applications easily to different type of files, such as Microsoft Office or PDF files.

Analytics Tools from SAP

Figure 10.4 shows an overview of SAP's analytics tools, which have been divided into SAP PLM 7.02 (SAP ERP reporting), SAP NetWeaver BW, and SAP BusinessObjects BI. Before we look at these individually, let's first fit them into the end-to-end process for Integrated Product Development and briefly explore the history of these solutions. We hope to provide you with background on why name changes have caused some confusion in the past and to provide you with the correct acronyms used today.

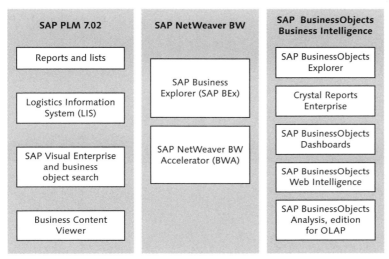

Figure 10.4 Business Intelligence Product Analytics Tools

So far we've been focusing on the different processes and tools for SAP PLM, of which Integrated Product Development is an important one. Figure 10.5 shows this process, illustrated with call-outs to indicate which SAP analytics tools are used or expected to be used during the various steps. We'll introduce you to those different solutions in this chapter.

Putting SAP Analytics Tools in Context

SAP PLM 7.02 offers some very good reporting and analytic tools out of the box that, because they're embedded with SAP ERP, don't require configuration and data sourcing activities. In particular, operational reporting at the component level has been quite comprehensive and provides several flexible reporting tools such as selection and layout options. If you use SAP often, you should familiarize yourself with its capabilities. Section 10.1.2 will give you an overview of the options available.

During SAP PLM implementations several years ago, many users found the reporting and analyzing capabilities to be complicated, difficult to adjust to specific requirements, and visually unattractive—especially at a management level or across functional components. The introduction of a dedicated business warehouse tool in 1997 through the Business Warehouse Information System (known as BIW) proved to be a good change of direction to address these challenges. A new release became available almost every year. In 2001, its name changed to Business Warehouse (BW), and, in 2005, the name was again changed, this time to Business Intelligence (BI). Section 10.3.1 will describe the current SAP NetWeaver BW.

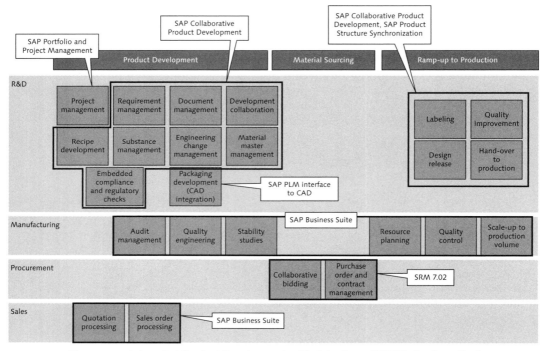

Figure 10.5 Integrated Product Development with Adoption of SAP Technology Platform

In 2007, SAP strengthened its product portfolio within business intelligence even further by acquiring the French company Business Objects. They were known for several business intelligence products, such as Enterprise Reporting (which became SAP Crystal Reports) for accessing, formatting, and delivering information to large populations of users, and Data Visualization (known as Xcelsius, and then Dashboards) for supporting creation of flash dashboards and dynamic charts and graphics. Section 10.3.2 will give you an overview and short introduction to the SAP BusinessObjects BI solutions; because it's such a large portfolio, more details weren't feasible to address in the scope of this book.

SAP used the term "Business Intelligence" in 2008 for both the SAP BusinessObjects BI solutions and the SAP NetWeaver BW solution, which caused confusion in the SAP community. To address this problem, the term Business Intelligence (BI) is now associated only with the solutions from the SAP BusinessObjects portfolio. SAP NetWeaver BI (which itself was replaced) is no longer being used. Instead, we refer to the following products:

- SAP NetWeaver Business Warehouse (SAP NetWeaver BW)
- SAP Business Explorer (SAP BEx)
- SAP NetWeaver Business Warehouse Accelerator

Let's now return to the final two processes of product intelligence, which came after SAP Visual Enterprise and reporting, querying, and analyzing.

10.1.3 Enabling Enterprise and Business Object Search

SAP NetWeaver Search and Classification (called TREX) provides searching capabilities so you can find information in both structured and unstructured data. TREX provides SAP applications with services for searching and classifying large collections of documents and for searching and aggregating business objects, providing a powerful search engine. (TREX actually stands for Text Retrieval and Information Extraction, which isn't a trade name registered with SAP and therefore isn't further used on SAP sources.) The TREX engine is a stand-alone component that is part of SAP NetWeaver but can be used in a range of system environments, although it's often used in combination with other SAP products such as SAP ERP and SAP Project and Portfolio Management (PPM).

Business applications can use this search engine service (SES) to index and search for specific business objects. It allows you to retrieve business objects such as business documents (e.g., project charters or work orders), master data (e.g., materials), analytics, documents, discussions, or manuals through the interface of choice (such as the SAP GUI, the Web Dynpro UI, the SAP NetWeaver Portal, or SAP NetWeaver Enterprise Search). Figure 10.6 shows an example in which a search term is looking across multiple product objects (in this example, searched across materials, BOMs, and routings), which leads to the following search results.

Figure 10.6 Searching Across Objects within the SAP NetWeaver Business Client (NWBC)

10.2   Standard Reporting in SAP ERP

SAP PLM 7.02 offers some very good reporting and analytic tools out of the box that don't require any configuration and data sourcing activities because they are embedded within SAP ERP.

We'll begin by detailing the standard available reporting options, followed by the Logistics Information Warehouse (LIS, the dedicated information warehouse for all the logistics components within SAP PLM and SAP ERP). Finally, we'll cover the Business Context Viewer (BCV), which was recently introduced as part of SAP ERP 6, EHP 4. BCV gives you a product-centric view of any product-related transaction by adding a side panel with business intelligence about the product you're viewing. This provides you with easy and quick access to product data and analytics from a single view, making it easier to access this information and make informed decisions.

10.2.1 Standard Reports and Lists

You can view the master data and the transactions that have been captured in SAP PLM in their respective component via a report or list, either during or after performing the operational task. Other areas might also have relevant reports—for example, maintenance and project key users can employ several FI–CO report options that include information about the planned and actual costs to the work orders or projects. The FI–CO order cost reports can be set up with the appropriate authorization, so the key user is just authorized for his own area.

If, as an SAP PLM user, you use the different reports and lists available, we recommend that you spend time understanding the general available functions— such as how to create your personal or company-wide selection variants and layouts, how to select functions such as multiple selections with inclusions and exclusions, and how to use reporting functions such as sorting, subtotals, exporting to Microsoft Office, graphics creation, and so on. Understanding the possibilities and being able to set up your own variants and layouts can save you time, make you more efficient, and improve your user experience.

Figure 10.7 and Figure 10.8 show you an example of a notification list, which is used by most of the SAP PLM areas. Within the selection screen you enter the selection parameters to narrow down the number of hits in the worklist.

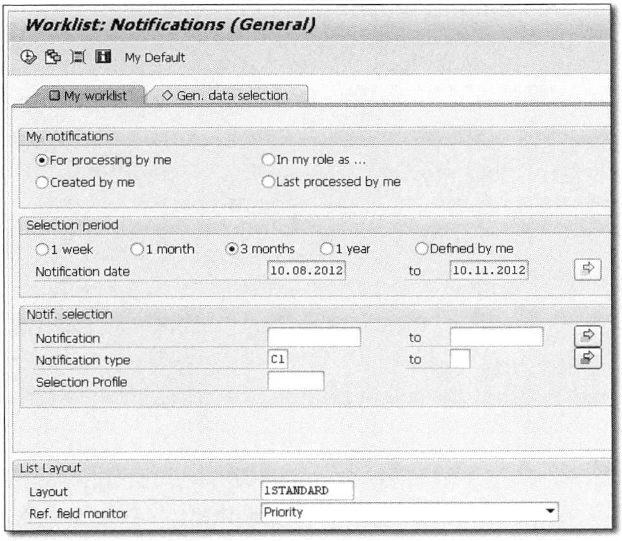

Figure 10.7 Selection of Data

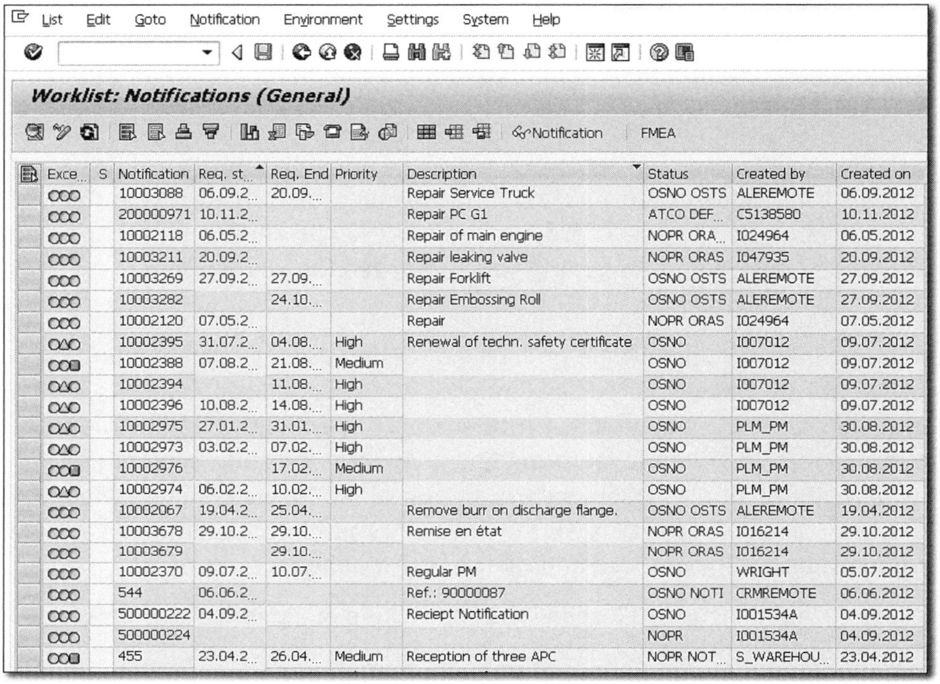

List Edit Goto Notification Environment Settings System Help

Worklist: Notifications (General)

Notification FMEA

Exce...	S	Notification	Req. st...	Req. End	Priority	Description	Status	Created by	Created on
		10003088	06.09.2...	20.09....		Repair Service Truck	OSNO OSTS	ALEREMOTE	06.09.2012
		200000971	10.11.2...			Repair PC G1	ATCO DEF...	C5138580	10.11.2012
		10002118	06.05.2...			Repair of main engine	NOPR ORA...	I024964	06.05.2012
		10003211	20.09.2...			Repair leaking valve	NOPR ORAS	I047935	20.09.2012
		10003269	27.09.2...	27.09....		Repair Forklift	OSNO OSTS	ALEREMOTE	27.09.2012
		10003282		24.10....		Repair Embossing Roll	OSNO OSTS	ALEREMOTE	27.09.2012
		10002120	07.05.2...			Repair	NOPR ORAS	I024964	07.05.2012
		10002395	31.07.2...	04.08....	High	Renewal of techn. safety certificate	OSNO	I007012	09.07.2012
		10002388	07.08.2...	21.08....	Medium		OSNO	I007012	09.07.2012
		10002394		11.08....	High		OSNO	I007012	09.07.2012
		10002396	10.08.2...	14.08....	High		OSNO	I007012	09.07.2012
		10002975	27.01.2...	31.01....	High		OSNO	PLM_PM	30.08.2012
		10002973	03.02.2...	07.02....	High		OSNO	PLM_PM	30.08.2012
		10002976		17.02....	Medium		OSNO	PLM_PM	30.08.2012
		10002974	06.02.2...	10.02....	High		OSNO	PLM_PM	30.08.2012
		10002067	19.04.2...	25.04....		Remove burr on discharge flange.	OSNO OSTS	ALEREMOTE	19.04.2012
		10003678	29.10.2...	29.10....		Remise en état	NOPR ORAS	I016214	29.10.2012
		10003679		29.10....			NOPR ORAS	I016214	29.10.2012
		10002370	09.07.2...	10.07....		Regular PM	OSNO	WRIGHT	05.07.2012
		544	06.06.2...			Ref.: 90000087	OSNO NOTI	CRMREMOTE	06.06.2012
		500000222	04.09.2...			Reciept Notification	OSNO	I001534A	04.09.2012
		500000224					NOPR	I001534A	04.09.2012
		455	23.04.2...	26.04....	Medium	Reception of three APC	NOPR NOT...	S_WAREHOU...	23.04.2012

Figure 10.8 Worklist

This example differentiates between a personalized worklist (the My worklist tab) or a general worklist (the Gen. data selection tab), but whether this feature is available depends on the report you run. The same can be said about which specific selection options are available. Usually a report can be executed by first entering the selection parameters. Figure 10.7 shows the selection parameters for a notification list, where My notifications are chosen for the past 3 months, of Notification type C1. After the selection parameters are finalized, you can execute the report via the Execute button (press F8).

After execution, the report results will be shown (see Figure 10.8). Notice that various general reporting functions are often available; these may vary based on the specific transaction, such as sorting, making a graphic, filtering, exporting to Microsoft Excel, and printing.

The results of the notification list shown in Figure 10.9 have been used to represent the division of the different priorities of the selected notifications in a pie chart.

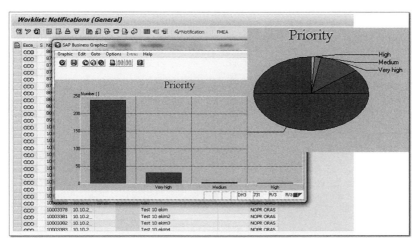

Figure 10.9 Using Results to Create Graphics

10.2.2 Reporting in SAP EHS with WII Integration

Within SAP EHS, reports are used to provide outputs based on the specification database, phrases, and other SAP components, and often contain graphic symbols. To allow you to change layouts of reports easily, a modified version of Microsoft Word called Windows Word Processor Integration (WWI) has been incorporated into SAP EHS. Because SAP EHS often handles and includes information that is critical to ensure both people's safety and safe handling of dangerous or hazardous goods, the reports generated with WWI have rigorous version control; colors are used for changes and release procedures via a status network to manage the correctness of the report. A report worklist is used and automatically updated with affected reports when a relevant specification or phrase has changed. You can make reports available on paper or electronically store them by using the SAP Document Management System (SAP DMS). Before you can run a report, you need to follow the process represented in Figure 10.10.

The first basic step is to create and adjust the reporting template, including the cover sheet, generation variant, report template, and cover sheet template. Next you'll focus on the report itself by requesting the report, generating it, checking the content, and releasing it. The system will automatically highlight reports for which certain details are missing—for example, when a description in a particular language or a symbol is missing—to allow you to update the required information in the system.

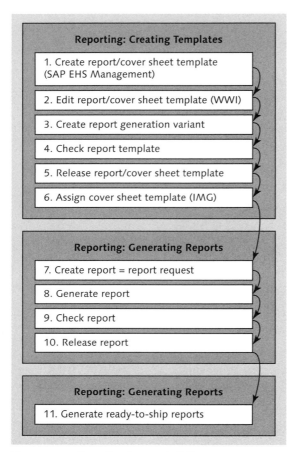

Figure 10.10 Reporting Process in WII

After the report has been generated successfully, you can incorporate a number of releases or checkpoints depending on the number of business partners that need to sign off on the report (e.g., the toxicologist, the dangerous goods manager, and the product manager). Once released, the report will receive the Completed status and will be assigned a version. Different report types are supported within WWI, such as the report template (SBV), report body (SBR), final report (SBE), cover sheet template (DBV), cover sheet final version (DBE), receipt acknowledgement template (EBV), receipt acknowledgement final version (EBE), and inbound document (IBD). You can also manage imported reports, originated from an external system via report management.

10.2.3   Reporting in Logistics Information System

The logistics applications from SAP PLM, such as SAP Plant Maintenance (SAP PM) and SAP Project System (SAP PS), all include an application-specific information system. The applications in the Logistics Information System (LIS) are usually named after their component names followed by "information system," such as the Sales Information System (SIS), the Plant Maintenance Information System (PMIS), and the Quality Management Information System (QMIS), as shown in Figure 10.11. The figure also outlines the three different modules available per information system, which we'll briefly introduce.

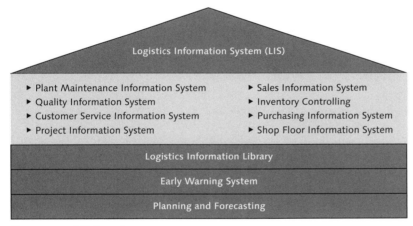

Figure 10.11 LIS Overview

The LIS consists of the following three components that provide you with several techniques to evaluate data:

► **Logistics Information Library**
   This data warehouse allows you to evaluate standard analysis, where you view aggregated information using key figures and characteristics. This is the part of the LIS that we'll be focusing on.

► **Early Warning System**
   This is the part of the LIS through which you focus on problem areas that need your attention. The "problem area" is defined by the setup of an exception and, after this situation occurs, allows you to detect the exception and correct this undesirable situation by supporting decision making. An example of an SAP PM exception could be to alert plant section supervisors when the actual costs

on an SAP PM work order exceed planned costs by 10%. An example of a project-related exception is alerting the project stakeholder when the budget is at 95%. Within SAP Quality Management (QM), an exception rule could be set up so that if the number of complaints of a product exceeds 20, the product manager is notified.

▶ **Planning and Forecasting**
The planning and forecasting area allows you to create plan and forecast data. It's often used in Sales and Operations Planning (S&OP), where you can create a sales forecast to determine the sales quantities of a product group or material. The forecasts are generated based on the historical consumption of materials (or reference materials in case of a new product) and aggregated up to the product group level. Multiple planning methods are supported. Because the planning and forecasting is often used by components that aren't part of SAP PLM, such as SAP Sales and Distribution (SD) and Production, we won't discuss it further.

The individual information systems can be found in the SAP menu of the respective component via the main INFORMATION SYSTEM folder (except for QM, which is in the QUALITY CONTROL folder). All these different logistics reports can also be found and accessed through the SAP menu LOGISTICS • LOGISTICS CONTROLLING.

The information systems are all based on the same data warehouse principle, so they offer similar basic functions. The LIS data warehouse system has been around for a long time and consists of numerous reports, which can be very beneficial for organizations to provide insights and analytics on operations.

Two downsides to the LIS are that it lacks that "wow" factor to impress decision makers, and it isn't easy to quickly change or expand an existing report in a user-friendly manner because it requires extensive knowledge to do so. Another important thing to point out is that although LIS is still being supported, SAP won't further develop or expand on it and has focused its attention on SAP NetWeaver BW and SAP BusinessObjects tools instead, which are described in Section 10.3. These tools are also better suited for the scenario described, so feel free to skip this section if that is what you're looking for. LIS has been included for completeness and because data can be extracted from it when using SAP NetWeaver BW or SAP BusinessObjects.

When accessing reports from LIS, again you'll first be asked to provide the selection parameters such as the characteristic you want to analyze, the time frame, and additional parameters, including exceptions, which is similar to the regular list reports. After execution, the report will become visible. The report will show you the key figures (includes aggregated information such as number of notifications, number of work orders, number of breakdowns, total actual costs, etc.) for your selected characteristics (master data and organizational elements).

Figure 10.12 shows an example of a PMIS report selection screen, followed by the analysis per piece of equipment (the characteristic) for the following key figures:

▶ Number of breakdowns

▶ Mean Time to Repair (MTTR), which is the time period in which the object was not operational in hours

▶ Mean Time between Repair (MTBR), which is the time period in which object was fully operational in hours for the selected equipment

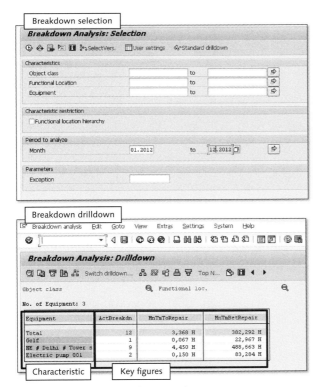

Figure 10.12 PMIS Breakdown Analysis

Several functions can be performed on the reports. Figure 10.13 shows an example of performing an ABC analysis; other functions include creating top *n* list, making a graphical representation, setting up selection versions, using drilldown functions, creating a cumulative frequency curve or a correlation curve, performing classification, and making comparisons.

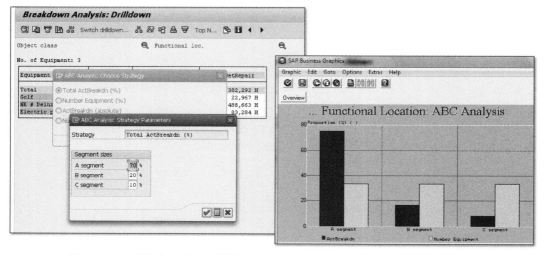

Figure 10.13 ABC Analysis in PMIS

The data warehouse model used in LIS consists of three levels as represented in Figure 10.14:

- ▶ **Online transaction processing (OLTP)**
  The lowest level consists of large quantities of master and process data based on the update rules as defined within the LIS information structures and provides the basis for obtaining information.

- ▶ **Data Warehouse**
  This level breaks down this data into a few meaningful database tables, which are referred to as information structures (InfoStructure). These InfoStructures get either updated in real time in parallel of the operational transaction or periodically through the communication interface, which consists of the communication structures and update rules. The InfoStructures contain aggregated statistical information per characteristic.

▶ **Online analytical processing (OLAP)**
The top level is the business intelligence level, which offers wide ranging options for effectively analyzing and presenting statistical data. Functions such as ABC analysis, top *n* lists, classification, comparison, correlation, and so on are offered.

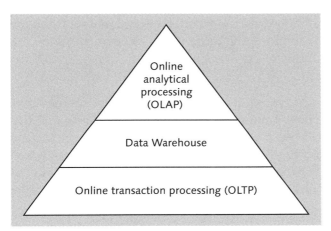

Figure 10.14 Logistic Information System Levels

When you want to get a better understanding of LIS, its concepts, how certain key figures are calculated, and so on, you can go to *http://help.sap.com* and follow the path: SAP BUSINESS SUITE • SAP ERP ECC • LOGISTICS GENERAL LO • LOGISTICS INFORMATION SYSTEM (LO-LIS), or you can find out more in the resources provided in Appendix A and Appendix B of this book.

10.2.4 Business Context Viewer (BCV)

You can use the Business Context Viewer (BCV) to access a fully flexible and changeable side panel without any development. You can easily set up a personalized BCV panel using the configuration wizard; the guided activity pattern proposes logical defaults where possible. It's available on SAP NetWeaver Business Client 3.5 for Desktop (NWBC), which needs to run on SAP ERP 6 EPH 6, although any version of SAP ERP 6 can be used as a source. (For additional information on technical requirements, please refer to the SAP Service Marketplace for SAP PLM and/or the online help covering the NWBC side panel.)

The BCV is the analytics tool from SAP PLM 7.01 onward; note that it was offered under the name Product Centric View (PCV) when it was introduced in SAP ERP 6 EHP 4 and has since been renamed to BCV in EHP 6. It enhances existing SAP transactions by providing embedded analytics through a side panel within the SAP PLM UI based on the context of the transaction. The analytical data is directly visible on the screen via a flexible side panel called a BCV quick view. These BCV quick views include queries, dashboards, and favorites because end users can run analytics in real-time data (using BAPI technology) or reports from SAP NetWeaver BW or SAP BusinessObjects BI applications. The search capabilities are based on SAP NetWeaver Enterprise Search via TREX, as described earlier.

The frontend can provide an analytic view in which you can influence the representation of the selected analytical information. You can show charts and lists, change query settings and selection parameters, export to Excel, print the list, and access navigation and drilldown capabilities. The BCV quick views provide you with context-sensitive analytics and supplementary information based on the business transaction. BCV quick views consist of three tabs, as shown in Figure 10.15:

▶ **Previews**
This tab allows you to see previews for charts and lists.

▶ **Query Views**
This hierarchical list gives you access to queries via the quick view; click on the query to open the analytical view.

▶ **Dashboards**
This tab can be used to arrange different information related to a specific SAP PLM object in one overview. Dashboards allow you to arrange and compose product information on one page, providing comparisons based on data from different sources, which can be shared among team members.

Table 10.1 provides you with an overview of the functions offered from the BCV.

Functions	Details on Functions
Chart types	▶ Line chart ▶ Column chart ▶ Stacked column chart

Table 10.1 BCV Functions

Functions	Details on Functions
Chart types (Cont.)	▶ Pie chart ▶ Bubble chart ▶ Gantt chart ▶ A vs. B chart
Extended settings for charts	▶ Label handling (dynamic data) ▶ Multiple y-axes ▶ 3D chart ▶ Color palette usage ▶ Values for start/end points (axes) ▶ Zoom
Export functionality	▶ Table to Excel ▶ Chart to GIF file
Integration for Xcelsius dashboards	▶ Runs in Flash island ▶ Easy configuration (no ABAP necessary) ▶ Field mapping ▶ No SAP BusinessObjects BI/SAP NetWeaver BW necessary
Printing capabilities	▶ Table ▶ Chart ▶ Dashboard

Table 10.1 BCV Functions (Cont.)

Figure 10.15 shows an example of the use of the BCV during the display material transaction (Transaction MM03), showing you the standard available quick views, which include the outstanding quality notifications, sales orders, material stock, material where used in BOMs, production orders, and purchase orders.

When you're seeing a quick view that requires your further attention, you can open the graph through an *analytic view* (which is another type of view area). You can personalize the analytic view, for example, by changing the table or chart (line, column, stacked, pie, bubble, Gantt, A vs. B, and time scatter) or exporting the input parameters to Excel tables or GIF files charts, printing, or drilling down.

Figure 10.16 shows the analytic view for material stock.

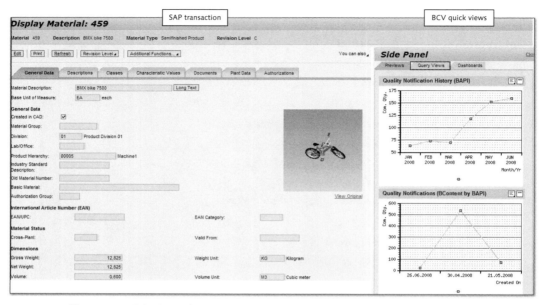

Figure 10.15 BCV Example

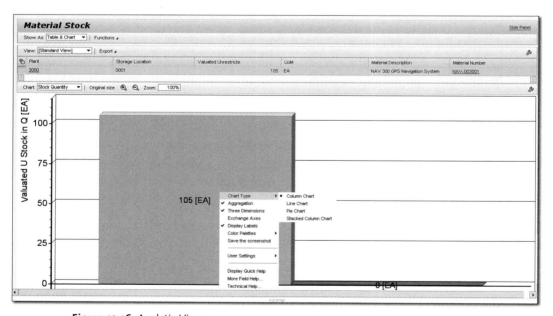

Figure 10.16 Analytic View

Figure 10.17 shows an example of the BCV cockpit. Through this cockpit, you can configure and use your favorite content (e.g., query views, dashboards, and snapshots) without starting the BCV side panel or dashboard application. It integrates to an SAP BusinessObjects Dashboards dashboard without any coding. You can ensure appropriate authorizations by using user roles and access control lists (ACLs). Personalization can take place through a configuration wizard, which guides you through the steps required and prefills logical default values where possible.

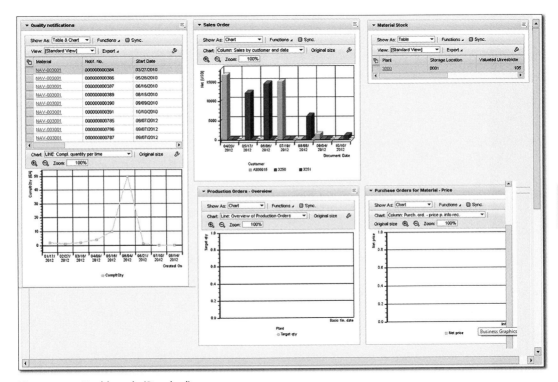

Figure 10.17 Dashboards (Standard)

BCV is delivered with the predefined BI Content for SAP PLM via the Business Configuration Sets (BC Sets) shown in Table 10.2.

SAP PLM Object	Data Provision Technology	Description
PLM Content General	BC Set	(/PLMI/BCV_BC_PLM_GENERAL)
PLM Content for BI	BC Set	(/PLMI/BCV_BC_PLM_BI)
PLM Content for PDCE	BC Set	(/PLMI/BCV_BC_PLM_PDCE)
PLM Content for Process Industry	BC Set	(/PLMI/BCV_BC_PLM_RCP)
Document	Workflow	Workflows for Document
Document	BAPI	Last Released Version for Document
Change Number	Workflow	Workflows for Change Numbers
Recipe	Classic InfoSet	Materials Assigned to Input Substance
Recipe	Classic InfoSet	Materials Assigned to Output Substance
Recipe	Classic InfoSet	Recipes Related to Change Number
Recipe	Classic InfoSet	Where-Used List of Recipe
Recipe	Classic InfoSet	Calculated Price of Each Ingredient
Recipe	Classic InfoSet	Min. – Max. – Current Quantity for Items
Recipe	Classic InfoSet	Composition Quantities
Recipe	Classic InfoSet	Ingredient Quantities
Recipe	Classic InfoSet	Formula Item Quantities
Recipe	Classic InfoSet	Validity of Recipe Versions
Recipe	Classic InfoSet	Costs of Recipe Versions
C-projects	Classic InfoSet	Availability of a Business Partner in PPM
C-projects	Classic InfoSet	Staffing of a Business Partner in PPM
C-projects	Classic InfoSet	Role Demand in PPM
C-projects	Classic InfoSet	Role Staffing in PPM

Table 10.2 BCV Predefined Content

SAP PLM Object	Data Provision Technology	Description
Rapid Planning Matrix (RPM)	Classic InfoSet	Bucket Financial Data
RPM	Classic InfoSet	PPM Capacity Planning Data in PPM 5.0
RPM	Classic InfoSet	PPM Financial Planning Data in PPM 5.0
RPM	Classic InfoSet	PPM Initiatives Data
RPM	Classic InfoSet	PPM Initiatives Data in PPM 5.0 for Complex Column Chart
RPM	Classic InfoSet	PPM Initiatives Data at PPM 5.0 for Complex Gantt Chart
RPM	Classic InfoSet	Item Financial Data
RPM	Classic InfoSet	Bucket Financial Data by Time Line
RPM	Classic InfoSet	Initiative Financial Data by Time Line
RPM	Classic InfoSet	Item Financial Data by Time Line
RPM	Classic InfoSet	PPM Item Data in PPM 5.0
RPM	Classic InfoSet	PPM Item Data for Complex Chart in PPM 5.0
RPM	Classic InfoSet	Phase/Decision Point Data in PPM 5.0 for Complex Gantt Chart
RPM	Classic InfoSet	PPM Financial Project Cost Data in PPM 5.0
RPM	Classic InfoSet	PPM Financial project Cost data in PPM 5.0 for Complex Column
RPM	Classic InfoSet	PPM What if – Original and Simulated Items Data
RPM	Classic InfoSet	PPM What if – Items Data for Complex Column Chart
RPM	Classic InfoSet	PPM What if – Items Data for Complex Gantt Chart
Material	BI	Material Cost Analysis Search via SAP Business-Objects BI

Table 10.2 BCV Predefined Content (Cont.)

SAP PLM Object	Data Provision Technology	Description
Material	BI	Stock Overview Search via SAP Business-Objects BI
Material	BAPI	Quality Notification Search via BAPI
Material	BAPI	Sales Order Search for Customer via BAPI
Material	BAPI	Sales Order Search for Material via BAPI
Material	SAP NetWeaver Enterprise Search	Material Search via SAP NetWeaver Enterprise Search
Material	SES	Material Search via Search Engine Service (SES)
Material	Classic InfoSet	Stock for Material from Local ERP System
Material	BAPI	Production Orders for Material
Material	BAPI	Purchase Orders for Material
Material	BAPI	Product Design Cost Estimating (PDCE) Product Costing Data for Material
Material	ES	Material Where-Used in BOM
Material	Workflow	Workflows for Material
Product Structure Management (PSM)	PSM can use all of the material search connectors listed above	
PSM	Workflow	Workflows for Product Structure Component

Table 10.2 BCV Predefined Content (Cont.)

Let's briefly touch on the technical requirements of BCV configuration. SAP NetWeaver Business Client 3.5 for Desktop provides the side panel area, which requires the roles and tagging rules. The application system with the SAP GUI transactions needs to have conversion service in the side panel area. The NWBC needs to run on the SAP ERP 6, EHP 6 environment. The SAP ERP backend needs to be SAP ERP 6, but it isn't required to be on the same enhancement level—that is, a lower level is also supported (see Figure 10.18).

Before you can use the BCV, it needs to be configured, which is done through a bottom-up configuration, starting with the search connector (which enables connection to the data provider), followed with the BCV query defining the data selection, finishing with the query view that defines the graphical representation. After these have been set up, the BCV side panel becomes available with the different tabs (PREVIEWS, QUERY VIEWS, and DASHBOARDS) as shown in Figure 10.18.

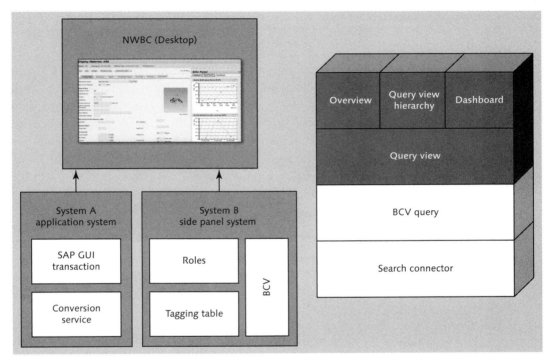

Figure 10.18 BCV Technical Requirements

10.3   Reporting with Comprehensive SAP Products

This section is dedicated to the additional reporting tools of SAP NetWeaver BW and SAP BusinessObjects BI. SAP NetWeaver BW will be explained by going through its architecture and data flow, describing its data model, and finally discussing how reports are run. For the SAP BusinessObjects solutions, it isn't possible to go into similar detail due to the large number of solutions and the diversity and complexity of these solutions. Instead, Section 10.3.2 will solely provide an overview of the SAP BusinessObjects solutions, give a general introduction, and show you some examples.

10.3.1 SAP NetWeaver BW

SAP NetWeaver BW is an analytic and business planning solution targeted to handle, interpret, and analyze a large volume of business data to support decision making. The reporting, analysis, and interpretation of business data is of central importance to a company in guaranteeing its competitive edge, optimizing processes, and enabling it to react quickly and in line with the market. SAP NetWeaver BW is offered as part of the business intelligence solutions.

Although SAP NetWeaver BW contains valuable integration tools and BI Content for SAP solutions such as SAP PLM and SAP ERP, its data warehouse concept with open architecture allows you to source data from any external data source systems. A *data warehouse* serves to integrate data from heterogeneous sources; transform, consolidate, clean up, and store this data; and stage it efficiently for analysis and interpretation purposes. As a user, you can run the reports efficiently via multiple user-friendly working environments. These reports can be flexibly distributed to the various participants in the decision-making process by email or in a corporate portal, for example.

The following section is written based on SAP NetWeaver Release 7.3 EHP 1, and SAP BusinessObjects BI content Release Add-on 7.47 SP02. Note that the data model has changed from previous versions. SAP NetWeaver BW is also offered through SAP HANA, an in-memory technology focused on enhancing the performance of SAP NetWeaver BW. In particular, SAP HANA makes it possible to efficiently process demanding scenarios with unpredictable query types, high data volumes, high query frequency, and complicated calculations.

Before we take a look at some example reports from SAP NetWeaver BW, it's worthwhile to introduce you to SAP NetWeaver BW's architecture and the simplest data flow option. Then we'll briefly go through the data model to explain the most commonly used BW terms, such as the InfoCube and its structure, which will be supported by two example InfoCubes both from the SAP PLM area. Then we'll explain how to access and run some reports, including a few example SAP NetWeaver BW reports from the SAP PLM area.

The objective of this section is to provide you with the general SAP NetWeaver BW concepts and a functional introduction to SAP NetWeaver BW. For more details about administration and development, visit the *http://help.sap.com* site, navigate to SAP NETWEAVER • SAP NETWEAVER BUSINESS WAREHOUSE, and then select the SAP NetWeaver BW version that is relevant for you.

Architecture

SAP NetWeaver BW provides you with the capabilities to extract, restructure, and reformat source data to run efficient and user-friendly analyses. Before you can generate reports or queries, the data required from the source systems need to be extracted, transformed, consolidated, cleaned up, and stored.

To adequately meet requirements regarding consistency and flexibility, SAP NetWeaver BW has a layered architecture, which contains data in differing levels of granularity. The following layers have been identified and represented in Figure 10.19, but keep in mind that these are largely conceptual. In reality the boundaries are often not as clear (they are fluid).

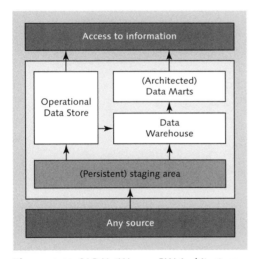

Figure 10.19 SAP NetWeaver BW Architecture

- ▶ **Persistent staging area (PSA)**
  The layer in which the data is first stored when extracted from the source system.

- ▶ **Data warehouse**
  The layer in which the data is stored after the first transformation and cleanup activities. It consists of integrated, granular, historic, stable data without modification for usage (hence, also referred to as neutral).

- ▶ **Architected data marts**
  The layer that contains the most multidimensional analysis structures focused

on data analysis requirements. These structures are called architected data marts and are based on a universally consistent data model.

▶ **Operational data store**
The layer that supports operative data analysis so that it's available on a continual basis or at short intervals. It can be used to forward operational data to the data warehouse layer; however, the operational data is often more detailed and contains all the data, whereas the data in the warehouse is, for example, just the end-of-day status.

You can perform reporting, planning, and analyzing activities either via the operational data store (for operational reporting) or via the architected data marts (for the management reporting and planning activities such as simulations and budgeting calculations).

Data Flow

Figure 10.20 shows the simplest possible data flow. In reality, the data transfer process (DTP) is often repeated several times.

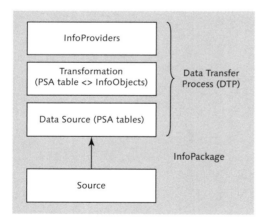

Figure 10.20 SAP NetWeaver BW Data Flow

In a load process, the data from the source is transferred via an InfoPackage from the source system into the PSA in a PSA table, which is a transparent, flat database table. Next, the DTP loads data from one physical data store (the PSA table) into the next data store, which is called an *InfoProvider* in SAP NetWeaver BW. During this transfer, transformation rules map the fields from the source data store (the

PSA table) to the InfoObjects of the target data store (the InfoProvider). The Info-Providers representing the data view (similar to the PMIS InfoStructure) need to be filled, cleansed, consolidated, and integrated with the required data from the source systems, which is performed via a comprehensive DTP. The details of this process fall outside the scope of this book, but Figure 10.21 shows an example of the data flow from an SAP ERP source system to an SAP NetWeaver BW InfoProvider. The 0QM_C07 InfoCube shown here is one of the many InfoCubes that SAP NetWeaver BW offers through its BI Content. As you can see, the InfoCube is filled by using the InfoSources containing the following:

- InfoSource Quality Notifications – Activities
- InfoSource Maintenance Notifications – Activities
- InfoSource Service Notifications – Activities

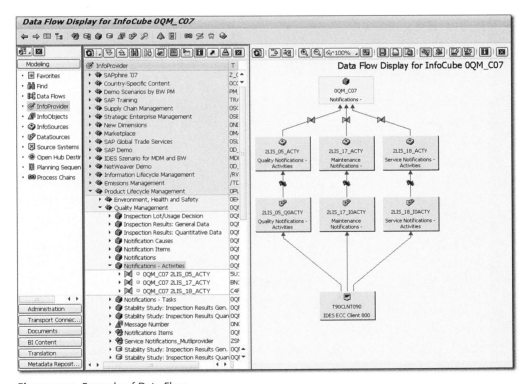

Figure 10.21 Example of Data Flow

Data Model

During the transfer process, the InfoObjects of the target data store (the InfoProvider) are filled. InfoObjects are the smallest data units used in SAP NetWeaver BW and are divided into the following three types:

► **Key figure**
Provides transactional data—such as quantities, amounts, number of items, sales volumes, or figures—to be analyzed.

► **Characteristics**
Contains master data in the form of attributes, text, or hierarchies, which can be used to sort the dataset (e.g., product, customer group, fiscal year, period, or region).

► **Units**
Contains the context of the values of the key figures, such as currencies and unit of measure.

Reports or queries are performed based on InfoProviders that represent the *data view* (also being referred to as the physical *data store*), similar to the InfoStructure within LIS. Data stores consist of a key and a data area, which can contain key figures or characteristics. Commonly used InfoProviders include the InfoCube, MultiProviders, InfoSets, HybridProviders, and CompositeProviders. Of these, we'll only discuss InfoCubes in detail.

Modeling of a multidimensional store is implemented using InfoCubes. An *InfoCube* is a data container used for reports and analyses, which contain ordered characteristics and key figures; they are referred to as *InfoObjects* in SAP NetWeaver BW.

An InfoCube is a set of relational tables generated based on an enhanced star schema. The star schema indicates that it consists of a large fact table with the InfoCube's key figures and multiple surrounding dimension tables containing the InfoCube's characteristics. For queries on an InfoCube, the facts and key figures are automatically aggregated (summation, minimum, or maximum) if necessary. The dimensions combine characteristics that logically belong together—such as a customer dimension consisting of the customer number, customer group, and the steps of the customer hierarchy, or a product dimension consisting of the product number, product group, and brand—and refer to master data. The facts are the key figures to be evaluated, the fact table, and the dimensions that are optimized for efficient data analysis. Figure 10.22 illustrates the structure of the InfoCube.

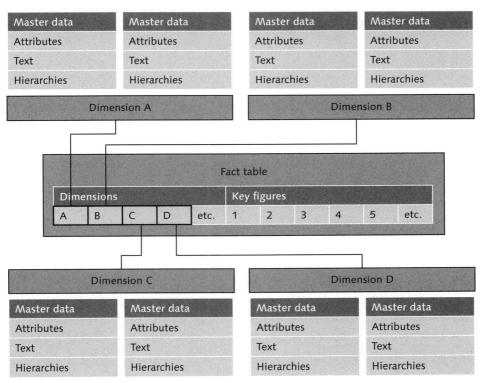

Figure 10.22 InfoCube Structure

Figure 10.23 offers an example based on an existing InfoCube. InfoCube 0QM_C07 Notification Activities is part of the business intelligence content for SAP Enterprise Asset Management (SAP EAM). We selected this InfoCube as an example because it contains notification activities; the notification document is used by most SAP PLM components.

0QM_C07 notification activities consists of four dimensions in Figure 10.24: TIME, MATERIAL, FUNCTIONAL LOCATION, and EQUIPMENT. These master data objects have their own dimension table(s); for example, the dimension time has day or months, where the material dimension has the attributes material group, material type, and so on. The fact table consists of all four dimensions and the single key figure: number of activities. Table 10.3 provides you with same examples of dimensions and key figures for each of the SAP PLM solutions as covered in this book, merely to provide relevant examples for all areas.

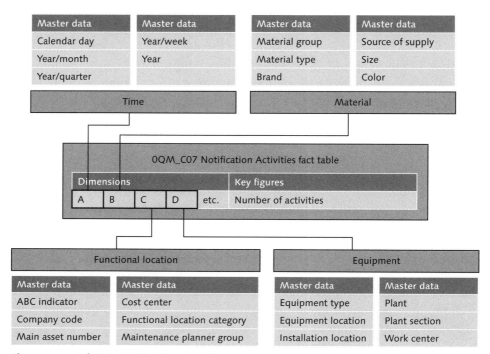

Figure 10.23 InfoCube Notification Activities

Component	Object	Example
SAP Plant Maintenance (SAP PM)	Dimensions	▶ Maintenance planning plant/planner group ▶ Functional location ▶ Equipment ▶ Assembly ▶ Order type ▶ Maintenance activity type ▶ SAP PM processing phase ▶ Planning indicator ▶ Plant ▶ Work center ▶ Controlling area

Table 10.3 Examples of Dimension and Key Figures per SAP PLM Solution

Component	Object	Example
SAP Plant Maintenance (SAP PM) (Cont.)	Dimensions (Cont.)	▶ Currency type ▶ Time ▶ Data package ▶ Unit
	Key figures	▶ Planned work for operation ▶ Number of orders ▶ Number of orders with status completed ▶ Number of orders to be executed immediately ▶ Number of orders completed on schedule ▶ Number of orders with status not executed ▶ Number of orders with status outstanding ▶ Number of planned orders ▶ Lead time for order in calendar days ▶ Total actual costs ▶ Total planned cost ▶ Actual work for operation
SAP Project Systems (SAP PS)	Dimensions	▶ Project definition ▶ Work Breakdown Structure (WBS) ▶ Network ▶ Network activity ▶ Activity element ▶ Milestone ▶ Controlling area
	Key figures	▶ Duration ▶ Billable days external ▶ Billable days internal ▶ Chargeable days ▶ Investment days

Table 10.3 Examples of Dimension and Key Figures per SAP PLM Solution (Cont.)

Component	Object	Example
SAP Project Systems (SAP PS) (Cont.)	Key figures (Cont)	The key figures featured here are all percentage values compared to the available days of the productive employees. Investment days, in this example, contain training, education, sales, and learning on the job activities, which can't be charged on a consulting project.
SAP Quality Management (QM)	Dimensions	▸ Cause ▸ Time ▸ Problem ▸ Object part ▸ Plant and material ▸ Assembly ▸ Customer ▸ Notification number ▸ Vendor
	Key figures	▸ Number of causes ▸ Number of activities ▸ Quality score ▸ Number of lots ▸ Number of accepted lots ▸ Number of rejected lots
SAP Environment, Health, and Safety Management (SAP EHS Management)	Dimensions	▸ Date ▸ Time ▸ Specification ▸ Material ▸ Work area ▸ Operation status ▸ Accident ▸ Safety measure

Table 10.3 Examples of Dimension and Key Figures per SAP PLM Solution (Cont.)

Component	Object	Example
SAP Environment, Health, and Safety Management (SAP EHS Management) (Cont.)	Key figures	▶ Warehouse stock ▶ Stock receipts ▶ Stock issues ▶ Average mass ▶ Number of accidents ▶ Number of safety measures
SAP Project and Portfolio Management (PPM)	Dimensions	▶ Time ▶ Collaboration ▶ Area
	Key figures	▶ Number of collaborations ▶ Number of areas ▶ Number of folders ▶ Number of users
PPM–Project Management	Dimensions	▶ Time ▶ Objects ▶ Role ▶ Date ▶ Project charter
	Key figures	▶ Staffed required capacity ▶ Project role assignment work

Table 10.3 Examples of Dimension and Key Figures per SAP PLM Solution (Cont.)

For more documentation, go to the *http://help.sap.com* and choose SAP NET-WEAVER • BI CONTENT 7.06.

Figure 10.24 shows the original InfoCube from within the SAP NetWeaver BW system through the Data Warehousing Workbench (DWB).

The SAP Business Content (BI Content) is shipped as an add-on and comes with a large amount of predefined business content. BI Content is a preconfigured set of role- and task-related information models that are based on consistent metadata in SAP NetWeaver BW that enable selected roles within a company with the information that the roles need to perform their tasks. The BI Content is created based on the years of project experiences from SAP and its partners. This allows you to leverage these experiences, minimize implementation cost, and accelerate implementation time. You can choose to work directly with the delivered BI Content without any modifications, or you can modify the content to meet your organization's specific requirements and merely use it as a template. (At time of publication, the most recent BI Content add-on was 7.06.)

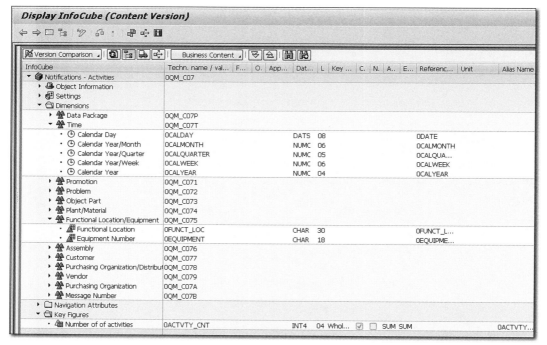

Figure 10.24 InfoCube OQM_C07

The BI Content (or information models) consists of a wide range of objects, such as the InfoObjects, transformations, InfoProvider (InfoCubes and DataStore Objects [DSOs]), roles, and even data mining tools, queries, workbooks, and web templates. It even contains SAP Crystal Reports (BI Content Extension) and SAP BusinessObjects Dashboards (BI Content Extension), which might support customers looking to use SAP BusinessObjects.

Table 10.4 provides you with an overview of the available InfoCubes for the SAP PLM-relevant components.

Functional Area	InfoCubes Available
SAP Environment, Health, and Safety Management (SAP EHS Management)	▶ Specification and Material/Stock Movements
SAP Quality Management (QM)	▶ Inspection Lot/Usage Decision ▶ Inspection Results General Data ▶ Inspection Results Quantitative Data ▶ Notification Causes ▶ Notification Items ▶ Notifications ▶ Notification Activities ▶ Notification Tasks ▶ Stability Study: Inspection Results General ▶ Stability Study: Inspection Results Quantity Data
SAP Plant Maintenance (SAP PM)	▶ Budget Data for Plant Maintenance ▶ Equipment Dismantling at Functional Locations ▶ Maintenance Orders: Costs and Allocations ▶ Maintenance Orders: Operations ▶ Maintenance Orders: Scheduling ▶ Measurement Result ▶ Plant Maintenance Orders ▶ Simulated Plant Maintenance Costs
SAP Project System (SAP PS)	▶ PS Claims ▶ PS Controlling ▶ PS Controlling New ▶ PS Dates ▶ PS Earned Value ▶ PS Residual Order Plan

Table 10.4 SAP PLM-Relevant InfoCubes

Functional Area	InfoCubes Available
SAP Project and Portfolio Management (PPM)	► Actual and Planned Work
	► Assigned Work and Staffed Requirements Capacities
	► Costs from R/3
	► Collaboration Cube
	► Key Figures for Project Charter

Table 10.4 SAP PLM-Relevant InfoCubes (Cont.)

For more information on additional BI Content, please go to SAP NetWeaver • SAP NetWeaver Business Warehouse • Business Content at *http://help.sap.com.*

Running Reports

SAP NetWeaver BW supports multiple user interfaces to run reports, which have been represented in Figure 10.25. We'll walk through each of these user interfaces now.

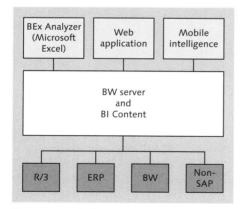

Figure 10.25 SAP NetWeaver BW Overview at a Glance

SAP Business Explorer (SAP BEx) provides flexible reporting and analysis tools for strategic analyses, operational reporting, and decision-making support within an organization. SAP BEx allows a broad spectrum of users access to information in SAP NetWeaver BW using the SAP NetWeaver Portal, the intranet (web application design), or mobile technologies. SAP BEx includes query, reporting, and analysis functions, and, as an employee with the appropriate access authorization, you can evaluate past or current data on various levels of detail. Figure 10.26 and Figure 10.27 offer examples of SAP BEx reports for project management.

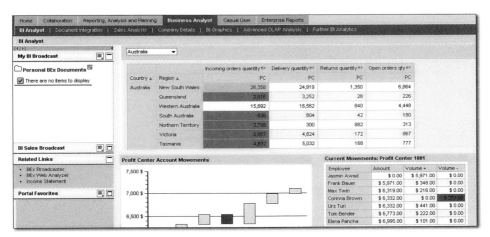

Figure 10.26 Sales Order BEx Analysis (BI Map; 01 BI Analyst 2)

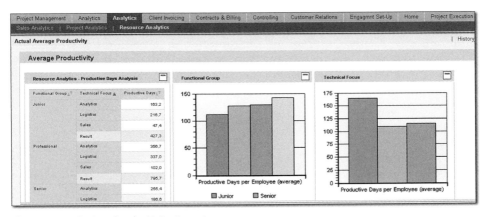

Figure 10.27 Project Productivity Report

You can flexibly adjust or create a query by using simple drag-and-drop functions to add characteristics, key figures, or rows. Based on where you're positioned within the query, you can right-click to reach reporting functions such as filtering, sorting, or creating exceptions. Figure 10.28 shows an example of a project analysis where exceptions have been defined for the project's overall status, date status, and budget status. This gives you the ability to look into the areas that require your attention further.

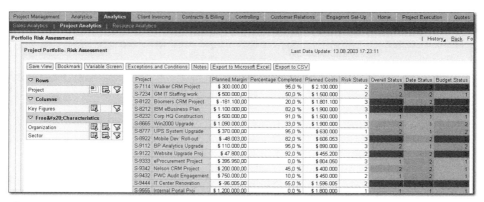

Figure 10.28 Project Risk Assessment with Exceptions

SAP BEx can be used via web environments such as the SAP NetWeaver Portal or via Excel. Figure 10.29 shows an Excel report.

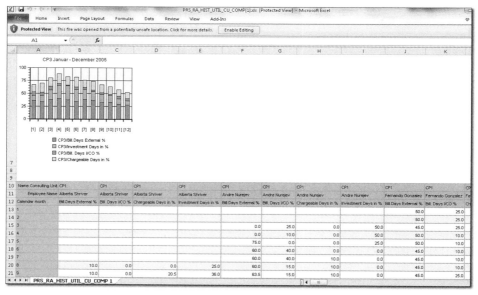

Figure 10.29 Excel Report

The SAP BEx report designer allows you to design and format reports according to the appropriate standards. Figure 10.30 shows the creation of an income statement, for example.

All financial figures in mio €	Variance in M€ vs Last Cycle	Variance in M€ vs Previous Year	Variance in M€ vs Budget	Variance in % vs Last Cycle	Variance in % vs Previous Year	Variance in % vs Budget	Sales Plan
Total Revenues	**39.7**	**39.7**	**58.3**	**4.9 %**	**4.9 %**	**7.4 %**	**$ 602,566.1**
Total Net Sales	**37.7**	**37.7**	**57.4**	**4.7 %**	**4.7 %**	**7.3 %**	**$ 692,436.85**
Indirect Sales	1.8	1.8	2.1	59.8 %	59.8 %	79.4 %	$ 636,663
Sales to Other Division	0.5	0.5	-0.6	7.5 %	7.5 %	-8.0 %	$ 529,280
Sales to Own Division	35.5	35.5	55.9	4.5 %	4.5 %	7.2 %	$ 650.000.100
Total Other Revenues from Indirect Sales	2.0	2.0	0.9	59.7 %	59.7 %	19.0 %	$ 547.254.100
Revenues from Indirect Sales Royalties	0.5	0.5	0.2	22.7 %	22.7 %	6.2 %	$ 123.542.000
Revenues From Tele Sales	1.4	1.4	0.5	100.0 %	100.0 %	58.5 %	$ 457.000.542
Other Revenues from Indirect Sales	0.1	0.1	0.2	10.9 %	10.9 %	18.2 %	$ 651.123.541
Total Costs	**-46.3**	**-46.3**	**-30.5**	**-11.4 %**	**-11.4 %**	**-7.3 %**	**$ 452.000.00**
Total Costs for Production	**-47.1**	**-47.1**	**-30.5**	**-12.1 %**	**-12.1 %**	**-7.5 %**	**$ 398.800.456**
Costs Own Division	-2.8	-2.8	-2.4	-44.7 %	-44.7 %	-36.6 %	$ 320.120.000
Manufacturing Costs	0.8	-0.8	2.5	-19.5 %	19.5 %	44.4 %	$ 707,426
Variances & Write-offs	2.3	2.3	-4.5	11.7 %	11.7 %	-35.3 %	$ 746,296

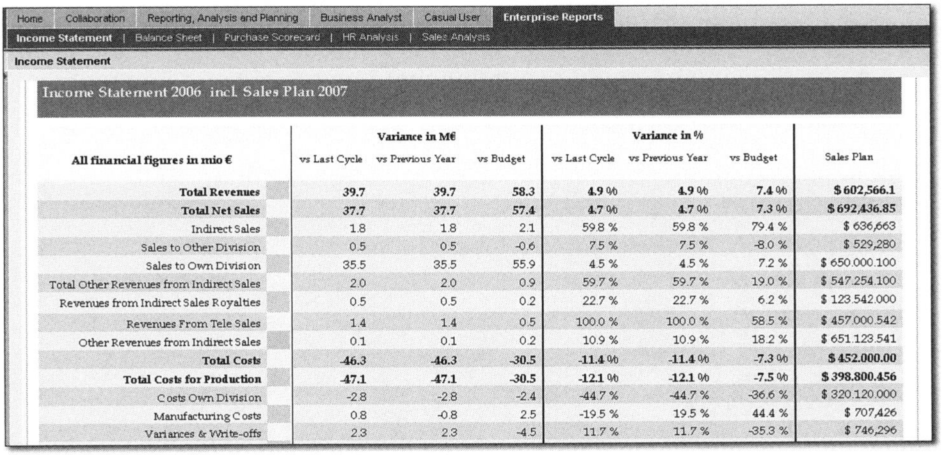

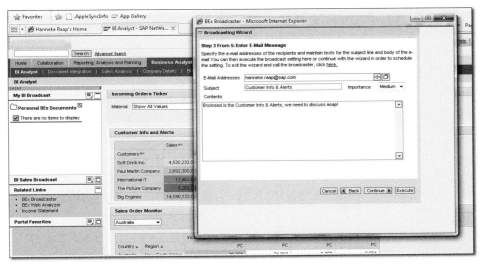

Figure 10.30 SAP BEx Report Designer

You can use the SAP BEx information broadcasting capabilities to distribute BI Content from SAP NetWeaver BW by email either as static report formats (e.g., a PDF) or via links with live data. You can also publish it to the SAP NetWeaver Portal. Figure 10.31 shows an example of broadcasting using the SAP BEx BROADCASTING WIZARD.

Figure 10.31 Broadcasting (in MAP BI – 02 Broadcasting 1) Wizard

SAP BEx includes the capability to produce geographical analysis to visualize content such as sales figures via color coding onto a map. Figure 10.32 shows how sales figures are represented per sales region.

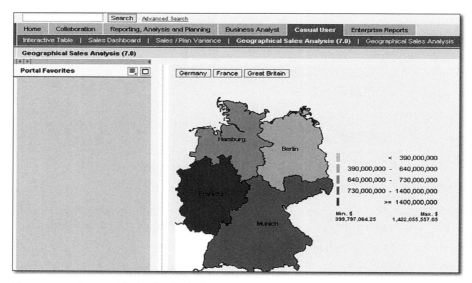

Figure 10.32 Geographical Sales Analysis

This section has offered only a brief functional introduction to the SAP NetWeaver BW. For more details, consult the SAP site (*www.sap.com*) and navigate to SAP NETWEAVER • SAP NETWEAVER BUSINESS WAREHOUSE. Select the SAP NetWeaver BW version that is relevant for you. Also check out the resources that are presented in Appendix A and Appendix B of this book.

> **Note**
>
> For a compressive insight into SAP NetWeaver BW, please refer to *SAP NetWeaver BW 7.3 — Practical Guide* by Amol Palekar, Bharat Patel, and Shreekant Shiralkar (SAP PRESS, 2012), *SAP NetWeaver BW and SAP BusinessObjects: The Comprehensive Guide* by Heilig et al. (SAP PRESS, 2012).

10.3.2 SAP BusinessObjects

SAP BusinessObjects BI offerings supplement the SAP NetWeaver BW capabilities, offering tools and applications to provide appropriate information to business users allowing them to gain insight, share these insights with colleagues across corporate environments, make fact-based informed decisions, and adjust strategies. Figure 10.33 shows how the SAP BEx user segments are expanded by SAP Crystal Reports, Dashboards and SAP BusinessObjects Analytics, and how two entirely new user segments have been added—the Web Intelligence and SAP BusinessObjects Explorer segment. You can easily access relevant information when and wherever you need it to better understand your business, act quickly and confidently, and ultimately achieve remarkable results. Business users, report designers, data managers, and administrators can use web-enabled clients or Windows-based clients to access the tools.

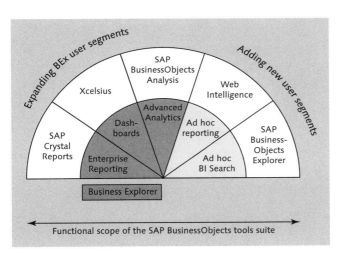

Figure 10.33 How SAP NetWeaver BW and SAP BusinessObjects BI Supplement Each Other

Using SAP BusinessObjects BI can offer the following benefits:

▶ Provide intuitive, self-service access to business information.

▶ Enable informed and rapid decisions based on reliable and real-time business data.

▶ Maximize visibility into the performance of your business network.

▶ Simplify deployment and optimized use of IT infrastructure and resources.

SAP BusinessObjects BI is one of the most important SAP BusinessObjects product offerings. It covers a wide range of processes from search and navigation to advanced analytics, reporting and analysis, interactive analysis, dashboards and visualization, data exploration, information infrastructure management, and advanced analytics. Figure 10.34 gives you an overview of the entire SAP BusinessObjects BI product portfolio available today based on the function.

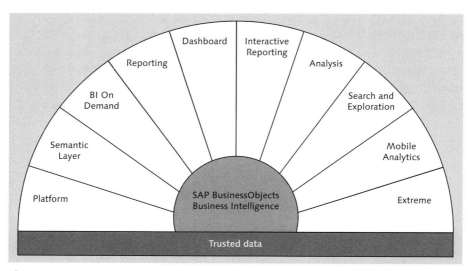

Figure 10.34 SAP BusinessObjects BI Solution Overview

Table 10.5 breaks down the SAP BusinessObjects BI solution into area and function to show which products are offered. The focus of this section and area of the book is on SAP BusinessObjects BI's core functions: reporting, dashboards and analytics, and data discovery, which were given asterisks in the table.

Area	Function	Product Description
Core	Core platform	▶ SAP BusinessObjects BI 4.0
	Semantic layer	▶ SAP BusinessObjects BI 4.0
	Platform customization	▶ SAP BusinessObjects BI 4.0
	BI on-demand	▶ SAP BusinessObjects BI On-Demand, powered by SAP HANA
	Reporting	▶ SAP Crystal Reports* ▶ SAP BusinessObjects Web Intelligence*
	Dashboards	▶ SAP BusinessObjects Dashboards*
	Analytics	▶ SAP BusinessObjects Analysis for Microsoft Office ▶ SAP BusinessObjects Analysis for OLAP*

Table 10.5 SAP BusinessObjects BI Solutions

Area	Function	Product Description
Creative	Data discovery	▶ SAP BusinessObjects Explorer* ▶ SAP Visual Enterprise
Mobile analytics	Mobile analytics	▶ SAP BusinessObjects Mobile Analytics Suite
Extreme	Big data, real-time, insight to action	▶ SAP BusinessObjects BI 4.0, powered by SAP HANA
	Predictive analysis	▶ SAP BusinessObjects Predictive Analysis (initial release)
Social	Social	▶ SAP BusinessObjects BI 4.0

Table 10.5 SAP BusinessObjects BI Solutions (Cont.)

Figure 10.35 places the SAP BusinessObjects BI solutions in the pyramid based on the technical knowledge capability required of the user to effectively utilize them. For example, Crystal Reports and dashboards use guided procedures, as opposed to the SAP BEx or OLAP, where the user navigates through the solution freely through an interactive experience.

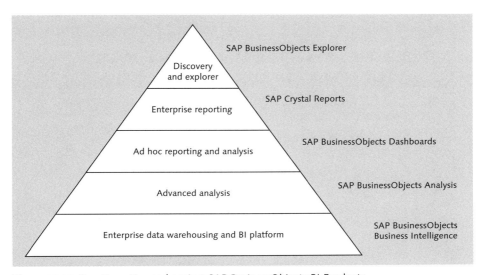

Figure 10.35 Functions Mapped against SAP BusinessObjects BI Products

Let's walk through these tools now.

SAP BusinessObjects Explorer (once known as Polestar) is a data discovery application that provides you quick access to the SAP BusinessObjects BI environment and intuitive search and exploration capabilities. Through search, you can find relevant data held within consistent, meaningful datasets known as *information spaces*, which you can filter and drill down into to find your answers. When you find the appropriate information, you can use the advanced visualizations or charts to attain the information quickly in the most appropriate format.

SAP Crystal Reports allows you to design, explore, visualize, and deliver reports via the web or embedded in enterprise applications and provides the industry standard for enterprise reporting. It's a dynamic and powerful reporting solution and is designed to use virtually any data source to help you produce the reports you want, making it available to a large number of end users to multiple destinations. It can tightly integrate with the SAP Business Suite and is optimized to use business warehouse objects such as InfoCubes, queries, DSOs, and InfoSets. Additionally you can use SAP Crystal Reports for operational reporting through a direct connection to the SAP Business Suite. Figure 10.36 shows how a business analyst has created a project report and has broadcasted this to the SAP NetWeaver Portal, so it can be accessed by the authorized project employees. Figure 10.37 shows a Crystal Report with the project size per customer.

Figure 10.36 Broadcasted Report to SAP NetWeaver Portal

786

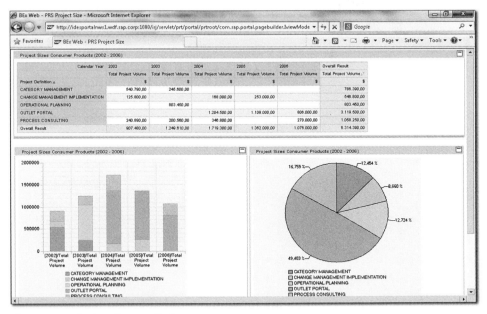

Figure 10.37 Project Size per Customer

SAP BusinessObjects Web Intelligence (also referred to as "WebI") is the solution used to produce web-based intuitive ad hoc queries and analyses. It ensures that your deployment meets performance demands and supports standardization efforts by providing an integrated analysis tool for all users. It's a very agile and easy-to-use solution because it provides self-services to perform ad hoc reporting and apply report formatting and analysis for the casual user, enabling a simple and consistent user experience over any data. SAP BusinessObjects Web Intelligence is available both as a client tool of the SAP BusinessObjects BI platform and as a stand-alone product. It can also be referred to as interactive analysis in this release. Figure 10.38 shows an example of a project-related WebI report.

SAP BusinessObject Dashboards provides superior, highly interactive dashboard capabilities and sophisticated visual presentations (data visualization). The dashboards are offered via an intuitive and easy-to-use point-and-click interface. It can be deployed on a variety of tools, such as the web, desktop, or Microsoft Office documents. Its intuitive Windows interface allows you to build interactive models of data and formulas from Excel spreadsheets. These models can then be exported in multiple formats to meet your specific business needs and be used by other individuals in your organization.

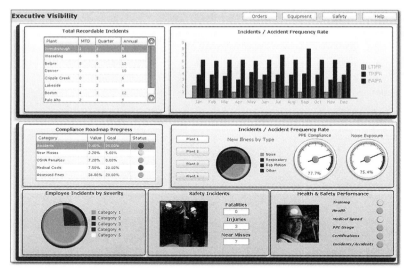

Figure 10.38 BCV Dashboard Executive Visibility

The dashboard in Figure 10.39 gives you an overview of the most important information for the group of products that this product manager is responsible for. A product manager can drill down into a specific product and can display its dashboard by simply clicking on the product.

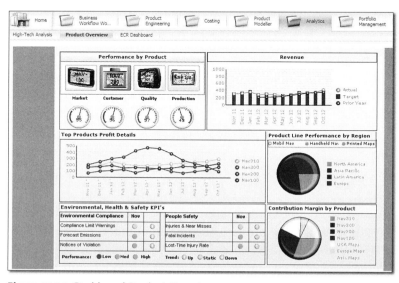

Figure 10.39 Dashboard Product Overview

SAP BusinessObjects Analysis, edition for OLAP, is an advanced AJAX-based online analysis tool allowing analysis of multidimensional (OLAP) data sources. Its web client can be used to perform business and financial analyses, where information from different systems can be combined.

The report designer can use the more advanced OLAP capabilities, allowing for more comprehensive analytic options. Figure 10.40 shows a split pie and a polar chart that have been created with SAP BusinessObjects Analysis, edition for OLAP, based on project sales data from the SAP Business Suite.

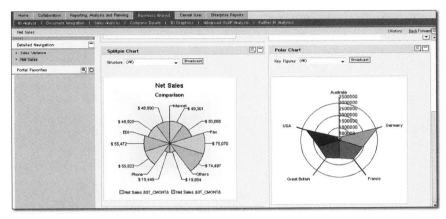

Figure 10.40 Advanced OLAP Query

SAP BusinessObjects BI provides an enterprise data warehousing and business intelligence platform. It's a flexible, scalable, and reliable solution for reporting, analysis, and information delivery, allowing the delivery of reports to users via any web application such as the intranet, Internet, or corporate portal. The platform includes or interacts with most SAP BusinessObjects tools and has an adaptive service-oriented architecture.

SAP BusinessObjects BI is available in two editions:

▶ SAP BusinessObjects Analysis, edition for OLAP

▶ SAP BusinessObjects Analysis, edition for Microsoft Office

SAP BusinessObjects Analysis, edition for OLAP, helps you gain insight into business data and make intelligent decisions that impact corporate performance. The edition for OLAP is accessed from the SAP BusinessObjects BI Launch Pad in a web browser.

The SAP BusinessObjects Analysis for Microsoft Office edition integrates SAP BusinessObjects Analysis with Excel and PowerPoint.

SAP Crystal Reports and SAP BusinessObject Dashboards are delivered as part of the SAP Business Suite version 7 and onward. Similar to the BI Content, Crystal Reports and Dashboards-specific content will also become available for customers.

System Architecture

When you're using SAP ERP, SAP NetWeaver BW, and SAP BusinessObjects BI, your system landscape will consist of the following elements as represented simply in Figure 10.41:

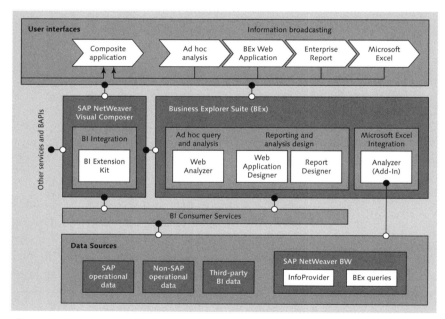

Figure 10.41 System Architecture

▶ **Data sources**
Starting from the bottom, several data sources can be used such as any SAP operational system or non-SAP system.

▶ **Business Explorer Suite**
Allows you to perform ad hoc queries and analysis, to design any reports and broadcast them, and integrate to Excel via the add-in.

▶ **SAP NetWeaver Visual Composer**
Provides the SAP BusinessObjects BI integration via the BI Extension Kit.

▶ **User interfaces**
The different user interfaces, such as composite application, ad hoc analysis, SAP BEx web application, enterprise report, and Excel, allow the user to view the reports generated.

10.3.3 Future Outlook

SAP PLM will continue to focus on SAP BusinessObjects BI and SAP NetWeaver BW solutions to provide the different user groups of product data with the appropriate information to support decision making and adjust product strategies and the company's direction. The solution offerings will be standardized and simplified to include the best of both worlds. The products will be continuously improved, innovated, and further embedded into SAP PLM and the SAP Business Suite as per the 2012 SAP Business Intelligence Roadmap published on the SAP Service Marketplace.

Of course, the roadmap has not been carved into stone yet; SAP's projections are subject to various risks and uncertainties and can change over time. So make sure to check the latest information on business analytics on the SAP Service Marketplace (*http://service.sap.com/bi*) and on the SAP Help portal (*http://help.sap.com*).

10.4 Summary

This product insight and analytics chapter has introduced you to the business processes focused on product intelligence. First we described the business process covering the SAP 3D Visual Enterprise; this solution provides the means to combine business data with visual data—for example, in maintenance you can include technical drawings during the performance of a maintenance activity.

We next discussed the business processes for reporting, querying, and analyzing, covering how and with which solutions you can generate reports and queries. The solutions were categorized into two main areas: standard reporting in SAP ERP and reporting with comprehensive SAP products. The section finished with the process covering SAP NetWeaver Enterprise Search and business object search, which enables organizations to search product data across multiple objects.

Section 10.2 elaborated on the SAP ERP reporting means, discussing the standard list reports with selection and layout options, the Windows Word Processor Integration in SAP EHS (which is specifically targeted to be used to report on data from the specification), the embedded data warehouse offered through the Logistical Information System, and the Business Content Viewer (which provides users with an embedded side panel with product analytics when running a transaction). This section included the history and explanation of the acronyms used within the SAP BusinessObjects BI area, which, due to overlap, is worth understanding.

Section 10.3 explained the two comprehensive SAP reporting tools offered in addition to standard tools: SAP NetWeaver BW and SAP BusinessObjects BI. Before you can run reports in SAP NetWeaver BW, you have to ensure the data warehouse has the appropriate business data to run reports on, which is why we briefly talked about the architecture, the data flow, and the data model. The SAP BusinessObjects solutions both expand the existing SAP BEx user segment by adding additional enterprise reports, dashboard, and advanced analytics, and add two new user segments through SAP BusinessObjects Web Intelligence and SAP BusinessObjects Explorer.

This book has taken you on a journey through the entire product portfolio available within the SAP Business Suite specifically targeted at SAP Product Lifecycle Management.

11 Conclusion

Let's conclude with a brief summary and take-away points for each of the chapters. We'll also explain how and where to find more resources per topic and will give an overview of the outlook for SAP PLM in the future.

Chapter 1: Product Lifecycle Management

Chapter 1 introduced product lifecycle management as a concept, offered a brief history of the space, described the current trends and challenges companies are facing, and listed some important benefits customers can expect when implementing SAP PLM. The product portfolio it covered provided you with an understanding of the different solutions offered under the SAP PLM Solution Map.

Chapter 2: Product Management

This chapter covered the creative part of the product lifecycle and followed the structure of the New Product Development and Introduction (NPDI) pyramid to highlight the solutions available for each tier.

Product Innovation Management

Product innovation management is supported by defining your product strategy via pathways and strategy maps using SAP Strategy Management. To protect your intellectual property, you need to implement SAP Governance, Risk, and Compliance (SAP GRC) functions and processes to fully ensure that your product complies with regulations and company policies and to introduce controls to mitigate your organization's product-related risks.

Planning and Management

We covered the management and monitoring capabilities regarding product portfolio, initiatives, and new product proposals in SAP Project and Portfolio Management (PPM).

Functional Execution

PPM can be fed by using code name "Edison" or SAP Product Definition to capture all product ideas, prioritize them, assign them to teams, and collect and analyze data to prepare for the market launch management phase. All of these are functional execution solutions, which is the last tier in the NPDI pyramid.

The chapter finished with the new product introductions process. Although this process varies per customer, depending on the industry and the complexity of the innovation process, the SAP PLM solution, in combination with SAP Supply Chain Management (SAP SCM) manufacturing solutions, offers an end-to-end solution for all variations.

Both Chapter 3 and Chapter 4 offered information about product master data and its related required business processes and scenarios.

Chapter 3: Product Data Management

This chapter focused on the core product master data elements, which were split into the following areas.

Product Master Data

We explained all of the master data objects that can be used to describe a product—that is, the material, the bill of material (BOM), the routings, task lists, and work centers. If you use multiple objects to represent a product, and the same people are responsible for maintaining these master data elements, you should consider using the Integrated Product Development tools. Integrated Product Development tools allow you to access and work on multiple objects simultaneously when your product is the central object.

Apart from using the SAP Graphical User Interface (SAP GUI), you can also use the SAP NetWeaver Portal, which delivers two separate interfaces based on industry focus with the current SAP PLM version (7.02) — one for discrete products and another for process industries. In the future, SAP may pursue a single interface independent of industry.

Document Management

SAP Document Management System (SAP DMS) allows you to store and access important digitally available data such as design drawings, photographs, and business documents. This solution includes the expected features of any document management solution, such as document approvals, check in and check out of documents, and version management, with the added main benefit of being integrated into other SAP solution areas. This provides you with direct access to the documents from within a product master or product master BOM, for example. Because it's part of SAP, you can leverage the technical capabilities of workflow, SAP Engineering Change Management (ECM), and SAP Office. However, apart from being integrated within the SAP Business Suite, it also is possible to set up integration to externally involved systems such as integration to Microsoft Office, CAD systems, geographical information systems (GIS), product data systems, and archive solutions.

Product Costing

This section explained how SAP PLM supports different costing methods depending on when costing is made and which data is available for costing at that particular time.

Specification Management and Recipe Management

This solution was originally targeted mainly at customers in the process industry, but it's now considered a cross-industry solution. Through Specification Management and Recipe Management, you can define a recipe and the ingredients that make up your product to support the product development process. By defining substances, you can describe products and product ingredients in greater detail, as opposed to using the material master. It allows you to manage product safety, Dangerous Goods Management, Industrial Hygiene and Safety, waste management, occupational health management, and Recipe Management functions.

Chapter 4: Product Variants, Classification, and Collaboration

Chapter 4 continued with the master data objects available to represent the product and its parts by explaining two optional master data capabilities: product classification and product Variant Configuration. The chapter finished with the business processes (department specific) and scenarios (across multiple departments) that focus on product data collaboration between stakeholders.

Product Classification

You can enrich product master data through SAP Classification (CA) by defining your own specific product fields. As a cross-application component, its concept and data model can be used in multiple components to enrich master data objects or transactions, such as in SAP Plant Maintenance (SAP PM) and SAP Customer Service (SAP CS) to enrich the technical objects and notifications types; in SAP Environment, Health, and Safety Management (SAP EHS Management) to enrich the substance data; and in SAP Project System (SAP PS) to enrich your projects and orders.

Product Variant Configuration

Variant Configuration is a great tool to use to model similar types of products easily to create all product variants possible from a technical and business point of view. It ensures that sales representatives can only offer and sell products that are valid and technically possible because the product variant includes the configuration restrictions and rules. Using Variant Configuration reduces the amount of master data maintenance to prevent data redundancy and to have one single source of the truth when it comes to product data. Note that Integrated Product and Process Engineering (iPPE) will become the standard modeling platform in the future for product development.

Product classification and product Variant Configuration have been described together in this chapter because they go hand in hand; product Variant Configuration uses CA to describe its product variants, which means the possibilities of product characteristics are endless.

The variant concept has been adopted and applied to configure other objects, such as the standard task list, the standard network, and the model specification (e.g., within SAP PM and within SAP PS).

Business Processes and Business Scenarios

The final section focused on the available business processes (department specific) and scenarios (across multiple departments) to facilitate collaboration on product data between stakeholders.

Chapter 5: Maintenance and Customer Service

Now that the product-specific master data objects have been described, including their business processes and business scenarios, the next topic focused on the next stage in the product lifecycle: the optimized asset operations and maintenance stage. This chapter has given you an overview of the functions and features that SAP CS and SAP PM offers during the post-sales process, when you've sold your product or assets to a customer (supported by SAP CS). The planning and execution of the maintenance and service activities on these assets are your responsibility, and, when necessary, you can charge the customer for these activities.

In contrast, SAP PM focuses on the maintenance and operations of your internal products or assets that are owned or leased by your company and for which you're responsible. Because SAP CS and SAP PM share most of their master data objects and their transactions, they have been described together.

The chapter first introduced SAP Enterprise Asset Management (SAP EAM) and detailed related benefits, supported maintenance activities, and strategies.

Master Data

This section focused on the master data in both areas referred to as technical objects, detailing objects such as the functional location and the equipment. It explained the common functions available for technical objects, such as categorization, classification, change management, data transfer, SAP DMS, business partners, status, permits, and SAP Customer Relationship Management (SAP CRM) integration and enhancement options.

Main Transactional Objects

This section gave an overview of the objects used when performing a transaction in SAP PM or SAP CS. It overviewed the structure and purpose of the object information, notification, work order, repair order, measurement documents, maintenance plan and strategy, service contracts, visualization and publications, and log book and shift reports.

Configuration Management

This section also explained how to use the configuration management verification process to check the actual technical object structure against an expected structure. Last, the section covered spare parts management, which included information about how spare parts can be generated and used with BOMs or maintenance catalogs.

Main Maintenance and Customer Service Processes

We focused on the main business processes, covering the organizational setup, master data maintenance (including handover and takeover), maintenance cost budgeting, corrective maintenance process (including its variations, breakdown and emergency), inspections, preventive maintenance, project-oriented maintenance, and returns and repairs. This section concluded with coverage of reporting and analysis.

Supplementary Maintenance and Customer Service Processes

The last section focused on the supplementary business processes, such as the capacity requirements planning processes, performing refurbishments, using Pool Asset Management (PAM) for loaning assets, work clearance maintenance, providing a safe working environment, warranty claim processing, and the lean scenario for simplified processes. Because using mobile devices in the field can substantially improve and shorten paper-based processes, the chapter also briefly touched on mobility.

Chapter 6: Product Compliance

The increasing number of laws and industry standards has made product compliance one of the SAP PLM topics that deserve the full attention of companies developing and producing products. SAP offers integrated and embedded product compliance business process, which is the focus of this chapter.

Environment, Health, and Safety

The SAP Environment, Health, and Safety Management (SAP EHS Management) component of SAP ERP covers product labeling, Hazardous Substance Management, Dangerous Goods Management, and SAP Waste and Recycling. You can use dashboards based on detailed product data to get insights into product compliance.

Operational Risk Management

The Operational Risk Management process allows you to manage product and asset risks through a closed-loop process, which includes worker safety. Operational Risk Management is an important integration between SAP EHS Management and SAP PM/SAP CS. Performing regular audits regarding the product's information and product-specific processes is another important area that ensures product compliance.

SAP Audit Management

This section focused on explaining how product audits can be planned, performed, and monitored by using Audit Management, a cross-application component.

Chapter 7: Project Management

Chapter 7 focused on the design, source, and make phases of a product, especially when these phases are done through a project-based methodology. Of course, this chapter is just an introduction to project management and SAP's products in this space, and an entire book can be written on the topic. The main aim of this chapter was to provide you with an understanding of the SAP solutions in the project management space and a high-level overview of their functions and features.

To this end, the chapter offered you a high-level perspective of these available project management products, their functions and features, the benefits their implementation can bring, and when they are recommended.

Project and Resource Management with SAP ERP

SAP PS, which is the application within SAP ERP, has been around for a while; it seamlessly works together with other areas such as your financial and controlling set up, including Investment Management, SAP DMS, procurement processes and material requirements planning (MRP), and SAP Inventory Management processes.

Project Management via PPM

SAP Project and Portfolio Management (PPM) is a somewhat younger application; it's web-enabled, is intuitive to use, and provides a number of exciting dashboards and reporting cockpits to enable a quick insight into the status of your projects and the portfolio to which they are assigned.

Project Collaboration

One fundamental part of successful project management is making sure you have the right tools to collaborate within a project team using resources from both inside and outside company firewalls. This need can be addressed by using the project collaboration scenarios from PPM.

External Project Management Applications

We described the integration to external project management software applications and introduced the SAP Enterprise Project Connection, a tool developed by SAP to be able to exchange project data from external project management tools.

The chapter established the project management-specific vocabulary and offered an initial introduction to their capabilities so you can efficiently browse SAP resources to find additional information. Appendix A and Appendix B include SAP courses and additional links as well.

Chapter 8: Product Quality and Product Change Management

The focus of Chapter 8 is on two additional processes within the main process of product development and collaboration: product quality management and SAP Engineering Change Management (ECM).

Product Quality Management

SAP Quality Management (QM) plays an important role during all of the different phases of a product's lifecycle to ensure and improve product quality by planning, performing, and recording quality checks and results along the way.

Master Data

This chapter introduced you to the QM master data objects, which are important during processes relevant for ensuring product quality. The data was grouped into three areas:

▶ **Logistics general master data**
The logistics general master data refers to master data objects from the other logistic components. It includes the material, customer, vendor, batches, quality information record (Q-info record) for sales and procurement, and quality certificates and documents.

▶ **Inspection planning master data**
The inspection planning master data is used to perform quality inspection planning. It covered the inspection plan, reference operation set, material specification, routing, task list, and master recipe.

▶ **Quality planning basic master data**
Quality planning basic master data covers master data that is required for quality planning and belongs within the QM component, specifically. It covered the catalog, set, master inspection characteristics, class characteristic, inspection methods, sample master data, work center, and production resource/tool (PRT)—all of which are quality planning basic master data elements.

Quality Management Business Processes

We continued with three business processes within QM:

▶ **Quality engineering**
First we described the Failure Mode and Effect Analysis (FMEA) and the setup of a control plan; both are important business processes to eliminate or reduce product weaknesses and set up appropriate actions and controls. We then continued with how the FMEA and control plan are part of the closed-loop inspection planning processes. Furthermore, the quality engineering process

includes product development via a product development project involving the appropriate quality gates and the execution of stability studies.

▶ **Quality assurance and control**
After your quality processes are in place, you must strive to maintain and improve the attained level of quality. Quality control involves inspections at all stages, continuous monitoring, and intervening quickly to deal with unexpected events. Quality assurance and control checks can be performed during any step within the logistics value chain with the goal of ensuring that the quality of a product conforms to the necessary quality standards.

▶ **Quality improvement**
The recording of any problems takes place during the quality improvement process. Quality improvement includes the recording of quality problems, such as problem solving by systematically determining their cause and solution and effective processing follow-up actions as a result of the problem. The quality notification process is available to document problems of any type for this purpose—especially problems related to poor quality of a product, such as processing complaints against suppliers and complaints from customers. It can also be used for processing an internal company problem relating to processes and products and for handling positive events, such as proposals for improvement.

Product Change Management

Product change management represents the definition and efficient management of engineering changes to ensure that your product data is up to date (i.e., representing the latest changes) and that product quality in all phases of the product lifecycle is met. Product change management is addressed by the SAP PLM component ECM (also is available within SAP ERP). It includes all types of changes (e.g., form, fit, and function) with processes and procedures that manage how changes are proposed, reviewed, approved, and incorporated into a product and its associated data items. The product change management was divided into the following two subsections:

▶ **Master data objects used for ECM**
This focuses on the master data objects used within ECM, which are the validity parameters, the engineering change record (ECR), and the engineering change order (ECO).

▶ **Business scenario for change and configuration management**
This business scenario was designed for all industries. It shows how engineers and central configuration management work together with the customer (either external or internal) who requires a change to allow changes to product master data. Although the business scenario uses the ECR/ECO as the object for change, a cut-down version of the scenario could be implemented with the use of the change master as the object for change.

Chapter 9: Relevant SAP PLM Additions

This chapter focused on two areas that aren't core to SAP PLM but often offer substantial benefits to manage within the same environment and leverage the integrated nature of SAP PLM and the SAP ERP core component abilities.

SAP Fleet Management

You can leverage SAP Fleet Management to support SAP EAM for your company's transportation means, from procuring the fleet, to maintaining and operating your fleet, to optimizing planning capabilities, to finally disposing of the fleet and starting the cycle again—using a single source of truth for all fleet items. SAP Fleet Management provides a holistic solution supporting all of the stages of your company's transportation means. There are three main functional areas of SAP Fleet Management:

▶ **Administration**
The fleet data model and detailed master data objects used to represent your organization's fleet, such as the equipment master and the fixed asset register.

▶ **Maintenance**
The maintenance-specific processes, such as maintenance engineering, incidents, preventive maintenance, spare parts, services, and warranty management.

▶ **Operations**
Fuel management, pool car management, and driver and transport scheduling.

SAP Mobility

Within SAP PLM, several business users and roles that were identified throughout this book may require offsite accessibility apart from the onsite office environment;

they need to be able to work outside of the office on different devices while still being able to perform business activities. We broke our discussion of mobility with SAP into two main sections:

▶ **SAP Mobile Platform**
We explained the current SAP Mobile technology platforms available (Syclo Agentry and Sybase Unwired Platform) that can mobilize your workforce. We also touched on SAP's anticipated future direction—toward a single SAP Mobile Platform that covers all apps and is based on cloud technology. This would allow you to extend the use of your business application to mobile devices so employees have access anywhere, anytime, and from any device to the relevant business data.

▶ **SAP Mobile apps**
We also described the different mobile apps available for mobile maintenance and operations crew via the Syclo work manager, service manager, rounds manager, and inventory manager. We also highlighted the business-to-employer (B2E) apps for raising a quality issue, an SAP EHS issue, and a timesheet, as well as the business analytics apps available for our reporting solutions.

Chapter 10: Product Insight and Analytics

This product insight and analytics chapter introduced you to the business processes focused on product intelligence and reporting.

Product Intelligence Business Processes

First we described the business process covering the SAP 3D Visual Enterprise, a solution that combines business data with visual data. Recall that as an example, you could include technical drawings during performance of a maintenance activity.

We next discussed the business processes for reporting, querying, and analyzing, covering how and with which solutions you can generate reports and queries. The solutions were categorized into two main areas: standard reporting in SAP ERP and reporting with comprehensive SAP products. The section finished with the process covering SAP NetWeaver Enterprise Search and business objects search, which enables organizations to search product data across multiple objects.

Standard Reporting in SAP ERP

This section elaborated on the SAP ERP reporting means, discussing the standard list reports with selection and layout options, the Windows Word Processor Integration (WWI) in SAP EHS Management (which is specifically targeted to report on data from the specification), the embedded data warehouse offered through the Logistical Information System (LIS), and the Business Context Viewer (BCV).

Reporting with Comprehensive SAP Products

In this section, we explained the two comprehensive SAP reporting tools offered in addition to standard tools: SAP NetWeaver BW and SAP BusinessObjects BI. Before you're able to run reports in SAP NetWeaver BW, you have to ensure the data warehouse has the appropriate business data to run reports on, which is why we briefly talked about the architecture, the data flow, and the data model. The SAP BusinessObjects solutions both expand the existing SAP BEx user segment by adding additional enterprise reports, dashboards, and advanced analytics, as well as two new user segments through Web Intelligence (WebI) and SAP Business-Objects Explorer.

Book Conclusion

The objective of this book was to give you a functional overview of the SAP PLM solutions available and an understanding of how the product lifecycle is supported in all stages of its life. Whether you're interested in the entire solution portfolio or only part of the portfolio, by reading this book entirely, you should be able to understand which solutions are available per the topic, but perhaps more importantly, how the different solutions are integrated and seamlessly work together to provide an end-to-end solution for all your product management stakeholders.

The book can assist organizations and users to determine whether the SAP PLM is the best solution for their enterprise. For existing SAP PLM or SAP Business Suite customers, hopefully it gave you an idea of how to optimize or extend your current solution footprint to get more benefits from an integrated solution.

Finally, this book should provide you with the correct context to dive deeper into a solution area after you've finished a chapter. For this purpose, we recommend you consult the appendices; Appendix A lists relevant SAP courses per chapter, and Appendix B offers additional resources. Of course, the support team at your nearest SAP office can provide additional information or give you a product demonstration.

Having worked with SAP products and customers for more than 15 years, I firmly believe that the best businesses run SAP. Of course, that isn't to say that its solutions and services will always be a perfect fit and never pose any challenges—but this is what makes my job as a consultant so rewarding.

My main motivation for writing this book was to share my knowledge of and experience with SAP PLM solutions with as many customers as possible. Writing this book—my first—has been both challenging and educational; it's my hope that the book will inspire you to keep learning and challenging yourself as well. I leave you with a quote from Google executive Eric Schmidt: "None of us is as smart as all of us."

Appendices

A   Relevant Courses per Chapter

Table A.1 includes an overview of the standard SAP courses available per chapter.

Chapter	Courses
Chapter 1, Product Lifecycle Management	▶ SAP01 SAP Overview ▶ SAP PLM Solution Overview ▶ PLM100 Lifecycle Data Management
Chapter 2, Product Management	▶ CPM210 SAP Strategy Management ▶ GRC100 Principles and Harmonization ▶ GRC300 SAP BusinessObjects Access Control – Implementation and Configuration ▶ GRC310 SAP GRC Access Control ▶ GRC330 SAP BusinessObjects Process Control ▶ GRC340 SAP BusinessObjects Risk Management
Chapter 3, Product Data Management	▶ PLM100 Lifecycle Data Management ▶ PLM110 Basic Data Part 1 (Material and BOM) ▶ PLM111 Basic Data Part 2 (Work Center and Routing) ▶ PLM112 Master Data ▶ PLM114 Basic Data for Manufacturing and Product Management ▶ PLM170 Integrated Product and Process Engineering ▶ PLM120 Document Management ▶ PLM130 Classification ▶ AC505 Product Cost Planning ▶ PLM160 and PLM16E Recipe Management
Chapter 4, Product Variants, Classification, and Collaboration	▶ PLM140 Variant Configuration (Part 1) ▶ PLM145 and PLM146 Variant Configuration (Part 2)

Table A.1 Relevant Courses per Chapter

Chapter	Courses
Chapter 5, Maintenance and Customer Service	▶ PLM300 Business Processes in Plant Maintenance ▶ PLM315 Maintenance Processing: Operational Functions ▶ PLM316 Maintenance Processing: Controlling and Reporting ▶ PLM310 Maintenance and Service Processing ▶ PLM301 Business Processes in Customer Service ▶ PLM330 Service Contracts ▶ PLM335 Service Processing
Chapter 6, Product Compliance	*Product Safety and Stewardship* ▶ EH103 EHS Management Essentials and Functions ▶ EH103a EHS Management Essentials and Functions Professional ▶ EH203 Product Safety ▶ EH203a Product Safety Professional ▶ EH253 Global Label Management ▶ EH253a Global Label Management Professional ▶ EH303 Dangerous Goods Management ▶ EH303a Dangerous Goods Management Professional ▶ EH913 WWI Layout ▶ EH913a WWI Layout Professional *SAP EHS Management for Product and Reach* ▶ RC102a SAP REACH Compliance Essential Functions (RC EF) ▶ RC102b SAP REACH Compliance Essential Functions (RC Proc) ▶ RC102c SAP REACH Compliance Essential Functions (RC Professional)

Table A.1 Relevant Courses per Chapter (Cont.)

Chapter	Courses
Chapter 6, Product Compliance (Cont.)	*Environmental Performance* ▶ EM101 Environmental Compliance ▶ EM201 Environmental Compliance Advanced Reporting ▶ EH103 EHS Management Essentials and Functions ▶ EH103a EHS Management Essentials and Functions (EEF Professional) ▶ EH603 Waste Management ▶ EH603a Waste Management (WA Professional)
Chapter 7, Project Management	*SAP ERP* ▶ ACA020 Investment Management ▶ CA500 Cross Application Time Sheets ▶ PLM200 Business Processes in Project Management ▶ PLM210 Project Management – Structures ▶ PLM220 Project Management – Logistics ▶ PLM230 Project Management – Controlling ▶ PLM235 Project Controlling with Work Breakdown Structures ▶ PLM240 Project Management – Reporting *SAP Project and Portfolio Management (PPM)* ▶ PLM510 c-Projects and c-folders ▶ PLM512 c-Folders
Chapter 8, Product Quality and Product Change Management	*Change Management* ▶ PLM100 Lifecycle Data Management (Change Management) ▶ PLM150 Change and Configuration Management

Table A.1 Relevant Courses per Chapter (Cont.)

Chapter	Courses
Chapter 8, Product Quality and Product Change Management (Cont.)	*SAP Quality Management (QM)* ▶ PLM400 Business Processes in Quality Management ▶ PLM405 Quality Inspections ▶ PLM410 Quality Notifications ▶ PLM420 Quality Management in Production ▶ PLM412 Quality Planning and Inspections ▶ SNC100 Supplier Collaboration with SAP SNC
Chapter 9, Relevant SAP PLM Additions	*SAP Fleet Management* ▶ None available *Mobility* ▶ MOB01 Mobility Fundamentals and Best Practices ▶ SUP120 Sybase Unwired Platform 2.0 Architectures and Technical Overview ▶ SUP512 Moving to Sybase Unwired Platform 2.0
Chapter 10, Product Insight and Analytics	*Reporting* ▶ PLM 240 Project Management – Reporting *SAP NetWeaver BW – Courses with prefix "BW"* ▶ BW001 SAP NetWeaver Business Warehouse ▶ BW361 Business Warehouse Accelerator *SAP BusinessObjects – Courses with prefix "BO"* ▶ BO100 SAP BusinessObjects BI Solution with SAP NetWeaver BW

Table A.1 Relevant Courses per Chapter (Cont.)

You can find a detailed description of training online at *https://training.sap.com/us/en/courses-and-curricula/product-lifecycle-management*. Apart from these standard training courses, SAP Education can also deliver tailor-made workshops, so contact your nearest SAP location for more details, if required.

B   Additional SAP PLM Resources

The objective of this appendix is to help identify where current or prospective customers (Table B.1) and SAP employees and partners (Table B.2) can find additional help or information.

Name	Site	Menu or Quicklink
SAP Help Portal	*http://help.sap.com*	SAP Business Suite > SAP Product Lifecycle Management
Company website	*www.sap.com/plm*	Contact regional business development/ pre-sales/consulting/marketing ▶ *https://www.sap.com/contactsap* ▶ *http://www.sap.com/contactsap/directory/index.epx* ▶ *https://www.sap.com/solutions* ▶ *http://www.sap.com/solutions/analytics/business-intelligence/esri-gis/index.epx*
SAP Service Marketplace	*http://service.sap.com* Quicklink (URL + link; for example, RKT is *http://service.sap.com/RKT*)	*RKT* (business maps), *PLM, findinnovation* (road maps), *usergroups, quicklinks, CATS, PAM* (Product Availability Matrix), *solutionmanager, swcat* (SAP Software Catalog), *RDS-PLM* (Rapid Deployment Solutions for PLM), *SCL* (Scenario and Process Component List), *solutions, solutions/business-process/product-lifecycle-management, roadmap, xapps, xcqm, swdc* (software downloads)
SAP Community Network	*http://scn.sap.com*	*http://scn.sap.com/community/plm* *http://scn.sap.com/community/eam*
SAP Developer Network	*http://sdn.sap.com*	*http://www.sdn.sap.com/irj/bpx/plm*
SAP Training	*http://training.sap.com*	
SAP Partners	*sappartneredge.com*	

Table B.1 Current and Prospective Customers

Name	Site	Menu or Quicklink
SAP Solution Manager	Local environment	The SAP Solution Manager contains valuable solution and business process information
Corporate portal		SMI, SMART, Ramp-Up Knowledge Transfer, Field Services Portal, SDN
Overview of solution offerings	*https://portal. wdf.sap.corp/go/ salesportfolio*	
Assets	*http://smartdirec- tory.sap.corp*	
SAP wiki pages	*https://wiki.sdn. sap.com/*	

Table B.2 References for SAP Employees

C   The Author

Hanneke Raap is a senior SAP consultant at SAP with 15 years of project experience in the Product Lifecycle Management and Supply Chain Management areas. She has been working on SAP implementations across a range of industries, including retail, engineering and construction, telecommunications, utilities, defense, customer products, and the public sector. She has been involved as a consultant, team lead, integration specialist, and solution architect during at least ten full-cycle project implementations in dozens of different countries, mainly in Europe, Australia, and New Zealand. Apart from consulting, she is passionate about sharing her knowledge by teaching, writing, conducting presentations, and providing product demonstrations.

Index

Interested in reading more?

Please visit our website for all new
book and e-book releases from SAP PRESS.

www.sap-press.com